COLLEGE ACCOUNTING

ELEVENTH EDITION

PARTS 1-2-3

Arthur E. Carlson, PhD

Professor of Accounting
School of Business Administration
Washington University, St. Louis

James A. Heintz, DBA, CPA

Associate Professor of Accounting
Indiana University
Bloomington, Indiana

A. B. Carson, PhD, CPA

Late Professor Emeritus of Accounting
University of California, Los Angeles

Published by

A10 **SOUTH-WESTERN PUBLISHING CO.**

CINCINNATI   WEST CHICAGO, ILL.   DALLAS   PELHAM MANOR, N.Y.   PALO ALTO, CALIF.

PREFACE

College Accounting is for students of accounting, business administration, and secretarial science. An understanding of the principles of business accounting is essential for anyone who aspires to a successful career in business, in many of the professions, and in numerous branches of government. Those who manage or operate a business, its owners, its prospective owners, its present and prospective creditors, governmental taxing authorities, and other government agencies have need for various types of information. Accounting systems are designed to fill such needs. The particular practices followed are tailored to meet the requirements and the circumstances in each case. However, the same accounting principles underlie all of the practices — just as the same principles of structural engineering apply to the construction of a one-car frame garage and of a fifty-floor steel and concrete office building.

This eleventh edition of College Accounting continues the pattern of earlier editions — explanations of principles with examples of practices. Numerous forms and documents are illustrated. Because the terminology of accounting is undergoing gradual change, the currently preferred terms are used throughout the textbook. Diagrams and color are used both to facilitate understanding and, in the case of many of the color illustrations, to conform to practice. New features of this eleventh edition include "Chapter Objectives" at the beginning of each chapter, "Building Your Accounting Knowledge" review questions at the end of each chapter section (there are one or more sections per chapter), and "Expanding Your Business Vocabulary" terms at the end of each chapter. The vocabulary terms are referenced to the textbook pages on which they appear.

Two entirely new chapters have been added to this edition: Chapter 14 on Internal Accounting Control, and Chapter 30 on Accounting for Changing Prices. In addition, the material on accounting for merchandise has been split into two chapters: Chapter 6 on Accounting for Purchases of Merchandise, and Chapter 7 on Accounting for Sales of Merchandise. Chapter 24 on Accounting for Corporate Bonds has been revised to include the increasingly popular effective interest method. Chapter 26 has been expanded to include a simplified introduction to consolidated financial statements. Chapters 27 and 28 have been revised to accommodate a job-order manufacturing business (Hartup Tool, Inc.), and Chapter 29 is exclusively devoted to an expanded analysis of financial statements.

The textbook is organized to facilitate the use of various supplementary learning aids. Workbooks containing study assignments correlated with the chapter sections are available. Each workbook study assignment (called a report) includes an exercise on principles and one or more problems bearing on the material discussed in the related section of the textbook. A compilation of check figures for selected workbook problems is available for distribution to students. Additional accounting problems to be used for either supplementary or remedial work are included following Chapters 5, 10, 15, 20, 25, and 30. Four practice sets (the latter two of which are completely new) are available: the first involves the accounting records of a professional person (John H. Roberts, a management consultant), the second involves the accounting records of a retail clothing store (Boyd's Clothiers), the third involves the accounting records of a wholesale and retail bakery business (the partnership of Fishler & Marvon), and the fourth involves the accounting records of an incorporated job-order manufacturing business (Hartup Tool, Inc.). These sets provide realistic work designed to test the student's ability to apply the knowledge of the principles of accounting which has been gained from studying the textbook and completing the workbook assignments. Upon completion of each practice set, a test is provided to determine the student's ability to interpret intelligently the records and financial statements of the enterprise. An expanded comprehensive periodic testing program is provided. Tests are available for use following completion of Chapters 2, 5, 7, 10, 13, 15, 17, 20, 23, 25, 28, and 30.

The authors acknowledge their indebtedness and express their appreciation to the considerable number of accounting instructors, business executives, accountants, and other professional people whose suggestions contributed to the preparation of this textbook.

A. E. Carlson

J. A. Heintz

A. B. Carson

CONTENTS   PARTS 1–2–3

CHAPTER 1

THE NATURE OF BUSINESS ACCOUNTING

CHAPTER OBJECTIVES

The objectives of this chapter are to enable you:

▶ To describe business accounting as it applies to profit-seeking enterprises.

▶To define certain business accounting terms.

▶To explain how selected business transactions affect the business entity, using the accounting equation.

▶To explain the nature of the income statement and the balance sheet, and how they relate to one another.

▶To explain the double-entry framework.

▶To explain the function of the trial balance.

The purpose of business accounting is to provide information about the current financial operations and condition of an enterprise to individuals, agencies, and organizations who have the need and the right to be so informed. These interested parties normally include:

(1) The **owners** of the business — both present and prospective.
(2) The **managers** of the business — managers may or may not own the business. (Often, but not always, the owners and the managers are the same persons.)

1

(3) The **creditors**, or **suppliers**, of the business — both present and prospective. Creditors or suppliers are those who supply goods and services on credit — meaning that payment need not be made on the date of purchase. The creditor category also includes banks and individuals who lend money to the business.

(4) **Government agencies** — local, state, and national. For purposes of either regulation or taxation — sometimes both — various governmental agencies must be given certain financial information.

In connection with many businesses, some or all of the following also make use of accounting information: customers or clients, labor unions, competitors, trade associations, stock exchanges, commodity exchanges, financial analysts, and financial writers.

Although the information needed by all types of users is not identical, most want data regarding (1) the results of operations — net income or loss — for the current period and (2) the financial status of the business as of a recent date. The demand for the greatest quantity and variety of information usually comes from the managers of the business. They constantly need up-to-the-minute information about the financial activities of every department in their organization. Because accounting relates to so many phases of business, it is not surprising that there are several fields of accounting specialization such as tax work, cost accounting, information systems design and installation, management services, and budget preparation.

Many accountants have but one employer whereas others become qualified as public accountants and offer their services as independent contractors or consultants. Public accountants perform various functions. One of their major activities is auditing. This involves the application of standard testing and checking procedures to the records of an enterprise to be certain that acceptable accounting policies and practices have been consistently followed. The purpose of the audit is to provide an independent opinion that the financial information about a business is fairly presented. Public accountants frequently extend their activities into the area of "management services" — a term that covers a variety of specialized consulting assignments. Some states license individuals as **Public Accountants** or **Registered Accountants**, although this practice is declining. All states grant the designation of **Certified Public Accountant** (CPA) to those who meet various prescribed requirements, including the passing of a uniform examination prepared by the American Institute of Certified Public Accountants. A uniform examination is also offered in numerous cities throughout the country by the Institute of Management Accounting of the National Association of Accountants, leading to the designation of **Certified Management Accountant** (CMA). This certificate is designed to give professional status to one-employer accountants.

All of the foregoing comments have related to accounting and accountants in connection with profit-seeking organizations. There are thousands of not-for-profit organizations such as governments, educational institutions, churches, and hospitals that also need to accumulate and dispense information. These organizations also engage a large number of accountants. While the "rules of the game" are somewhat different for not-for-profit organizations, much of the record keeping is identical with that found in profit-seeking organizations.

The accountant has the task of accumulating and dispensing the financial information needed by users. Since such activities touch upon nearly every aspect of the business operation and since financial information is communicated in accounting terms, accounting is said to be the "language of business." Anyone intending to engage in any type of business activity is well advised to learn this language.

THE ACCOUNTING PROCESS

Business accounting may be defined as the art of analyzing and recording financial transactions and certain business-related economic events in a manner that (1) classifies and summarizes the information and (2) reports and interprets the results. The accounting process itself provides the basis for this definition.

Analyzing is the first step in the accounting process. The accountant must look at a transaction or event that has occurred and determine its fundamental significance to the business so that the information may be properly processed.

Recording traditionally meant writing something by hand. Much of the record keeping in accounting still is done manually, however, technological advances have introduced a variety of bookkeeping machines which typically combine the major attributes of typewriters, calculators, and electronic printing. Today the initial processing sometimes takes the form of holes punched in certain places on a card or a paper tape, of invisible magnetized spots on a special type of tape, or of special characters that can be magnetically or electronically "read" from source documents and thus used to feed information into an electronic computer. Because of the multiple ways information may be processed, the term "data entry" may be substituted for the term "recording" in the accounting process.

Classifying relates to the process of sorting or grouping like things together rather than merely keeping a simple, diary-like narrative record of numerous and varied transactions and events.

Summarizing is the process of bringing together various items of information to determine or explain a result.

Final processing, or **reporting**, refers to the process of communicating the results. In accounting, it is common to use tabular arrangements rather than narrative-type reports. Sometimes, a combination of the two is used.

Interpreting refers to the steps taken to direct attention to the significance of various matters and relationships. Percentage analyses and ratios often are used to help explain the meaning of certain related bits of information. Footnotes to financial reports and special captions may also be valuable in the interpreting phase of accounting.

ACCOUNTING AND BOOKKEEPING

A person involved with or responsible for such functions as forms and records design, accounting policy making, data analysis, report preparation, and report interpretation may be referred to as an accountant. A person who records or enters information in accounting records may be referred to as a bookkeeper. Bookkeeping is the recording phase of the accounting process. That term goes back to the time when formal accounting records were in the form of books — pages bound together. While this still is sometimes the case, modern practice favors the use of loose-leaf or computer-generated records and cards. When the language catches up with practice, the designation "record keeper" or information processor may replace "bookkeeper."

ACCOUNTING ELEMENTS

A business entity is a particular individual, association, or other organization for which formal records are kept and periodic reports are made. Properties of value that are owned by a business entity are called assets.

Assets. Properties such as money, accounts receivable, merchandise, furniture, fixtures, machinery, buildings, and land are common examples of business assets. An account receivable is an unwritten promise by a customer to pay at a later date for goods sold or for service rendered.

It is possible to conduct a business or a professional practice with very few assets. A doctor of medicine, for example, may have relatively few assets, such as money, accounts receivable, instruments, laboratory equipment, and office equipment. In many cases, a variety of assets are necessary. A merchant must have a large selection of merchandise to sell and store equipment with which to display the merchandise. A manufacturer must have an inventory of parts and materials, tools and various sorts of machinery with which to make or assemble the product.

Liabilities. A legal obligation of a business to pay a debt is a business liability. Debts can be paid with money, goods, or services, but usually are paid in cash. Liabilities represent one type of ownership interest in a business — an outside interest.

The most common liabilities are accounts payable and notes payable. An account payable is an unwritten promise to pay a supplier for property purchased on credit or for a service rendered. Formal written promises to pay suppliers or lenders specified sums of money at definite future times are known as notes payable. A business also may have one or more types of taxes payable classified as a liability.

Owner's Equity. The amount by which the business assets exceed the business liabilities is termed the owner's equity in the business. The word "equity" used in this sense represents a second type of ownership interest in a business — an inside interest. The terms proprietorship, net worth, or capital are sometimes used as synonyms for owner's equity. If there are no business liabilities, the owner's equity in the business is equal to the total amount of the assets of the business.

A business that is owned by one person traditionally is called a proprietorship. The person owning the interest in a business is known as the proprietor. A distinction must be made between the business assets and liabilities and nonbusiness assets and liabilities that a proprietor may have. For example, the proprietor probably owns a home, clothing, and a car, and perhaps owes the dentist for medical service. These are personal, nonbusiness assets and liabilities. The formal accounting records for the enterprise will relate to the business entity only; any nonbusiness assets and liabilities of the proprietor should be excluded. While the term "owner's equity" can be used in a very broad sense, its use in accounting is nearly always limited to the meaning: business assets minus business liabilities.

Frequent reference will be made to the owner's acts of investing money or other property in the business and to the withdrawal of money or other property from the business. In either case, property is changed from the category of a nonbusiness asset to a business asset or vice versa. These distinctions are important if the owner is going to make decisions based on the financial condition and results of the business apart from nonbusiness affairs.

THE ACCOUNTING EQUATION

The relationship between the three basic accounting elements can be expressed in the form of a simple equation known as the **accounting equation**.

> **ASSETS = LIABILITIES + OWNER'S EQUITY**

This equation reflects the fact that outsiders and insiders have an interest in all of the assets of a business. When the amounts of any two of these elements are known, the third can always be calculated.

> **LIABILITIES = ASSETS – OWNER'S EQUITY**
>
> **OWNER'S EQUITY = ASSETS – LIABILITIES**

For example, Nancy Deppen has business assets on December 31 in the sum of $30,200. The business liabilities on that date consist of $1,200 owed for supplies purchased on account and $1,500 owed to a bank on a note. The owner's equity element of the business may be calculated by subtracting the total liabilities from the total assets, $30,200 − $2,700 = $27,500. These facts about the business can also be expressed in equation form as follows:

> **ASSETS = LIABILITIES + OWNER'S EQUITY**
> $30,200 $2,700 $27,500

A closer examination of the owner's equity will show how the equation maintains equality. One way to increase the owner's equity in the business is to increase the assets. To increase the assets and owner's equity, Deppen may (1) invest more money or other property in the business or (2) operate the business profitably.

For example, if one year later the assets are $45,700 and the liabilities are $2,600, the status of the business would be as follows:

$$\begin{array}{ccc} \text{ASSETS} & = & \text{LIABILITIES} & + & \text{OWNER'S EQUITY} \\ \$45,700 & & \$2,600 & & \$43,100 \end{array}$$

The fact that Deppen's equity in the business had increased by $15,600 (from $27,500 to $43,100) does not prove that she had made a profit (often called net income) equal to the increase. Increases and decreases in owner's equity must be analyzed. If the records indicated that she invested additional money during the year in the amount of $7,000 and did not withdraw any funds for personal use, the remainder of the increase in her equity ($8,600) would have been due to profit (net income).

If the records indicated she invested no additional funds, withdrew assets in an amount of $9,400 cash for personal use, and increased her equity by $25,000 as a result of a profitable operation, the net effect would also account for the $15,600 ($25,000 − $9,400) increase. It is essential that the business records show the changes in owner's equity due to events that are part of regular business operations and the changes in owner's equity due to investments and withdrawals of assets by the owner.

TRANSACTIONS

Any activity of an enterprise which involves the exchange of values is referred to as a transaction. These values frequently are expressed in terms of money. Buying and selling property and performing services are common transactions. The following typical transactions are analyzed to show that each represents an exchange of values.

Typical Transactions	Analysis of Transactions
(1) Purchased equipment for cash, $1,250.	Money was exchanged for equipment.
(2) Received cash in payment of professional fees, $300.	Professional service was rendered in exchange for money.
(3) Paid office rent, $250.	Money was exchanged for the right to use property.
(4) Paid an amount owed to a supplier, $700.	Money was given in settlement of a debt that may have resulted from the purchase of property on account or from services rendered by a supplier.
(5) Paid wages in cash, $150.	Money was exchanged for services rendered.
(6) Borrowed $3,000 at a bank giving a 9 percent interest-bearing note due in 30 days.	A liability known as a note payable was incurred in exchange for money.
(7) Purchased office equipment on account, $500.	A liability known as an account payable was incurred in exchange for office equipment.

EFFECT OF TRANSACTIONS ON THE ACCOUNTING EQUATION

Each transaction affects one or more of the three basic accounting elements. For example, in transaction (1) the purchase of equipment for cash represents both an increase and a decrease in assets. The assets increased because equipment was acquired; the assets decreased because cash was disbursed. The office equipment in transaction (7) had been purchased on account, thereby creating a liability. The transaction results in an increase in assets (equipment) with a corresponding increase in liabilities (accounts payable). Neither of these transactions has any effect upon the owner's equity element of the equation.

The effect of any transaction on the basic elements of the accounting equation may be indicated by increasing or decreasing a specific asset, liability or owner's equity account. To illustrate: assume that Edward Foote, an attorney, decided to go into practice for himself. During the first month of this venture (June, 1982), the following transactions relating to the practice took place:

Transaction (a)

An Increase in an Asset Offset by an Increase in Owner's Equity

Foote opened a bank account with a deposit of $8,000. This transaction caused the new business to receive the asset cash; and since Foote contributed the assets, the owner's equity element was increased by the same amount. As a result of this transaction, the equation for the business would appear as follows:

ASSETS		LIABILITIES + OWNER'S EQUITY
Cash	=	Edward Foote, Capital
(a) $8,000		$8,000

Transaction (b)

An Increase in an Asset Offset by an Increase in a Liability

Foote purchased office equipment (desk, chairs, file cabinet, etc.) for $4,100 on 30 days credit. This transaction caused the asset office equipment to increase by $4,100 and resulted in an equal increase in the liability accounts payable. Updating the foregoing equation by this (b) transaction gives the following result:

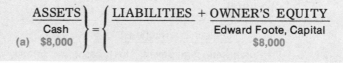

ASSETS			LIABILITIES	+ OWNER'S EQUITY
Cash	+ Office Equipment		Accounts Payable	Edward Foote, Capital
Bal. $8,000		=		$8,000
(b)	$4,100		$4,100	
Bal. $8,000	$4,100		$4,100	$8,000

Transaction (c)

An Increase in One Asset Offset by a Decrease in Another Asset

Foote purchased office supplies (stationery, legal pads, pencils, etc.) for cash, $640. This transaction caused a $640 increase in the asset office supplies that exactly offset the $640 decrease in the asset cash. The effect on the equation is as follows:

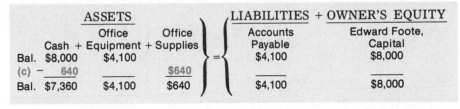

	ASSETS			LIABILITIES + OWNER'S EQUITY	
		Office	Office	Accounts	Edward Foote,
	Cash +	Equipment +	Supplies	Payable	Capital
Bal.	$8,000	$4,100		$4,100	$8,000
(c)	− 640		$640		
Bal.	$7,360	$4,100	$640	$4,100	$8,000

Transaction (d)

A Decrease in an Asset Offset by a Decrease in a Liability

Foote paid $2,500 on account to the company from which the office equipment was purchased. (See Transaction (b).) This payment caused the asset cash and the liability accounts payable both to decrease $2,500. The effect on the equation is as follows:

	ASSETS			LIABILITIES + OWNER'S EQUITY	
		Office	Office	Accounts	Edward Foote,
	Cash +	Equipment +	Supplies	Payable	Capital
Bal.	$7,360	$4,100	$640	$4,100	$8,000
(d)	− 2,500			− 2,500	
Bal.	$4,860	$4,100	$640	$1,600	$8,000

Transaction (e)

An Increase in an Asset Offset by an Increase in Owner's Equity Resulting from Revenue

Foote received $1,800 cash from a client for professional services. This transaction caused the asset cash to increase $1,800, and since the cash was received for services performed by the business, the owner's equity increased by the same amount. The effect on the equation is as follows:

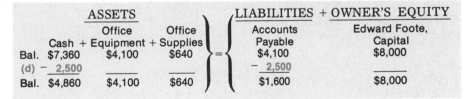

	ASSETS			LIABILITIES + OWNER'S EQUITY	
		Office	Office	Accounts	Edward Foote,
	Cash +	Equipment +	Supplies	Payable	Capital
Bal.	$4,860	$4,100	$640	$1,600	$8,000
(e)	1,800				1,800
Bal.	$6,660	$4,100	$640	$1,600	$9,800

Transaction (f)

A Decrease in an Asset Offset by a Decrease in Owner's Equity Resulting from Expense

(1) Foote paid $350 for office rent for June. This transaction caused the asset cash to be reduced by $350 with an equal reduction in owner's equity. The effect on the equation is as follows:

	ASSETS				LIABILITIES	+	OWNER'S EQUITY
	Cash	+	Office Equipment	+ Office Supplies	Accounts Payable		Edward Foote, Capital
Bal.	$6,660		$4,100	$640	$1,600		$9,800
(f1)	− 350						− 350
Bal.	$6,310		$4,100	$640	$1,600		$9,450

(2) Foote paid a bill for telephone service, $42. This transaction, like the previous one, caused a decrease in the asset cash with an equal decrease in the owner's equity. The effect on the equation is as follows:

	ASSETS				LIABILITIES	+	OWNER'S EQUITY
	Cash	+	Office Equipment	+ Office Supplies	Accounts Payable		Edward Foote, Capital
Bal.	$6,310		$4,100	$640	$1,600		$9,450
(f2)	− 42						− 42
Bal.	$6,268		$4,100	$640	$1,600		$9,408

THE FINANCIAL STATEMENTS

A set of records that make up an accounting information system is maintained to fill a variety of needs. Foremost is to provide source data for use in preparing various reports, including those referred to as financial statements. The two most important of these are the income statement and the balance sheet.

The Income Statement. The income statement, sometimes called the profit and loss statement or operating statement, shows the net income (net profit) or net loss for a specified period of time and how it was calculated. A very simple income statement has been prepared relating to the business of Edward Foote for the first month's operation, June, 1982. This statement contains information that was obtained by analysis of the changes in the owner's equity element of the business for the month. This element went from zero to $9,408. Part of this increase, $8,000, was due to the initial investment made by Foote. Since an investment is not classified as income or expense to the business, it is not considered in the income statement. The remainder of the increase, $1,408, was due to Foote's earning income and incurring expense. Transaction (e) involved revenue of $1,800; transactions (f1) and (f2) involved expenses of $350 and $42, respectively. Taken together, these transactions explain the net income of $1,408, as it appears in the statement below:

EDWARD FOOTE, ATTORNEY Income Statement For the Month of June, 1982		
Professional fees..		$1,800
Expenses:		
Rent expense...	$350	
Telephone expense...	42	392
Net income for month..		$1,408

The Balance Sheet. The balance sheet, sometimes called a statement of financial condition or statement of financial position, shows the assets, liabilities, and owner's equity of a business at a specified date. A balance sheet for Foote's business as of June 30, 1982, is shown below.

EDWARD FOOTE, ATTORNEY Balance Sheet June 30, 1982			
Assets		**Liabilities**	
Cash	$ 6,268	Accounts payable.................	$ 1,600
Office supplies......................	640	**Owner's Equity**	
Office equipment.................	4,100	Edward Foote, capital..........	9,408
		Total liabilities and	
Total assets..........................	$11,008	owner's equity..................	$11,008

BUILDING YOUR ACCOUNTING KNOWLEDGE

1. Identify the four types of information users found in connection with virtually every business enterprise.
2. Which group of information users demands the greatest quantity and variety of information? Why?
3. Why is accounting called the "language of business?"
4. What is the major difference between a management accountant and a public accountant?
5. Identify the six major phases of the accounting process, and indicate what is done in each phase.

6. Why is it necessary to distinguish between the business assets and liabilities and the nonbusiness assets and liabilities of the single proprietor?
7. In what other way than by making a profit can the owner's equity be increased?
8. In what other way than by suffering a loss can the owner's equity be decreased?

Report No. 1-1

> A workbook of study assignments is provided for use with this textbook. Each study assignment is referred to as a report. The work involved in completing Report No. 1-1 requires a knowledge of the principles developed in the preceding textbook discussion. Before proceeding with the following discussion, complete Report No. 1-1 in accordance with the instructions given in the study assignments.

THE DOUBLE-ENTRY FRAMEWORK

The meanings of the terms asset, liability, and owner's equity were explained in the preceding pages. Examples were given to show how each business transaction causes a change in one or more of the three basic accounting elements. Transaction **(a)** shown on page 8 involved an increase in an asset with a corresponding increase in owner's equity. Transaction **(b)** involved an increase in an asset which caused an equal increase in a liability. Transaction **(c)** involved an increase in one asset which was offset by a decrease in another. Each of the transactions illustrated a dual effect. This is always true. A change, increase or decrease, in any asset, any liability, or in owner's equity is always accompanied by an offsetting change within the basic accounting elements.

The fact that each transaction has two aspects — a dual effect upon the accounting elements — provides the basis for what is called double-entry bookkeeping. This term describes a processing system that involves recording the two aspects that are involved in every transaction. Double entry does not mean that a transaction is recorded twice; instead, it means that both of the two aspects of each transaction are recorded.

Double entry is known to have been practiced for at least 500 years. The method has endured largely because it has several virtues; it is orderly, fairly simple, and very flexible. There is no transaction that cannot be recorded in a double-entry manner. Double entry promotes accuracy. Its use makes it impossible for certain types of error to remain undetected for very long. For example, if one aspect of a transaction is properly recorded but the other aspect is overlooked, it will soon be found that the records as a whole are "out of balance." The accountant then knows that something is wrong, checks the transaction to discover the trouble and then makes the needed correction.

THE ACCOUNT

It has been explained previously that the assets of a business may consist of a number of items, such as cash, accounts receivable, merchandise, equipment, buildings, and land. The liabilities may consist of one or more items, such as accounts payable and notes payable. A separate record should be kept of each asset and of each liability. Later it will be shown that a separate record should also be kept of the increases and decreases in owner's equity.

A form or record used to keep track of the increases and decreases in each item that result from business transactions is known as an account. There are many types of account forms in general use. They may be ruled on sheets of paper and bound in a book form or kept in a loose-leaf binder; they may be ruled on cards and kept in a file of some sort; or they may be developed as computer print-outs. An illustration of a standard account form is shown below:

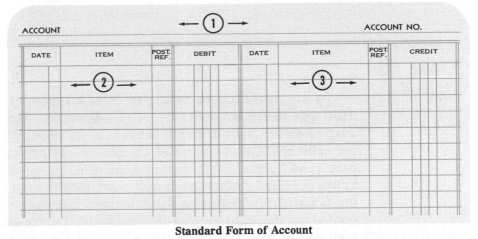

Standard Form of Account

The three major parts of the standard account form are **(1)** the title and the account number, **(2)** the debit side, and **(3)** the credit side. This account form is designed to facilitate the recording of the essential information regarding each transaction that affects the account. Each account should be given an appropriate title that will indicate whether it is an asset, a liability, or an owner's equity account. Before any entries are recorded in an account, the title and number of the account should be entered on the horizontal line at the top of the form. The standard account form is divided into two equal parts or sections which are ruled identically to facilitate recording increases and decreases. The left side is called the debit side, while the right side is called the credit side. The Date columns are used for recording the dates of transactions. The Item columns may be used for entering a brief description of a transaction when deemed necessary. The Posting Reference columns will be discussed later. The amount column on the left is headed "Debit" while that on the right is headed "Credit." The Debit and Credit columns are used for recording the amounts of transactions.

To determine the balance of an account at any time, it is necessary only to total the amounts in the Debit and Credit columns, and calculate the difference between the two totals. To save time, a T account is commonly used for instructional purposes. It consists of a two-line drawing resembling the capital letter T and is sometimes referred to as a skeleton form of account.

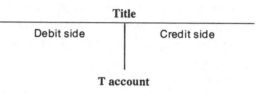

T account

DEBITS AND CREDITS

To debit an account means to enter an amount on the left or debit side of the account. To credit an account means to enter an amount on the right or credit side of the account. The abbreviation for debit is Dr. and for credit Cr. (based on the Latin terms "debere" and "credere"). Sometimes the word charge is used as a substitute for debit. Increases in assets are recorded on the left side of the accounts; increases in liabilities and in owner's equity are recorded on the right side of the accounts. Decreases in assets are recorded on the right side of the accounts; decreases in liabilities and in owner's equity are recorded on the left side of the accounts. Recording increases and decreases in the accounts in this manner will reflect the basic equality of assets to liabilities plus owner's equity (Assets = Liabilities + Owner's Equity); at the same time it will maintain equality between the total amounts debited to all accounts and the total amounts credited to all accounts (Debits = Credits). These basic relationships may be illustrated in the following manner:

ASSETS	=	LIABILITIES + OWNER'S EQUITY

All Asset Accounts		**All Liability Accounts**	
Debit to enter increases (+)	Credit to enter decreases (−)	Debit to enter decreases (−)	Credit to enter increases (+)

		All Owner's Equity Accounts	
		Debit to enter decreases (−)	Credit to enter increases (+)

TOTAL DEBITS	=	TOTAL CREDITS

USE OF ASSET, LIABILITY, AND OWNER'S EQUITY ACCOUNTS

To illustrate the application of the double-entry process, the transactions discussed on pages 8–10 will be analyzed and their effect on the accounting elements will be indicated by showing the proper entries in T accounts. As before, the transactions are identified by letters; dates are omitted intentionally.

Transaction (a)

An Increase in an Asset Offset by an Increase in Owner's Equity

Edward Foote, an attorney, started a business by investing $8,000 in cash.

Cash		Edward Foote, Capital	
(a) 8,000			(a) 8,000

Analysis: As a result of this transaction the business acquired an asset, cash. The amount of money invested represents Foote's equity in the business; thus the amount of the asset cash is equal to the owner's equity in the business. Separate accounts are kept for the asset cash and for the owner's equity. To record the transaction as an increase in an asset and an increase in owner's equity, the cash account was debited and Foote's capital account was credited for $8,000.

Transaction (b)

An Increase in an Asset Offset by an Increase in a Liability

Purchased office equipment (desk, chairs, file cabinet, etc.) for $4,100 on 30 days' credit.

Office Equipment		Accounts Payable	
(b) 4,100			(b) 4,100

Analysis: As a result of this transaction the business acquired a new asset, office equipment. The debt incurred as a result of purchasing the equipment on 30 days' credit is a liability, accounts payable. Thus, the outside interest in the business has increased by $4,100. Separate accounts are kept for office equipment and for accounts payable. The purchase of office equipment caused an increase in the assets of the business. Therefore, the asset account, Office Equipment, was debited for $4,100. The purchase also caused an increase in a liability. Therefore the liability account, Accounts Payable was credited for $4,100.

Transaction (c)

An Increase in One Asset Offset by a Decrease in Another Asset

Purchased office supplies (stationery, legal pads, pencils, etc.) for cash, $640.

Cash			Office Supplies	
(a) 8,000	(c) 640		(c) 640	

Analysis: As a result of this transaction the business acquired a new asset, office supplies. The addition of this asset was offset by a decrease in the asset cash. Notice there is no change in total assets. To enter the transaction properly, Office Supplies was debited and Cash was credited for $640. This is the second entry in the cash account; the account was previously debited for $8,000 when Transaction (a) was recorded.

It is proper to enter office supplies as an asset at the time of purchase even though they will become an expense when used. The procedure in accounting for supplies used will be discussed later.

Transaction (d)

A Decrease in an Asset Offset by a Decrease in a Liability

Paid $2,500 on account to the company from which the office equipment was purchased. (See Transaction (b).)

	Cash				Accounts Payable		
(a)	8,000	(c)	640	(d)	2,500	(b)	4,100
		(d)	2,500				

Analysis: This transaction resulted in a decrease in the liability accounts payable with a corresponding decrease in the asset cash; hence, it was recorded by debiting Accounts Payable and by crediting Cash for $2,500. Note that this is the second entry in the accounts payable account and the third entry in the cash account. At this point in time, the outside interest in the business has decreased by $2,500.

REVENUE AND EXPENSE

The owner's equity element of a business entity or professional enterprise may be increased in two ways as follows:

(1) The owner may invest additional money or other property in the enterprise. Such investments result in an increase both in the assets of the enterprise and in the owner's equity, but they do not further enrich the owner. More property merely is invested in the enterprise and less property outside of the enterprise.

(2) Revenue may be derived from sales of goods or services, or from other sources.

As used in accounting, the term revenue in nearly all cases refers to an increase in the owner's equity in a business resulting from transactions involving asset inflows except the investment of assets in the business by its owner. In most cases, an increase in owner's equity due to revenue results from an addition to the assets without any change in the liabilities. Often it is cash that is increased. However, an increase in cash and other assets can occur in connection with several types of transactions that do not involve revenue. For this reason, revenue is often defined in terms of a change in owner's equity rather than a change in assets. Any transaction that causes owner's equity to increase, except for investments in the business by its owner, involves revenue.

The owner's equity element of a business entity or professional enterprise may be decreased in two ways as follows:

(1) The owner may withdraw assets (cash or other property) from the business enterprise.
(2) Expenses may be incurred in operating the enterprise.

As used in accounting, the term expense in nearly all cases means a decrease in the owner's equity in a business caused by transactions involving asset outflows other than a withdrawal by the owner. When an expense is incurred, either the assets are reduced or the liabilities are increased. In either event, owner's equity is reduced. If a transaction causing a reduction is not a withdrawal of assets by the owner, an expense is incurred. Common examples of expense are rent of office or store, salaries of employees, telephone service, supplies consumed, and many types of taxes.

If during a specified period of time, the total increases in owner's equity resulting from revenue exceed the total decreases resulting from expenses, it may be said that the excess represents the net income or net profit for the period.

Revenue > Expenses = Net Profit

On the other hand, if the expenses of the period exceed the revenue, such excess represents a net loss for the period.

Expenses > Revenue = Net Loss

The time interval used in the measurement of net income or net loss can be determined by the owner. It may be a month, a quarter (three months), a year, or some other period of time. Any accounting period of twelve months' duration is usually referred to as a fiscal year. The fiscal year frequently coincides with the calendar year.

Transactions involving revenue and expense always cause a change in the owner's equity element of an enterprise. Such changes could be recorded by debiting an account called Owner's Equity for expense and crediting it for revenue. If this practice were followed, however, the credit side of the owner's equity account would contain a mixture of increases due to revenue and to the investment of assets in the business by the owner, while the debit side would contain a mixture of decreases due to expenses and to the withdrawal of assets from the business by the owner. In order to determine the net income or the net loss for each accounting period, a careful analysis of the owner's equity account would be required. It is, therefore, better practice to record revenue and expenses in separate accounts.

When a transaction produces revenue, the amount of the revenue should be credited to an appropriate revenue account. When a transaction involves expense, the amount of the expense should be debited to an appropriate expense account. The relationship of these accounts to the owner's equity account and the application of the debit and credit theory to the accounts are indicated in the following diagram:

All Owner's Equity Accounts

Debit	Credit
to enter	to enter
decreases	increases
(−)	(+)

All Expense Accounts

Debit	Credit
to enter	to enter
increases	decreases
(+)	(−)

All Revenue Accounts

Debit	Credit
to enter	to enter
decreases	increases
(−)	(+)

The revenue and expense accounts are called temporary owner's equity accounts because it is customary to close them (set their balances back to zero) at the end of each accounting period. It is important to recognize that the credit side of each revenue account is serving temporarily as a part of the credit side of the owner's equity account. Increases in owner's equity are entered as credits. Thus increases in owner's equity resulting from revenue should be credited to revenue accounts. The debit side of each expense account is serving temporarily as a part of the debit side of the owner's equity account. Decreases in owner's equity are entered as debits. Thus decreases in owner's equity resulting from expense should be debited to expense accounts.

USE OF REVENUE AND EXPENSE ACCOUNTS

To illustrate the application of the double-entry process in recording transactions that affect revenue and expense accounts, the transactions that follow will be analyzed and their effect on the accounting elements will be indicated by showing the proper entries in T accounts. These transactions represent a continuation of the transactions completed by Edward Foote, an attorney, in the conduct of his practice. (See pages 15–17 for Transactions (a) to (d).)

Transaction (e)

An Increase in an Asset Offset by an Increase in Owner's Equity Resulting from Revenue

Received $1,800 in cash from a client for professional services rendered.

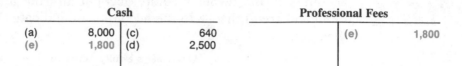

Cash				Professional Fees	
(a)	8,000	(c)	640		
(e)	1,800	(d)	2,500	(e)	1,800

Analysis: This transaction results in an increase in the asset cash with a corresponding increase in owner's equity because of revenue from professional fees. To record the transaction properly, Cash was debited and an appropriate account for the revenue was credited for $1,800. Accounts should always be given a descriptive title that will aid in classifying them in relation to the accounting elements. In this case the revenue account was given the title, Professional Fees. Note that this is the fourth entry in the cash account and the first entry in the account, Professional Fees.

Transaction (f)

A Decrease in an Asset Offset by a Decrease in Owner's Equity Resulting from Expense

(1) Paid $350 for office rent for one month.

Cash				Rent Expense	
(a)	8,000	(c)	640	(f1)	350
(e)	1,800	(d)	2,500		
		(f1)	350		

Analysis: This transaction resulted in a decrease in the asset cash with a corresponding decrease in owner's equity because of expense. To record the transaction properly, Rent Expense was debited and Cash was credited for $350. This is the first entry in the rent expense account and the fifth entry in the cash account.

(2) Paid bill for telephone service, $42.

Cash				Telephone Expense	
(a)	8,000	(c)	640	(f2)	42
(e)	1,800	(d)	2,500		
		(f1)	350		
		(f2)	42		

Analysis: This transaction is identical with the previous one except that telephone expense rather than rent expense was the reason for the decrease in owner's equity. To record the transaction properly, Telephone Expense was debited and Cash was credited for $42. This is the first entry in the telephone expense account and the sixth entry in the cash account.

THE TRIAL BALANCE

It is a fundamental principle of double-entry bookkeeping that the sum of the assets is always equal to the sum of the liabilities and owner's equity. In order to maintain this equality in recording transactions, the sum of the debit entries must always be equal to the sum of the credit entries. To determine whether this equality has been maintained, it is customary to take a trial balance periodically. A trial balance is a list of all of the accounts showing the title and balance of each account. The balance of any account is the amount of difference between the total debits and the total credits to that account. To determine the balance of each account, the debit and credit amount columns should be totaled. This procedure is called footing the amount columns as illustrated below:

Cash			
(a)	8,000	(c)	640
(e)	1,800	(d)	2,500
6,268	*9,800*	(f1)	350
		(f2)	42
			3,532

If there is only one item entered in a column, no footing is necessary. To find the balance of an account, it is necessary only to determine the difference between the footings by subtraction.

Since asset and expense accounts are debited for increases, these accounts normally have debit balances. Since liability, owner's equity, and revenue accounts are credited to record increases, these accounts normally have credit balances. The balance of an account should be entered on the side of the account that has the larger total. The footings and balances of accounts should be entered in small figures just below the last entry. A pencil is generally used for this purpose. If the two footings of an account are equal in amount, the account is said to be in balance.

The accounts of Edward Foote are reproduced on page 22. To show their relationship to the fundamental accounting equation, the accounts are arranged in three columns under the headings of Assets, Liabilities, and Owner's Equity. The footings and the balance are printed in italics. Note the position of the footings directly under the debit and credit amount columns of the cash account, and the position of the balance on the left side of the cash account. (The balance of the accounts payable account is shown on the credit side in italics.) It is not necessary to enter the balances of the other accounts because there are entries on only one side of those accounts.

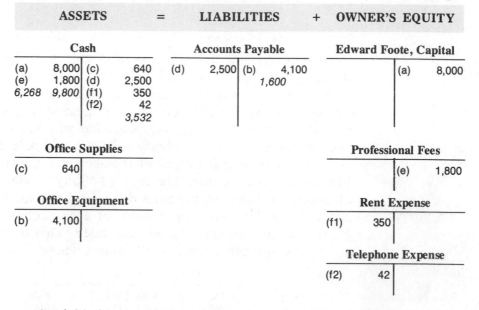

A trial balance of Edward Foote's accounts is shown below. The trial balance was taken on June 30, 1982; therefore, this date is

Edward Foote, Attorney
Trial Balance
June 30, 1982

Account	Dr. Balance	Cr. Balance
Cash	6268 00	
Office Supplies	640 00	
Office Equipment	4100 00	
Accounts Payable		1600 00
Edward Foote, Capital		8000 00
Professional Fees		1800 00
Rent Expense	350 00	
Telephone Expense	42 00	
	11400 00	11400 00

Edward Foote's Trial Balance

shown on the third line of the heading. The trial balance shows that the debit and credit totals are equal in amount. This is proof that in recording Transactions (a) to (f) inclusive the total of the debits was equal to the total of the credits.

A trial balance is not a formal statement or report. Normally, it is never seen by anyone except the accountant or bookkeeper. It is used as an aid in preparing the income statement and the balance sheet. If the trial balance is studied in conjunction with the income statement and the balance sheet shown on page 11, it will be seen that those statements could have been prepared quite easily from the information that this trial balance provides.

BUILDING YOUR ACCOUNTING KNOWLEDGE

1. Identify at least three ways in which account record forms may be developed and kept.
2. What is the standard form of account designed to facilitate?
3. What are the three major parts of the standard account form?
4. Explain the basis of the abbreviations "Dr." for debit and "Cr." for credit.
5. What word is sometimes used as a substitute for debit?
6. In most cases an increase in owner's equity due to revenue results from what event?
7. When an expense is incurred, what may be the effect on the assets? What may be the effect on the liabilities?
8. What is the purpose of the trial balance?

Report No. 1-2

> *Refer to the study assignments and complete Report No. 1-2 in accordance with the instructions given therein. The work involved in completing the assignment requires a knowledge of the principles developed in the preceding discussion. Any difficulty experienced in completing the report will indicate a lack of understanding of these principles. In such event further study, using the vocabulary words on page 24, should be helpful. After completing the report, you may continue with the textbook discussion in Chapter 2 until the next report is required.*

EXPANDING YOUR BUSINESS VOCABULARY

What is the meaning of each of the following terms?

account (p. 13)
accountant (p. 4)
accounting equation (p. 6)
account payable (p. 5)
account receivable (p. 4)
assets (p. 4)
auditing (p. 2)
balance (p. 21)
balance sheet (p. 11)
bookkeeper (p. 4)
business accounting (p. 3)
business entity (p. 4)
capital (p. 5)
charge (p. 14)
credit (p. 14)
credit balances (p. 21)
debit (p. 14)
debit balances (p. 21)
double-entry bookkeeping
    (p. 12)
expense (p. 18)
fiscal year (p. 18)
footing (p. 21)

in balance (p. 21)
income statement (p. 10)
information processor (p. 4)
liability (p. 5)
net income (p. 18)
net loss (p. 18)
net worth (p. 5)
notes payable (p. 5)
operating statement (p. 10)
owner's equity (p. 5)
profit and loss statement (p. 10)
proprietorship (p. 5)
revenue (p. 17)
statement of financial condition
    (p. 11)
statement of financial position
    (p. 11)
temporary owner's equity
    accounts (p. 19)
transaction (p. 7)
trial balance (p. 21)
T account (p. 14)

CHAPTER 2

ACCOUNTING PROCEDURE

CHAPTER OBJECTIVES

The objectives of this chapter are to enable you:

▶ To recognize the flow of the financial data in an accounting information system — the basic accounting cycle.

▶ To explain the purpose of a book of original entry.

▶ To describe the chart of accounts as a means of classifying financial information, using an account numbering system.

▶ To perform the journalizing and posting process.

▶ To prepare the income statement and the balance sheet.

The principles of double-entry bookkeeping were explained and illustrated in the preceding chapter. To avoid complicating these principles, the mechanics of collecting and classifying information about business transactions were ignored. In actual practice, the first record of a transaction, sometimes called the source document, is in the form of a business paper, such as a check stub, receipt, cash register tape, sales ticket, or purchase invoice. The information supplied by source documents is an aid in analyzing transactions to determine their effect upon the accounts.

JOURNALIZING TRANSACTIONS

The record or book in which the first formal double-entry record of a transaction is made is called a journal. The act of recording transactions in a journal is called journalizing. It is necessary to analyze each transaction before it can be journalized properly. The purpose of a series of journal entries is to provide a chronological record of all transactions completed by the business showing the date of each transaction, titles of the accounts to be debited and credited, and the amounts of the debits and credits. The journal then provides all the information needed to transfer the debits and credits to the proper accounts. When the accounts are grouped together, they collectively comprise a ledger. The flow of data concerning transactions can be illustrated in the following manner:

Business transactions are
evidenced by various
SOURCE DOCUMENTS ⟶ The source documents provide the information needed to enter the transactions in a
JOURNAL ⟶ The journal provides the information needed to transfer the debits and credits to the accounts which collectively comprise a
LEDGER

SOURCE DOCUMENTS

The term source document covers a wide variety of forms and papers. Almost any document that provides information about a business transaction can be called a source document

SOURCE DOCUMENTS

Examples:	*Provide information about:*
(1) Check stubs or carbon copies of checks	Cash disbursements
(2) Receipt stubs, carbon copies of receipts, cash register tapes, or memos of cash register totals	Cash receipts
(3) Copies of sales tickets or sales invoices issued to customers or clients	Sales of goods or services
(4) Purchase invoices received from suppliers	Purchases of goods or services

THE JOURNAL

A journal is commonly referred to as a book of original entry because the first formal accounting record of a transaction is made in a journal from source document information. The format of the pages of a journal varies with the type and size of an enterprise and the nature of its operations. Although a wide variety of journals are used in business, the simplest form of journal is a two-column journal. A standard form of such a journal is illustrated below. A two-column journal has only two amount columns, one for debit amounts and one for credit amounts. In the illustration, the columns have been numbered to facilitate the following discussion.

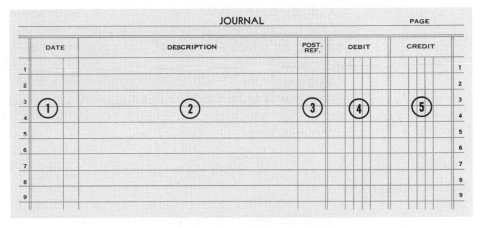

Standard Two-Column Journal

Column 1 is the Date column. The year is written in small figures at the top of the column immediately below the column heading and need only be repeated at the top of each new page unless an entry for a new year is made farther down on the page. The Date column is a double column, the perpendicular single rule being used to separate the month from the day. Thus in writing the date, the name of the month should be written or abbreviated to the left of the single line. The number designating the day of the month should be written to the right of this line. The name of the month need only be shown for the first entry on a page unless an entry for a new month is made farther down on the page.

Column 2 is generally referred to as the Description or explanation column. The Description column is used to record the titles of the accounts affected by each transaction, together with a description of the transaction. Two or more accounts are affected by each transaction, and the titles of all accounts must be recorded. The titles of the accounts debited are written first, followed by the titles of the accounts credited. A separate line should be used for each account title. The titles of the accounts to be debited are written at the extreme left of the column, while the titles of the accounts to be credited are usually indented one-half inch (about 1.3 centimeters). The description should be written immediately following the credit entry and indented an additional one-half inch.

Column 3 is the Posting Reference column sometimes referred to as a folio column. No entries are made in this column at the time of journalizing the transactions; such entries are made only at the time of posting which is the process of entering the debit and credit elements in the proper accounts in the ledger. This procedure will be explained in detail later in this chapter.

Column 4, the Debit amount column, is a column in which the amount that is to be debited to an account should be written on the same line on which the title of that account appears in the description column.

Column 5, the Credit amount column, is a column in which the amount that is to be credited to an account should be written on the same line on which the title of that account appears in the description column.

JOURNALIZING

Journalizing involves recording the significant information concerning each transaction either (1) at the time the transaction occurs or (2) subsequently, but in the chronological order in which it and the other transactions occurred. For every transaction, the entry should record the date, the title of each account affected, the amounts, and a brief description. Before a transaction can be entered properly, it must be analyzed in order to determine:

(1) Which accounts are affected by the transaction.
(2) What effect the transaction has upon each of the accounts involved, that is, whether the balance of each affected account is increased or decreased.

To illustrate the journalizing process, assume that a business purchased a calculator on June 20 for $95 in cash. The asset accounts affected are Office Equipment and Cash. Office Equipment was increased and Cash was decreased upon purchase of the calculator. The following information would be recorded in a two-column journal:

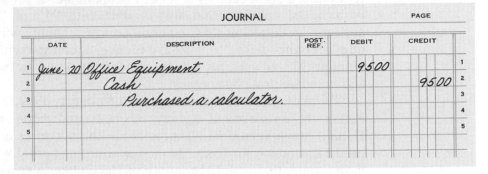

DATE	DESCRIPTION	POST. REF.	DEBIT	CREDIT	
1	June 20 Office Equipment		9500		1
2	Cash			9500	2
3	Purchased a calculator.				3
4					4
5					5

JOURNAL   PAGE

THE CHART OF ACCOUNTS

In analyzing a transaction prior to journalizing it, the accountant or bookkeeper must know which accounts are being kept. When an accounting system is established for a new business, the first step is to decide which accounts are required. The accounts used will depend upon the information needed or desired. Ordinarily, it is desirable to keep a separate account for each type of asset and each type of liability, since it is certain that information will be desired in regard to what is owned and what is owed. A permanent owner's equity or capital account should be kept in order that information may be available as to the owner's interest in the business. Furthermore, it is advisable to keep separate accounts for each type of revenue and each kind of expense. The revenue and expense accounts are temporary accounts that are used in recording increases and decreases in owner's equity from day-to-day business transactions apart from changes caused by the owner's investments and withdrawals. The specific accounts to be kept for recording increases and decreases in owner's equity depend upon the nature and sources of the revenue and the nature of the expenses incurred in earning the revenue.

A professional person or an individual engaged in operating a small enterprise may need to keep relatively few accounts. On the other hand, a large business may need to keep a great many accounts because of the complexity of the operation. Regardless of the number, accounts can be segregated into the three major classes, assets, liabilities, and owner's equity, and should be grouped according to these classes in the ledger. Assets accounts are placed first, liability accounts second, and owner's equity accounts, including revenue and expense accounts, last. A list of all the accounts used by a business is called a chart of accounts. It has become a general practice to give each account a number and to keep the accounts in numerical order. The numbering usually follows a consistent pattern and becomes a code. For example, asset accounts may be assigned numbers that always start with ''1'' or ''2,'' liability accounts with ''3'' or ''4,'' owner's equity accounts with ''5,'' revenue accounts with ''6,'' and expense accounts with ''8.'' The number ''7'' is used for a type of account found in merchandising and manufacturing businesses.

To illustrate, assume that on December 1, 1982, Donald Mays enters the employment agency business under the name of The Donald Mays Personnel Agency. Since the accounts are to be kept on the calendar-year basis, the first accounting period will be for one month only, that is, for the month of December. A two-column journal and a ledger will be used. Mays realizes that there will not be a need for many accounts at present because the business is new but that additional accounts may be added as the need arises. A chart of the accounts for the agency is shown below:

THE DONALD MAYS PERSONNEL AGENCY
CHART OF ACCOUNTS

Assets*
- 111 Cash
- 181 Office Supplies
- 211 Office Equipment

Liabilities
- 318 Accounts Payable

Owner's Equity
- 511 Donald Mays, Capital
- 511.1 Donald Mays, Drawing**

Revenue
- 611 Placement Fees

Expenses
- 821 Rent Expense
- 822 Salary Expense
- 823 Travel and Entertainment Expense
- 824 Telephone Expense
- 825 Office Supplies Expense
- 839 Miscellaneous Expense

*Words in heavy type represent headings and not account titles.
**The number of this account will have four digits with a decimal point separating the third and fourth digits. The first three digits will be the same as the capital account to indicate that its balance is subtracted from the capital account balance on the balance sheet. A similar procedure will be followed for all accounts whose balances are subtracted from other related account balances on the financial statements.

JOURNALIZING PROCEDURE ILLUSTRATED

To illustrate journalizing procedures, the transactions completed by The Donald Mays Personnel Agency through December 31, 1982, will be journalized. A narrative of the transactions follows which provides all of the information needed in journalizing the transactions. Some of the transactions are analyzed to explain their effect upon the accounts. The analysis will immediately follow the journal entry.

THE DONALD MAYS PERSONNEL AGENCY

NARRATIVE OF TRANSACTIONS

Wednesday, December 1, 1982

Mays invested $3,500 cash in a business enterprise to be known as The Donald Mays Personnel Agency.

	DATE	DESCRIPTION	POST. REF.	DEBIT	CREDIT	
		JOURNAL			PAGE 1	
1	1982 Dec. 1	Cash		350000		1
2		Donald Mays, Capital			350000	2
3		Original investment				3
4		in personnel agency.				4
5						5

Analysis: As a result of this transaction, the business acquired the asset cash in the amount of $3,500. Since Mays contributed this asset, the transaction caused an increase of $3,500 in owner's equity. Accordingly, the entry to record the transaction is a debit to Cash and a credit to Donald Mays, Capital, for $3,500.

Note that the following steps are involved:

(1) Since this was the first entry on the journal page, the year is written at the top of the Date column.
(2) The month (abbreviated) and day are written on the first line in the Date column.
(3) The title of the account to be debited, Cash, is written on the first line at the extreme left of the Description column. The amount of the debit, $3,500, is written on the same line in the Debit column.
(4) The title of the account to be credited, Donald Mays, Capital, is written on the second line indented one-half inch from the left side of the Description column. The amount of the credit, $3,500, is written on the same line in the Credit column.
(5) The explanation of the entry is started on the next line indented an additional one-half inch. The second line of the explanation is also indented the same distance as the first.

Friday, December 3

Paid office rent for December, $400.

5	1982 Dec. 3	Rent Expense		40000		5
6		Cash			40000	6
7		Paid December rent.				7

Analysis: This transaction resulted in an increase in an expense, with a corresponding decrease in the asset cash. The increase in the expense represents a decrease in owner's equity. The transaction is recorded by debiting Rent Expense and by crediting Cash for $400.

Mays ordered several pieces of office equipment. Since the dealer did not have in stock what Mays wanted, the articles were ordered from the factory. Delivery is not expected until the latter part of the month. Pending arrival of the equipment, the dealer loaned Mays some used office equipment. No entry is required until the new equipment is received.

Monday, December 6

Purchased office supplies from the Clark Peeper Co. on account, $327.

8	6 Office Supplies		327 00		8
9	Accounts Payable			327 00	9
10	Clark Peeper Co.				10

Analysis: In this transaction, the business acquired a new asset which represented an increase in the total assets. A liability was also incurred because of the purchase on account. The transaction is recorded by debiting Office Supplies and crediting Accounts Payable for $327. As these supplies are consumed, the amount will become an expense of the business.

Tuesday, December 7

Paid the Continental Telephone Co. $35 covering the cost of installing a telephone in the office, together with the first month's service charges payable in advance.

11	7 Telephone Expense		35 00		11
12	Cash			35 00	12
13	Paid telephone bill.				13

Analysis: This transaction caused an increase in an expense and a corresponding decrease in the asset cash. The transaction is recorded by debiting Telephone Expense and by crediting Cash for $35.

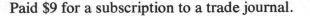

Wednesday, December 8

Paid $9 for a subscription to a trade journal.

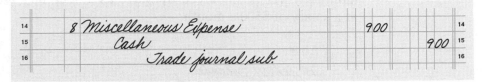

14	8 Miscellaneous Expense		9 00		14
15	Cash			9 00	15
16	Trade journal sub.				16

Analysis: This transaction resulted in an increase in an expense and a corresponding decrease in the asset cash. The transaction is recorded by debiting Miscellaneous Expense and by crediting Cash for $9.

Thursday, December 9

Received $250 from Bradley Swalwell for placement services rendered.

17	9 Cash		250 00		17
18	Placement Fees			250 00	18
19	Bradley Swalwell.				19

Analysis: This transaction resulted in an increase in the asset cash with a corresponding increase in revenue from placement fees. The transaction is recorded by debiting Cash and by crediting Placement Fees for $250. In keeping the accounts, Mays follows the practice of not recording revenue until it is received in cash. This practice is common to professional and personal service enterprises.

Friday, December 10

Paid the Aldine Travel Service $165 for an airplane ticket to be used the next week for an employment agency convention trip.

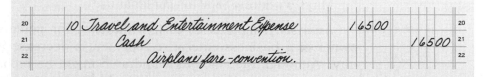

20	10 Travel and Entertainment Expense		165 00		20
21	Cash			165 00	21
22	Airplane fare - convention.				22

Analysis: This transaction resulted in an increase in an expense and a corresponding decrease in the asset cash. The transaction is recorded by debiting Travel and Entertainment Expense and by crediting Cash for $165.

Wednesday, December 15

Paid Mary Wurtz $250 covering her salary for the first half of the month: Wurtz is employed by Mays as a secretary and bookkeeper at a salary of $500 a month.

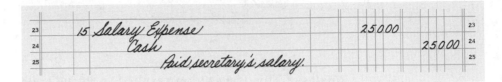

Analysis: This transaction resulted in an increase in salary expense with a corresponding decrease in the asset cash. The transaction is recorded by debiting Salary Expense and by crediting Cash for $250. (The matter of payroll taxes is purposely ignored at this point. These taxes will be discussed in detail in Chapter 4.)

Note that the Posting Reference column has been left blank in the eight preceding journal entry illustrations. This is because the column is not used until the amounts are posted to the accounts in the ledger, a process to be described starting on page 38. Account numbers are shown in the Posting Reference column of the journal illustrated on pages 36 and 37, since the illustration shows how the journal appears after the posting has been completed.

The journal entries for the following transactions (as well as for those to this point) are illustrated on pages 36 and 37.

Monday, December 20

Received $600 from Robert Lewis for placement services rendered.

Wednesday, December 22

Mays withdrew $800 for personal use.

Analysis: Amounts of cash withdrawn for personal use by the owner of a business enterprise represent a decrease in owner's equity. Although the amounts withdrawn might be recorded as debits to the owner's capital account, it is better practice to record withdrawals in a separate account, Donald Mays, Drawing, since this makes it easier to summarize the owner's withdrawals. This transaction is recorded in the journal by debiting Donald Mays, Drawing, and by crediting Cash for $800.

Friday, December 24

Received $700 from Leesa Gornish for services rendered.

Tuesday, December 28

Paid $60 membership dues in the National Placement Officers' Association.

Wednesday, December 29

Received the office equipment ordered December 3. These items were purchased on account from the Shaw-Walker Office Equipment Co. for $3,050. The dealer removed the used equipment that had been loaned to Mays.

Thursday, December 30

Paid the Clark-Peeper Co. $327 for the office supplies purchased on December 6.

Analysis: This transaction caused a decrease in the liability accounts payable with a corresponding decrease in the asset cash. The transaction is recorded by debiting Accounts Payable and by crediting Cash for $327.

Received from Ellen Lim $550 for placement services rendered.

Friday, December 31

Paid Wurtz $250 covering her salary for the second half of the month.
Office supplies used during the month, $55.

Analysis: By referring to the transaction of December 6, it will be noted that office supplies amounting to $327 were purchased and were recorded as an asset. By taking an inventory, counting the supplies in stock at the end of the month, Mays was able to determine that the expense of supplies used during the month amounted to $55. The total expenses for the month of December would not be reflected properly if the supplies used during the month were not taken into consideration. Therefore, the expense of supplies used is recorded by debiting the expense account, Office Supplies Expense, and by crediting the asset account, Office Supplies, for $55.

Note that in the journal illustrated on pages 36 and 37 there are no blank lines between the entries. Some bookkeepers leave a blank

	JOURNAL			PAGE 1

	DATE	DESCRIPTION	POST. REF.	DEBIT	CREDIT	
1	1982 Dec. 1	Cash	111	350000		1
2		Donald Mays, Capital	511		350000	2
3		Original investment				3
4		in personnel agency.				4
5	3	Rent Expense	821	40000		5
6		Cash	111		40000	6
7		Paid December rent.				7
8	6	Office Supplies	181	32700		8
9		Accounts Payable	318		32700	9
10		Clark-Peeper Co.				10
11	7	Telephone Expense	824	3500		11
12		Cash	111		3500	12
13		Paid telephone bill.				13
14	8	Miscellaneous Expense	839	900		14
15		Cash	111		900	15
16		Trade journal sub.				16
17	9	Cash	111	25000		17
18		Placement Fees	611		25000	18
19		Bradley Swalwell.				19
20	10	Travel and Entertainment Expense	823	16500		20
21		Cash	111		16500	21
22		Airplane fare, convention.				22
23	15	Salary Expense	822	25000		23
24		Cash	111		25000	24
25		Paid secretary's salary.				25
26	20	Cash	111	60000		26
27		Placement Fees	611		60000	27
28		Robert Lewis.				28
29	22	Donald Mays, Drawing	511.1	80000		29
30		Cash	111		80000	30
31		Withdrawn for personal use.				31
32	24	Cash	111	70000		32
33		Placement Fees	611		70000	33
34		Leesa Gornish.				34
35	28	Miscellaneous Expense	839	6000		35
36		Cash	111		6000	36
37		N.P.O.A. dues.				37
38	29	Office Equipment	211	305000		38
39		Accounts Payable	318		305000	39
40		Shaw-Walker Office Equip. Co.		1014600	1014600	40

The Donald Mays Personnel Agency Journal
(continued on next page)

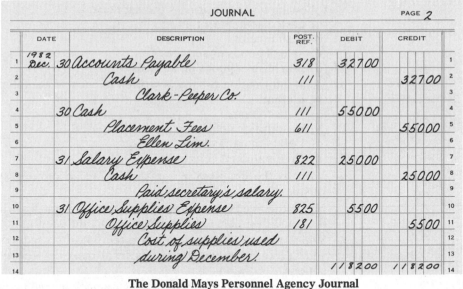

DATE	DESCRIPTION	POST. REF.	DEBIT	CREDIT	
1982 Dec. 30	Accounts Payable	318	32700		1
	Cash	111		32700	2
	Clark-Peeper Co.				3
30	Cash	111	55000		4
	Placement Fees	611		55000	5
	Ellen Lim				6
31	Salary Expense	822	25000		7
	Cash	111		25000	8
	Paid secretary's salary				9
31	Office Supplies Expense	825	5500		10
	Office Supplies	181		5500	11
	Cost of supplies used				12
	during December				13
			118200	118200	14

The Donald Mays Personnel Agency Journal
(concluded)

line after the explanation of each entry. This practice is acceptable, though not recommended, because it provides an opportunity for dishonest persons to alter one or more entries.

PROVING THE JOURNAL

Because a double entry is made for each transaction, the equality of debit and credit entries on each page of the journal may be proved merely by totaling the amount columns. The total of each column is entered as a footing immediately under the last entry. When a page of the journal is filled, the footings may be entered just under the last single horizontal ruled line at the bottom of the page as shown in the illustration on page 36. When it is desirable to prove the equality of debits and credits on a page that is not filled, the footings should be entered immediately under the last entry as shown in the above illustration.

BUILDING YOUR ACCOUNTING KNOWLEDGE

1. Where is the first formal accounting record of a transaction usually made?

2. Name a source document that provides information about each of the following types of business transactions:
   (a) cash disbursement
   (b) cash receipt
   (c) sale of goods or services
   (d) purchase of goods or services

3. What information usually is written in each of the following columns of the journal?
   (a) Date column
   (b) Description column
   (c) Debit amount column
   (d) Credit amount column

4. What is the first step in establishing an accounting system for a new business?

5. Name the five types of financial statement items for which it is ordinarily found desirable to keep separate accounts.

6. Which two types of accounts are temporarily used to record increases and decreases in owner's equity from most day-to-day business transactions?

7. In what order are the accounts customarily placed in the ledger?

Report No. 2-1

> *Refer to the study assignments and complete Report No. 2-1. To complete this assignment correctly, the principles developed in the preceding discussion must be understood. Review the text assignment if necessary. After completing the report, continue with the following textbook discussion until the next report is required.*

POSTING TO THE LEDGER; THE TRIAL BALANCE

The purpose of a journal is to provide a chronological record of financial transactions expressed as debits and credits to accounts. Accounts are kept to supply management with desired information in summary form. Collectively, the accounts are known as the general ledger, or often simply as "the ledger." The account forms may be on sheets of paper or on cards. When on sheets of paper, the sheets may be bound in book form or kept in a loose-leaf binder. Usually a separate page or card is used for each account. The accounts should be classified properly in the ledger; that is, the asset accounts should be grouped together, the liability accounts together, and the owner's equity accounts together. Proper grouping of the accounts in the ledger is an aid in preparing the various reports desired by the owner. Mays decided to keep all of the accounts for the personnel agency in a loose-leaf ledger. The numbers shown in the agency's chart of accounts on page 30 were used as a guide in arranging the accounts in the ledger. The ledger is reproduced on pages 41–43. Note that the accounts are in numerical order.

Since Mays makes few purchases on account, a separate account is not kept for each supplier. When invoices are received for items purchased on account, the invoices are checked and entered in the journal by debiting the proper accounts and by crediting Accounts Payable. The credit balance of Accounts Payable indicates the total amount owed to suppliers. After each invoice is recorded, it is filed in an unpaid invoice file, where it remains until it is paid in full. When an invoice is paid in full, it is removed from the unpaid invoice file and then filed under the name of the supplier for future reference. The balance of the accounts payable account may be proved at any time by determining the total of the unpaid amounts of the invoices.

POSTING

The process of transferring information from the journal to the ledger is known as posting. All amounts entered in the journal should be posted to the accounts kept in the ledger in order to summarize the results. Such posting may be done daily or at frequent intervals. The ledger is not a reliable source of information until all of the transactions recorded in the journal have been posted. Since the accounts provide the information needed in preparing financial statements, an accurate posting procedure must be maintained.

Posting from the journal to the ledger involves entering the following information in the accounts:

(1) The date of each transaction.
(2) The amount of each transaction.
(3) The page of the journal from which each transaction is posted.

The posting procedure also requires that after the page of the journal has been posted to the ledger account, the number of that account should be entered in the Posting Reference column in the journal so as to provide a cross-reference between the journal and the ledger.

The first entry of the agency to be posted from the journal occurred on December 1, 1982, and required a debit to cash of $3,500.

The posting is, as illustrated below, accomplished by (1) entering the year, "1982," the month, abbreviated "Dec.," and the day, "1," in the Date column of the cash account, (2) entering the amount, $3,500, in the Debit column, (3) entering the number "1" in the Posting Reference column since the posting came from Page 1 of the journal, and (4) entering the cash account number 111 in the Posting Reference column of the journal on the same line as the debit to Cash for $3,500. The same pattern is followed in posting the credit part of the entry, $3,500, to Donald Mays, Capital, Account No. 511.

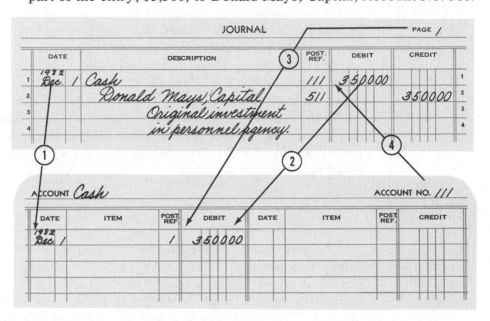

Reference to the journal of The Donald Mays Personnel Agency (reproduced on pages 36 and 37) and its ledger (reproduced on pages 41–43) will indicate that a similar procedure is followed in posting every amount from the journal. Note also that in the ledger, the year "1982" is entered only at the top of each Date column, and that the month "Dec." is entered only with the first posting to an account.

ACCOUNT *Cash*   ACCOUNT NO. *111*

DATE	ITEM	POST. REF.	DEBIT	DATE	ITEM	POST. REF.	CREDIT
1982 Dec. 1		1	3500 00	1982 Dec. 3		1	400 00
9		1	250 00	7		1	35 00
20		1	600 00	8		1	9 00
24		1	700 00	10		1	165 00
30	3,304.00	2	550 00	15		1	250 00
			5600 00	22		1	800 00
				28		1	60 00
				30		2	327 00
				31		2	250 00
							2296 00

ACCOUNT *Office Supplies*   ACCOUNT NO. *181*

DATE	ITEM	POST. REF.	DEBIT	DATE	ITEM	POST. REF.	CREDIT
1982 Dec. 6	272.00	1	327 00	1982 Dec. 31		2	55 00

ACCOUNT *Office Equipment*   ACCOUNT NO. *211*

DATE	ITEM	POST. REF.	DEBIT	DATE	ITEM	POST. REF.	CREDIT
1982 Dec. 29		1	3050 00				

ACCOUNT *Accounts Payable*   ACCOUNT NO. *318*

DATE	ITEM	POST. REF.	DEBIT	DATE	ITEM	POST. REF.	CREDIT
1982 Dec. 30		2	327 00	1982 Dec. 6		1	327 00
				29	3,050.00	1	3050 00
							3377 00

ACCOUNT *Donald Mays, Capital*   ACCOUNT NO. *511*

DATE	ITEM	POST. REF.	DEBIT	DATE	ITEM	POST. REF.	CREDIT
				1982 Dec. 1		1	3500 00

The Donald Mays Personnel Agency Ledger
(continued on next page)

ACCOUNT	Donald Mays, Drawing						ACCOUNT NO. 511.1	
DATE	ITEM	POST. REF.	DEBIT	DATE	ITEM	POST. REF.	CREDIT	
1982 Dec. 22		1	800 00					

ACCOUNT	Placement Fees						ACCOUNT NO. 611	
DATE	ITEM	POST. REF.	DEBIT	DATE	ITEM	POST. REF.	CREDIT	
				1982 Dec. 9		1	250 00	
				20		1	600 00	
				24		1	700 00	
				30		2	550 00	
							2 1 0 0 00	

ACCOUNT	Rent Expense						ACCOUNT NO. 821	
DATE	ITEM	POST. REF.	DEBIT	DATE	ITEM	POST. REF.	CREDIT	
1982 Dec. 3		1	400 00					

ACCOUNT	Salary Expense						ACCOUNT NO. 822	
DATE	ITEM	POST. REF.	DEBIT	DATE	ITEM	POST. REF.	CREDIT	
1982 Dec. 15		1	250 00					
31		2	250 00					
			5 0 0 00					

ACCOUNT	Travel and Entertainment Expense						ACCOUNT NO. 823	
DATE	ITEM	POST. REF.	DEBIT	DATE	ITEM	POST. REF.	CREDIT	
1982 Dec. 10		1	165 00					

The Donald Mays Personnel Agency Ledger
(continued)

| ACCOUNT *Telephone Expense* | | | | | | | ACCOUNT NO. *824* |
DATE	ITEM	POST. REF.	DEBIT	DATE	ITEM	POST. REF.	CREDIT
1952 Dec. 7		1	35 00				

| ACCOUNT *Office Supplies Expense* | | | | | | | ACCOUNT NO. *825* |
DATE	ITEM	POST. REF.	DEBIT	DATE	ITEM	POST. REF.	CREDIT
1952 Dec. 31		2	55 00				

| ACCOUNT *Miscellaneous Expense* | | | | | | | ACCOUNT NO. *839* |
DATE	ITEM	POST. REF.	DEBIT	DATE	ITEM	POST. REF.	CREDIT
1952 Dec. 8		1	9 00				
28		1	60 00				
			69 00				

The Donald Mays Personnel Agency Ledger
(concluded)

As seen from the preceding discussion, when the posting is completed, the same information is provided in both the journal and the ledger as to the date, the amount, and the effect of each transaction. A cross-reference from each book to the other book is provided by the Posting Reference column. Each entry in the journal may be traced to the ledger by referring to the account numbers indicated in the Posting Reference column of the journal. The cross reference also makes it possible to trace the entry in the ledger to the journal by referring to the page indicated in the Posting Reference column. By referring to pages 36 and 37, it will be seen that the account numbers were inserted in the Posting Reference column. This was done as each part of the posting was completed.

THE TRIAL BALANCE

As indicated in Chapter 1, the purpose of a trial balance is to prove that the totals of the debit and credit balances in the ledger are equal. In a double-entry framework, equality of debit and credit balances in the ledger must be maintained. A trial balance may be taken daily, weekly, monthly, or whenever desired. Before taking a trial balance, all transactions should be journalized and the posting should be completed in order that the effect of all transactions to date will be reflected in the ledger accounts.

Footing Accounts. Prior to taking a trial balance it is necessary to (1) foot — add the amounts recorded on the debit and credit side of each account and (2) determine the balance of the account. The footing process is illustrated below. The footings are recorded immediately below the last item in both the debit and credit amount columns of the account. The footings should be written in small figures close to the preceding line so that they will not interfere with the recording of an item on the next ruled line. At the same time, the balance (the difference between the footings) is computed and recorded in small figures in the Item column of the account on the side with the larger footing. In other words, if an account has a debit balance, the balance should be written in the Item column on the debit or left side of the account just below the line on which the last regular entry appears and in line with the footing. If the account has a credit balance, the balance should be written in the Item column on the credit or right side of the account just below the line in which the last regular entry appears.

ACCOUNT *Cash*							ACCOUNT NO. *111*
DATE	ITEM	POST. REF.	DEBIT	DATE	ITEM	POST. REF.	CREDIT
1982 Dec. 1		1	3 5 0 0 00	1982 Dec. 3		1	4 0 0 00
9		1	2 5 0 00	7		1	3 5 00
20		1	6 0 0 00	8		1	9 00
24		1	7 0 0 00	10		1	1 6 5 00
30		2	5 5 0 00	15		1	2 5 0 00
	3,504.00		5 6 0 0 00	22		1	8 0 0 00
				28		1	6 0 00
				30		2	3 2 7 00
				31		2	2 5 0 00
							2 2 9 6 00

Reference to the accounts kept in the ledger shown on pages 41–43 reveals that the accounts have been footed and shows how the footings and the balances are recorded. When only one item has been posted to an account, regardless of whether it is a debit or a credit amount, no footing is necessary.

Care should be used in computing the balances of the accounts. If an error is made in adding the amount columns or in determining the difference between the footings, the error will be carried to the trial balance and considerable time may be required to locate the mistake. Most accounting errors result from carelessness. For example, a bookkeeper may write an account balance on the wrong side of an account by mistake or may enter figures so illegibly that they may be misread later. Neatness in writing the amounts is just as important as accuracy in determining the footings and the balances.

Preparing the Trial Balance. It is important that the following procedure be followed in preparing a trial balance:

(1) Head the trial balance showing (a) the name of the individual, firm, or organization, (b) the title of the report, "Trial Balance," and (c) the date. The date shown is the day of the last transaction that is included in the accounts, which is usually the last day of a month. A December 31 trial balance might be prepared by the bookkeeper on January 3, however, the accounts should reflect only transactions through December 31.

(2) List the account titles in order, showing each account number.

(3) Record the account balances, entering debit balances in the left amount column and credit balances in the right amount column.

(4) Add the columns and record the totals, ruling a single line across the amount columns above the totals and a double line below the totals in the manner shown in the illustration below.

Account	Acct. No.	Dr. Balance	Cr. Balance
Cash	111	330400	
Office Supplies	181	27200	
Office Equipment	211	305000	
Accounts Payable	318		305000
Donald Mays, Capital	511		350000
Donald Mays, Drawing	511.1	80000	
Placement Fees	611		210000
Rent Expense	821	40000	
Salary Expense	822	50000	
Travel and Entertainment Expense	823	16500	
Telephone Expense	824	3500	
Office Supplies Expense	825	5500	
Miscellaneous Expense	839	6900	
		865000	865000

Donald Mays Personnel Agency
Trial Balance
December 31, 1982

Model Trial Balance

A trial balance is usually prepared on ruled paper though it can be written on plain paper if desired. The illustration on page 45 shows the trial balance as of December 31, 1982, of the ledger of The Donald Mays Personnel Agency.

Even though the trial balance indicates that the ledger is in balance, there still may be errors in the ledger. For example, if a journal entry has been made in which the wrong accounts were debited or credited, or if an item has been posted to the wrong account, the ledger will still be in balance. It is important, therefore, that extreme care be used in preparing the journal entries and in posting them to the ledger accounts.

BUILDING YOUR ACCOUNTING KNOWLEDGE

1. What useful purpose is served by proper grouping of the accounts in the ledger?
2. When does the ledger become a reliable source of information?
3. Name the three elements of information normally entered in each ledger account involved in the posting process.
4. What information is entered in the Posting Reference column of the journal as each amount is posted to the proper account in the ledger?
5. Where should the footings of an account be recorded?
6. Where should the balance of an account be recorded?
7. Explain why there still may be errors in the ledger even though the trial balance indicates that the ledger is in balance. Give examples of two such types of errors.

Report No. 2-2

> *Refer to the study assignments and complete Report No. 2-2. To complete this assignment correctly, the principles developed in the preceding discussion must be understood. Review the text assignment if necessary. After completing the report, continue with the following textbook discussion until the next report is required.*

THE FINANCIAL STATEMENTS

The transactions completed by The Donald Mays Personnel Agency during the month of December were recorded in a two-column journal (see pages 36 and 37). The debits and credits were subsequently posted to the proper accounts in a ledger (see pages 41–43). At the end of the month, a trial balance was taken as a means of proving that the equality of debits and credits had been maintained throughout the journalizing and posting process (see page 45).

Although the trial balance of The Donald Mays Personnel Agency taken as of December 31 contains a list of all of the accounts, shows the amounts of their debit and credit balances, and proves the equality of these debit and credit balances, it does not clearly present all of the information that Mays may need regarding either the results of operations during the month or the status of the business at the end of the month. To meet these needs, it is usual practice to prepare two financial statements — the income statement and the balance sheet.

THE INCOME STATEMENT

An income statement is an itemized statement that provides information regarding the results of operations during a specified period of time. It is a statement of the changes in owner's equity resulting from the revenue and expenses of a specific period (month, quarter, or year). Such changes are entered originally in temporary owner's equity accounts known as revenue and expense accounts. Changes in owner's equity resulting from investments or withdrawals of assets by the owner are not included in the income statement because they involve neither revenue nor expense.

The **heading** of an income statement consists of the following:

(1) The name of the business.
(2) The title of the statement.
(3) The period of time covered by the statement.

The **body** of an income statement consists of (1) an itemized list of the sources and amounts of revenue received during the period, and (2) an itemized list of the various expenses incurred during the period. The income statement reflects the matching concept (matching the revenues and expenses of a business on a periodic basis). It is said that this matching process is the "heart" of income measurement.

An income statement prepared from The Donald Mays Personnel Agency trial balance showing the results of operations for the month ended December 31, 1982, is reproduced at the top of page 48.

The financial statements usually are prepared first on ruled paper. Such handwritten copies may then be typed so that a number

Donald Mays Personnel Agency
Income Statement
For the Month Ended December 31, 1982

Revenue:			
Placement fees			$2100 00
Expenses:			
Rent expense	$400 00		
Salary expense	500 00		
Travel and entertainment expense	165 00		
Telephone expense	35 00		
Office supplies expense	55 00		
Miscellaneous expense	69 00		
Total expenses			1224 00
Net income			$876 00

Income Statement

of copies will be available for those who are interested in examining the statements. Since the typewritten copies are not on ruled paper, dollar signs are included in the handwritten copy so that the typist will understand just when they are to be inserted. Note that a dollar sign is placed beside the first amount in each column and the first amount below a ruling in each column. The income statement illustrated above is shown on two-column ruled paper; however, the columns do not have any debit-credit significance. The only source of revenue was placement fees that amounted to $2,100. The total expenses for the month amounted to $1,224. The revenue exceeded the expenses by $876. This represents the amount of the net income for the month. If the total expenses had exceeded the total revenue, the excess would have represented a **net loss** for the month. The information provided by the income statement of The Donald Mays Personnel Agency may be summarized in equation form as follows:

REVENUE − EXPENSES = NET INCOME
$2,100 $1,224 $876

It is apparent that the income statement is more informative than the trial balance as to the results of operations for December. The trial balance contains the necessary data for preparing the income statement, but the income statement presents the data in a more meaningful way.

THE BALANCE SHEET

The balance sheet is an itemized statement of the assets, liabilities, and owner's equity of a business enterprise as of a specified date. Its purpose is to provide information regarding the status of these basic accounting elements as of the close of business on the date indicated in the heading.

The **heading** of a balance sheet contains the following:

(1) The name of the business.
(2) The title of the statement.
(3) The date of the statement as of the close of business on that day.

The **body** of a balance sheet consists of an itemized list of the assets, the liabilities, and the owner's equity, the latter being the difference between the total amount of the assets and the total amount of the liabilities. A balance sheet for The Donald Mays Personnel Agency showing the status of the business when it closed on December 31, 1982, is reproduced on pages 50 and 51. The balance sheet illustrated is arranged like a standard account with the assets listed on the left side and the liabilities and owner's equity listed on the right side. The information provided by the balance sheet of The Donald Mays Personnel Agency may be summarized in equation form as follows:

$$\text{ASSETS} = \text{LIABILITIES} + \text{OWNER'S EQUITY}$$
$$\$6,626 \qquad\quad \$3,050 \qquad\qquad\qquad \$3,576$$

The trial balance was the source of the information needed in listing the assets and liabilities in the balance sheet. The amount of the owner's equity may be calculated by subtracting the total liabilities from the total assets. Thus, Mays' equity as of December 31, 1982, is as follows:

Total assets	$6,626
Less total liabilities	3,050
Owner's equity	$3,576

The owner's equity may also be determined by taking into consideration the following factors:

(1) The **amount invested** in the enterprise by Mays on December 1, as shown by the capital account.
(2) The amount of the **net income** of The Donald Mays Personnel Agency for December, as shown by the income statement.
(3) The total **amount withdrawn** for personal use during December, as shown by Mays' drawing account.

Donald Mays		
Balance		
December		
Assets		
Cash	$3304 00	
Office supplies	272 00	
Office equipment	3050 00	
Total assets		$6626 00

Balance Sheet — Account Form *(Left Page)*

The trial balance on page 45 shows that Mays' equity in The Donald Mays Personnel Agency on December 1 amounted to $3,500. This is indicated by the credit balance of the capital account. The income statement on page 48 shows that the net income of the agency for December amounted to $876. The trial balance also shows that the amount withdrawn by Mays for personal use during the month amounted to $800. This is indicated by the debit balance of the drawing account. On the basis of this information, Mays' equity in The Donald Mays Personnel Agency as of December 31, 1982, is as follows:

Amount of capital, December 1		$3,500
Net income for December	$876	
Less amount withdrawn for personal use during the month	800	76
Capital as of close of business, December 31		$3,576

BUILDING YOUR ACCOUNTING KNOWLEDGE

1. What is the purpose of an income statement?
2. Why are changes in owner's equity resulting from investments or withdrawals of assets by the owner not included in the income statement?
3. What are the three parts of the heading of an income statement?

Personnel Agency
Sheet
31, 1982

Liabilities			
Accounts payable		$3050 00	
Total liabilities			$3050 00
Owner's Equity			
Donald Mays, capital			
Capital, Dec. 1, 1982		$3500 00	
Net income	$876.00		
Less withdrawals	800.00		
Net increase		76 00	
Capital, Dec. 31, 1982			3576 00
Total liabilities and owner's equity			$6626 00

Balance Sheet — Account Form *(Right Page)*

4. What is the purpose of a balance sheet?
5. What are the three parts of the heading of a balance sheet?
6. What is the source of information for preparing both the income statement and the balance sheet?
7. Owner's equity can be calculated by subtracting total liabilities shown by the balance sheet from total assets shown by the balance sheet. What three factors may be used to prove the amount of owner's equity calculated in this manner?

Report No. 2-3

Refer to the study assignments and complete Report 2-3. This assignment provides a test of your ability to apply the principles developed in Chapters 1 and 2 of this textbook. The textbook and the study assignments go hand in hand, each serving a definite purpose in the learning process. Inability to solve correctly any problem included in the report indicates that you have failed to master the principles developed in the textbook. Further study, with the aid of the vocabulary list on page 52, should be helpful in this regard. After completing the report, you may proceed with Chapter 3 until the next report is required.

EXPANDING YOUR BUSINESS VOCABULARY

What is the meaning of each of the following terms:

balance (p. 44)
balance sheet (p. 49)
book of original entry (p. 27)
capital account (p. 29)
chart of accounts (p. 29)
Credit amount column (p. 28)
Date column (p. 27)
Debit amount column (p. 28)
Description column (p. 27)
foot (p. 44)
general ledger (p. 38)

income statement (p. 47)
journal (p. 26)
journalizing (p. 26)
matching concept (p. 47)
owner's equity (p. 29)
posting (p. 39)
Posting Reference column
 (p. 28)
source document (p. 26)
two-column journal (p. 27)

CHAPTER 3

ACCOUNTING FOR CASH

CHAPTER OBJECTIVES

The objectives of this chapter are to enable you:

▶ To explain the meanings of the term "cash" as it is used in accounting.

▶ To describe **internal control** as it relates to the handling of cash.

▶ To explain the operation of a petty cash fund and to prepare a special multicolumn record of cash disbursements.

▶ To describe banking procedures relating to the use of commercial bank checking accounts, and to prepare a bank statement reconciliation.

In the preceding chapters, the purpose and nature of business accounting, transaction analysis, and the framework of double entry bookkeeping were introduced. Explanations and illustrations were given of (1) **journalizing** (recording transactions in a general journal — a book of original entry), (2) **posting** (transferring the entries to the accounts that, taken together, comprise the general ledger), (3) taking a trial balance, and (4) using the latter to prepare an income statement and a balance sheet (two basic and important financial statements).

This chapter is devoted to a discussion of the handling of and accounting for cash receipts and cash disbursements, including various considerations that are involved when cash is kept in a commercial bank.

CASH RECEIPTS AND CASH DISBURSEMENTS

The term "cash" has several different, though not totally dissimilar, meanings. In a very narrow sense, cash means currency and coins. In a broader sense, cash includes checks, drafts, and money orders. All of these, including currency and coins, are sometimes called cash items. Usually, any reference to the cash receipts of a business relates to the receipt of checks, drafts, and money orders payable to the business, as well as to the receipt of currency and coins. The cash account balance, as well as the amount shown for cash in a balance sheet, normally includes cash and cash items on hand plus the amount on deposit in a bank checking account. In some cases, the balance sheet figure for cash includes amounts on deposit in more than one bank. On the balance sheet, it is rather rare to make a distinction between "cash on hand" and "cash in bank," but sometimes this is done.

A good policy for a business enterprise to adopt is one which requires that all cash and cash items which it receives be deposited in a bank. When this is done, its total cash receipts will equal its total deposits in the bank. It is also a good policy to make arrangements with the bank so that all checks and other cash items received by the business from customers or others in the usual course of business will be accepted by the bank for deposit only. This will cause the records of cash receipts and disbursements of the business to agree item by item with the bank's record of deposits and withdrawals.

THE CASH ACCOUNT

The cash account is debited when cash is increased and credited when cash is decreased. This account normally has a debit balance.

Cash Receipts. Cash and cash items received by a business are known as cash receipts. It is vital that an accurate and timely record be kept of cash receipts. When the volume of the receipts is large both in number and in amount, procedures designed to reduce the danger of mistake and embezzlement (the unauthorized taking of business cash by an employee) should be followed. When numerous receipts of currency and coins from customers are given in person for goods or services just received, it is customary to use a cash register. Such a machine provides a listing of amounts recorded as the money is received. A cash register may have the capability of accumulating subtotals that permit classification of amounts — sales by departments or products, for example.

When money comes in by mail (nearly always checks), a pre-supplied form showing the remitter's name, address, and the amount on the enclosed check or money order is usually enclosed. A good example of this is the top part of a monthly statement that the customer has received as shown below.

	PHONE NUMBER	DATE
Dr. Hugh Embertson 925 Hemlock St. San Francisco, CA 94127-1011	583-2791	06 01 82

MAKE CHECKS PAYABLE TO THE ABOVE.
TO INSURE PROPER CREDIT
PLEASE RETURN THIS PORTION IN THE ENCLOSED ENVELOPE.

ACCOUNT NO.	PATIENT	PLEASE PAY THIS AMOUNT
636412	Scott Swanson	

RETAIN BOTTOM PORTION FOR INCOME TAX PURPOSES.
IT WILL BE THE ONLY RECORD WHICH YOU WILL RECEIVE.
(SEE REVERSE SIDE FOR INSTRUCTIONS)

TEAR HERE   TEAR HERE

ACCOUNT NUMBER	PATIENT NAME & RESPONSIBLE PARTY	PHONE NUMBER	DATE
636412	Scott Swanson Gilbert J. Swanson	624-5643	06 01 82

DATE MO DAY YR	DESCRIPTION	AMOUNT
04 17 82	INITIAL OFFICE VISIT, EXAM	500.00
04 21 82	Tonsillectomy	
04 26 82	Post-op office visit	
04 27 82	Medical insurance filed $500	
05 15 82	Received on account	500.00 CR

	BALANCE DUE
Hugh Embertson, MD INC	-0-

DISREGARD THIS STATEMENT IF IT HAS BEEN PAID WITHIN THE LAST 10 DAYS.

Sometimes a written receipt must be prepared by the business. A carbon copy of the receipt or the returned portion of the monthly statement provides the source document for the cash received. In any case, the initial record of each amount received should be prepared by someone other than the bookkeeper to provide good internal control. The money received, including checks and money orders, is placed in the custody of whoever is authorized to handle bank deposits and cash on hand. The bookkeeper uses the initial records in preparing proper journal entries for cash receipts. Under such a plan, the bookkeeper does not actually handle any cash; instead cash receipts are entered from records prepared by other persons. The procedure of having transactions involving cash handled by two or more persons reduces the danger of embezzlement and is one of the important features of a system of internal control.

Cash Disbursements. Cash and cash items paid by a business are known as cash disbursements. Disbursements may be made in cash or by bank check. When a disbursement is made in cash, a receipt or a receipted voucher should be obtained as evidence of the payment. When a disbursement is made by bank check, it is not necessary to obtain a receipt since the canceled check that is returned by the bank serves as a receipt.

Proving Cash. The process of determining whether the amount of cash, both on hand and in the bank, is the same amount that exists on the accounting records is called proving cash. Cash should be proved at least once a week and, more often if the volume of cash transactions is large. The first step is to determine from the records the amount of the cash account balance. The most recent cash account balance is calculated by adding the total of the receipts to the opening balance and subtracting the total of the payments. The result should be equal to the amount of cash on deposit in the bank as reflected in the checkbook stubs plus the total of currency, coins, checks, and money orders on hand. An up-to-date record of cash in bank is maintained — usually by using check stubs to show deposits as well as checks drawn, and the resulting balance after each deposit made or check drawn. (See check stubs illustrated on page 71.) The amount of cash on hand must be determined by actual count.

Cash Short and Over. If the effort to prove cash is not successful, it means that either (1) the records of receipts, disbursements, and cash on deposit contain one or more recording errors, (2) the physical count of cash not deposited is incorrect, or (3) a shortage or an overage exists. If verifications of the records and the cash count do not uncover any error, it is evident that some mistake must have been made in handling cash.

Finding that cash is slightly short or over is not unusual. If there are numerous cash transactions, it is difficult to avoid occasional errors in making change. There is always the danger of shortages due to dishonesty, but most discrepancies are the result of mistakes. Many businesses have a special ledger account entitled Cash Short and Over which is used to keep track of day-to-day shortages and overages of cash. If, in the effort to prove cash, it is found that a shortage exists, the amount is treated as a cash disbursement transaction involving a debit to Cash Short and Over. Any overage discovered is regarded as a cash receipt transaction involving a credit to Cash Short and Over. By the end of the fiscal year, it is likely that the cash short and over account will have both debits and credits. If the total of the debits exceeds the total of the credits, the balance represents an expense or loss; if the reverse is the case, the balance represents revenue.

THE PETTY CASH FUND

When all cash receipts are deposited in a bank, an office fund known as a petty cash fund may be established for paying small items. ("Petty" means small or little.) Such a fund eliminates the necessity of writing checks for small amounts.

Operating a Petty Cash Fund. To establish a petty cash fund, a check is written for the amount that is to be set aside in the fund. The amount may be $50, $100, $125, or any amount considered necessary. The check is made payable to the person who will have custody of the fund. That person's name, followed by a comma and the words, "Petty Cashier" appears on the check as the payee. When the check is cashed by the bank, the money is placed in a cash drawer, a cash register, or a safe at the depositor's place of business; and a designated individual in the office is authorized to make payments from the fund. The person responsible for the fund should be able to account for the full amount of the fund at any time.

Disbursements from the fund should not be made without obtaining some sort of receipt. A special form of receipt, showing the name of the payee, the purpose of the payment, and the account to be charged for each petty cash disbursement, is known as a petty cash voucher. A form of petty cash voucher is shown on page 58. Such a voucher should be used for each expenditure.

The check written to establish the petty cash fund may be entered in the journal by debiting Petty Cash Fund and by crediting Cash. When it is necessary to replenish the fund, the petty cashier usually prepares a statement of the expenditures, properly classi-

Petty Cash Voucher

No. _4_   Date _December 14, 1982_

Paid to _Barbara K. Moran_   Amount

For _American Red Cross_ | 15 | 00 |

Charge to _Charitable Contributions Expense_

Payment received:

Barbara K. Moran Approved by _Al Boes_

Petty Cash Voucher

fied. A check is then written for the exact amount of the total expenditures. This check is entered in the journal by debiting the proper accounts indicated in the statement and by crediting Cash.

To illustrate, assume that on July 1, Marcia's Boutique established a petty cash fund for $75, and that on July 31 the fund was replenished for $62.50 after classifying and totaling the petty cash vouchers. The journal entries to record these transactions are:

July	1	Petty Cash Fund	75.00	
		Cash		75.00
		To establish petty cash fund.		
	31	Automobile Expense	14.00	
		Supplies Expense..	26.00	
		Postage Expense..	19.00	
		Miscellaneous Expense	3.50	
		Cash		62.50
		Replenishment of petty cash fund.		

The petty cash fund is thus a revolving fund. The petty cash account balance does not change in amount unless the fund is increased or decreased. The actual amount of cash in the fund plus the total of the petty cash vouchers should be equal to the amount originally deposited to the petty cash fund. This commonly used method for handling petty cash is referred to as the imprest method.

Petty Cash Disbursements Record. When a petty cash fund is maintained, it is good practice to keep a formal record of all disbursements from the fund. The petty cash disbursements record is a special multicolumn record that supplements the regular accounting records. No posting is done from this special record. Various types of records have been designed for this purpose. One of the standard forms is illustrated on pages 60 and 61. The headings of the Distribution columns may vary with each enterprise, depending upon the desired classification of the expenditures. The headings represent accounts that eventually are to be charged for the expenditures. The desired headings may either be printed on the form or they may be written in. Often account numbers instead of account titles are used in the headings to indicate the accounts to be charged.

The petty cashier should have a document for each disbursement made from the petty cash fund. Whether or not a receipt or receipted invoice is obtained, the petty cashier should prepare a voucher. The vouchers should be numbered consecutively.

A typical petty cash disbursement record is reproduced on pages 60 and 61. It is a part of the records of Al Boes, a business consultant. Since Boes is out of the office much of the time, a petty cash fund is provided from which the secretary is authorized to make petty cash disbursements not to exceed $25 each. A narrative of the petty cash transactions completed by Pauline Curtis, Boes' secretary, during the month of December follows:

AL BOES

NARRATIVE OF PETTY CASH TRANSACTIONS

Dec. 1 Issued check for $125 payable to Pauline Curtis, Petty Cash Fund Cashier. The check is cashed and the proceeds placed in a petty cash fund.

> This transaction is recorded in the journal by debiting Petty Cash Fund and by crediting Cash. A memorandum entry is also made in the Description column of the petty cash disbursements record reproduced on pages 60 and 61.

	JOURNAL				PAGE	
DATE	DESCRIPTION	POST. REF.	DEBIT	CREDIT		
1	Dec. 1	Petty Cash Fund		125 00		1
2		Cash			125 00	2
3		To establish petty				3
4		cash fund.				4
5						5
6						6
7						7

During the month of December, the following disbursements were made from the petty cash fund:

PAGE		PETTY CASH DISBURSEMENTS				
	DAY	DESCRIPTION	VOU. NO.	TOTAL AMOUNT	Tel. Exp.	Auto Exp.
1		AMOUNTS FORWARDED				
2	1	Received in fund		125.00		
3	6	Automobile repairs	1	16 40		16 40
4	7	Client luncheon	2	11 50		
5	13	Al Boes, personal use	3	25 00		
6	14	American Red Cross	4	15 00		
7	15	Typewriter repairs	5	8 75		
8	17	Traveling expense	6	9 25		
9	20	Washing automobile	7	4 50		4 50
10	22	Postage expense	8	1 50		
11	23	Salvation Army	9	8 00		
12	27	Postage stamps	10	15 00		
13	28	Long distance call	11	3 60 / 118 50	3 60	20 90
14				118 50	3 60	20 90
15	31	Balance		6.50		
16	31	Received in fund		118.50		
17		Total		125.00		
18						
19						
20						
21						

Al Boes' Petty Cash Disbursements Record (Left Page)

6 Paid $16.40 to Jim Smith of Smith's Auto for having the company automobile serviced. Petty Cash Voucher No. 1.

7 Reimbursed Boes $11.50 for the amount spent in entertaining a client at lunch. Petty Cash Voucher No. 2.

13 Gave Boes $25 for personal use. Petty Cash Voucher No. 3.

This item is entered in the Amount column provided at the extreme right of the petty cash disbursements record since no special distribution column has been provided for recording amounts withdrawn by the owner for personal use.

14 Gave the American Red Cross a $15 donation. Petty Cash Voucher No. 4.

15 Paid $8.75 for typewriter repairs. Petty Cash Voucher No. 5.

17 Reimbursed Boes $9.25 for traveling expenses. Petty Cash Voucher No. 6.

FOR MONTH OF *December* 19**82**   PAGE *1*

DISTRIBUTION OF DEBITS

	Post. Exp.	Char. Cont. Exp.	Travel & Ent. Exp.	Misc. Exp.		Account	Amount	
1								1
2								2
3								3
4			11 50					4
5						Al Boes, Drawing	25 00	5
6		15 00						6
7				8 75				7
8			9 25					8
9								9
10	1 50							10
11		8 00						11
12	15 00							12
13								13
14	16 50	23 00	20 75	8 75			25 00	
	16 50	23 00	20 75	8 75			25 00	14
15								15
16								16
17								17
18								18
19								19
20								20
21								21

Al Boes' Petty Cash Disbursements Record (Right Page)

20 Paid $4.50 to Mike Butler of Glow Car Care for having the company automobile washed. Petty Cash Voucher No. 7.

22 Paid $1.50 for mailing a package. Petty Cash Voucher No. 8.

23 Donated $8 to the Salvation Army. Petty Cash Voucher No. 9.

27 Paid $15 for postage stamps. Petty Cash Voucher No. 10.

28 Reimbursed Boes $3.60 for a long distance telephone call made from a booth. Petty Cash Voucher No. 11.

Proving the Petty Cash Disbursements Record. To prove the petty cash disbursements record, it is first necessary to foot all of the amount columns. The sum of the footings of the Distribution columns should equal the footing of the Total Amount column. After proving the footings, the totals are recorded and the record is ruled as shown in the illustration. The illustration shows that a total of $118.50 was paid out during December. Since this is an appropriate time to replenish the petty cash fund, the following statement of the disbursements for December is prepared:

STATEMENT OF PETTY CASH DISBURSEMENTS FOR DECEMBER

Telephone Expense	$ 3.60
Automobile Expense	20.90
Postage Expense	16.50
Charitable Contributions Expense	23.00
Travel and Entertainment Expense	20.75
Miscellaneous Expense	8.75
Al Boes, Drawing	25.00
Total disbursements	$118.50

The statement of petty cash disbursements provides the information for the issuance of a check for $118.50 to replenish the petty cash fund. On December 31, Boes issued a check for $118.50 payable to Pauline Curtis, Petty Cashier to replenish the petty cash fund. This transaction was recorded as a compound entry in the journal by debiting the proper accounts and by crediting Cash for the total amount of the expenses. A compound entry is one that affects more than two accounts, with the sum of the debits equal to the sum of the credits. Such an entry is usually required for petty cash fund replenishment. The entry is posted from the journal to the affected ledger accounts.

	JOURNAL				PAGE 15
DATE	DESCRIPTION	POST. REF.	DEBIT	CREDIT	
19-- Dec. 31	Telephone Expense		3 60		1
	Automobile Expense		20 90		2
	Postage Expense		16 50		3
	Charitable Contributions Expense		23 00		4
	Travel and Entertainment Expense		20 75		5
	Miscellaneous Expense		8 75		6
	Al Boes, Drawing		25 00		7
	Cash			1 1850	8
	Replenishment of				9
	petty cash fund.				10
					11

After footing and ruling the petty cash disbursements record, the balance in the fund and the amount received to replenish the fund may be recorded in the Description column below the ruling as shown in the illustration. It is customary to carry the total forward to the top of a new page as a memorandum entry before recording any of the transactions for the following month.

BUILDING YOUR ACCOUNTING KNOWLEDGE

1. What is the usual source documentation of cash receipts when they are numerous and given in person? What form of source documentation usually accompanies money that comes in by mail?
2. Why should transactions involving cash be handled by two or more persons?
3. Why is it not unusual to find that the cash balance at the end of the day is slightly short or over?
4. What does a debit balance in the cash short and over account represent? What does a credit balance in this account represent?
5. What is the purpose of a petty cash fund?
6. What should be obtained from the receiving party each time a petty cash disbursement is made?
7. From what source is the information for issuing a check to replenish the petty cash fund obtained?

Report No. 3-1

> *Refer to the study assignments and Complete Report No. 3-1. After completing the report, proceed with the textbook discussion until the next report is required.*

BANKING PROCEDURES

A bank is a financial institution that receives deposits, lends money, makes collections, and renders other services, such as providing vaults for the safekeeping of valuables and handling trust funds for its customers. Most banks offer facilities for both checking accounts and savings accounts.

CHECKING ACCOUNT

The majority of all money payments in the United States are made by checks. Commercial paper drawn on funds in a bank account and payable on demand is called a check. It involves three original parties: (1) the depositor who orders the bank to pay a certain amount of money is known as the drawer; (2) the bank in which the drawer has money on deposit is known as the drawee; and (3) the person directed to receive the money is known as the payee. The drawer and payee may be the same person, though the payee named in such a case usually is "Cash," or the name of the drawee bank.

A check is negotiable (meaning that the right to receive the money can be transferred to someone else) if it complies with the following requirements: (1) it is in writing; (2) it is signed by the drawer; (3) it contains an unconditional order to pay a specified amount of money; (4) it is payable on demand; and (5) it is payable to the order of another party or to the bearer. The payee transfers the right to receive the money by indorsing the check. This procedure requires writing his or her name and sometimes other pertinent information on the back of the check. If the payee simply signs on the back of the check, customarily near the left end, the signature is called a blank indorsement. This makes the check payable to any bearer. If there are added words such as "For deposit," "Pay to any bank or banker," or "Pay to Mel Blank only," it is called a restrictive indorsement. A widely used business practice when indorsing checks for deposit is to use a rubber stamp similar to that illustrated below.

PAY TO THE
FIRST NATIONAL BANK
IN ST. LOUIS
FOR DEPOSIT ONLY

H. H. ROBERTSON

No. 648 $\frac{80\text{-}482}{810}$

January 2 19 *82*

Robertson $800 $\frac{00}{}$

$\frac{00}{100}$ DOLLARS

M. L. Lipton

⑆ 13 5832 3 ⑈

Restrictive Indorsement for Deposit (Rubber Stamp)

Important factors in connection with a checking account are: (1) opening the account, (2) making deposits, (3) making withdrawals, (4) recording bank transactions, and (5) reconciling the bank statement.

Opening a Checking Account. To open a checking account with a bank, it is necessary to obtain the approval of an official of the bank and to make an initial deposit. Money, checks, bank drafts, money orders, and other cash items usually are accepted for deposit, subject to their verification as to amount and validity.

Banks usually require new depositors to sign their names on a card or form as an aid in verifying the depositor's signature on checks that may be issued, on cash items that may be indorsed for deposit, and on other business papers that may be presented to the bank. The form a depositor signs to give the bank a sample signature is called a signature card. If desired, depositors may authorize others to sign checks and other business forms on their behalf. A person who is so authorized is required to sign the depositor's name along with his or her own signature on a signature card and on all documents subsequently executed on behalf of the depositor. To aid in identification, the depositor's social security number is also shown. A signature card is one of the safeguards that a bank uses to protect its own interests as well as the interests of its depositors.

Making Deposits. To make a deposit with a bank, it is necessary to use certain forms prescribed by that bank and to observe the rules of the bank with regard to acceptable and unacceptable deposit items. In preparing the deposit, paper money should be arranged in the order of the denominations, the smaller denominations being placed on top. The bills should be all stacked face up and top up. Coins (pennies, nickels, dimes, quarters, half dollars and dollars) that are to be deposited in considerable quantities should be wrapped in coin wrappers, which the bank provides, unless the bank has a coin-sorting machine. The name and account number of the depositor should be written on the outside of each coin wrapper as a means of identification in the event that a mistake has been made in counting the coins. All checks being deposited must be indorsed. The indorsement on the check illustrated on page 64 was made by means of a rubber stamp.

Deposit Ticket. A printed form with a detailed listing of items being deposited is called a deposit ticket. Banks provide these forms for depositors. A filled-in deposit ticket, typical of the type that most banks provide, is reproduced on page 66. Note that the number of the depositor's account is preprinted at the bottom in

Deposit ticket			4-5 / 810

		Amount	
Currency		$ 822	00
Coin		38	27
Checks	4-5	290	40
List checks singly	80-459	620	00
	4-97	560	00
Be sure all items are endorsed			
Total		2,330	67

First National Bank in St. Louis   First Union Group
St. Louis, Missouri

October 13, 1982

For credit of

H. H. ROBERTSON
2650 S. Hanley Rd.
St. Louis, MO 63144-9892

⑆081000058⑆ 13 6725 4⑈

Deposit Ticket

numbers that can be "read" by electronic equipment used by banks. These numbers are called **MICR numbers**, which stands for magnetic ink character recognition. This series of digits, which is also preprinted at the bottom of all of the depositor's checks, is actually a code used in sorting and routing deposit slips and checks. In the first set of digits, 081000058, the first "8" indicates that the bank is in the Eighth Federal Reserve District. The third digit "1" is the reserve bank or branch serving the district. The fourth digit "0" indicates whether the item is for immediate credit or deferred credit. The number "5" is a number assigned to the First National Bank in St. Louis. The last number "8" is known as a check digit and is used to verify the accuracy of the eight preceding digits in computer processing. Because this numbering method was established by the American Bankers Association, code numbers used in sorting and routing deposit tickets are also known as **ABA numbers**. The second set of digits, 13-6725-4, is the number assigned by the First National Bank in St. Louis to H. H. Robertson's account.

It is common practice to prepare deposit tickets in duplicate so that one copy, when receipted by the bank teller, may be retained by the depositor. In preparing a deposit ticket, the date should be written in the space provided. The amounts of cash represented by currency and by coins should be entered in the amount column of the deposit ticket on the lines provided for these items.

Each check to be deposited should be listed on a separate line of the deposit ticket as shown in the illustration. In listing checks on the deposit ticket, the instructions of the bank should be observed in describing the checks for identification purposes. Banks usually prefer that depositors identify checks being deposited by showing the ABA number of the bank on which the check is drawn. The ABA number for the first check listed on the deposit ticket is $\frac{4-5}{810}$. The number "4" is the number assigned to the city in which the bank is located and the number "5" is assigned to the specific bank. The denominator "810" is the check routing number, but only the numerator is used in identifying the deposit.

The total of the cash and other items deposited should be entered on the deposit tickets. The deposit tickets, prepared in duplicate, together with the cash and the other items deposited, should be delivered to the receiving teller of the bank. The teller processes the deposit tickets and returns the duplicate to the depositor.

A depositor may personally obtain cash at the time of making a deposit by indicating on the deposit slip the portion of the total of items listed to be returned to him or her, with the remainder to constitute the deposit. Alternatively, a check may be drawn payable to the depositor, or usually, just to "Cash."

If a duplicate deposit ticket is not used, the bank may provide the depositor with a machine-printed receipt for each deposit. Some banks use automatic teller machines in preparing the receipts. The use of such machines saves the time required to make the manual entries and eliminates the need for making duplicate copies of deposit tickets. Such machines are not only timesaving, but they also promote accuracy in the handling of deposits. A deposit that consists exclusively of checks often is mailed to the bank with a single deposit ticket. Later, a machine-printed deposit receipt and a new deposit envelope are mailed back to the depositor.

The deposits handled by each teller during the day may be accumulated in the automatic teller machine so that at the end of the day the total amount of the deposits received by the teller is automatically recorded by the machine. This amount may be proved by counting the cash and cash items accepted by a teller for deposit during the day.

Dishonored Checks. A check that a bank refuses to pay is described as a dishonored check. A depositor guarantees all items deposited and is liable to the bank for the amount involved if any item is not honored when presented for payment. When a check or other cash item is deposited with a bank and is not honored upon presentation to the bank upon which it is drawn, the depositor's bank may charge the amount of the dishonored item to the depositor's account or may present it to the depositor for reimbursement. It is not uncommon for checks that have been deposited to be returned to the depositor for various reasons accompanied with a debit advice. As indicated on the debit advice shown below, the most common reason for checks being returned unpaid is that they are NSF checks ("not sufficient funds" remain in the drawer's account to cover them).

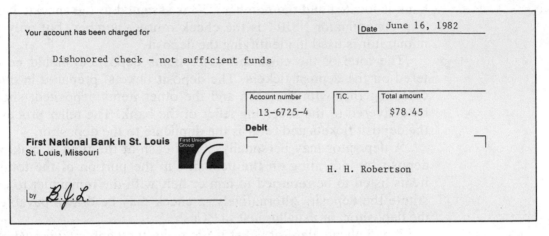

Your account has been charged for |Date June 16, 1982

Dishonored check – not sufficient funds

Account number   T.C.   Total amount
13-6725-4 $78.45

Debit

First National Bank in St. Louis   First Union Group
St. Louis, Missouri

H. H. Robertson

by *B.J.L.*

Debit Advice

Issuance of a check on a bank without sufficient funds on deposit with that bank to cover the check when it is presented for payment is called an overdraft. Under the laws of most states, issuance of such a check is illegal. When a dishonored check is charged to the depositor's account, the amount should be deducted from the balance shown on the depositor's checkbook stub.

Most overdraft checks are not the result of any dishonest intent on the part of the drawer of such checks. Either the depositor thought that there was money in the account when the check was written, due to an error in keeping the checkbook, or expected to get a deposit to the bank in time to "cover" the check before it reached the bank for payment. It is commonly considered to be something of a disgrace to the drawer of a check if the bank will not honor (pay) it. In recent years, many banks have made available plans that guarantee that all checks, within prescribed limits as to amount, will be honored even if the depositor's balance is too low. This amounts to a prearrangement with the bank to make a loan to the depositor. These plans have been given names such as "Ready Reserve Account," "Instant Cash," and others. Arrangements of this sort are parts of larger plans that involve such things as picture checks, no minimum balance requirement, bank statements that list checks paid in numerical order, check guarantee cards, travelers checks without fee, safe-deposit boxes, and even bank credit cards. The bank may charge a monthly fee for any or all of these services.

Such comprehensive plans are not widely subscribed to by businesses (in contrast to individuals).

Postdated Checks. Checks dated after the date that the check was written and issued are known as postdated checks. For example, a check written and issued on March 1 is dated March 15. The recipient of the postdated check should not deposit it before the date specified on the check (March 15) because it is not legally acceptable as cash until that date. One reason for issuing a postdated check may be that the maker does not have sufficient funds in the bank at the time of issuance which in this case is March 1, but expects to have a sufficient amount on deposit by the time the check is presented for payment on or after the date of the check (March 15). When a postdated check is presented to the bank on which it is drawn and payment is not made, it is handled by the bank in the same manner as any other dishonored check and the payee should treat it as a dishonored check. Generally, it is not considered good practice for a business to issue postdated checks.

Making Deposits by Mail. As indicated earlier, bank deposits may be made either over the counter or by mail. The over-the-counter method of making deposits is frequently used, but it may not always be convenient to make deposits over the counter. If the depositor lives at a great distance from the bank, it may be more convenient to make deposits by mail. When deposits are made by mail, the bank may provide the depositor with a supply of deposit tickets, a self-addressed, prestamped envelope, and a form which is subsequently returned with a machine-printed receipt for the deposit.

Night Deposits. Many banks provide night deposit service. A common practice is for the bank to have a night safe with an opening on the exterior of the bank building. Upon signing a night depository contract, the bank supplies the depositor with a key to the outside door of the safe, together with a bag that has an identifying number and in which valuables may be placed, and two keys to the bag itself. Once the depositor places the bag in the night deposit safe, it cannot be retrieved because it moves to a vault in the bank that is accessible to bank employees only. Since only the depositor is provided with keys to the bag, the depositor or an authorized representative must go to the bank to unlock the bag. The depositor may or may not deposit the funds that had been placed previously in the night deposit safe.

Night deposit banking service is especially valuable to those individuals and concerns that accumulate cash and other cash items which they cannot take to the bank during regular banking hours and that do not have safe facilities in their own places of business.

Making Withdrawals. The amount deposited in a bank checking account may be withdrawn either by the depositor or by any other person who is properly authorized to make withdrawals from the depositor's account. Such withdrawals are accomplished by the use of checks signed by the depositor or by others having the authority to sign checks drawn on the account.

Checkbook. Checks used by businesses are usually bound in the form of a book with two or three blank checks to a page and perforated so that they may be removed singly. Checks may be provided by the bank (often for a charge) or purchased directly from firms that specialize in the manufacture of check forms.

To the left of each check is a small form called a check stub that contains space to record all relevant information about the check. Sometimes the depositor is provided with a checkbook that, instead of containing stubs, is accompanied by a small register book in which the relevant information is noted. The information contained on the stub or on the register includes the check number, date, payee, amount, the purpose of the check and often the account to be charged, along with the bank balance before the check was issued, current deposits if any, and the resulting balance after issuing the check.

The depositor's name and address normally are printed on each check and the MICR numbers are shown along the bottom edge. Often the check number is preprinted in the upper right corner. Sometimes, checks come bound in the form of a pad. There may be a blank page after each check for use in making a carbon copy of the check. The carbon copy is not a check; it is merely a copy of what was typed or written on the original check and provides the essential information for recording an entry in the formal records.

Writing a Check. The first step in writing a check is to complete the check stub or check register. This plan insures that the drawer will retain a record of each check issued. Second, the name of the payee is written on the check. Third, the amount of the check is written on the check in both figures and words. If the amount shown on the check in figures does not agree with the amount shown in words, the bank usually contacts the drawer for the correct amount or returns the check unpaid.

Care must be used in writing the amount on the check in order to avoid any possibility that the payee or a subsequent holder may change the amount. If the instructions given on page 71 are followed in the preparation of a check, it will be difficult to change the amount.

(1) The amount shown in figures should be written so that there is no space between the dollar sign and the first digit of the amount.

(2) The amount stated in words should be written beginning at the extreme left on the line provided for this information. The cents should be written in the form of a common fraction; if the check is for an even number of dollars, use two ciphers or the word "no" as the numerator of the fraction. If a vacant space remains, a line should be drawn from the amount stated in words to the word "Dollars" on the same line with it, as illustrated below.

Checks and Stubs

A machine frequently used to write or print the amount of a check in figures and in words is known as a checkwriter. The use of a checkwriter is desirable because it practically eliminates the possibility of changing the amount of a check.

As the fourth step in writing a check, the purpose for which a check is drawn is often noted in the lower left-hand corner of the check itself. Indicating the purpose on the check provides information for the benefit of the payee and provides a specific receipt for the drawer. In the fifth step, the signature of the drawer is written on the lower right hand corner of the check in the same manner as on the signature card.

Each check issued by a depositor will be returned by the bank on which it is drawn after the check has been paid. Canceled checks are returned to the depositor with the bank statement, which is usually rendered each month. Canceled checks will have been indorsed by the payee and any subsequent holders. They constitute receipts that the depositor should retain for future reference. They may be attached to the stubs from which they were removed originally or they may be filed.

Electronic Processing of Checks. It is now nearly universal practice to use checks that, like deposit tickets, can be processed by MICR (magnetic ink character recognition) equipment. Imprinted in magnetic ink along the lower margin of the check is a series of numbers or digits in the form of a code that indicates (1) the identity of the Federal Reserve district in which the bank is located and a routing number, (2) the identity of the bank, and (3) the account number assigned to the depositor. Sometimes the check number is also shown. In processing checks with electronic equipment, the first bank that handles the check imprints the amount in magnetic ink characters to further aid in the processing of the check. The amount is printed directly below the signature line in the lower right-hand corner of the check.

Checks imprinted with the bank's number, the depositor's number, and the amount — all in MICR characters — can be posted electronically to the customer's account. The two checks reproduced on page 71 illustrate magnetic ink characters along the lower margins, as well as check stubs properly completed.

Recording Banking Transactions. A depositor should keep a record of the transactions completed with the bank. The checkbook stubs, as shown in the illustration on page 71, serve this purpose. The record consists of detailed information concerning each check written and an amount column in which are recorded (1) the balance brought forward, (2) the amount of deposits to be added, and (3) the amount of each check to be subtracted. The purpose is to keep a detailed record of deposits made and checks issued and to indicate the balance in the checking account after each check is drawn.

As the amount of each check is recorded in the journal, a check mark is placed immediately after the account title written on the stub to indicate that the check has been recorded. When the canceled check is subsequently received from the bank, the amount shown on the stub may be checkmarked to indicate that the canceled check has been received.

Records Kept by a Bank. The usual transactions completed by a bank with a depositor are:

(1) Accepting deposits made by the depositor.
(2) Paying checks issued by the depositor.
(3) Lending money to the depositor.
(4) Collecting the amounts of various kinds of commercial paper, such as matured notes or bonds, for the account of the depositor.

The bank keeps an account for each depositor. Each transaction affecting the depositor's account is recorded by either debiting or crediting the depositor's account, depending upon the effect of the transaction.

When a bank accepts a deposit, the account of the depositor is credited (increased) for the amount of the deposit. The deposit increases the bank's liability to the depositor. When the bank pays a check that has been drawn on the bank, it debits (decreases) the account of the depositor for the amount of the check. If the bank makes a collection for the depositor, the net amount of the collection is credited to the account. At the same time, the bank notifies the depositor that the collection has been made using a form similar to the one shown below.

Credit
Your account has been credited for

Date April 19, 1982

Redemption of Treasury Bill $15,000.00
Less collection charge 15.00

Account number	T.C.	Total amount
13-6725-4		$14,985.00

H. H. ROBERTSON

First National Bank in St. Louis
St. Louis, Missouri

First Union Group

by *R. A. R.*

Credit Advice

Bank Statement. A statement of account rendered to each depositor once a month by a bank is called a bank statement. An illustration of a widely used form of bank statement is shown on page 74. Some banks provide statements that also present information

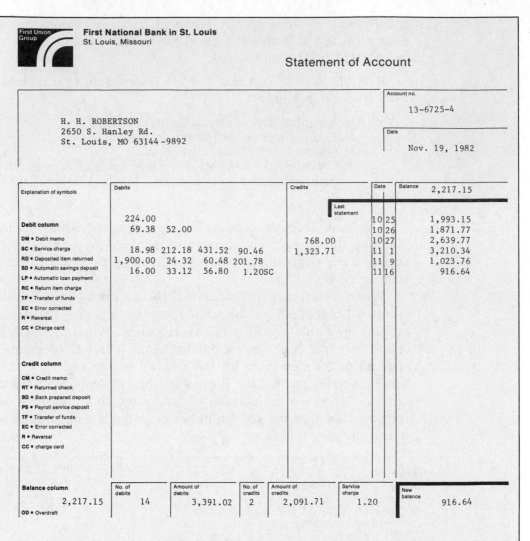

First National Bank in St. Louis
St. Louis, Missouri

First Union Group

Statement of Account

H. H. ROBERTSON	Account no. 13-6725-4
2650 S. Hanley Rd.	
St. Louis, MO 63144-9892	Date Nov. 19, 1982

Explanation of symbols	Debits	Credits	Date	Balance 2,217.15
		Last statement		
Debit column	224.00		10 25	1,993.15
	69.38 52.00		10 26	1,871.77
DM • Debit memo		768.00	10 27	2,639.77
SC • Service charge	18.98 212.18 431.52 90.46	1,323.71	11 1	3,210.34
RD • Deposited item returned	1,900.00 24.32 60.48 201.78		11 9	1,023.76
SD • Automatic savings deposit	16.00 33.12 56.80 1.20SC		11 16	916.64
LP • Automatic loan payment				
RC • Return item charge				
TF • Transfer of funds				
EC • Error corrected				
R • Reversal				
CC • Charge card				
Credit column				
CM • Credit memo				
RT • Returned check				
BD • Bank prepared deposit				
PS • Payroll service deposit				
TF • Transfer of funds				
EC • Error corrected				
R • Reversal				
CC • charge card				

Balance column	No. of debits	Amount of debits	No. of credits	Amount of credits	Service charge	New balance
2,217.15	14	3,391.02	2	2,091.71	1.20	916.64
OD • Overdraft						

Bank Statement

regarding savings accounts and loan accounts, for those depositors who have such accounts. Very commonly, however, a separate statement is furnished for each type of account.

The statement illustrated is for a checking account. It is a report showing (1) the balance on deposit at the beginning of the period, (2) the amount of deposits made during the period (credits), (3) the amounts of checks honored during the period (debits), (4) other items charged to the depositor's account during the period, and (5) the balance on deposit at the end of the period. With the bank statement, the depositor also receives all checks paid by the bank during the period, together with any other vouchers representing items charged to the account.

Reconciling the Bank Statement. A depositor ordinarily keeps one or more records of bank-related transactions. A bank also keeps records of transactions with each depositor. The depositor's records of transactions with the bank should be brought into agreement with the bank's records of transactions with the depositor at periodic intervals — usually once a month.

As soon as possible after a bank statement is received, the depositor should try to make it agree with the bank balance record kept on the check stubs, a procedure known as reconciling the bank statement. The balance shown on the bank statement may not be the same as the amount shown on the check stubs for one or more of the following reasons:

(1) Checks issued during the period may not have been presented to the bank for payment before the statement was prepared. These are known as outstanding checks. Some of the checks issued may fall into this category.

(2) Deposits may not have been recorded by the bank on the bank statement. These are known as deposits in transit. Such a deposit may have been mailed, or placed in the night depository and not recorded by the bank until the day following the date of the statement.

(3) The bank may have credited the depositor's account for an amount collected, but the depositor may not as yet have noted it on the check stubs since the credit advice has not yet been received.

(4) Service charges or other charges may appear on the bank statement that the depositor has not recorded on the check stubs.

(5) The depositor may have erred in keeping the bank account record.

(6) The bank may have erred in keeping its account with the depositor.

Each bank usually provides a form for completing the bank reconciliation on the back of the bank statement. If a depositor is unable to reconcile the bank statement, a report on the matter should be made to the bank immediately.

A suggested procedure in reconciling the bank statement is enumerated below:

(1) The amount of each deposit recorded on the bank statement is checked with the amount recorded on the check stubs. Any deposit recorded on the check stub but not recorded on the bank statement should be added to the bank statement balance as a deposit in transit.

(2) The amount of each canceled check is compared both with the amount recorded on the bank statement and with the amount recorded on the depositor's check stubs. When making this comparison, it is a good plan to place a check mark by the amount recorded on each check stub to indicate that the canceled check has been returned by the bank and its amount verified.

(3) The outstanding checks are listed, totaled, and deducted from the bank balance. The information needed for this list may be obtained by examining the check stubs and noting the amounts that have not been checkmarked.

(4) The amounts of any items listed on the bank statement that represent credits or charges to a depositor's account which have not been entered on the check stubs are added to or deducted from the balance on the check stubs and are recorded in the journal that is being used to record cash receipts and disbursements.

(5) Any error discovered on the check stubs or bank statement will require an adjustment to the check stub balance or bank balance depending on the nature of the error. A journal entry will also be necessary to correct for any check stub errors.

After completion of the foregoing procedure, the adjusted balance shown on the check stubs should equal the adjusted bank balance. A reconciliation of the bank balance shown in the statement reproduced on page 74 with the most recent check stub balance is presented below.

H. H. ROBERTSON
Reconciliation of Bank Statement
November 19, 1982

(1) Balance, November 19, per bank statement..............		$ 916.64
(2) Add deposit, November 19...		729.81
		$1,646.45
(3) Less checks outstanding, November 19:		
No. 426...	$136.00	
No. 429...	27.84	
No. 431...	272.40	436.24
(4) Adjusted bank balance...		$1,210.21
(5) Balance, November 19, per check stub		$1,211.50
(6) Less: Bank service charge..	$ 1.20	
(7) Error on stub for Check No. 404	.09	1.29
(8) Adjusted check stub balance......................................		$1,210.21

In making the reconciliation of the H. H. Robertson bank statement as of November 19, 1982, the following steps, which correspond with the numbers in the reconciliation, were completed:

(1) The November 19 bank balance, $916.64, was copied from the bank statement.

(2) A deposit of $729.81, placed in the night depository on November 19 and therefore not shown on the bank statement, was added to the November 19 bank balance to agree with the check stub that reflected the deposit on that date.

(3) The outstanding Checks Nos. 426, 429, and 431 were listed, totaled, and $436.24 was subtracted from the bank balance. These checks had not been presented to the bank for payment and thus were not returned with the bank statement.

(4) The adjusted bank balance as of the close of business November 19, was calculated as $1,210.21.

(5) The check stub balance as of November 19 was copied from the last check stub bearing that date, in the amount of $1,211.50.

(6) A bank service charge of $1.20 shown at the bottom of the bank statement was subtracted from the check stub balance.

(7) A checkbook error was discovered. Check No. 404 was written for $18.98 and recorded in the check stub as $18.89. This error required the check stub balance to be decreased by $.09.

(8) The adjusted check stub balance as of the close of business, November 19, was calculated as $1,210.21 and was equal to the adjusted November 19 bank balance.

In step number 6 above, a bank service charge was mentioned. A service charge may be made by a bank for the handling of checks and other items. The basis and the amount of such charges vary with different banks in different localities.

When a bank statement indicates that a service charge has been made, the depositor should record the amount of the service charge by debiting an expense account, such as Miscellaneous Expense, and by crediting Cash.

Miscellaneous Expense	1.20	
Cash		1.20
Bank service charge for November.		

The error noted in step number 7 above was discovered when the canceled checks that were returned with the bank statement were matched against the check stubs. It was found that, although Check No. 404 had been written for $18.98, the amount was shown as $18.89 on its stub. This is called a transposition error, because the "9" and the "8" were transposed; i.e., their order was reversed. On Stub No. 404, and the others that followed, the bank balance shown was $.09 overstated. The correct amount, $18.98, should be shown on Stub No. 404, and the bank balance shown on the stub of the last check used should be corrected by reducing the amount by $.09. If Check No. 404 was in payment of a telephone bill, an entry should be made debiting Telephone Expense and crediting Cash. Alternatively, since such a small amount was involved, the debit might be made to Miscellaneous Expense.

Telephone Expense or Miscellaneous Expense.................................	.09	
Cash...		.09
Correction of checkbook error.		

KEEPING A LEDGER ACCOUNT FOR EACH BANK

As explained previously, the depositor may keep a checkbook for each bank account. The depositor may also keep a ledger account for each bank. The title of such an account usually is the name of the bank. Sometimes, more than one account is kept with a bank, in which case each account should be correctly labeled. Such terms as "commercial," "executive," and "payroll" are used to identify the accounts.

The bank account is debited for the amount of each deposit and should be credited for the amount of each check written. The account should also be debited or credited for any other items that may have been handled directly by the bank, including collections and service charges.

When both a cash on hand account and a bank account are kept in the ledger, the following procedure should be observed in recording transactions affecting these accounts:

(1) Cash receipts are recorded as debits in the cash on hand account.
(2) Cash payments and bank deposits are recorded as credits to the cash on hand account.
(3) Cash deposits and bank collections are recorded as debits to the bank account.
(4) Checks written and bank charges are recorded as credits to the bank account.

Cash on Hand		First National Bank in St. Louis	
Debit	Credit	Debit	Credit
(1) For all receipts of cash and cash items.	(2) For all payments in cash. For all bank deposits.	(3) For all deposits. For collection of amounts for the depositor.	(4) For all checks written. For all service charges. For all other charges such as for dishonored checks.

Under this method of accounting for cash and banking transactions, the cash on hand account will be in balance when all cash on hand has been deposited in the bank. When the account is in balance, it means that the account has a zero balance since the total of the debits is equal to the total of the credits. To prove the balance of the cash on hand account at any time, it is necessary only to count the cash and cash items on hand and to compare the total with the cash on hand account balance. To prove the bank account balance, it is necessary to reconcile the bank statement in the same manner in which it was reconciled when only a memorandum record of bank transactions was kept on the check stubs.

The cash on hand account can be dispensed with when a bank account is kept in the ledger and all cash receipts are deposited in the bank. All disbursements except small expenditures made from a petty cash fund are made by check. Daily, or at frequent intervals, the receipts are deposited in the bank. If all cash received during the month has been deposited before the books are closed at the end of the month, the total amount of the bank deposits will equal the total cash receipts for the month. If all disbursements made during the month are made by check, the total amount of checks issued will be the total disbursements for the month.

SAVINGS ACCOUNT

When a savings account is opened in a bank, a signature card must be signed by the depositor. By signing the signature card, the depositor agrees to abide by the rules and regulations of the bank. These rules and regulations vary with different banks and may be altered and amended from time to time. At this time, a passbook may be given to the depositor. This is a small book in which the bank teller enters the date and amount of each deposit or withdrawal and initials the entry. The passbook is to be presented at the bank or mailed to the bank along with a deposit or withdrawal slip, each time money is deposited or withdrawn from the account. An alternative practice for depositing or withdrawing money from a savings account is to give the depositor a small register for recording deposits and withdrawals and a pad of deposit-withdrawal forms. This procedure eliminates the use of the passbook. Each time a deposit or withdrawal from savings is made, the appropriate part of one of the forms is filled in, signed, recorded in the register and presented or mailed to the bank with deposit items or other documents. The bank gives a machine-printed receipt to the depositor or returns it by mail. There should be a separate savings account in the ledger to record these activities. Sometimes, the name of the bank is in the title of the account, for example, "First National Bank in St. Louis — Savings Account."

At least once each quarter, the bank mails a credit advice to the depositor, indicating the amount of interest credited to the account. This should be entered in the depositor's register upon receipt. The depositor should also record the amount in the business accounts by a debit to the savings account and by a credit to Interest Earned. The interest is revenue earned whether withdrawn or not and is taxable to the depositor.

First National Bank in St. Louis — Savings Account........................	xxx	
Interest Earned		xxx
Quarterly interest earned.		

Traditionally, the principal differences between a savings account and a checking account are that interest is paid regularly by the bank on a savings account and withdrawals from a savings account may be made at the bank or by mail by the depositor or an authorized agent. Depositors use checking accounts primarily as a convenient means of making payments, while savings accounts are used primarily as a means of accumulating funds with interest.

An increasingly common practice is for the bank to combine savings and checking accounts and get depositor permission to make automatic transfers of funds from the savings portion to the checking portion whenever the latter falls below a specified minimum balance. This amounts to giving the depositor an interest-earning checking account.

BUILDING YOUR ACCOUNTING KNOWLEDGE

1. Name the five requirements with which a check must comply in order to be negotiable.
2. Why do banks usually require a new depositor to fill out a signature card? Why may more than one name appear on a signature card?
3. What is the reason for preparing a deposit ticket in duplicate?
4. Describe the use of MICR numbers in the electronic processing of checks.
5. Name the five major dollar amounts summarized on a bank statement.
6. If a depositor is unable to reconcile a bank statement, what should be done?
7. What journal entry should a depositor make when a bank statement indicates that there has been a service charge?
8. What is the primary purpose of a savings account? Are savings accounts in frequent use by businesses?

Report No. 3-2

> *Refer to the study assignments and complete Report No. 3-2. This assignment provides a test of your ability to apply the principles developed in the first three chapters of the textbook. Further study, with the aid of the vocabulary list below, may be helpful in this regard. After completing the report, you may proceed with the textbook discussion in Chapter 4 until the next report is required.*

EXPANDING YOUR BUSINESS VOCABULARY

What is the meaning of each of the following terms?

ABA numbers (p. 66)
automatic teller machine (p. 67)
bank statement (p. 73)
blank indorsement (p. 64)
cash (p. 54)
cash disbursements (p. 56)
cash receipts (p. 54)
cash register (p. 55)
Cash Short and Over (p. 57)
check (p. 63)
check stub (p. 70)
checkwriter (p. 71)
compound entry (p. 62)
debit advice (p. 67)
deposit ticket (p. 65)
deposits in transit (p. 75)
dishonored check (p. 67)
drawee (p. 64)
drawer (p. 63)
embezzlement (p. 54)

imprest method (p. 58)
indorsing (p. 64)
MICR numbers (p. 66)
NSF checks (p. 68)
negotiable (p. 64)
outstanding checks (p. 75)
overdraft (p. 68)
passbook (p. 79)
payee (p. 64)
petty cash disbursements record (p. 58)
petty cash fund (p. 57)
petty cash voucher (p. 57)
postdated checks (p. 69)
proving cash (p. 56)
reconciling the bank statement (p. 75)
restrictive indorsement (p. 64)
signature card (p. 65)
transposition error (p. 77)

CHAPTER 4

PAYROLL ACCOUNTING

CHAPTER OBJECTIVES

The objectives of this chapter are to enable you:

▶ To explain and perform the three major functions of payroll accounting: **(1)** determination of employee earnings and deductions, **(2)** determination of employer payroll taxes, and **(3)** proper recording of the expenses, liabilities, and cash disbursements in connection with (1) and (2).

▶ To explain those government laws and regulations that primarily affect payroll accounting.

▶ To describe and prepare selected forms and records that are required or desirable in payroll accounting.

▶ To explain selected manual and mechanical record-keeping methods used in the payroll area.

Employers need to maintain detailed and accurate payroll accounting records for both financial and legal reasons. The financial reason is simply that payroll expenditures represent a major part of the total expenditures of most companies. Payroll accounting records provide data useful in the analysis, classification, and control of these expenditures. In addition, payroll accounting information is invaluable in contract discussions with labor unions, in the settlement of company-union grievances, and in determining employee pension benefits.

The legal reason for maintaining payroll accounting records is that employers are required by federal, state, and local laws to do so. Companies must accumulate payroll data both for the business as a whole and for each employee. Clearly, accurate payroll accounting is essential to the survival of most businesses.

EMPLOYEE EARNINGS AND DEDUCTIONS

The first step in determining the amount to be paid to an employee is to calculate the employee's total or gross earnings for the pay period. The second step is to determine the amounts of deductions that are required either by law or by specific agreement between the employer and the employee. Depending upon a variety of circumstances, either or both of these steps may be relatively simple or quite complicated. An examination of the factors that must be considered in performing these two steps follows.

EMPLOYEES AND INDEPENDENT CONTRACTORS

Not every individual who performs services for a business is considered to be an employee. A public accountant, lawyer, or management consultant who sells services to a business does not necessarily become its employee. Neither does a plumber nor an electrician who is hired to make specific repairs or installations on business property. These people are told what to do, but not how to do it, and the compensation that they receive for their services is called a fee. Any person who agrees to perform a service for a fee and is not subject to the control of those for whom the service is performed is called an independent contractor.

In contrast, an employee is one who is under the control and direction of an employer with regard to the performance of services. The difference between an independent contractor and an employee is an important legal distinction. The nature and extent of the responsibilities of a contractor and a client to each other and to third parties are quite different from the mutual obligations of an employer and the employee. Of particular importance for payroll accounting purposes is the fact that the various government laws and regulations regarding employee deductions, employer payroll taxes, records, and reports apply only to employees.

TYPES OF COMPENSATION

Compensation for managerial or administrative services usually is called salary. A salary normally is expressed in terms of a month or a year. Compensation either for skilled or for unskilled labor usually is referred to as wages. Wages ordinarily are expressed in terms of hours, weeks, or pieces of accomplishment. The terms salaries and wages often are used interchangeably in practice.

Supplements to basic salaries or wages of employees include bonuses, commissions, cost-of-living adjustments, pensions, and profit sharing plans. Compensation also may take the form of goods, lodging, meals, or other property, and as such is measured by the fair market value of the property or service given in payment for the employee's efforts. This chapter demonstrates proper accounting for basic salaries and wages of employees paid in cash.

DETERMINATION OF TOTAL EARNINGS

An employee's earnings commonly are based on the time worked during the payroll period. Sometimes earnings are based on units of output or of sales during the period. Compensation based on time requires a record of the time worked by each employee. If there are only a few employees, a record of times worked may be kept in a memorandum book. Where there are many employees, time clocks commonly are used to record time spent on the job each day. With time clocks, a time card is provided for each employee and the clock is used to record arrival and departure times on the card. Alternatively, plastic cards or badges with holes punched in them for basic employee data are now being used in computer-based timekeeping systems. Whatever method is used, the total time worked during the payroll period must be computed.

Employees often are entitled to compensation at more than their regular rate of pay for work during certain hours or on certain days. If the employer is engaged in Interstate Commerce, the Federal Fair Labor Standards Act (commonly known as the Wages and Hours Law) provides that all employees covered by the Act must be paid one and one-half times the regular rate for all hours worked over 40 per week. Labor-management agreements often require extra pay for certain hours or days. In such cases, hours worked in excess of eight per day or work on Sundays and specified holidays may be paid for at higher rates.

To illustrate, assume that the company which employs Donald Schramm pays time and a half for all hours worked in excess of 40 per week and double time for work on Sunday. Schramm's regular rate is $8 per hour; and during the week ended April 15, Schramm worked nine hours each day Monday through Friday, six hours on Saturday and four on Sunday. Schramm's total earnings for the week ended April 15, are computed as follows:

40 hours @ $8	$320
11 hours @ $12	132*
4 hours (on Sunday) @ $16	64
Total earnings for the week	$516

*Schramm worked 9 hours each day Monday through Friday and 6 hours on Saturday — a total of 51 hours. Forty hours would be paid for at the regular rate and 11 hours at time and a half.

An employee who is paid a regular monthly or annual salary may also be entitled to premium pay for any overtime. If this is the case, it is necessary to compute the regular hourly rate of pay before computing the overtime rate. To illustrate, assume that Linda Herer receives a regular salary of $1,400 a month and that Herer is entitled to overtime pay at the rate of one and one-half times the regular hourly rate for any time worked in excess of 40 hours per week. Herer's overtime pay is computed as follows:

$1,400 × 12 months	$16,800 annual pay
$16,800 ÷ 52 weeks	$323.08 pay per week
$323.08 ÷ 40 hours	$8.08 pay per regular hour
$8.08 × 1½	$12.12 overtime pay per hour

DEDUCTIONS FROM TOTAL EARNINGS

An employee's take-home or net pay typically is significantly less than the total earnings or gross pay described above. The difference between an employee's gross and net pay generally can be explained by three factors: (1) employee FICA (Federal Insurance Contributions Act) tax withheld by the employer, (2) employee federal income taxes (and state and city income taxes where applicable) withheld by the employer, and (3) other deductions based on special agreements between the employer and the employee.

Employees' FICA Tax Withheld. The Federal Insurance Contributions Act (FICA) requires most employers to withhold certain amounts from employees' earnings for contributions to the old-age, survivors, and disability insurance (OASDI) and health insurance for the aged (HIP) programs. These withheld amounts are commonly referred to as FICA taxes.

Each employee is required to have a social security number for payroll accounting purposes. A completed form SS-5, the official form used in applying for an account number is illustrated below:

Application for Social Security Number (Form SS-5)

The earnings base against which the FICA tax is applied and the tax rate have been changed several times since the law was first enacted and are subject to change by Congress at any time in the future. These base and rate changes, however, do not affect the accounting principles and procedures for payroll. Therefore, for the sake of convenience in this chapter, the rate is assumed to be 5.6 percent of taxable wages paid during the calendar year for OASDI plus 1.4 percent for HIP for a total FICA rate of 7.0%. It is also assumed that the first $30,000 of earnings paid to each employee in any calendar year is taxable. Any amount of compensation paid in excess of $30,000 is assumed to be exempt from the tax.

State and Local Taxes. In addition to the federal requirements described above, a few states require employers to withhold a percentage of the employees' wages for unemployment compensation benefits or for disability benefits. In some states and cities, employers are also required to withhold a percentage of the employees' wages for other types of payroll taxes.

Employees' Income Tax Withheld. Under federal law, employers are required to withhold certain amounts from the total earnings of each employee to be applied toward the payment of the employee's federal income tax. The amount to be withheld each pay period is based on (1) the total earnings of the employee, (2) the marital status of the employee, (3) the number of withholding allowances claimed by the employee, and (4) the length of the employee's pay period.

Each employee is required to furnish the employer with an Employee's Withholding Allowance Certificate, Form W-4, showing marital status and the number of allowances claimed. The marital status of the taxpayer and the number of allowances claimed determine the dollar amount of earnings subject to withholding tax. According to 1979 federal income tax laws, $2,300 for single taxpayers and $3,400 for married taxpayers is excluded from withholding tax. These amounts on which no withholding tax is levied are known as zero bracket amounts, that is, they represent income brackets or levels at which the withholding tax is zero. A withholding allowance is an allowance of $1,000 on which no federal income tax is withheld from the employee's pay. Each federal income taxpayer is permitted one personal withholding allowance and one for each dependent who qualifies, that is, the taxpayer is entitled to one or more exemptions of $1,000 each from federal income tax based on family status and dependency relationships. The law specifies the relationship that must exist, the extent of support required, and the amount of support that must be provided in order for a person to qualify as a dependent.

In addition to these withholding allowances for personal and dependent exemptions, a taxpayer can qualify for two other types of withholding allowances. First, one special withholding allowance can be claimed by each single taxpayer who has only one job, or each married taxpayer whose spouse is not employed. Second, additional withholding allowances are permitted to taxpayers who anticipate large itemized deductions. In order to claim one or more additional withholding allowances, an employee's expected total earnings and itemized deductions for the coming year have to be estimated. Based on these expected total earnings and itemized deductions, the schedule and table illustrated on page 89 are used to determine the number of additional withholding allowances to which the employee is entitled.

An allowance certificate completed by John Anthony Indiman is shown on page 88.

To illustrate the use of the schedule and table, John Indiman is married, has a spouse who is not employed, and has one dependent child. Indiman expects earnings of $24,500 and itemized deductions of $4,500 in the coming year. As computed in the schedule, Indiman is therefore entitled to 1 additional withholding allowance. On line 1 of the W-4 form, Indiman claims 5 allowances, calculated as follows:

Form **W-4**	Department of the Treasury—Internal Revenue Service
(Rev. October 1979)	**Employee's Withholding Allowance Certificate**

Print your full name ▶ JOHN ANTHONY INDIMAN   Your social security number ▶ 307 78 3813

Address (including ZIP code) ▶ 925 LINCOLN AVE., ST. LOUIS, MO 63120-4752

Marital status: ☐ Single   ☒ Married   ☐ Married, but withhold at higher Single rate

Note: *If married, but legally separated, or spouse is a nonresident alien, check the single block.*

1 Total number of allowances you are claiming (from line F of the worksheet on page 2)   5

2 Additional amount, if any, you want deducted from each pay (if your employer agrees) . . . . $ –0–

3 I claim exemption from withholding because (see instructions and check boxes below that apply):

  a ☐ Last year I did not owe any Federal income tax and had a right to a full refund of **ALL** income tax withheld, **AND**

  b ☐ This year I do not expect to owe any Federal income tax and expect to have a right to a full refund of **ALL** income tax withheld. If both

    a and b apply, enter "EXEMPT" here . . . . ▶

  c If you entered "EXEMPT" on line 3b, are you a full-time student? . . . .   ☐ Yes ☐ No

Under the penalties of perjury, I certify that I am entitled to the number of withholding allowances claimed on this certificate, or if claiming exemption from withholding, that I am entitled to claim the exempt status.

Employee's signature ▶ *John A. Indiman*   Date ▶ JANUARY 4 , 19 82

Employer's name and address (including ZIP code) **(FOR EMPLOYER'S USE ONLY)**   Employer identification number

Withholding Allowance Certificate (Form W-4)

Personal allowances:
  Self... 1
  Wife... 1   2

Special withholding allowance................. 1
Allowance for dependent........................... 1
Additional withholding allowance............. 1
Total withholding allowances.................... 5

Most employers use the wage-bracket method of determining the amount of tax to be withheld from an employee's pay by tracing the employee's gross pay for a specific time period into the appropriate wage-bracket table provided by the Internal Revenue Service. These tables cover monthly, semimonthly, biweekly, weekly, and daily or miscellaneous periods, and there are separate tables for single and married taxpayers. Copies may be obtained from any local Internal Revenue Service office. A portion of a weekly income tax wage-bracket withholding table for married persons is illustrated on page 89. To use this table, assume that John Indiman (who claims 5 allowances) had gross earnings of $375 for the week ending December 17, 1982. On the line showing the tax on wages of "at least $370, but less than $380," in the column headed "5 withholding allowances," $41.50 is given as the amount to be withheld.

Whether the wage-bracket method or some other method is used in computing the amount of tax to be withheld, the sum of the taxes withheld from an employee's wages only approximates the tax on actual income derived solely from wages. An employee may be liable for a tax larger than the amount withheld. This additional tax will be remitted with the employee's federal income tax return. On the other hand, the amount of the taxes withheld by the employer may be greater than the employee's actual tax liability. In such an event, the employee will be entitled to a refund of the excess taxes withheld, or the excess can be applied to the employee's tax liability for the following year.

Several states and cities have adopted state and city income tax procedures. Some of these states and cities supply employers with withholding allowance certificate forms and income tax withholding tables that are similar in concept and appearance to those used by the federal Internal Revenue Service. Other states determine the amount to be withheld merely by applying a fixed percentage to the federal withholding amount.

Other Deductions. In addition to the compulsory deductions from employee earnings for FICA and income taxes, there are many

WEEKLY Payroll Period — Employee MARRIED — In Effect January 1, 1980 *

And the wages are-		And the number of withholding allowances claimed is—										
At least	But less than	0	1	2	3	4	5	6	7	8	9	10 or more
		The amount of income tax to be withheld shall be—										
125	130	12.20	9.30	6.40	3.50	.70	0	0	0	0	0	0
130	135	13.10	10.10	7.20	4.30	1.40	0	0	0	0	0	0
135	140	14.00	10.80	7.90	5.00	2.20	0	0	0	0	0	0
140	145	14.90	11.60	8.70	5.80	2.90	0	0	0	0	0	0
145	150	15.80	12.40	9.40	6.50	3.70	.80	0	0	0	0	0
150	160	17.20	13 70	10.60	7.70	4.80	1.90	0	0	0	0	0
160	170	19.00	15 50	12.10	9.20	6.30	3.40	.50	0	0	0	0
170	180	20.80	17.30	13.80	10.70	7.80	4.90	2.00	0	0	0	0
180	190	22.60	19 10	15.60	12.20	9.30	6.40	3.50	.60	0	0	0
190	200	24.40	20 90	17.40	14.00	10.80	7.90	5.00	2.10	0	0	0
200	210	26.20	22.70	19.20	15.80	12.30	9.40	6.50	3.60	.80	0	0
210	220	28.10	24.50	21.00	17.60	14.10	10.90	8.00	5.10	2.30	0	0
220	230	30.20	26.30	22.80	19.40	15.90	12.50	9.50	6.60	3.80	.90	0
230	240	32.30	28.30	24.60	21.20	17.70	14.30	11.00	8.10	5.30	2.40	0
240	250	34.40	30.40	26.40	23.00	19.50	16.10	12 60	9.60	6.80	3.90	1.00
250	260	36.50	32 50	28.50	24.80	21.30	17.90	14.40	11.10	8.30	5.40	2.50
260	270	38.60	34.60	30.60	26.60	23.10	19.70	16.20	12.70	9.80	6.90	4.00
270	280	40.70	36 70	32.7?	28.60	24.90	21.50	18.00	14.50	11.30	8.40	5.50
280	290	42.80	38 80	34.80	30.70	26.70	23.30	19.80	16.30	12.90	9.90	7.00
290	300	45.10	40.90	36.90	32.80	28.80	25.10	21.60	18.10	14.70	11.40	8.50
$300	$310	$47 50	$43 00	$39 00	$34 90	$30 90	$26 90	$23 40	$19 90	$16.50	$13 00	$10.00
310	320	49 90	45 30	41 10	37 00	33.00	28 90	25 20	21 70	18 30	14 80	11.50
320	330	52 30	47 70	43 20	39 10	35 10	31 00	27 00	23 50	20 10	16 60	13 20
330	340	54 70	50 10	45 50	41 20	37 20	33 10	29 10	25 30	21 90	18 40	15 00
340	350	57 10	52 50	47 90	43 30	39 30	35 20	31 20	27 20	23 70	20 20	16 80
350	360	59 50	54 90	50 30	45 70	41 40	37 30	33 30	29 30	25 50	22 00	18 60
360	370	61 90	57 30	52 70	48 10	43 50	39 40	35 40	31 40	27 30	23 80	20 40
370	380	64 60	59 70	55 10	50 50	45 90	41 50	37 50	33 50	29 40	25 60	22 20
380	390	67 40	62 10	57 50	52 90	48 30	43 70	39 60	35 60	31 50	27 50	24 00
390	400	70 20	64 80	59 90	55 30	50 70	46 10	41 70	37 70	33 60	29 60	25 80

*As of the date of printing, the above Weekly Federal Income Tax Withholding Table is the most current available.

Portion of Weekly Federal Income Tax Wage-Bracket Withholding Table for Married Persons

other possible deductions that generally are voluntary and depend on specific agreements between the employee and employer. Some examples of these deductions are for:

(1) United States savings bond purchases.
(2) Life, accident or health insurance premiums.
(3) Union dues.
(4) Pension plan payments.
(5) Charitable contributions.

PAYROLL RECORDS

The needs of management and the requirements of various federal and state laws make it necessary for employers to keep records that will provide the following information for each employee:

(1) Name, address, and social security number.
(2) The gross amount of earnings, the date of payment, and the period of employment covered by each payroll.
(3) The gross amount of earnings accumulated since the first of the year.
(4) The amount of any taxes or other items withheld.

Regardless of the number of employees or type of business, three types of payroll records usually need to be prepared by the employer. They are: (1) the payroll register or payroll journal; (2) the payroll check with earnings statement attached; and (3) the earnings record of the individual employee (on a weekly, monthly, quarterly, or annual basis). These records can be prepared either by manual or by automated methods.

Record-Keeping Methods. A purely manual system is one in which all records, journals and ledgers are handwritten. Such systems are rare today. Even very small businesses use cash registers, desk calculators and other machines in performing accounting tasks. In this sense, virtually all accounting systems today are at least partially automated, i.e., they use some kind of machines in the accounting process.

In a manual system, all employee data on the payroll records, such as name, address, social security number, pay rate, hours worked, current earnings, and taxes withheld, are determined, calculated, and recorded manually. In such a system, it often is necessary to record the same data a number of times. For example, identical employee earnings amounts would be recorded on the payroll register, paycheck, and earnings record.

Automated systems can be broken down into two types: mechanical and electronic. A mechanical system is one in which various types of accounting machines are used for posting accounts, billing customers, recording payroll, and printing paychecks. An electronic system is one in which data are processed by electronic computers. On the following pages, a payroll register, payroll check, and individual employee's earnings record that were prepared using an accounting machine are illustrated.

In a mechanical system, much of the payroll information is recorded simultaneously on the payroll register, paycheck, and earnings record. This is an example of the write-it-once principle. It is often desirable to record data on a number of documents and records at the same time, because each time the same information is recopied there is another chance for an error. Many accounting machines are available that perform these functions. Most of these machines also are capable of performing the arithmetic operations necessary in preparing the payroll. Each pay period, accounting personnel still need to provide input to the machines indicating information such as employee name, social security number, gross earnings, taxes withheld, and other deductions.

In a system using electronic computers, not only are the payroll register, paycheck, and earnings record generated simultaneously, but a number of inputs need not be repeated each pay period. Computers have the ability to store internally large amounts of information, such as employee names, social security numbers, withholding allowances, pay rates, FICA and income tax withholding rates, and earnings to date. They also can perform arithmetic and logic functions required in payroll accounting. In a given pay period, based on inputs of employee social security numbers and hours worked, the computer can determine the employee names and other data and calculate gross earnings, all appropriate deductions, and net pay. The computer would then print the paychecks, the payroll register, and updated employee's earnings records.

Both mechanical and electronic processing systems are also available through companies external to an employer's business. These companies, known as service bureaus (or automation companies), perform payroll accounting, among other accounting functions, for businesses on a contract basis. A common approach is for the employer to provide a service bureau with whatever inputs the employer would need if the payroll were being prepared on the employer's own mechanical or electronic payroll system. The service bureau then processes these inputs and provides the employer with the completed payroll register, paychecks, and updated employee earnings records.

Computers are also used with payroll accounting systems on a time sharing basis. This refers to the use of a single computer by a number of small- to medium-sized businesses who share time on the computer. Thus it is possible for businesses that cannot afford their own computer to have the use of one by sharing it with other companies. Companies using time sharing have record keeping and processing situations similar to those for companies having their own computers. The main difference is that communication between time sharing users and the computer is normally by means of special telephone lines, remote computer terminals, and other electronic devices at each business location.

An important point to note in connection with this discussion of payroll record-keeping methods is that the same inputs and outputs are required in each of the three systems. Even given an electronic computer with substantial data stored in its memory, the inputs required for payroll processing have to be provided to the system at some point in time. The outputs in the form of a payroll register, paychecks, and employee earnings records are basically the same under each of the three systems. This means that the illustrations of payroll records under any of these systems are quite similar. For the sake of convenience and in order to avoid duplication, the illustrations in this chapter are based on a mechanical system only. The forms and procedures illustrated are equally applicable to a manual or an electronic system.

Payroll Register. A payroll register is a multicolumn form used to assemble, compute, and summarize the data required at the end of each payroll period. The payroll register used by Central States Diversified, Inc., for the payroll period ended December 17, 1982, is

PAYROLL

| NAME | EMPLOYEE NUMBER | NUMBER OF ALLOW. | MARITAL STATUS | EARNINGS | | | | TAXABLE EARNINGS | |
				REGULAR	OVERTIME	TOTAL	CUMULATIVE TOTAL	UNEMPLOYMENT COMP.	FICA
Becker, Mark P.	1	3	M	280.00		280.00	14,000.00		280.00
Gardner, Debra	2	1	S	320.00	35.00	355.00	17,400.00		355.00
Indiman, John A.	3	5	M	375.00		375.00	19,025.00		375.00
McGrath, Martin D.	4	2	M	590.00	60.00	650.00	30,840.00		
Reiss, Wanda T.	5	2	M	300.00		300.00	15,000.00		300.00
Sorenson, Shawn	6	2	S	400.00	45.00	445.00	21,850.00		445.00
Wight, Albert J.	7	3	M	350.00		350.00	18,220.00		350.00
Zimmer, Joel F.	8	1	S	260.00		260.00	5,200.00	260.00	260.00
				2,875.00	140.00	3,015.00	141,535.00	260.00	2,365.00

Payroll Register — Machine Prepared (Left Page)

illustrated on page 92 and below. The columnar headings are basically self-explanatory. Detailed information on earnings, taxable earnings, deductions, and net pay is summarized for each employee.

Central States Diversified, Inc., has eight employees. Debra Gardner and Joel Zimmer each claim only one allowance because each has two jobs. Shawn Sorenson claims two allowances because she has only one job. Martin McGrath and Wanda Reiss each claim only two withholding allowances because their spouses also work. Mark Becker and Albert Wight each get the special withholding allowance, but none as yet has any children.

Only the first $30,000 of earnings received in any calendar year is subject to FICA tax. As indicated in the taxable earnings columns, McGrath's earnings for the week ending December 17 are exempt from the FICA tax because earnings totaling $30,000 have already been taxed. In addition to their use in determining the employees' FICA tax, the columns for taxable earnings are needed for determining the employer's payroll taxes. These taxes are discussed on pages 102–104.

Regular deductions are made from the earnings of employees for FICA tax, federal income tax, and city earnings tax. In addition, voluntary deductions are made for the company pension plan (which is a voluntary plan), health insurance, the company credit union, and for the United Way contribution, according to agreement with individual employees. Gardner and McGrath have each authorized Central States Diversified, Inc., to withhold $15 each week for their United Way contributions. After the data for each employee have been entered, the amount columns in the payroll register must be footed and the footings verified as shown on page 94.

REGISTER

			DEDUCTIONS							
FICA TAX	FEDERAL INC. TAX	CITY TAX	PENSION PLAN	HEALTH INS.	CREDIT UNION	UNITED WAY	TOTAL	DATE	NET PAY	CK. NO.
19.60	30.70	5.60	8.00		6.25		70.15	Dec. 17, '82	209.85	301
24.85	72.00	7.10			6.25	15.00	125.20	Dec. 17, '82	229.80	302
26.25	41.50	7.50		8.00			83.25	Dec. 17, '82	291.75	303
	141.70	13.00	10.50	9.00	6.25	15.00	195.45	Dec. 17, '82	454.55	304
21.00	39.00	6.00	10.50	9.00	6.25		91.75	Dec. 17, '82	208.25	305
31.15	98.80	8.90	7.00				145.85	Dec. 17, '82	299.15	306
24.50	45.70	7.00		8.00	6.25		91.45	Dec. 17, '82	258.55	307
18.20	43.80	5.20					67.20	Dec. 17, '82	192.80	308
165.55	513.20	60.30	36.00	34.00	31.25	30.00	870.30		2,144.70	

Payroll Register — Machine Prepared (Right Page)

Regular earnings		$2,875.00
Overtime earnings		140.00
Gross earnings		$3,015.00
Deductions:		
FICA tax	$165.55	
Federal income tax	513.20	
City earnings tax	60.30	
Pension plan	36.00	
Health insurance premiums	34.00	
Credit union	31.25	
United Way	30.00	870.30
Net amount of payroll		$2,144.70

Whether the payroll system is manual or automated, this footing and verification process must be performed in order to make certain that there is no error in the payroll register. An error could cause the payment of an incorrect amount to an employee or remittance of an incorrect amount to the companies or government agencies for whom funds are deducted from the employees' gross pay.

Payroll Check. Employees may be paid in cash or by check. In some cases today, the employee does not even handle the paycheck. Rather, salary is paid via a direct deposit of the check by the employer at the employee's bank. The employee receives the deduction stub from the check and a copy of the deposit slip. Payment by check or direct deposit is strongly preferred because it provides better accounting control. Many businesses prepare a single check for the net amount of the total payroll and deposit it in a special payroll bank account. Individual paychecks are then drawn on that account for the amount due to each employee. Data needed to prepare an individual paycheck for each employee are contained in the payroll register. (In an automated system, the paychecks would normally be prepared at the same time as the payroll register.) The employer furnishes a statement of payroll deductions to each employee along with each wage payment. Paychecks with detachable stubs, like the one for John Indiman illustrated on page 95, are widely used for this purpose. Before such a check is cashed, the stub should be detached and retained by the employee as a permanent record of earnings and payroll deductions.

Employee's Earnings Record. A separate record of each employee's earnings, called an employee's earnings record, is kept in order to provide the information needed in preparing the various federal, state, and local reports required of employers. A mechanically prepared employee's earnings record used by Central States Diversified, Inc., for John A. Indiman during the last two quarters of the current calendar year is illustrated on pages 96 and 97.

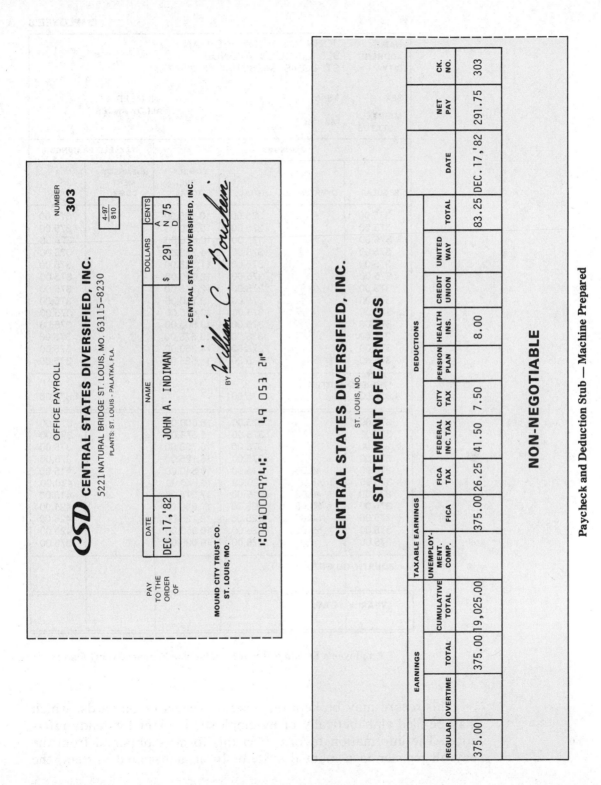

Paycheck and Deduction Stub — Machine Prepared

NAME	JOHN ANTHONY INDIMAN	
ADDRESS	925 LINCOLN AVENUE	
CITY	ST. LOUIS, MISSOURI 63120-4752	

SEX	Male	NUMBER OF ALLOWANCES
MARITAL STATUS	Married	5

EARNINGS				TAXABLE EARNINGS	
REGULAR	OVERTIME	TOTAL	CUMULA-TIVE TOTAL	UNEMPLOY-MENT COMP.	FICA
375.00		375.00	10,125.00		375.00
375.00		375.00	10,500.00		375.00
375.00		375.00	10,875.00		375.00
375.00		375.00	11,250.00		375.00
375.00		375.00	11,625.00		375.00
375.00		375.00	12,000.00		375.00
375.00		375.00	12,375.00		375.00
375.00		375.00	12,750.00		375.00
375.00		375.00	13,125.00		375.00
375.00		375.00	13,500.00		375.00
375.00		375.00	13,875.00		375.00
375.00		375.00	14,250.00		375.00
375.00		375.00	14,625.00		375.00
THIRD QUARTER 4,875.00		4,875.00			4,875.00
375.00		375.00	15,000.00		375.00
375.00		375.00	15,375.00		375.00
375.00		375.00	15,750.00		375.00
375.00		375.00	16,125.00		375.00
375.00	40.00	415.00	16,540.00		415.00
375.00	45.00	420.00	16,960.00		420.00
375.00	40.00	415.00	17,375.00		415.00
375.00	50.00	425.00	17,800.00		425.00
375.00	50.00	425.00	18,225.00		425.00
375.00	50.00	425.00	18,650.00		425.00
375.00		375.00	19,025.00		375.00
FOURTH QUARTER					
YEARLY TOTAL					

Employee's Earnings Record — Machine Prepared (Left Page)

This record may be kept on separate sheets or on cards, which may be filed alphabetically or by employee number for ready reference. The information recorded on this form is obtained from the payroll register in a manual system. In an automated system, the

EARNINGS RECORD

DEPARTMENT	Maintenance	SOCIAL SECURITY NUMBER	307-78-3813
OCCUPATION	Service	DATE OF BIRTH	September 19, 1960
PAY RATE	$375 Weekly	DATE EMPLOYED	January 3, 1979
EMPLOYEE NO.	3	DATE EMPLOYMENT TERMINATED	

			DEDUCTIONS							
FICA TAX	FEDERAL INC. TAX	CITY TAX	PENSION PLAN	HEALTH INS.	CREDIT UNION	UNITED WAY	TOTAL	DATE	NET PAY	CK. NO.
26.25	41.50	7.50		8.00			83.25	July 9, '82	291.75	119
26.25	41.50	7.50		8.00			83.25	July 16, '82	291.75	127
26.25	41.50	7.50		8.00			83.25	July 23, '82	291.75	135
26.25	41.50	7.50		8.00			83.25	July 30, '82	291.75	143
26.25	41.50	7.50		8.00			83.25	Aug. 6, '82	291.75	151
26.25	41.50	7.50		8.00			83.25	Aug. 13, '82	291.75	159
26.25	41.50	7.50		8.00			83.25	Aug. 20, '82	291.75	167
26.25	41.50	7.50		8.00			83.25	Aug. 27, '82	291.75	175
26.25	41.50	7.50		8.00			83.25	Sept. 3, '82	291.75	183
26.25	41.50	7.50		8.00			83.25	Sept. 10, '82	291.75	191
26.25	41.50	7.50		8.00			83.25	Sept. 17, '82	291.75	199
26.25	41.50	7.50		8.00			83.25	Sept. 24, '82	291.75	207
26.25	41.50	7.50		8.00			83.25	Oct. 1, '82	291.75	215
341.25	539.50	97.50		104.00			1,082.25		3,792.75	
26.25	41.50	7.50		8.00			83.25	Oct. 8, '82	291.75	223
26.25	41.50	7.50		8.00			83.25	Oct. 15, '82	291.75	231
26.25	41.50	7.50		8.00			83.25	Oct. 22, '82	291.75	239
26.25	41.50	7.50		8.00			83.25	Oct. 29, '82	291.75	247
29.05	50.90	8.30		8.00			96.25	Nov. 5, '82	318.75	255
29.40	53.90	8.40		8.00			99.10	Nov. 12, '82	320.90	263
29.05	50.90	8.30		8.00			96.25	Nov. 19, '82	318.75	271
29.75	53.30	8.50		8.00			99.55	Nov. 26, '82	325.45	279
29.75	53.30	8.50·		8.00			99.55	Dec. 3, '82	325.45	287
29.75	53.30	8.50		8.00			99.55	Dec. 10, '82	325.45	295
26.25	41.50	7.50		8.00			83.25	Dec. 17, '82	291.75	303

Employee's Earnings Record — Machine Prepared (Right Page)

employee's earnings record can be updated simultaneously with the preparation of the payroll register.

Indiman's earnings for the last half of the year up to December 17 are shown on this form. The entry for the pay period ended December 17 is posted from the payroll register illustrated on pages 92 and 93.

The payroll register is a summary of the earnings of all employees for each pay period, while the earnings record is a summary of the annual earnings of each employee. The earnings record illustrated on pages 96 and 97 is designed so that quarterly and yearly totals can be accumulated. Thus the form provides a complete record of the earnings of an employee for the year — information that is needed in preparing an annual report to the employee and the Internal Revenue Service on a form called a Wage and Tax Statement. This report is explained in the following section. The earnings record also provides information on an employee's quarterly earnings, which is needed for filing quarterly reports to government agencies on various forms. These reports will be discussed later in this chapter.

WAGE AND TAX STATEMENT

Not later than January 31 of each year, the law requires employers to furnish each employee from whom income taxes have been withheld an annual report called a Wage and Tax Statement, Form W-2, showing the total amount of wages paid and the amount of such tax withheld during the preceding calendar year. A completed form W-2 is illustrated on page 99. If the employee's wages are subject to FICA tax as well as federal, state, or local income tax, the employer must report total wages paid and the amounts deducted both for income tax and for FICA tax. Information for this purpose is contained in the employee's earnings record.

The employer's identification number appearing on the Wage and Tax Statement is an an identification number assigned to the employer by the Internal Revenue Service. An employer who employs one or more persons must file for an identification number. This number must be shown on all reports required of Central States Diversified, Inc., under the Federal Insurance Contributions Act.

Wage and Tax Statements must be prepared in quadruplicate. Copy A goes to the Social Security Administration. Copies B and C are furnished to the employee; Copy B must be sent in with the employee's federal income tax return, and Copy C is for the employee's files. Copy D is kept by the employer as part of the accounting records. In states or cities which have state or city income tax withholding laws, two more copies are furnished. Copy 1 is sent by the employer to the appropriate state or city tax department, and Copy 2 is sent by the employee with the state or city income tax return.

1 Control number	22222						

2 Employer's name, address, and ZIP code

Central States Diversified, Inc.
5221 Natural Bridge
St. Louis, MO 63115-8230

3 Employer's identification number 43-0211630

4 Employer's State number 21-686001

5 Stat. em-ployee | De-ceased | Pension plan | Legal rep. | 942 emp. | Sub-total | Cor-rection | Void

6 •

7 Advance EIC payment

8 Employee's social security number 307-78-3813

9 Federal income tax withheld $2,224.00

10 Wages, tips, other compensation $19,775.00

11 FICA tax withheld $1,384.25

12 Employee's name (first, middle, last)
John Anthony Indiman

13 FICA wages $19,775.00

14 FICA tips

16 Employer's use

925 Lincoln Ave.
St. Louis, MO 63120-4752

17 State income tax

18 State wages, tips, etc.

19 Name of State

20 Local income tax $395.50

21 Local wages, tips, etc. $19,775.00

22 Name of locality St. Louis Co.

15 Employee's address and ZIP code

Form **W-2 Wage and Tax Statement 1982**   Copy A For Social Security Administration
• See Instructions for Forms W-2 and W-2P   Department of the Treasury Internal Revenue Service

Wage and Tax Statement (Form W-2)

ACCOUNTING FOR EMPLOYEE EARNINGS AND EARNINGS DEDUCTIONS

In accounting for employee earnings and deductions from earnings, it is desirable to keep separate accounts for (1) earnings and (2) earnings deductions. Various account titles are used in recording wages, such as Payroll Expense, Salaries Expense, and Salaries and Commissions Expense. The accounts needed in recording earnings deductions depend upon what deductions are involved. It helps in understanding the accounting for these deductions if we recognize that in withholding amounts from employees' earnings, the employer basically is serving as an agent for various groups such as the federal government, insurance companies, and labor unions. Amounts that are withheld and deducted from an employee's gross earnings must be paid by the employer to these groups. Therefore, a separate account should be kept for the liability incurred under each type of deduction, such as employee income tax, FICA tax, and insurance premiums. Examples of several of the major accounts involved in payroll accounting and of a typical journal entry for payroll are presented in the following sections.

Payroll Expense. This is an expense account which is debited for the total amount of the gross earnings of all employees for each pay period. Sometimes separate payroll accounts are kept for the employees of different departments. Thus separate accounts may be kept for Office Salaries Expense, Sales Salaries Expense, and Factory Payroll Expense.

Payroll Expense

Debit	
to record gross earnings of employees for each pay period.	

FICA Tax Payable. This is a liability account which is credited for (1) the FICA tax withheld from employees' earnings and (2) the FICA tax imposed on the employer. FICA taxes imposed on the employer are discussed later in the chapter. The account should be debited for amounts paid to the Internal Revenue Service. When all of the FICA taxes have been paid, the account should be in balance.

FICA Tax Payable

Debit	Credit
to record payment of FICA tax previously withheld or imposed.	to record FICA taxes (1) withheld from employees' earnings and (2) imposed on the employer.

Employees Income Tax Payable. This is a liability account which should be credited for the total income tax withheld from employees' earnings. The account is debited for amounts paid to a bank depository for the Internal Revenue Service. When all of the income taxes withheld have been paid, the account will be in balance. A city or state earnings tax payable account is used in a similar manner.

Employees Income Tax Payable

Debit	Credit
to record payment of income tax previously withheld.	to record income tax withheld from employees' earnings.

Other Deductions. Pension Plan Deductions Payable is a liability account which is credited with amounts withheld from employees' earnings for any pension plan contributions. The account should be debited for the subsequent payment of these amounts to the pension plan trustee. Accounts for health insurance premiums payable, credit union contributions payable, and United Way contributions payable are similarly used.

Journalizing Payroll Transactions. The information needed to properly record the payment of employee wages and salaries is contained in the payroll register. The totals at the bottom of the columns of the payroll register on pages 92 and 93 provide the basis for the following two-column journal entry to record wages paid on December 17, 1982:

Dec. 17	Payroll Expense	3,015.00
	FICA Tax Payable	165.55
	Employees Income Tax Payable	513.20
	City Earnings Tax Payable................................	60.30
	Pension Plan Deductions Payable....................	36.00
	Health Insurance Premiums Payable...............	34.00
	Credit Union Contributions Payable................	31.25
	United Way Contributions Payable..................	30.00
	Cash	2,144.70
	Payroll for week ended December 17.	

These amounts are posted to payroll expense and liability accounts such as those illustrated in the preceding paragraphs.

BUILDING YOUR ACCOUNTING KNOWLEDGE

1. Why is it important for payroll accounting purposes to distinguish between an employee and an independent contractor?
2. Name three factors that generally explain the difference between an employee's gross pay and net pay.
3. Identify the four factors that determine the amount of federal income tax that is withheld from an employee's pay each pay period.
4. What factors determine the number of withholding allowances to which a taxpayer is entitled?
5. Identify the three types of payroll records usually needed by an employer.
6. Describe the information contained in the payroll register.
7. Why is it important to foot and verify the footings of the payroll register after the data for each employee have been entered?
8. Distinguish between the payroll register and the employee earnings record.
9. Explain what an employer does with the amounts withheld from an employee's pay.

Report No. 4-1

> *Complete Report No. 4-1 in the study assignments and submit your working papers to the instructor for approval. After completing the report, continue with the following textbook discussion until the next report is required.*

PAYROLL TAXES IMPOSED ON THE EMPLOYER

The various taxes discussed thus far have had one thing in common — they all were levied on the employee. The employer withholds them from the employees' earnings only for the purpose of subsequently paying them to some agency or organization. They do not represent any additional expense of the employer.

In addition to these employee taxes, however, certain taxes are also imposed directly on the employer for various purposes, such as: old-age, survivors, and disability insurance benefits; hospital insurance benefits for the aged; and unemployment, relief, and welfare. Most employers are subject to payroll taxes imposed under the Federal Insurance Contributions Act (FICA) and the Federal Unemployment Tax Act (FUTA). An employer may also be subject to the payroll tax imposed under the unemployment compensation laws of one or more states. This tax is commonly called a State Unemployment Tax. All of these employer taxes do represent additional payroll expenses of the employer, as will be demonstrated in subsequent sections.

EMPLOYER'S FICA TAX

The taxes imposed under the Federal Insurance Contributions Act are levied on employers for exactly the same amounts as employees. As explained on page 86, the rate and the taxable earnings base of the tax may be changed by Congress at any time. It was assumed in this chapter that the combined rate (OASDI and HIP) is 7 percent and the base is $30,000. Thus the employer would be required to pay the employer's share of the FICA tax at a rate of 7% on the first $30,000 of each employee's earnings. Any amount of earnings paid to an employee during a year in excess of $30,000 is exempt from FICA tax. (Note that a total of 14% of each employee's taxable earnings — the employer's share and the employee's share — must be paid periodically to an authorized bank or the Internal Revenue Service.)

EMPLOYER'S FUTA TAX

Under the Federal Unemployment Tax Act, a payroll tax, called the FUTA tax, is levied on employers for the purpose of financing the cost of administering the federal-state unemployment compensation program. This tax is levied only on employers and is not deducted from employees' earnings. Employers who employ one or more persons for at least one day in each of 20 or more calendar weeks in a calendar year, or who pay wages of $1,500 or more in any calendar quarter are subject to this tax. The federal law imposes a specific rate of tax on a specific earnings base but allows a substantial credit against this levy for amounts paid into state unemployment compensation programs. Since all states have such programs, the amounts actually paid to the federal government by most employers are substantially less than the legal maximum. Most of the total amount of tax levied under the FUTA program typically is paid to the state governments.

As in the case of the FICA tax, Congress can and does change both the rate and the taxable base of the FUTA tax from time to time. For the purpose of this discussion, a rate of 3.4 percent with a credit of 2.7 percent for payments to state unemployment programs is assumed. The difference, 0.7 percent (3.4%–2.7%) is the effective federal rate. It is further assumed that the taxable base is the first $6,000 of compensation paid to each employee during the calendar year. Note that both the rate and base are substantially lower than the 7 percent and $30,000 for the FICA tax. It is also important to note that all of the payroll taxes relate to gross wages paid — not to wages earned. Sometimes wages are earned in one quarter or year, but not paid until the following period.

EMPLOYER'S STATE UNEMPLOYMENT TAX

All of the states and the District of Columbia have enacted unemployment compensation laws providing for the payment of benefits to qualified unemployed workers. The cost of administering the state unemployment compensation laws is borne by the federal government. Under the federal law an appropriation is made for each year by the Congress from which grants are made to the states to meet the proper administrative costs of their unemployment compensation laws. As a result of this provision, the entire amount paid into the state funds may be used for the payment of benefits to qualified workers. While in general there is considerable uniformity in the provisions of the state laws, there are many variations in coverage, rates of tax imposed, and benefits payable to qualified workers. The date of payment of unemployment taxes also varies from state to state, and a penalty generally is imposed on the employer for late payment. Not all employers covered by the Federal Unemployment Tax Act are covered by the unemployment compensation laws of the states in which they have employees. But most employers of one or more individuals are covered by the federal law.

There are frequent changes in the state laws with respect to coverage, contribution rates required, eligibility to receive benefits, and amounts of benefits payable. In this discussion, it is assumed that the state tax rate is 2.7 percent of the first $6,000 of wages paid each employee each year. However, under the laws of most states there is a merit-rating system which provides a tax-saving incentive to employers to stabilize employment. Under this system, an employer's rate may be considerably less than the maximum rate if steady work is provided for the employees, i.e., if none or very few of the employer's workers have applied for unemployment compensation. If an employer qualifies for a lower state rate, the full credit of 2.7 percent would still be allowed in computing the federal unemployment tax due.

To illustrate the merit-rating system and the functioning of the federal-state unemployment tax program as a whole, assume that an employer has a favorable merit rating and is required to pay only 1.0 percent rather than 2.7 percent to the state government. If an employee earns $4,000, this employer would be required to pay a total of $68 in unemployment taxes; $40 to the state government and $28 to the federal government, calculated as follows:

Taxable earnings		$4,000
State unemployment tax rate		× 1.0%
State unemployment tax		$ 40
Taxable earnings		$4,000
Total FUTA rate	3.4%	
Credit for state program	2.7%	
		× 0.7%
Federal unemployment tax		$ 28

ACCOUNTING FOR EMPLOYER PAYROLL TAXES

In accounting for employer payroll taxes, it is acceptable either to use separate accounts for FICA Tax Expense, FUTA Tax Expense, and State Unemployment Tax Expense, or to record all of these taxes in a single account such as Payroll Taxes Expense. Liabilities for FICA, FUTA, and state unemployment taxes normally should be recorded in separate accounts. Examples of the payroll taxes expense and liability accounts and a typical journal entry for payroll taxes are presented in the following sections.

Payroll Taxes Expense. All of the payroll taxes imposed on an employer under the federal and state social security laws are an expense of the employer. For the purpose of this discussion, it is assumed that a single account entitled Payroll Taxes Expense is used in summarizing such taxes. This is an expense account which is debited for all payroll taxes imposed on the employer.

Payroll Taxes Expense

Debit
to record FICA, FUTA, and state unemployment taxes imposed on the employer.

FICA Tax Payable. This is the same liability account that was illustrated on page 100 and was used to recognize the FICA tax withheld from employees' earnings. As used here, the account is credited to record the FICA tax imposed on the employer. The account is debited when the tax is paid to the Internal Revenue Service. When all of the FICA taxes have been paid, the account should be in balance.

FICA Tax Payable

Debit	Credit
to record payment of FICA tax.	to record FICA taxes (1) withheld from employees' earnings and (2) imposed on the employer.

FUTA Tax Payable. In recording the federal unemployment tax, it is customary to keep a separate liability account entitled FUTA Tax Payable. This is a liability account which is credited for the tax imposed on employers under the Federal Unemployment Tax Act. The account is debited for amounts paid to apply on such taxes. When all of the FUTA taxes have been paid, the account should be in balance.

FUTA Tax Payable

Debit	Credit
to record payment of FUTA tax.	to record FUTA tax imposed on the employer.

State Unemployment Tax Payable. In recording the tax imposed under state unemployment compensation laws, it is customary to keep a separate liability account entitled State Unemployment Tax Payable. This is a liability account which is credited for the tax imposed on employers under the state unemployment compensation laws. The account is debited for the amount paid to apply on such taxes. When all of the state taxes have been paid, the account should be in balance. Some employers who are subject to taxes imposed under the laws of several states keep a separate liability account for the tax imposed by each state.

State Unemployment Tax Payable

Debit	Credit
to record state unemployment tax paid.	to record state unemployment tax imposed on the employer.

Journalizing Employer's Payroll Taxes. The payroll taxes imposed on employers may be recorded periodically, such as monthly or quarterly. It is more common to record such taxes at the time that wages are paid so that the employer's liability for such taxes and related expenses may be recorded in the same period as the wages on which the taxes are based.

The information needed to properly record employer payroll taxes is contained in the payroll register such as the one illustrated on pages 92 and 93. The totals at the bottom of the two columns for "Taxable Earnings" headed "Unemployment Comp." and "FICA" indicate the total employee earnings on which employer taxes would be levied. The FICA taxable earnings for the pay period involved amounted to $2,365.00. Assuming that the combined rate of the tax imposed on the employer was 7 percent, which is the same as the rate of the tax imposed on each employee, the tax would amount to $165.55. The only earnings in the payroll register that were subject to unemployment compensation taxes were Zimmer's earnings for the year because they had not exceeded the $6,000 taxable base. Zimmer just started working for Central States Diversified, Inc., on August 1, 1982. Federal and state unemployment taxes in this situation can be computed as follows:

State unemployment tax, 2.7% of $260 .... $7.02
FUTA tax, 0.7% of $260 .... 1.82
Total unemployment taxes $8.84

The following two-column journal entry would therefore be made to record employer payroll taxes expense on wages paid on December 17. These amounts would be posted to payroll taxes expense and liability accounts such as those illustrated in the preceding paragraphs.

Dec. 17   Payroll Taxes Expense 174.39
          FICA Tax Payable 165.55
          FUTA Tax Payable 1.82
          State Unemployment Tax Payable 7.02
          Employer payroll taxes for the week ended De-
          cember 17.

An alternative approach employed by some businesses is to record employer payroll taxes only when they are paid. Under this approach, the above entry would not be made on December 17. Rather, at the time the employer payroll taxes were paid, an entry would be made debiting Payroll Taxes Expense and crediting Cash (or Bank) for the total amount of the employer payroll taxes. The business illustrated in the following chapter accounts for employer payroll taxes in this manner.

It is important to note in these illustrations the total cost incurred by an employer in order to employ a person. The employer must of course pay the gross wages of an employee, either in whole or in part to the employee, or in part to various government agencies and other organizations. In addition to these gross wages, however, the employer must pay payroll taxes on wages paid to an employee up to certain dollar limits. To illustrate this point, assume that an employee earns $20,000 for a year. The total cost of this employee to the employer can be calculated as follows:

Gross wages $20,000.00
Employer FICA tax, 7% of $20,000 ....   1,400.00
State unemployment tax, 2.7% of $6,000 ....   162.00
FUTA tax, 0.7% of $6,000 ....   42.00
                                                 $21,604.00

Thus, the total cost to an employer of employing a person whose salary is $20,000 is not $20,000, but $21,604.00. Employer payroll taxes clearly are a signficant cost of doing business.

FILING RETURNS AND MAKING PAYROLL TAX PAYMENTS

Employer responsibilities for filing reports and making payroll tax payments can be broken down into two areas: (1) responsibility with respect to FICA and federal income taxes, and (2) responsibility with respect to state and federal unemployment taxes. These two areas are discussed in the following sections.

Responsibilities for FICA and Federal Income Taxes. Federal reporting and payment regulations deal jointly with requirements for employee FICA taxes withheld, federal income taxes withheld, and employer FICA taxes. When the cumulative amount withheld from employees for FICA and income tax purposes plus the cumulative amount of employer FICA tax exceeds certain specified dollar amounts as of particular dates, an employer is required to deposit the amount in a District Federal Reserve Bank or some other authorized depository. The dollar amounts and dates have been changed several times in recent years and are subject to change at any time in the future. In general, large employers are required to make deposits about every four days. Medium-size employers generally are required to make deposits by the 15th of each month. In contrast, very small employers may need to make a deposit only at the end of each quarter. For the sake of convenience in this chapter, it is assumed that the cumulative amount of FICA and income taxes at the end of each month must be deposited by the 15th of the following month.

At the time any one of these tax deposits is made, the employer should submit to the depository bank a completed copy of the Federal Tax Deposit — Withheld Income and FICA Taxes, Form 501. An example of this form is shown on page 109.

To illustrate the accounting procedure for recording the payment of employees' FICA and income taxes withheld and employer's FICA tax, assume that on February 15, Central States Diversified, Inc., issued a check in payment of the following taxes imposed with respect to wages paid during the first four payroll weeks of January:

Employees' income tax withheld from wages		$1,875.90
FICA tax:		
Withheld from employees' wages	$789.45	
Imposed on employer	789.45	1,578.90
Amount of check		$3,454.80

The journal entry to properly record this transaction would be as follows:

Feb. 15	FICA Tax Payable	1,578.90	
	Employees Income Tax Payable	1,875.90	
	Cash		3,454.80
	Remitted $3,454.80 in payment of taxes.		

Another major form that the employer must file in connection with employee FICA and income taxes withheld and cumulative employer FICA taxes is Form 941. This is the Employer's Quarterly

FEDERAL TAX DEPOSIT OF: WITHHELD INCOME AND FICA TAX

REPORT ON IRS RETURN	NAME OF BANK	AMOUNT OF DEPOSIT	
	GUARANTY NATIONAL	3,454	80
		DOLLARS	CENTS
941	CENTRAL STATES DIVERSIFIED, INC.		
	5221 NATURAL BRIDGE		
501	ST. LOUIS, MO 63115-8230		
FTD Form			

Employer Identification Number
43-0211630
1 37 43
JAN 83
Tax Period Ending

DEPARTMENT OF THE TREASURY - FISCAL SERVICE
Bureau of Government Financial Operations - FTD Form Rev. Oct. 1977

THE DEPARTMENT OF THE TREASURY 1789

ENTER AMOUNT OF DEPOSIT AND NAME OF BANK WHERE DEPOSITED IN SPACE ABOVE

The space below may be used by depositaries for MICR encoding

Bank Name/Date Stamp

Federal Tax Deposit Form (Form 501)

Federal Tax Return which must be filed with the Internal Revenue Service during the month following the end of each quarter. A completed copy of Form 941 which would be used by Central States Diversified, Inc., on April 15, 1983, to file for the quarter ended April 1, 1983, is shown on page 110. This form summarizes employee FICA and federal income taxes withheld and employer FICA taxes due for the quarter. Portions of the information needed to complete Form 941 are obtained from the payroll register.

Responsibilities for State and Federal Unemployment Taxes. The amount of the tax imposed on employers under the state unemployment compensation laws must be remitted to the proper state office during the month following the close of each calendar quarter. Each state provides an official form to be used in making a return of the taxes due. To illustrate the accounting procedure for recording the payment of state unemployment taxes, assume that a check for $629.70 was issued on April 30 in payment of state unemployment compensation taxes on wages paid during the preceding quarter ended April 1. This transaction would be recorded properly with the following two-column journal entry:

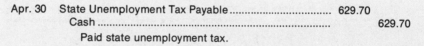

Apr. 30	State Unemployment Tax Payable	629.70	
	Cash		629.70
	Paid state unemployment tax.		

Federal unemployment tax must be computed on a quarterly basis. If the amount of the employer's liability under the Federal Unemployment Tax Act during any quarter is more than $100, the

[¶ 208] 151 4-81 [Form 941] 1175

Form **941**
(Rev. March 1981)
Department of the Treasury
Internal Revenue Service

Employer's Quarterly Federal Tax Return

T			
FF			
FD			
FP			
I			
T			

Your name, address, employer identification number, and calendar quarter of return. (If not correct, please change.)

Name (as distinguished from trade name): Central States Diversified, Inc.
Date quarter ended: March 31, 1983
Trade name, if any: Central States
Employer identification number: 43-0211630
Address and ZIP code: 5221 Natural Bridge, St. Louis, MO 63115-8230

If address is different from prior return, check here ▶ ☐

1	Number of employees (except household) employed in the pay period that includes March 12th (complete first quarter only)	8	
2	Total wages and tips subject to withholding, plus other compensation →	36,675	00
3	Total income tax withheld from wages, tips, annuities, sick pay, gambling, etc.	6,084	70
4	Adjustment of withheld income tax for preceding quarters of calendar year	-0-	
5	Adjusted total of income tax withheld →	6,084	70
6	Taxable FICA wages paid $ 36,675.00 times 14.0% = TAX	5,134	50
7 a	Taxable tips reported $ times 7.0% = TAX	-0-	
b	Tips deemed to be wages (see instructions) $ times 7.0% = TAX	-0-	
8	Total FICA taxes (add lines 6, 7a, and 7b) →	5,134	50
9	Adjustment of FICA taxes (see instructions)	-0-	
10	Adjusted total of FICA taxes →	5,134	50
11	Total taxes (add lines 5 and 10)	11,219	20
12	Advance earned income credit (EIC) payments, if any (see instructions)	-0-	
13	Net taxes (subtract line 12 from line 11)	11,219	20

▶ ☐ Check if you are a first-time 3-banking-day depositor (see Specific Instructions on page 6).

Record of Federal Tax Deposits

Deposit period ending:		a. Tax liability for period	b. Date of deposit	c. Amount deposited
Overpayment from previous quarter				
I First month total	I	3,454.80	Feb. 15	3,454.80
Second month of quarter: 1st through 3rd day	I			
4th through 7th day	J	863.10		
8th through 11th day	K	863.00		
12th through 15th day	L			
16th through 19th day	M	861.80		
20th through 22nd day	N			
23rd through 25th day	O	862.40		
26th through last day	P			
II Second month total	II	3,450.30	Mar. 15	3,450.30
III Third month total	III	4,314.10	Apr. 15	4,314.10
IV Total for quarter (add items I, II, and III)		11,219.20		11,219.20
V Final deposit made for quarter. (Enter 0 if included in item IV.)				-0-
VI Total deposits for quarter. Add items IV and V. Enter here and on line 14 on next page				11,219.20

13 a	Net taxes. Enter amount from line 13 on front	11,219	20
14	Total deposits for quarter. Enter amount from item VI on front	11,219	20
15	Undeposited taxes due (subtract line 14 from line 13a). Pay to Internal Revenue Service and enter here ▶	-0-	
16	If line 14 is more than line 13a, enter overpayment here ▶ $ and check if to be: ☐ Applied to next return, or ☐ Refunded.		
17	Number of Forms W–4 enclosed. Do not send originals. (See General and Specific Instructions.)		
18	If you are not liable for returns in the future, write "FINAL" (see instructions) ▶ Date final wages paid ▶		

Under penalties of perjury, I declare that I have examined this return, including accompanying schedules and statements, and to the best of my knowledge and belief it is true, correct, and complete.

Date ▶ April 15, 1983 Signature ▶ *William C. Boucheen* Title ▶ Treasurer

Please file this form with your Internal Revenue Service Center (see instructions on "Where to File").

[¶ 208]

Employer's Quarterly Federal Tax Return and Quarterly Report (Form 941)

total must be paid to a Federal Reserve Bank or some other authorized depository by the last day of the first month following the close of the quarter. If the amount is $100 or less, no deposit is necessary, but this amount must be added to the amount subject to deposit for the next quarter. When a federal unemployment tax deposit is made, the employer should submit to the bank a completed copy of the Federal Tax Deposit form, Form 508. This form is similar to Form 501, which was illustrated on page 109.

In addition to these quarterly reports and deposits, employers are required to submit an annual report of federal unemployment tax on Form 940 to the District Director of Internal Revenue by the end of the month following the close of the calendar year. Form 940 is not illustrated here. Any federal unemployment tax due for the last quarter or for other periods during the year would be submitted with Form 940.

To illustrate the accounting procedure for payment of federal unemployment tax, assume that a check for $138.30 was issued on January 31 in payment of federal unemployment tax on wages paid during the preceding quarter ended December 31. This transaction would be recorded properly with the following two-column journal entry:

Jan. 31	FUTA Tax Payable	138.30	
	Cash		138.30
	Paid federal unemployment tax.		

BUILDING YOUR ACCOUNTING KNOWLEDGE

1. Why do employer payroll taxes represent an additional expense to the employer whereas, the various employee payroll taxes do not?
2. What is the purpose of the FUTA tax and who must pay it?
3. Why is most of the total amount of the tax levied under the FUTA program typically paid to the state governments?
4. Describe how a state merit-rating system works to reduce an employer's unemployment tax rate.
5. Identify all items that are debited or credited to the FICA Tax Payable account.
6. Explain why an employee whose gross salary is $16,000 costs an employer more than $16,000 to employ.
7. What is the purpose of the Employer's Quarterly Federal Tax Return Form 941?
8. What accounts are affected when employer payroll tax expenses are properly recorded?

Report No. 4-2

> Complete Report No. 4-2 in the study assignments and sub-mit your working papers to the instructor for approval. After completing the report, you may continue with the textbook discussion in Chapter 5 until the next report is required.

EXPANDING YOUR BUSINESS VOCABULARY

What is the meaning of each of the following terms?

additional withholding
  allowances (p. 87)
automated systems (p. 91)
direct deposit (p. 94)
electronic system (p. 91)
employee (p. 83)
employee's earnings record
  (pp. 90, 94)
employer's identification
  number (p. 98)
fee (p. 83)
FICA taxes (p. 85)
FUTA tax (p. 102)
gross pay (p. 85)
independent contractor (p. 83)
manual system (p. 90)

mechanical system (p. 91)
merit-rating system (p. 104)
net pay (p. 85)
payroll register (pp. 90, 92)
salary (p. 84)
service bureaus (p. 91)
special withholding allowance
  (p. 87)
State Unemployment Tax
  (p. 102)
time sharing (p. 92)
wage-bracket method (p. 88)
wages (p. 84)
withholding allowance (p. 87)
write-it-once principle (p. 91)
zero-bracket amounts (p. 87)

CHAPTER 5

ACCOUNTING FOR A PERSONAL SERVICE ENTERPRISE

CHAPTER OBJECTIVES

The objectives of this chapter are to enable you:

▶ To combine the basic ideas, procedures, forms, and records that have been described and illustrated thus far into a real-world accounting system.

▶ To explain and prepare a multicolumn book of original entry (the combination journal) and a four-column form of balance-column ledger.

▶ To describe the cash basis of accounting and to recognize the limits of its application.

▶ To explain and perform the following end-of-period steps in the accounting process:
  (1) Determining needed adjustments to the accounts.
  (2) Preparing an end-of-period work sheet.
  (3) Preparing financial statements with the aid of the work sheet.
  (4) Journalizing and posting adjusting entries.
  (5) Journalizing and posting closing entries.
  (6) Preparing a post-closing trial balance.

A **personal service enterprise** is one in which the principal source of revenue is compensation for services rendered to a business firm or to a person. This is in contrast to a **mercantile enterprise** which buys merchandise for resale and a **manufacturing enterprise** which makes and sells one or more products. There are two major types of personal service enterprises:

(1) Business enterprises
(2) Professional enterprises

Personal service **business enterprises** include real estate, insurance, advertising, transportation, storage, entertainment, brokerage, and various other firms. Personal service **professional enterprises** include attorneys, physicians, dentists, public accountants, management consultants, engineers, architects, artists, and educators. The principal source of revenue for individuals engaged in these two types of enterprises is usually the compensation received for rendering personal services.

THE CASH BASIS OF ACCOUNTING FOR A PERSONAL SERVICE ENTERPRISE

Accounting for revenue on a cash basis, **cash basis revenue**, means that no record of revenue is made in the accounts until the cash is received for the services performed. Some services may be rendered in one period but the revenue from them will not be accounted for until received in the succeeding period. The business or professional person using the cash basis of accounting takes the view that there is no revenue until it is received in such a form that it can be spent. One cannot "spend" the promise of a customer or client to pay some money.

The cash basis is widely used in accounting for the revenue of a personal service enterprise. It is acceptable for federal and state income tax purposes. Under this basis, revenue is recognized not only when cash is received but also when certain other types of transactions or events occur. For example, any property or service that is accepted in lieu of cash for services rendered is treated as revenue to the extent of its fair market value at the time received. Revenue from interest on a savings account is said to be a **constructive receipt** if it is credited to the depositor's account or set apart so that it can be drawn upon. Such interest need not actually be received in cash or be withdrawn immediately.

Accounting for expenses on the cash basis, **cash basis expense**, generally means that expenses are not recorded in the accounts until paid for in cash. Consequently, a certain expense may be incurred in one period and recorded in the accounts in the succeeding period. In the case of many expenses of a recurring nature, however, this situation is not considered to be a significant problem. If, for example, twelve monthly telephone bills of about the same amount are paid during each year, little importance is attached to the fact that the bill that is paid and recorded as an expense in January is really for service that was received in December.

An exception to the cash basis of accounting for expenses is made in connection with most plant and equipment. For example, it would be unreasonable to consider the entire cost of a building or piece of equipment to be an expense of the period in which these assets were purchased. It is expected that these assets will serve for a number of years. Their cost less any expected scrap or salvage value should be allocated over their estimated useful lives. The part of the original cost of the asset that is assigned to each period expected to benefit from its use is described as depreciation expense. Such expense cannot be calculated with precise accuracy. Still, this allocation results in a far more equitable periodic net income (profit) or loss measurement than one that simply considers the costs of such assets to be entirely expenses of the period in which they were purchased.

Another exception to the cash basis of accounting for expenses is sometimes made in connection with supplies purchased and later used. If the amount of money so invested is substantial and at the end of the accounting period a considerable quantity of expensive supplies is still on hand, an effort is made to determine the cost of those items which are on hand, so that only the cost of the supplies used will be treated as an expense of the period. If both the quantity and the cost of the items on hand at the end of an accounting period are small, the usual practice is to consider the total cost of all items purchased during that accounting period to be an expense of that period.

ILLUSTRATION OF ACCOUNTING PROCEDURE

As an aid in applying the principles and procedures involved in keeping the accounts of a personal service enterprise on the cash basis, a system of accounts for John H. Roberts, a management consultant, will be described. While certain distinctive problems may arise in keeping the accounts of any specific enterprise, it will be found that the principles are generally the same; hence, the system of accounts used by Roberts may readily be adapted to the needs of any personal service enterprise regardless of whether it is of a professional or a business nature.

CHART OF ACCOUNTS

Roberts' chart of accounts is reproduced below. Note that all account numbers beginning with 1 and 2 relate to assets; 3, liabilities; 5, owner's equity; 6, revenue; and 8, expenses. Account numbers that have four digits with a decimal point between the third and fourth digits represent contra accounts meaning "opposite" or "offsetting" accounts. A contra account is used with a related account to bring about a decrease in the net amount of the two account balances. This system of account numbering permits the addition of new accounts as they may be needed without disturbing the numerical order of the existing accounts.

Most of the accounts in the chart have been discussed and their use illustrated in the preceding chapters. Three notable exceptions are: Accumulated Depreciation — Office Equipment (No. 211.1), Depreciation Expense (No. 827), and Expense and Revenue Summary (No. 531). Each of these will be explained and its use illustrated as the need for the account arises in the narrative of transactions on pages 120–128. Except for Depreciation Expense, every debit to an expense account arises in connection with a cash dis-

---

JOHN H. ROBERTS, MANAGEMENT CONSULTANT
CHART OF ACCOUNTS

Assets*
111   County Bank
112   Petty Cash
211   Office Equipment
211.1 Accumulated Depreciation —
        Office Equipment

Liabilities
311   FICA Tax Payable
314   Employees Income Tax Payable

Owner's Equity
511   John H. Roberts, Capital
511.1 John H. Roberts, Drawing
531   Expense and Revenue
        Summary

Revenue
611   Professional Fees

Expenses
821   Rent Expense
822   Salary Expense
823   Travel and Entertainment
        Expense
824   Telephone Expense
825   Forms and Supplies Expense
826   Automobile Expense
827   Depreciation Expense
828   Insurance Expense
829   Charitable Contributions
        Expense
831   Payroll Taxes Expense
839   Miscellaneous Expense

*Words in bold type represent headings and not account titles.

bursement. Note that there is no asset account for forms and supplies. In this illustration, the cost of all business forms and supplies purchased is debited (charged) to Forms and Supplies Expense, Account No. 825. The cost of any unused forms and supplies that may be on hand at the end of the year is ignored because such quantities normally are very small. The car that Roberts uses for business purposes is leased. The monthly car rental and the cost of gasoline, oil, lubrication, washing, and automobile insurance are charged to Automobile Expense, Account No. 826. The cost of all other types of insurance that relate to the enterprise, such as workers' compensation, "errors and omissions" insurance (normally carried by management consultants), and fire insurance on the office equipment and contents, is charged to Insurance Expense, Account No. 828, when the premiums on the policies are paid.

BOOKS OF ACCOUNT

Roberts uses the following books of account:

(1) General books
  (a) Combination journal
  (b) General ledger
(2) Auxiliary records
  (a) Petty cash disbursements record
  (b) Employees' earnings records
  (c) Copies of statements rendered to clients (billings for fees) with collections noted thereon

Combination Journal. The two-column journal can be used to record every transaction of a business enterprise. However, in most businesses, there are many similar transactions that involve the same account or accounts. Outstanding examples are receipts and disbursements of cash. Suppose that in a typical month there are 30 transactions that result in an increase in cash and 40 transactions that cause a decrease in cash. In a two-column journal, this would require writing the word "Cash" (or "County Bank") 70 times, using a journal line each time. A considerable saving of time and space would result if two columns were added to the journal: one for debits to Cash (or County Bank) and the other for credits to Cash (or County Bank). Other Debit and Credit columns in the journal can be used for amounts that belong in other accounts. At the end of the month, the special columns for cash debits and credits are totaled. The total of the Cash Debit column is posted as one amount to the debit side of the cash account and the total of the Cash Credit column is posted as one amount to the credit side of the cash account. Thus, instead of receiving 70 postings, Cash receives only two, one debit and one credit. Posting would require much less time and the danger of posting error would be reduced.

There is no reason to limit special journal columns to those for cash. If there are other accounts frequently used in the recording of transactions, special columns may be used to assemble all amounts that have the same effect on the account. More space and time may be saved. A journal with such special columns, and in addition a General Debit column and a General Credit column to take care of changes in accounts infrequently involved, is called a combination journal.

Roberts uses a combination journal as the only book of original entry. This journal, a portion of which is reproduced below, has eight amount columns, two at the left and six at the right of the Description column. The headings of the amount columns (as they read from left to right on the journal page) are as follows:

> County Bank
> > Deposits Debit
> > Checks Credit
> General
> > Debit
> > Credit
> Professional Fees Credit
> Salary Expense Debit
> Wage Deductions
> > FICA Tax Payable Credit
> > Employees Income Tax Payable Credit

Each of the six special columns is justified because there are enough transactions requiring entries in the accounts indicated by each of the column headings to warrant this arrangement, which will save time and labor in the bookkeeping process. A narrative of transactions completed by Roberts during the month of December, 19--, is given on pages 120–128. These transactions are recorded in the combination journal on pages 124–127. Note that before any transactions are recorded in this journal, a memo notation of the bank balance at the start of the month, $4,993.65, is entered in the Description column just after the words "Amounts Forwarded."

General Ledger. Roberts uses a balance-column account form, which has four amount columns: a debit column, a credit column, and two balance columns — one for debit balances and one for credit balances.

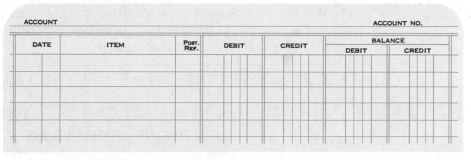

DATE	ITEM	Post. Ref.	DEBIT	CREDIT	BALANCE	
					DEBIT	CREDIT

Balance-Column Account Form

The standard two-column account form illustrated up to now is still used by some, but the four-column balance-column account form is used more frequently and has the advantage of providing a specific place for the account balance to be recorded after each amount is posted. Posting to the ledger may be done after each transaction, at the end of the week, or at month end. Roberts prefers to post the general column accounts of the combination journal at the end of the week and the column totals at the end of the month.

Roberts' general ledger is reproduced on pages 128–131. In each instance, the balance of the account as of December 1 has been entered. Two accounts are omitted: Expense and Revenue Summary (No. 531) and Depreciation Expense (No. 827). They are not included because neither had a balance on December 1, and neither received any debits or credits as a result of the cash receipt and disbursement transactions in December. These accounts are not used until the end-of-year process of adjusting and closing the accounts takes place. This procedure will be explained and illustrated on pages 138–139.

Auxiliary Records. The auxiliary records included in Roberts' system of accounts are not reproduced in this chapter. The petty cash disbursements record that is used as a source document to record the December 31 entry (see page 126) to replenish petty cash is almost identical in form to the one illustrated in Chapter 3 on pages

60–61. An employee's earnings record, similar to the one illustrated in Chapter 4 on pages 96 and 97, is maintained for each employee. Roberts has two employees: Dean McElroy, a full-time systems programmer, and Martha Jacobs, a part-time secretary. Roberts keeps a file for each client which includes, among other things, a copy of the contract or agreement with the client. This agreement stipulates the fee for the assignment and the time of payment (or payments, if the fee is to be paid in installments — which is the usual case). A carbon copy of each statement or billing for fees earned is placed in each client's file. When money is received from a client, the date and amount are noted on the copy of the billing in addition to the formal record made in the combination journal.

TRANSACTIONS AND ENTRIES DURING THE FISCAL PERIOD

JOHN H. ROBERTS, MANAGEMENT CONSULTANT
NARRATIVE OF TRANSACTIONS

Friday, December 3

Issued Check No. 321 for $514.59 to Dean McElroy, systems analyst and programmer, in payment of his salary for the week: $650 less income tax withholding, $135.41. McElroy's gross earnings from the start of the year reached $30,000 during the week ended November 27. Since that time, no FICA tax has been withheld.[1]

Since the individual posting of McElroy's salary is not required, a check mark was placed in the Posting Reference column of the combination journal at the time the transaction was recorded. The check mark notes that there is nothing recorded in the General Debit and Credit columns on that line.

Issued Check No. 322 for $157.62 to Martha Jacobs, secretary (part-time), in payment of her salary for the week: $200 less income tax withholding, $28.38, and FICA tax withholding, $14.

Issued Check No. 323 for $350 to J. C. Bowden for December office rent.

Note that the account title Rent Expense was recorded in the Description column and that $350 was debited in the General column and credited in the County Bank column. The rent expense ledger account has been debited as an end-of-week work activity

---

[1]Because the cash basis method of accounting is used, Roberts's share of FICA taxes and federal and state unemployment taxes are not recorded until they are actually paid. FICA taxes for both Roberts as an employer and the two employees normally are paid once each month. (See the second entry for December 14 on page 124.) Federal unemployment taxes normally are paid in January, and state unemployment taxes are paid in January, April, July, and October. In either of the latter two cases, the entry is a debit to Payroll Taxes Expense (No. 831) and a credit to County Bank (No. 111).

Payroll Taxes Expense.. xxx
  County Bank... xxx
  To pay federal and state unemployment taxes.

for $350 and the account number 821 has been recorded in the Posting Reference column of the combination journal.

END-OF-THE-WEEK WORK

(1) Proved the footings of the combination journal.

To be sure that the debits recorded in the journal are equal to the credits, the journal must be proved. Each amount column is footed and the sum of the footings of the debit columns and the sum of the footings of the credit columns compared. This is known as a proof of footings. The footings are recorded in small pencil figures immediately below the last regular entry. If these sums are not the same, the journal entries must be checked to discover and correct the errors. The footings should be proved frequently. When the transactions are numerous, it is advisable to prove the footings daily. The footings must be proved when a page of the journal is filled to be sure that no error is carried forward to a new page. Proof of the footings is essential at the end of the month before the journal is ruled or any column totals are posted. Below is a proof of the footings of Roberts' combination journal. As is common practice, the footings are proved using an adding machine. The first set of amounts is the totals of the two debit columns, followed by a second set of amounts which is the totals of the three credit columns. No entries had been made in the General Credit column at this point.

| | COUNTY BANK | | CK. NO. | DAY | DESCRIPTION | POST REF | GENERAL | | PROFESSIONAL FEES CR. | SALARY EXPENSE DR. | WAGE DEDUCTIONS | |
	DEPOSITS DR.	CHECKS CR.					DEBIT	CREDIT			FICA TAX PAY. CR.	EMP. INC. TAX PAY. CR.
1					AMOUNTS FORWARDED *Balance 4,993.65*							
2		514 59	321	3	*Dean McElroy*	✓				650 00		135 41
3		157 62	322	3	*Martha Jacobs*	✓				200 00	14 00	28 38
4		350 00	323	3	*Rent Expense*	821	350 00					
		3,971.44					*350 00*			*850 00*	*14 00*	*163 79*

(2) Proved the bank balance (Beginning balance, $4,993.65 − cash credits $1,022.21 = $3,971.44, end-of-week balance), and entered the new balance in the Description column following the third transaction of December 3.

Monday, December 6

Received a check for $1,200 from R. A. Bauer, a client, and deposited it in the bank.

In the journal on page 122, note that the client's name is written in the Description column and that a check mark is placed in the Posting Reference column.

Wednesday, December 8

Issued Check No. 324 for $54.80 to Evelyn York, an insurance agent, in payment of the one-year premium on a fire insurance policy covering Roberts' office equipment and contents.

Friday, December 10

Issued Check No. 325 for $514.59 to Dean McElroy and Check No. 326 for $157.62 to Martha Jacobs in payment of salaries for the week.

END-OF-THE-WEEK WORK

(1) Proved the footings of the combination journal. Total debits ($1,200 + $404.80 + $1,700 = $3,304.80) equal total credits ($1,749.22 + $1,200 + $327.58 + $28 = $3,304.80).

(2) Proved the bank balance ($4,993.65 + $1,200 − $1,749.22 = $4,444.43), and entered the new balance in the Description column following the second transaction of December 10.

(3) Posted the entry from the General Debit column of the combination journal to the proper general ledger account. (Note that there was one such posting and that the account number, 828, was entered in the Posting Reference column.)

28 PAGE				COMBINATION JOURNAL					FOR MONTH OF December 19 — —		PAGE 28	
COUNTY BANK		CK NO.	DAY	DESCRIPTION	POST REF	GENERAL		PROFESSIONAL FEES CR.	SALARY EXPENSE DR.	WAGE DEDUCTIONS		
DEPOSITS DR.	CHECKS CR.					DEBIT	CREDIT			FICA TAX PAY. CR.	EMP. INC. TAX PAY. CR.	
5	1 2 0 0 0 0			6	R. A. Bauer	✓			1 2 0 0 0 0				5
6		5 4 8 0	324	8	Insurance Expense	828	5 4 8 0						6
7		5 1 4 5 9	325	10	Dean McElroy	✓				6 5 0 0 0		1 3 5 4 1	7
8	1 2 0 0 0 0	1 5 7 6 2	326	10	Martha Jacobs	✓		4,444.43	4 0 4 8 0	1 2 0 0 0 0	2 0 0 0 0 1 7 0 0 0 0	1 4 0 0 2 8 0 0	2 8 3 8 3 2 7 5 7	8

Monday, December 13

Issued Check No. 327 for $93.61 to Moore Business Forms Co. in payment for supplies.

Received a check for $9 from Evelyn York, the insurance agent, to whom Roberts had sent a check (No. 324) on December 8 in the amount of $54.80 in payment of the premium on a fire insurance policy covering office equipment and contents. The check for $9 was accompanied by a letter from York explaining that a clerical error was made in preparing the invoice for the policy. The correct amount was $45.80 — not $54.80. Roberts' check for $54.80 had been deposited before the mistake was discovered. Accordingly, York sent the check for $9 as a refund of the excess premium and the check was deposited in the bank.

This insurance premium refund check was recorded in the combination journal by a debit to County Bank, Account No. 111, and a credit to Insurance Expense, Account No. 828, in the amount of $9. Since the entry to record Check No. 324 has already been posted as a debit to Insurance Expense, this manner of handling was required. Note that the error resulted from the fact that the clerk in York's office had made a transposition error — a mistake well known to bookkeepers and accountants. The intention was to write or type $45.80 but $54.80 was written instead. The "4" and the "5" were placed in the wrong order — they were transposed.

Tuesday, December 14

Received a check for $1,500 from G. A. Barger, a client, and deposited it in the bank.

Issued Check No. 328 for $767.16 to the County Bank, a United States depository, in payment of the following taxes:

Employees' income tax withheld during November		$655.16
FICA tax imposed:		
On employees (withheld during November)	$56.00	
On the employer	56.00	112.00
Total		$767.16

This disbursement involved three factors in addition to the decrease in the bank balance: (1) payment of the recorded liability, Employees Income Tax Payable, Account No. 314, of $655.16; (2) payment of the recorded liability, FICA Tax Payable, Account No. 311, of $56; and (3) payment of the unrecorded liability of $56, the employer's FICA tax relating to the taxable earnings paid in November. To record the transaction correctly, the first two amounts ($655.16 and $56) are debited to the proper liability accounts, since the tax liability was being decreased, and the third amount is debited to Payroll Taxes Expense, Account No. 831, resulting in an increase in the employer's expenses. Note that three lines were needed in the combination journal. A Tax Deposit Form was presented at the bank in payment of the taxes. The stub attached to the form was filled out and retained as a record of the deposit.

Wednesday, December 15

Issued Check No. 329 for $1,800 to Roberts for personal use.

Thursday, December 16

Issued Check No. 330 for $102.20 to the Executive Auto Leasing Co. in payment of one month's rent of the leased automobile used by Roberts for business purposes.

This disbursement was recorded by a debit to Automobile Expense, Account No. 826.

Friday, December 17

Issued Check No. 331 for $514.59 to Dean McElroy and Check No. 332 for $157.62 to Martha Jacobs in payment of salaries for the week.

Issued Check No. 333 for $100 to American Lung Association.

END-OF-THE-WEEK WORK

(1) Proved the footings of the combination journal. (2) Proved the bank balance ($2,418.25). (3) Posted each entry individually from the General Debit and General Credit columns of the combination journal to the proper general ledger accounts. When the entry of December 14 relating to Check No. 328 was posted, debits were made to Employees Income Tax Payable, Account No. 314, and

FICA Tax Payable, Account No. 311, which caused those accounts to be in balance.

Monday, December 20

Issued Check No. 334 for $45.38 to Tom's Service Center in payment for gasoline, oil, and lubrication purchased on credit during the past month. All of these purchases related to the expense of operating the leased automobile used for business purposes.

Issued Check No. 335 for $18.25 to Eppler-Marstan Typewriter Service in payment of charges for cleaning and repairing office typewriter.

28 PAGE COMBINATION JOURNAL

	COUNTY BANK		CK. NO.	DAY	DESCRIPTION	POST. REF.	
	DEPOSITS DR.	CHECKS CR.					
1					AMOUNTS FORWARDED *Balance 4,993.65*		1
2		514 59	321	3	Dean McElroy	✓	2
3		157 62	322	3	Martha Jacobs	✓	3
4		350 00 *1,022.21*	323	3	Rent Expense	821	4
5	1 200 00			6	R. A. Bauer *3,971.44*	✓	5
6		54 80	324	8	Insurance Expense	828	6
7		514 59	325	10	Dean McElroy	✓	7
8	*1,200.00*	157 62 *1,749.22*	326	10	Martha Jacobs	✓	8
9		93 61	327	13	Forms and Supplies Expense *4,444.43*	825	9
10	9 00			13	Insurance Expense	828	10
11	1 500 00			14	G. A. Barger	✓	11
12		767 16	328	14	Employees Income Tax Payable	314	12
13					FICA Tax Payable	311	13
14					Payroll Taxes Expense	831	14
15		1 800 00	329	15	John H. Roberts, Drawing	511.1	15
16		102 20	330	16	Automobile Expense	826	16
17		514 59	331	17	Dean McElroy	✓	17
18		157 62	332	17	Martha Jacobs	✓	18
19	*2,709.00*	100 00 *5,284.40*	333	17	Charitable Contributions Expense *12,418.25*	829	19
20		45 38	334	20	Automobile Expense	826	20
21		18 25	335	20	Miscellaneous Expense	839	21
22		43 35	336	21	Telephone Expense	824	22
23	1 800 00			22	Mary Berthold	✓	23
24		91 18	337	23	Forms and Supplies Expense	825	24
25		514 59	338	24	Dean McElroy	✓	25
26	*4,509.00*	157 62 *6,154.77*	339	24	Martha Jacobs	✓	26
27	4 509 00	6 154 77			Carried Forward *3,347.55*		27
28							28

Combination Journal (Left Page)

The amount of this check was charged to Miscellaneous Expense, Account No. 839.

Tuesday, December 21

Issued Check No. 336 for $43.35 to Missouri Bell Telephone Co. in payment of statement just received showing charges for local and long-distance business calls, during the past month.

Wednesday, December 22

Received a check for $1,800 from Mary Berthold, a client, and deposited it in the bank.

FOR MONTH OF *December*   19 — —   PAGE *28*

	GENERAL		PROFESSIONAL FEES CR.	SALARY EXPENSE DR.	WAGE DEDUCTIONS	
	DEBIT	CREDIT			FICA TAX PAY. CR.	EMP. INC. TAX PAY. CR.
1						
2				650 00		135 41
3				200 00	14 00	28 38
4	350 00					
5			1200 00	550 00	14 00	163 79
6	54 80					
7				650 00		135 41
8			1200 00	200 00	14 00	28 38
9	93 61					
10		9 00				
11			1500 00			
12	655 16					
13	56 00					
14	56 00					
15	1800 00					
16	102 20					
17				650 00		135 41
18				200 00	14 00	28 38
19	100 00	9 00	2700 00	2550 00	42 00	491 37
20	45 38					
21	18 25					
22	43 35					
23			1800 00			
24	91 18					
25				650 00		135 41
26				200 00	14 00	28 38
27	3465 93	9 00	4500 00	3400 00	56 00	655 16
28						

Combination Journal (Right Page)

Thursday, December 23

Issued Check No. 337 for $91.18 to Corporate Business Systems in payment for supplies purchased.

Friday, December 24

Issued Check No. 338 for $514.59 to Dean McElroy and Check No. 339 for $157.62 to Martha Jacobs in payment of salaries for the week. (See explanation relating to Checks Nos. 321 and 322 issued on December 3.)

END-OF-THE-WEEK WORK

(1) Proved the footings of the combination journal. (2) Proved the bank balance ($3,347.88). (3) Posted each entry individually from the General Debit column of the combination journal.

Because a page of the combination journal was filled after Check No. 339 was recorded, the footings of the columns were proved and recorded as totals on the last line of the page, and the words "Carried Forward" were written in the Description column. The totals were entered in the appropriate columns on the top line of the next page. The bank balance was entered in the Description column of the new page just after the words "Amounts Forwarded."

29 PAGE				COMBINATION JOURNAL		
COUNTY BANK		CK. NO.	DAY	DESCRIPTION	POST. REF.	
DEPOSITS DR.	CHECKS CR.					
4 5 0 9 00	6 1 5 4 77		24	AMOUNTS FORWARDED *Balance 3,347.88*		1
	1 1 4 10	340	29	*Travel & Entertainment Expense*	823	2
1 1 0 0 00			30	*Arva Haines*	✓	3
	7 7 96	341	31	*John H. Roberts, Drawing*	511.1	4
				Travel & Entertainment Expense	823	5
				Forms and Supplies Expense	825	6
				Automobile Expense	826	7
				Charitable Contributions Expense	829	8
				Miscellaneous Expense	839	9
	5 1 4 59	342	31	*Dean McElroy*	✓	10
	1 5 7 62	343	31	*Martha Jacobs*	✓	11
5 6 0 9 00	7 0 1 9 04			*3,583.61*		12
5 6 0 9 00	7 0 1 9 04					12
(111)	(111)					13

Combination Journal (Left Page) *(concluded)*

Wednesday, December 29

Issued Check No. 340 for $114.10 to Glen Echo Country Club in payment of food and beverage charges for one month.

The amount of this check was charged to Travel and Entertainment Expense, Account No. 823. Roberts uses the facilities of the club to entertain prospective clients.

Thursday, December 30

Received a check for $1,100 from Arva Haines, a client, and deposited it in the bank.

Friday, December 31

Issued Check No. 341 for $77.96 to replenish the petty cash fund. Following is a summary of the petty cash disbursements for the month of December prepared from the Petty Cash Disbursements Record:

John H. Roberts, Drawing	$17.50
Travel and Entertainment Expense	27.80
Forms and Supplies Expense	12.75
Automobile Expense	5.25
Charitable Contributions Expense	8.50
Miscellaneous Expense	6.16
Total disbursements	$77.96

FOR MONTH OF *December* 19 - -   PAGE 29

	GENERAL DEBIT	GENERAL CREDIT	PROFESSIONAL FEES CR.	SALARY EXPENSE DR.	FICA TAX PAY. CR.	EMP. INC. TAX PAY. CR.	
1	3 46593	900	4 50000	3 40000	5600	65516	1
2	1 1410						2
3	-		1 10000				3
4	1750						4
5	2780						5
6	1275						6
7	525						7
8	850						8
9	616						9
10				65000		13541	10
11	3 65799	900	5 60000	20000	1400	2838	11
12	3 65799	900	5 60000	4 25000	7000	81895	12
13	(↙)	(↙)	(611)	(822)	(311)	(314)	13

Combination Journal (Right Page) *(concluded)*

Issued Check No. 342 for $514.59 to Dean McElroy and Check No. 343 for $157.62 to Martha Jacobs in payment of salaries for the week. (See explanation relating to Checks No. 321 and 322 issued on December 3.)

ROUTINE-END-OF-THE-MONTH WORK

(1) Proved the footings and entered the totals in the combination journal. (2) Proved the bank balance ($3,583.61). (3) Completed the individual posting from the General Debit column of the combination journal. (4) Completed the summary posting of the six special-column totals of the combination journal and ruled the journal as

ACCOUNT *County Bank*   ACCOUNT NO. *111*

DATE	ITEM	POST. REF.	DEBIT	CREDIT	BALANCE DEBIT	BALANCE CREDIT
Dec. 1	Balance	✓			4993 65	
31		CJ29	5609 00		10602 65	
31		CJ29		7019 04	3583 61	

ACCOUNT *Petty Cash Fund*   ACCOUNT NO. *112*

DATE	ITEM	POST. REF.	DEBIT	CREDIT	BALANCE DEBIT	BALANCE CREDIT
Dec. 1	Balance	✓			160 00	

ACCOUNT *Office Equipment*   ACCOUNT NO. *211*

DATE	ITEM	POST. REF.	DEBIT	CREDIT	BALANCE DEBIT	BALANCE CREDIT
Dec. 1	Balance	✓			1692 060	

ACCOUNT *Accumulated Depreciation -- Office Equipment*   ACCOUNT NO. *211.1*

DATE	ITEM	POST. REF.	DEBIT	CREDIT	BALANCE DEBIT	BALANCE CREDIT
Dec. 1	Balance	✓				5634 45

John H. Roberts, Management Consultant — General Ledger

illustrated on pages 124–127. Note that the number of the account to which the total is posted was written in parentheses just below the total, and that check marks are placed below the General Debit and General Credit column totals in parentheses to indicate that these amounts were not posted. Also note that the ledger accounts were balanced at the time that they were posted. (5) Prepared a trial balance of the ledger accounts.

Usually a trial balance at the end of a month is prepared using two-column paper. However, because Roberts has chosen the calendar year for the fiscal year (a common, but by no means universal practice), the trial balance at the end of December is placed in the first two amount columns of a form known as a work sheet. The need for and preparation of a work sheet is explained and illustrated on pages 132–136.

ACCOUNT *FICA Tax Payable*   ACCOUNT NO. *311*

DATE	ITEM	POST. REF.	DEBIT	CREDIT	BALANCE DEBIT	BALANCE CREDIT
19-- Dec. 1	Balance	✓				5600
14		CJ28	5600		-0-	-0-
31		CJ29		7000		7000

ACCOUNT *Employees Income Tax Payable*   ACCOUNT NO. *314*

DATE	ITEM	POST. REF.	DEBIT	CREDIT	BALANCE DEBIT	BALANCE CREDIT
19-- Dec. 1	Balance	✓				65516
14		CJ28	65516		-0-	-0-
31		CJ29		81895		81895

ACCOUNT *John H. Roberts, Capital*   ACCOUNT NO. *511*

DATE	ITEM	POST. REF.	DEBIT	CREDIT	BALANCE DEBIT	BALANCE CREDIT
19-- Dec. 1	Balance	✓				1030680

ACCOUNT *John H. Roberts, Drawing*   ACCOUNT NO. *511.1*

DATE	ITEM	POST. REF.	DEBIT	CREDIT	BALANCE DEBIT	BALANCE CREDIT
19-- Dec. 1	Balance	✓			3000800	
15		CJ28	180000		3180800	
31		CJ29	1750		3182550	

John H. Roberts, Management Consultant — General Ledger *(Continued)*

ACCOUNT *Professional Fees*   ACCOUNT NO. *611*

DATE	ITEM	POST. REF.	DEBIT	CREDIT	BALANCE DEBIT	BALANCE CREDIT
19-- Dec. 1	Balance	✓				8441600
31		CJ29		560000		9001600

ACCOUNT *Rent Expense*   ACCOUNT NO. *821*

DATE	ITEM	POST. REF.	DEBIT	CREDIT	BALANCE DEBIT	BALANCE CREDIT
19-- Dec. 1	Balance	✓			385000	
3		CJ28	35000		420000	

ACCOUNT *Salary Expense*   ACCOUNT NO. *822*

DATE	ITEM	POST. REF.	DEBIT	CREDIT	BALANCE DEBIT	BALANCE CREDIT
19-- Dec. 1	Balance	✓			3346400	
31		CJ29	425000		3771400	

ACCOUNT *Travel and Entertainment Expense*   ACCOUNT NO. *823*

DATE	ITEM	POST. REF.	DEBIT	CREDIT	BALANCE DEBIT	BALANCE CREDIT
19-- Dec. 1	Balance	✓			277681	
29		CJ29	11410		289091	
31		CJ29	2780		291871	

ACCOUNT *Telephone Expense*   ACCOUNT NO. *824*

DATE	ITEM	POST. REF.	DEBIT	CREDIT	BALANCE DEBIT	BALANCE CREDIT
19-- Dec. 1	Balance	✓			61690	
21		CJ28	4335		66025	

ACCOUNT *Forms and Supplies Expense*   ACCOUNT NO. *825*

DATE	ITEM	POST. REF.	DEBIT	CREDIT	BALANCE DEBIT	BALANCE CREDIT
19-- Dec. 1	Balance	✓			217775	
13		CJ28	9361		227136	
23		CJ28	9118		236254	
31		CJ29	1275		237529	

John H. Roberts, Management Consultant — General Ledger (*Continued*)

ACCOUNT *Automobile Expense*   ACCOUNT NO. *826*

DATE	ITEM	POST. REF.	DEBIT	CREDIT	BALANCE DEBIT	BALANCE CREDIT
19-- Dec. 1	Balance	✓			194390	
16		CJ28	10220		204610	
20		CJ28	4538		209148	
31		CJ29	525		209673	

ACCOUNT *Insurance Expense*   ACCOUNT NO. *828*

DATE	ITEM	POST. REF.	DEBIT	CREDIT	BALANCE DEBIT	BALANCE CREDIT
19-- Dec. 1	Balance	✓			26780	
8		CJ28	5480		32260	
13		CJ28		900	31360	

ACCOUNT *Charitable Contributions Expense*   ACCOUNT NO. *829*

DATE	ITEM	POST. REF.	DEBIT	CREDIT	BALANCE DEBIT	BALANCE CREDIT
19-- Dec. 1	Balance	✓			61600	
17		CJ28	10000		71600	
31		CJ29	850		72450	

ACCOUNT *Payroll Taxes Expense*   ACCOUNT NO. *831*

DATE	ITEM	POST. REF.	DEBIT	CREDIT	BALANCE DEBIT	BALANCE CREDIT
19-- Dec. 1	Balance	✓			304450	
14		CJ28	5600		310050	

ACCOUNT *Miscellaneous Expense*   ACCOUNT NO. *839*

DATE	ITEM	POST. REF.	DEBIT	CREDIT	BALANCE DEBIT	BALANCE CREDIT
19-- Dec. 1	Balance	✓			22850	
20		CJ28	1825		24675	
31		CJ29	616		25291	

John H. Roberts, Management Consultant — General Ledger *(Concluded)*

> *Study Assignment: Report No. 5-1, Part B, Problem 1, in the study assignments may be completed at this time at the option of your instructor.*

WORK AT CLOSE OF THE FISCAL PERIOD

As soon as possible after the end of the fiscal period, the owner (or owners) of an enterprise wants to be provided with (1) an income statement covering the period just ended, and (2) a balance sheet as of the last day of the period. To provide these statements, the accountant must consider certain matters that have not been recorded in the daily routine of entering events. For example, in the case of Roberts' enterprise, depreciation of office equipment for the past year is one such matter. Furthermore, the revenue accounts, the expense accounts, and the account showing the owner's withdrawals have performed their function for the period just ended (in this case, the calendar year) and need to be made ready to receive the entries of the new period. In the language of accountants and bookkeepers, "the books must be adjusted and closed." Actually, only the temporary owner's equity accounts — those for revenue, expense and the owner's drawings — are closed, but the remark quoted is widely used to describe what takes place at this time.

THE END-OF-PERIOD WORK SHEET

To facilitate (1) the preparing of the financial statements, (2) the making of needed adjustments in the accounts, and (3) the closing of the temporary owner's equity accounts, it is common practice to prepare an end-of-period work sheet. Because of the nature of Roberts' enterprise, an eight-column work sheet is adequate. Note that

John H. Roberts, Management Consultant
Work Sheet
For the Year Ended December 31, 19--

ACCOUNT TITLE	ACCT. NO.	TRIAL BALANCE		ADJUSTMENTS		INCOME STATEMENT		BALANCE SHEET	
		DEBIT	CREDIT	DEBIT	CREDIT	DEBIT	CREDIT	DEBIT	CREDIT

the heading states that it is for the year ended December 31, 19––. The income statement columns relate to the full year, and the balance sheet columns show the financial position as of the last day of the fiscal period.

The first pair of columns of the work sheet illustrated on page 135 shows the trial balance taken after the routine posting for the month of December has been completed. Note that the account Depreciation Expense (No. 827) is included in the list of accounts and account numbers even though the account has no balance at this point. The second pair of columns, headed "Adjustments," shows the manner in which the expense of estimated depreciation of office equipment for the year affects the accounts. The trial balance shows that the account Office Equipment (No. 211) has a balance of $16,920.60, and that the balance of the account Accumulated Depreciation — Office Equipment (No. 211.1) is $5,634.45. No new equipment was purchased during the year and there were no sales or retirements of such property during the year. Accordingly, the balances of these two accounts have not changed during the year. The two accounts are closely related: the debit balance of the office equipment account indicates the cost of the assets, and the credit balance of the accumulated depreciation account indicates the amount of this cost that has been charged off as depreciation in past years — that is, to January 1 of the current year. The difference between the cost of the asset and the accumulated depreciation, $11,286.15 ($16,920.60 − $5,634.45) is described as the undepreciated cost of the office equipment. This amount is also called the book value of the equipment. A better description of the difference is "cost yet to be charged to expense."

Since the year has just ended, it is necessary to record as an expense the estimated depreciation for the year. Roberts estimates that the various items of office equipment have average useful lives of ten years and that any scrap or salvage value at the end of that time is likely to be so small that it can be ignored. Accordingly, estimated depreciation expense for the year is calculated to be $1,692.06 ($16,920.60 ÷ 10 years). This expense needs to be entered on the work sheet so that it will be considered when the financial statements are prepared. Later it will be journalized and posted to the ledger accounts. As illustrated on page 134, the record is made on the work sheet as follows: $1,692.06 is written in the Adjustments Debit column on the line for Depreciation Expense and the same amount is written in the Adjustments Credit column on the line for Accumulated Depreciation. Since there are no more adjustments, the Debit and Credit columns are totaled.

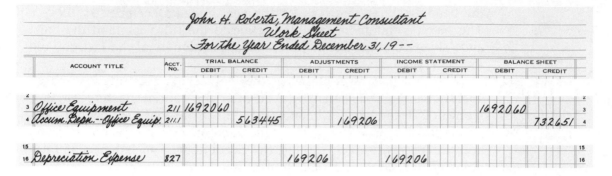

John H. Roberts, Management Consultant
Work Sheet
For the Year Ended December 31, 19--

ACCOUNT TITLE	ACCT. NO.	TRIAL BALANCE DEBIT	TRIAL BALANCE CREDIT	ADJUSTMENTS DEBIT	ADJUSTMENTS CREDIT	INCOME STATEMENT DEBIT	INCOME STATEMENT CREDIT	BALANCE SHEET DEBIT	BALANCE SHEET CREDIT
3 Office Equipment	211	1692060						1692060	
4 Accum. Depn.--Office Equip.	211.1		563445		169206				732651
16 Depreciation Expense	827			169206		169206			

The next step is to combine each amount in the Trial Balance columns with the amount, if any, in the Adjustments columns and to extend the total into the Income Statement or Balance Sheet columns. Revenue and expense account balances are extended to the Income Statement columns and balance sheet account balances to the Balance Sheet columns. Note that the new amount for Accumulated Depreciation — Office Equipment, $7,326.51 ($5,634.45 + $1,692.06) appears in the Balance Sheet Credit column, and that the depreciation expense of $1,692.06 appears, along with all other expenses, in the Income Statement Debit column.

Each of the last four columns is then totaled. The total of the Income Statement Credit column exceeds the total of the Income Statement Debit column by $33,967.45 — the calculated net income for the year. That amount, so designated, is placed in the Income Statement Debit column to bring the pair of Income Statement columns into balance. When the same amount, $33,967.45, is placed in the Balance Sheet Credit column, the last pair of columns is brought into balance. The final totals of the last four columns are entered at the bottom of the work sheet.

John H. Roberts, Management Consultant
Work Sheet
For the Year Ended December 31, 19--

ACCOUNT TITLE	ACCT. NO.	TRIAL BALANCE DEBIT	TRIAL BALANCE CREDIT	ADJUSTMENTS DEBIT	ADJUSTMENTS CREDIT	INCOME STATEMENT DEBIT	INCOME STATEMENT CREDIT	BALANCE SHEET DEBIT	BALANCE SHEET CREDIT
21		10684620	10684620	169206	169206	5604855	9001600	5248971	1852226
22 Net income						3396745			3396745
23						9001600	9001600	5248971	5248971

The reason for adding the net income for the year, $33,967.45, to the Balance Sheet Credit column causing its total to equal the total of the Balance Sheet Debit column is explained as follows. The

John H. Roberts, Management Consultant
Work Sheet
For the Year Ended December 31, 19--

	ACCT. NO.	TRIAL BALANCE DEBIT	TRIAL BALANCE CREDIT	ADJUSTMENTS DEBIT	ADJUSTMENTS CREDIT	INCOME STATEMENT DEBIT	INCOME STATEMENT CREDIT	BALANCE SHEET DEBIT	BALANCE SHEET CREDIT	
Country Bank	111	358361						358361		1
Petty Cash Fund	112	16000						16000		2
Office Equipment	211	1692060						1692060		3
Accum. Depr.—Office Equip.	211.1		563445		169206				732651	4
FICA Tax Payable	311		7000						7000	5
Employees Income Tax Pay.	314		81895						81895	6
John H. Roberts, Capital	511		1030680						1030680	7
John H. Roberts, Drawing	511.1	3182550						3182550		8
Professional Fees	611		9001600				9001600			9
Rent Expense	821	420000				420000				10
Salary Expense	822	3771400				3771400				11
Travel + Entertainment Exp.	823	291871				291871				12
Telephone Expense	824	66025				66025				13
Forms + Supplies Expense	825	237529				237529				14
Automobile Expense	826	209673				209673				15
Depreciation Expense	827			169206		169206				16
Insurance Expense	828	31360				31360				17
Charitable Contrib. Exp.	829	72450				72450				18
Payroll Taxes Expense	831	310050				310050				19
Miscellaneous Expense	839	25291				25291				20
		10846420	10846420	169206	169206	5604855	9001600	5248971	1852226	21
Net Income						3396745			3396745	22
						9001600	9001600	5248971	5248971	23
										24
										25

John H. Roberts, Management Consultant — End-of-Period Work Sheet

amounts for the assets and liabilities in the last pair of columns are up-to-date amounts. However, the Roberts equity account is not up-to-date. In this example, the equity account of $10,306.80 reflects the balance of the account at the beginning of the year. It is affected during the year by withdrawals and net income. The contra owner's equity withdrawals of $31,825.50 has been recorded in the debit column of the Balance Sheet to offset the equity account. It is also necessary to record the net income of $33,967.45 in the credit column of the Balance Sheet to show the increase in the owner's equity due to the successful operation of the business during the year. The explanation is that there has been a profit from operations during the year (increasing owner's equity) as well as withdrawals for personal expenses (decreasing owner's equity) that have caused the owner's equity element to adjust to $12,448.75. This can be expressed in the form of the following equation:

Owner's Equity at Start of Period	+	Net Income for the Period	+ Investments	− Withdrawals	=	Owner's Equity at End of Period
$10,306.80	+	$33,967.45	+ 0	− $31,825.50	=	$12,448.75

The correct amounts for assets and liabilities and two of the three factors (owner's equity at start of period and withdrawals) needed to determine the correct amount of the owner's equity as of December 31, are already in the Balance Sheet columns. Therefore, the amount of the third factor — the net income for the year — has to be included so that those columns will reflect the basic equation: Assets = Liabilities + Owner's Equity.

The Financial Statements. The work sheet supplies all of the information needed to prepare an income statement and a balance sheet. These statements for Roberts' enterprise are shown on page 137.

Three features of the balance sheet should be noted:

(1) Its format is the report form of balance sheet — the liabilities and the owner's equity sections are shown below the assets section. An alternative is the account form of balance sheet, in which the assets are at the left, and the liabilities and the owner's equity sections are at the right. (See the balance sheet of The Donald Mays Personnel Agency on pages 50–51.)

(2) The assets are classified on the basis of whether they are current or property, plant and equipment. Current assets include cash and any other assets that will be converted into cash within one year or the normal operating cycle of the business, whichever is longer. This cycle is the period of time required to purchase supplies and services and convert them back into cash. Roberts' enterprise does not have any current assets

JOHN H. ROBERTS, MANAGEMENT CONSULTANT
Income Statement
For the Year Ended December 31, 19--

Professional fees..		$90,016.00
Professional expenses:		
Rent expense...	$ 4,200.00	
Salary expense	37,714.00	
Travel and entertainment expense	2,918.71	
Telephone expense...	660.25	
Forms and supplies expense.....................................	2,375.29	
Automobile expense	2,096.73	
Depreciation expense	1,692.06	
Insurance expense..	313.60	
Charitable contributions expense.............................	724.50	
Payroll taxes expense..	3,100.50	
Miscellaneous expense..	252.91	
Total professional expenses		56,048.55
Net income		$33,967.45

John H. Roberts, Management Consultant — Income Statement

JOHN H. ROBERTS, MANAGEMENT CONSULTANT
Balance Sheet
December 31, 19--

Assets

Current assets:		
Cash		$ 3,743.61
Property, plant, and equipment assets:		
Office equipment..	$16,920.60	
Less accumulated depreciation...............	7,326.51	9,594.09
Total assets		$13,337.70

Liabilities

Current liabilities:		
FICA tax payable	$ 70.00	
Employees income tax payable	818.95	
Total current liabilities.........................		$ 888.95

Owner's Equity

John H. Roberts, capital:			
Capital, January 1, 19--...........................		$10,306.80	
Net income for year...................................	$33,967.45		
Less withdrawals....................................	31,825.50	2,141.95	
Capital, December 31, 19--		12,448.75	
Total liabilities and owner's equity.............		$13,337.70	

John H. Roberts, Management Consultant — Balance Sheet

other than cash. The amount shown includes both cash in bank and petty cash. The property, plant, and equipment assets are those which are expected to serve for many years.

(3) All of the liabilities are classified as current, since they must be paid in the near future. Certain types of obligations are classified as long-term, but Roberts has no debts of this type.

Rounded Amounts in Statements and Schedules. The foregoing income statement and balance sheet could be presented by rounding to the nearest dollar. The rule adopted for rounding is: If the cents in the amount are 50 or more, raise the first digit left of the decimal point by one; if 49 or less, drop the cents. Thus, $23.62 would become $24; $23.35 would become $23.

Adjusting Entries for a Personal Service Enterprise. The amounts in the financial statements must agree with the ledger account balances. To speed up the preparation of the statements, a work sheet was used to adjust accounts and accumulate income statement and balance sheet information. Subsequently, adjustments will have to be formally recorded in the journal and posted to the accounts. This is accomplished by posting the journal entry that is shown in the partial combination journal illustration on page 140. The two accounts affected by the entry, Depreciation Expense (No. 827) and Accumulated Depreciation — Office Equipment (No. 211.1), are reproduced below as they appear after the entry is posted. After this posting is completed, the balance of the depreciation expense account agrees with the amount shown in the income statement, and the balance of the accumulated depreciation account is the same as the amount shown in the balance sheet.

ACCOUNT *Depreciation Expense*   ACCOUNT NO. 827

DATE	ITEM	POST. REF.	DEBIT	CREDIT	BALANCE DEBIT	BALANCE CREDIT
19-- Dec. 31		cj30	169206		169206	
31		cj30		169206	-0-	-0-

ACCOUNT *Accumulated Depreciation -- Office Equipment*   ACCOUNT NO. 211.1

DATE	ITEM	POST. REF.	DEBIT	CREDIT	BALANCE DEBIT	BALANCE CREDIT
19-- Dec. 1	Balance	✓				563445
31		cj30		169206		732651

Closing Entries for a Personal Service Enterprise. As in the case of the adjusting entry, the closing entries are made as of December

31. Note that the work sheet provides all of the data needed to prepare the adjusting and closing entries. The purpose and use of Expense and Revenue Summary, Account No. 531, as its name indicates, is to summarize the amounts of expense and revenue which are reasons for changes in owner's equity that are not the result of investments and withdrawals by the owner.

The revenue and expense accounts and the account for John H. Roberts, Drawing (No. 511.1) have served their purpose for the year 19--, and the balance of each of these accounts needs to be reduced to zero in order to make the accounts ready for entries in the following year. The expense and revenue summary account will assist in closing the expense and revenue accounts.

The procedures for closing the temporary accounts under the double-entry system are:

(1) For expense accounts with debit balances: debit the expense and revenue summary account and credit the temporary account for its balance.
(2) For revenue accounts with credit balances: debit the account for its balance and credit Expense and Revenue Summary.
(3) Close the expense and revenue summary account to the John H. Roberts capital account.
(4) Close the John H. Roberts drawing account to the capital account.

ACCOUNT *John H. Roberts, Drawing*   ACCOUNT NO. 511.1

DATE	ITEM	POST. REF.	DEBIT	CREDIT	BALANCE DEBIT	BALANCE CREDIT
19-- Dec. 1	Balance	✓			3000800	
15		CJ28	180000		3180800	
31		CJ29	1750		3182550	
31		CJ30		3182550	-0-	-0-

ACCOUNT *Expense and Revenue Summary*   ACCOUNT NO. 531

DATE	ITEM	POST. REF.	DEBIT	CREDIT	BALANCE DEBIT	BALANCE CREDIT
19-- Dec. 31		CJ30		9001600		9001600
31		CJ30	5604855			3396745
31		CJ30	3396745		-0-	-0-

The net effect is an increase in the credit balance of the account for John H. Roberts, Capital (No. 511) of $2,141.95 — the excess of net income for the year, $33,967.45, over withdrawals for the year, $31,825.50. This result is accomplished by means of four entries illustrated in the combination journal shown on page 140:

(1) The $90,016 credit balance of Professional Fees, Account No. 611, is closed to (transferred to the credit side of) Expense and Revenue Summary, Account No. 531.

(2) The debit balances of all eleven expense accounts (Nos. 821 through 829, 831, and 839) which, in total, amounted to $56,048.55, are closed to (transferred to the debit side of) Expense and Revenue Summary (No. 531).

(3) The result of entries (1) and (2) is a credit balance of $33,967.45 — the net income for the year — in Expense and Revenue Summary (No. 531). This was closed to John H. Roberts, Capital (No. 511).

(4) The $31,825.50 debit balance of John H. Roberts, Drawing, Account No. 511.1, was closed to John H. Roberts, Capital (No. 511).

COMBINATION JOURNAL FOR MONTH OF *December* 19 - -   PAGE 30

	DAY	DESCRIPTION	POST. REF.	GENERAL DEBIT	GENERAL CREDIT	
1		AMOUNTS FORWARDED				1
2	31	*Adjusting Entry*				2
3		Depreciation Expense	827	169206		3
4		Accumulated Depn.--Office Equip.	211.1		169206	4
5						5
6	31	*Closing Entries*				6
7		Professional Fees	611	9001600		7
8		Expense and Revenue Summary	531		9001600	8
9		Expense and Revenue Summary	531	5604855		9
10		Rent Expense	821		420000	10
11		Salary Expense	822		3771400	11
12		Travel & Entertainment Expense	823		291871	12
13		Telephone Expense	824		66025	13
14		Forms and Supplies Expense	825		237529	14
15		Automobile Expense	826		209673	15
16		Depreciation Expense	827		169206	16
17		Insurance Expense	828		31360	17
18		Charitable Contributions Expense	829		72450	18
19		Payroll Taxes Expense	831		310050	19
20		Miscellaneous Expense	839		25291	20
21		Expense and Revenue Summary	531	3396745		21
22		John H. Roberts, Capital	511		3396745	22
23		John H. Roberts, Capital	511	3182550		23
24		John H. Roberts, Drawing	511.1		3182550	24
25				21354956	21354956	25

John H. Roberts, Management Consultant — Adjusting and Closing Entries

Balancing the Closed Accounts. After posting the closing entries, all of the temporary owner's equity accounts are closed, and they are balanced in the manner illustrated below and on pages 142–143. (Note that zeros are entered in the Debit Balance and Credit Balance columns in each account on the line with the closing entry.)

ACCOUNT *Professional Fees*   ACCOUNT NO. *611*

DATE		ITEM	POST. REF.	DEBIT	CREDIT	BALANCE DEBIT	BALANCE CREDIT
19-- Dec.	1	Balance	✓				8441600
	31		CJ29		560000		9001600
	31		CJ30	9001600		-0-	-0-

ACCOUNT *Rent Expense*   ACCOUNT NO. *821*

DATE		ITEM	POST. REF.	DEBIT	CREDIT	BALANCE DEBIT	BALANCE CREDIT
19-- Dec.	1	Balance	✓			385000	
	3		CJ28	35000		420000	
	31		CJ30		420000	-0-	-0-

ACCOUNT *Salary Expense*   ACCOUNT NO. *822*

DATE		ITEM	POST. REF.	DEBIT	CREDIT	BALANCE DEBIT	BALANCE CREDIT
19-- Dec.	1	Balance	✓			3346400	
	31		CJ29	425000		3771400	
	31		CJ30		3771400	-0-	-0-

ACCOUNT *Travel and Entertainment Expense*   ACCOUNT NO. *823*

DATE		ITEM	POST. REF.	DEBIT	CREDIT	BALANCE DEBIT	BALANCE CREDIT
19-- Dec.	1	Balance	✓			277681	
	29		CJ29	11410		289091	
	31		CJ29	2780		291871	
	31		CJ30		291871	-0-	-0-

John H. Roberts, Management Consultant — Closed General Ledger Accounts

ACCOUNT *Telephone Expense*   ACCOUNT NO. *824*

DATE	ITEM	POST. REF.	DEBIT	CREDIT	BALANCE DEBIT	BALANCE CREDIT
19-- Dec. 1		✓			61690	
21		CJ28	4335		66025	
31		CJ30		66025	-0-	-0-

ACCOUNT *Forms and Supplies Expense*   ACCOUNT NO. *825*

DATE	ITEM	POST. REF.	DEBIT	CREDIT	BALANCE DEBIT	BALANCE CREDIT
19-- Dec. 1		✓			217775	
13		CJ28	9361		227136	
23		CJ28	9118		236254	
31		CJ29	1275		237529	
31		CJ30		237529	-0-	-0-

ACCOUNT *Automobile Expense*   ACCOUNT NO. *826*

DATE	ITEM	POST. REF.	DEBIT	CREDIT	BALANCE DEBIT	BALANCE CREDIT
19-- Dec. 1	Balance	✓			194390	
16		CJ28	10220		204610	
20		CJ28	4538		209148	
31		CJ29	525		209673	
31		CJ30		209673	-0-	-0-

ACCOUNT *Depreciation Expense*   ACCOUNT NO. *827*

DATE	ITEM	POST. REF.	DEBIT	CREDIT	BALANCE DEBIT	BALANCE CREDIT
19-- Dec. 31		CJ30	169206		169206	

ACCOUNT *Insurance Expense*   ACCOUNT NO. *828*

DATE	ITEM	POST. REF.	DEBIT	CREDIT	BALANCE DEBIT	BALANCE CREDIT
19-- Dec. 1	Balance	✓			26780	
8		CJ28	5480		32260	
13		CJ28		900	31360	
31		CJ30		31360	-0-	-0-

John H. Roberts, Management Consultant — Closed General Ledger Accounts
(continued)

ACCOUNT *Charitable Contributions Expense*					ACCOUNT NO. *829*	
DATE	ITEM	POST. REF.	DEBIT	CREDIT	BALANCE DEBIT	BALANCE CREDIT
19-- Dec. 1	Balance	✓			61600	
17		CJ28	10000		71600	
31		CJ29	850		72450	
31		CJ30		72450	-0-	-0-

ACCOUNT *Payroll Taxes Expense*					ACCOUNT NO. *831*	
DATE	ITEM	POST. REF.	DEBIT	CREDIT	BALANCE DEBIT	BALANCE CREDIT
19-- Dec. 1	Balance	✓			304450	
14		CJ28	5600		310050	
31		CJ30		310050	-0-	-0-

ACCOUNT *Miscellaneous Expense*					ACCOUNT NO. *839*	
DATE	ITEM	POST. REF.	DEBIT	CREDIT	BALANCE DEBIT	BALANCE CREDIT
19-- Dec. 1	Balance	✓			22850	
20		CJ28	1825		24675	
31		CJ29	616		25291	
31		CJ30		25291	-0-	-0-

John H. Roberts, Management Consultant — Closed General Ledger Accounts
(concluded)

Updating Owner's Equity Accounts. After the temporary owner's equity accounts are closed, the permanent owner's equity accounts are updated to prepare them to receive entries in the next fiscal period. Only one of Roberts' owner's equity accounts needs to be updated: John H. Roberts, Capital, Account No. 511. This account is shown below as it appears after the third and fourth closing entries illustrated on page 140 are posted.

ACCOUNT *John H. Roberts, Capital*					ACCOUNT NO. *511*	
DATE	ITEM	POST. REF.	DEBIT	CREDIT	BALANCE DEBIT	BALANCE CREDIT
19-- Dec. 1	Balance	✓				1030680
31		CJ30		3396745		4427425
31		CJ30	3182550			1244875

John H. Roberts, Management Consultant — Updating Owner's Equity

Post-Closing Trial Balance. After posting the closing entries, it is advisable to take a post-closing trial balance to prove the equality of the debit and credit balances in the general ledger accounts. The post-closing trial balance of Roberts' ledger is shown below:

Account	Acct. No.	Dr. Balance	Cr. Balance
John H. Roberts, Management Consultant			
Post-Closing Trial Balance			
December 31, 19--			
County Bank	111	3 583 61	
Petty Cash Fund	112	160 00	
Office Equipment	211	16 920 60	
Accumulated Depreciation -- Office Equip.	211.1		7 326 51
FICA Tax Payable	311		70 00
Employees Income Tax Payable	314		818 95
John H. Roberts, Capital	511		12 448 75
		20 664 21	20 664 21

John H. Roberts, Management Consultant — Post-Closing Trial Balance

THE ACCOUNTING CYCLE

The steps involved in handling all of the transactions and events completed during an accounting period, beginning with recording in a book of original entry and ending with a post-closing trial balance, are referred to collectively as the accounting cycle. This chapter has illustrated a complete accounting cycle. A brief summary of the various steps follows:

(1) Journalize the transactions.
(2) Post to the ledger accounts.
(3) Take a trial balance.
(4) Determine the needed adjustments.
(5) Complete an end-of-period work sheet.
(6) Prepare an income statement and a balance sheet.
(7) Journalize and post the adjusting and closing entries.
(8) Balance the closed accounts and update certain owner's equity accounts.
(9) Take a post-closing trial balance.

In visualizing the accounting cycle, it is important to realize that steps (3) through (9) in the foregoing list are performed as of the last day of the accounting period. This does not mean that they are done on the last day. The accountant or bookkeeper may not be able to do any of these things until the first few days (sometimes weeks) of the next period. Nevertheless, the work sheet, statements, and entries are prepared or recorded as of the closing date. While the journalizing of transactions in the new period proceeds in regular fashion, entries relating to the new period are normally not posted to the general ledger until the steps relating to the period just ended have been completed.

BUILDING YOUR ACCOUNTING KNOWLEDGE

1. How does a personal service enterprise differ from a mercantile enterprise? From a manufacturing enterprise?
2. Describe the process of accounting for revenue on a cash basis.
3. Describe the process of accounting for expenses on a cash basis.
4. What is the chief advantage of John H. Roberts' system of account numbering?
5. How does the use of the combination journal save time and space in entering cash transactions?
6. What is the principal advantage of the four-column balance-column account form over the standard two-column account form?
7. Name two elements that are normally added to and one element that is normally deducted from owner's equity at the start of the fiscal period to produce owner's equity at the end of the fiscal period.
8. List the nine steps in John H. Roberts' accounting cycle.

Report No. 5-1

> *Complete Report No. 5-1 in the study assignments and submit your working papers to the instructor for approval. After completing the report you will then be given instructions as to the work to be done next.*

EXPANDING YOUR BUSINESS VOCABULARY

What is the meaning of each of the following terms?

account form of balance sheet (p. 136)
accounting cycle (p. 144)
balance-column account form (p. 119)

book value (p. 133)
business enterprises (p. 114)
cash basis expense (p. 114)
cash basis revenue (p. 114)
combination journal (p. 118)

constructive receipt (p. 114)
contra accounts (p. 116)
current assets (p. 136)
depreciation expense (p. 115)
end-of-period work sheet
   (p. 132)
manufacturing enterprise
   (p. 114)
mercantile enterprise (p. 114)
personal service enterprise
   (p. 114)

post-closing trial balance
   (p. 144)
professional enterprises (p. 114)
proof of footings (p. 121)
property, plant and equipment
   assets (p. 138)
proved (p. 121)
report form of balance sheet
   (p. 136)
transposition error (p. 122)
undepreciated cost (p. 133)

CHAPTERS 1–5

SUPPLEMENTARY PRACTICAL ACCOUNTING PROBLEMS

The following problems supplement those in Reports 1-1 through 5-1 of the Part 1 Study Assignments. These problems are numbered to indicate the chapter of the textbook with which they correlate. For example, Problem 1-A and Problem 1-B correlate with Chapter 1. Loose-leaf stationery should be used in solving these problems. The paper required includes plain ruled paper, two-column journal paper, two-column and three-column statement paper, ledger paper, and work sheet paper.

Problem 1-A   Accounting elements — equation form

S. Bail owns an insurance agency. As of December 31, Bail owned the following property that related to the business: Cash, $1,794; office equipment, $3,210; and an automobile, $5,240. At the same time, Bail owed business creditors $1,730.

Required: (1) On the basis of the above information, compute the amounts of the accounting elements and show them in equation form. (2) Assume that during the following year there is an increase in Bail's business assets of $2,190 and a decrease in the business liabilities of $225. Indicate the changes in the accounting elements by showing them in equation form after the changes have occurred.

Problem 1-B   T account format; trial balance

M. Bass, a real estate agent who has been employed by a large local firm, decides to go into business. Bass' business transactions for the first month of operations were as follows:

(a) Bass invested $18,000 cash in the business. ✓

(b) Paid office rent for one month, $360.

(c) Purchased office equipment from the Hillenbrand Office Equipment Co. (a supplier), $2,990 on account.

(d) Paid telephone bill, $46.

(e) Received $3,250 for services rendered to C. Feaster.

(f) Paid $1,600 to the Hillenbrand Office Equipment Co., on account.

(g) Received $1,900 for services rendered to M. Greer.

(h) Paid $750 salary to office secretary.

Required: (1) On a plain sheet of paper, rule eight T accounts and enter the following titles: Cash; Office Equipment; Accounts Payable; M. Bass, Capital; Professional Fees; Rent Expense; Telephone Expense; and Salary Expense. (2) Record the foregoing transactions directly in the accounts. (3) Foot the accounts and enter the balances where necessary. (4) Prepare a trial balance of the accounts, using a sheet of two-column journal paper.

Problem 2-A   Journal entries

Following is a narrative of the transactions completed by M. A. Dupre, accounting systems consultant, during the first month of Dupre's business operations:

Oct.   1   Dupre invested $12,000 cash in the business.

       1   Paid office rent, $300.

       3   Purchased office furniture for $2,025.

       3   Paid $38.50 for installation of telephone and for one month's service.

       4   Received $500 from Bender Lumber Co. for consulting services rendered.

       5   Purchased stationery and supplies on account from V. W. Hayes Stationery Co., $284.60.

       6   Paid $14 for subscription to an accounting systems magazine. (Charge Miscellaneous Expense.)

       8   Paid $80 to Dr. Robert Burns, a dentist, for dental service performed for Dupre.
(Note: This is equivalent to a withdrawal of $80 by Dupre for personal use. Charge to drawing account.)

     10   Received $350 from Sherwood Green, Inc., for professional services rendered.

     12   Paid $147 for an airplane ticket for a business trip.

     14   Paid other traveling expenses, $79.15.

     19   Received $300 from Bedford Electric Co. for professional services rendered.

     20   Paid account of V. W. Hayes Stationery Co. in full, $284.60.

     31   Paid $540 monthly salary to secretary.

     31   Office supplies used during the month were $68.

Required: Journalize the foregoing transactions, using a sheet of two-column journal paper. Number the pages and use both sides of the sheet, if necessary. Select the account titles from the chart of accounts shown below.

Chart of Accounts

Assets
111   Cash
112   Stationery and Supplies
211   Office Furniture

Liabilities
311   Accounts Payable

Owner's Equity
511   M. A. Dupre, Capital
511.1 M. A. Dupre, Drawing

Revenue
611   Professional Fees

Expenses
811   Rent Expense
812   Telephone Expense
813   Traveling Expense
814   Salary Expense
815   Miscellaneous Expense
816   Stationery and Supplies Expense

After journalizing the transactions, prove the equality of the debits and credits by footing the amount columns. Enter the footings in pencil immediately under the line on which the last entry appears.

Problem 2-B   Journal entries, posting, trial balance

T. F. Holihen is a real estate appraiser. Following is the trial balance of Holihen's business taken as of September 30, 19––.

T. F. HOLIHEN, APPRAISER
Trial Balance
September 30, 19––

Cash	111	2,146.16	
Office Equipment	211	1,310.00	
Automobile	221	5,680.00	
Accounts Payable	311		2,474.38
T. F. Holihen, Capital	511		6,032.85
T. F. Holihen, Drawing	511.1	3,820.00	
Professional Fees	611		9,600.00
Rent Expense	811	3,420.00	
Telephone Expense	812	286.10	
Electric Expense	813	264.05	
Automobile Expense	814	558.76	
Charitable Contributions Expense	815	404.00	
Miscellaneous Expense	816	218.16	
		18,107.23	18,107.23

A narrative of the transactions completed by Holihen during the month of October follows below and on page 150.

Oct. 1   (Saturday) Paid one month's rent, $380.
      3   Paid telephone bill, $29.50.
      3   Paid electric bill, $28.15.

Oct. 5 Received $550 from First National Bank for services rendered.
      7 Paid a garage bill, $42.80.
     10 Received $360 from G. Ruebeck for services rendered.
     12 Paid Buchanan Furniture Store, $89.75. (Charge to Holihen's drawing account.
     15 Holihen withdrew $300 for personal use.
     17 Paid Doyle's Office Supply, $190 on account.
     19 Received $280 from Eastside Development Co. for services rendered.
     24 Gave the American Cancer Society $40.
     26 Paid the American Appraisal Institute $80 for annual membership dues and fees.
     29 Received $225 from Fountain Federal Savings and Loan for professional services.
     31 Holihen withdrew $350 for personal use.

Required: (1) Journalize the October transactions, using a sheet of two-column journal paper. Number the pages and use both sides of the sheet, if necessary. Foot the amount columns. (2) Open the necessary accounts, using the standard account form of ledger paper. Allow one page for each account. Record the October 1 balances as shown in the September 30 trial balance and post the journal entries for October. (3) Foot the ledger accounts, enter the balances, and prove the balances by taking a trial balance as of October 31. Use a sheet of two-column journal paper for the trial balance.

Problem 2-C   Income statement and balance sheet

THE R. N. MYERS AGENCY
Trial Balance
March 31, 19––

Cash	111	6,744.20	
Stationery and Supplies	112	1,476.10	
Office Furniture	211	4,104.80	
Notes Payable	311		1,590.00
Accounts Payable	312		1,830.48
R. N. Myers, Capital	511		8,475.29
R. N. Myers, Drawing	511.1	1,612.76	
Professional Fees	611		4,059.45
Rent Expense	811	360.00	
Telephone Expense	812	54.85	
Salary Expense	813	702.00	
Traveling Expense	814	782.68	
Stationery and Supplies Expense	815	49.11	
Miscellaneous Expense	816	68.72	
		15,955.22	15,955.22

Required: (1) Prepare an income statement for The R. N. Myers Agency showing the results of the first month of operations, March. Use a sheet of two-column statement paper for the income statement. (2) Prepare a balance sheet in account form showing the financial condition of the agency as of March 31. Two sheets of two-column statement paper may be used for the balance sheet. List the assets on one sheet and the liabilities and owner's equity on the other sheet.

Problem 3-A   Journalizing; posting; trial balance

Phyllis Plant operates a day-care center for children of working mothers. The only book of original entry for the business is a two-column journal and the standard form of account in the general ledger is used. Following is the trial balance of the business taken as of November 30.

PHYLLIS PLANT DAY-CARE CENTER
Trial Balance
November 30, 19––

Cash	111	3,000.00	
Equipment	211	625.00	
Accounts Payable	311		195.50
Phyllis Plant, Capital	511		2,354.79
Phyllis Plant, Drawing	511.1	1,900.00	
Day-Care Fees	611		8,200.00
Rent Expense	811	4,400.00	
Telephone Expense	812	234.60	
Electric Expense	813	310.44	
Supplies Expense	814	175.00	
Miscellaneous Expense	815	92.00	
Cash Short and Over	816	13.25	
		10,750.29	10,750.29

NARRATIVE OF TRANSACTIONS FOR DECEMBER

Dec. 1 (Thursday) Paid December rent in advance, $400.
  1 Paid electric bill, $29.50.
  2 Paid telephone bill, $21.90.
  2 Received cash and checks for day-care services, $210.
  6 Paid $14.60 for repair of broken window.
  8 Plant withdrew $200 for personal use.
  9 Received cash and checks for day-care services, $195.
  13 Purchased new table and chairs from Lilwon Furniture Co. on credit, $85.
  16 Received cash and checks for day-care services, $200.
  19 Paid $5 for having snow shoveled.
  20 Paid $17.85 for supplies.
  22 Paid Ubrakum Furniture Co. $80 on account.
  23 Received cash and checks for day-care services, $180.
  27 Plant withdrew $200 for personal use.
  30 Received cash and checks for day-care services, $85.

Dec. 30   In attempting to prove cash, it was found that there was a cash shortage of $4.50. The cause of the shortage could not be determined.

Required: (1) Journalize the December transactions. For the journal use two sheets of two-column journal paper and number the pages, 11 and 12. (2) Open the necessary ledger accounts. Allow one page for each account and number the accounts. Record the December 1 balances and post the journal entries. Foot the journal. (3) Take a trial balance.

Problem 3-B   Bank reconciliation

Tom Steinmetz, who owns a bicycle shop, completed the following transactions with the Greenwood State Bank during the month of July:

July 3 (Monday) Balance in bank per record kept on check stubs $5,500.00	July 11 Check No. 218.... $ 180.00
3 Deposit 2,900.00	11 Check No. 219.... 98.10
3 Check No. 208.... 456.70	13 Check No. 220.... 859.50
3 Check No. 209.... 50.00	14 Check No. 221.... 86.30
4 Check No. 210.... 850.00	14 Check No. 222.... 446.49
4 Check No. 211.... 230.00	14 Deposit 766.28
5 Check No. 212.... 260.00	17 Check No. 223.... 250.00
6 Check No. 213.... 170.00	18 Check No. 224.... 520.30
7 Check No. 214.... 321.10	21 Check No. 225.... 149.90
7 Check No. 215.... 100.00	21 Deposit 1,492.00
7 Check No. 216.... 196.00	24 Check No. 226.... 64.82
7 Deposit 569.30	25 Check No. 227.... 271.66
10 Check No. 217.... 968.04	27 Check No. 228.... 545.95
	28 Check No. 229.... 460.00
	31 Check No. 230.... 925.77
	31 Deposit 1,520.68

Required: (1) Prepare a record of the bank account as it would appear on the check stubs from July 24 through July 31. (2) Prepare a reconciliation of the bank statement for July which indicated a balance of $4,411.39 on July 31, with Checks Nos. 216, 226, 229, and 230 outstanding. The July 31 deposit is not shown on the bank statement, and a service charge of $2.15 has been deducted.

Problem 3-C   Petty cash disbursements; statement of petty cash disbursements

Nancy Bonsell, a beauty shop owner, had a balance of $200 in the petty cash fund as of April 1. During April the following petty cash transactions were completed.

Apr. 2 (Thursday) Paid $6.45 for typewriter repairs. Petty Cash Voucher No. 41.

Apr.   6   Paid for long-distance telephone call, $3.75. Petty Cash Voucher No. 42.

      8   Gave $12 for Girl Scout cookies. Petty Cash Voucher No. 43.

      9   Paid garage for washing car, $4.50. Petty Cash Voucher No. 44.

    12   Gave Bonsell's son $15. (Charge to Nancy Bonsell, Drawing.) Petty Cash Voucher No. 45.

    14   Paid for postage stamps, $18. Petty Cash Voucher No. 46.

    17   Paid for newspaper for month, $4.80. Petty Cash Voucher No. 47.

    22   Paid for window washing, $8.50. Petty Cash Voucher No. 48.

    27   Paid Hoosier Motor Club $25 for dues. (Charge to Nancy Bonsell, Drawing.) Petty Cash Voucher No. 49.

    28   Paid for car oil and lubrication, $19.50. Petty Cash Voucher No. 50.

    30   Rendered report of petty cash expenditures for month and received the amount needed to replenish the petty cash fund.

Required: (1) Record the foregoing transactions in a petty cash disbursements record, distributing the expenditures as follows (a page of work sheet paper may be used):

Nancy Bonsell, Drawing	Postage Expense
Automobile Expense	Miscellaneous Expense
Telephone Expense	

(2) Prove the petty cash disbursements record by footing the amount columns and proving the totals. Enter the totals and rule the amount columns with single and double lines. (3) Prepare a statement of the petty cash disbursements for April. (4) Bring down the balance in the petty cash fund below the ruling in the Description column. Enter the amount received to replenish the fund and record the total.

Problem 4-A   Payroll register

Following is a summary of the hours worked, rates of pay, and other relevant information concerning the employees of The St. Joe Mineral Co., Robert W. Burns, owner, for the week ended Saturday, November 6. Employees are paid at the rate of time and one half for all hours worked in excess of 8 in any day or 40 in any week.

No.	Name	Allowances Claimed	Hours Worked M T W T F S						Regular Hourly Rate	Cumulative Earnings Jan. 1–Oct. 30
1	Bowen, Michael F. ...	1	8	8	8	8	8	6	$5.00	$9,110
2	Hanson, John A.	5	8	9	8	8	8	4	5.25	9,530
3	Malone, Sherri M.	3	8	8	8	8	8	0	5.10	9,325
4	Moore, Ann M...........	2	8	8	8	9	8	4	4.90	8,600
5	Tomita, Lyanne	1	8	8	8	8	8	4	5.15	9,290
6	Yarbrough, James....	3	8	8	8	8	6	0	5.40	9,750

Bowen and Moore each have $6 withheld this payday for group life insurance. Hanson and Yarbrough each have $5 withheld this payday for private hospital insurance. Tomita has $10 withheld this payday as a contribution to the United Way.

Required: (1) Using plain ruled paper size 8½" by 11", rule a payroll register form similar to that reproduced on pages 92 and 93, and insert the necessary columnar headings. Enter on this form the payroll for the week ended Saturday, November 6. Refer to the Weekly Income Tax Table on page 89 to determine the amounts to be withheld from the wages of each worker for income tax purposes. All of Burns' employees are married. Seven percent of the taxable wages of each employee should be withheld for FICA tax. Checks Nos. 611 through 616 were issued to the employees. Complete the payroll record by footing the amount columns, proving the footings, entering the totals, and ruling. (2) Assuming that the wages were paid on November 10, record the payment on a sheet of two-column journal paper.

Problem 4-B   Journal entries — payroll and payroll taxes

The Castleton Square Store employs twelve people. They are paid by checks on the 15th and last working day of each month. The entry to record each payroll includes the liabilities for the amounts withheld. The expense and liabilities arising from the employer's payroll taxes are recorded on each payday.

Following is a narrative of the transactions completed during the month of January that relate to payrolls and payroll taxes:

Jan. 15 Payroll for first half of month:

Total salaries..		$5,320.00
Less amounts withheld:		
FICA tax	$372.40	
Employees' income tax	856.10	1,228.50
Net amount paid		$4,091.50

15 Payroll taxes imposed on employer:
FICA tax, 7%
State unemployment tax, 2%
FUTA tax, 0.7%

29 Paid $3,175.30 for December's payroll taxes:
FICA tax, $1,472.90
Employees income tax withheld, $1,702.40

29 Paid state unemployment tax for quarter ended December 31, $624.45.

29 Paid balance due on FUTA tax for last half of year ended December 31, $298.85.

Jan. 30 Payroll for last half of month:

Total salaries...		$5,390.00
Less amounts withheld:		
FICA tax	$377.30	
Employees' income tax	859.70	1,237.00
Net amount paid......................................		$4,153.00

　　30 Payroll taxes imposed on employer:
　　　　All salaries taxable; rates same as on January 15.

Required: (1) Journalize the foregoing transactions, using two-column general journal paper. (2) Foot the debit and credit amount columns as a means of proof.

Problem 5-A Combination journal

Frank Neal operates a janitorial service. Neal's revenue consists entirely of compensation for personal services rendered, and accounts are kept on the cash basis. The chart of accounts is as follows:

Assets
111　Cash
211　Cleaning Equipment
211.1 Accumulated Depreciation —
　　　Cleaning Equipment
231　Truck
231.1 Accumulated Depreciation —
　　　Truck

Liabilities
311　FICA Tax Payable
312　Employees Income Tax Payable

Owner's Equity
511　Frank Neal, Capital
511.1 Frank Neal, Drawing
521　Expense and Revenue Summary

Revenue
611　Cleaning Fees

Expenses
811　Salary Expense
812　Telephone Expense
813　Supplies Expense
814　Repairs Expense
815　Truck Expense
816　Depreciation Expense
817　Payroll Taxes Expense
818　Miscellaneous Expense

The following transactions were completed by Neal during the month of June, 19––.

June　3 Issued Check No. 261 for $180 to Sherington's Cleaning Supplies for cleaning supplies.
　　　4 Issued Check No. 262 for $38 to Missouri Bell Telephone Co. for telephone service.
　　　6 Received check for $310 from St. Charles School for services rendered.
　　　10 Received check for $340 from Whitesides Clothiers for services rendered.
　　　12 Issued Check No. 263 for $61 to Sturgeon's Garage for servicing truck.

June 14 Issued Check No. 264 for $249 to part-time assistant Michael Losch in payment of salary for first half of month: $300 less income tax withholding, $30, and FICA tax withholding, $21.

14 Received check for $265 from Oliver's Skateboard Park for services rendered.

18 Issued Check No. 265 for $95 for cleaning supplies.

20 Issued Check No. 266 for $87 to Bob's Fixit Shop for repairs to cleaning equipment.

21 Issued Check No. 267 for $150 to Frank Neal for personal use.

25 Received check for $325 from Schramm's Refinishing Shop for services rendered.

27 Issued Check No. 268 for $69 to Sturgeon's Garage for gasoline bill.

28 Issued Check No. 269 for $249 to part-time assistant Michael Losch in payment of salary for second half of month. (See explanation of Check No. 264 issued on June 14.)

Required: (1) Prepare a combination journal with eight amount columns and record Frank Neal's June transactions. The headings of the amount columns are as follows:

First National Bank
   Deposits 111 Dr.
   Checks   111 Cr.

General
   Debit
   Credit

Cleaning Fees   611 Cr.

Salary Expense 811 Dr.

Wage Deductions
   FICA Tax Payable 311 Cr.
   Employees Income Tax Payable 312 Cr.

The balance in the First National Bank Account on June 1 is $2,410.

(2) Foot and prove the combination journal. (3) Record all appropriate posting references in the combination journal, assuming all general ledger posting had been completed.

Problem 5-B   Work sheet; adjusting entries; income statement and balance sheet

Donna Taylor is a lawyer engaged in professional practice. Taylor's revenue consists entirely of compensation for personal services rendered, and accounts are kept on the cash basis. The trial balance for the current year ending December 31 appears on page 157.

Required: (1) Prepare an eight-column work sheet making the necessary entries in the Adjustments columns to record the depreciation of the following assets:

Office equipment, 10%, $618.20
Automobiles, 25%, $2,930.00

(2) Prepare the following financial statements:

(a) An income statement for the year ended December 31.
(b) A balance sheet in report form as of December 31.

DONNA TAYLOR, LAWYER
Trial Balance
December 31, 19--

Cash	111	10,280.36	
Office Equipment	231	6,182.00	
Accumulated Depreciation — Office Equipment	231.1		618.20
Automobiles	241	11,720.00	
Accumulated Depreciation — Automobiles	241.1		2,930.00
Accounts payable	311		2,437.20
FICA Tax Payable	312		252.80
Employees Income Tax Payable	313		270.50
Donna Taylor, Capital	511		13,809.26
Donna Taylor, Drawing	511.1	20,000.00	
Professional Fees	611		58,140.00
Rent Expense	811	8,400.00	
Salary Expense	812	18,000.00	
Automobile Expense	813	1,310.40	
Depreciation Expense	814		
Payroll Taxes Expense	815	1,207.70	
Charitable Contributions Expense	816	550.00	
Miscellaneous Expense	817	807.50	
		78,457.96	78,457.96

Problem 5-C   Work sheet; adjusting and closing entries; financial statements

Steve Grela operates a commuter helicopter service between La-Guardia and Kennedy airports and downtown New York. A trial balance of Grela's general ledger accounts is reproduced on page 158.

Required: (1) Prepare an eight-column work sheet making the necessary adjustments to record the depreciation of long-term assets as shown below.

Property	Rate of Depreciation	Amount of Depreciation
Office equipment	10%	$ 770
Air service equipment	15%	52,143

(2) Prepare an income statement for the year ended December 31.
(3) Prepare a balance sheet in report form as of December 31. (4) Using two-column journal paper, prepare the entries required:

    (a) To adjust the general ledger accounts so that they will be in agreement with the financial statements.
    (b) To close the temporary owner's equity accounts on December 31. (Use account No. 521 for Expense and Revenue Summary.)

Foot the amount columns of the journal.

GRELA'S HELICOPTER SERVICE
Trial Balance
December 31, 19––

Cash	111	23,899.00	
Office Equipment	231	7,700.00	
Accumulated Depreciation — Office Equipment	231.1		1,540.00
Air Service Equipment	241	347,620.00	
Accumulated Depreciation — Air Service Equipment	241.1		104,286.00
Accounts Payable	311		18,007.00
FICA Tax Payable	312		875.00
Employees Income Tax Payable	313		840.00
Steve Grela, Capital	511		139,449.00
Steve Grela, Drawing	511.1	26,000.00	
Commuter Revenue	611		269,045.00
Rent Expense	811	20,160.00	
Salary Expense	812	50,400.00	
Office Expense	813	3,975.00	
Air Service Expense	814	49,964.00	
Depreciation Expense	815		
Payroll Taxes Expense	816	3,554.00	
Charitable Contributions Expense	817	560.00	
Miscellaneous Expense	818	210.00	
		534,042.00	534,042.00

CHAPTER 6

ACCOUNTING FOR PURCHASES OF MERCHANDISE

CHAPTER OBJECTIVES

The objectives of this chapter are to enable you:

▶ To explain why the cash basis of periodic income determination usually is unsuited to a merchandise business, and why the accrual basis gives a more meaningful measure of periodic income.

▶ To define the terms **purchases**, **purchases returns and allowances**, **merchandise inventory**, and **cost of goods sold**.

▶ To describe and use the following source documents:

(1) Purchase requisition
(2) Purchase order
(3) Purchase invoice

(4) Freight bill
(5) Credit memorandum

▶ To define **trade discounts**, **cash discounts**, and the most common **terms of purchase**.

▶ To explain and use a special journal for purchases of merchandise.

▶ To describe subsidiary records that support amounts in general ledger accounts, specifically —

(1) A file of unpaid suppliers invoices — the "invoice" method, or
(2) A subsidiary accounts payable ledger — the "ledger account" method.

In the preceding chapter, accounting practices suitable for a personal service enterprise were discussed and illustrated. Except for depreciation, the net income for the year was calculated on the cash basis where revenue is not recorded until money is received for the service performed. Similarly, most expenses were not recorded until paid in cash, even though many of the payments were for items of value received and consumed in a prior period or for things to be received and consumed in a later period. An exception to this practice was made for depreciation, since it is unrealistic to consider the entire cost of an asset such as office equipment (expected to be used for many years) to be an expense only of the month or year of purchase. The cost of plant and equipment assets is spread as expense over their expected useful lives.

The cash basis, even when slightly modified, is not technically perfect; but it has the virtues of simplicity and ease of understanding. This basis has proved to be quite satisfactory for most personal service enterprises. In the case of business enterprises whose major activity is the purchase of merchandise for resale, however, the cash basis of periodic income determination usually does not give a meaningful or useful measure of net income or net loss. There are two reasons why this is true: (1) Merchandising businesses commonly purchase and sell merchandise "on account" or "on credit" — meaning that payment is postponed a few days or weeks. The amount of cash paid or collected in any accounting period is almost never the same as the amount of purchases or sales of that period. (2) Merchandising businesses normally start and end each period with a stock of goods on hand for resale, and the dollar amount of this stock is not likely to be the same at both points of time.

A stock of goods held for resale at any time in the normal course of business is known as merchandise inventory. Determining the value of this inventory at the beginning, during, and at the end of the accounting period is an important factor in the periodic determination of net income for a merchandising business. Net purchases is the cost of merchandise purchased during the period less (1) the cost of goods returned to suppliers because they have proved to be unsatisfactory or unwanted, and (2) the amount of any allowances (price reductions for damaged or defective goods received) made by suppliers.

In recording transactions concerned with purchases of merchandise, it is desirable to keep at least the following accounts:

(1) Purchases
(2) Purchases Returns and Allowances

The accrual basis of accounting, which will be discussed in detail in Chapter 8, requires that the cost of goods sold should be determined periodically in order that it can be matched against the net sales revenue of the related period. Cost of goods sold (really merchandise inventory expense) is simply defined by the following formula:

$$\begin{array}{c} \text{Cost of} \\ \text{Goods Sold} \end{array} = \begin{array}{c} \text{Merchandise} \\ \text{Inventory,} \\ \text{Beginning of Period} \end{array} + \text{Net Purchases} - \begin{array}{c} \text{Merchandise} \\ \text{Inventory,} \\ \text{End of Period} \end{array}$$

SOURCE DOCUMENTS AND ASSOCIATED RECORDS FOR PURCHASES

Merchandise for resale and other property for use in the operation of a business enterprise may be purchased either for cash or on account. In a small enterprise the buying may be done by the owner or by an employee, and may require only part-time attention. In a large enterprise a purchasing department may be maintained with a manager and staff who devote their entire time to buying activities. The successful operation of a purchasing department requires an efficient organization as well as the proper equipment.

THE PURCHASE REQUISITION

A form used to request the responsible person or department to purchase merchandise or other property is known as a purchase requisition. Such requests may come from any person or department of an enterprise. Purchase requisitions should be numbered consecutively to prevent the loss or misuse of the forms. Usually they are prepared in duplicate, with the original copy going to the person responsible for purchasing and the duplicate copy being retained by the person or department originating the requisition.

A purchase requisition is reproduced on page 162. The requisition specifies merchandise wanted in women's wear. The merchandising business known as Boyd's Clothiers is organized into several store areas. Requisitions for merchandise originate with the salespersons responsible for the particular areas. After the purchase requisition shown in the illustration was approved by Boyd, an order was placed with Huk-A-Poo, Inc., a manufacturer of women's blouses, as indicated by the memorandum at the bottom of the form. The purchase requisition, when approved, is the authority to order the merchandise or other property described in the requisition.

Purchase Requisition

THE PURCHASE ORDER

A written order by the buyer for merchandise or other property specified in the buyer company's purchase requisition is known as a purchase order. A purchase order may be prepared on a printed stock form, on a specially designed form, or on an order blank furnished by a supplier of goods or services. Purchase orders should be numbered consecutively. Usually they are prepared with multiple copies. The original copy goes to the supplier or vendor — the person or firm from whom the merchandise or other property is ordered. Sometimes the duplicate copy also goes to the supplier. If this is the case, this copy — called the "acknowledgment copy" — will have a space for the supplier's signature to indicate the acceptance of the order. Such acceptance creates a formal contract. The signed acknowledgment copy is then returned to the ordering firm. Sometimes a copy of the purchase order is sent to the salesperson or department of the company that requisitioned the purchase. In many organizations a copy of the purchase order is sent to a receiving clerk. Some firms require that the accounting department receive a copy of the purchase order to provide a basis for verifying the charges made by the supplier. A variety of practices are followed with respect to requisitioning purchases, placing orders, checking goods received and charges made, recording purchases, and paying suppliers. Each business adopts procedures best suited to its particular needs.

A purchase order is reproduced below. The quantity and the description of the merchandise ordered are the same as were specified in the purchase requisition reproduced on page 162. The unit prices shown in the purchase order are those quoted by the supplier and it is expected that the merchandise will be billed at such prices.

BOYD'S clothiers

600 Olive Street, St. Louis, Missouri 63101-2356

PURCHASE ORDER NO. 312

DATE March 26, 19-- DELIVER BY April 12, 19--

TERMS 8/10, n/30

SHIP BY Hulsey Transfer Co.

FOB St. Louis

TO
Huk-A-Poo, Inc.
1411 Broadway
New York, NY 10012-1209

QUANTITY	DESCRIPTION	UNIT PRICE
10	Women's Blouses, small, No. B121	9.50
10	Women's Blouses, medium, No. B123	9.50
10	Women's Blouses, large, No. B125	9.50

Lynn C. Boyd

Purchase Order

THE PURCHASE INVOICE

A source document prepared by the seller that lists the items shipped, their cost, and the method of shipment is commonly referred to as an invoice. From the viewpoint of the seller, it is considered a sales invoice; from the viewpoint of the buyer, it is considered a purchase invoice.

A purchase invoice may be received by the buyer before or after delivery of the merchandise or other property ordered. As invoices are received, it is customary to number them consecutively. These numbers should not be confused with the suppliers' numbers, which represent their sale numbers. After being numbered, each purchase invoice is compared with a copy of the purchase order to determine that the quantity, description, prices, and the terms agree and that the method of shipment and the date of delivery conform to the instructions and specifications. A separate approval form may be used, or approval may be stamped on the invoice by means of a rubber stamp. If a separate approval form is used, it may be stapled to or pasted on the invoice form.

An example of a purchase invoice is reproduced below. A rubber stamp was used to imprint the approval form on the face of the invoice. When the merchandise is received, the salesperson may compare the contents of the shipment with a copy of the purchase order, or may prepare a receiving report indicating the contents of the shipment. In the latter event, the receiving report and the purchase order must be compared by someone from either the purchasing or the accounting area. After the prices and extensions are verified, the purchase invoice is recorded by entering it in the purchases journal and then posting it to the proper supplier's account in the accounts payable ledger. The invoice is then held in an unpaid invoice file until it is paid.

		Invoice No.	2541	
	Huk-A-Poo, Inc.	Salesperson	O'Toole	
	1411 Broadway	Cust. Order No.	312	
	New York, NY 10012-1209	Shipped Via	Truck	
		Terms	8/10, n/30	
		F.O.B.	Factory	

Sold To	Date
Boyd's Clothiers 600 Olive Street St. Louis, MO 63101-2356	March 29, 19--

Quan.	Item	Style No.	Unit Price	Amount
5*	Women's blouses, small	B121	9.50	$ 47.50
10	Women's blouses, medium	B123	9.50	95.00
10	Women's blouses, large	B125	9.50	95.00
				$237.50
5*	Women's blouses, small, back ordered. Will ship 4/14.			

Date received............
Received by.............
Items OK................
Prices OK...............
Ext. and total OK.......
Invoice no..............
FOB.....................
Fr. bill no.............
Fr. charge..............
Appr. for paymt.........

Purchase Invoice

Back Orders. If the supplier is unable to ship immediately a part or all of the merchandise ordered, the portions not shipped are known as back orders. Nevertheless, the supplier may send an invoice for the complete order, indicating on it what has been back ordered and when such items will be shipped. The purchase invoice reproduced on page 164 indicates that while 10 small size women's blouses were ordered, only 5 were shipped by Huk-A-Poo, Inc. Notice of this shortage was indicated on the invoice. In this instance, only the items shipped were billed.

Trade Discounts. Many manufacturers and wholesalers quote list prices (printed) which are subject to special discounts. Special discounts on list prices granted to customers to encourage their patronage are known as trade discounts. Such arrangements make possible the publication of catalogs with quotations of prices that will not be subject to frequent changes. Some firms, such as those dealing in hardware and jewelry, publish catalogs listing thousands of items. Such catalogs are costly, and considerable loss might be involved when price changes occur if it were not for the fact that discount rates may be changed without changing the list or catalog prices. This practice also has the advantage of permitting retail dealers to display catalogs to their customers without revealing what the items of merchandise cost the dealers.

When an invoice is subject to a trade discount, the discount is usually shown as a deduction from the total amount of the invoice. For example, if the invoice shown on page 164 had been subject to a trade discount of 10 percent, the discount would be stated in the body of the invoice in the manner shown below:

	Huk-A-Poo, Inc. 1411 Broadway New York, NY 10012-1209	Invoice No. 2541 Salesperson O'Toole Cust. Order No. 312 Shipped Via Truck Terms 8/10, n/30 F.O.B. Factory

Sold To

Boyd's Clothiers
600 Olive Street
St. Louis, MO 63101-2356

Date

March 29, 19--

Quan.	Item	Style No.	Unit Price	Amount
5*	Women's blouses, small	B121	9.50	$ 47.50
10	Women's blouses, medium	B123	9.50	95.00
10	Women's blouses, large	B125	9.50	95.00
				$237.50
			Less 10% discount	23.75
				$213.75

Date received.......... March 31
Received by..........
Items OK..........
Prices OK..........
Ext. and total OK..........
Invoice no.......... 47730
FOB.......... 5 10
Fr. bill no.......... LOB
Fr. charge..........
Appr. for paymt..........

| 5* | Women's blouses, small, back ordered. Will ship 4/14. | | | |

In recording such an invoice, the amount to be entered in the books is the net amount, $213.75, after deducting the trade discount of $23.75. Trade discounts represent a reduction in the price of the merchandise and should not be entered in the accounts of either the seller or the buyer.

Sometimes a series or chain of trade discounts is allowed. For example, if the list prices are subject to discounts of 20, 10, and 5 percent, each discount is computed separately on the successive net amounts. Assume that the gross amount of an invoice is $100 and discounts of 20, 10, and 5 percent are allowed. The net amount is determined as follows:

Gross amount of invoice	$100.00
Less 20%	20.00
Balance	$ 80.00
Less 10%	8.00
Balance	$ 72.00
Less 5%	3.60
Net amount	$ 68.40

In recording this invoice only the net amount, $68.40, is entered.

Cash Discounts. Many firms follow the practice of allowing cash discounts, which are discounts from quoted prices, as an inducement for prompt payment of invoices. The terms of payment should be clearly indicated on the invoice. The terms specified on the invoice reproduced on page 164 are "8/10, n/30." This means that a discount of 8 percent will be allowed if payment is made within 10 days from the date of the invoice (March 29), that is, if payment is made by April 8.

If the invoice is paid on or before April 8, 8 percent of $237.50, or $19, is deducted and a check for $218.50 may be issued in full settlement of the invoice. After April 8, no discount will be allowed, and the total amount of $237.50 must be paid not later than 30 days after the date of invoice, that is, by April 28.

Cash discounts usually are not recorded at the time of recording purchase invoices, even though it may be the policy of a firm to pay all invoices in time to get the benefit of any cash discounts offered. For example, the invoice reproduced on page 164 was recorded in the books for $237.50. The cash discount taken at time of payment on or before April 8 was accounted for by crediting a purchases discount account at the time of recording the check issued in settlement of the invoice. At the end of the period, the credit balance of the purchases discount account is shown in the income statement as a deduction from the cost of goods purchased.

Sometimes an invoice is subject to both trade and cash discounts. In such cases the trade discount should be deducted from the gross amount of the invoice before the cash discount is computed and deducted. For example, if the invoice reproduced on page 165 were subjected to a trade discount of 10 percent and the terms were 8/10, n/30, the net amount payable within 10 days from the date of the invoice should be computed in the following manner:

Amount of invoice..	$237.50
Less trade discount, 10%	23.75
Amount subject to cash discount........................	$213.75
Less cash discount, 8%	17.10
Net amount payable...	$196.65

Usually an entire invoice must be paid within the time specified to obtain the benefit of any cash discount offered. However, in some instances, the purchaser is allowed the usual cash discount for partial payment of an invoice within the time specified. Thus, if instead of paying the entire invoice of Huk-A-Poo, Inc., Boyd's Clothiers made a payment of $131.10 on the invoice by April 8, Huk-A-Poo, Inc., might agree to allow Boyd's Clothiers the cash discount of 8 percent. In this case, the amount of the discount is computed in the following manner:

100% = Amount for which Boyd's Clothiers should receive credit
100% − 8% = 92%
$131.10 ÷ 92% = $142.50
$142.50 − $131.10 = $11.40 discount

This transaction should be recorded on the books of Boyd's Clothiers by debiting Accounts Payable for $142.50, by crediting Purchases Discount for $11.40, and by crediting the bank account for $131.10.

Purchase Invoice Terms. The terms commonly used in connection with purchase invoices are interpreted as follows:

30 days	The amount of the invoice must be paid within 30 days from its date.
2/10, n/30	A discount of 2% is allowed if payment is made within 10 days from the date of the invoice; otherwise, the total amount of the invoice must be paid within 30 days from its date.
2/EOM, n/60	A discount of 2% is allowed if payment is made before the end of the month; otherwise, the total amount of the invoice must be paid within 60 days from its date.

4/10, EOM	A discount of 4% is allowed if payment is made within 10 days after the end of the current month.
COD	Collect on delivery. The amount of the invoice must be paid at the time the merchandise is delivered.
FOB Shipping Point	Free on board at point of origin of the shipment. Under such terms the buyer must pay all transportation costs and assume all risks from the time the merchandise is accepted for shipment by the carrier.
FOB Destination	Free on board at destination of the shipment. The seller will pay the transportation costs and will assume all responsibility for the merchandise until it reaches the carrier's delivery point at destination.

COD Purchases. Merchandise or other property may be purchased on COD terms, that is, collect on delivery or cash on delivery. COD shipments may be received by parcel post, express, or freight. When shipments are received by parcel post or express, the recipient must pay for the property at the time of delivery. The bill may include transportation charges and COD fees. In any event, the total amount paid represents the cost of the property purchased.

When COD shipments are made by freight, the amount to be collected by the transportation company is entered immediately below the description of the merchandise on the bill. A copy of the sales invoice may be inserted in an envelope which is pasted to the outside of the package, carton, or case. The transportation company then collects the amount specified, plus a COD collection fee, at the time of delivering the merchandise, and remits the amount to the shipper.

THE FREIGHT BILL

At the time merchandise or other property is delivered to a transportation company for shipment, an agent of the transportation company prepares a document known as a waybill which describes the shipment, shows the point of origin and destination, and indicates any special handling that may be required. The original copy is forwarded to the agent of the transportation company at the station to which the shipment is directed. When the shipment arrives at the destination, a bill for the transportation charges is prepared, which is known as a freight bill. Sometimes the recipient of the shipment is required to pay the freight bill before the property can be obtained. A reproduction of a freight bill is presented on page 169.

TO	Boyd's Clothiers 600 Olive St. St. Louis, MO 63101-2356		Broadway at Poplar, St. Louis, Missouri 63102-6363 **Hulsey Transfer Co.**			
		ORIGINAL FREIGHT BILL		NUMBER 375485		
		CODE 3	TERMINAL St. Louis		SHIPPER NO. C 02473	
FROM	Hanes Corporation Winston Salem, NC 27102-7022	FOR OFFICE USE ONLY CL NAME			PRO DIV	
		DATE March 31, 19--				
PIECES	DESCRIPTION	WEIGHT	RATE	PREPAID	COLLECT	
3	Cartons Hosiery	3#	1.65		4.95	
		C. O. D. AMOUNT		FEE	DRIVER COLLECT	
ARTICLES LISTED HAVE BEEN RECEIVED IN GOOD CONDITION BY *A. S.* DATE April 1						

Freight Bill

Trucking companies usually make what is known as a "store-to-door delivery." Freight shipments made by railroad or airline may also be delivered to the recipient's place of business at no extra charge. In case such service is not rendered by the transportation company, it may be necessary for the recipient to employ a local drayage company to transport the merchandise from the freight station to the place of business. In such a case, the drayage company will submit a bill for its services, which is known as a drayage bill.

THE CREDIT MEMORANDUM

Ordinarily the buyer expects to receive the merchandise or other property ordered and pays for it at the agreed price in accordance with the terms specified in the purchase invoice. However, part or all of the merchandise or other property may be returned to the supplier for various reasons, such as the following:

(1) It may not conform to the specifications in the purchase order.
(2) A mistake may have been made in placing the order and the supplier may give permission for it to be returned.
(3) It may have been delayed in shipment and thus, the buyer cannot dispose of it. This sometimes happens with seasonal goods, such as some of the style merchandise handled by Boyd's Clothiers.

If the merchandise received is unsatisfactory or the prices charged are not in accord with an existing agreement or with previous quotations, an adjustment may be made that is referred to as an allowance.

When merchandise is to be returned to the supplier for credit, a charge-back invoice — essentially, a formal request for credit to be granted by the supplier — is usually issued by the buyer for the purchase price of the merchandise returned. Upon receipt of the merchandise, the supplier usually issues a document, known as a credit memorandum, confirming the amount of the credit allowed. A filled-in credit memorandum is reproduced below. This form indicates that Huk-A-Poo, Inc., has given Boyd's Clothiers credit for the return of two large-size women's blouses.

Credit Memorandum

Huk-A-Poo, Inc.
1411 Broadway
New York, NY 10012-1209

Date: April 7, 19--

To: Boyd's Clothiers
600 Olive St.
St. Louis, MO 63101-2356

We Credit Your Account As Follows

Description	Quantity	Unit Price	Extension	Total
Women's Blouses, Large, No. B125	2	9.50	19.00	19.00

Credit Memorandum

BUILDING YOUR ACCOUNTING KNOWLEDGE

1. What are two major reasons why the cash basis of accounting does not result in meaningful income or loss determination for a merchandising business?
2. What is the formula for the simple determination of the cost of goods sold?

3. Why should purchase requisitions be numbered consecutively?
4. Why should a purchase invoice be compared with a copy of the related purchase order after having been numbered consecutively upon receipt?
5. How is a trade discount usually shown on an invoice?
6. Is a cash discount usually recorded at the time of purchase or at the time of settlement of the invoice?
7. If an invoice is subject to both trade and cash discounts, which type of discount should be deducted from the gross invoice amount first?
8. When does a supplier usually issue a credit memorandum?

Report No. 6-1

> *Complete Report No. 6-1 in the study assignments and submit your working papers to the instructor for approval. Then continue with the following textbook discussion until Report No. 6-2 is required.*

ACCOUNTING PROCEDURES FOR PURCHASES

The word purchase can refer to the act of buying almost anything or, if used as a noun, to the thing that is bought. In connection with the accounting for a merchandising business, however, the term usually refers to merchandise. A reference to "purchases for the year," unless qualified in some way, relates to the merchandise purchased for resale, stock in trade.

PURCHASES ACCOUNT

The purchases account is a temporary owner's equity account in which the cost of all merchandise purchased during the accounting period is recorded. The account is debited for the cost of the merchandise purchased. If the purchase is for cash, the cash account is credited; if purchased on account, Accounts Payable should be credited. For example, Boyd's Clothiers purchased from Huk-A-Poo, Inc., merchandise on account for $357.

Purchases	
Debit to record the cost of merchandise purchased.	

Purchases	357	
Accounts Payable		357

The purchases account may also be debited for any transportation charges, such as freight, express, and parcel post charges, that increase the cost of the merchandise purchased. The common practice, however, is to charge these items to a separate account.

PURCHASES RETURNS AND ALLOWANCES ACCOUNT

The purchases returns and allowances account is a temporary owner's equity account in which purchases returns and allowances are recorded. The account is credited for the cost of any merchandise returned to suppliers and for any allowances received from suppliers that decrease the cost of the merchandise purchased. The offsetting debit is to Accounts Payable if the goods were purchased on account, or to Cash if a refund is received because the purchase was originally for cash. Allowances may be received from suppliers for merchandise delivered in poor condition or for merchandise that does not meet specifications as to quality, weight, size, color, grade, or style.

Purchases Returns and Allowances

	Credit
	to record the cost of merchandise returned and allowances received.

Although purchases returns and allowances may be credited directly to Purchases, it is better to credit the account Purchases Returns and Allowances. There will then be a record of the amount of gross purchases and the total amount of returns and allowances. If returns and allowances are large in proportion to gross purchases, a weakness in purchasing operations is indicated. It may be that better sources of supply should be sought or that purchase specifications should be stated more clearly.

As an example, consider the credit memorandum for $19 illustrated on page 170 that was received from Huk-A-Poo, Inc., for two large-size women's blouses that were returned by Boyd's Clothiers. This should be recorded in the combination journal on a single line, using the General Credit and Accounts Payable Debit columns. "Purchases Returns and Allowances" should be written in the Description column. The equivalent entry, in two-column journal form, is as follows:

Accounts Payable..	19	
Purchases Returns and Allowances...		19

If a separate accounts payable ledger is kept, this amount should also be posted as a debit to the individual account of Huk-A-Poo, Inc., in that ledger. This procedure will be discussed further in the next section.

ACCOUNTS PAYABLE

In order that the owner or manager may know both the amount owed to the individual suppliers (sometimes referred to as "creditors"), and the total amount owed to all suppliers, it is advisable to keep an individual record of each supplier and a summary or controlling ledger account. A summary account in the general ledger that represents the total liability to all the suppliers at any point in time is known as Accounts Payable. The credit balance of the account at the beginning of the period represents the total amount owed to suppliers from prior accounting periods. During the period, the account is credited for the amount of any transactions involving increases and is debited for the amount of any transactions involving decreases in the amounts owed to suppliers. At the end of the period, the credit balance of the liability account again represents the total amount owed to all the suppliers.

It is also necessary to keep a record of the transactions completed with each supplier in order that information may be readily available as to the amount owed to each supplier and as to when each invoice should be paid. Two widely used methods of accounting for purchases on account are described in the following paragraphs.

The Invoice Method. Under this method, it is customary to keep a chronological record of the purchase invoices received and to file them systematically by due date in an "unpaid invoices" file. All other documents representing transactions completed with suppliers are filed with the purchase invoices. After an invoice is paid, it is filed alphabetically by supplier name in a "paid invoices" file. In this way, the "unpaid invoices" file represents a detailed listing of the liabilities to individual suppliers for individual invoices. The total amount of unpaid invoices should equal the balance in the accounts payable account. Special filing equipment facilitates the use of this method.

The Ledger Account Method. Under this method, a chronological record of the purchase invoices received from each supplier is kept in an individual ledger account. A separate ledger containing individual accounts with suppliers arranged in alphabetical order is called a subsidiary accounts payable ledger.

PURCHASES JOURNAL

All of the transactions of a merchandising business can be recorded in an ordinary two-column general journal or in a combination journal. However, in many enterprises purchase transactions occur frequently. Since most purchases are made on account, such transactions may be recorded advantageously in a special journal. A journal designed for recording only purchases of merchandise on account is called a purchases journal. A sample purchases journal is illustrated below.

	DATE	INVOICE NO.	FROM WHOM PURCHASED	POST. REF.	AMOUNT	
			PURCHASES JOURNAL		PAGE 7	
1	1982 Mar. 4	58	Hanes Corporation	✓	290 10	1
2	9	59	Julius Resnick, Inc.	✓	930 00	2
3	18	60	Damon, Inc.	✓	359 00	3
4	31	61	Huk-A-Poo, Inc.	✓	237 50	4
5	31		Purchases Dr. - Accounts Payable Cr.	711/315	1 816 60	5
6						6
7						7

Purchases Journal

Note that in recording each purchase, the following information is entered in the purchases journal:

    (1) Date on which the invoice is received
    (2) Number of the invoice, i.e., the number assigned by the buyer
    (3) From whom purchased (the supplier)
    (4) Amount of the invoice

With this form of purchases journal, each transaction can be recorded on one horizontal line.

If an individual ledger account is not kept with each supplier, the purchase invoices should be filed immediately after they have been recorded in the purchases journal. It is preferable that they are filed according to due date in an unpaid invoice file. If an individual ledger account is kept with each supplier, the invoices normally are used to post to the supplier accounts, after which the invoices are properly filed.

The unpaid invoice file is usually arranged with a division for each month with folders numbered 1 to 31 in each division. This makes it possible to file each unpaid invoice according to its due date which facilitates payment of the invoices on or before their due dates. Since certain invoices may be subject to discounts if paid within a specified time, it is important that they are handled in such a manner that payment is made in sufficient time to get the benefit of the discounts.

If a partial payment is made on an invoice, a notation of the payment should be made on the invoice, and it should be retained in the unpaid invoice file until paid in full. If credit is received because of returns and allowances, a notation of the amount of the credit should also be made on the invoice so that the adjusted balance due will be indicated. When the invoice is paid in full, the payment should be noted on the invoice, and the invoice then transferred from the unpaid invoice file to the paid invoice file. It is considered a good policy to pay each invoice in full. Paying specific invoices in full simplifies record keeping for both the buyer and the seller.

The folders in the paid invoice file are usually arranged in alphabetic order according to the names of suppliers. This facilitates the filing of all paid invoices, and all other vouchers or documents representing transactions with suppliers, in such a manner that a complete history of the business done with each supplier is maintained.

POSTING FROM THE PURCHASES JOURNAL

At the end of the month, the Amount column of the purchases journal is totaled and the ruling completed as illustrated. A process referred to as summary posting is then performed by posting the total of the purchases on account for the month to the ledger as a debit to Purchases and as a credit to Accounts Payable. The titles of both accounts and the posting reference may be entered on one horizontal line of the purchases journal as shown in the illustration. A proper cross-reference should be provided by entering the page of the purchases journal preceded by the initial "P" in the Posting Reference column of the ledger account and by entering the account number in the Posting Reference column of the purchases journal.

The summary posting from Boyd's Clothiers purchases journal to the ledger accounts on March 31 is illustrated on page 176.

The Invoice Method. Under the invoice method of accounting for purchases on account, individual posting from the purchases journal is not required. When this plan is followed, it is customary to place

ACCOUNT	Accounts Payable					ACCOUNT NO. 318	
						BALANCE	
DATE	ITEM	POST. REF.	DEBIT	CREDIT		DEBIT	CREDIT
1982 Mar. 31		P7		181660			181660

ACCOUNT	Purchases					ACCOUNT NO. 711	
						BALANCE	
DATE	ITEM	POST. REF.	DEBIT	CREDIT		DEBIT	CREDIT
1982 Mar. 31		P7	181660			181660	

General Ledger Accounts After Posting from Purchases Journal

a check mark in the Posting Reference column of the purchases journal at the time each invoice is entered.

The Ledger Account Method. If an individual ledger account is kept for each supplier, all transactions representing either increases or decreases in the amount owed to each supplier should be posted individually to the proper account. The posting may be done by hand or electronic machines. If posting is done by hand, it may be completed either directly from the purchase invoices and other vouchers or documents representing the transactions, or it may be completed from the books of original entry. If posting is done with the aid of electronic machines, it will usually be completed directly from the purchase invoices and other vouchers or documents. In either case, as the individual supplier accounts are posted, a check mark ($\sqrt{}$) should be placed in the Posting Reference column of the purchases journal. The ledger account method of accounting for Accounts Payable will be explained in detail in Chapter 8.

SCHEDULE OF ACCOUNTS PAYABLE

A list showing the amount due to each supplier as of a specified date is known as a schedule of accounts payable. It is usually advisable to prepare such a schedule at the end of each month. An example for Boyd's Clothiers as of March 31, 1982, is provided on page 177. Such a schedule can be prepared easily from the list of supplier accounts in the subsidiary accounts payable ledger or by going through the unpaid invoice file and listing the names of the suppliers and the amount due to each. If the total of the schedule does not agree with the balance of the summary accounts payable account, the error may be in either the subsidiary ledger, the file, or the summary ledger account. The subsidiary ledger could be incorrect because of an error in posting. The file may be incorrect in that one or more paid invoices have not been removed or one or more unpaid ones are missing. Another possibility is that a memorandum of a partial payment was overlooked in preparing the list. The accounts payable account could be incorrect because of an error in posting or because of an error in a journal from which the total purchases was posted. In any event, the postings, journals, and invoices must be checked until the reason for the discrepancy is found so that the necessary correction can be made.

Boyd's Clothiers

Schedule of Accounts Payable

March 31, 1982

Damon, Inc.		35900
Hanes Corporation		29010
Huk-A-Poo, Inc.		23750
Julius Resnick, Inc		93000
		181660

Boyd's Clothiers — Schedule of Accounts Payable

CASH PURCHASES

Cash purchases of merchandise are entered in the combination journal by debiting the purchases account and by crediting the bank account. Usually cash purchases are not posted to the individual accounts of suppliers. However, if it is desired to post cash purchases to the individual accounts of suppliers, such transactions may be entered both in the purchases journal and in the combination journal. In other words, invoices received in connection with cash purchases may be recorded in the same manner as invoices for purchases on account. Boyd's Clothiers follow the practice of entering cash purchases of merchandise in the combination journal and purchases on account in the purchases journal.

COD PURCHASES

When property is purchased on COD terms, the total amount paid represents the cost of the property. Since payment must be made before possession of the property can be obtained, it is customary to treat such transactions the same as cash purchases. Thus the check issued in payment of a COD purchase is entered in the combination journal by debiting the proper account and by crediting the bank account. The proper account to debit depends upon the kind of property purchased. If merchandise is purchased, the purchases account is debited for the cost of the merchandise and the transportation account is debited for the amount of any transportation charges paid. If plant or equipment assets are purchased, the proper asset account is debited for the total cost, including COD fees and transportation charges. If supplies are purchased, the proper supplies account is debited for the total cost of the supplies, including COD fees and transportation charges.

TRANSPORTATION CHARGES

Express and freight charges may be prepaid by the shipper or may be paid by the buyer at the time of delivery. Parcel post charges must be prepaid by the shipper. Store-to-door delivery of freight shipments may be made by the transportation companies. However, when freight shipments are not delivered to the buyer's place of business by the transportation company, the buyer either calls for the goods at a nearby freight station or employs a truck to deliver the goods.

Transportation Charges Prepaid. If the transportation charges are prepaid by the shipper, the amount may or may not be added to the invoice, depending upon the terms of the sale. If the shipper has quoted prices FOB destination, it is understood that the prices quoted include transportation charges either to the buyer's place of business or to a nearby freight station and that no additional charge will be made for any transportation charges paid by the shipper.

If the shipper has quoted prices FOB shipping point , it is understood that the prices quoted do not include the transportation charges and that the buyer is expected to pay the transportation costs. If these transportation charges are prepaid by the shipper, the charges will be added to the invoice, and the shipper will be reimbursed by the buyer when the invoice is paid.

Transportation Charges Collect. If prices are quoted FOB shipping point and shipment is made collect, the buyer pays the transportation charges before obtaining possession of the shipment. Such transportation charges represent an addition to the cost of the merchandise or other property purchased. The method of recording the transportation charges in this case is the same as if the charges had been prepaid by the shipper and added to the invoice.

If prices are quoted FOB destination but for some reason shipment is made collect, the buyer pays the transportation charges to obtain possession of the shipment. In such cases the transportation charges paid by the buyer are recorded as a debit to the account of the supplier from whom the merchandise or other property was ordered. In other words, the payment of the transportation charges in such case should be treated the same as a partial payment of the amount due the shipper.

Transportation Accounts. As previously explained, transportation charges applicable to merchandise purchased may be recorded by debiting the purchases account. However, it is common practice to record transportation charges on incoming merchandise in a separate account, which may be entitled Freight In or Transportation In. Under these circumstances, a special Freight In or Transportation In column is included in the purchases journal for this purpose, or this type of transaction can be recorded in a two-column general journal. This account is treated as a subdivision of the purchases account and the balance must be taken into consideration as an addition to purchases in computing the cost of goods sold at the close of each accounting period.

Transportation charges applicable to equipment assets, such as office equipment, store equipment, or delivery equipment, are treated as an addition to the cost of the equipment. It is immaterial whether the freight charges are prepaid by the shipper and added to the invoice or whether shipment is made collect. If the freight is prepaid and added to the invoice, the total cost, including the invoice price and the transportation charges, is recorded as a debit to the equipment asset account in one amount. On the other hand, if shipment is made freight collect, the amount of the invoice and the amount of the freight charges are posted as separate debits to the equipment asset account.

Parcel Post Insurance. Merchandise or other property mailed parcel post may be insured against loss or damage in transit. Such insurance may be purchased from the government through the post office, or it may be purchased from private insurance companies. If the cost of insurance is charged to the customer and is added to the invoice, it represents an addition to the cost of the merchandise or other property purchased. Thus, if an invoice is received for merchandise purchased and the merchandise is billed at a total cost of $175 plus postage of $2 and insurance of 60 cents, the total cost of the merchandise is $177.60.

The cost of insurance seldom is recorded separately on the books of the buyer, but either is charged directly to the purchases account or is included with transportation charges and charged to Freight In.

The purchaser may indicate in placing an order that the merchandise is not to be insured. When this is indicated, the purchaser implies a willingness to assume the risk for any loss or damage sustained to the merchandise in transit. Title to merchandise ordinarily passes to the purchaser when it is placed in the hands of the carrier for delivery.

BUILDING YOUR ACCOUNTING KNOWLEDGE

1. Describe briefly how each of the following accounts is used: (1) Purchases (2) Purchases Returns and Allowances
2. Discuss the two major methods of keeping records of the transactions completed with individual suppliers.
3. List four items of information about each purchase normally entered in the purchases journal.
4. In what journal does Boyd's Clothiers record cash purchases?
5. Are COD purchases handled the same as cash purchases or the same as purchases on account?
6. If transportation charges are billed collect under normal FOB shipping point terms, what do such charges represent as far as the buyer is concerned?
7. If transportation charges are billed collect under FOB destination terms, how should the buyer treat the payment of these charges?
8. Indicate two alternative means of recording the cost of parcel post insurance.

Report No. 6-2

> *Complete Report No. 6-2 in the study assignments and submit your working papers to the instructor for approval. Then continue with the textbook discussion in Chapter 7 until Report No. 7-1 is required.*

EXPANDING YOUR BUSINESS
VOCABULARY

What is the meaning of each of the following terms?

Accounts Payable (p. 173)

allowance (p. 170)

back orders (p. 165)

cash discounts (p. 166)

charge-back invoice (p. 170)

COD (p. 168)

cost of goods sold (p. 161)

credit memorandum (p. 170)

drayage bill (p. 169)

FOB destination (p. 178)

FOB shipping point (p. 178)

freight bill (p. 168)

invoice (p. 163)

list prices (p. 165)

merchandise inventory (p. 160)

net purchases (p. 160)

purchase (p. 171)

purchase invoice (p. 163)

purchase order (p. 162)

purchase requisition (p. 161)

purchases journal (p. 174)

receiving report (p. 164)

sales invoice (p. 163)

schedule of accounts payable (p. 176)

stock in trade (p. 171)

subsidiary accounts payable ledger (p. 174)

summary posting (p. 175)

supplier or vendor (p. 162)

trade discounts (p. 165)

waybill (p. 168)

CHAPTER 7

ACCOUNTING FOR SALES OF MERCHANDISE

CHAPTER OBJECTIVES

The objectives of this chapter are to enable you:

▶ To define the terms **sales**, **sales returns and allowances**, **net sales**, and **gross margin (gross profit)**.

▶ To describe the various types of sales, including cash sales, sales on account, bank credit card sales, COD sales, sales "on approval," "layaway" sales, installment sales, and consignment sales.

▶ To describe retail sales taxes and the related accounting procedure.

▶ To describe commonly followed practices in processing incoming orders for merchandise, including the use of the following source documents:

    (1) Customer purchase order
    (2) Sales ticket or invoice
    (3) Credit memorandum

▶ To explain and use a special journal for sales of merchandise.

▶ To describe subsidiary records, specifically:

    (1) A file of uncollected charge sale tickets — the "sales ticket" method
    (2) A subsidiary accounts receivable ledger — the "ledger account" method

In the calculation of periodic income under the accrual basis, realized revenue of a period is matched with the expenses reasonably assignable to that period. Realized revenue means the receipt of cash or a collectible claim to cash arising from the sale of something of value — usually goods.

In the case of merchants, the process of determining periodic net income starts with an important dimension of accrual accounting for merchants — the calculation of what is called the gross margin. Gross margin (also known as gross profit) is the difference between net sales and cost of goods sold. Net sales is the gross amount of revenue from sales (1) less the sales price of any goods returned by customers because the merchandise was found to be unsatisfactory or unwanted for some reason, and (2) less any reductions in price (allowances) given to customers rather than having the goods returned. Cost of goods sold is determined by adding the amount of beginning inventory to the net purchases (purchases less purchases returns and allowances) and then subtracting the amount of ending inventory. To illustrate the calculation of the gross margin, consider the following circumstances:

Sales price of all goods sold and delivered to customers during the current period	$102,000
Sales price of goods returned by customers	7,000
Cost of merchandise (goods) on hand, beginning of period	15,000
Cost of merchandise purchased during the period	80,000
Cost of goods returned to the supplier or allowances made by the supplier (not ordered, damaged or soiled, etc.)	4,000
Cost of merchandise (goods) on hand, end of period	18,000

If the relevant information in the foregoing array of data is assembled in the proper fashion, the gross margin for the period is calculated to be $22,000, as follows:

Sales			$102,000
Less sales returns and allowances			7,000
Net sales			$ 95,000
Cost of goods sold:			
Merchandise inventory, beginning of period		$15,000	
Add purchases	$80,000		
Less purchases returns and allowances	4,000		
Net purchases		76,000	
Merchandise available for sale		$91,000	
Less merchandise inventory, end of period		18,000	73,000
Gross margin on sales			$ 22,000

Cash disbursements during the period for goods purchased both in prior periods and the current period amounted to $71,000. Cash received from customers during the period in payment for sales both of prior periods and the current period amounted to $84,000. Note that the movement of cash is not relevant to the calculation of the gross margin on sales. This is in accordance with the accrual basis of accounting, examination of which began in Chapter 6, continues in this chapter, and will be conducted in detail in Chapter 8.

In recording transactions concerned with sales of merchandise, it is desirable to keep at least the following accounts:

(1) Sales
(2) Sales Returns and Allowances
(3) Sales Tax Payable

SOURCE DOCUMENTS AND ASSOCIATED RECORDS FOR SALES

In order to understand the role of the various source documents and associated records for sales, it is helpful to know the nature of the underlying sales transactions. A variety of types of sales may be identified in the retail business world.

TYPES OF SALES

Eight of these types of sales will be discussed here: (1) cash sales; (2) sales on account; (3) bank credit card sales; (4) COD sales; (5) sales on approval; (6) layaway sales; (7) installment sales; and (8) consignment sales.

Cash Sales. Some businesses sell merchandise for cash only, while others sell merchandise either for cash or on account. A variety of practices are followed in the handling of cash sales. If such transactions are numerous, it is probable that one or more types of cash registers will be used. In this instance the original record of the sales is made in the register. Often, registers have the capability of accumulating more than one total. This means that by using the proper key, each amount that is punched in the register can be classified by type of merchandise, by department, or by salesperson. Where sales tax is involved, the amount of the tax may be separately recorded. In accounting terms, a cash sale means that the asset Cash is increased by a debit and the income account Sales and a liability account Sales Tax Payable are credited.

In many retail establishments the procedure in handling cash sales is for the salesclerks to prepare sales tickets in triplicate. (Sales tickets will be discussed and illustrated in a subsequent section.) Sometimes the preparation of the sales tickets involves the use of a cash register that prints the amount of the sale directly on the ticket. Modern electronic cash registers serve as input terminals that are "on line" with computers, that is, in direct communication with the central processor. At the end of each day the cash received is compared with the record that the register provides. The receipts may also be compared with the total of the cash-sales tickets, if the system makes use of the latter.

Sales on Account. Sales on account are often referred to as "charge sales" because the seller exchanges merchandise for the buyer's promise to pay. In accounting terms, this means that the asset Accounts Receivable of the seller is increased by a debit or charge, and the income account Sales is increased by a credit. Selling goods on account is common practice at the retail level of the distribution process. Firms that sell goods on account should investigate the financial reliability of those to whom they sell. A business of some size may have a separate credit department whose major function is to establish credit policies and decide upon requests for credit from persons and firms who wish to buy goods on account. Seasoned judgment is needed to avoid a credit policy that is so stringent that profitable business may be refused, or a credit policy that is so liberal that uncollectible account losses may become excessive.

Generally, no goods are delivered until the salesclerk has been assured that the buyer has established credit — that there is an account for this customer with the company. In the case of many retail businesses, customers with established credit are provided with credit cards or charge plates, which provide evidence that the buyer has an account. These are used in mechanical or electronic devices to print the customer's name and other identification on the sales tickets. In the case of merchants who commonly receive a large portion of their orders by mail or by phone, this confirmation of the buyer's status can be handled as a matter of routine before the goods are delivered.

Bank Credit Card Sales. The use of bank credit cards in connection with retail sales of certain types of goods and service is a common practice. The two most widely used credit cards of this type in the United States are the VISA card and the MasterCard. The former was started by the Bank of America in California. That bank now franchises numerous banks in other localities to offer the program. Likewise, several thousand banks participate in the Master-Card program. The two systems have much in common.

Participating banks encourage their depositors and other customers to obtain the cards by supplying the necessary information to establish their credit reliability. When this is accomplished, a small plastic card containing the cardholder's name, an identifying number, and an expiration date is issued to the applicant.

Merchants and other businesses are invited to participate in the program. If certain conditions are met, the bank will accept for deposit completed copies of the prescribed form of sales invoice (also sometimes called "ticket," or "draft") for goods sold or services rendered to cardholders and evidenced by the invoices bearing the card imprints and the buyers' signatures. The bank, in effect, either "buys" the tickets at a discount (commonly 3 percent, though it may be more or less depending upon various factors) immediately, or gives the merchant immediate credit for the full amount of the tickets, and, once a month, charges the merchant's account with the total amount of the discount at the agreed rate. The latter practice is more common.

For the merchant, bank credit card sales are nearly the equivalent of cash sales. The service is performed or the goods are sold; and the money is secured. It is then up to the bank to collect from the buyer or bear the loss, if the account proves to be uncollectible.

In most respects, accounting for bank credit card sales is very much the same as accounting for regular cash sales. A regular sales ticket may be prepared as well as the credit card form of invoice. Usually the transactions are accounted for as sales for the full price with the amount of the discount being treated as an expense when the bank makes the monthly charge.

Sales made by certain types of businesses that use other forms of retail credit cards — notably those of petroleum companies, and businesses participating in the "American Express," "Carte Blanche," and "Diner's Club" programs, are similar in many respects to bank credit card sales.

COD Sales. Merchandise or other property may be sold on COD terms. Under this arrangement, payment must be made at the time the goods are delivered to the buyer by the seller or the agent. The agent usually is an employee of the seller but may also be a messenger, the post office, an express company, or any common carrier (railroad, truck line, airline, etc.).

In retail merchandising, COD sales tickets are segregated each day and a COD list is prepared for control purposes. The merchandise is then delivered to the customer and the sale price is collected upon delivery. When the money is turned in to the seller, the driver or other agent is given credit for the collection on the COD list and the sale is recorded in the same manner as a cash sale. If, for any reason, the customer refuses to accept the merchandise, it is returned to stock and the sale is canceled. Under this plan of handling

COD sales, title to the merchandise does not pass to the customer until the goods are delivered and collection has been made; therefore, the merchandise is considered to be part of the inventory of the seller until a remittance is received.

Sales on Approval. Sales that give the customer the right to return the goods within a specified time are called sales on approval. The sale is not complete until the customer either retains the goods or returns them. Such sales may be treated as ordinary charge sales, and any returns may be handled as ordinary sales returns. On the other hand, sales on approval may be handled the same as ordinary cash sales. Under this plan a memorandum record of the sale is kept until it is definitely known that the goods will be retained by the customer. The customer must either pay for the goods or return them by a specified date. When a remittance is received, the sale is recorded.

Layaway Sales. Sales on approval should not be confused with layaway sales. Layaway sales may be made for cash or on account, but in either case the customer agrees to call later for the goods. Sometimes a deposit is made by the buyer with the understanding that the merchandise will be held until some future date, at which time the buyer either calls for the merchandise or requests that the merchandise be delivered. If instead of calling for the merchandise, the customer requests delivery on a COD basis, a COD slip is made for the proper amount. When the remittance is received, it is recorded in the same manner as if the customer had called for the merchandise and paid cash.

Accounting for deposits on layaway sales is not uniform, but the usual method is to record the deposits in the same manner as cash sales. When this plan is used, a charge sales ticket is prepared for the balance due and is recorded by debiting a special accounts receivable control account and crediting the sales account. Individual accounts with layaway customers may be kept in a special subsidiary ledger, sometimes referred to as a layaway ledger.

At the end of the accounting period, the total amount due from customers who made deposits on layaway sales is treated as ordinary accounts receivable. The cost of the merchandise that is being held for future delivery is not included in the inventory because it is considered to be the property of the customer.

Installment Sales. The term installment sales is applied to a variety of arrangements in which the purchaser of goods (and sometimes services) makes a so-called "down payment" and agrees to pay the remainder of the sales price in fractional, periodic amounts over an extended period of time. These arrangements might also be viewed as "installment payments." From the standpoint of the seller, such transactions often are equivalent to cash or bank credit card sales. Frequently, some type of financial institution is a party to the transaction at the outset. The seller gets the money immediately; thus the buyer becomes a borrower who must make payments to a bank or finance company. Interest is always involved. In other cases, the seller does acquire a receivable, but soon "sells" it to a financial institution. Often, the seller must guarantee the collectibility of the receivable. In some cases, the seller "carries the account" and the buyer makes periodic payments directly to the business from whom the goods were purchased. Usually, the payments include an interest component.

If the seller does carry the account, it is desirable to use a special form of subsidiary ledger account that is designed to facilitate recording installment transactions. The subsidiary accounts comprise what is called an "installment ledger" that contains the details of the general ledger account titled Installment Accounts Receivable. At one time, the accounting for installment sales entailed a somewhat complicated procedure that was based on the idea that no gross margin on such sales should be taken into income calculations until the money was received. Each dollar collected, whether from down payment or periodic installments, was considered to be partly a recovery of the cost of what was sold and partly gross margin. If the collection period extended over several years, the recognition of the gross margin on the sale would be spread over those years. This procedure, called the "installment method," is no longer considered to be an acceptable accounting practice except in special and unusual circumstances. Normal practice is to regard installment sales as regular sales on account, that is, all revenue from an installment sale is considered to be realized at the point of sale. For income tax purposes, however, the installment method may be used. Using this method in the calculation of taxable income permits the postponement of payment of taxes until the year that the money is received.

Consignment Sales. An arrangement in which one business, known as the consignor, ships goods to another business, known as the consignee, without any change in the legal ownership of the goods, is called a consignment sale. The consignee acts as an agent for the consignor and attempts to sell the goods, usually at prices specified by the consignor. If the goods are sold the consignee receives an agreed commission, which is deducted from the proceeds of the sales when remittance of the amount due is made to the consignor. Consigned goods in the hands of the consignee at the end of the accounting period are a part of the consignor's inventory until sold and should be included in that account balance. Sale of such goods is recorded by the consignor when they are sold by the consignee.

Sometimes, each party keeps a set of formal memorandum accounts for consignment transactions. In other cases, no formal records are made until the goods have been sold. Consignment selling is not a widespread practice.

RETAIL SALES TAX

A tax imposed by many cities and states upon the sale of tangible personal property at retail is known as a retail sales tax. The tax usually is a percentage of the gross sales price or the gross receipts from sales. Retail sales taxes may also include taxes imposed upon persons engaged in furnishing services at retail, in which case the tax is a percentage of the gross receipts for furnishing such services. The rates of the tax vary considerably. In most states the tax is a general sales tax. However, in some states the tax is imposed only on specific items, such as automobiles, cosmetics, radio and television sets, and playing cards.

To avoid fractions of cents and to simplify the determination of the tax, it is customary to use a sales tax table or schedule. For example, where the rate is 5 percent, the tax may be calculated as shown in the following schedule:

Amount of Sale	Amount of Tax
1¢ to 10¢	None
11¢ to 29¢	1¢
30¢ to 49¢	2¢
50¢ to 69¢	3¢
70¢ to 89¢	4¢
90¢ to $1.09	5¢

and so on

The amount of the tax imposed under the schedule approximates the legal rate. Retail sales tax reports accompanied by remittances for the amounts due must be filed periodically, either monthly or quarterly, depending upon the law of the state or city in which the business is located.

CUSTOMER PURCHASE ORDER

Sales by merchants may be made in response to purchase orders received by mail or telephone. Orders received by mail may be written on the purchase order form, letterhead, or other stationery of the buyer or on an order blank furnished by the seller. An illustration of a typical purchase order form was shown on page 163. It is probable that upon receiving this order, a rubber stamp impression with spaces to show the date received, credit approval, approval of prices shown, and date of billing was placed on its face. In the process of handling the order, the person or persons involved make appropriate notations. Orders received by telephone are carefully recorded on forms provided for that purpose.

Procedure for Handling Incoming Purchase Orders. The procedure in handling purchase orders varies widely with different firms. It is important that there should be a well-organized plan, the purpose of which is to promote efficiency and to maintain an internal check that will tend to prevent mistakes in handling orders. The following five steps constitute the heart of such a plan.

(1) Interpretation. Each purchase order received should be interpreted as to (a) identity of the customer and (b) quantity and description of items ordered. Orders may be received from old or new customers. Sometimes it is difficult to identify a new customer, particularly if there had been no previous correspondence or the customer had not been contacted by the seller's representative. In some cases identification of the items ordered is difficult because customers frequently are careless in describing the merchandise wanted. Different items of merchandise may be specified by name or stock number. Care should be used to make sure that the stock number agrees with the description of the item.

(2) Transportation. In handling each purchase order, it is necessary to determine how shipment will be made and how the transportation charges will be handled. Shipment may be made by parcel post, express, or freight. Parcel post packages may be insured. Express shipments may be made by rail or air. Freight shipments may be made by rail, air, truck, or water.

The transportation charges must be prepaid on shipments made by parcel post. The transportation charges on express and freight shipments may be prepaid by the shipper or may be paid by the customer upon receipt of the shipment. When transportation charges are prepaid by the shipper, they may or may not be added to the invoice, depending upon whether prices have been quoted FOB shipping point or FOB destination.

If shipment is made by freight, it is also necessary to determine the routing of the shipment. The buyer may specify how shipment should be made. When the buyer does not indicate any preference, the shipper must determine whether to make shipment by rail, truck, air, or water, and also frequently must make a choice of transportation companies to be used. Shipment to certain points may be made via a variety of different trucking companies, airlines, or railroads.

A retail merchant like Boyd's Clothiers would seldom incur transportation charges in connection with its sales. If any such charges are incurred, they may be charged to an operating expense account entitled Freight Out and recorded in the combination journal.

(3) Credit Approval. All purchase orders received that involve credit in any form should be referred to the store manager or credit department for approval before being billed or shipped. COD orders should also be so approved because some customers have a reputation for not accepting COD shipments which are then returned at the seller's expense. Customers who abuse the COD privilege may be required thereafter to send cash with the order, either in full or part payment. Some firms follow a policy of requiring part payment in cash with all orders for merchandise to be shipped COD.

(4) Verification of Purchase Orders. The unit prices specified on purchase orders should be verified, the proper extensions should be made, and the total should be recorded. Persons performing this function usually use either mechanical or electronic calculating machines.

(5) Billing. The next step in the handling of an order is billing or preparing the sales ticket .or invoice. The sales ticket or invoice usually is prepared on a typewriter, billing machine, or computer-printer. Sales invoices should be numbered consecutively. By using carbon paper or some other duplicating device, additional copies may be prepared. At least three copies usually are considered necessary. The original should go to the customer as an acknowledgment of the order; a copy should go to accounting personnel for recording purposes; and a copy should be used as authority for packing and shipping the merchandise.

Additional copies of the sales ticket or invoice may also be used for the following purposes by larger organizations:

(1) One copy may go to the salesperson in whose territory the sale is made.
(2) One copy may go to a branch office, if the sale is made in a territory served by such an office.
(3) One copy may serve as a label to be pasted on the carton or package in which shipment is made. Usually this copy is perforated so that only that part containing the name and the address of the customer is used.

SALES TICKET

The first record or source document of a sales transaction is called a sales ticket or sales invoice. Whether merchandise is sold for cash or on account, a sales ticket should be prepared. When the sale is for cash, the ticket may be printed by the cash register at the time that the sale is keyed in. However, some stores prefer to use handwritten sales tickets whether the sale is for cash or on account. The same flexibility does not prevail in recording charge sales; instead, a sales ticket or charge slip must be prepared for every sale on account. Each salesperson is usually provided with a separate pad of sales tickets. Each pad bears a different number that identifies the clerk. The individual sales tickets are also numbered consecutively. This facilitates sorting the tickets by clerks if it is desired to compute the amount of goods sold by each clerk.

The sales ticket illustrated below shows the type of information usually recorded.

Sales Ticket

When merchandise is sold for cash in a state or a city which has a retail sales tax, the transaction results in an increase in the asset cash offset by an increase in sales revenue and an increase in the liability sales tax payable. Such transactions should be recorded by debiting Cash for the amount received and by crediting Sales for the sales price of the merchandise, excluding any sales tax, and crediting Sales Tax Payable for the amount of the tax collected. When merchandise is sold on account in such a state or city, the transaction results in an increase in the asset accounts receivable offset by an increase in sales revenue and an increase in the liability sales tax payable. Such transactions should be recorded by debiting Accounts Receivable for the total amount charged to the customer and by crediting Sales for the amount of the sale and crediting Sales Tax Payable for the amount of the related tax.

An alternative procedure that is permissible under some sales tax laws is to credit the total of both the sales and the tax to the sales account in the first place. Periodically — usually at the end of each month — a calculation is made to determine how much of the balance of the sales account is presumed to be tax, and an entry is made to remove this amount from the sales account and transfer it to the sales tax payable account. Suppose, for example, that the tax rate is 5 percent, and that the sales account includes the tax collected or charged, along with the amount of the sales. In this event, 100/105 of the balance of the account is presumed to be the amount of the sales, and 5/105 of the balance is the amount of the tax. If the sales account had a balance of $10,500, the tax portion would be $500 (5/105 of $10,500). A debit to Sales and a credit to Sales Tax Payable of $500 would remove the tax from the sales account and transfer it to the sales tax payable account.

Discounts. Trade discounts allowed on sales are usually shown as deductions in arriving at the total of the sales ticket or invoice. Such discounts should not be entered in the accounts of the seller, as they represent merely a reduction in the selling price of the merchandise to avoid overly frequent publication of suppliers' catalogs.

Cash discounts offered should be indicated in the terms. Retail merchants seldom allow cash discounts to their customers but their suppliers commonly allow cash discounts to merchants as an inducement for prompt payment of sales invoices. Cash discounts should be ignored at the time of recording sales invoices, for it cannot be known at that time whether the customers will pay the invoices in time to get the discounts offered. Any cash discount that is deducted from an invoice by the customer when making a remittance normally is regarded by the seller as a reduction in gross sales (similar to sales returns and allowances). Some accountants accept the view that sales discounts are expenses, but to most accountants it seems more logical to regard such discounts as a reduction of sales price. Accordingly, the debit balance of the sales discount account is shown as a subtraction from sales in the income statement.

CREDIT MEMORANDUM

Merchandise may be returned by the customer for a credit or the customer may ask for an allowance representing a reduction in the price of the merchandise. If credit is given for merchandise returned or an allowance is made, it is customary to issue a credit memorandum for the amount involved. A filled-in copy of a credit memorandum issued by Boyd's Clothiers, authorizing the return of a suit by J. E. Buelt, and granting credit for the price of the suit and the sales tax, is reproduced below.

CREDIT MEMORANDUM

BOYD'S clothiers
600 Olive Street, St. Louis, Missouri 63101-2356

DATE *Mar. 19, 19--*   NO. *78*

NAME *J. E. Buelt*

ADDRESS *9140 Fox Estates*

CITY *St. Louis, MO 63126-4131*

SALES NUMBER		OK *Boyd*		
CASH REFUND	MDSE ORDER	CHARGE	GIFT	AMOUNT *$204.75*

QUAN.	ARTICLES	AMOUNT	
1	*Men's suit, 40R*	*195*	*00*
	Tax	*9*	*75*
		204	*75*

Two hundred four 75/00 ~~~~ DOLLARS

REASON *Cut improperly*

REC'D STOCK BY *J. A. Anderson*

x *J. E. Buelt*
CUSTOMER'S SIGNATURE

Credit Memorandum

BUILDING YOUR ACCOUNTING KNOWLEDGE

1. What is the focus of the effort in the calculation of periodic income under the accrual basis of accounting?
2. In what two ways does a bank accept for deposit copies of bank credit card sales invoices or tickets?
3. In what ways do layaway sales differ from sales on approval?
4. Describe the major ways in which financial institutions may get involved in installment sales transactions.
5. Briefly describe the nature of consignment sales.
6. What is the usual basis of measurement for a retail sales tax?
7. What two major aspects of each purchase order should be interpreted?
8. If a sales ticket is prepared in triplicate, what distribution should be made of the copies?
9. Under what circumstances is it customary for a seller of merchandise to issue a credit memorandum?

Report No. 7-1

> *Refer to the study assignments and complete Report No. 7-1. After completing the report, continue with the textbook discussion until the next report is required.*

ACCOUNTING PROCEDURES FOR SALES

In recording transactions arising from merchandising activities, it is desirable to keep certain accounts, including accounts for sales, for sales tax payable, and for sales returns and allowances. A discussion of these accounts, together with a discussion of the sales journal, follows.

SALES ACCOUNT

The sales account is a temporary owner's equity account in which the revenue resulting from sales of merchandise is recorded. The account is credited for the selling price of all merchandise sold during the accounting period. If sales are for cash, the credit to Sales is offset by a debit to Cash; if the sales are on account, the debit is made to an asset account, Accounts Receivable.

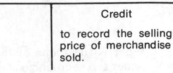

Sales	
	Credit
	to record the selling price of merchandise sold.

SALES TAX PAYABLE ACCOUNT

Where sales tax is imposed on merchandise sold, it is advisable to keep an account for Sales Tax Payable. This is a liability account which is credited for the amount of tax collected or imposed on sales. The account should be debited for the amount of the tax paid to the proper taxing authority or adjustment of tax on merchandise returned by customers. A credit balance in the account at any time indicates the amount of the liability to the tax authority for taxes collected or imposed.

Sales Tax Payable	
Debit	Credit
to record payment of tax to the proper taxing authority or adjustment of tax on merchandise returned by customers.	to record tax collected or imposed on sales.

Sales tax accounting may be complicated by such factors as (1) sales returns and allowances and (2) exempt sales. As mentioned above, if the tax is recorded at the time the sale is recorded, it will be necessary to adjust for the tax when recording sales returns and allowances. If some sales are exempt from the tax, it will be necessary to distinguish between the taxable and the nontaxable sales. A common example of nontaxable sales is sales to out-of-state customers.

SALES RETURNS AND ALLOWANCES ACCOUNT

This account is a temporary owner's equity account in which sales returns and allowances are recorded. The account is debited for the selling price (less sales tax) of any merchandise returned by customers or for any allowances made to customers that decrease the selling price of the merchandise sold. The offsetting credit is to Accounts Receivable if the goods are sold on account, or to Cash if a refund was made because the sale was originally for cash. Such allowances may be granted to customers for merchandise delivered in poor condition or for merchandise that does not meet specifications as to quality, weight, size, color, grade, or style.

Sales Returns and Allowances	
Debit	
to record returns and allowances.	

While sales returns and allowances can be debited directly to Sales, it is better to debit Sales Returns and Allowances. The accounts will then show both the amount of gross sales and the amount of returns and allowances. If returns and allowances are large in proportion to gross sales, a weakness in the merchandising operations is indicated; and the trouble should be determined and corrected.

As an example of accounting for sales returns and allowances, consider the credit memorandum illustrated on page 194 for $204.75 which was issued to J. E. Buelt for one men's suit returned (sales price of merchandise, $195; tax, $9.75). In the combination journal, this transaction was recorded on two lines, using the General Debit and Accounts Receivable Credit columns. "Sales R. & A. — J. R. Buelt" was written in the Description column on the first line, and "Sales Tax Payable" was written in the Description column on the second line. In two-column journal form, the equivalent entry is as follows:

Sales Returns and Allowances	195.00	
Sales Tax Payable	9.75	
Accounts Receivable		204.75

If a separate accounts receivable ledger is kept, the amount of $204.75 should also be posted to the credit of the individual account with J. E. Buelt in that ledger. This procedure will be discussed further in the next section.

ACCOUNTS RECEIVABLE

In order that the owner or manager of an enterprise may know the total amount due from charge customers at any time, it is advisable to keep a summary ledger account known as Accounts Receivable. At the beginning of the period, the debit balance of the account represents the total amount due from customers. During the period, the account was debited for the amount of any transactions involving increases and was credited for the amount of any transactions involving decreases in the amounts due from customers. At the end of the period, the debit balance of the account again represents the total amount due from charge customers.

It is also necessary to keep some record of the transactions completed with each customer in order that information may be readily available at all times as to the amount due from each customer. The following methods of accounting for charge sales are widely used:

The Sales Ticket Method. This method is similar to the invoice method of accounting for purchases, discussed in Chapter 6, pages 175–176. Under this method, it is customary to file the charge sales tickets systematically. All other related documents representing transactions with customers should be filed with the appropriate sales tickets. Special filing equipment facilitates the use of this method. In some cases, a chronological record of the charge sales tickets is kept as a means of control.

The Ledger Account Method. This method is similar to the ledger account method of accounting for purchases, discussed in Chapter 6, page 176. Under this method it is customary to keep a chronological record of the charge sales tickets. An individual ledger account with each customer is also kept. A separate ledger containing individual accounts with customers arranged in alphabetical order is called a subsidiary accounts receivable ledger. Special equipment may be used in maintaining a permanent file of the charge sales tickets and other documents supporting the records.

Under either of these methods of accounting for transactions with charge customers, it is necessary that a sales ticket or charge slip be made for each sale on account. In making a charge sales ticket the date, the name and address of the customer, the quantity, a description of the items sold, the unit prices, the total amount of the sale, and the amount of the sales tax should be recorded.

A three-column account form frequently is used for accounts receivable and accounts payable subsidiary ledgers. Such an account form has only one balance column, which usually is a debit balance in customers' accounts and a credit balance in suppliers' accounts. As each item is posted, the balance should be extended immediately so that it will be up to date at all times.

SALES JOURNAL

Transactions involving the sale of merchandise on account can be recorded in an ordinary two-column general journal or in a combination journal. However, in merchandising businesses where

many sales transactions are made on account, such transactions
may be recorded advantageously in a special journal. A journal designed for recording only sales on account is called a sales journal. If
the business is operated in an area where no sales taxes are imposed, all sales on account can be recorded in a sales journal with
only one amount column as illustrated below.

	DATE	SALE NO.	TO WHOM SOLD	POST. REF.	AMOUNT	
1						1
2						2
3						3
4						4

SALES JOURNAL   PAGE

Sales Journal Without Sales Taxes

If the business is operated in an area where sales taxes are imposed, a sales journal with three amount columns, such as the one
illustrated below, is more appropriate.

SALES JOURNAL   PAGE 16

	DATE	SALE NO.	TO WHOM SOLD	POST REF.	ACCOUNTS RECEIVABLE DR.	SALES CR.	SALES TAX PAYABLE CR.	
	1982							
1	Mar. 5	7842	G. J. Wood	✓	173 25	165 00	8 25	1
2	10	7288	Darlene Green	✓	56 39	53 70	2 69	2
3	13	824C	Julia Millman	✓	154 88	147 50	7 38	3
4	16	7870	J. J. Anders	✓	138 60	132 00	6 60	4
5	19	827C	K. E. Vivian	✓	263 55	251 00	12 55	5
6	25	7308	I. J. Zuckerman	✓	573 30	546 00	27 30	6
7	31	7918	G. L. Sachs	✓	140 70	134 00	6 70	7
8					1500 67 1500 67	1429 20 1429 20	71 47 71 47	8
9					(131)	(611)	(321)	9

Sales Journal With Sales Tax

The transactions recorded in the journal were completed by Boyd's
Clothiers, retail merchants, during the month of March. The store is

located in a state that imposes a tax of 5 percent on the retail sale of all merchandise whether sold for cash or on account.

Note that the following information regarding each charge sales ticket is recorded in the sales journal:

(1) Date
(2) Number of the sales ticket and salesclerk code
(3) To whom sold (the customer)
(4) Amount charged to customer
(5) Amount of sale
(6) Amount of sales tax

With this form of sales journal, each transaction can be recorded on one horizontal line. The sales ticket should provide all the information needed in recording each charge sale.

If an individual ledger account is not kept with each customer, the charge sales tickets should be filed by customer's name after they have been recorded in the sales journal. There are numerous types of trays, cabinets, and files on the market that are designed to facilitate the filing of charge sales tickets by customer name. Such devices are designed to save time, to promote accuracy, and to provide a safe means of keeping a record of the transactions with each charge customer. If an individual ledger account is kept with each customer, the sales tickets normally are used to post the customer accounts. They should then be properly filed.

When a customer makes a partial payment on an account, the amount of the payment should be noted on the most recent charge sales ticket and the new balance should be indicated. Sales tickets paid in full should be receipted and may either be given to the customer or be transferred to another file for future reference. If a customer is given credit for merchandise returned or because of allowances, a notation of the amount of credit should be made on the most recent charge sales ticket and the new balance indicated. If a credit memorandum is issued to a customer, it should be prepared in duplicate and the carbon copy should be attached to the sales ticket on which the amount is noted.

POSTING FROM THE SALES JOURNAL

At the end of the month, the amount columns of the sales journal are footed in small figures. The sum of the totals of the credit columns should be equal to the total of the debit column. The totals are then entered in full-size figures and the ruling completed as illustrated. The totals should be posted to the general ledger accounts indicated in the column headings. This summary posting should be completed in the following order:

(1) Post the total of the Accounts Receivable Dr. column to the debit of Accounts Receivable.
(2) Post the total of the Sales Cr. column to the credit of Sales.
(3) Post the total of the Sales Tax Payable Cr. column to the credit of Sales Tax Payable.

A proper cross-reference should be provided by entering the page of the sales journal preceded by the initial "S" in the Posting Reference column of the ledger and by entering the account number immediately below the column total of the sales journal. The proper method of completing the summary posting from Boyd's Clothiers' sales journal on March 31 is shown in the accounts affected as illustrated below.

ACCOUNT Accounts Receivable					ACCOUNT NO. 131	
DATE	ITEM	POST. REF.	DEBIT	CREDIT	BALANCE DEBIT	CREDIT
1982 Mar. 31		S16	150067		150067	

ACCOUNT Sales Tax Payable					ACCOUNT NO. 321	
DATE	ITEM	POST. REF.	DEBIT	CREDIT	BALANCE DEBIT	CREDIT
1982 Mar. 31		S16		7147		7147

ACCOUNT Sales					ACCOUNT NO. 611	
DATE	ITEM	POST. REF.	DEBIT	CREDIT	BALANCE DEBIT	CREDIT
1982 Mar. 31		S16		142920		142920

General Ledger Accounts After Posting from Sales Journal

The Sales Ticket Method. Under the sales ticket method of accounting for sales on account, individual posting from the sales journal is not required. When this plan is followed, it is customary to place a check mark in the Posting Reference column of the sales journal at the time of entering each sale.

The Ledger Account Method. If an individual ledger account is kept for each customer, all transactions representing either increases or decreases in the amount due from each customer should be posted individually to the proper account. The posting may be done by hand or by posting machines. If the posting is done by hand, it may be completed either directly from the charge sales tickets or other documents representing the transactions, or from the books of original entry. If the posting is done with posting machines, it will usually be completed directly from the charge sales tickets and other documents. In either case, as the individual customer accounts are posted, a check mark ($\checkmark$) is placed in the Posting Reference column of the sales journal. The ledger account method of accounting for accounts receivable will be explained in detail in Chapter 8.

SCHEDULE OF ACCOUNTS RECEIVABLE

A list of customers showing the amount due from each as of a specified date is known as a schedule of accounts receivable. It is usually advisable to prepare such a schedule at the end of each month. An example for Boyd's Clothiers as of March 31, 1982, is provided below.

Boyd's Clothiers — Schedule of Accounts Receivable

This schedule can be prepared easily from the list of customer accounts in the accounts receivable subsidiary ledger or by going through the sales ticket file and listing the names of the customers and the amount due from each. If the total does not agree with the balance of the summary accounts receivable account, the error may be in the subsidiary ledger, the file, or the ledger account. The subsidiary ledger could be in error because of an error in posting. The file may be incorrect in that either one or more sales tickets on which collection has been made have not been removed or one or more uncollected ones are missing. Another possibility is that a memorandum of a partial collection was overlooked in preparing the list. The accounts receivable account could be incorrect because of an error in posting or because of an error in a journal from which the totals were posted. In any event, the postings, journals, and sales tickets must be reviewed until the reason for the discrepancy is found so that the necessary correction can be made.

BUILDING YOUR ACCOUNTING KNOWLEDGE

1. Describe how each of the following accounts is used:
   (1) Sales   (2) Sales Tax Payable   (3) Sales Returns and Allowances
2. Discuss the sales ticket method of keeping records of the transactions completed with individual customers.
3. Discuss the ledger account method of keeping records of the transactions completed with individual customers.
4. List six items of information about each sale normally entered in the sales journal.
5. In what order should the summary posting from the sales journal to the general ledger be completed?
6. If the schedule of accounts receivable does not agree in total with the balance of the summary accounts receivable account, what major error possibilities exist?

Report No. 7-2

> *Refer to the study assignments and complete Report No. 7-2. After completing the report, you may proceed with the textbook discussion in Chapter 8 until the next report is required.*

EXPANDING YOUR BUSINESS VOCABULARY

What is the meaning of each of the following terms?

Accounts Receivable (p. 197)   allowances (p. 183)

consignee (p. 188)
consignment sale (p. 188)
consignor (p. 188)
cost of goods sold (p. 183)
credit cards or charge plates (p. 185)
gross margin or gross profit (p. 183)
Installment Accounts Receivable (p. 188)
installment sales (p. 187)
layaway ledger (p. 187)
layaway sales (p. 187)
net sales (p. 183)

realized revenue (p. 183)
retail sales tax (p. 189)
sales invoice (p. 192)
sales journal (p. 199)
sales on approval (p. 187)
sales ticket (p. 192)
schedule of accounts receivable (p. 202)
subsidiary accounts receivable ledger (p. 198)

CHAPTER 8

ACCRUAL ACCOUNTING
APPLIED TO A SMALL
RETAIL BUSINESS

CHAPTER OBJECTIVES

The objectives of this chapter are to enable you:

▶ To apply accrual accounting and the record-keeping phases of the accounting cycle to a small retail business.

▶ To explain the application of accounting principles in accounting for:

(1) Uncollectible accounts.
(2) Prepaid expenses.
(3) Depreciation.

▶ To explain the nature of and accounting for purchases discount in a small retail business setting.

▶ To describe the accounts receivable and accounts payable control accounts in the general ledger, and the three-column account form of their related subsidiary ledgers.

▶ To explain and prepare a charge customer's statement of account.

A business enterprise that purchases and sells goods on account, maintains a stock of merchandise, and has property, plant or equipment assets must account for periodic income or loss on the accrual basis. This is necessary to measure the success of the business and to comply with federal and state income tax laws. Several features of accrual accounting were introduced in the preceding chapters. A more detailed consideration of these procedures and the introduction of other major practices that constitute accrual accounting will be presented here and in the two following chapters. As an aid in applying the principles and procedures involved in keeping the accounts of a merchandising business on the accrual basis, a system of accounts for a retail clothing business called Boyd's Clothiers, owned and operated by Lynn C. Boyd, will be described. While specific problems may arise in keeping the accounts of a particular enterprise, it should be recognized that most of the principles and procedures discussed and illustrated for Boyd's Clothiers are equally applicable to many other types of business.

PRINCIPLES AND PROCEDURES

The discussion will continue to be a blend of accounting principles and bookkeeping practices. It is important to keep in mind that the principles relate to goals and objectives while bookkeeping practices are designed to attain these goals and objectives. Procedures such as double entry and the use of source documents, journals, and ledger accounts are employed to make the record-keeping process complete, orderly, and as error-free as possible. While most accounting principles are broad enough to allow considerable flexibility, it is in the area of bookkeeping practices that wide latitude is found. Within limits, the records for each business can be styled to meet the particular requirements of the management.

ACCRUAL ACCOUNTING

In the opening pages of Chapters 6 and 7, brief mention was made of the accrual basis of accounting, which consists of recording revenue in the period in which it is earned and recording expenses in the period in which they are incurred. The receipt or disbursement of cash in the same period may or may not be involved. Revenue generally is recognized when services are performed or goods are provided, and is considered to be earned when, in exchange for something of value, money is received or a legal claim to money comes into existence. To a merchant, this normally means the time when the customer buys goods and either pays or agrees to pay for them. In terms of changes in the accounting elements, revenue arises or accrues when an increase in cash or a receivable causes an increase in owner's equity, except in cases where the increase is due to an investment of assets in the business by the owner. In comparable terms, expense accrues or is incurred when either a reduction of an asset (asset ouflow) or an increase in a liability causes the owner's equity to be reduced (except in cases where the owner's withdrawal of assets reduces the owner's equity). Expenses should be recognized when goods or services are consumed.

The accrual basis of accounting is widely used by enterprises because it involves the period-by-period matching of revenue with the expenses that caused or aided in producing that revenue. The revenue from sales, for example, must be matched against the cost of the goods sold and the various other expenses that were incurred in conducting the business. A simple matching of cash received from customers during a period with the cash paid for goods purchased in that period would be almost meaningless in most cases. The collections might relate to sales of a prior period and the payments to purchases of the current period, or vice versa. The expense related to most property, plant or equipment assets does not arise when they are acquired. The expense occurs as the assets' usefulness is gradually exhausted. In computing net income for a specified period, the accrual basis recognizes changes in many types of assets and liabilities — not just changes in the cash account.

In keeping business records, accountants must think in terms of time intervals, and must be sure that revenue and expense are accounted for in the proper accounting period. Certain types of revenue and expense do not have to be recognized at the precise moment this revenue or expense arises. For example, the wages of an employee literally accrue minute by minute during each working day but no record is made of the expense until it is paid at the end of the period. If the employee is not paid by the end of the period, the accountant should record the payroll expense and the liability that has accrued up to that time. There may be a lag in recording revenue and expense within the accounting period, but steps must be taken at the end of the period to record all revenue earned and expenses incurred. These steps consist of making what are called end-of-period adjustments in the accounts. It should be mentioned, however, that adjustments normally are not made for trivial amounts. The practice of ignoring matters that are too small to make any significant difference is an application of the concept of materiality. Just how small is "too small" is a question that requires judgment on the part of the accountant.

ACCOUNTING FOR UNCOLLECTIBLE ACCOUNTS RECEIVABLE

Businesses that sell goods or services on account realize that from time to time some of the customers do not pay all that they owe. The amounts that cannot be collected from charge customers are called uncollectible accounts expense, bad debts expense or loss from uncollectible accounts. The amount of such expense depends to a large degree upon the credit policy of the business. The seller should seek to avoid the two extremes of either having such a liberal credit policy that uncollectible accounts become excessive or having such a tight credit policy that uncollectible accounts are minimized at the sacrifice of a larger volume of sales and greater net income.

One method of accounting for uncollectible accounts receivable is to recognize the related expense only when a customer's account actually becomes uncollectible, by a debit to Uncollectible Accounts Expense and a credit to Accounts Receivable. A better accounting method is to estimate the amount of uncollectible account losses that will eventually result from the sales of a period and to treat the estimated amount of expected losses as an expense of that same period. This treatment will result in better periodic matching of revenue and expense. In this case, the procedure is to use a contra account entitled Allowance for Doubtful Accounts or Allowance for Bad Debts. The allowance for doubtful accounts is contra to the accounts receivable account, which means its balance will be deducted from the total of the accounts receivable. Any account having a balance which is intended to be deducted from another related account balance for financial statement purposes is known as a contra account.

At the end of the accounting period, an estimate of the expected uncollectible account losses is made based on the sales on account. The adjusting entry is made by debiting Uncollectible Accounts Expense and crediting Allowance for Doubtful Accounts. To illustrate, assume that in view of past experience it is expected that there will be a loss due to uncollectible accounts of an amount equal to one half of one percent of the sales on account during the year. If the sales on account amounted to $100,000, the estimated uncollectible account losses would be $500 ($100,000 × .005), which should be recorded as follows:

Dec. 31	Uncollectible Accounts Expense	500	
	Allowance for Doubtful Accounts...............................		500
	Uncollectible accounts expense provision for the year.		

The amount of the debit balance in the uncollectible accounts expense account is reported in the income statement as an operating expense. The amount of the credit balance in the allowance for doubtful accounts is reported in the balance sheet as a deduction from the receivables.

Another technique sometimes used in arriving at the end-of-period adjustment for uncollectible accounts involves aging the receivables. A detailed analysis is made of the receivables to see what proportions are for recent charges — those that are less than a month old, 30–60 days old, 61–90 days old, etc. Then, guided by past experience, estimates are made of the probable amounts that are likely to be uncollectible for each of the age groups. Generally, the longer a charge has been on the books, the less likely it is that it will ever be collected. The estimates can be totaled to arrive at an amount deemed necessary to have as the end-of-period (credit) balance in the allowance for doubtful accounts. An adjustment is made to give the allowance account the indicated balance.

To illustrate, assume that after aging the accounts it is estimated that $500 will not be collected. Assume also that the allowance account has an existing credit balance of $50. It would appear, in T account form, as follows:

Allowance for Doubtful Accounts

	Bal. 50

This means that the adjusting entry must be for the amount of $450 to bring the allowance account to the desired credit balance. The entry would be as follows:

Dec. 31	Uncollectible Accounts Expense	450	
	Allowance for Doubtful Accounts...............................		450
	To adjust accounts receivable for uncollectible accounts.		

After posting the $450 adjusting entry, the two accounts involved will appear, in T account form, as follows:

Uncollectible Accounts Expense		**Allowance for Doubtful Accounts**	
Dec. 31 450		Bal. 50	
		Dec. 31 450	
		500	

Many accountants think that the best way to show the net amount of receivables on the balance sheet is gross receivables less allowance for doubtful accounts. This is a realistic estimate of net realizable value (realizable cash value) of the receivables.

Accounts receivable	$60,000	
Less allowance for doubtful accounts	500	$59,500

It should be apparent that the credit part of the adjusting entry cannot be made directly to a specific receivable account because, at the time the entry is made, there is no way of knowing exactly which debtors will not pay. Experience gives virtual assurance that some of the amounts due from customers will be uncollectible but only time will reveal which ones.

When it is determined that a certain account will not be collected, an entry should be made to write off the account and to charge the loss against the allowance. For example, on April 22 of the next year, it is determined that $75 owed by L. R. Cleavelin cannot be collected due to either death or bankruptcy. Whatever the circumstance, if it is fairly certain that the amount can never be collected, the following journal entry should be made:

Apr. 22	Allowance for Doubtful Accounts	75	
	Accounts Receivable		75
	To write off account of L. R. Cleavelin found to be uncollectible.		

Sometimes, the allowance for doubtful accounts will show a debit balance at the end of the accounting period. This happens when the total amount of estimated uncollectible customers' accounts for the year is smaller than the total amount actually written off during the year. When this condition is encountered, the adjusting entry for estimated uncollectible accounts must (1) cover the debit balance, and (2) provide for the expected uncollectible account losses of the coming year.

In still other cases, the allowance account may have a large credit balance, which means that the amount of write-offs was not as large as was expected. Very often, this is handled by making the amount of the adjustment for the year just ended smaller than it otherwise would be. Alternatively, the beginning-of-period balance in the allowance for doubtful accounts may have been corrected by means of a separate adjusting entry. The end-of-period adjusting entry for the expected uncollectible account losses can then be made in the normal manner.

ACCOUNTING FOR PREPAID EXPENSES

The term prepaid expense is used to describe an item that was purchased and considered to be an asset when acquired, but which will be consumed or used up in the near future and thus becomes an expense. Supplies of various sorts and prepaid (unexpired) insurance are good examples. At the end of the period, the portions of such assets that have expired or have been consumed must be determined and entries made debiting the proper expense accounts and crediting the proper prepaid expense accounts. For example, a company purchased office supplies for $750 and a three-year fire insurance policy for $300. The entry would appear as follows:

Office Supplies...	750	
Prepaid Insurance..	300	
Cash		1,050
To record the purchase of office supplies and insurance.		

If at the end of the accounting period a physical count indicated that there were $125 of office supplies on hand, it can be determined that $625 ($750 − $125) of supplies would have been used. The following adjusting entry should be made:

Office Supplies Expense..	625	
Office Supplies..		625
To record office supplies used.		

If the insurance policy had been in effect since the beginning of the fiscal year, $100 ($300 ÷ 3 years) of the prepaid insurance would have been consumed during the year. The following adjusting journal entry should be made:

Insurance Expense...	100	
Prepaid Insurance..		100
To record insurance expired for the year.		

The chart of accounts for Boyd's Clothiers includes two prepaid expense accounts: Supplies, Account No. 181, and Prepaid Insurance, Account No. 184. These accounts are classified as assets in the chart of accounts. The supplies account is debited for the cost of supplies purchased. At the end of the year, the account should be credited for the cost of supplies used during the year with an offsetting debit to Supplies Expense, Account No. 825. The prepaid insurance account is debited for the cost of the insurance purchased during the year. At the end of the year, the account is credited for the portion of the cost that relates to the year then ending with an offsetting debit to Insurance Expense, Account No. 828.

ACCOUNTING FOR DEPRECIATION

Depreciation accounting is the process of allocating the cost of plant and equipment assets to the periods expected to benefit from the use of these assets. Most of such assets eventually become useless to the business because they either wear out or become inadequate or obsolete. Sometimes all of these causes combine to make the assets valueless except, perhaps, for some small salvage value as scrap or junk.

Generally, in computing depreciation, no consideration is given to what these assets might bring if they were to be sold. Assets of this type are acquired to be used and not to be sold. During their useful lives any resale value is of no consequence unless the business is about to cease. For a going business, the idea is to allocate the net cost of an asset over the years that it is expected to serve. Net cost means original cost less estimated scrap or salvage value. Usually, there is no way of knowing just how long an asset will serve the business. It is therefore apparent that depreciation expense can be no more than an estimate. However, with past experience as a guide, the estimates can be reasonably reliable.

There are several ways of calculating the periodic depreciation write-off. In the traditional straight-line method, the net cost (original cost less any expected scrap value) of an asset is divided by the number of years that the asset is expected to serve, to arrive at the amount of depreciation expense each year. Because the estimated scrap or salvage value is typically quite small, it is often ignored and the entire original cost of the asset is allocated. Thus, it is common practice to express depreciation as a percentage of the original cost of the asset. For example, in the case of an asset with a 10-year life, 10 percent of the original cost should be written off each year. If it has a 20-year life, 5 percent should be written off.

In 1954, the Internal Revenue Code was revised to permit taxpayers to use depreciation methods that involve larger depreciation charges in the earlier years of the life of an asset in calculating net income subject to tax. These methods primarily are useful only in the case of new assets. These reducing-charge methods permit large write-offs in the early years and successively smaller write-offs each succeeding year. However, the straight-line method has been very popular in the past. One of its virtues is simplicity. The straight-line method of accounting for depreciation is used by Boyd's Clothiers.

Depreciation expense is recorded by an end-of-period adjusting entry that involves debiting one or more depreciation expense accounts and crediting one or more accumulated depreciation (sometimes called Allowance for Depreciation) accounts. For example, assume that a company purchased a lawn tractor for $3,000 at the beginning of the year, and estimates that it has a useful life of 6 years with no salvage value. The annual depreciation of the lawn tractor under the straight-line method of depreciation would be $500 ($3,000 ÷ 6 years). The entry upon purchase of the equipment would be:

Equipment — Tractor	3,000	
Cash		3,000
To record purchase of equipment.		

The adjusting entry to record depreciation at the end of the year would be:

Depreciation Expense	500	
Accumulated Depreciation — Equipment		500
To record annual depreciation of equipment.		

The accumulated depreciation account is a contra account — which means that its balance will be deducted from the related asset that is being depreciated. In theory, there would be no objection to making the credits directly to the asset accounts themselves in the same way that the asset accounts for prepaid expenses are credited to record their decreases. However, in order that the original cost of the assets will be clearly revealed, portions of the cost written off are credited to the contra accounts. The amounts of the credit balances of the contra accounts are reported in the balance sheet as deductions from the costs of the assets to which they relate.

Equipment	$3,000	
Less accumulated depreciation	500	$2,500

The credit balances in the accumulated depreciation accounts increase year by year. When these amounts are equal to the cost of the related assets, no more depreciation may be taken.

The similarities and differences between the allowance for doubtful accounts and the accumulated depreciation account should be recognized. Both contra asset accounts are credited by adjusting entries at the end of the period. In both cases, the offsetting debits go to expense accounts. In both cases, the balances in the contra accounts are shown in the balance sheet as subtractions from the amounts of the assets to which they relate. However, Allowance for Doubtful Accounts is decreased or debited whenever an uncollectible account materializes and it is necessary to write off the account. The credit balance of the allowance for doubtful accounts does not continually increase. If it does, this indicates that the estimate of uncollectible account losses has been excessive. In contrast, the credit balances of the accumulated depreciation accounts get larger year by year. The credit balances remain in these accounts for as long as the assets to which they relate are kept in service.

Note also that the purposes of the two contra accounts are not the same. When the balance of the allowance for doubtful accounts is subtracted from the balance of the accounts receivable account, the result is an estimate of how much will be collected from customers — the net realizable value of the receivables. However, when the balance of the accumulated depreciation account is subtracted from the balance of the related asset account, the result is the cost not yet charged to depreciation expense, and will represent the current value of the asset only by sheer coincidence.

Since Boyd's Clothiers has only store equipment that is subject to depreciation, there is only one contra account, Accumulated Depreciation — Store Equipment, Account No. 211.1. Depreciation expense is debited to an account so named, Account No. 827.

ACCOUNTS WITH SUPPLIERS AND CUSTOMERS

When the character of the enterprise and the volume of business are such that it is necessary to keep relatively few accounts, it may be satisfactory to keep all of the accounts together in a single general ledger, which may be bound, loose-leaf, or a set of cards. As explained in Chapters 6 and 7, a record of the amounts due to suppliers for purchases on account and the amounts due from customers for sales on account may be kept without maintaining a separate ledger account for each supplier and for each customer. A file of unpaid suppliers' invoices and another of sales tickets for sales on account may suffice. However, many merchants prefer to keep a separate ledger account for each supplier and for each customer.

Subsidiary Ledgers. When the volume of business and the number of transactions warrant, it may be advisable to subdivide the ledger. In this case, it usually is considered advisable to segregate the accounts with customers and the accounts with suppliers from the other accounts and keep them in separate ledgers called subsidiary ledgers. Separate ledgers containing individual accounts with customers and suppliers are known as accounts receivable subsidiary ledgers and accounts payable subsidiary ledgers, respectively.

Three-Column Account Form. A special account form known as the three-column account form is widely used in keeping the individual accounts with customers and suppliers. While the standard account form shown in the illustration on page 27, or the four-column form illustrated on page 119, may be used, the three-column account form shown on page 215 is in frequent use for such accounts. Note that three parallel amount columns are provided for recording debits, credits, and balances. The nature of the account determines whether its normal balance is a debit or a credit. Accounts with customers usually have debit balances; accounts with suppliers nearly always have credit balances. After each entry, the new balance may be determined and recorded in the Balance column, or if preferred, the balance may be determined and recorded at the end of each month.

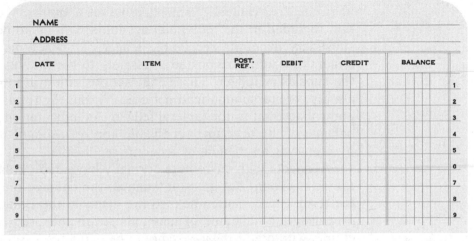

Three-Column Account Form

Control Accounts. When subsidiary ledgers are kept for suppliers and for customers, it is customary to keep control accounts for the subsidiary ledgers in the general ledger. Thus, accounts with suppliers are kept in a subsidiary accounts payable ledger, and the control account, Accounts Payable, is kept in the general ledger. Accounts with customers are kept in a subsidiary accounts receivable ledger, and the control account, Accounts Receivable, is kept in the general ledger. The use of control accounts in the general ledger makes it possible to take a trial balance of the general ledger accounts without referring to the subsidiary ledgers.

Accounts Payable Control. A general ledger account, called Accounts Payable — Control, provides a summary of the information recorded in the individual accounts with suppliers kept in the subsidiary accounts payable ledger. Transactions affecting suppliers' accounts are posted separately to the individual accounts in the subsidiary ledger. These transactions either are also posted separately, or are summarized periodically and the totals posted, to the control account in the general ledger. As indicated in Chapter 6, the balance of the accounts payable control account may be proved by preparing a schedule of accounts payable.

Accounts with suppliers normally have credit balances. If a supplier's account has a debit balance, the balance may be circled or the term "Dr." written next to the figure in the Balance column. In preparing the schedule of accounts payable, the total of the accounts with debit balances should be deducted from the total of the accounts with credit balances, and the difference should agree with the balance of the accounts payable control account.

Accounts Receivable Control. A general ledger account, called Accounts Receivable — Control, provides a summary of the information recorded in the individual accounts with customers kept in the subsidiary accounts receivable ledger. Transactions affecting customers' accounts are posted separately to the individual accounts in the subsidiary ledger. These transactions either are also posted separately, or are summarized periodically and the totals posted, to the control account in the general ledger. As indicated in Chapter 7, the balance of the accounts receivable control account may be proved by preparing a schedule of accounts receivable.

Accounts with customers normally have debit balances. If a customer's account has a credit balance, the balance may be circled or the term "Cr." written next to the figure in the Balance column. In preparing the schedule of accounts receivable, the total of the accounts with credit balances should be deducted from the total of the accounts with debit balances and the difference should agree with the balance of the accounts receivable control account.

POSTING TO INDIVIDUAL ACCOUNTS

It is necessary to post all the amounts that represent increases or decreases to the accounts of each supplier and each customer.

Supplier Accounts. A list of vouchers or other documents that usually represent transactions completed with suppliers is shown below. The usual posting reference is also indicated.

Transaction	Voucher or Document	Posting Reference
Purchase	Purchase invoice No. 1	P1
Return or allowance	Charge-back invoice No. 1	CB1
Payment on account	Check stub No. 1	Ck1

The purchase invoices and charge-back invoices are usually numbered consecutively as they are received or issued. These numbers should be not confused with the numbers used by the supplier. The check stub is numbered consecutively to agree with the number of the checks issued. As the direct posting is completed, the proper cross-reference should be made in the Posting Reference column of the account and on the voucher or other document. If a loose-leaf ledger is used and accounts with suppliers are kept in alphabetic order, the posting is indicated by means of a distinctive check mark on the voucher or other document.

Customer Accounts. A list of vouchers or other documents that usually represent transactions completed with customers is shown below. The usual posting reference is also indicated.

Transaction	Voucher or Document	Posting Reference
Sale	Sales ticket No. 1	S1
Return or allowance	Credit memo No. 1	CM1
Collection on account	Remittance received	C

The sales tickets usually are prepared in duplicate or triplicate and are numbered consecutively. Each salesperson may use a different series of numbers. One copy of the sales ticket is retained for the use of the bookkeeper and another copy is given to the customer. Credit memorandums issued to customers in connection with sales returns or allowances usually are prepared in duplicate and are numbered consecutively. One copy of the credit memorandum goes to the customer and the other copy is retained for the use of the bookkeeper. Remittances received from customers may consist of cash or cash items, such as checks, bank drafts, and money orders. When the remittance is in the form of cash, it is customary to issue a receipt. The receipt may be issued in duplicate, in which case the duplicate copy will provide the information needed for the purpose of posting to the customer's account. Sometimes, receipt stubs are used to record the information for posting purposes. When the remittance is in the form of a check, it is not necessary to issue a receipt as the canceled check will serve as a receipt for the customer.

Posting of a credit to the customer's account may be made directly from the check or from a list of checks received. Sometimes all remittances received daily are listed in such a manner as to provide the information needed for posting purposes. When this plan is followed, the bookkeeper need not handle the remittances at all. It is a common practice to use a form of monthly statement of account, the upper portion of which contains the customer's name and address. This portion is detached and returned along with the remittance. The customer notes the amount of the remittance on this slip of paper which then contains all the information needed to post the correct credit to the proper subsidiary ledger account. If the customer does not return the top part of the statement, a receipt or memo is prepared to serve the same purpose. This procedure is especially suitable when it is possible to separate the functions of (1) handling the cash and cash items, and (2) recording the credits to the customers' accounts. As the direct posting is completed, the proper cross-reference should be made in the Posting Reference column of the account and on the voucher or other document. If a loose-leaf ledger is used and accounts with customers are kept in alphabetic order, the posting may be indicated by means of a distinctive check mark or by initialing the voucher or other document.

Accountants generally prefer to post from the basic documents rather than from the books of original entry to the individual accounts with suppliers and customers because such procedure provides better control and promotes accuracy. When a purchase invoice is recorded in a purchases journal by one person and is posted directly from the invoice to the proper supplier's account by another person, it is unlikely that both persons will make the same mistake. Even if the posting is done by the person who also keeps the purchases journal, there is less likelihood of making a mistake than when the posting is done from the journal entry. If a mistake was made in recording the amount of the invoice in the purchases journal, the same mistake would almost certainly be made in posting from the purchases journal to the supplier's account. The same reasoning may be applied to the recording of sales transactions and all other transactions that affect accounts with suppliers and customers.

STATEMENT OF ACCOUNT

When merchandise is sold on account, it is customary to send a monthly bill to each charge customer. An itemized bill, showing the amount still owed from the previous month and the detailed charges and credits to the customer's account during the current month, is known as a statement of account. Usually the statements are mailed as soon as they can be completed following the close of each month or at a time during the month determined by the billing cycle. The use of "billing cycles" is limited, generally, to businesses with hundreds or thousands of customers. In order that statements may be mailed promptly, some firms follow the policy of including transactions completed up to the 25th of the preceding month or five days before the close of the customer's billing cycle. When a remittance is not received from the customer within the usual credit period, a copy of the statement of account may be referred to the credit department for such action as the credit manager may wish to take.

A filled-in copy of a statement of account is reproduced below. This is a statement of the account of C. W. Reed for the month ended October 31. It shows (1) the balance at the beginning of the month amounting to $83.90; (2) a charge of $225.23 (for a sale of $214.50 plus tax of $10.73) made on October 22; (3) a credit of $200 for cash received on October 27; and (4) the balance at the close of the month amounting to $109.13. Note that the customer is asked to tear off the upper portion of the statement and to return it along with the remittance.

STATEMENT

BOYD'S clothiers

600 Olive Street, St. Louis, Missouri 63101-2356

C. W. REED
761 Cella
St. Louis, MO 63124-3301

▼ PLEASE DETACH THIS PORTION AND RETURN WITH YOUR REMITTANCE.

DATE	DESCRIPTION	CHARGES	CREDITS	BALANCE
Oct. 1			BALANCE FORWARD	83.90
22	Mdse.	225.23		309.13
27	Cash		200.00	109.13

Statement of Account

BUILDING YOUR ACCOUNTING KNOWLEDGE

1. When should revenue be recognized in accrual accounting?
2. When should expense be recognized in accrual accounting?

3. Why is it considered better accounting to estimate the amount of uncollectible accounts receivable in advance rather than wait until they
become certain?

4. Why is the allowance for doubtful accounts called a contra account?

5. What is the journal procedure when it is determined that a particular
customer's account will not be collected?

6. What is meant by the "net cost" of a depreciable asset?

7. Why is the amount of depreciation only an estimate?

8. What are the major differences between the allowance for doubtful accounts and the accumulated depreciation account?

Report No. 8-1

> *Complete Report No. 8-1 in the study assignments and sub-
> mit your working papers to the instructor for approval. After
> completing the report, continue with the following textbook
> discussion until the next report is required.*

ILLUSTRATION OF ACCOUNTING PROCEDURE

To apply accrual accounting and the record-keeping phases of
the accounting cycle, the transactions of Boyd's Clothiers, a small
retail business, will be discussed and illustrated in this chapter and
in the next two chapters.

THE CHART OF ACCOUNTS

The importance of classifying accounts was discussed and illustrated in preceding chapters. A chart of accounts is an orderly and
systematic list of accounts that identifies each account by means of
an assigned number used to assist in locating the account in the
ledger. The chart of accounts for the retail business of Boyd's Clothiers is shown on the following page.

The pattern of numbers or code shown in the illustration is fairly
typical of the arrangement used by many businesses. However, numerous variations are possible. Sometimes letters as well as
numbers are made a part of the code. When numbers are used, it is
not uncommon for special columns in journals to be headed by just

BOYD'S CLOTHIERS
CHART OF ACCOUNTS

Assets*

Cash
- 111 First National Bank
- 112 Petty Cash Fund

Receivables
- 131 Accounts Receivable
    - 131.1 Allowance for Doubtful Accounts

Merchandise Inventory
- 161 Merchandise Inventory

Prepaid Expenses
- 181 Supplies
- 184 Prepaid Insurance

Property, Plant, and Equipment
- 211 Store Equipment
    - 211.1 Accumulated Depreciation — Store Equipment

Liabilities
- 311 FICA Tax Payable
- 312 FUTA Tax Payable
- 313 State Unemployment Tax Payable
- 314 Employees Income Tax Payable
- 315 Accrued Bank Credit Card Payable
- 316 Notes Payable
- 317 Accrued Interest Payable
- 318 Accounts Payable
- 321 Sales Tax Payable

Owner's Equity
- 511 Lynn C. Boyd, Capital
- 511.1 Lynn C. Boyd, Drawing
- 531 Expense and Revenue Summary

Revenue
- 611 Sales
    - 611.1 Sales Returns and Allowances

Cost of Goods Sold
- 711 Purchases
    - 711.1 Purchases Returns and Allowances
    - 711.2 Purchases Discount

Operating Expenses
- 821 Rent Expense
- 822 Salaries and Commissions Expense
- 823 Heating and Lighting Expense
- 824 Telephone Expense
- 825 Supplies Expense
- 826 Advertising Expense
- 827 Depreciation Expense
- 828 Insurance Expense
- 829 Charitable Contributions Expense
- 831 Payroll Taxes Expense
- 832 Bank Credit Card Expense
- 833 Uncollectible Accounts Expense
- 839 Miscellaneous Expense

Other Expenses
- 911 Interest Expense

*Words in bold type represent headings and not account titles.

the account number, rather than the name of the account. In a system of records that requires numerous accounts, the use of account numbers virtually displaces account names except for statement purposes. Furthermore, in recent years account numbers have become essential to the development of a computer-based accounting system.

The nature of many of the accounts included in the chart of accounts for Boyd's Clothiers should be apparent because they have been described in preceding chapters and their use has been illustrated. In addition, the chart includes certain accounts that are needed in recording several types of transactions and events that were described in the first section of this chapter.

Note that the general ledger illustrated on pages 240–247 does not include accounts numbers 315, 317, 531, 825, 827, 828, and 833. This is because these accounts are not needed to record routine transactions. When the matter of adjusting entries and closing entries is discussed and illustrated in the following chapters, these accounts will be shown.

BOOKS OF ACCOUNT

The books of account used by Boyd's Clothiers, owned and operated by Lynn C. Boyd, are discussed and illustrated on the following pages. The records include:

Books of Original Entry	Books of Final Entry	Auxiliary Records
Combination journal	General ledger	Petty cash disbursements
Purchases journal	Accounts receivable ledger	record
Sales journal	Accounts payable ledger	Checkbook
		Employees' earnings records

With the exception of the checkbook and the employees' earnings records, the above records are illustrated on pages 235–253 of this chapter.

Combination Journal. The combination journal used in Boyd's Clothiers is similar to the one illustrated on pages 124–127. However, in Boyd's journal, special columns are provided for credits to Purchases Discount, Accounts Receivable, Sales, and Sales Tax Payable, and for charges to Accounts Payable. Boyd's follows the practice of depositing all cash receipts in a checking account at the First National Bank and making all disbursements by check (except for the payment of small items, which may be paid from a petty cash fund, and a few charges made directly by the bank). The posting to the bank account is from the combination journal. The bank account is debited for the total receipts (deposits) and credited for the total disbursements (checks and bank charges).

All items entered in the General Debit and Credit columns of the combination journal are posted individually to the proper accounts in the general ledger. No individual posting to the general ledger is required from any of the other amount columns. Instead, the totals of these columns are posted at the end of the month.

Purchases Journal. The purchases journal used in Boyd's Clothiers is the same as the one illustrated on page 174 and described in detail in Chapter 6. All transactions involving the purchase of merchandise on account are recorded in this journal. Because the posting of the individual credits to the accounts with suppliers is done directly from the purchase invoices, the only posting required from the purchases journal is the total purchases for each month. This involves a debit to Purchases, Account No. 711, and a credit to Accounts Payable, Account No. 318.

Sales Journal. The sales journal used in Boyd's Clothiers is the same as the one illustrated on page 199 and described in detail in Chapter 7. All transactions involving the sale of merchandise **on account** are recorded in this journal. Because the posting of individual charges to the accounts with customers is done directly from the sales tickets, the only posting required from the sales journal is the total sales for each month. This involves a debit to Accounts Receivable, Account No. 131, and credits to Sales, Account No. 611, and to Sales Tax Payable, Account No. 321.

General Ledger. A general ledger with the accounts arranged in numerical order is used. A chart of accounts appears on page 221. The four-column account form is used in the general ledger.

Accounts Receivable Ledger. An accounts receivable ledger with the accounts for customers arranged in alphabetic order is used. The three-column account form is used in this ledger. Posting to the individual accounts with customers is done directly from the sales tickets or other documents. As each item is posted, the balance is extended immediately so that reference to the account of any customer at any time will reveal without any delay the amount due. This is important since it is often necessary to determine the status of a particular customer's account before extending additional credit.

Accounts Payable Ledger. An accounts payable ledger with the accounts for suppliers arranged in alphabetic order is used. The three-column account form is used in this ledger also. Posting to the individual accounts with suppliers is done directly from the invoices or other documents. As each item is posted, the balance is extended immediately so that reference to the account of any supplier at any time will reveal the amount owed to that supplier.

Auxiliary Records. As previously stated, certain auxiliary records are used, including a petty cash disbursements record and a checkbook. The form of petty cash disbursements record is similar to that illustrated on pages 60 and 61. A record of deposits made and checks issued is kept on the check stubs as well as in the combination journal. At the end of each month, when the summary posting from the combination journal is completed, the balance of the bank checking account in the ledger should be the same as the balance recorded on the check stubs. The earnings records maintained for each of Boyd's four employees are similar to the one illustrated on pages 96 and 97.

ACCOUNTING PROCEDURE

The books of account containing a record of the transactions completed during the month of December are reproduced on pages 235–253. These books include the combination journal, the purchases journal, the sales journal, the petty cash disbursements record, the general ledger, the accounts receivable ledger, and the accounts payable ledger. Before recording the transactions for December, the balance of the bank checking account was entered in the combination journal and the balance in the petty cash fund was entered in the petty cash disbursements record. The balance at the beginning of the month of December is shown in each of the accounts in the general, accounts receivable, and accounts payable ledgers. These balances, along with those at the end of the month, are summarized in the trial balance and schedules reproduced on pages 253–255.

Following is a narrative of the transactions completed during December. Transactions that have not been previously introduced are analyzed to show their effect upon the accounts.

BOYD'S CLOTHIERS

NARRATIVE OF TRANSACTIONS

Wednesday, December 1

Issued checks as follows:

No. 757, Dolan Realty Co., $900, in payment of December rent.

No. 758, The Penn-Central Transportation Co., $69.14, in payment of freight on merchandise purchased.

No. 759, Aris Glove Co., $429, in payment of invoice of November 5, no discount.

Note that all three checks were recorded in the combination journal. Check No. 757 was recorded by debiting Rent Expense, Account No. 821, and crediting the bank account. Check No. 758 was recorded by debiting Purchases, Account No. 711, and by crediting the bank account. Since the freight charge increases the cost of the merchandise, the purchases account was debited. Note that the account titles were written in the Description column. The account numbers were inserted in the Posting Reference column when the individual posting was completed at the end of the week.

Check No. 759 was recorded by debiting Accounts Payable and crediting the bank account, the name of the supplier being written in the Description column. A check mark was placed in the Posting Reference column to indicate that checks issued to suppliers are not posted individually from the combination journal. These checks are posted directly to the proper suppliers' accounts in the accounts payable ledger from the information on the check stubs.

Thursday, December 2

Received the following invoices for merchandise purchased on account:

Daniel Hays Co., Johnstown, NY 12095-1001, $296, per Invoice No. 194 of November 30. Terms, net 30 days.

Hanes Corporation, Winston-Salem, NC 27102-7022, $967, per Invoice No. 195 of November 30. Terms, 8/10 EOM.

Julius Resnick, Inc., 46 E. 32d St., New York, NY 10016-1619, $1,934, per Invoice No. 196 of November 30. Terms, 3/10 EOM.

Note that after receiving the merchandise and checking the invoices, transactions were recorded in the purchases journal. Check marks were placed in the Posting Reference column to indicate that individual posting is not done from the purchases journal. The invoices were then posted directly to the credit of the three suppliers' accounts in the accounts payable ledger, after which the invoices were filed in an unpaid invoice file according to their due dates.

Friday, December 3

Received check from D. P. Walsh, $412.40.

Note that the credit was immediately posted to the customer's account. The remittance was then recorded in the combination journal by debiting the bank account and crediting Accounts Receivable. The name of the customer was written in the Description column. Since the credit had already been posted to the customer's account, a check mark was placed in the Posting Reference column.

Received a notice from the First National Bank that $306.05 had been deducted from the account of Boyd's Clothiers, representing a discount of 3 percent of the net amount of Visa and MasterCard vouchers that were deposited by Boyd's relating to such sales (less credits issued to customers for returns) during the preceding month.

Note that this was recorded in the combination journal as a debit to Bank Credit Card Expense, Account No. 832, and a credit in the Bank column. (Even though the reduction in the Bank balance was not accomplished by issuing a check, the effect was the same. A subtraction of the amount was made on the next check stub.)

Saturday, December 4

Sold merchandise on account as follows:

No. 271A, D. P. Walsh, 113 Grether, St. Louis, MO 63135-4725, $562.10, tax, $28.11.

No. 257B, J. J. Anders, 11939 Rocky, St. Louis, MO 63141-1353, $110.66, tax, $5.53.

No. 235C, J. L. Burnett, 15 Forester, St. Louis, MO 63011-2631, $699.34, tax, $34.97.

Unless otherwise specified, all customer charge accounts are payable by the 10th of the following month. No cash discount is allowed. Note that these transactions were recorded in the sales journal. A check mark was placed in the Posting Reference column to indicate that individual posting is not done from the sales journal. The sales tickets were then posted directly to the proper customers' accounts in the accounts receivable ledger, after which each ticket was filed under the name of the customer for future reference. The numbers of the sales tickets indicate that there are four salespersons identified by the letters A, B, C, and D. Each of these persons uses a separate pad of sales tickets numbered consecutively.

Cash (including bank credit card) sales for the week:

Salesperson	Merchandise	Tax	Total
A	$ 728.13	$ 36.41	$ 764.54
B	660.56	33.03	693.59
C	902.82	45.14	947.96
D	544.60	27.23	571.83
	$2,836.11	$141.81	$2,977.92

As each cash sale was completed, a sales ticket and a Visa or Master Card ticket, if necessary, were prepared. The ticket provides the information needed in recording the amount of the sale on the cash register. Each amount was added to the previous total of cash sales made by each salesperson on an electronic accumulator in the register. Usually the total cash sales are recorded daily, but to save time and avoid unnecessary duplication of entries, the total cash sales are here recorded at the end of each week and on the last day of the month. This transaction was recorded in the combination journal by debiting the bank account for $2,977.92 and crediting Sales for $2,836.11 and Sales Tax Payable for $141.81.

END-OF-THE-WEEK WORK

(1) Proved the footings of the combination journal. (2) Deposited $3,390.32 in the First National Bank and proved the bank balance, $17,679.77. (3) Posted each entry individually from the General Debit and Credit columns of the combination journal to the proper general ledger accounts. (4) Proved the footings of the sales journal.

Monday, December 6

Issued checks as follows:

No. 760, Brown Shoe Co., $598.78, in payment of invoice of November 27, $611 less discount of $12.22.

No. 761, Damon, Inc., $562.12, in payment of invoice of November 27, $598 less discount of $35.88.

No. 762, El Jay Co., $2,702.96, in payment of invoice of November 29, $2,938 less discount of $235.04.

No. 763, Marx Neuman Co., $1,019.20, in payment of invoice of November 27, $1,040 less discount of $20.80.

No. 764, Schoeneman, Inc., $1,466.40, in payment of invoice of November 29, $1,560 less discount of $93.60.

No. 765, Smart Pants, Inc., $1,636.68, in payment of invoice of November 27, $1,779 less discount of $142.32.

Each check was recorded in the combination journal by crediting the bank account, crediting Purchases Discount in the column provided, and debiting Accounts Payable for the gross amount. The name of the supplier was written in the Description column and a check mark was placed in the Posting Reference column to indicate that the posting to the individual supplier's account in the accounts payable ledger was not made from this journal. The check stubs provided the information for posting. In posting to the suppliers' accounts, one line was used for the amount of the check and another for the amount of the discount.

Bought merchandise from Damon, Inc., 16 E. 34th St., New York, NY 10016-3141, $1,495, per Invoice No. 197 of December 4. Terms, 6/10, n/30.

Sold merchandise on account as follows:

No. 259B, J. F. Yager, 5 Brookston Ct., Kirkwood, MO 63122-3074, $138.22, tax, $6.91.

Issued checks as follows:

No. 766, Globe Publishing Co., $79.35, in payment for circulars to be used for advertising purposes.

No. 767, State Treasurer, $1,185.78, in payment of sales taxes for November.

Both checks were recorded in the combination journal by debiting the proper accounts and crediting the bank account. Check No. 766 was charged to Advertising Expense, and Check No. 767 was charged to Sales Tax Payable. The numbers of the checks were written in the Check No. column and the titles of the accounts to be charged were written in the Description column.

Tuesday, December 7

Made petty cash disbursements as follows:

Postage stamps, $15. Petty Cash Voucher No. 63.
Messenger fee, $4.50. Petty Cash Voucher No. 64.

All disbursements from the petty cash fund are recorded in the petty cash disbursements record. This record is ruled so as to facilitate the classification of each expenditure. Note that the cost of the postage stamps was recorded as a charge to Supplies, Account No. 181, and the messenger fees were charged to Miscellaneous Expense, Account No. 839.

Wednesday, December 8

Issued checks as follows:

No. 768, Daniel Hays Co., $889, in payment of invoice of November 15, no discount.

No. 769, Hanes Corporation, $889.64, in payment of invoice of November 30, $967 less discount of $77.36.

No. 770, Julius Resnick, Inc., $1,875.98, in payment of invoice of November 30, $1,934 less discount of $58.02.

A customer who used a MasterCard to purchase a dress (sales price, $109.95, sales tax, $5.50) two days before, returned it because it was the wrong color. Boyd agreed to take it back and prepared a MasterCard credit ticket for the full amount, $115.45.

Since the original transaction had been handled as a cash sale, the return was recorded in the combination journal as a credit of $115.45 in the Bank column with a debit of $109.95 to Sales Returns and Allowances, Account No. 611.1, and a debit of $5.50 to Sales Tax Payable, Account No. 321. (At the next bank deposit, the amount of the credit ticket will be treated as a deduction from the amount of the tickets being deposited.)

Thursday, December 9

Issued Check No. 771 for $650.92 to the First National Bank, a U.S. depository, in payment of the following taxes:

Employees' income tax withheld during November.................		$281.20
FICA tax imposed:		
On employees (withheld during November).........................	$184.86	
On the employer	184.86	369.72
Total		$650.92

This transaction resulted in a decrease in FICA tax payable and employees income tax payable with a corresponding decrease in the bank account. This was recorded in the combination journal by debiting FICA Tax Payable for $369.72 and Employees Income Tax Payable for $281.20 and crediting the bank account for $650.92.

Sold merchandise on account as follows:

No. 243D, R. D. Williams, 617 Rebecca, St. Charles, MO 63301-3122, $319.85, tax, $15.99.

Friday, December 10

Received the following remittances from customers:

J. E. Buelt, $400, on account.
L. V. Freeman, $300, on account.
K. E. Vivian, $106.74, in full settlement of account.

Saturday, December 11

Cash and bank credit card sales for the week:

Salesperson	Merchandise	Tax	Total
A	$1,079.16	$ 53.96	$1,133.12
B	1,579.57	78.98	1,658.55
C	947.45	47.37	994.82
D	535.08	26.75	561.83
	$4,141.26	$207.06	$4,348.32

END-OF-THE-WEEK WORK

(1) Proved the footings of the combination journal. (2) Deposited $5,039.61 ($5,155.06 − $115.45 credit of December 8) in the First National Bank and proved the bank balance, $9,162.57. (3) Posted each entry individually from the General Debit and Credit columns of the combination journal to the proper general ledger accounts. (4) Proved the footings of the petty cash disbursements record and proved the balance of the petty cash fund, $130.50. (5) Proved the footings of the sales journal.

Monday, December 13

Received the following invoices for merchandise purchased on account:

Aris Glove Co., 10 E. 38th St., New York, NY 10016-6310, $536.25, per Invoice No. 198 of December 10. Terms, net 30 days.

El Jay Co., 411 Anderson, Fairview, NJ 07022-2710, $2,203.50, per Invoice No. 199 of December 10. Terms, 8/10, n/30.

Huk-A-Poo, Inc., 411 Broadway, New York, NY 10012-1209, $706.85, per Invoice No. 200 of December 11. Terms, 8/10, n/30.

Tuesday, December 14

Issued Check No. 772 to Damon, Inc., $1,405.30, in payment of invoice of December 4, $1,495 less discount of $89.70.

Made the following disbursements from the petty cash fund:

Boy Scouts of America, $10. Petty Cash Voucher No. 65.

Lynn C. Boyd, $20, for personal use. Petty Cash Voucher No. 66.

Wednesday, December 15

Issued Check No. 773 payable to Payroll for $848.96.

Boyd's follows the policy of paying employees on the 15th and last day of each month. The following statement was prepared from the payroll record:

PAYROLL STATEMENT FOR PERIOD ENDED DECEMBER 15

Total wages and commissions earned during period		$1,160.50
Employees' taxes to be withheld:		
Employees' income tax	$230.30	
FICA tax, 7% of $1,160.50	81.24	311.54
Net amount payable to employees		$ 848.96
Employer's payroll taxes:		
FICA tax, 7% of $1,160.50		$ 81.24
Unemployment compensation taxes —		
State unemployment tax, 2.7% of $136.20		3.68
FUTA tax, 0.7% of $136.20		.95
Total		$ 85.87

None of the earnings of the four employees has reached the $30,000 point. Accordingly, all of the wages and commissions earned during the period are subject to the FICA tax. All but one employee (a part-time employee) reached the $6,000 maximum state unemployment and FUTA tax limits in an earlier month. As a result, only $136.20 of wages and commissions earned during the period is subject to these unemployment taxes.

Two entries were required to record the payroll in the combination journal — one to record the total earnings of the employees, the amounts withheld for FICA tax and income tax, and the net amount paid; the other to record the payroll taxes imposed on the employer.

Thursday, December 16

Received the following remittances from customers:

J. F. Yager, $277.58, on account.
S. W. Novak, $480.87, in full settlement of account.
C. E. Wuller, $477.84, in full settlement of account.

Since a page of the combination journal was filled at this point, the totals of the amount columns were recorded on the double ruled line at the bottom of the page, after which they were carried forward and entered at the top of the next page.

Friday, December 17

Sold merchandise on credit as follows:

No. 239C, K. E. Vivian, 1830 Patterson Rd., Florissant, MO 63031-1830, $428.90, tax $21.45.

No. 246D, E. E. Palmer, 1129 Mackinac, St. Louis, MO 63141-3031, $88.60, tax $4.43.

No. 277A, W. R. Price, 1629 Rathford Ct., St. Louis, MO 63141-3563, $200.35, tax, $10.02.

Saturday, December 18

Issued checks as follows:

No. 774, El Jay Co., $2,027.22, in payment of invoice of December 10, $2,203.50 less discount of $176.28.

No. 775, Huk-A-Poo, Inc., $650.30, in payment of invoice of December 11, $706.85 less discount of $56.55.

Cash and bank credit card sales for the week:

Salesperson	Merchandise	Tax	Total
A	$1,277.25	$ 63.86	$1,341.11
B	1,041.70	52.09	1,093.79
C	929.20	46.46	975.66
D	1,092.05	54.60	1,146.65
	$4,340.20	$217.01	$4,557.21

END-OF-THE-WEEK WORK

(1) Proved the footings of the combination journal. (2) Deposited $5,793.50 in the First National Bank and proved the bank balance, $10,024.29. (3) Posted each entry individually from the General Debit and Credit columns of the combination journal to the proper general ledger accounts. (4) Proved the footings of the petty cash disbursements record and proved the balance of the petty cash fund, $100.50. (5) Proved the footings of the sales journal.

Monday, December 20

Issued Charge-Back Invoice No. 181 for $85 to Aris Glove Co., for merchandise returned; to be applied on Invoice No. 198 received on December 13.

This transaction was recorded in the combination journal by debiting Accounts Payable and crediting Purchases Returns and Allowances. It was also posted directly to the account of the Aris Glove Co. in the accounts payable ledger from the charge-back invoice.

Tuesday, December 21

Issued Check No. 776 for $1,500 to Boyd for personal use.
Made petty cash disbursements as follows:

Advertising, $9.75. Petty Cash Voucher No. 67.
Supplies, $12.50. Petty Cash Voucher No. 68.
Miscellaneous expense, $2.25. Petty Cash Voucher No. 69.

Wednesday, December 22

Issued Check No. 777 for $21.85 to United Parcel Service in payment of statement for delivery service for month ended December 15.

Few of the customers of Boyd's Clothiers wish to have their purchases delivered. In some special circumstances, one of the employees handles deliveries. In some cases, United Parcel Service is used. Since the monthly amount is small, Miscellaneous Expense is debited when the charge is paid.

Thursday, December 23

Sold merchandise on credit as follows:

No. 262B, D. P. Walsh, 113 Grether, St. Louis, MO 63135-4725, $24.10, tax, $1.21.
No. 249D, C. W. Reed, 761 Cella, St. Louis, Mo 63124-3301, $248.85, tax, $12.44.
No. 256C, L. V. Freeman, 7362 S. Yorkshire, St. Louis, MO 63126-1416, $23.35, tax, $1.17.

Friday, December 24

Received the following remittances from customers:

W. R. Price, $150, on account.
C. W. Reed, $400, on account.

Made petty cash disbursements as follows:

Advertising, $7.25. Petty Cash Voucher No. 70.
Supplies, $13.73. Petty Cash Voucher No. 71.
Miscellaneous expense, $4.35. Petty Cash Voucher No. 72.

Cash and bank credit card sales for the 5-day period:

Salesperson	Merchandise	Tax	Total
A	$ 861.68	$ 43.08	$ 904.76
B	939.80	46.99	986.79
C	436.70	21.84	458.54
D	695.90	34.80	730.70
	$2,934.08	$146.71	$3,080.79

END-OF-THE-WEEK WORK

(1) Proved the footings of the combination journal. (2) Deposited $3,630.79 in the First National Bank and proved the bank balance, $12,133.23. (3) Posted each entry individually from the General Debit and Credit columns of the combination journal to the proper general ledger accounts. (4) Proved the footings of the petty cash disbursements record and proved the balance of the petty cash fund, $50.67. (5) Proved the footings of the sales journal.

Monday, December 27

Issued Credit Memorandum No. 22 for $29.35 to W. R. Price for merchandise returned. (Sales price of merchandise, $27.95; tax, $1.40.)

Issued Check No. 778 for $547.70 to the Globe Publishing Co. in payment of advertising bill.

Received a notice from the First National Bank that $480.87 had been deducted from the account of Boyd's Clothiers, because a check from S. W. Novak deposited a few days before had not been paid by Novak's bank due to insufficient funds. Novak's check was enclosed with the notice.

The amount of the check was debited immediately to Novak's account in the accounts receivable ledger with the notation "NSF" (not sufficient funds). An entry was made in the combination journal debiting Accounts Receivable with a credit in the Bank column. A deduction was made on the following check stub.

Tuesday, December 28

Issued checks as follows:

No. 779, The Ozark Bell Telephone Co., $41.80, for telephone service.

No. 780, The Central States Gas & Electric Co., $95.26, for gas and electricity.

No. 781, Daniel Hays Co., $296, in payment of invoice of November 30, no discount.

Wednesday, December 29

Received invoice from Jacob Siegel Co., 4725 N. Broad St., Philadelphia, PA 19141-1612, $1,690, for merchandise purchased per Invoice No. 201 of December 27. Terms, 6/10, n/30.

Thursday, December 30

Received the following invoices:

Brown Shoe Co., 8300 Maryland Ave., St. Louis, MO 63105-3101, $915 per invoice No. 202 of December 27. Terms 2/10, n/30.

El Jay Co., 411 Anderson, Fairview, NJ 07022-2710, $880 per Invoice No. 203 of December 27. Terms 8/10, n/30.

Hanes Corporation, Winston-Salem, NC 27102-7022, $193.40 per Invoice No. 204 of December 27. Terms 8/10, EOM.

Marx Neuman Co., 9 W. 57th St., New York, NY 10019-2111, $785 per Invoice No. 205 of December 27. Terms 2/10, n/30.

Webster Safe & Lock Co., 916 Washington Ave., St. Louis, MO 63101-3011, $730, safe purchased per invoice of December 29. Terms 2/30, n/60.

The first four invoices were recorded in the purchases journal in the usual manner. The invoice received from the Webster Safe & Lock Co. was recorded in the combination journal by debiting Store Equipment and crediting Accounts Payable. In this enterprise, the purchases journal is used only for recording invoices covering merchandise purchased on account.

Friday, December 31

Cash and bank credit card sales:

Salesperson	Merchandise	Tax	Total
A	$ 554.33	$27.72	$ 582.05
B	369.05	18.45	387.50
C	346.95	17.35	364.30
D	321.60	16.08	337.68
	$1,591.93	$79.60	$1,671.53

Issued Check No. 782 payable to Payroll for $845.33.

PAYROLL STATEMENT FOR PERIOD ENDED DECEMBER 31

Total wages and commissions earned during period		$1,149.50
Employees' taxes to be withheld:		
Employees' income tax	$223.70	
FICA tax, 7% of $1,149.50	80.47	304.17
Net amount payable to employees		$ 845.33
Employer's payroll taxes:		
FICA tax, 7% of $1,149.50		$ 80.47
Unemployment compensation taxes —		
State unemployment tax, 2.7% of $134.90		3.64
FUTA tax, 0.7% of $134.90		.94
Total		$ 85.05

Issued Check No. 783 for $99.33 to replenish the petty cash fund.

STATEMENT OF PETTY CASH DISBURSEMENTS FOR DECEMBER

Lynn C. Boyd, drawing...	$20.00
Supplies..	41.23
Advertising expense	17.00
Charitable contributions expense...	10.00
Miscellaneous expense..	11.10
Total disbursements	$99.33

Before the above statement was prepared, the totals of the petty cash disbursements record were entered, and the record was ruled with single and double lines. The balance was then brought down below the double rules. The amount received to replenish the fund was added to the balance and the total, $150, was entered in the Description column.

The amount of the check issued was entered in the combination journal by debiting the proper accounts and crediting the bank account. It should be remembered that no posting is done from the petty cash disbursements record; the proper accounts will be charged for the petty cash disbursements when the posting is completed from the combination journal.

ROUTINE END-OF-THE-MONTH WORK

(1) Proved the footings and entered the totals in the combination journal and the sales journal; entered the total in the purchases journal. (2) Deposited $1,671.53 in the First National Bank and proved the bank balance, $11,398.47. (3) Completed the individual posting from the General Debit and Credit columns of the combination journal. (4) Completed the summary posting of the columnar totals of the combination journal, the purchases journal, and the sales journal to the proper accounts in the general ledger. (5) Ruled the combination journal, the purchases journal, and the sales journal. (6) Prepared a trial balance and schedules of accounts receivable and accounts payable.

	DATE	INVOICE NO.	FROM WHOM PURCHASED	POST. REF.	AMOUNT	
PURCHASES JOURNAL					PAGE 32	
1	19-- Dec. 2	194	Daniel Hays Co.	✓	29600	1
2	2	195	Hanes Corporation	✓	96700	2
3	2	196	Julius Resnick, Inc.	✓	193400	3
4	6	197	Damon, Inc.	✓	149500	4
5	13	198	Aris Glove Co.	✓	53625	5
6	13	199	El Jay Co.	✓	220350	6
7	13	200	Huk-A-Poo, Inc.	✓	70685	7
8	29	201	Jacob Siegel Co	✓	169000	8
9	30	202	Brown Shoe Co.	✓	91500	9
10	30	203	El Jay Co.	✓	88000	10
11	30	204	Hanes Corporation	✓	19340	11
12	30	205	Marx Neuman Co.	✓	78500	12
13			Purchases Dr. - Accounts Payable Cr.	711/318	1260200	13
14						14
15						15
16						16

Boyd's Clothiers — Purchases Journal

	DATE	SALE NO.	TO WHOM SOLD	POST. REF.	ACCOUNTS RECEIVABLE DR.	SALES CR.	SALES TAX PAYABLE CR.	
SALES JOURNAL							PAGE 44	
1	19-- Dec. 4	271D	D. P. Walsh	✓	59021	56210	2811	1
2	4	257B	J. J. Anders	✓	11619	11066	553	2
3	4	235C	J. L. Burnett	✓	73431	69934	3497	3
4	6	259B	J. F. Yager	✓	14513	13822	691	4
5	9	243B	R. D. Williams	✓	33584	31985	1599	5
6	17	239C	K. E. Vivian	✓	45035	42890	2145	6
7	17	246B	E. E. Palmer	✓	9303	8860	443	7
8	17	277D	W. H. Price	✓	21037	20035	1002	8
9	23	262B	D. P. Walsh	✓	2531	2410	121	9
10	23	249B	C. W. Reed	✓	26129	24885	1244	10
11	23	256C	L. V. Freeman	✓	2452	2335	117	11
12					298655	284432	14223	12
13					(131)	(611)	(321)	13
14								14
15								15
16								16

Boyd's Clothiers — Sales Journal

47 PAGE   COMBINATION JOURNAL

	FIRST NATIONAL BANK		PURCHASES DISCOUNT CR.	CK. NO.	DAY	DESCRIPTION	POST. REF.	
	DEPOSITS DR.	CHECKS CR.						
1						AMOUNTS FORWARDED *Balance 15,993.64*		1
2		90000		757	1	Rent Expense	821	2
3		6914		758	1	Purchases	711	3
4		42900		759	1	Aris Glove Co.	✓	4
5	41240				3	D. P. Walsh	✓	5
6		30605			3	Bank Credit Card Expense	832	6
7	297792 339032				4	Cash + bank credit card sales for wk. 17,679.77	✓	7
8		170419 59878	1222	760	6	Brown Shoe Co.	✓	8
9		56212	3588	761	6	Damon, Inc.	✓	9
10		270296	23504	762	6	El Jay Co	✓	10
11		101920	2080	763	6	Mary Neuman Co.	✓	11
12		146640	9360	764	6	Shoeneman, Inc.	✓	12
13		163668	14232	765	6	Smart Pants, Inc.	✓	13
14		7935		766	6	Advertising Expense	826	14
15		118578		767	6	Sales Tax Payable	321	15
16		88900		768	8	Daniel Hays Co.	✓	16
17		88964	7736	769	8	Hanes Corporation	✓	17
18		187598	5802	770	8	Julius Resnick, Inc.	✓	18
19		11545			8	Sales Returns + Allowances	611.1	19
20						Sales Tax Payable	321	20
21		65092		771	9	FICA Tax Payable	311	21
22						Employees Income Tax Pay.	314	22
23	40000				10	J. E. Buelt	✓	23
24	30000				10	L. V. Freeman	✓	24
25	10674				10	K. E. Vivian	✓	25
26	434832 854588				11	Cash + bank credit card sales for wk. 9,162.57	✓	26
27		1587645 140530	67524 8970	772	14	Damon, Inc.	✓	27
28		84896		773	15	Salaries + Commissions Exp.	822	28
29						FICA Tax Payable	311	29
30						Employees Income Tax Pay.	314	30
31					15	Payroll Taxes Expense	831	31
32						FICA Tax Payable	311	32
33						FUTA Tax Payable	312	33
34						State Unemployment Tax Pay.	313	34
35	27758				16	J. F. Yager	✓	35
36	48087				16	S. W. Novak	✓	36
37	47784				16	C. E. Wuller	✓ 5,144.60	37
38	975167 978167	1763071	76494		16	Carried forward		38

Boyd's Clothiers — Combination Journal (Left Page)
(continued on next page)

FOR MONTH OF *December*　19 - -　　　PAGE 47

	GENERAL		ACCOUNTS PAYABLE DR.	ACCOUNTS RECEIVABLE CR.	SALES CR.	SALES TAX PAYABLE CR.	
	DEBIT	CREDIT					
1							1
2	90000						2
3	6914						3
4			42900				4
5				41240			5
6	30605						6
7					283611	14181	7
8	127519		42900	41240	283611	14181	8
9			61100 59800				9
10			293800				10
11			104000				11
12			156000				12
13			177900				13
14	7935						14
15	118578						15
16			88900				16
17			96700				17
18			193400				18
19	10995						19
20	550						20
21	36972						21
22	28120						22
23				40000			23
24				30000			24
25				10674			25
26	350669		1274500	121914	414126 697737	20706 34887	26
27			149500				27
28	116050						28
29		8124					29
30		23030					30
31	8587						31
32		8124					32
33		95					33
34		368					34
35				27758			35
36				48087			36
37				47784			37
38	455306	39741	1424000	245543	697737	34887	38

Boyd's Clothiers — Combination Journal (Right Page)
(continued on next page)

48 PAGE   COMBINATION JOURNAL

	FIRST NATIONAL BANK		PURCHASES DISCOUNT CR.	CK. NO.	DAY	DESCRIPTION	POST. REF.	
	DEPOSITS DR.	CHECKS CR.						
1	978167	1763071	76494			AMOUNTS FORWARDED		1
2		202722	17628	774	18	El Jay Co.	✓	2
3		65030	5655	775	18	Huk-A-Poo, Inc.	✓	3
4	455721				18	Cash + bank credit card sales for wk. 10,024.29	✓	4
5	1433855	2030523	99777		20	Purch. R. + A. - Aris Glove Co.	711.1	5
6		150000		776	21	Lynn C. Boyd, Drawing	511.1	6
7		2185		777	22	Miscellaneous Expense	839	7
8	15000				24	W. R. Price	✓	8
9	40000				24	C. W. Reed	✓	9
10	308079				24	Cash + bank credit card sales for wk. 12,133.28	✓	10
11	1796967	2153008	99777		27	Sales R. + A. - W. R. Price	611.1	11
12						Sales Tax Payable	321	12
13		54770		778	27	Advertising Expense	826	13
14		48087			27	Accounts Rec. - S. W. Novak	131	14
15		4180		779	28	Telephone Expense	824	15
16		9526		780	28	Heating + Lighting Exp.	823	16
17		29600		781	28	Daniel Hays Co.	✓	17
18					31	Store Equipment	211	18
19						Accts. Pay. - Webster Safe + Lock Co.	318	19
20	167153				31	Cash + bank credit card sales for wk.	✓	20
21		84533		782	31	Salaries + Commissions Exp.	822	21
22						FICA Tax Payable	311	22
23						Employees Income Tax Pay.	314	23
24					31	Payroll Taxes Expense	831	24
25						FICA Tax Payable	311	25
26						FUTA Tax Payable	312	26
27						State Unemployment Tax Pay.	313	27
28		9933		783	31	Lynn C. Boyd, Drawing	511.1	28
29						Supplies	181	29
30						Advertising Expense	826	30
31						Charitable Contributions Exp.	829	31
32	1964120	2423637	99777			Miscellaneous Expense 11,398.47	839	32
33	1964120	2423637	99777					33
34	(111)	(111)	(711.2)					34

Boyd's Clothiers — Combination Journal (Left Page)
(concluded)

FOR MONTH OF *December* 19 – –   PAGE *48*

	GENERAL DEBIT	GENERAL CREDIT	ACCOUNTS PAYABLE DR.	ACCOUNTS RECEIVABLE CR.	SALES CR.	SALES TAX PAYABLE CR.	
1	455306	39741	1424000	245543	697737	34887	1
2			220350				2
3			70685				3
4					434020	21701	4
5	455306	39741 / 8500	1716035 / 8500	245543	1131757	56588	5
6	150000						6
7		2185					7
8				15000			8
9				40000			9
10					293408	14671	10
11	607491 / 2795	43241	1729535	300543 / 2935	1425165	71259	11
12		140					12
13	54770						13
14	48087						14
15		4180					15
16		9526					16
17			29600				17
18	73000						18
19		73000					19
20					159193	7960	20
21	114950						21
22		8047					22
23		22370					23
24	8505						24
25		8047					25
26		94					26
27		364					27
28	2000						28
29	4123						29
30	1700						30
31	1000						31
32	1110						32
33	983377 / 933377	160163	1753135	303478	1584358	79219	33
34	(✓)	(✓)	(318)	(131)	(611)	(321)	34

Boyd's Clothiers — Combination Journal (Right Page)
(concluded)

PAGE 28   PETTY CASH DISBURSEMENTS

	DAY	DESCRIPTION		VOU. NO.	TOTAL AMOUNT	511.1	181	
1		AMOUNTS FORWARDED	150.00					1
2	7	Postage stamps		63	15 00		15 00	2
3	7	Messenger fee		64	4 50			3
4	14	Boy Scouts of America	130.50	65	19 50 / 10 00		15 00	4
5	14	Lynn C. Boyd, personal use		66	20 00	20 00		5
6	21	Advertising	100.50	67	49 50 / 9 75	20 00	15 00	6
7	21	Supplies		68	12 50		12 50	7
8	21	Miscellaneous expense		69	2 25			8
9	24	Advertising		70	7 25			9
10	24	Supplies		71	13 73		13 73	10
11	24	Miscellaneous expense		72	4 35			11
12			50.67		99 33 / 99 33	20 00	41 23 / 41 23	12
13	31	Balance	50.67					13
14	31	Received in fund	99.33					14
15		Total	150.00					15
16								16

Boyd's Clothiers — Petty Cash Disbursements Record (Left Page)

ACCOUNT *First National Bank*   ACCOUNT NO. 111

DATE	ITEM	POST. REF.	DEBIT	CREDIT	BALANCE DEBIT	BALANCE CREDIT
19-- Dec. 1	Balance	✓			1599364	
31		CJ48	1964120			
31		CJ48		2423637	1139847	

ACCOUNT *Petty Cash Fund*   ACCOUNT NO. 112

DATE	ITEM	POST. REF.	DEBIT	CREDIT	BALANCE DEBIT	BALANCE CREDIT
19-- Dec. 1	Balance	✓			15000	

Boyd's Clothiers — General Ledger

FOR MONTH OF December 19--						PAGE 28
DISTRIBUTION OF DEBITS						
826	829	839			ACCOUNT	AMOUNT
1						1
2						2
3		450 450				3
4	10 00					4
5						5
6 9 75	10 00	4 50				6
7						7
8		2 25				8
9 7 25						9
10						10
11		4 35				11
12 1700 1700	1000 1000	1110 1110				12
13						13

Boyd's Clothiers — Petty Cash Disbursements Record (Right Page)

ACCOUNT Accounts Receivable					ACCOUNT NO. 131	
DATE	ITEM	POST. REF.	DEBIT	CREDIT	BALANCE DEBIT	BALANCE CREDIT
19-- Dec. 1	Balance	✓			3855 79	
27		CJ48	480 87			
31		S44	2986 55			
31		CJ48		3034 78	4288 43	

ACCOUNT Allowance for Doubtful Accounts					ACCOUNT NO. 131.1	
DATE	ITEM	POST. REF.	DEBIT	CREDIT	BALANCE DEBIT	BALANCE CREDIT
19-- Dec. 1	Balance	✓				76 99

Boyd's Clothiers — General Ledger
(continued)

ACCOUNT *Merchandise Inventory*   ACCOUNT NO. 161

DATE	ITEM	POST. REF.	DEBIT	CREDIT	BALANCE DEBIT	BALANCE CREDIT
19-- Dec. 1	Balance	✓			3592210	

ACCOUNT *Supplies*   ACCOUNT NO. 181

DATE	ITEM	POST. REF.	DEBIT	CREDIT	BALANCE DEBIT	BALANCE CREDIT
19-- Dec. 1	Balance	✓			29936	
31		CJ48	4123		34059	

ACCOUNT *Prepaid Insurance*   ACCOUNT NO. 184

DATE	ITEM	POST. REF.	DEBIT	CREDIT	BALANCE DEBIT	BALANCE CREDIT
19-- Dec. 1	Balance	✓			73140	

ACCOUNT *Store Equipment*   ACCOUNT NO. 211

DATE	ITEM	POST. REF.	DEBIT	CREDIT	BALANCE DEBIT	BALANCE CREDIT
19-- Dec. 1	Balance	✓			654110	
31		CJ48	73000		727110	

ACCOUNT *Accumulated Depreciation - Store Equipment*   ACCOUNT NO. 211.1

DATE	ITEM	POST. REF.	DEBIT	CREDIT	BALANCE DEBIT	BALANCE CREDIT
19-- Dec. 1	Balance	✓				112070

Boyd's Clothiers — General Ledger
(continued)

ACCOUNT _FICA Tax Payable_   ACCOUNT NO. _311_

DATE		ITEM	POST. REF.	DEBIT	CREDIT	BALANCE DEBIT	BALANCE CREDIT
19-- Dec.	1	Balance	✓				36972
	9		CJ47	36972		-0-	-0-
	15		CJ47		8124		
	15		CJ47		8124		
	31		CJ48		8047		
	31		CJ48		8047		32342

ACCOUNT _FUTA Tax Payable_   ACCOUNT NO. _312_

DATE		ITEM	POST. REF.	DEBIT	CREDIT	BALANCE DEBIT	BALANCE CREDIT
19-- Dec.	1	Balance	✓				10785
	15		CJ47		95		
	31		CJ48		94		10974

ACCOUNT _State Unemployment Tax Payable_   ACCOUNT NO. _313_

DATE		ITEM	POST. REF.	DEBIT	CREDIT	BALANCE DEBIT	BALANCE CREDIT
19-- Dec.	1	Balance	✓				14010
	15		CJ47		368		
	31		CJ48		364		14742

ACCOUNT _Employees Income Tax Payable_   ACCOUNT NO. _314_

DATE		ITEM	POST. REF.	DEBIT	CREDIT	BALANCE DEBIT	BALANCE CREDIT
19-- Dec.	1	Balance	✓				28120
	9		CJ47	28120		-0-	-0-
	15		CJ47		23030		
	31		CJ48		22370		45400

Boyd's Clothiers — General Ledger
(continued)

ACCOUNT *Notes Payable*   ACCOUNT NO. 316

DATE	ITEM	POST. REF.	DEBIT	CREDIT	BALANCE DEBIT	BALANCE CREDIT
19-- Dec. 1	Balance	✓				400000

ACCOUNT *Accounts Payable*   ACCOUNT NO. 318

DATE	ITEM	POST. REF.	DEBIT	CREDIT	BALANCE DEBIT	BALANCE CREDIT
19-- Dec. 1	Balance	✓				984400
31		CJ48		73000		
31		P32		1260200		
31		CJ48	1753135			564465

ACCOUNT *Sales Tax Payable*   ACCOUNT NO. 321

DATE	ITEM	POST. REF.	DEBIT	CREDIT	BALANCE DEBIT	BALANCE CREDIT
19-- Dec. 1	Balance	✓				118578
6		CJ47	118578		-0-	-0-
8		CJ47	550			
27		CJ48	140			
31		S44		14223		
31		CJ48		79219		92752

ACCOUNT *Lynn C. Boyd, Capital*   ACCOUNT NO. 511

DATE	ITEM	POST. REF.	DEBIT	CREDIT	BALANCE DEBIT	BALANCE CREDIT
19-- Dec. 1	Balance	✓				3313590

ACCOUNT *Lynn C. Boyd, Drawing*   ACCOUNT NO. 511.1

DATE	ITEM	POST. REF.	DEBIT	CREDIT	BALANCE DEBIT	BALANCE CREDIT
19-- Dec. 1	Balance	✓			2912750	
21		CJ48	150000			
31		CJ48	2000		3064750	

Boyd's Clothiers — General Ledger
(continued)

ACCOUNT *Sales*   ACCOUNT NO. 611

DATE		ITEM	POST. REF.	DEBIT	CREDIT	BALANCE	
						DEBIT	CREDIT
19-- Dec.	1	Balance	✓				24255537
	31		S44		284432		
	31		CJ48		1584358		26124327

ACCOUNT *Sales Returns and Allowances*   ACCOUNT NO. 611.1

DATE		ITEM	POST. REF.	DEBIT	CREDIT	BALANCE	
						DEBIT	CREDIT
19-- Dec.	1	Balance	✓			371130	
	8		CJ47	10995			
	27		CJ48	2795		384920	

ACCOUNT *Purchases*   ACCOUNT NO. 711

DATE		ITEM	POST. REF.	DEBIT	CREDIT	BALANCE	
						DEBIT	CREDIT
19-- Dec.	1	Balance	✓			15406694	
	1		CJ47	6914			
	31		P32	1260200		16673808	

ACCOUNT *Purchases Returns and Allowances*   ACCOUNT NO. 711.1

DATE		ITEM	POST. REF.	DEBIT	CREDIT	BALANCE	
						DEBIT	CREDIT
19-- Dec.	1	Balance	✓				215160
	20		CJ48		8500		223660

ACCOUNT *Purchases Discount*   ACCOUNT NO. 711.2

DATE		ITEM	POST. REF.	DEBIT	CREDIT	BALANCE	
						DEBIT	CREDIT
19-- Dec.	1	Balance	✓				899865
	31		CJ48		99777		999642

Boyd's Clothiers — General Ledger
(continued)

ACCOUNT *Rent Expense*   ACCOUNT NO. 821

DATE	ITEM	POST. REF.	DEBIT	CREDIT	BALANCE DEBIT	BALANCE CREDIT
19-- Dec. 1	Balance	✓			990000	
1		CJ47	90000		1080000	

ACCOUNT *Salaries and Commissions Expense*   ACCOUNT NO. 822

DATE	ITEM	POST. REF.	DEBIT	CREDIT	BALANCE DEBIT	BALANCE CREDIT
19-- Dec. 1	Balance	✓			2540135	
15		CJ47	116050			
31		CJ48	114950		2771135	

ACCOUNT *Heating and Lighting Expense*   ACCOUNT NO. 823

DATE	ITEM	POST. REF.	DEBIT	CREDIT	BALANCE DEBIT	BALANCE CREDIT
19-- Dec. 1	Balance	✓			89227	
28		CJ48	9526		98753	

ACCOUNT *Telephone Expense*   ACCOUNT NO. 824

DATE	ITEM	POST. REF.	DEBIT	CREDIT	BALANCE DEBIT	BALANCE CREDIT
19-- Dec. 1	Balance	✓			44220	
28		CJ48	4180		48400	

ACCOUNT *Advertising Expense*   ACCOUNT NO. 826

DATE	ITEM	POST. REF.	DEBIT	CREDIT	BALANCE DEBIT	BALANCE CREDIT
19-- Dec. 1	Balance	✓			1068575	
6		CJ47	7935			
27		CJ48	54770			
31		CJ48	1700		1132980	

Boyd's Clothiers — General Ledger
(continued)

ACCOUNT *Charitable Contributions Expense*   ACCOUNT NO. *829*

DATE		ITEM	POST. REF.	DEBIT	CREDIT	BALANCE	
						DEBIT	CREDIT
19-- Dec.	1	Balance	✓			44850	
	31		CJ48	1000		45850	

ACCOUNT *Payroll Taxes Expense*   ACCOUNT NO. *831*

DATE		ITEM	POST. REF.	DEBIT	CREDIT	BALANCE	
						DEBIT	CREDIT
19-- Dec.	1	Balance	✓			221428	
	15		CJ47	8587			
	31		CJ48	8505		238520	

ACCOUNT *Bank Credit Card Expense*   ACCOUNT NO. *832*

DATE		ITEM	POST. REF.	DEBIT	CREDIT	BALANCE	
						DEBIT	CREDIT
19-- Dec.	1	Balance	✓			283390	
	3		CJ47	30605		313995	

ACCOUNT *Miscellaneous Expense*   ACCOUNT NO. *839*

DATE		ITEM	POST. REF.	DEBIT	CREDIT	BALANCE	
						DEBIT	CREDIT
19-- Dec.	1	Balance	✓			59956	
	22		CJ48	2185			
	31		CJ48	1110		63251	

ACCOUNT *Interest Expense*   ACCOUNT NO. *911*

DATE		ITEM	POST. REF.	DEBIT	CREDIT	BALANCE	
						DEBIT	CREDIT
19-- Dec.	1	Balance	✓			15092	

Boyd's Clothiers — General Ledger
(concluded)

NAME J. J. Anders
ADDRESS 11939 Rocky, St. Louis, MO 63141-1353

	DATE	ITEM	POST. REF.	DEBIT	CREDIT	BALANCE	
1	19-- Dec. 4		S25T8	11619		11619	1

NAME J. E. Buelt
ADDRESS 9140 Fox Estates, St. Louis, MO 63126-4431

	DATE	ITEM	POST. REF.	DEBIT	CREDIT	BALANCE	
1	19-- Dec. 1	Dr. Balance	✓			79932	1
2	10		C		40000	39932	2

NAME J. L. Burnett
ADDRESS 15 Forester, St. Louis, MO 63011-2631

	DATE	ITEM	POST. REF.	DEBIT	CREDIT	BALANCE	
1	19-- Dec. 4		S235C	73431		73431	1

NAME L. V. Freeman
ADDRESS 7362 S. Yorkshire, St. Louis, MO 63126-1416

	DATE	ITEM	POST. REF.	DEBIT	CREDIT	BALANCE	
1	19-- Dec. 1	Dr. Balance	✓			56212	1
2	10		C		30000	26212	2
3	23		S256C	2452		28664	3

NAME S. W. Novak
ADDRESS 216 Hawkesbury, St. Louis, MO 63135-2463

	DATE	ITEM	POST. REF.	DEBIT	CREDIT	BALANCE	
1	19-- Dec. 1	Dr. Balance	✓			48087	1
2	16		C		48087	-0-	2
3	27	NSF		48087		48087	3

NAME E. E. Palmer
ADDRESS 1129 Mackinac, St. Louis, MO 63141-3031

	DATE	ITEM	POST. REF.	DEBIT	CREDIT	BALANCE	
1	19-- Dec. 1	Dr. Balance	✓			14580	1
2	17		S246D	9303		23883	2

Boyd's Clothiers — Accounts Receivable Ledger

NAME *W. R. Price*
ADDRESS *1629 Rathford Court, St. Louis, MO 63141-3563*

	DATE	ITEM	POST. REF.	DEBIT	CREDIT	BALANCE	
1	19-- Dec. 1	Dr. Balance	✓			18485	1
2	17		S277a	21037		39522	2
3	24		C		15000	24522	3
4	27		CM22		2935	21587	4

NAME *C. W. Reed*
ADDRESS *761 Cella, St. Louis, MO 63124-3301*

	DATE	ITEM	POST. REF.	DEBIT	CREDIT	BALANCE	
1	19-- Dec. 1	Dr. Balance	✓			40827	1
2	23		S249D	26129		66956	2
3	24		C		40000	26956	3

NAME *K. E. Vivian*
ADDRESS *1830 Patterson Rd., Florissant, MO 63031-1830*

	DATE	ITEM	POST. REF	DEBIT	CREDIT	BALANCE	
1	19-- Dec. 1	Dr. Balance	✓			10674	1
2	10		C		10674	-0-	2
3	17		S239C	45035		45035	3

NAME *D. P. Walsh*
ADDRESS *113 Grether, St. Louis, MO 63135-4725*

	DATE	ITEM	POST. REF.	DEBIT	CREDIT	BALANCE	
1	19-- Dec. 1	Dr. Balance	✓			41240	1
2	3		C		41240	-0-	2
3	4		S271a	59021		59021	3
4	23		S262B	2531		61552	4

NAME *R. D. Williams*
ADDRESS *617 Rebecca, St. Charles, MO 63301-3122*

	DATE	ITEM	POST. REF.	DEBIT	CREDIT	BALANCE	
1	19-- Dec. 9		S243D	33584		33584	1

Boyd's Clothiers — Accounts Receivable Ledger
(continued)

NAME *C. E. Wuller*

ADDRESS *10711 St. Mathew Ln., St. Ann, MO 63074-4119*

	DATE	ITEM	POST. REF.	DEBIT	CREDIT	BALANCE	
1	19-- Dec. 1	Dr. Balance	✓			477 84	1
2	16		C		477 84	–0–	2

NAME *J. F. Yager*

ADDRESS *5 Brookston Ct., Kirkwood, MO 63122-3074*

	DATE	ITEM	POST. REF.	DEBIT	CREDIT	BALANCE	
1	19-- Dec. 1	Dr. Balance	✓			277 58	1
2	6		S259B	145 13		422 71	2
3	16		C		277 58	145 13	3

Boyd's Clothiers — Accounts Receivable Ledger
(concluded)

NAME *Aris Glove Co.*

ADDRESS *10 East 38th St., New York, NY 10016-6310*

	DATE	ITEM	POST. REF.	DEBIT	CREDIT	BALANCE	
1	19-- Dec. 1	Cr. Balance				429 00	1
2	1		Ck759	429 00		–0–	2
3	13	12/10 – n/30	P198		536 25	536 25	3
4	20		CB181	85 00		451 25	4
5							5

NAME *Brown Shoe Co.*

ADDRESS *8300 Maryland Ave., St. Louis, MO 63105-3101*

	DATE	ITEM	POST. REF.	DEBIT	CREDIT	BALANCE	
1	19-- Dec. 1	Cr. Balance				611 00	1
2	6		Ck760	598 78			2
3	6	Discount		12 22		–0–	3
4	30	12/27 – 2/10, n/30	P202		915 00	915 00	4
5							5

Boyd's Clothiers — Accounts Payable Ledger

NAME *Damon, Inc.*
ADDRESS *16 E. 34th St., New York, N.Y. 10016-3141*

	DATE	ITEM	POST. REF.	DEBIT	CREDIT	BALANCE	
1	19-- Dec. 1	Cr. Balance				598 00	1
2	6		Ck 761	562 12			2
3	6	Discount		35 88		-0-	3
4	6	12/4 - 6/10, n/30	P197		1495 00	1495 00	4
5	14		Ck 772	1405 30			5
6	14	Discount		89 70		-0-	6

NAME *El Jay Co.*
ADDRESS *411 Anderson, Fairview, N.J. 07022-2710*

	DATE	ITEM	POST. REF.	DEBIT	CREDIT	BALANCE	
1	19-- Dec. 1	Cr. Balance				2938 00	1
2	6		Ck 762	2702 96			2
3	6	Discount		235 04		-0-	3
4	13	12/10 - 8/10, n/30	P199		2203 50	2203 50	4
5	18		Ck 774	2027 22			5
6	18	Discount		176 28		-0-	6
7	30	12/27 - 8/10, n/30	P203		880 00	880 00	7

NAME *Hanes Corporation*
ADDRESS *Winston - Salem, N.C. 27102-7022*

	DATE	ITEM	POST. REF.	DEBIT	CREDIT	BALANCE	
1	19-- Dec. 2	11/30 - 8/10 EOM	P195		967 00	967 00	1
2	8		Ck 769	889 64			2
3	8	Discount		77 36		-0-	3
4	30	12/27 - 8/10 EOM	P204		193 40	193 40	4

NAME *Daniel Hays Co.*
ADDRESS *Johnstown, N.Y. 12095-1001*

	DATE	ITEM	POST. REF.	DEBIT	CREDIT	BALANCE	
1	19-- Dec. 1	Cr. Balance				889 00	1
2	2	11/30 - n/30	P194		296 00	1185 00	2
3	8		Ck 768	889 00		296 00	3
4	28		Ck 781	296 00		-0-	4

Boyd's Clothiers — Accounts Payable Ledger
(continued)

NAME *Huk-A-Poo, Inc.*
ADDRESS *411 Broadway, New York, NY 10012-1209*

	DATE	ITEM	POST. REF.	DEBIT	CREDIT	BALANCE	
1	19-- Dec. 13	12/11 – 8/10, n/30	P200		706 85	706 85	1
2	18		Ck 775	650 30			2
3	18	Discount			56 55	–0–	3

NAME *Mary Neuman Co.*
ADDRESS *9 W. 57th St., New York, NY 10019-2111*

	DATE	ITEM	POST. REF.	DEBIT	CREDIT	BALANCE	
1	19-- Dec. 1	Cr. Balance				1040 00	1
2	6		Ck 763	1019 20			2
3	6	Discount		20 80		–0–	3
4	30	12/27 – 2/10, n/30	P205		785 00	785 00	4

NAME *Julius Resnick, Inc.*
ADDRESS *46 E. 32d St., New York, NY 10016-1619*

	DATE	ITEM	POST. REF.	DEBIT	CREDIT	BALANCE	
1	19-- Dec. 2	11/30 – 3/10 EOM	P196		1934 00	1934 00	1
2	8		Ck 770	1875 98			2
3	8	Discount		58 02		–0–	3

NAME *Schoeneman, Inc.*
ADDRESS *Box 17, Owings Mills, MD 21117-1914*

	DATE	ITEM	POST. REF.	DEBIT	CREDIT	BALANCE	
1	19-- Dec. 1	Cr. Balance				1560 00	1
2	6		Ck 764	1466 40			2
3	6	Discount		93 60		–0–	3

NAME *Jacob Siegel Co.*
ADDRESS *4725 N. Broad St., Philadelphia, PA 19141-1612*

	DATE	ITEM	POST. REF.	DEBIT	CREDIT	BALANCE	
1	19-- Dec. 29	12/27 – 6/10, n/30	P201		1690 00	1690 00	1

Boyd's Clothiers — Accounts Payable Ledger
(continued)

	DATE	ITEM	POST. REF.	DEBIT	CREDIT	BALANCE	
	19--						
1	Dec. 1	Cr. Balance				1 77900	1
2	6		Ck 765	1 63668			2
3	6	Discount		1 4232		-0-	3

NAME *Smart Pants, Inc.*
ADDRESS *1407 Broadway, New York, N.Y. 10012-3126*

	DATE	ITEM	POST. REF.	DEBIT	CREDIT	BALANCE	
	19--						
1	Dec. 30	12/29 - 2/30, n/60	CJ 48		7 3000	7 3000	1
2							2
3							3

NAME *Webster Safe & Lock Co.*
ADDRESS *916 Washington Ave., St. Louis, MO 63101-3011*

Boyd's Clothiers — Accounts Payable Ledger
(concluded)

Boyd's Clothiers
Schedule of Accounts Receivable

	Nov. 30, 19--	Dec. 31, 19--
J. J. Anders		1 16 19
J. E. Buelt	79932	3 9932
J. L. Burnett		7 3431
L. V. Freeman	5 6212	2 8664
S. W. Novak	4 8087	4 8087
E. E. Palmer	1 4580	2 3883
W. R. Price	1 8485	2 1587
C. W. Reed	4 0827	2 6956
K. E. Vivian	1 0674	4 5035
D. P. Walsh	4 1240	6 1552
R. D. Williams		3 3584
C. E. Wuller	4 7784	
J. F. Yager	2 7758	1 4513
	3 85579	4 28843
	3 85579	4 28843

Boyd's Clothiers — Schedule of Accounts Receivable

Boyd's Clothiers
Trial Balance

Account	Acct. No.	November 30, 19-- Debit	November 30, 19-- Credit	December 31, 19-- Debit	December 31, 19-- Credit
First National Bank	111	1599364		1139847	
Petty Cash Fund	112	15000		15000	
Accounts Receivable	131	385579		428843	
Allow. for Doubt. Accts.	131.1		7699		7699
Merchandise Inventory	161	3592210		3592210	
Supplies	181	29936		34059	
Prepaid Insurance	184	73140		73140	
Store Equipment	211	654110		727110	
Accum. Depr.-Store Equip.	211.1		112070		112070
FICA Tax Payable	311		36972		32342
FUTA Tax Payable	312		10785		10974
State Unemp. Tax Pay.	313		14010		14742
Employees Inc. Tax Pay.	314		28120		45400
Notes Payable	316		400000		400000
Accounts Payable	318		984400		564465
Sales Tax Payable	321		118578		92752
Lynn C. Boyd, Capital	511		3313590		3313590
Lynn C. Boyd, Drawing	511.1	2912750		3064750	
Sales	611		24255537		26124327
Sales Ret. and Allow.	611.1	371130		384920	
Purchases	711	15406694		16673808	
Pur. Ret. and Allow.	711.1		215160		223660
Purchases Discount	711.2		899865		999642
Rent Expense	821	990000		1080000	
Sal. and Comm. Expense	822	2540135		2771135	
Heating & Light Expense	823	89227		98753	
Telephone Expense	824	44220		48400	
Advertising Expense	826	1068575		1132980	
Charitable Cont. Expense	829	44850		45850	
Payroll Taxes Expense	831	221428		238520	
Bank Credit Card Exp.	832	283390		313995	
Miscellaneous Expense	839	59956		63251	
Interest Expense	911	15092		15092	
		30396786	30396786	31941663	31941663
		30396786	30396786	31941663	31941663

Boyd's Clothiers — Trial Balance

Boyd's Clothiers *Schedule of Accounts Payable*	*Nov. 30, 19--*	*Dec. 31, 19--*
Aris Glove Co.	429 00	451 25
Brown Shoe Co.	611 00	915 00
Damon, Inc.	598 00	
El Jay Co.	2938 00	880 00
Hanes Corporation		193 40
Daniel Hays Co.	889 00	
Mark Neuman	1040 00	785 00
Schoeneman, Inc.	1560 00	
Jacob Siegel Co.		1690 00
Smart Pants, Inc.	1779 00	
Webster Safe & Lock Co.		730 00
	9844 00	5644 65
	9844 00	5644 65

Boyd's Clothiers — Schedule of Accounts Payable

BUILDING YOUR ACCOUNTING KNOWLEDGE

1. Why are account numbers more widely used than account names in a system of records requiring numerous accounts?
2. In addition to the two special columns used in recording banking transactions, name five other special columns found in Boyd's combination journal.
3. What kinds of transactions are recorded in Boyd's purchases journal?
4. What kinds of transactions are recorded in Boyd's sales journal?
5. What are the names and account forms of the three ledgers used by Boyd?
6. What are the three auxiliary records maintained by Boyd?
7. Why are check marks placed in the Posting Reference columns of Boyd's purchases and sales journals?
8. Why are check marks placed below the totals of the General Debit and Credit columns of Boyd's combination journal?

Report No. 8-2

> Complete Report No. 8-2 in the study assignments and submit your working papers to the instructor for approval. After completing this report, continue with the textbook discussion in Chapter 9 until the next report is required.

EXPANDING YOUR BUSINESS VOCABULARY

What is the meaning of each of the following terms?

Accounts Payable — Control (p. 215)

Accounts Receivable — Control (p. 216)

accrual basis of accounting (p. 206)

bad debts expense (p. 208)

chart of accounts (p. 220)

contra account (p. 208)

control accounts (p. 215)

depreciation accounting (p. 211)

end-of-period adjustments (p. 207)

loss from uncollectible accounts (p. 208)

materiality (p. 207)

net cost (p. 212)

prepaid expense (p. 210)

reducing-charge methods (p. 212)

statement of account (p. 218)

straight-line method (p. 212)

subsidiary ledgers (p. 214)

three-column account form (p. 214)

uncollectible accounts expense (p. 208)

CHAPTER 9

THE PERIODIC SUMMARY

CHAPTER OBJECTIVES

The objectives of this chapter are to enable you:

▶ To prepare a ten-column end-of-year work sheet for a retail business, including the following adjustments:

(1) The two adjustments needed to combine the beginning and ending merchandise inventory components of cost of goods sold.
(2) The adjustment needed to recognize accrued interest payable.
(3) The adjustment needed to recognize accrued bank credit card payable.
(4) The two adjustments needed to recognize the cost of supplies and insurance premiums applicable to the year just ended.
(5) The two adjustments needed to recognize the amount of uncollectible accounts expense expected to result from the past year's charge sales and the amount of depreciation of property, plant, and equipment assets during the past year.

▶ To prepare the financial statements of a retail merchandising business.

▶ To analyze financial statements using some basic techniques.

▶ To describe the business owner's, as distinguished from the business', responsibility for income and self-employment taxes.

One of the major reasons for keeping accounting records is to accumulate information that will make it possible to prepare periodic summaries for (1) the revenue and expenses of the business during a specified period and (2) the assets, liabilities, and owner's equity of the business at a specified date. A trial balance of the general ledger accounts provides most of the information that is required for these summaries (the income statement and the balance sheet). However, the trial balance does not supply the data in a form that is easily interpreted, nor does it reflect changes in the accounting elements that have not been represented by ordinary business transactions. Therefore, at the end of a fiscal period, it is necessary (1) to determine the kinds and amounts of changes that the accounts do not reflect and adjust the accounts accordingly and (2) to recast the information into the form of an income statement and a balance sheet. These two steps are often referred to as the periodic summary.

END-OF-PERIOD WORK SHEET

It has already been mentioned that an end-of-period work sheet is a device that assists the accountant in three ways. It facilitates (1) the preparation of the financial statements, (2) the making of needed adjustments in the accounts, and (3) the closing of the temporary owner's equity accounts. In most cases, management is interested in reviewing the income statement and the balance sheet as soon as possible after the period has ended.

Work sheets are not financial statements; they are devices used to assist the accountant in performing certain tasks. Ordinarily, it is only the accountant who uses a work sheet. For this reason, a work sheet is usually prepared in pencil.

A WORK SHEET FOR A RETAIL STORE

While an end-of-period work sheet can be in any one of several forms, a common and widely used arrangement involves ten amount columns consisting of five pairs. The first pair of amount columns is for the trial balance. The data to be recorded consist of the name, number, and debit or credit balance of each account. Debit balances should be entered in the left-hand column and credit balances in the right-hand column. The second pair of amount columns is used to record end-of-period adjustments. The third pair of amount columns is used to show the account balances as adjusted. This pair of amount columns is headed "Adjusted Trial Balance" because its purpose is to show that the debit and credit account balances as adjusted are equal in amount. The fourth pair of columns is for the adjusted balances of the expense and revenue accounts and is headed "Income Statement" since the amounts shown will be reported in that statement. The fifth and last pair is headed "Balance Sheet" and shows the adjusted account balances that will be reported in that statement. A ten-column end-of-year work sheet for Boyd's Clothiers is illustrated on pages 260 and 261.

To illustrate the preparation and use of the end-of-period work sheet, the example of the accounts of Boyd's Clothiers will be continued. The journals and ledgers for this business for the month of December were reproduced in the preceding chapter. In this chapter, the income statement for the year and the balance sheet at the end of the year are reproduced, and the use of a work sheet as a device for summarizing the data to be presented in those statements will be demonstrated.

THE WORK SHEET FOR BOYD'S CLOTHIERS

Following is a description and discussion of the steps taken in the preparation of the work sheet on pages 260 and 261. Each step should be studied carefully with frequent reference to the work sheet.

Trial Balance Columns. The trial balance of the general ledger accounts as of December 31 is entered in the first pair of amount columns. This trial balance is the same as the one shown on page 254 except that all of the account titles shown in the chart of accounts on page 221 are included in the work sheet list even though some of the accounts have no balances at this point.

The Trial Balance Debit and Credit columns are then totaled. The totals should be equal. If not, the discrepancy must be found and corrected before the preparation of the work sheet can proceed.

Adjustments Columns. The second pair of amount columns on the work sheet is used to record entries that reflect the changes that occurred during the year in some of the accounting elements. In this case, adjustments are needed: (a) and (b) to remove the amount of the beginning-of-year merchandise inventory and to record the amount of the end-of-year inventory; (c) to record the amount of interest expense incurred but not paid; (d) to record the amount of bank credit card expense for December that will not be deducted from the bank account until early in the following month; (e) and (f) to record the portions of supplies used and prepaid insurance expired during the year; (g) to record the estimated amount of expected uncollectible accounts expense; and (h) to record the estimated depreciation expense for the year.

Eight complete entries are made in the Adjustments columns to reflect these changes. When an account is debited or credited, the

Boyd's Clothiers
Work Sheet
For the Year Ended December 31, 19 --

Account	Acct. No.	Trial Balance Debit	Trial Balance Credit	Adjustments Debit	Adjustments Credit	Adjusted Trial Balance Debit	Adjusted Trial Balance Credit	Income Statement Debit	Income Statement Credit	Balance Sheet Debit	Balance Sheet Credit
First National Bank	111	1,139847				1,139847				1,139847	
Petty Cash Fund	112	15000				15000				15000	
Accounts Receivable	131	428843				428843				428843	
Allowance for Doubtful Accts.	131.1		7699		(a) 32628		40327				40327
Merchandise Inventory	141	3,592210		(b) 3,259625	(a) 3,592210	3,259625				3,259625	
Supplies	151	34059			(c) 26059	8000				8000	
Prepaid Insurance	161	73140			(f) 36570	36570				36570	
Store Equipment	184	727110				727110				727110	
Accum. Depr.--Store Equip.	211		112070		(e) 65411		177481				177481
FICA Tax Payable	211.1		32342				32342				32342
FUTA Tax Payable	311		10974				10974				10974
State Unemployment Tax Pay.	312		14742				14742				14742
Employees Income Tax Pay.	313		45400				45400				45400
Accrued Bank Credit Card Pay.	314				(d) 27250		27250				27250
Notes Payable	315		400000				400000				400000
Accrued Interest Payable	316				(c) 4978		4978				4978
Accounts Payable	317		564465				564465				564465
Sales Tax Payable	318		92752				92752				92752
Lynn O. Boyd, Capital	321		33,13590				33,13590				33,13590
Lynn O. Boyd, Drawing	511	3,064750				3,064750				3,064750	
Expense & Revenue Summary	531			(a) 3,592210	(b) 3,259625	3,592210	3,259625	3,592210	3,259625		
Sales	611		26,124327				26,124327		26,124327		
Sales Returns & Allowances	611.1	384920				384920		384920			
Purchases	711	16,673808				16,673808		16,673808			
Purchases Returns & Allowances	711.1		223660				223660		223660		
Purchases Discount	711.2		999642				999642		999642		
Rent Expense	521	1,080000				1,080000		1,080000			

Account Title	Acct. No.	Trial Balance Debit	Adjustments Debit	Adjusted Trial Balance Debit	Income Statement Debit	Income Statement Credit	Balance Sheet Debit	Balance Sheet Credit
Salaries + Commissions Exp.	822	2771135		2771135	2771135			
Heating + Lighting Expense	823	98753		98753	98753			
Telephone Expense	824	48400		48400	48400			
Supplies Expense	825	1132980		1132980	1132980			
Advertising Expense	826		(a) 26059	26059	26059			
Depreciation Expense	827		(a) 65411	65411	65411			
Insurance Expense	828		(b) 36570	36570	36570			
Charitable Contributions Exp.	829	45850		45850	45850			
Payroll Taxes Expense	831	238520		238520	238520			
Bank Credit Card Expense	832	313995	(a) 27250	341245	341245			
Uncollectible Accounts Exp.	833		(g) 32628	32628	32628			
Miscellaneous Expense	839	63251		63251	63251			
Interest Expense	911	15092	(c) 4978	20070	20070			
		31941663	7044731	35331555	26651810	30607254	8679745	4724301
Net Income					3955444			3955444
					30607254	30607254	8679745	8679745

Boyd's Clothiers — Ten Column Work Sheet

amount is entered on the same horizontal line as the name of the account and in the appropriate Adjustments Debit or Credit column. Each adjusting entry made on the work sheet is identified by a small letter in parentheses to facilitate cross-reference. Following is an explanation of each entry:

Entry (a)

Expense and Revenue Summary	35,922.10	
Merchandise Inventory		35,922.10

This entry is the first of two entries that adjust for the cost of goods sold. In order to remove the amount of the beginning merchandise inventory from the asset account and at the same time include it in the determination of net income for the current year, Expense and Revenue Summary, Account No. 531, is debited and Merchandise Inventory, Account No. 161, is credited for $35,922.10. This amount had been in the merchandise inventory account as a debit since the accounts were adjusted as of December 31, a year ago. The amount of the beginning merchandise inventory is debited to Expense and Revenue Summary because it is, in effect, a part of the cost of goods sold.

Entry (b)

Merchandise Inventory	32,596.25	
Expense and Revenue Summary		32,596.25

The second entry of this two-step procedure that adjusts for the cost of goods sold records the calculated cost of the merchandise on hand December 31 — often referred to as the year-end inventory. The calculation was based on a physical count of the merchandise in stock at the close of the year. The cost of the merchandise in stock at year end is recorded by debiting Merchandise Inventory, Account No. 161, and crediting Expense and Revenue Summary, Account No. 531, for $32,596.25. The amount of ending inventory is credited to Expense and Revenue Summary because this amount is, in effect, a deduction in the calculation of the cost of goods sold, as shown below:

Merchandise inventory, January 1			$ 35,922.10
Purchases		$166,738.08	
Less: Purchases returns and allowances	$2,236.60		
Purchases discounts	9,996.42	12,233.02	
Net purchases			154,505.06
Merchandise available for sale			$190,427.16
Less merchandise inventory, December 31.			32,596.25
Cost of goods sold			$157,830.91

It is the portion of the merchandise available for sale, defined as beginning inventory plus net purchases, that is still on hand at year end.

Entry (c)

Interest Expense	49.78	
Accrued Interest Payable		49.78

This entry records the accrued interest expense that was incurred but not paid by debiting Interest Expense, Account No. 911, and by crediting Accrued Interest Payable, Account No. 317, for $49.78. The $4,000 note payable in the December 31 trial balance represents an 8 percent, 6-month note dated November 5. Interest on this note at the rate of 8 percent per year for 56 days (November 5 to December 31) is $49.78.

Entry (d)

Bank Credit Card Expense	272.50	
Accrued Bank Credit Card Payable		272.50

This entry records the expense of the deduction that will be made by the bank during January for Visa and MasterCard vouchers deposited during December. These amounted to $9,083.45. The bank will deduct 3 percent of this amount, or $272.50 ($9,083.45 × .03), from the checking account. Since this $272.50 is really an expense for the year just ended, the adjustment is needed to include the expense in the calculation of net income for the past year. The adjustment is recorded by a debit to Bank Credit Card Expense, Account No. 832, and a credit to Accrued Bank Credit Card Payable, Account No. 315.

Entry (e)

Supplies Expense	260.59	
Supplies		260.59

This entry records the calculated cost of the supplies used during the year by debiting Supplies Expense, Account No. 825, and crediting Supplies, Account No. 181, for $260.59. This amount was determined as follows: The December 31 trial balance shows that Supplies has a debit balance of $340.59, which is the cost of supplies on hand at the start of the year, plus the cost of supplies purchased during the year. A physical count made of the supplies on December 31 determined the cost of the supplies on hand to be $80. Thus, the cost of the supplies used during the year amounted to $260.59 ($340.59 − $80).

Entry (f)

Insurance Expense	365.70	
Prepaid Insurance		365.70

This entry records the insurance expense for the year by debiting Insurance Expense, Account No. 828, and crediting Prepaid Insurance, Account No. 184, for $365.70. The December 31 trial balance shows that Prepaid Insurance has a debit balance of $731.40. This amount is the cost of a two-year policy dated January 2 of the year under consideration. By December 31, one year had elapsed; therefore one half of the premium paid had become an expense.

Entry (g)

Uncollectible Accounts Expense	326.28	
Allowance for Doubtful Accounts		326.28

This entry records the estimated uncollectible accounts expense for the year by debiting Uncollectible Accounts Expense, Account No. 833, and crediting Allowance for Doubtful Accounts, Account No. 131.1 for $326.28. Guided by past experience, Boyd's estimated that uncollectible account losses will be approximately one percent of the total sales on account for the year. Investigation of the records revealed that such sales amounted to $32,627.53. One percent of this amount is $326.28.

Entry (h)

Depreciation Expense	654.11	
Accumulated Depreciation — Store Equipment		654.11

This entry records the calculated depreciation expense for the year by debiting Depreciation Expense, Account No. 827, and crediting Accumulated Depreciation — Store Equipment, Account No. 211.1 for $654.11. The December trial balance shows that Store Equipment has a debit balance of $7,271.10. This balance represents the $6,541.10 cost of various items of property that have been owned the entire year plus the $730 cost of the safe that was purchased on December 30. Boyd's follows the policy of not calculating any depreciation on assets that have been owned for less than a month. Thus, depreciation expense for the year on store equipment relates to property costing $6,541.10 that had been owned for the entire year. This equipment is being depreciated at the rate of 10 percent a year, or $654.11 ($6,541.10 × .10).

After making the required entries in the Adjustments columns of the work sheet, the columns are totaled to prove the equality of the debit and credit entries.

Adjusted Trial Balance Columns. The third pair of amount columns of the work sheet is for the adjusted trial balance, which is a trial balance after the adjustments have been applied. To determine the balance of each account after making the required adjustments, it is necessary to take into consideration the amounts recorded in the first two pairs of amount columns (Trial Balance and Adjustments columns).

When an account balance is not affected by entries in the Adjustments columns, the amount in the Trial Balance columns is extended directly to the Adjusted Trial Balance columns. When an account balance is affected by an entry in the Adjustments columns, the balance to be recorded in the Adjusted Trial Balance columns is increased or decreased by the amount of the adjusting entry. For example, Accumulated Depreciation — Store Equipment is listed in the Trial Balance Credit column as $1,120.70. Since there is an entry of $654.11 in the Adjustments Credit column, the amount extended to the Adjusted Trial Balance Credit column is $1,774.81 ($1,120.70 + $654.11). Prepaid Insurance is listed in the Trial Balance Debit column as $731.40. Since there is an entry of $365.70 in the Adjustments Credit column, the amount extended to the Adjusted Trial Balance Credit column is $365.70 ($731.40 − $365.70).

There is one exception to the procedure just described. It relates to the debit and the credit in the Adjustments columns for Expense and Revenue Summary, Account No. 531. While $3,325.85 is the excess of the $35,922.10 debit (the amount of the beginning-of-year merchandise inventory) over the $32,596.25 credit (the amount of the end-of-year merchandise inventory) and this excess amount can be extended to the Adjusted Trial Balance Debit column, it is better to extend both the debit and credit amounts into the Adjusted Trial Balance columns. The reason is that both amounts are used in the preparation of the income statement and, therefore, both amounts should appear in the Income Statement columns.

The Adjusted Trial Balance columns are then totaled to prove the equality of the debits and the credits.

Income Statement Columns. The fourth pair of columns of the work sheet shows the amounts that will be reported in the income statement. The manner of extending both the debit and credit amounts on the line for Expense and Revenue Summary was mentioned previously. The amounts for sales, purchases returns and allowances, and purchases discount are extended to the Income Statement Credit column. The amounts for sales returns and allowances, purchases, and all expenses are extended to the Income Statement debit column.

The Income Statement columns are then totaled. The difference between the totals of these columns is the net income or net loss during the accounting period. If the total of the credits exceeds the total of the debits, the difference represents the increase in owner's equity due to net income; if the total of the debits exceeds the total of the credits, the difference represents the decrease in owner's equity due to net loss.

The Income Statement columns of Boyd's Clothiers work sheet on pages 260–261 show that the total of the credits amounts to $306,072.54 and the total of the debits amounts to $266,518.10. The difference, $39,554.44, is the net income for the year.

Balance Sheet Columns. The fifth pair of columns of the work sheet shows the amounts that will be reported in the balance sheet. The Balance Sheet columns are totaled. The difference between the totals of these columns also is the amount of net income or net loss for the accounting period. If the total of the debits exceeds the total of the credits, the difference represents net income; if the total of the credits exceeds the total of the debits, the difference represents net loss. This difference should be the same as the difference between the totals of the Income Statement columns.

The Balance Sheet columns of the work sheet of Boyd's Clothiers show that the total of the debits amounts to $86,797.45 and the total of the credits amounts to $47,243.01. The difference of $39,554.44 represents the amount of net income for the year.

Completing the Work Sheet. The difference ($39,554.44) between the totals of the Income Statement columns and the totals of the Balance Sheet columns is recorded on the next horizontal line below the totals. Since the difference represents net income, it is recorded in the Income Statement Debit and in the Balance Sheet Credit columns. If a net loss resulted, the amount would be so designated and entered in the Income Statement Credit and in the Balance Sheet Debit columns. After the net income (or net loss) has been entered, a double line is ruled immediately below the totals.

Proving the Work Sheet. The work sheet provides proof of the arithmetical accuracy of the data that it summarizes. The totals of the Trial Balance columns, the Adjustments Columns, and the Adjusted Trial Balance columns must be equal. The amount of the difference between the totals of the Income Statement columns must be exactly the same amount as the difference between the totals of the Balance Sheet columns.

The reason why the same amount will balance both the Income Statement columns and the Balance Sheet columns is provided by an understanding of (1) the real nature of net income (or net loss) and (2) the basic difference between the income statement accounts and the balance sheet accounts. The reality of net income is that the assets have increased, or that the liabilities have decreased, or that some combination of both events has taken place during a period of time. Most of these changes are recorded day after day in the asset and liability accounts in order that they may be kept up to date. However, the effect of the changes on the owner's equity element is not recorded in the permanent owner's equity account. Instead, the changes are recorded in the temporary owner's equity accounts — the revenue and expense accounts.

At the end of the period after the asset and liability accounts have been adjusted, each of these accounts reflects all of the changes of the period. In contrast, all of the changes in owner's equity for the period are reflected in the revenue and expense accounts and in the drawing account.

As applied to the work sheet, this means that the Balance Sheet column totals are out of balance by the amount of the change in owner's equity due to net income or net loss for the period involved. In other words, the asset and liability accounts reflect the net income of the period, but the owner's capital account at this point does not. It is only after the temporary accounts are closed at the end of the period and the amount of the net income for the period has been transferred to the owner's capital account that this account reflects the net income of the period.

The owner's capital account lacks two things to bring its balance up to date: (1) the decrease due to any withdrawals during the period, which is reflected in the debit balance of the drawing account and (2) the increase due to any net income (or the decrease due to any net loss) for the period. On the work sheet, the debit balance of the drawing account is extended to the Balance Sheet Debit column. Thus, all that is needed to cause the Balance Sheet columns to be equal is the amount of the net income (or loss) for the year — the same amount that is the difference between the totals of the Income Statement columns.

BUILDING YOUR ACCOUNTING KNOWLEDGE

1. In what three ways does an end-of-period work sheet assist the accountant?
2. Explain the purpose of each of the eight adjustments on the Boyd's Clothiers' work sheet.

3. Why are both the debit and credit amounts in the Adjustments columns on the Expense and Revenue Summary line of the work sheet extended to the Adjusted Trial Balance columns?

4. What two amounts from the Income Statement Debit column are added and what two amounts from the Income Statement Credit column are then subtracted to determine the amount of merchandise available for sale?

5. What amount from the Income Statement Credit column is subtracted from the merchandise available for sale to calculate the cost of goods sold?

6. What does the difference between the totals of the Income Statement columns represent? What does the difference between the Balance Sheet column totals represent?

7. What two things does the owner's capital account lack to bring its balance up to date?

Report No. 9-1

> Complete Report 9-1 in the study assignments and submit your working papers to the instructor for approval. After completing the report, continue with the following textbook discussion until the next report is required.

THE FINANCIAL STATEMENTS

The financial statements usually include (1) an income statement and (2) a balance sheet. The purpose of an income statement is to summarize the results of operations during an accounting period. The income statement provides information as to the sources of revenue, types of expenses, and the amount of the net income or the net loss for the period. The purpose of a balance sheet is to provide information as to the status of a business at a specified date. The balance sheet shows the kinds and amounts of assets and liabilities and the owner's equity in the business at a specified point in time — usually at the close of business on the last date of the accounting period.

THE INCOME STATEMENT

A formal statement of the results of the operation of a business during an accounting period is called an income statement. Other titles commonly used for this statement include profit and loss statement, income and expense statement, and operating statement. The purpose of the statement is to show the types and amounts of revenue and expenses that the business had during the accounting period involved, and the resulting net income or net loss for this period.

Importance of the Income Statement. The income statement is generally considered to be the most important financial statement of a business. A business normally cannot survive for very long unless it makes a profit. The income statement is essentially a "report card" of the enterprise. The statement provides a basis for judging the overall effectiveness of the management. Decisions as to whether to continue a business, to expand it, or to contract it are often based upon the results as reported in the income statement. Actual and potential creditors are interested in income statements because one of the best reasons for extending credit or for making a loan is that the business is profitable.

Various government agencies are interested in income statements of businesses for a variety of reasons. Regulatory bodies are concerned with the earnings of the enterprises they regulate, such as airlines, banks, insurance companies, public utilities and railroads, because a part of the regulation usually relates to the prices, rates, or fares that may be charged. If the enterprise is either exceptionally profitable or unprofitable, some change in the allowed prices or rates may be needed. Income tax authorities — federal, state, and local — have an interest in business income statements. Net income determination for tax purposes differs somewhat from the calculation of net income for financial reporting purposes, but for a variety of reasons, the tax authorities are interested in both sets of calculations.

Form of the Income Statement. It is essential that the income statement be properly headed. The name of the business (or of the individual if it is a professional practice or is named for the owner) should be shown first. The name of the statement is then shown followed by the period of time that the statement covers, for example, "For the Year Ended December 31, 1982."

The body of the income statement depends, in part, upon the type of business. Two types of income statement forms are commonly used — the single step and the multiple step. The single-step form of income statement lists all revenue items and their total first, followed by all expense items and their total, to produce a difference which is either net income or net loss.

The multiple-step form of income statement is commonly used for merchandising businesses. The name "multiple-step" is applied because the final net income is calculated on a step-by-step basis. The amount of gross sales is shown first with sales returns and allowances deducted, resulting in a difference called net sales. Cost of goods sold is next subtracted to arrive at gross margin (sometimes called gross profit). The portion of the statement down to this point is sometimes called the "trading section." Operating expenses are listed next, and the total of their amounts is subtracted from the gross margin to arrive at the amount of operating income. Finally, the amounts of any other revenue are added and any other expenses are subtracted to arrive at the final amount of net income (or net loss).

Very often, the accountant prepares the original statement in pencil or ink on ruled paper. This is used by the typist in preparing typewritten copies to be presented to the owners of a business and to potential creditors or other interested parties. The income statement for Boyd's Clothiers for the year ended December 31, 19––, is shown on the next page. The information needed in preparing the statement was obtained from the work sheet shown on pages 260 and 261. Note that the operating expenses are arranged in descending size order (except for Miscellaneous Expense), which is a fairly common approach.

THE BALANCE SHEET

A formal statement of the assets, liabilities, and owner's equity of a business at a specified date is known as a balance sheet. The title of the statement had its origin in the equality of the elements, that is, the sum of the assets equals the sum of the liabilities and owner's equity. Sometimes, the balance sheet is called a statement of assets and liabilities, a statement of condition, or a statement of financial position. Various other titles are used occasionally.

Importance of the Balance Sheet. The balance sheet of a business is of considerable interest to various parties for several reasons. The owner or owners of a business are interested in the kinds and amounts of assets and liabilities and the amount of the owner's equity or capital element.

Creditors of the business are interested in the financial position of the enterprise, particularly as it pertains to the claims they have and the prospects for prompt payment. Potential creditors are concerned about the financial position of the business. Their decision as to whether to extend credit or to make loans to the business may depend, in large part, upon the condition of the enterprise as revealed by a balance sheet.

Persons considering buying an ownership interest in a business are greatly interested in the character and amount of the assets and

BOYD'S CLOTHIERS
Income Statement
For the Year Ended December 31, 19--

Operating revenue:			
Sales			$261,243.27
Less sales returns and allowances			3,849.20
Net sales			$257,394.07
Cost of goods sold:			
Merchandise inventory, January 1		$ 35,922.10	
Purchases	$166,738.08		
Less: Purchases returns and allowances	$2,236.60		
Purchases discount	9,996.42	12,233.02	
Net purchases		154,505.06	
Merchandise available for sale		$190,427.16	
Less merchandise inventory, December 31		32,596.25	
Cost of goods sold			157,830.91
Gross margin on sales			$ 99,563.16
Operating expenses:			
Salaries and commissions expense		$ 27,711.35	
Advertising expense		11,329.80	
Rent expense		10,800.00	
Bank credit card expense		3,412.45	
Payroll taxes expense		2,385.20	
Heating and light expense		987.53	
Depreciation expense		654.11	
Telephone expense		484.00	
Charitable contributions expense		458.50	
Insurance expense		365.70	
Uncollectible accounts expense		326.28	
Supplies expense		260.59	
Miscellaneous expense		632.51	
Total operating expenses			59,808.02
Operating income			$ 39,755.14
Other expenses:			
Interest expense			200.70
Net income			$ 39,554.44

Boyd's Clothiers — Income Statement

liabilities, in addition to their interest in the future earnings possibilities.

Finally, various regulatory bodies are interested in the financial position of the businesses that are under their jurisdiction.

Form of the Balance Sheet. It is essential that the balance sheet be properly headed. The name of the business (or the name of the individual if it is a professional practice or is named for the owner), should be shown first. This is followed by the name of the statement — usually just "Balance Sheet," and then the date — month, day, and year. It must be remembered that a balance sheet relates to a particular moment of time.

Traditionally, balance sheets have been presented either in account form or in report form. Each of these forms was discussed briefly on page 136 of Chapter 5. In the account form, the assets are listed on the left side of the page or on the left of two facing pages, and the liabilities and owner's equity are listed on the right. This form is similar to the debit-side and credit-side arrangement of the standard ledger account. The balance sheet of Boyd's Clothiers as of December 31, 19––, in account form is reproduced on pages 274 and 275. The data for the preparation of the statement were taken from the work sheet.

When the report form of the balance sheet is followed, the assets, liabilities, and owner's equity elements are exhibited in that order on the page. The balance sheet of John H. Roberts, Management Consultant, was shown in report form on page 137. This arrangement is generally preferable if the statement is to be typed on regular letter-size paper (8½″ × 11″).

Classification of Data in the Balance Sheet. The purpose of the balance sheet and of all other financial statements and reports is to convey as much information as possible. This aim is furthered by the classification of the data being reported. As applied to the balance sheet, it has become almost universal practice to classify both assets and liabilities into those that are considered current and those that are considered noncurrent or long-term (sometimes called "fixed").

Current Assets. Current assets include cash and all other assets that may be reasonably expected to be converted to cash or sold or consumed within one year or the normal operating cycle of the business, whichever is longer. In a merchandising business, the current assets usually include cash, receivables (such as accounts receivable), merchandise inventory, and temporary investments. Prepaid expenses, such as unused supplies and unexpired insurance, are also generally treated as current assets. This is not because these items will be realized in cash, but because they will probably be consumed in a relatively short time.

The asset, cash, may be represented by one or more accounts, such as bank checking accounts, bank savings accounts, or a petty cash fund. The Boyd's Clothiers balance sheet on pages 274–275 shows that cash is listed at $11,548.47, which is made up of two items as shown in the work sheet on pages 260–261: the balance in the checking account at the First National Bank, $11,398.47, and the amount of the petty cash fund, $150.

Temporary investments are those assets that have been acquired with money that would otherwise have been temporarily idle and unproductive. Such investments usually take the form of corporate stocks, bonds, notes, or any of several types of government bonds, notes, or bills. Quite often, the policy is to invest in securities that can be liquidated in a short time with little chance of loss. The account entitled Marketable Securities is frequently used to describe temporary investments.

Assets of the same type may be owned by a business for many years. Under such circumstances, they would be classified as long-term investments and included in a separate asset classification entitled Investments. The intention of the business indicates whether the investments are to be classified as temporary and included in the current assets as marketable securities or considered as long-term investments and included in a separate asset classification entitled Investments. Presently, Boyd's Clothiers has no investments.

Property, Plant, and Equipment. Assets that are used in the operation of a business, such as land, buildings, office equipment, store equipment, and delivery equipment are called property, plant, and equipment. Of these assets, only land is permanent; however, all of these assets have a useful life that is comparatively long.

The balance sheet of Boyd's Clothiers shows that store equipment is the only such asset. The amount of the accumulated depreciation is shown as a deduction from the cost of the equipment. The difference represents the undepreciated cost of the equipment which is the amount that will be written off as depreciation expense in future periods.

Current Liabilities. Current liabilities include those obligations that will be due within one year or the normal operating cycle of the business, whichever is longer, and paid with monies provided by the current assets. As of December 31, the current liabilities of Boyd's Clothiers consist of FICA tax payable, FUTA tax payable, state unemployment tax payable, employees income tax payable, accrued bank credit card payable, notes payable, accrued interest payable, accounts payable, and sales tax payable.

Long-Term Liabilities. Long-term liabilities include those obligations that will extend beyond one year or one normal operating cycle, whichever is longer. The most common long-term liability is a mortgage payable.

Mortgage Payable is an account that is used to reflect a debt or an obligation that is secured by a mortgage on certain property. A mortgage is a written agreement specifying that if the borrower does

		BOYD'S Balance December
Assets		
Current assets:		
Cash..		$11,548.47
Accounts receivable..	$4,288.43	
Less allowance for doubtful accounts..................	403.27	3,885.16
Merchandise inventory..		32,596.25
Supplies...		80.00
Prepaid insurance		365.70
Total current assets		$48,475.58
Property, plant, and equipment:		
Store equipment...	$7,271.10	
Less accumulated depreciation	1,774.81	
Total property, plant, and equipment................		5,496.29
Total assets...		$53,971.87

Boyd's Clothiers — Balance Sheet (Left Side)

not repay a debt, the lender has the right to take over the property to satisfy the debt. When the debt is paid, the mortgage becomes void. A mortgage payable is similar to an account payable or a note payable except that the creditor holds the mortgage as security for the payment of the debt. Usually, debts secured by mortgages run for a longer period of time than ordinary notes payable or accounts payable. A mortgage payable is classified as a long-term liability if the maturity date extends beyond one year or the normal operating cycle of the business, whichever is longer. Boyd's Clothers has no long-term liabilities.

Owner's Equity. Accounts relating to the owner's equity element may be either permanent or temporary. The permanent owner's equity accounts which are used to accumulate the results of the operations of a particular enterprise are determined by the type of organization, that is, whether the enterprise is organized as a sole proprietorship, as a partnership, or as a corporation.

In a sole proprietorship, one or more accounts representing the owner's interest or equity in the assets may be kept. The chart of accounts on page 221 shows that the following accounts are classified as owner's equity accounts for Lynn C. Boyd:

CLOTHIERS
Sheet
31, 19--

Liabilities

Current liabilities:
FICA tax payable... $ 323.42
FUTA tax payable...   109.74
State unemployment tax payable...........................   147.42
Employees income tax payable..............................   454.00
Accrued bank credit card payable 272.50
Notes payable 4,000.00
Accrued interest payable 49.78
Accounts payable... 5,644.65
Sales tax payable...   927.52

   Total current liabilities.. $11,929.03

Owner's Equity

Lynn C. Boyd, capital:
Capital, January 1... $33,135.90
Net income... $39,554.44
Less withdrawals.................................. 30,647.50   8,906.94

Capital, December 31 ....   42,042.84
Total liabilities and owner's equity........................... $53,971.87

Boyd's Clothiers — Balance Sheet (Right Side)

                 Lynn C. Boyd, Capital — Account No. 511
                 Lynn C. Boyd, Drawing — Account No. 511.1
                 Expense and Revenue Summary — Account No. 531

      Account No. 511 reflects the amount of Boyd's equity. It may be increased by additional investments and net income for the accounting period of the enterprise; it may be decreased by withdrawals and by sustaining a net loss for the accounting period. Except for additional investments, there will be no change in the balance of this account during the accounting period, in which case the balance represents the owner's investment in the business as of the beginning of the accounting period and until such time as the books are closed at the end of the accounting period.

      Account No. 511.1 is Boyd's drawing account. This account is charged for any withdrawals of cash or other property for personal use. It is a temporary account in which a record is kept of the owner's personal drawings during the accounting period. Ordinarily such drawings are made in anticipation of earnings rather than as withdrawals of capital. The balance of the account, as shown by the trial balance at the close of an accounting period, represents the total amount of the owner's drawings during the period.

The work sheet shown on pages 260 and 261 reveals that the balance of Boyd's drawing account is listed in the Balance Sheet Debit column. This is because there is no provision on a work sheet for making deductions from owner's equity except by listing them in the Debit column. Since the balance of the owner's capital account is listed in the Balance Sheet Credit column, the listing of the balance of the owner's drawing account in the Debit column is equivalent to deducting the amount from the balance of the owner's capital account.

Account No. 531 is used only at the close of the accounting period to adjust the merchandise inventory account and summarize the temporary owner's equity accounts. Sometimes this account is referred to as a clearing account. No entries appear in this account before the books are adjusted and closed at the end of the accounting period.

The owner's equity section of the balance sheet of Boyd's Clothiers is arranged to show the major changes that took place during the year in the owner's equity element of the business. Boyd's interest in the business amounted to $33,135.90 at the beginning of the period. The interest increased $39,554.44 as the result of profitable operations and decreased $30,647.50 as the result of withdrawals during the year. Thus, the owner's equity element of the business on December 31 amounted to $42,042.84 ($33,135.90 + $39,554.44 − $30,647.50).

ANALYSIS OF FINANCIAL STATEMENTS

There are various procedures employed to assist in the interpretation of income statements.

Income Statement Analysis. Income statements may be presented for two or more periods of comparable length in comparative form. The figures for the two periods are shown in adjacent columns and a third column shows the amount of increase or decrease in each element. This will call attention to changes of major significance.

Another analytical device is to express all or at least the major items on the statement as a percent of net sales and then to compare these percentages for two or more periods. The income statement of Boyd's Clothiers on page 271 is used to illustrate this approach. If the net sales of $257,394.07 for the year just ended are treated as 100 percent, the cost of goods sold, which amounted to $157,830.91, is equal to 61.32 percent ($157,830.91 ÷ $257,394.07) of net sales; the gross margin on sales, which amounted to $99,563.16, is equal to

38.68 percent of net sales; operating expenses, which amounted to $59,808.02, are equal to 23.24 percent of net sales; operating income (gross margin less operating expenses), which amounted to $39,755.14, is equal to 15.44 percent of net sales; and net income, which amounted to $39,554.44, is equal to 15.37 percent of net sales.

Net sales	$257,394.07	100.00%
Less cost of goods sold	157,830.91	61.32
Gross margin on sales	$ 99,563.16	38.68
Operating expenses	59,808.02	23.24
Operating income	$ 39,755.14	15.44
Interest expense	200.70	.07
Net income	$ 39,554.44	15.37

A comparison of these percentages with the same data for one or more prior years would reveal trends that would be of interest, and perhaps of real concern, to the management of the business.

Balance Sheet Analysis. The information provided by a balance sheet can be analyzed in several ways to assist in judging the financial position and soundness of the business. A few of the major analytical procedures will be briefly considered.

A balance sheet as of one date may be compared with a balance sheet as of another date to determine the amount of the increase or the decrease in any of the accounts or groups of accounts. Sometimes, balance sheets as of two or more dates are prepared in comparative form by listing the amounts as of different dates in parallel columns. Thus, if balance sheets as of the close of two consecutive calendar years are compared, it is possible to determine the amount of the increase or the decrease during the intervening period in any of the accounts or groups of accounts involved. If the comparison reveals an increase in accounts receivable, it may indicate either a business expansion or that collections were not as favorable as they were during the preceding period. If the comparison reveals an increase in accounts payable, it may indicate either business expansion or an inability to pay current bills because of insufficient cash. If the comparison reveals an increase in the current assets without a corresponding increase in the current liabilities, it may indicate an improved financial position or status.

Too much emphasis should not be placed upon an increase or decrease in cash. Some individuals are inclined to judge the results of operations largely by the cash balance. This practice may be misleading. The net results of operations can be properly determined only by the comparison of all assets and liabilities.

The ability of a business to meet its current obligations may be determined largely by an analysis of its current assets and current liabilities. In a merchandising enterprise in which the capital in-vested is a material revenue-producing factor, the current ratio, which is the ratio of the current assets to the current liabilities, may be important.

$$\text{Current ratio} = \frac{\text{Current assets}}{\text{Current liabilities}}$$

The balance sheet shown on pages 274 and 275 reveals that the total current assets amount to $48,475.58 and the total current liabil-ities amount to $11,929.03, a ratio of over 4 to 1 ($48,475.58 ÷ $11,929.03). The total assets amount to $53,971.87 and the total lia-bilities amount to $11,929.03, a ratio of over 4.5 to 1. These ratios are sufficiently high to indicate a very favorable financial position.

Banks often consider the ratio of current assets to current liabili-ties when considering the advisability of making a loan. It is not expected that the property, plant and equipment assets will be sold to realize sufficient funds with which to pay a short-term loan. If the balance sheet seems to indicate that a sufficient amount of cash will not be realized from the collection of accounts receivable or from the sales of service or merchandise to repay a loan at maturity, the bank may consider the loan inadvisable.

Other measures sometimes used in analyzing a firm's ability to meet its current obligations are the quick ratio and the amount of working capital. Quick assets include cash and all other current assets that are readily realizable in cash, such as accounts receiv-able, and temporary investments in the form of marketable securi-ties and short-term certificates of deposit. The ratio of quick assets to current liabilities is called the quick ratio.

$$\text{Quick ratio} = \frac{\text{Quick assets}}{\text{Current liabilities}}$$

The balance sheet shown on pages 274 and 275 reveals total quick assets of $15,433.63 and a quick ratio of 1.29 to 1 ($15,433.63 ÷ $11,929.03). This means that quick assets are more than adequate to meet current obligations.

The excess of the amount of current assets over the amount of current liabilities is called working capital or net current assets.

Working Capital = Current assets − Current liabilities

Working capital is an indicator of the funds available with which to carry on current business operations. Boyd's working capital at year-end amounts to $36,546.55 ($48,475.58 − $11,929.03), which is nearly 87% of owner's equity.

It is difficult to estimate what the proper current ratio, quick ratio, or amount of working capital should be, because of the variations in enterprises and industries. A 2 to 1 ratio of current assets to current liabilities may be more than sufficient in some enterprises but entirely insufficient in others. In the milk distribution business, for example, a 1 to 1 ratio of current assets to current liabilities is considered satisfactory. The reasons are that very little capital is tied up in inventory, the amount of accounts receivable is comparatively small, and the terms on which the milk is purchased from farmers are such that settlements are slow and comparatively large amounts are due to farmers at all times. Another reason is that a large amount of capital is invested in property, plant and equipment assets, such as equipment for treating the milk and delivering it to customers.

Generally, the ratio of current assets to current liabilities should be maintained in a range from 2 to 1 to 5 to 1. While a standard ratio cannot be established for all enterprises, a knowlege of the working capital requirements of a particular enterprise will be helpful in determining what the ratio of current assets to current liabilities should be.

Interstatement Analysis. A comparison of the relationships between certain amounts in the income statement and certain amounts in the balance sheet may be informative. A good example of this type is the ratio of net income to owner's equity in the business, which is known as return on owner's equity.

$$\text{Return on owner's equity} = \frac{\text{Net income}}{\text{Owner's equity}}$$

The owner's equity of Boyd's Clothiers was $33,135.90 on January 1. The net income for the year of $39,554.44 is nearly 120 percent ($39,554.44 ÷ $33,135.90) of the owner's equity. A comparison of this ratio with the return on owner's equity in prior years should be of interest to the owner. It may also be of interest to compare the return on owner's equity of Boyd's Clothiers with the same ratio for other stores of comparable nature and size. It is important to note, however, that the net income of Boyd's Clothiers was computed without regard to any salary or other compensation for the services of Boyd. In comparing the results of operations of Boyd's Clothiers with those of other retail clothing businesses, some appropriate adjustment of the salary and other compensation data might be needed to make the comparison valid.

Another ratio involving both balance sheet and income statement accounts is the rate of inventory turnover for each accounting period — the number of times the merchandise available for sale is turned during the accounting period. The rate of inventory turnover is determined by the following:

$$\frac{\text{Cost of goods sold for the period}}{\text{Average inventory}}$$

If inventory is taken only at the end of each accounting period, the average inventory for the period may be calculated by adding the beginning and ending inventories and dividing their sum by two. The turnover of Boyd's Clothiers for the year ended December 31, is computed as follows:

Beginning inventory $35,922.10
Ending inventory 32,596.25
Cost of goods sold for the period 157,830.91

$$\text{Average inventory} = \frac{\text{Beginning inventory (\$35,922.10)} + \text{Ending inventory (\$32,596.25)}}{2}$$

$$= \$34,259.18$$

$$\text{Rate of turnover} = \frac{\text{Cost of goods sold for the period (\$157,830.91)}}{\text{Average inventory (\$34,259.18)}} = 4.6$$

This calculation indicates that, on the average, the merchandise turns over about once every 2½ months. A careful analysis of the theory involved in computing the rate of turnover will indicate that the greater the physical volume of unit sales, the smaller the margin need be on each dollar of sales to produce a satisfactory dollar amount of gross margin.

INCOME AND SELF-EMPLOYMENT TAXES

The discussion of accounting for the revenue and expenses of a business enterprise has included frequent references to income tax considerations. It is important to note than an unincorporated business owned by one person is not taxed. The owner — not the business — is subject to income taxes. Business revenue and business expenses must be reported on the owner's personal tax return regardless of the amount of money or other property that was withdrawn from the business during the year. As mentioned on pages 5–6 of Chapter 1, in the case of a sole proprietorship, there is no legal distinction between the business and its owner.

To bring a large class of self-employed individuals into the federal social security program, the law requires all self-employed persons (except those specifically exempted) to pay a self-employment tax. The rate of tax is about 2 percent more than the prevailing FICA rate, but the base of the self-employment income tax is the same as the base for the FICA tax. If it is assumed that the combined FICA tax rate is 7 percent, the self-employment income tax rate would be about 9 percent on the assumed base of $30,000. Self-employment income means the net income of a trade or business conducted by an individual or a partner's distributive share of the net income of a partnership whether or not any cash is distributed. Earnings of less than $400 from self-employment are ignored. The actual rate and base of the tax may be changed by Act of Congress at any time.

A taxable year for the purpose of the tax on self-employment income is the same as the taxpayer's taxable year for federal income tax purposes. The self-employment tax is reported along with the regular federal income tax. For calendar-year taxpayers, the tax return and full or final payment are due on April 15 following the close of the year. Like the personal income tax, the self-employment tax is treated as a personal expense of the owner, and thus its cost would not appear on the financial statements of the business. If the taxes are paid with business funds, the amount should be charged to the owner's drawing account and will thus appear on the balance sheet opposite the "Less withdrawals" caption.

BUILDING YOUR ACCOUNTING KNOWLEDGE

1. Explain why the income statement is essentially a "report card" of the enterprise.
2. Describe the nature of the two forms of income statement.
3. How did the title "balance sheet" originate?
4. What is the major difference between the two forms of balance sheet?
5. What determines the permanent owner's equity accounts used to accumulate the results of operations of a particular enterprise?
6. What are the two major analytical devices used to assist in the interpretation of income statements?
7. Explain why it is difficult to say what is a proper ratio of current assets to current liabilities.
8. Describe the use of the return on owner's equity ratio; the use of rate of inventory turnover.
9. How should the amount of the self-employment tax be accounted for if the tax is paid with business funds?

Report No. 9-2

> Complete Report No. 9-2 in the study assignments and submit your working papers to the instructor for approval. After completing the report, you may continue with the textbook discussion in Chapter 10 until the next report is required.

EXPANDING YOUR BUSINESS VOCABULARY

What is the meaning of each of the following terms?

account form (p. 272)

adjusted trial balance (p. 265)

balance sheet (p. 270)

clearing account (p. 276)

current assets (p. 272)

current liabilities (p. 273)

current ratio (p. 278)

gross margin (p. 270)

income statement (p. 268)

income and expense statement (p. 268)

inventory turnover (p. 280)

long-term liabilities (p. 273)

Marketable Securities (p. 273)

merchandise available for sale (p. 263)

mortgage (p. 273)

Mortgage Payable (p. 273)

multiple-step (p. 269)

net current assets (p. 278)

net sales (p. 270)

operating income (p. 270)

operating statement (p. 268)

periodic summary (p. 258)

profit and loss statement (p. 268)

property, plant, and equipment (p. 273)

quick assets (p. 278)

quick ratio (p. 278)

report form (p. 272)

return on owner's equity (p. 279)

self-employment income (p. 281)

single-step (p. 269)

statement of assets and liabilities (p. 270)

statement of condition (p. 270)

statement of financial position (p. 270)

temporary investments (p. 273)

undepreciated cost (p. 273)

work sheet (p. 258)

working capital (p. 278)

CHAPTER 10

ADJUSTING AND CLOSING ACCOUNTS AT END OF ACCOUNTING PERIOD

CHAPTER OBJECTIVES

The objectives of this chapter are to enable you:

▶ To explain and perform the steps in the accounting cycle that are needed to:

(1) Journalize and post the adjusting entries and update the ledger account balances.
(2) Journalize and post the closing entries and update the ledger account balances.
(3) Take a post-closing trial balance.
(4) Journalize and post reversing entries.

As explained in the preceding chapter, the adjustment of certain accounts at the end of the accounting period is required because changes that have occurred during the period are not reflected in the accounts. Since the purpose of the temporary owner's equity accounts is to assemble information relating to a specified period of time, the balances of these accounts must be closed out at the end of the period to prepare the accounts for the following period.

ADJUSTING ENTRIES

Entries required at the end of an accounting period to bring certain account balances up to date are known as adjusting entries. In preparing the work sheet for Boyd's Clothiers (reproduced on pages 260 and 261), adjustments were made to accomplish the following purposes:

(1) To transfer the amount of the merchandise inventory at the beginning of the accounting period to the expense and revenue summary account.

(2) To record the calculated cost of the merchandise inventory at the end of the accounting period.

(3) To record the amount of interest accrued on notes payable.

(4) To record the amount of accrued bank credit card payable.

(5) To record the cost of supplies used during the year.

(6) To record the amount of insurance premium expired during the year.

(7) To record the amount of uncollectible accounts estimated to result from the sales on account made during the year.

(8) To record the estimated amount of depreciation of property, plant and equipment (store equipment) for the year.

The effect of these adjustments was reflected in the financial statements reproduced on pages 271 and 274–275. To bring the ledger into agreement with the financial statements, the adjustments should be recorded in the proper accounts. It is customary, therefore, at the end of each accounting period to journalize the adjustments and post them to the proper accounts.

JOURNALIZING THE ADJUSTING ENTRIES

Adjusting entries may be recorded in either a general journal or a combination journal. If the entries are made in a combination journal, the only amount columns used are the General Debit and Credit columns. A portion of a combination journal showing the adjusting entries of Boyd's Clothiers is reproduced on the next page. It should be noted that when adjusting entries are recorded in the combination journal, they are entered in exactly the same manner as they would be entered in a general journal. Since the heading "Adjusting Entries" explains the nature of the entries, a separate explanation of each adjusting entry is unnecessary. The information needed in journalizing the adjustments was obtained from the Adjustments columns of the work sheet reproduced on pages 260 and 261. The account numbers were not entered in the Posting Reference column at the time of journalizing but were entered when the posting was completed.

DAY	DESCRIPTION	POST. REF.	GENERAL DEBIT	GENERAL CREDIT	
	COMBINATION JOURNAL FOR MONTH OF *December* 19-- PAGE *49*				
1	AMOUNTS FORWARDED				1
2	*31*	*Adjusting Entries*				2
3		*Expense and Revenue Summary*	531	3592210		3
4		*Merchandise Inventory*	161		3592210	4
5		*Merchandise Inventory*	161	3259625		5
6		*Expense and Revenue Summary*	531		3259625	6
7		*Interest Expense*	911	4978		7
8		*Accrued Interest Payable*	317		4978	8
9		*Bank Credit Card Expense*	832	27250		9
10		*Accrued Bank Credit Card Payable*	315		27250	10
11		*Supplies Expense*	825	26059		11
12		*Supplies*	181		26059	12
13		*Insurance Expense*	828	36570		13
14		*Prepaid Insurance*	184		36570	14
15		*Uncollectible Accounts Expense*	833	32628		15
16		*Allowance for Doubtful Accounts*	131.1		32628	16
17		*Depreciation Expense*	827	65411		17
18		*Accum. Depn. -- Store Equipment*	211.1	7044731	65411 7044731	18
19						19
20						20
21						21
22						22
23						23

Boyd's Clothiers — Adjusting Entries

POSTING THE ADJUSTING ENTRIES

The adjusting entries are posted individually to the proper ledger accounts. The accounts of Boyd's Clothiers that were affected by the adjusting entries are reproduced on pages 286–288. The entries in the accounts for December transactions that were posted prior to the adjusting entries are the same as in the accounts reproduced on pages 240–247. The number of the combination journal page on which the adjusting entries are recorded was entered in the Posting Reference column of the general ledger accounts, and the account numbers were entered in the Posting Reference column of the combination journal as the posting was completed. This provided a cross-reference in both books.

ACCOUNT *Allowance for Doubtful Accounts*   ACCOUNT NO. *131.1*

DATE	ITEM	POST. REF.	DEBIT	CREDIT	BALANCE DEBIT	BALANCE CREDIT
Dec. 1	Balance	✓				7699
31		CJ49		32628		40327

ACCOUNT *Merchandise Inventory*   ACCOUNT NO. *161*

DATE	ITEM	POST. REF.	DEBIT	CREDIT	BALANCE DEBIT	BALANCE CREDIT
Dec. 1	Balance	✓			3592210	
31		CJ49		3592210		
31		CJ49	3259625		3259625	

ACCOUNT *Supplies*   ACCOUNT NO. *181*

DATE	ITEM	POST. REF.	DEBIT	CREDIT	BALANCE DEBIT	BALANCE CREDIT
Dec. 1	Balance	✓			29936	
31		CJ48	4123		34059	
31		CJ49		26059	8000	

ACCOUNT *Prepaid Insurance*   ACCOUNT NO. *184*

DATE	ITEM	POST. REF.	DEBIT	CREDIT	BALANCE DEBIT	BALANCE CREDIT
Dec. 1	Balance	✓			73140	
31		CJ49		36570	36570	

ACCOUNT *Accumulated Depreciation – Store Equipment*   ACCOUNT NO. *211.1*

DATE	ITEM	POST. REF.	DEBIT	CREDIT	BALANCE DEBIT	BALANCE CREDIT
Dec. 1	Balance	✓				112070
31		CJ49		65411		177481

ACCOUNT *Accrued Bank Credit Card Payable*   ACCOUNT NO. *315*

DATE	ITEM	POST. REF.	DEBIT	CREDIT	BALANCE DEBIT	BALANCE CREDIT
Dec. 31		CJ49		27250		27250

Boyd's Clothiers — General Ledger Accounts After Posting Adjusting Entries

ACCOUNT *Accrued Interest Payable*   ACCOUNT NO. *317*

DATE	ITEM	POST. REF.	DEBIT	CREDIT	BALANCE DEBIT	BALANCE CREDIT
19-- Dec. 31		CJ49		4978		4978

ACCOUNT *Expense and Revenue Summary*   ACCOUNT NO. *531*

DATE	ITEM	POST. REF.	DEBIT	CREDIT	BALANCE DEBIT	BALANCE CREDIT
19-- Dec. 31		CJ49	3592210			
		CJ49		3259625		

ACCOUNT *Supplies Expense*   ACCOUNT NO. *825*

DATE	ITEM	POST. REF.	DEBIT	CREDIT	BALANCE DEBIT	BALANCE CREDIT
19-- Dec. 31		CJ49	26059		26059	

ACCOUNT *Depreciation Expense*   ACCOUNT NO. *827*

DATE	ITEM	POST. REF.	DEBIT	CREDIT	BALANCE DEBIT	BALANCE CREDIT
19-- Dec. 31		CJ49	65411		65411	

ACCOUNT *Insurance Expense*   ACCOUNT NO. *828*

DATE	ITEM	POST. REF.	DEBIT	CREDIT	BALANCE DEBIT	BALANCE CREDIT
19-- Dec. 31		CJ49	36570		36570	

ACCOUNT *Bank Credit Card Expense*   ACCOUNT NO. *832*

DATE	ITEM	POST. REF.	DEBIT	CREDIT	BALANCE DEBIT	BALANCE CREDIT
19-- Dec. 1	Balance	✓			283390	
3		CJ47	30605		313995	
31		CJ49	27250		341245	

Boyd's Clothiers — General Ledger Accounts After Posting Adjusting Entries
(continued)

ACCOUNT *Uncollectible Accounts Expense*   ACCOUNT NO. *833*

DATE	ITEM	POST. REF.	DEBIT	CREDIT	BALANCE DEBIT	BALANCE CREDIT
19-- Dec. 31		CJ49	32628		32628	

ACCOUNT *Interest Expense*   ACCOUNT NO. *911*

DATE	ITEM	POST. REF.	DEBIT	CREDIT	BALANCE DEBIT	BALANCE CREDIT
19-- Dec. 1	Balance	✓			15092	
31		CJ49	4978		20070	

Boyd's Clothers — General Ledger Accounts After Posting Adjusting Entries
(concluded)

BUILDING YOUR ACCOUNTING KNOWLEDGE

1. Give a brief explanation of the purpose of each of the eight end-of-period adjusting entries made by Boyd's Clothiers.
2. In what two types of journals may adjusting entries be recorded?
3. What amount columns are used when adjusting entries are recorded in a combination journal?
4. Where is the information obtained that is needed in journalizing the adjustments?
5. When is the account number of each adjusted ledger account entered in the Posting Reference column of the combination journal?
6. In the posting process, how is a cross-reference provided both to the combination journal and to the general ledger?

Report No. 10-1

> *Complete Report No. 10-1 in the study assignments and submit your working papers to the instructor for approval. Continue with the following textbook discussion until Report No. 10-2 is required.*

CLOSING PROCEDURE

After the adjusting entries have been posted, all of the temporary owner's equity accounts should be closed. This means that the accountant must close out (1) the balance of each account that enters into the calculation of the net income (or net loss) for the accounting period and (2) the balance of the owner's drawing account. The purpose of the closing procedure is to transfer the balances of the temporary owner's equity accounts to the permanent owner's equity account, and entries made to accomplish this are known as closing entries. This is accomplished by debiting or crediting each account involved with an offsetting credit or debit to the permanent owner's equity account, or to a summarizing account called Expense and Revenue Summary (sometimes called **Income Summary**, **Profit and Loss Summary**, or just **Profit and Loss**). The resulting balance of the expense and revenue summary account, which is the net income or net loss for the period, is then transferred to the permanent owner's equity account.

The final step in the closing procedure is to transfer the balance of the owner's drawing account to the permanent owner's equity account. After the temporary owner's equity and drawing accounts are transferred to the permanent owner's equity account, only the asset accounts, the liability accounts, and the permanent owner's equity account will have balances. The sum of the balances of the asset accounts (less balances of any contra accounts) will be equal to the sum of the balances of the liability accounts plus the balance of the permanent owner's equity account. The accounts will agree exactly with what is shown in the balance sheet as of the close of the period. The balance sheet of Boyd's Clothiers as of December 31, reproduced on pages 274 and 275, will show that the assets, liabilities, and owner's equity as of December 31 may be expressed in equation form as follows:

ASSETS	=	LIABILITIES	+	OWNER'S EQUITY
$53,971.87		$11,929.03		$42,042.84

JOURNALIZING THE CLOSING ENTRIES

Closing entries, like adjusting entries, are recorded in either a general journal or a combination journal. If the entries are made in a combination journal, only the General Debit and Credit columns are used. A portion of a combination journal showing the closing entries for Boyd's Clothiers is shown on the next page. Since the heading "Closing Entries" explains the nature of the entries, a separate explanation of each closing entry is not necessary. The information required in preparing the closing entries was obtained from the Income Statement columns of the work sheet illustrated on pages 260 and 261.

			GENERAL	
DAY	DESCRIPTION	POST. REF.	DEBIT	CREDIT
1	AMOUNTS FORWARDED			
2	31 *Closing Entries*			
3	*Sales*	611	26124327	
4	*Purchases Returns and Allowances*	711.1	223660	
5	*Purchases Discount*	711.2	999642	
6	*Expense and Revenue Summary*	531		27347629
7	*Expense and Revenue Summary*	531	23059600	
8	*Sales Returns and Allowances*	611.1		384920
9	*Purchases*	711		16673808
10	*Rent Expense*	821		1080000
11	*Salaries and Commissions Expense*	822		2771135
12	*Heating and Lighting Expense*	823		98753
13	*Telephone Expense*	824		48400
14	*Supplies Expense*	825		26059
15	*Advertising Expense*	826		1132980
16	*Depreciation Expense*	827		65411
17	*Insurance Expense*	828		36570
18	*Charitable Contributions Expense*	829		45850
19	*Payroll Taxes Expense*	831		238520
20	*Bank Credit Card Expense*	832		341245
21	*Uncollectible Accounts Expense*	833		32628
22	*Miscellaneous Expense*	839		63251
23	*Interest Expense*	911		20070
24	*Expense and Revenue Summary*	531	3955444	
25	*Lynn C. Boyd, Capital*	511		3955444
26	*Lynn C. Boyd, Capital*	511	3064750	
27	*Lynn C. Boyd, Drawing*	511.1		3064750
28			57427423	57427423

COMBINATION JOURNAL FOR MONTH OF *December* 19--   PAGE *50*

Boyd's Clothiers — Closing Entries

The first closing entry was made to close the sales, purchases returns and allowances, and purchases discount accounts. Since these accounts have credit balances, each account must be debited for the amount of its balance in order to close it. The debits to these three accounts are offset by a credit of $273,476.29 to Expense and Revenue Summary.

The second closing entry was made to close the sales returns and allowances, purchases, and all of the expense accounts. Since these accounts have debit balances, each account must be credited for the amount of its balance in order to close it. The credits to these accounts are offset by a debit of $230,596.00 to Expense and Revenue Summary.

The posting of the first two adjusting entries and the first two closing entries causes the expense and revenue summary account to have a credit balance of $39,554.44, which is the net income for the year. At this point, the account has served its purpose and must be closed. The third closing entry accomplishes this by debiting the expense and revenue summary account and crediting Lynn C. Boyd, Capital, for $39,554.44. The fourth closing entry was made to close the Lynn C. Boyd drawing account. Since this account has a debit balance, it must be credited to close it. The offsetting entry is a debit of $30,467.50 to Lynn C. Boyd, Capital.

The account numbers shown in the Posting Reference column were not entered at the time of journalizing the closing entries. They were entered as the posting was completed.

ACCOUNT *Lynn C. Boyd, Capital*   ACCOUNT NO. 511

DATE	ITEM	POST. REF.	DEBIT	CREDIT	BALANCE DEBIT	BALANCE CREDIT
19-- Dec. 1	Balance	✓				33 135 90
31		CJ50		39 554 44		
31		CJ50	30 647 50			42 042 84

Boyd's Clothiers — Partial General Ledger

POSTING THE CLOSING ENTRIES

Closing entries are posted in the usual manner and proper cross-references are provided by using the Posting Reference columns of the combination journal and the ledger accounts. After all the closing entries are posted, the accounts affected appear as shown on pages 292–296. Note that as each account was closed, the "no balance" symbol "—0—" was placed in each column.

Observe that the first two adjusting entries described and illustrated on pages 284–285 serve to adjust the merchandise inventory account by removing the amount of the beginning inventory and by recording the amount of the ending inventory. These two entries also facilitate the closing process in that they cause the two amounts that enter into the calculation of net income or net loss to be entered in the Expense and Revenue Summary. Once the expense and revenue summary account has been closed to the owner's equity account, the income and expense accounts are ready to perform their function in the following period.

ACCOUNT *Lynn C. Boyd, Drawing*   ACCOUNT NO. *511.1*

DATE	ITEM	POST. REF.	DEBIT	CREDIT	BALANCE DEBIT	BALANCE CREDIT
19-- Dec. 1	Balance	✓			2912750	
21		CJ48	150000			
31		CJ48	2000		3064750	
31		CJ50		3064750	-0-	-0-

ACCOUNT *Expense and Revenue Summary*   ACCOUNT NO. *531*

DATE	ITEM	POST. REF.	DEBIT	CREDIT	BALANCE DEBIT	BALANCE CREDIT
19-- Dec. 31		CJ49	3592210			
31		CJ49		3259625		
31		CJ50		27347629		
31		CJ50	23059600			
31		CJ50	3955444		-0-	-0-

ACCOUNT *Sales*   ACCOUNT NO. *611*

DATE	ITEM	POST. REF.	DEBIT	CREDIT	BALANCE DEBIT	BALANCE CREDIT
19-- Dec. 1	Balance	✓				24255537
31		S44		284432		
31		CJ48		1584358		26124327
31		CJ50	26124327		-0-	-0-

ACCOUNT *Sales Returns and Allowances*   ACCOUNT NO. *611.1*

DATE	ITEM	POST. REF.	DEBIT	CREDIT	BALANCE DEBIT	BALANCE CREDIT
19-- Dec. 1	Balance	✓			371130	
8		CJ47	10995			
27		CJ48	2795		384920	
31		CJ50		384920	-0-	-0-

ACCOUNT *Purchases*   ACCOUNT NO. *711*

DATE	ITEM	POST. REF.	DEBIT	CREDIT	BALANCE DEBIT	BALANCE CREDIT
19-- Dec. 1	Balance	✓			15406694	
1		CJ47	6914			
31		P32	1260200		16673808	
31		CJ50		16673808	-0-	-0-

Boyd's Clothiers — Partial General Ledger (*continued*)

ACCOUNT *Purchases Returns and Allowances*   ACCOUNT NO. *711.1*

DATE		ITEM	POST. REF.	DEBIT	CREDIT	BALANCE DEBIT	BALANCE CREDIT
19-- Dec.	1	Balance	✓				215160
	20		CJ48		8500		223660
	31		CJ50	223660		-0-	-0-

ACCOUNT *Purchases Discount*   ACCOUNT NO. *711.2*

DATE		ITEM	POST. REF.	DEBIT	CREDIT	BALANCE DEBIT	BALANCE CREDIT
19-- Dec.	1	Balance	✓				899865
	31		CJ48		99777		999642
	31		CJ50	999642		-0-	-0-

ACCOUNT *Rent Expense*   ACCOUNT NO. *821*

DATE		ITEM	POST. REF.	DEBIT	CREDIT	BALANCE DEBIT	BALANCE CREDIT
19-- Dec.	1	Balance	✓			990000	
	2		CJ47	90000		1080000	
	31		CJ50		1080000	-0-	-0-

ACCOUNT *Salaries and Commissions Expense*   ACCOUNT NO. *822*

DATE		ITEM	POST. REF.	DEBIT	CREDIT	BALANCE DEBIT	BALANCE CREDIT
19-- Dec.	1	Balance	✓			2540135	
	15		CJ47	116050			
	31		CJ48	114950		2771135	
	31		CJ50		2771135	-0-	-0-

ACCOUNT *Heating and Lighting Expense*   ACCOUNT NO. *823*

DATE		ITEM	POST. REF.	DEBIT	CREDIT	BALANCE DEBIT	BALANCE CREDIT
19-- Dec.	1	Balance	✓			89227	
	28		CJ48	9526		98753	
	31		CJ50		98753	-0-	-0-

Boyd's Clothiers — Partial General Ledger (*continued*)

ACCOUNT *Telephone Expense*   ACCOUNT NO. 824

DATE	ITEM	POST. REF.	DEBIT	CREDIT	BALANCE DEBIT	BALANCE CREDIT
19-- Dec. 1	Balance	✓			442 20	
28		CJ48	41 80		484 00	
31		CJ50		484 00	-0-	-0-

ACCOUNT *Supplies Expense*   ACCOUNT NO. 825

DATE	ITEM	POST. REF.	DEBIT	CREDIT	BALANCE DEBIT	BALANCE CREDIT
19-- Dec. 31		CJ49	260 59		260 59	
31		CJ50		260 59	-0-	-0-

ACCOUNT *Advertising Expense*   ACCOUNT NO. 826

DATE	ITEM	POST. REF.	DEBIT	CREDIT	BALANCE DEBIT	BALANCE CREDIT
19-- Dec. 1	Balance	✓			10 685 75	
6		CJ47	79 35			
27		CJ48	547 70			
31		CJ48	17 00		11 329 80	
31		CJ50		11 329 80	-0-	-0-

ACCOUNT *Depreciation Expense*   ACCOUNT NO. 827

DATE	ITEM	POST. REF.	DEBIT	CREDIT	BALANCE DEBIT	BALANCE CREDIT
19-- Dec. 31		CJ49	654 11		654 11	
31		CJ50		654 11	-0-	-0-

ACCOUNT *Insurance Expense*   ACCOUNT NO. 828

DATE	ITEM	POST. REF.	DEBIT	CREDIT	BALANCE DEBIT	BALANCE CREDIT
19-- Dec. 31		CJ49	365 70		365 70	
31		CJ50		365 70	-0-	-0-

Boyd's Clothiers — Partial General Ledger (continued)

ACCOUNT *Charitable Contributions Expense*   ACCOUNT NO. *829*

DATE		ITEM	POST. REF.	DEBIT	CREDIT	BALANCE	
						DEBIT	CREDIT
19-- Dec.	1	Balance	✓			44850	
	31		CJ48	1000		45850	
	31		CJ50		45850	-0-	-0-

ACCOUNT *Payroll Taxes Expense*   ACCOUNT NO. *831*

DATE		ITEM	POST. REF.	DEBIT	CREDIT	BALANCE	
						DEBIT	CREDIT
19-- Dec.	1	Balance	✓			221428	
	15		CJ47	8587			
	31		CJ48	8505		238520	
	31		CJ50		238520	-0-	-0-

ACCOUNT *Bank Credit Card Expense*   ACCOUNT NO. *832*

DATE		ITEM	POST. REF.	DEBIT	CREDIT	BALANCE	
						DEBIT	CREDIT
19-- Dec.	1	Balance	✓			283390	
	3		CJ47	30605		313995	
	31		CJ49	27250		341245	
	31		CJ50		341245	-0-	-0-

ACCOUNT *Uncollectible Accounts Expense*   ACCOUNT NO. *833*

DATE		ITEM	POST. REF.	DEBIT	CREDIT	BALANCE	
						DEBIT	CREDIT
19-- Dec.	31		CJ49	32628		32628	
	31		CJ50		32628	-0-	-0-

ACCOUNT *Miscellaneous Expense*   ACCOUNT NO. *839*

DATE		ITEM	POST. REF.	DEBIT	CREDIT	BALANCE	
						DEBIT	CREDIT
19-- Dec.	1	Balance	✓			59956	
	22		CJ48	2185			
	31		CJ48	1110		63251	
	31		CJ50		63251	-0-	-0-

Boyd's Clothiers — Partial General Ledger (*continued*)

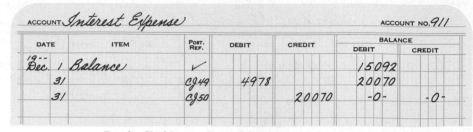

Boyd's Clothiers — Partial General Ledger (*concluded*)

POST-CLOSING TRIAL BALANCE

A trial balance of the general ledger accounts taken after the temporary owner's equity accounts have been closed is usually referred to as a post-closing trial balance. The purpose of the post-closing trial balance is to prove that the general ledger is in balance at the beginning of a new accounting period before any transactions for the new accounting period are recorded.

The post-closing trial balance contains the same accounts and amounts that appear in the Balance Sheet columns of the work sheet, except that (1) the owner's drawing account is omitted because it has been closed, and (2) the owner's capital account has been adjusted for the amount of the net income (or net loss) and the amount of drawings.

A post-closing trial balance of the general ledger of Boyd's Clothiers is shown on page 297. The post-closing trial balance may be dated either as of the close of the old accounting period or as of the beginning of the new accounting period. In this illustration, the trial balance is dated December 31, 19––, the end of the period.

COMPLETING THE ACCOUNTING CYCLE

In Chapter 5, pages 144 and 145, the nine steps involved in handling the effect of all transactions and events completed during an accounting period, beginning with entries in the books of original entry and ending with the post-closing trial balance, were referred to collectively as the accounting cycle. A tenth step — journalizing and posting reversing entries — needs to be added if the accrual basis of accounting is being used.

Reversing Entries for Accrual Adjustments. The purposes of reversing entries are (1) to make possible the recording of the transac-

| Boyd's Clothiers
Post-Closing Trial Balance
December 31, 19--			
Account	Acct. No.	Dr. Balance	Cr. Balance
First National Bank	111	1139847	
Petty Cash Fund	112	15000	
Accounts Receivable	131	428843	
Allowance for Doubtful Accounts	131.1		40327
Merchandise Inventory	161	3259625	
Supplies	181	8000	
Prepaid Insurance	184	36570	
Store Equipment	211	727110	
Accumulated Depr.--Store Equipment	211.1		177481
FICA Tax Payable	311		32342
FUTA Tax Payable	312		10974
State Unemployment Tax Payable	313		14742
Employees Income Tax Payable	314		45400
Accrued Bank Credit Card Payable	315		27250
Notes Payable	316		400000
Accrued Interest Payable	317		4978
Accounts Payable	318		564465
Sales Tax Payable	321		92752
Lynn C. Boyd, Capital	511		4204284
		5614995	5614995

Boyd's Clothiers — Post-Closing Trial Balance

tions of the succeeding accounting period in a routine manner, (2) to assure that the proper amount of revenue is credited to the period in which it is earned, and (3) to assure that the proper amount of expense is charged to the period in which it is incurred.

A case in point is interest expense. Assume that interest of $50 had accrued on a $3,500 loan in the year 1982. To adjust for the interest expense for 1982, Interest Expense must be debited and Accrued Interest Payable must be credited, as follows:

Interest Expense	50	
Accrued Interest Payable		50

To simplify the entry for the payment of the note and interest in 1983, the adjusting entry for 1982 needs to be reversed at the beginning of the 1983 accounting period by debiting Accrued Interest Payable and crediting Interest Expense, as follows:

Accrued Interest Payable... 50	
Interest Expense	50

Thus, if cash of $3,575 is disbursed in 1983, in payment of the note and interest that has accrued in prior and present periods, a simple entry can be recorded by debiting Notes Payable and Interest Expense and crediting Cash (or Bank), as shown:

Notes Payable 3,500	
Interest Expense 75	
Cash (Bank)	3,575

As a result of this entry and the reversing entry made at the beginning of the period, the interest expense account will have a balance of $25, as shown below. This $25 is the correct amount of interest expense on this loan to be charged to 1983.

Interest Expense

Interest paid	Accrued from prior accounting period (reversing entry)
75	50
Bal. 25	

Note that if the 1982 adjusting entry had not been reversed, it would be necessary to debit the accrued interest payable account for $50 as well as debit the interest expense account for the $25 interest accrued in 1983 at the time the note was paid.

Journalizing the Reversing Entries. Reversing entries, like adjusting and closing entries, may be recorded in either a general journal or a combination journal. If the entries are made in a combination journal, the only amount columns used are the General Debit and Credit columns. A portion of a combination journal showing the reversing entries of Boyd's Clothiers is reproduced below. Usually

	DAY	DESCRIPTION	POST. REF.	GENERAL DEBIT	GENERAL CREDIT	
1		AMOUNTS FORWARDED				1
2	1	Reversing Entries				2
3		Accrued Interest Payable	317	4978		3
4		Interest Expense	911		4978	4
5		Accrued Bank Credit Card Payable	315	27250		5
6		Bank Credit Card Expense	832		27250	6
				322228	322228	

COMBINATION JOURNAL FOR MONTH OF *January* 19 – –   PAGE *51*

Boyd's Clothiers — Reversing Entries

the reversing entries are made immediately after closing the books at the end of an accounting period. However, it is customary to date the entries as of the first day of the succeeding accounting period. Thus, the reversing entries for Boyd's Clothiers are dated January 1. Since the heading "Reversing Entries" explains the nature of the entries, a separate explanation of each reversing entry is unnecessary. Each of the reversing entries shown is discussed in the following section.

Posting the Reversing Entries. Reversing entries are posted in the usual manner and proper cross-references are provided by using the Posting Reference columns of the combination journal and the ledger accounts. After the reversing entries have been posted, the accounts affected appear as shown on page 301.

Accrued Interest Payable. The adjusting entry on December 31 for Boyd's Clothiers reproduced on page 285 shows that Interest Expense, Account No. 911, was debited and Accrued Interest Payable, Account No. 317, was credited for $49.78 to record the interest accrued on a 6-month, 8 percent interest-bearing note for $4,000 issued on November 5. To reverse the adjusting entry it is necessary to debit Accrued Interest Payable, Account No. 317, and to credit Interest Expense, Account No. 911, for $49.78. The accounts affected by the entry are reproduced below.

ACCOUNT *Accrued Interest Payable*   ACCOUNT NO. 317

DATE	ITEM	POST. REF.	DEBIT	CREDIT	BALANCE DEBIT	BALANCE CREDIT
19-- Dec. 31		CJ49		49 78		49 78
19-- Jan. 1		CJ51	49 78		-0-	-0-

ACCOUNT *Interest Expense*   ACCOUNT NO. 911

DATE	ITEM	POST. REF.	DEBIT	CREDIT	BALANCE DEBIT	BALANCE CREDIT
19-- Dec. 1	Balance	✓			150 92	
31		CJ49	49 78		200 70	
31		CJ50		200 70	-0-	-0-
19-- Jan. 1		CJ51		49 78		49 78

Boyd's Clothiers — Accrued Interest Payable and Interest Expense
After Posting of Reversing Entry

Note that after posting the reversing entry, the account Accrued Interest Payable has a zero balance and the account Interest Expense has a credit balance of $49.78. If the note for $4,000 plus interest is paid on May 5, the payment will amount to $4,160 ($4,000, principal of note, plus $160, interest at 8 percent for 6 months). The payment is recorded by a debit to Notes Payable, Account No. 316 for $4,000 and Interest Expense, Account No. 911, for $160 and a credit to First National Bank, Account No. 111, for $4,160. After posting this entry, the interest expense account will have a debit balance of $110.22 ($160 minus $49.78). This balance of $110.22 represents the amount of interest expense incurred in the year in which the note matures. If the adjusting entry is not reversed, an analysis would have to be made before recording the payment on May 5 to determine the amount of interest expense incurred in the preceding year and the amount of interest expense incurred in the current year. It would be necessary to debit Accrued Interest Payable for $49.78 and Interest Expense for $110.22 so that each year might be charged with the correct interest expense. If the adjustment is reversed, however, this analysis becomes unnecessary.

The reversal procedure is particularly useful if the year-end adjustment for interest expense, incurred but not paid, relates to interest accrued on several interest-bearing obligations. When the adjustment is reversed, all future payments of interest can be debited to the interest expense account without any concern as to when each amount paid was incurred. The portion of any payments that is an expense of the new period will automatically emerge as the balance of the interest expense account.

Accrued Bank Credit Card Payable. The adjusting entry for Boyd's Clothiers shows that Bank Credit Card Expense, Account No. 832, was debited and Accrued Bank Credit Card Payable, Account No. 315, was credited for $272.50 to record the expense for December which the bank will not deduct from Boyd's checking account until early in January. The reversing entry is a debit to the accrual account, Accrued Bank Credit Card Payable (No. 315), and a credit to the expense account, Bank Credit Card Expense (No. 832), for $272.50. The result of the reversing entry is to remove the credit balance in the liability account and give the expense account a credit balance of $272.50. The accounts after the reversing entry has been posted are shown on page 301.

The entry to record the bank's deduction for this expense is a debit to Bank Credit Card Expense and a credit to the bank account. If this entry is made in early January for the calculated amount, $272.50, the expense account will be in balance, which reflects the

ACCOUNT *Accrued Bank Credit Card Payable*   ACCOUNT NO. *315*

DATE	ITEM	POST. REF.	DEBIT	CREDIT	BALANCE DEBIT	BALANCE CREDIT
19-- Dec. 31		CJ49		272 50		272 50
19-- Jan. 1		CJ51	272 50		-0-	-0-

ACCOUNT *Bank Credit Card Expense*   ACCOUNT NO. *832*

DATE	ITEM	POST. REF.	DEBIT	CREDIT	BALANCE DEBIT	BALANCE CREDIT
19-- Dec. 1	Balance	✓			2833 90	
3		CJ47	306 05		3139 95	
31		CJ49	272 50		3412 45	
31		CJ50		3412 45	-0-	-0-
19-- Jan. 1		CJ51		272 50		272 50

**Boyd's Clothiers — Accrued Bank Credit Card Payable and
Bank Credit Card Expense After Posting of Reversing Entry**

fact that this amount is an expense of the year just ended, not of the new year. If the reversing entry had not been made, the accountant would have had to remember that the January debit had to be different from the other eleven months. This is not a serious problem, but it is better whenever possible not to disturb the regular routine of recording transactions. Reversing entries for accrued expense and revenue help to accomplish this objective.

BUILDING YOUR ACCOUNTING KNOWLEDGE

1. What amount columns are used when closing entries are recorded in a combination journal?
2. Where is the information obtained that is needed in journalizing the closing entries?
3. Explain the function of each of the four closing entries made by Boyd's Clothiers.
4. What is the purpose of a post-closing trial balance?
5. In what two ways does the information in the post-closing trial balance differ from the information in the Balance Sheet columns of the work sheet?
6. What is the tenth and last step in the accounting cycle?
7. What is the purpose of reversing entries for accruals?
8. What is the customary date for reversing entries?

Report No. 10-2

> *Complete Report No. 10-2 in the study assignments and submit your working papers to the instructor for approval. You will then be given instructions as to the work to be done next.*

EXPANDING YOUR BUSINESS VOCABULARY

What is the meaning of each of the following terms?

accounting cycle (p. 296)	post-closing trial balance
adjusting entries (p. 284)	(p. 296)
closing entries (p. 289)	reversing entries (p. 296)

CHAPTERS 6–10

SUPPLEMENTARY PRACTICAL ACCOUNTING PROBLEMS

Problem 6-A   Purchases journal; summary posting to general ledger

Charlotte Zietlow decides to open a general merchandise store under the name of Goods Store. The books of original entry consist of three different journals including a purchases journal. Zietlow uses the invoice method of accounting for purchases on account. Since Goods Store has just started operations, the first page in the July purchases journal is Page 1.

The following transactions relating to purchases occurred during the month of July.

July   5   Received Invoice No. 1 dated July 2 from Club Metalware, Inc., for merchandise purchased, $184.75. Terms, 30 days.

        7   Received Invoice No. 2 dated July 6 from Oriental Tea Co. for merchandise purchased, $112.50. Terms, 10 days.

        8   Received Invoice No. 3 dated July 7 from Reese Co. for merchandise purchased, $269.00. Terms, 30 days.

     12   Received Invoice No. 4 dated July 9 from Nashville Woodwork Co. for merchandise purchased, $258.65. Terms, 10 days.

     15   Received Invoice No. 5 dated July 14 from Bloomington Wholesalers for merchandise purchased, $225.50. Terms, 15 days.

     16   Received Invoice No. 6 dated July 14 from Bedford Kitchens, Inc., for merchandise purchased, $397.90. Terms, 2/10, net/30.

     21   Received Invoice No. 7 dated July 20 from Club Metalware, Inc., for merchandise purchased, $216.20. Terms, 30 days.

     26   Received Invoice No. 8 dated July 23 from Arts International for merchandise purchased, $305.45. Terms, 30 days.

     29   Received Invoice No. 9 dated July 28 from Opus Stoneware Co. for merchandise purchased, $288.75. Terms, 2/10, net/30.

Required: (1) Record each transaction in a purchases journal, using a sheet of paper ruled like that shown in the illustration on page 174. (2) Foot and rule the purchases journal. (3) Open accounts for Purchases, Account No. 711 and Accounts Payable, Account No. 318, using the four-column ledger form. Complete the summary posting of the purchases journal for July.

Problem 6-B   Purchases journal or general journal; individual and summary posting to general ledger

Gerry Wiley operates an office furniture and supply store. The books of original entry consist of four different journals including a two-column general journal and a purchases journal. Wiley uses the invoice method of accounting for purchases on account. The first page of the general journal is page 6. The first page of the purchases journal is page 9. The selected general ledger accounts and their balances as of April 1 are listed below:

	Account	Balance — April 1
318	Accounts Payable	$ 5,491.10
711	Purchases	15,185.67
711.1	Purchases Returns and Allowances	402.50
721	Freight In	388.45

The following transactions related to purchases occurred during the month of April:

Apr. 2 Received Invoice No. 193 dated March 31 from Yawman & Erbe Co. for desks purchased, $1,327.00. Desks were shipped FOB shipping point; terms, 2/10, net/30.

5 Received freight bill from DC Trucking Co., $86.20, for delivery charges on the desks purchased from Yawman & Erbe Co.

6 Received Invoice No. 194 dated April 5 from Steno Supply Co. for memo books purchased, $106.95. Terms, 10 days.

9 Received Invoice No. 195 dated April 7 from Great Lakes Office Supply Co. for ledger outfits purchased, $269.00. Terms, 10 days.

12 Received Invoice No. 196 dated April 9 from Mohawk Chair, Inc., for chairs purchased, $826.46. Desks were shipped FOB destination so freight charges of $67.60 were not included in the invoice. Terms, 2/10, net/30.

14 Received Invoice No. 197 dated April 13 from Heywood Furniture Co. for tables purchased, $487.70. Terms, 45 days.

15 Received Invoice No. 198 dated April 14 from Chestnut Co. for chairs purchased, $358.00. Terms, 30 days.

19 Received a credit memorandum from Mohawk Chair Inc., for $117.50 for one chair returned because it had the wrong fabric.

21 Received Invoice No. 199 dated April 20 from Parker's for desk sets, $224.80. Terms, 10 days.

Apr. 23 Received a credit memorandum from Heywood Furniture Co. for $32.00, an allowance for damage during shipment of tables purchased on Invoice No. 197.

27 Received Invoice No. 200 dated April 26 from Yawman & Erbe Co. for filing cabinets purchased, $389.25. Cabinets were shipped FOB shipping point and a separate freight bill for $42.90 was received with the invoice. Terms, 2/10, net/30. (Two entries are required.)

28 Received Invoice No. 201 dated April 27 from High Point Furniture Co. for desks purchased, $750.00. Terms, 60 days.

30 Received Invoice No. 202 dated April 28 from Olivetti Underwood Corp. for typewriters purchased, $1,114.00. Terms, 2/10, net/30.

Required: (1) Record each transaction in a purchases journal, using a sheet of paper ruled like that shown in the illustration on page 174, or in a two-column journal, using a sheet of paper ruled like that shown in the illustration on page 27. (2) Foot and rule the purchases journal. (3) Open accounts for the four accounts indicated above with the related balances, using the four-column ledger form. Complete the summary posting of the purchases journal and the individual posting of the general journal for April.

Problem 7-A   Sales journal; summary posting to general ledger

Jan Powell operates an auto parts store under the name of The Havit Store. The books of original entry consist of three different journals including a sales journal. Powell uses the sales ticket method of accounting for sales on account. The first page in the October sales journal is Page 10.

The following sales transactions on account occurred during the month of October:

Oct. 5 Sold merchandise on account to C. L. Martus, $61.90, tax, $3.10. Sale No. 109.

7 Sold merchandise on account to W. P. Keim, $91.85, tax, $4.59. Sale No. 110.

8 Sold merchandise on account to M. S. Hannah, $59.95, tax, $3.00. Sale No. 111.

12 Sold merchandise on account to J. M. Howard, $116.50, tax, $5.83. Sale No. 112.

16 Sold merchandise on account to G. A. Lents, $88.25, tax, $4.41. Sale No. 113.

21 Sold merchandise on account to A. P. Day, $72.40, tax, $3.62. Sale No. 114.

26 Sold merchandise on account to B. C. Subrin, $106.00, tax, $5.30. Sale No. 115.

29 Sold merchandise on account to K. T. Palumbo, $58.90, tax, $2.95. Sale No. 116.

Required: (1) Record each transaction in the sales journal, using a sheet of paper ruled like that shown in the illustration at the bottom of page 199. (2) Foot and rule the sales journal. (3) Open accounts for Sales, Account No. 611, Accounts Receivable, Account No. 131, and Sales Tax Payable, Account No. 321, using the four-column ledger form. Complete the summary posting of the sales journal for October.

Problem 7-B   Sales journal; combination journal; individual and summary posting to general ledger

C. R. Dorbin operates a clothing store under the name of The Westbury Store. The books of original entry include a sales journal, a purchases journal and a combination journal. This problem involves the use of the sales journal and combination journal only.

For the sales journal, use a sheet of paper ruled like that shown at the bottom of page 199. For the combination journal, use a sheet of paper like that shown in the illustration on pages 236 and 237. The Check No. column will not be used in this problem. Assume that the first page of each journal in July is page 9. The following accounts are used:

111	Cash	511	C. R. Dorbin, Capital
131	Accounts Receivable	611	Sales
321	Sales Tax Payable	611.1	Sales Returns and Allowances

The following selected transactions were completed during the month of July:

July 1 Invested $10,000 in the business.
2 Sold merchandise on account to P. D. Hiland, $91.15, tax, $4.56. Sale No. 104.
5 Sold merchandise on account to B. A. Dorbin, $97.25, tax, $4.86. Sale No. 105.
6 P. D. Hiland returned goods for credit. Sales price, $23.00, tax, $1.15.
9 Sold merchandise on account to D. C. Hunt, $146.37, tax, $7.32. Sale No. 106.
13 Received $71.60 from P. D. Hiland on account.
14 Sold merchandise on account to T. G. Walls, $70.56, tax, $3.53. Sale No. 107.
19 D. C. Hunt returned some merchandise for credit. Sales price, $17.15, tax, $.86.
21 Received $122.19 from D. C. Hunt on account.
26 Sold merchandise on account to S. L. Sparks, $42.85, tax, $2.14. Sale No. 108.
28 Sold merchandise on account to J. R. Miller, $26.32, tax, $1.32. Sale No. 109.

July   30   Sold merchandise on account to R. M. Stephens, $39.60, tax, $1.98. Sale No. 110.

Required: (1) Record each transaction in the proper journal. (2) Enter the totals and rule the sales journal and the combination journal. (3) Open the necessary accounts using the four-column form of ledger paper. Post the sales journal and combination journal entries for July.

There are no Supplementary Practical Accounting Problems for Chapter 8.

Problem 9-A   Adjustments in work sheet

John Schweisberg is in the business of retail heating and cooling. Merchandise is sold for cash and on account. On the next page is a reproduction of the Trial Balance columns of the work sheet for the year ended December 31. The following adjustments are to be made before the close of the accounting period:

(a) Merchandise inventory, end of year, $27,548.60.
(b) Accruals:
Interest accrued on notes payable, $39.61.
Accrued bank credit card payable, $223.29.
(c) Prepaid expenses:
Prepaid insurance unexpired, $604.80.
Supplies on hand, $129.00.
(d) Depreciation:
Store equipment, 10% a year, $950.00.
(e) Uncollectible accounts expense:
Increase allowance for doubtful accounts $173.00 to provide for estimated loss.

Required: Prepare a ten-column work sheet making the necessary entries in the Adjustments columns.

Note: Problems 9-B and 10A are also based on Schweisberg's work sheet. If these problems are to be solved, the work sheet prepared in Problem 9-A should be retained for reference until after they are solved, when the solutions of all three problems may be submitted to the instructor.

Problem 9-B   Financial statements

Refer to the work sheet for John Schweisberg (based on Problem 9-A) and from it prepare the following financial statements:
(1) An income statement for the year ended December 31.
(2) A balance sheet in account form as of December 31.

JOHN SCHWEISBERG
Work Sheet
For the Year Ended December 31, 19––

Account	Acct. No.	Trial Balance Debit	Trial Balance Credit
Bloomfield State Bank..	111	11,806.34	
Petty Cash Fund..	112	150.00	
Accounts Receivable	131	12,363.84	
Allowance for Doubtful Accounts.........................	131.1		107.40
Merchandise Inventory..	161	23,172.48	
Supplies..	181	388.80	
Prepaid Insurance...	184	1,209.60	
Store Equipment...	211	9,500.00	
Accumulated Depreciation — Store Equipment.....	211.1		950.00
FICA Tax Payable..	311		729.00
FUTA Tax Payable...	312		116.10
State Unemployment Tax Payable.........................	313		165.51
Employees Income Tax Payable...........................	314		796.50
Accrued Bank Credit Card Payable......................	315		
Notes Payable...	316		4,725.00
Accrued Interest Payable	317		
Accounts Payable	318		14,410.85
Sales Tax Payable	321		1,117.80
John Schweisberg, Capital	511		57,140.26
John Schweisberg, Drawing	511.1	16,200.00	
Expense and Revenue Summary..........................	521		
Sales...	611		111,099.60
Sales Returns and Allowances	611.1	386.64	
Purchases...	711	78,259.50	
Purchases Returns and Allowances......................	711.1		398.12
Rent Expense	811	6,480.00	
Advertising Expense..	812	842.40	
Salaries Expense...	813	25,920.00	
Payroll Taxes Expense	814	1,782.00	
Insurance Expense	815		
Supplies Expense	816		
Depreciation Expense	817		
Uncollectible Accounts Expense...........................	818		
Charitable Contributions Expense	819	540.00	
Bank Credit Card Expense...................................	821	2,467.26	
Miscellaneous Expense..	822	226.80	
Interest Expense	911	60.48	
		191,756.14	191,756.14

Problem 10-A   Adjusting, closing, and reversing entries

Refer to the work sheet for John Schweisberg (based on Problem 9-A) and prepare the general journal entries required: (1) To adjust the general ledger accounts so that they will be in agreement with the financial statements; (2) To close the temporary owner's equity accounts on December 31; and (3) To reverse the accrual adjustments as of January 1.

Problem 10-B   Complete accounting cycle

Myrtle Godbout, as a sole owner, operates a merchandising business known as Myrtle's Boutique. The business keeps a purchases journal, a sales journal, a combination journal, and a general ledger. While a petty cash fund is maintained, no payments are made from the fund in December.

For the combination journal, nine-column paper is used (3 columns on the left and 6 columns on the right) with headings arranged as follows:

(1) Deposits Dr.
(2) Checks Cr. } Bank
(3) Purchases Discount Cr.

(4) Debit } General
(5) Credit
(6) Accounts Payable Dr.
(7) Accounts Receivable Cr.
(8) Sales Cr.
(9) Sales Tax Payable Cr.

Number the pages of the journals as follows:

Purchases Journal ....Page 34
Sales Journal ....Page 46
Combination Journal ....Pages 49–51

The four-column form of ledger account is used. Individual accounts with customers and suppliers are not kept in ledger form; however, the purchase invoices and sales tickets are filed in such a manner that the amounts owed to suppliers and amounts due from customers can be determined at any time.

At the end of the eleventh month of this year, the trial balance appeared as shown on page 310. The following transactions occurred during the month of December:

NARRATIVE OF TRANSACTIONS FOR DECEMBER

Dec. 1 (Wednesday) Purchased merchandise from Berline Co., $2,250, Invoice No. 61, dated November 30. Terms, 6/10, n/30.

2 Paid the December rent, $1,125, Check No. 124.

2 Paid the telephone bill, $60, Check No. 125.

3 Paid Crowley Co. $2,106.25 in full settlement of December 1 balance. Check No. 126.

6 Sold merchandise on account to M. T. Collins, $187.50, tax, $9.38. Sale No. 121.

6 Purchased merchandise from the Jaycox Co., $1,650. Invoice No. 62, dated December 5. Terms, 30 days.

7 Received $281.25 from Bobbi Caffoe in full settlement of her account.

8 Paid Berline Co. $2,115 in settlement of their invoice of November 30, less 6% discount. Check No. 127.

8 Received $278.06 from Julia Weber in full settlement of her account.

MYRTLE'S BOUTIQUE
Trial Balance
November 30, 19—

Clayton Bank	111	17,617.13	
Petty Cash Fund	112	125.00	
Accounts Receivable	121	15,889.63	
Allowance for Doubtful Accounts	121.1		243.63
Merchandise Inventory	131	72,800.00	
Supplies	141	280.00	
Prepaid Insurance	151	1,662.50	
Store Equipment	211	6,650.00	
Accumulated Depreciation — Store Equipment	211.1		1,330.00
FICA Tax Payable	311		348.00
FUTA Tax Payable	312		99.13
State Unemployment Tax Payable	313		133.38
Employees Income Tax Payable	314		418.63
Accrued Bank Credit Card Payable	315		
Notes Payable	316		4,200.00
Accrued Interest Payable	317		
Accounts Payable	318		5,634.50
Sales Tax Payable	321		1,157.75
Myrtle Godbout, Capital	511		118,157.18
Myrtle Godbout, Drawing	511.1	15,750.00	
Expense and Revenue Summary	521		
Sales	611		292,880.00
Sales Returns and Allowances	611.1	442.38	
Purchases	711	221,200.00	
Purchases Returns and Allowances	711.1		493.88
Purchases Discount	711.2		385.00
Rent Expense	811	12,375.00	
Advertising Expense	812	8,437.50	
Salaries and Commissions Expense	813	45,250.00	
Payroll Taxes Expense	814	3,104.75	
Miscellaneous Expense	815	626.56	
Insurance Expense	816		
Supplies Expense	817		
Depreciation Expense	818		
Uncollectible Accounts Expense	819		
Bank Credit Card Expense	821	3,221.63	
Interest Expense	911	49.00	
		425,481.08	425,481.08

Dec. 9 Sold merchandise on account to Beth Willis, $71.63, tax $3.58. Sale No. 122.

   9 Received a notice from Clayton Bank that $440.31 had been deducted from the account of Myrtle's Boutique, representing a discount of 3 percent on the amount net of returns of Visa and MasterCard vouchers that had been deposited during November.

   10 Purchased merchandise from the Heerema Mfg. Co., $604. Invoice No. 63, dated December 9. Terms, 30 days.

Dec. 11   Sold merchandise on account to Nita Tosanguan, $188, tax, $9.40. Sale No. 123.

      13   Issued Check No. 128 to Clayton Bank, a U.S. depository, in payment of the following taxes:

(a) Employees' income tax withheld during November.....		$418.63
(b) FICA tax:		
On employees (withheld during November)..............	$174.00	
On the employer...	174.00	348.00
Total...		$766.63

     14   Sold merchandise on account to Julia Peet, $181.25, tax, $9.06. Sale No. 124.

     15   Issued Check No. 129 payable to State Treasurer for $1,157.75 for November sales tax.

     17   Myrtle Godbout withdrew $375 for personal use. Check No. 130.

     20   Gave Nita Tosanguan credit for $65.63 because a part of the merchandise sold to her on the eleventh was returned. (Sales price, $62.50, tax $3.13.)

     20   Sold merchandise on account to M. T. Collins, $106.25, tax, $5.31. Sale No. 125.

     21   Purchased merchandise from Barbie Brooks, Inc., $1,370.63. Invoice No. 64, dated December 20. Terms, 4/10, n/30.

     22   Received $131.77 from Nita Tosanguan for balance of Sale No. 123.

     23   Paid bill for advertising, $375. Check No. 131.

     24   Sold merchandise on account to Barbara Murphy, $282.19, tax, $14.11. Sale No. 126.

     27   Purchase merchandise from Berline Co. $1,927.38. Invoice No. 65, dated December 23. Terms, 2/10, n/30.

     27   Received a check for $125 from M. T. Collins to apply on account.

     27   Sold merchandise to Nita Tosanguan, $294.38, tax, $14.72. Sale No. 127.

     27   Sent the Heerema Mfg. Co. a check for $250 to apply on account. Check No. 132.

     28   Sold merchandise on account to Tracie Williams, $115.63, tax, $5.78. Sale No. 128.

     28   Purchased store equipment from the Mattoon Supply Co., $650. Terms, 60 days.

     29   Received $75.21 from Beth Willis in payment of Sale No. 122.

     29   Received credit from Berline Co. for $75 because a part of the merchandise purchased on the 27th was returned by agreement.

     29   Sold merchandise on account to Beth Willis, $153.13, tax, $7.66. Sale No. 129.

     31   Sundry cash and bank credit card sales for month, $18,018.50, tax, $900.93.

     31   Issued Check No. 133 payable to Payroll for $3,217.12.

PAYROLL STATEMENT FOR MONTH ENDED DECEMBER 31

Total salaries and commissions earned during period		$4,125.00
Employees' taxes to be withheld:		
(a) Employees' income tax	$619.13	
(b) FICA tax, 7%	288.75	907.88
Net amount payable to employees		$3,217.12
Employer's payroll taxes:		
(a) FICA tax, 7%		$ 288.75
(b) Unemployment compensation taxes:		
State, 2.7%	$111.38	
Federal, 0.7%	28.88	140.26
Total		$ 429.01

(In addition to recording the amounts withheld from employees' wages for FICA and income tax purposes, the payroll taxes imposed on the employer should also be recorded.)

The following adjustments are to be made before the close of business for the year ended December 31:

  (a) Merchandise inventory, end of year, $102,375.00.
  (b) Accruals:
      Interest accrued on notes payable, $42.00.
      Accrued bank credit card payable, $447.06.
  (c) Prepaid expenses:
      Prepaid insurance unexpired, $1,107.50.
      Supplies on hand, $87.50.
  (d) Depreciation:
      Store equipment, 10% a year, $665.00.
  (e) Uncollectible accounts expense:
      Increase allowance for doubtful accounts $369.88 to provide for estimated loss.

Required: (1) Journalize the December transactions. (2) Open the necessary ledger accounts and record the December 1 balances, using the November 30 trial balance as the source of the needed information. Complete the individual and summary posting from the books of original entry. (3) Take a trial balance of the general ledger accounts. (4) Prepare a ten-column work sheet making the required adjustments. (5) Prepare an income statement for the year ending December 31 and a balance sheet in report form as of December 31. (6) Record the adjusting entries in the combination journal and post. (7) Record the closing entries in the combination journal and post. (8) Place "no balance" symbols in the accounts that are in balance after the adjusting and closing entries have been posted. (9) Take a post-closing trial balance. (10) Record the necessary reversing entries as of January 1 in the combination journal and post. Place "no balance" symbols in the accounts that are in balance after the reversing entries have been posted.

CHAPTER 11

ACCOUNTING FOR NOTES AND INTEREST

CHAPTER OBJECTIVES

The objectives of this chapter are to enable you:

▶ To describe and explain the nature and use of promissory notes and compute any related interest on such notes.

▶ To describe and record transactions that involve notes receivable and to prepare a notes receivable register.

▶ To describe and record transactions that involve notes payable and to prepare a notes payable register.

▶ To explain and record end-of-period adjustments for:

(1) Interest earned but not yet collected, and
(2) Interest incurred but not yet paid.

▶ To describe and illustrate the various types of indorsement on notes.

A major characteristic of modern business is the extensive use of credit. Each day hundreds of millions of transactions involve the sale of goods or services in return for promises to pay at a later date. Sales of this type are said to be "on credit" or "on account," and are often described as charge sales. As mentioned in Chapter 7, to facilitate such transactions, the use of credit cards has become commonplace. The majority of credit transactions do not involve a written promise to pay a specified amount of money. Often, the buyer merely signs a sales slip or sales ticket that acknowledges the receipt of the merchandise or service. When opening an account, a form or document is signed that obligates the customer to pay for all purchases within a specific number of days after a bill for the purchases is received from the business.

THE PROMISSORY NOTE

While not nearly so commonplace as transactions that involve "open account" credit, or the use of bank credit cards, **promissory notes** (usually just called notes) are sometimes used. A promise to repay a borrowed sum of money nearly always takes the form of a note. The extension of credit for periods of more than 60 days, or for large amounts of money, may entail the use of notes. Such notes have certain legal characteristics that cause them to be negotiable commercial paper. In order to be considered **negotiable commercial paper**, a promissory note must evidence the following:

   (1) Be in writing and signed by the person or persons agreeing to make payment;
   (2) Be an unconditional promise to pay a certain amount of money;
   (3) Be payable either on demand or at a definite future time;
   (4) Be payable to the order of a specified person or firm, or to the bearer.

A promissory note is illustrated below. Observe that this note has all of the characteristics listed above. Jerald Kent is known as

$ 1,450.25   June 7   19 82

Ninety days   *after date*   I   *promise to pay to the order of*   Betsy Rand

One thousand four hundred fifty 25/100 ------- *Dollars*

Payable at   Tower Grove Bank

With interest at   8% per annum from date

No. 5   *Due* Sept. 5, 1982   *Jerald Kent*

Promissory Note

the maker of the note because he promises to pay a certain amount of money ($1,450.25) at a definite future time (90 days after June 7). Betsy Rand is called the payee of the note because she is the one who is to receive the specified amount of money. It should also be understood that to Jerald Kent it is a note payable while to Betsy Rand it is a note receivable.

Notes may be interest-bearing or non-interest-bearing. The note illustrated is interest-bearing, with interest at 8% per year. Sometimes no rate of interest is specified on the note; however, the transaction will entail some interest. For example, a borrower might give a $1,000 non-interest-bearing note, payable in 60 days to a bank in return for a loan of $985. The $15 difference between the amount received ($985) and the amount that must be repaid ($1,000) when the note matures will become, in reality, interest expense at maturity. Accounting for this type of transaction is explained on page 323.

CALCULATING INTEREST

In calculating interest on notes, it is necessary to take the following factors into consideration:

(1) The principal of the note.
(2) The rate of interest.
(3) The period of time involved.

The principal of the note is the face amount of the note that the maker promises to pay at maturity apart from any specified interest. The principal is the base on which the interest is calculated.

The rate of interest usually is expressed in the form of a percentage, such as 7 percent or 9 percent. Ordinarily the rate is an annual percentage rate, but in some cases the rate is quoted on a monthly basis, such as 1½ percent a month. A rate of 1½ percent a month is equivalent to a rate of 18 percent a year payable monthly. When a note is interest-bearing but the rate is not specified on the face of the note, it is subject to the legal rate, which varies under the laws of the different states.

The period of time of the note consists of the days or months from the date of issue of a note to the date of its maturity (or the interest payment date if it comes earlier). When the time is specified in months, the interest is calculated on the basis of months rather than days. For example, if a note is payable 3 months from date, the interest should be calculated on the basis of 3 months or ¼ of a year. However, when the time of a note is specified in days or when the due date is specified in a note, the interest should be computed using the exact number of days that will elapse from the date of the note to the date of its maturity. For example, if a $1,000, 8% note is dated April 1, and the due date is specified as July 1, the time should be computed as shown below:

Days in April	30
Deduct date of note, April 1	1
Days remaining in April	29
Add: Days in May	31
Days in June	30
Note matures on July	1
Total time in days	91

Notice that in this computation the date of maturity was counted but the date of the note was not counted. If the note had specified "3 months after date" instead of July 1, the interest should be computed on the basis of 90 days instead of 91 days since a month, when specified as such, is assumed to have 30 days.

In computing interest, it is customary to consider 360 days as a year. Most banks and business firms follow this practice, though some banks and government agencies use 365 days as the base in computing daily interest. In any case, the formula for computing interest is:

PRINCIPAL × RATE × TIME (usually a fraction of a 360-day year) = AMOUNT OF INTEREST

Thus, for the $1,000, 8% note mentioned above, interest on the due date would be $20.22 ($1,000 × 8% × 91/360).

In the case of long-term notes, the interest may be payable periodically, such as semiannually or annually.

The 60-Day, 6 Percent Method. There are short cuts that may be used in computing interest on the basis of a 360-day year. The interest on any amount for 60 days at 6 percent can be determined simply by moving the decimal point in the amount two places to the left. The reason for this is that 60 days is 1/6 of a year, and interest on any amount at 6 percent for 1/6 of a year is the same as the interest at 1 percent for a full year. Thus, the interest on $550 for 60 days at 6 percent is $5.50.

The 60-day, 6 percent method may be used to advantage in many cases even though the actual time may be other than 60 days and the actual rate other than 6 percent. The following examples will serve to illustrate this fact.

Factors

(1) Principal of note, $2,000
(2) Time, 30 days
(3) Rate of interest, 7%

Factors

(1) Principal of note, $3,000
(2) Time, 90 days
(3) Rate of interest, 9%

Calculation

Interest at 6% for 60 days = $20
Interest at 6% for 30 days = $10
Interest at 7% = 1 1/6 × $10 = $11.67

Calculation

Interest at 6% for 60 days = $30
Interest at 6% for 90 days = $45
Interest at 9% = 1 1/2 × $45 = $67.50

Sometimes it is helpful to determine the interest for 6 days at 6 percent and then use the result as the basis for calculating the actual interest. Since the interest on any sum for 6 days at 6 percent may be determined simply by moving the decimal point three places to the left, the interest on $1,000 at 6 percent for 6 days is $1. If the actual time is 24 days instead of 6 days, the interest will be four times $1 or $4. This method differs from the 60-day, 6 percent method only in that 6 days is used in the basic computation instead of 60 days.

Published tables are available for reference in determining the amount of interest on stated sums at different rates for any length of time. These tables are widely used by financial institutions and by other business firms.

ACCOUNTING FOR NOTES RECEIVABLE TRANSACTIONS

Businesses other than lending institutions such as commercial banks and savings and loan companies generally encounter four types of transactions involving notes receivable:

(1) Note received from customer to obtain an extension of time for payment of the obligation.
(2) Note collected at maturity.
(3) Note renewed at maturity.
(4) Note dishonored.

Note Received from Customer to Obtain an Extension of Time for Payment. To obtain an extension of time for the payment of an account, a customer may issue a note for all or part of the amount due. A merchant may be willing to accept the note because it is a written acknowledgment of the debt and undoubtedly will bear interest.

Assume that David Austin owes the Herbers Hardware Co. $832.16 on open account. The account is past due and Herbers insists upon a settlement. Austin offers to give a 60-day, 8 percent note dated May 12, and Herbers accepts Austin's offer. The note is recorded in the books of the Herbers Hardware Co. by the following two-column journal entry:

May 12	Notes Receivable...	832.16	
	Accounts Receivable...		832.16
	Received a note from David Austin.		

If instead of giving a note for the full amount, Austin gives a check for $32.16 and a note for the $800 balance, the transaction would be recorded in Herbers' books by the following two-column journal entry:

May 12	Cash	32.16	
	Notes Receivable...	800.00	
	Accounts Receivable...		832.16
	Received check and note from David Austin.		

The foregoing entry can be recorded in a combination journal, cash journal, or any other appropriate book of original entry. This observation applies to all illustrations of entries involving the receipt and disbursement of cash.

Note Collected at Maturity. When a note receivable matures, it may be collected by the holder or it may be left at a bank for collection. If the maker of the note resides in another locality, the note may be forwarded to a bank in that locality for collection. Usually the maker is notified a few days before the maturity of a note so that the maker may be reminded of the due date, the amount that must be paid, and where the amount is to be paid. When the bank makes the collection, it notifies the holder, on a form similar to the credit advice shown below, that the net amount has been credited to the holder's account.

ADVICE OF CREDIT	**First National Bank**
	Little Rock, Arkansas

TO Herbers Hardware Co.

Account No. 305-31599   July 11   19 82

WE CREDIT YOUR ACCOUNT AS FOLLOWS:

David Austin's note	$832.16
Interest for 60 days @8%	11.10
	$843.26	$ 833.26
Less collection charge	10.00

OFFSETTING DR.

APPROVED *L. Russell*

Credit Advice

To illustrate the necessary accounting procedure, assume that Herbers left Austin's 60-day, 8 percent note for $832.16 at the First

National Bank for collection, and on July 11 received notice that the note had been collected including the accrued interest of $11.10. The bank fee for collecting the note amounted to $10.

The transaction is recorded in Herbers' Books as follows:

July 11	Cash	833.26	
	Collection Expense	10.00	
	Notes Receivable		832.16
	Interest Earned		11.10
	Received credit for the proceeds of David Austin's note collected by the bank.		

Note Renewed at Maturity. If the maker of a note is unable to pay the amount due at maturity, it may be possible to renew all or part of the note. If, instead of paying the note for $832.16 at maturity, Austin is allowed to pay only the interest, $11.10, and give another note for 60 days at the same rate of interest, the transaction is recorded in the books of the Herbers Hardware Co. by the following two-column journal entry:

July 11	Cash	11.10	
	Notes Receivable (new note)	832.16	
	Notes Receivable (old note)		832.16
	Interest Earned		11.10
	Received a new note for $832.16 from David Austin in renewal of his note due today and $11.10 in cash for the interest on the old note.		

Note Dishonored. If the maker of a note refuses or is unable to pay or renew it at maturity, the note is said to be dishonored. It thereby loses the quality of negotiability which means that it loses its legal status as a note receivable. Usually the amount is transferred from the notes receivable account to the accounts receivable account pending final disposition of the obligation involved. For example, if Herbers is unable to collect the interest-bearing note for $832.16 received 60 days before from Austin, the following two-column journal entry is made in the books of the Herbers Hardware Co.:

July 11	Accounts Receivable	843.26	
	Notes Receivable		832.16
	Interest Earned		11.10
	David Austin's note dishonored.		

If the claim against Austin should turn out to be completely worthless, the $843.26 will be removed from the accounts receivable account and recognized as an uncollectible account expense. The manner of accounting for this type of transaction was discussed in Chapter 8.

NOTES RECEIVABLE REGISTER

When many notes are received in the usual course of business, it may be advisable to keep an auxiliary record. An auxiliary record of notes receivable that provides more detailed information than a ledger account is usually known as a notes receivable register. One form of a notes receivable register is reproduced below and on the following page. The notes recorded in the illustration were those received by the D. A. Simon Co. during the period indicated by the record. The information recorded in the register is obtained directly from the notes received. The notes are numbered consecutively as they are entered in the register. (This number should not be confused with the maker's number in the lower left-hand corner of the note, as shown in the illustration on page 314.) The due date of each note is calculated and entered in the proper When Due column. The interest to maturity is calculated and entered in the Interest Amount column. When a remittance is received in settlement of a note, the date is entered in the Date Paid column.

NOTES RECEIVABLE ACCOUNT

The information recorded in the notes receivable account should agree with that entered in the notes receivable register. The account shown at the top of page 321 contains a record of the notes that were entered in the notes receivable register of the D. A. Simon Co. Notice that each note is identified by the number assigned to the note. If the notes are not numbered, each note should be identified by writing the name of the maker in the Item column of the account.

PROVING THE NOTES RECEIVABLE ACCOUNT

Periodically (usually at the end of each month) the notes receivable account should be proved by comparing the balance of the ac-

PAGE 2			NOTES RECEIVABLE REGISTER					
DATE RECEIVED	No.	BY WHOM PAYABLE	WHERE PAYABLE			DATE MADE		
			BANK OR FIRM	ADDRESS		Mo.	Day	Year
1982 apr. 5	1	C. F. Pearson	First State Bank	Warrenton		apr. 5		'82
22	2	F. S. Stobie	County Bank	Clayton		apr. 22		'82
may 3	3	R. F. Adler	City Savings Bank	Moberly		may 3		'82
20	4	G. D. Stewart	Central Trust	Warrenton		may 20		'82
June 21	5	F. S. Stobie	County Bank	Clayton		June 21		'82

Notes Receivable Register (Left Page)

ACCOUNT Notes Receivable					ACCOUNT NO. 121		
DATE	ITEM	POST. REF.	DEBIT	CREDIT	BALANCE		
					DEBIT	CREDIT	
1982							
Apr. 5	No. 1	CJ3	42618		42618		
22	No. 2	CJ3	55000		97618		
May 3	No. 3	CJ4	72750		170368		
20	No. 4	CJ4	61000		231368		
June 2	No. 3	CJ5		72750	158618		
4	No. 1	CJ5		42618	116000		
21	No. 2	CJ5		55000	61000		
21	No. 5	CJ5	45000		106000		

count with the total of the notes owned as shown by the notes receivable register. A schedule of the notes owned on June 30 is given below. Notice that the total of this schedule is the same as the balance in the notes receivable account illustration.

SCHEDULE OF NOTES OWNED

No. 4 .... $ 610.00
No. 5 ....   450.00
$1,060.00

ACCRUED INTEREST RECEIVABLE

While interest on a note literally accrues day by day, it is impractical to keep a daily record of such accruals. If the life of a note receivable is within the accounting period, no record is made of the interest until the amount is received.

	WHEN DUE					NOTES RECEIVABLE REGISTER					PAGE 2	
TIME	J	J	J A	D	AMOUNT	INTEREST		DISCOUNTED		DATE PAID	REMARKS	
						RATE	AMT.	BANK	DATE			
60 da.	4				42618	7%	497			June 4		
60 da.	21				55000	8%	733			June 21	Renewal for $450	
30 da.	2				72750	8%	485			June 2	Sent for coll. 5/31	
90 da.			18		61000	8%	1220					
60 da.			20		45000	8%	600				Renewal of Note No. 2	

Notes Receivable Register (Right Page)

If, however, the business owns some interest-bearing notes receivable at the end of the accounting period, neither the net income for the period nor the assets at the end of the period will be correctly stated unless the interest accrued on notes receivable is taken into consideration. The amount of the accrued interest may be computed by reference to the notes themselves or to the record provided by a notes receivable register. The accounts are then adjusted by debiting Accrued Interest Receivable and by crediting Interest Earned for the amount of interest that has accrued to the end of the period. Assume that at the end of a fiscal year ending June 30, a business owns four interest-bearing notes as shown in the schedule below:

SCHEDULE OF ACCRUED INTEREST ON NOTES RECEIVABLE

Principal	Date of Issue	Rate of Interest	Days From Issue Date to June 30	Accrued Interest June 30
$600.00	April 14	8%	77	$10.27
400.00	May 3	9	58	5.80
485.30	May 28	8	33	3.56
600.00	June 11	8	19	2.53
Total accrued interest on notes receivable				$22.16

When the amount involved is so small, some accountants would ignore it on the ground of immateriality, but technical accuracy requires the following two-column journal entry as of June 30:

June 30	Accrued Interest Receivable..	22.16	
	Interest Earned..		22.16
	Interest accrued on notes receivable as of June 30.		

In preparing the financial statements at the end of the year, the balance of the interest earned account (which will include the $22.16 earned but not yet received) will be reported in the income statement, while the balance of the account, Accrued Interest Receivable, will be reported in the balance sheet as a current asset.

ACCOUNTING FOR NOTES PAYABLE TRANSACTIONS

There are generally four types of transactions involving notes payable:

(1) Note issued to a supplier to obtain an extension of time for payment of obligation.

(2) Note issued as security for cash loan.

(3) Note paid at maturity.

(4) Note renewed at maturity.

Note Issued to a Supplier to Obtain an Extension of Time for Payment. When a firm wishes to obtain an extension of time for the payment of an account, a note for all or part of the amount due may be acceptable to the supplier. Assume that Herbers Hardware Co. owes Wesley & Co. $567.40. By agreement, on June 11 Herbers issues to Wesley a check on the First National Bank for $67.40 and a 90-day, 8½ percent interest-bearing note for $500. This transaction is recorded in the books of the Herbers Hardware Co. by the following two-column journal entry:

June 11 Accounts Payable...	567.40	
Cash...		67.40
Notes Payable		500.00
Issued check for $67.40 and note for $500 to Wesley & Co.		

Note Issued as Security for Cash Loan. Many firms experience brief periods during the year in which receipts from customers are not adequate to finance their operations. During such periods, business firms commonly borrow money from banks on short-term notes to help finance their business operations. Assume that on June 15, Herbers borrows $5,000 from the First National Bank on a 60-day, 9 percent interest-bearing note. The transaction is recorded in two-column journal form as follows:

June 15 Cash..	5,000	
Notes Payable...		5,000
Borrowed $5,000 at the bank on a 60-day, 9% note.		

Commercial banks often deduct interest in advance, and this procedure is known as discounting. For example, instead of the transaction previously described, suppose that Herbers borrowed on a $5,000, 60-day, non-interest-bearing note which the bank discounted at 9 percent. The bank would calculate the implied interest on the note to maturity, known as bank discount, as $75 ($5,000 × 9% × 60/360) and deduct this amount from the $5,000 face of the note. Thus, the Herbers Hardware Co. would receive only $4,925 ($5,000 − $75), and the transaction would be recorded as follows:

June 15 Cash..	4,925	
Discount on Notes Payable...	75	
Notes Payable...		5,000
Discounted at 9%, a $5,000, 60-day, non-interest-bearing note.		

The $75 debit to the discount on notes payable account represents an offset to the $5,000 note payable, because Herber's liability at this time is only $4,925, which is the net amount received from the bank. Discount on Notes Payable is a contra-liability account. The $75 discount becomes interest expense when the note matures on August 14, and the $5,000 principal amount of the note is repaid. Accordingly, Herbers Hardware Co. will record the payment of the note at maturity by making the following two-column journal entry:

Aug. 14	Notes Payable	5,000	
	Interest Expense	75	
	Cash		5,000
	Discount on Notes Payable		75
	Paid 60-day, non-interest-bearing note due today, and recognized interest expense at 9%.		

Note that, even though the stated rate of interest was 9 percent in both cases, the money received was less in amount and therefore more expensive in the second case. In the first case, $5,000 was obtained for 60 days at a cost of $75 — exactly 9 percent ($75 ÷ $5,000 = 1.5% for 60 days; 9% for 360 days). In the second case, $75 was paid for the use of $4,925 for 60 days — a rate of nearly 9.14 percent, which is known as the effective rate of interest ($75 ÷ $4,925 = 1.523% for 60 days; 9.138% for 360 days).

Note Paid at Maturity. A note made payable to a bank for a loan commonly is paid at that bank upon maturity. When notes made payable to other payees mature, payment may be made directly to the holder or to a bank where the note was left for collection. The maker knows who the payee is but may not know who the holder is at maturity because the payee may have transferred the note to another party. When a note is left with a bank for collection, it is customary for the bank to mail the maker a notice of maturity. For example, assume that Wesley & Co. forwards the 90-day, 8½ percent note for $500 received from Herbers on June 11 to the First National Bank for collection. The bank would notify Herbers before the maturity date by sending a notice similar to the one reproduced at the top of page 325.

Upon receiving this notice, Herbers issues a check to the bank for $510.63 in payment of the note and interest. The transaction is recorded in the books of the Herbers Hardware Co. by the following two-column journal entry:

Sept. 9	Notes Payable	500.00	
	Interest Expense	10.63	
	Cash		510.63
	Paid note issued June 11 to Wesley & Co., plus interest.		

First National Bank
Little Rock, Arkansas

Your note described below will be due ───────

MAKER-COSIGNER-COLLATERAL	NUMBER	DATE DUE	PRINCIPAL	INTEREST	TOTAL
M. C. Herbers Herbers Hardware Co.	16930	9/9/82	$500.00	$10.63	$510.63

ENDORSER

TO _____

M. C. Herbers
Herbers Hardware Co.
1200 Oak Street
Little Rock, AR 72201-5687

Note: Please bring this notice with you.   PAYABLE AT   First National Bank

Notice of Maturity of Note

Note Renewed at Maturity. If the maker is unable to pay a note in full at maturity, it may be possible to renew all or a part of the note. For example, on September 9, Herbers might pay the $10.23 interest and $100 on the principal of the note ($500 issued to Wesley & Co. on June 11), and give a new 60-day, 8½ percent note for $400. This transaction should be recorded in the following two-column journal entry:

Sept. 9	Notes Payable (old note)	500.00	
	Interest Expense...	10.63	
	Cash..		110.63
	Notes Payable (new note)		400.00
	Issued a check for $110.63 and a note for $400 to Wesley & Co. in settlement of a note for $500 plus interest.		

NOTES PAYABLE REGISTER

When many notes are issued in the usual course of business, it may be advisable to keep an auxiliary record. An auxiliary record of notes payable that provides more detailed information than a ledger account is usually known as a notes payable register. One form of such a register is reproduced at the top of pages 326 and 327. The notes recorded in the illustration were those issued by the D. A. Simon Co. during the period indicated by the record.

PAGE /			NOTES PAYABLE REGISTER				
DATE ISSUED	No.	TO WHOM PAYABLE	WHERE PAYABLE			DATE MADE	
			BANK OR FIRM	ADDRESS		Mo.	Day	Year

1982							
Apr. 12	1	J. A. Kohl	First State Bank	Warrenton	Apr. 12	'82
May 11	2	County Bank	County Bank	Clayton	May 11	'82
June 1	3	Eliasson Brothers	County Bank	Clayton	June 1	'82

Notes Payable Register (Left Page)

The information recorded in the register may be obtained directly from the note before it is mailed or given to the payee, or from a note stub. Blank notes are usually made up in pads with stubs attached on which spaces are provided for recording such essential information as amount, payee, where payable, date, time, rate of interest, and number. The due date of each note is calculated and entered in the proper When Due column of the register. The interest at maturity is also calculated and entered in the Interest Amount column. When a note is paid, the date is entered in the Date Paid column.

NOTES PAYABLE ACCOUNT

The information recorded in the notes payable account should agree with that recorded in the notes payable register. The following account contains a record of the notes that were entered in the notes payable register of the D. A. Simon Co.

ACCOUNT Notes Payable					ACCOUNT NO. 316		
DATE	ITEM	POST. REF.	DEBIT	CREDIT	BALANCE		
					DEBIT	CREDIT	
1982							
Apr. 12	No. 1	cg3		196241		196241
May 11	No. 2	cg4		600000		796241
June 1	No. 3	cg5		103765		900006
11	No. 1	cg5	196241			703765

	WHEN DUE															AMOUNT	INTEREST		DATE PAID	REMARKS
NOTES PAYABLE REGISTER																			**PAGE** /	
TIME	J	F	M	A	M	J	J	A	S	O	N	D				AMOUNT	RATE	AMOUNT		
60 da.						11										196241	8%	2617	June 11	Settlement of Feb. 12 inv.
90 da.									9							600000	9%	13500		
30 da.							1									103765	10%	865		Settlement of Apr. 1 inv.

Notes Payable Register (Right Page)

PROVING THE NOTES PAYABLE ACCOUNT

Periodically (usually at the end of each month), the notes payable account is proved by comparing the balance of the account with the total notes outstanding as shown by the notes payable register. A schedule of the notes outstanding on June 30 is given below. Notice that the total of this schedule is the same as the balance in the notes payable account illustration.

SCHEDULE OF NOTES OUTSTANDING

No. 2	$6,000.00
No. 3	1,037.65
	$7,037.65

ACCRUED INTEREST PAYABLE

Neither the expenses for a period nor the liabilities at the end of the period will be correctly stated unless the interest accrued on notes payable is taken into consideration. The mechanics of calculating the amount of interest accrued on notes payable are the same as in the case of notes receivable. If a notes payable register is kept, it should provide the information needed in computing the amount of interest accrued on notes payable. If the total amount of such accrued interest was calculated to be $291.62, and the fiscal period ended June 30, the proper adjusting entry may be made in two-column journal form as follows:

June 30 Interest Expense..	291.62	
Accrued Interest Payable.......................................		291.62
Interest accrued on notes payable as of June 30.		

In preparing the financial statements at the end of the year, the balance of the interest expense account, which will include the $291.62 incurred but not yet paid, will be reported in the income statement, while the balance of the account, Accrued Interest Payable, will be reported in the balance sheet as a current liability.

INDORSEMENT OF NOTES

A promissory note is usually made payable to a specified person or firm, though some notes are made payable to "Bearer." If the note is payable to the order of a specified party, that party must indorse the note to transfer the promise to pay to another party. To indorse means to sign one's name as payee on the back of a note.

The two major types of indorsements are (1) the blank indorsement and (2) the special indorsement. The indorsement is called a blank indorsement when only the payee's name is signed on the left end of the back of the note. The indorsement is called a special indorsement if the words "Pay to the order of" followed by the name of a specified party and the payee's signature appear on the back of the note. The legal effect of both types of indorsement is much the same. However, a blank indorsement makes a note payable to the bearer, while a special indorsement identifies the party to whose order payment is made.

Under certain circumstances, the maker of a note may arrange for an additional party to join in the promise to pay, either as a cosigner or as an indorser of the note. A cosigner signs below the maker's signature on the face of the note. If the other party makes a blank indorsement on the back of the note, it is called an accommodation indorsement. In either event, the payee of the note has an additional person responsible for payment, which is intended to add security to the note.

If a partial payment is made on a note, it is common practice to record the date of the payment and the amount paid on the back of the note, which is called indorsing the payment.

Shown on page 329 is a reproduction of the back of a promissory note originally made payable to the order of Carr Trovillion. The maker of the note, Mike MacFarland, had Pamela Thomas become an accommodation indorser. Later, the payee, Trovillion, transferred the note to R. J. Frapart by a special indorsement. On may 14, $300 was paid on the note.

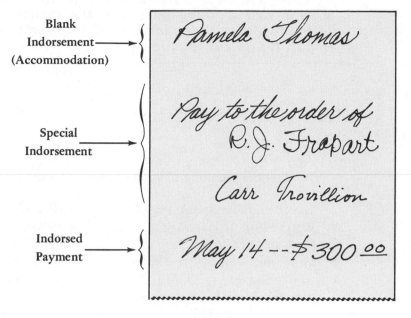

Blank Indorsement (Accommodation)

Special Indorsement

Indorsed Payment

Pamela Thomas

Pay to the order of
R. J. Frapart

Carr Trovillion

May 14 -- $300 00

Indorsements on Note

BUILDING YOUR ACCOUNTING KNOWLEDGE

1. What form does a promise to repay a borrowed sum of money nearly always take?
2. What are the four characteristics that a promissory note must evidence in order to be considered negotiable commercial paper?
3. What three factors must be taken into consideration in calculating interest on notes?
4. In computing the exact number of days of interest on a note, what date is counted? What date is not counted?
5. What number of days is considered as a year by most banks and business firms in computing interest?
6. What generally are the four types of transactions involving notes receivable and how do they differ from one another?
7. What generally are the four types of transactions involving notes payable and how do they differ from one another?
8. How are accrued interest receivable and accrued interest payable reported on the balance sheet?

Report No. 11-1

> Complete Report No. 11-1 in the study assignments and submit your working papers to the instructor for approval. Then proceed with the textbook discussion in Chapter 12 until Report No. 12-1 is required.

EXPANDING YOUR BUSINESS VOCABULARY

What is the meaning of each of the following terms?

accommodation indorsement (p. 328)
bank discount (p. 323)
blank indorsement (p. 328)
contra-liability (p. 324)
cosigner (p. 328)
discounting (p. 323)
dishonored (p. 319)
effective rate (p. 324)
indorse (p. 328)
indorsing the payment (p. 328)

maker of the note (p. 315)
negotiable commercial paper (p. 314)
notes payable register (p. 325)
notes receivable register (p. 320)
payee of the note (p. 315)
principal of the note (p. 315)
promissory notes (p. 314)
rate of interest (p. 315)
special indorsement (p. 328)
time of the note (p. 315)

CHAPTER 12

ACCOUNTING FOR INVENTORY AND PREPAID EXPENSES

CHAPTER OBJECTIVES

The objectives of this chapter are to enable you:

▶ To explain the nature and importance of the allocation of the total cost of merchandise acquired for sale between (1) the goods sold during the accounting period and (2) the goods on hand at the end of the period.

▶ To describe and contrast the two principal systems of accounting for inventory — the periodic system and the perpetual system.

▶ To perform the procedures involved in determining the end-of-period physical quantity of goods on hand, and to prepare an inventory sheet.

▶ To explain and contrast the specific identification, fifo, weighted average, and lifo bases of cost assignment to inventory; and to apply the lower of cost or market rule to the specific identification, fifo, and weighted average bases.

▶ To perform the gross margin and simplified retail methods of estimating the amount to be assigned to the end-of-period inventory.

▶ To explain and contrast the asset method and the expense method of accounting for supplies and prepayments.

Merchandise inventory and prepaid expenses have an important characteristic in common: both represent costs incurred in one accounting period that are expected in part to benefit the following period. Because the benefit is expected to be realized within a relatively short time, these assets are considered to be current rather than long-term. In most cases, the dollar amount of merchandise inventory is much larger than that for prepaid expenses. For this reason, accounting for merchandise inventory poses a much greater problem and receives much more attention.

MERCHANDISE INVENTORY

One of the major reasons for keeping accounting records is to determine the net income (or net loss) of a business on a periodic basis. If the business is engaged in the purchase and sale of merchandise, it is essential that the cost of all merchandise available for sale during the accounting period (goods on hand at the start of the period plus net purchases) be apportioned in a reasonable manner between the expense called cost of goods sold and the asset commonly called merchandise inventory. The routine bookkeeping procedure involved in accounting for merchandise, using accounts for purchases, purchases returns and allowances, purchases discount, and merchandise inventory, has been discussed and illustrated in preceding chapters. The problem of determining the quantity of goods on hand at the end of the period and of assigning cost to these goods remains to be considered.

TYPES OF INVENTORY SYSTEMS

There are two principal systems of accounting for inventory — the periodic system and the perpetual system. In the periodic system, the merchandise inventory account balance is merely a memorandum of the most recent physical inventory count, usually made only once a year when the stock is low or business is slow. As discussed in Chapter 6, the purchases account is debited with the cost of all goods bought at their respective invoice prices. As discussed in Chapter 7, the sales account is credited with the respective selling prices of all goods sold. The cost of goods sold is not determined until the end of the accounting period, at which time the following formula is applied:

Beginning Inventory	+	Net Purchases	−	Ending Inventory	= Cost of Goods Sold
(last year's physical count)		(account balance at end of this year)		(this year's physical count)	(for entire period)

Purchases returns and allowances and purchases discounts are subtracted from the purchases account to arrive at net purchases.

In the perpetual system, the merchandise inventory account is an active account. It is debited with the cost of all goods bought at their respective invoice prices, and credited with the assumed cost of all goods sold, as well as the cost of any inventory returns, allowances, or discounts. Thus, the balance of the account represents the cost of goods on hand at all times. No purchases or contra purchases accounts are kept. A cost of goods sold account is kept, and when goods are sold, it is debited for the same amount that Merchandise Inventory is credited. At the same time, a sales account is kept to receive credits at selling prices for all goods sold. Thus, two entries are required for each sale.

TAKING A PHYSICAL INVENTORY

Under the periodic inventory system, businesses do not maintain a record that shows the quantity and the cost of the merchandise on hand. Lacking such a record, the first step in attempting to apportion merchandise costs between sold and unsold goods consists of counting or measuring the goods that are on hand at the end of the period. This process is called taking a physical inventory.

Taking a physical inventory of a stock of merchandise can be a sizable task. Frequently, it is done after regular business hours. Some firms cease operations for a few days to take inventory. The ideal time to count the goods is when the quantity on hand is at its lowest level. If a fiscal year is selected so as to start and end at the time that the stock of goods is normally at its lowest level, it is known as a natural business year. Such a year is used by many businesses for accounting purposes.

It would be desirable if all goods on hand could be inventoried within a few hours. Extra help may be employed in order to take the inventory in as short a time as possible. Even if this is done, however, the taking of an inventory may require several days. If regular business is carried on during this time, special records must be kept of additions to and subtractions from the stock during the inventory-taking period. In this way, the quantities of goods that are on hand at the end of the last day of the fiscal period can be determined.

Various procedures are followed in taking an inventory so as to be sure that no items are missed, and that no items are included more than once. Frequently, persons taking inventory work in pairs; one counts the items and calls out the information to the other who records it. Usually this information is recorded on a special form. This form, known as an **inventory sheet** is arranged with columns to show the description of each type of item, the quantity on hand, the cost per unit, and the extension — the amount that results from multiplying the quantity by the unit cost. (The cost per unit usually is determined and the extensions completed after the count is finished.) Inventory sheets commonly provide spaces **(1)** to note the date of the inventory count, **(2)** to record the location of the items listed, and **(3)** to record the names or initials of the person who did the calling, the person who recorded the quantities, the person who entered the unit costs, the person who made the extensions, and the person who verified the information. A reproduction of part of an inventory sheet of a furniture store is shown below. Two extension columns are provided so that subtotals may be separated from extensions.

INVENTORY _July 31_   19 _82_   Page _1_

Sheet No. _____ _1_   Costed by _____ _R.E.V._

Called by _____ _M.L.W._   Department _____ _A_   Extended by _____ _R.E.V._

Entered by _____ _N.K._   Location _____ _Storeroom_   Examined by _____ _J.C.C._

Description	Quantity	Unit	Unit Cost	Extensions	
Table lamp	20	ea.	41.40	828.00	
Wall rack	18	ea.	7.60	136.80	
Bookcase	7	ea.	67.70	473.90	
End table	13	ea.	25.50	331.50	
Desk	6	ea.	83.10	498.60	
Total					3,434.70

Inventory Sheet

In taking a physical inventory, care must be exercised to be sure that only the goods that are the property of the firm are included. The two main problems in determining the items to be included in physical inventory are goods acquired and later sold on **consignment** and goods in transit. The important thing to remember about consignment goods is that they remain the property of the shipper (consignor) and should not be included in the inventory of the company holding the goods (consignee). Thus, if a company has acquired goods on consignment, they should not be included in that company's inventory. If a company has shipped goods on consignment for later sale, they should be included in that company's inventory.

In determining whether goods in transit at year end should be included in inventory, it is necessary to know the FOB terms. If goods are shipped FOB shipping point, the goods are the property of the buying company as soon as they are shipped. If goods are shipped FOB destination, the goods are not the property of the buying company until they are received.

ASSIGNING COST TO THE INVENTORY

After the quantities of goods owned have been determined at the end of the accounting period, the next step is to decide how much cost should be assigned to each unit. This might seem to be an easy, though perhaps a time-consuming job. If all purchases of the same article were made at the same price per unit, the unit cost times the number of units in the inventory would give the total cost to be assigned to those units. Frequently, however, identical articles are purchased at different times at different costs per unit. The question then arises as to which unit cost should be assigned to the goods in the inventory. If it is possible to separately identify and price items on hand when they are sold, this approach to cost assignment is preferred, and is known as specific identification costing. Often there is no way of knowing exactly which price was paid for the specific goods that are on hand. If so, one of three other bases of cost apportionment normally is adopted. These bases are (1) first-in, first-out costing, (2) weighted average costing, and (3) last-in, first-out costing.

Specific Identification Costing. A method of assigning merchandise cost which requires that each item that is sold and each item remaining in inventory be separately identified with respect to its purchase cost is called the specific identification method. This method is practical only for businesses in which sales volume is relatively low, inventory unit value is relatively high, and items can be distinguished easily from each other. Otherwise, record keeping becomes expensive and time consuming, if not impractical.

To illustrate how this method works, assume the following circumstances with respect to a particular article of merchandise:

	Units	Unit Price	Total Cost
On hand at start of period	400	$3.95	$1,580
Purchased during period:			
1st purchase	300	4.15	1,245
2d purchase	700	4.40	3,080
3d purchase	600	4.55	2,730
Number of units available for sale	2,000		$8,635
On hand at end of period	500		
Number of units sold during period	1,500		

Of the 1,500 units sold during the period, it is known for certain that 300 were from the beginning inventory, 200 were from the first purchase, 500 were from the second purchase, and 500 were from the last purchase. The cost of goods sold and the value of inventory at the end of the period are determined as follows:

	Cost of Goods Sold	Value of Ending Inventory
Beginning inventory	300 units @ $3.95 = $1,185	100 units @ $3.95 = $ 395
From 1st purchase	200 units @ 4.15 = 830	100 units @ 4.15 = 415
From 2d purchase	500 units @ 4.40 = 2,200	200 units @ 4.40 = 880
From 3d purchase	500 units @ 4.55 = 2,275	100 units @ 4.55 = 455
Total	1,500 units $6,490	500 units $2,145

First-In, First-Out Costing. Another widely used method of allocating merchandise cost is called the first-in, first-out or fifo method. This costing method assumes that the first goods bought were the first goods sold. As applied to the data given at the top of this page, the cost of goods sold and the value of inventory at the end of the period are determined as follows:

	Cost of Goods Sold	Value of Ending Inventory
Beginning inventory	400 units @ $3.95 = $1,580	—0—
From 1st purchase	300 units @ 4.15 = 1,245	—0—
From 2d purchase	700 units @ 4.40 = 3,080	—0—
From 3d purchase	100 units @ 4.55 = 455	500 units @ $4.55 = $2,275
Total	1,500 units $6,360	500 units $2,275

Note that the 500 items on hand at the end of the period are considered to be those most recently purchased. The term "fifo" relates to the goods sold during the accounting period and not to the goods in inventory at the end of the period. The term to reflect ending inventory valuation using the fifo concept would be more appropriately referred to as "lish," or "last-in, still here."

First in, first out costing is widely used because of two features: (1) Whenever the flow of merchandise can be controlled, the business will see to it that the older goods are moved out first. Thus fifo costing is often in harmony with the actual physical movement of the goods. (2) Fifo costing assigns the most recent purchase costs to the ending inventory shown in the balance sheet. This satisfies those accountants who contend that inventory should be shown on the balance sheet at the most current cost possible.

Another reason for the continuing widespread use of fifo costing is the reluctance of accountants to change a long-followed method of accounting when such a change would affect the comparability of their income calculations over a period of years. Consistency based on comparability is important in accounting. Firms that have used the fifo method for a long time are reluctant to abandon it.

Weighted Average Costing. Another method of allocating merchandise cost is called the weighted average cost method, also known as the average cost method. This costing method is based on the average cost of identical units.

Using the same data as shown at the top of page 336, the average cost of identical units is determined by dividing the total cost of units available for sale ($8,635) by the total number of units available for sale (2,000).

$$\frac{\$8,635 \text{ (cost of units available for sale)}}{2,000 \text{ (units available for sale)}} = \$4.3175 \text{ weighted average cost per unit}$$

The cost of goods sold and the value of the end-of-period inventory are calculated as follows:

Cost of goods sold	1,500 units @ $4.3175 =	$6,476.25
Value of ending inventory...	500 units @ 4.3175 =	2,158.75
Total.................................	2,000 units	$8,635.00

There is a logical appeal to the use of the weighted average basis to allocate cost between goods sold and goods on hand. In this example, one fourth (500) of the total units available (2,000) were unsold. The average cost basis assigns one fourth ($2,158.75) of the total cost ($8,635) to these goods.

Last-In, First-Out Costing. A fourth method of allocating merchandise cost is called the last-in, first-out or lifo method. It assumes that all of the sales in the period were made from the most recently purchased goods. As applied to the data given at the top of page 336, the cost of goods sold and the value of inventory at the end of the period are determined as follows:

	Cost of Goods Sold		Value of Ending Inventory	
Beginning inventory	—0—		400 units @ $3.95 = $1,580	
From 1st purchase.........	200 units @ $4.15 = $ 830		100 units @ 4.15 = 415	
From 2d purchase..........	700 units @ 4.00 = 3,080		—0—	
From 3d purchase..........	600 units @ 4.55 = 2,730		—0—	
Total...........................	1,500 units	$6,640	500 units	$1,995

Note that the 500 units on hand at the end of the period are considered to be the 400 units that were on hand at the start of the period plus 100 of the units from the first purchase. The term "lifo" relates to the goods sold during the accounting period and not to the goods in inventory at the end of the period. The term to reflect ending inventory using the lifo concept would be more appropriately referred to as "fish" or "first-in, still here."

Sometimes the lifo method has been justified on the grounds that the physical movement of goods in some businesses is actually last-in, first-out. This is rarely the case, but the method has become popular for other reasons. One persuasive argument for the use of the lifo method is that it matches the cost of the items purchased most recently against the current sales revenue. In many cases in which the lifo method is used, the calculated amount for inventory that has been sold, called cost of goods sold, is really the cost to replace the goods sold. When this amount is subtracted from sales revenue, the resulting gross margin figure is neither inflated nor deflated by gain or loss due merely to price changes. In the opinion of many accountants, this is proper and desirable.

Probably, the major reason for the growing popularity of the lifo method is the fact that when prices are rising, net income calculated by using the lifo method is smaller than the amount determined from using either the fifo or the weighted average method. As a result, the related income tax is smaller. The reverse would be true if prices were falling, but periods of falling prices have been few and brief in the past two centuries.

The lifo method is used by firms in many industries. Procedures have been developed to apply the lifo principle to situations in which the goods sold are not literally replaced. High-fashion merchandise is an example. Suitable adjustments are made to state costs on a lifo basis.

Opponents of the lifo method contend that its use causes old, out-of-date inventory costs to be shown in the balance sheet. The theoretical and practical merits of fifo and lifo are the subject of much professional debate.

Physical Flows and Cost Flows. It is important to recognize that of the four inventory costing methods described, only the specific identification costing method will necessarily reflect cost flows that match physical flows of goods. Each of the other three methods — fifo, weighted average, and lifo — is based on assumed cost flows which are not required to reflect the actual physical movement of goods within the company. Any one of the three assumed cost flow methods may be used under any physical flow conditions.

Comparison of Methods. To compare the results obtained by the use of the four cost assignment methods discussed, assume that the 1,500 units were sold for $9,000. The tabulation below contrasts the cost assigned to the ending inventory and cost of goods sold, and the resultant gross margin under each of the four methods. It must be remembered, however, that the example relates to a period in which costs and prices were rising.

	Fifo	Weighted Average	Specific Identification	Lifo
Sales	$9,000	$9,000	$9,000	$9,000
Cost of goods sold:				
Beginning inventory	$1,580	$1,580	$1,580	$1,580
Purchases	7,055	7,055	7,055	7,055
Merchandise available for sale	$8,635	$8,635	$8,635	$8,635
Less ending inventory	2,275	2,159	2,145	1,995
Cost of goods sold	$6,360	$6,476	$6,490	$6,640
Gross margin	$2,640	$2,524	$2,510	$2,360

Note that in all cases, the total cost of merchandise available for sale ($8,635) is the same. It is the apportionment between goods sold and goods on hand at the end of the period that differs. For example, under fifo costing, $6,360 is apportioned to cost of goods sold and $2,275 to ending inventory. Under conditions of rising prices, the gross margin is lowest if lifo is used because the most recent, and therefore the highest purchase costs are matched against sales revenue.

It is common practice to describe the methods that have been discussed as methods of inventory valuation. It should be apparent, however, that this process also values the cost of goods sold. The term "valuation" is somewhat misleading, since what is involved is really cost apportionment.

LOWER OF COST OR MARKET

It is a well-established tradition in accounting that unrealized gains should not be recorded except in very unusual cases. If the value of an asset increases while it is being held, no formal record of the gain is entered on the books because it has not been actually realized. On the other hand, if the value or usefulness of an asset declines while it is being held, it is generally considered proper to recognize and record the loss, even though it has not yet been realized. This is in keeping with the rule of conservatism, which states that gains should not be anticipated, but that all potential losses should be recognized.

The practice of assigning the lower of cost or market to the items that comprise the inventory of merchandise at the end of an accounting period is an important application of the rule of conservatism. Cost means the amount calculated using either the specific identification, fifo, or weighted average method. In determining the cost to be assigned to goods in an inventory, it is proper to assign to the goods on hand a fair share of any transportation costs that were incurred on goods purchased. In other words, cost means cost at the buyer's place of business, not cost at the supplier's shipping point. In some cases, transportation charges are an important part of the total cost of merchandise acquired. In addition, cost should be reduced by the amount of any purchases returns, allowances, or discounts taken.

Market means the cost to replace. It is the prevailing price in the market in which goods must be purchased — not the prevailing price in the market in which they are normally sold — that is involved. An improved statement of the practice is the lower of cost or cost to replace. Accountants have assigned upper and lower limits to the market value that may be used in particular cases. The meaning and calculation of these limits is a topic for a more advanced course. Suffice it to say that market may neither exceed the calculated upper limit nor be less than the calculated lower limit.

To illustrate the application of the lower of cost or market rule, assume the following end-of-period data with respect to an inventory consisting of three items:

Item	Recorded Purchase Cost	End-of-Period Market Value	Lower of Cost or Market
1	$ 6,000	$ 5,000	$ 5,000
2	7,000	8,000	7,000
3	5,000	4,500	4,500
	$18,000	$17,500	$16,500

The illustration demonstrates two possible ways of making the lower of cost or market calculation. First, the lower of cost or market rule can be applied to the total inventory, which in the above illustration would involve comparing $18,000 total cost with $17,500 total market value. Under the second approach, the rule is applied to each item in the inventory. In the above illustration, this would involve comparing $18,000 total cost with $16,500 lower of cost or market value. The difference between the cost and market value under either approach is considered a loss due to holding inventory and typically is included in cost of goods sold on the income statement.

Two restrictions on the use of the lower of cost or market rule for tax purposes should be observed: (1) The rule cannot be applied if the business uses lifo inventory costing. Users of lifo for tax purposes must make strict application of lifo costing rules to all business income calculations and financial reports.[1] (2) The rule must be consistently applied to each item in the inventory. It would not be appropriate to use the $17,500 total end-of-period market value in the previous example.

Since the merchandise will probably be sold for considerably more than either market or cost (however calculated), the reason for following a practice as conservative as the lower of cost or market rule may be questioned. Some firms assign cost — fifo or weighted average — to the ending inventory even if market is less. The purpose in using the lower of cost or market rule is to carry the goods into the next period with an assigned cost that will result in no less than an average or normal percentage of margin when the units are sold in the new period. If replacement cost has fallen, competition may cause some reduction in selling price.

THE GROSS MARGIN METHOD OF INVENTORY ESTIMATION

Taking a physical inventory may be such a sizable task that it is attempted only once a year. If interim income statements and balance sheets are to be prepared, the portions of the cost of goods available for sale during the interim period to be allocated to goods sold during the period and to goods on hand at the end of the period must be estimated. One way of doing this is to apply the gross margin method, in which the amount of sales during the period is reduced by the normal percentage of gross margin (gross profit) to determine the estimated cost of goods sold. Deducting this amount from the total cost of goods available for sale gives the estimated amount of the ending inventory.

To illustrate, assume the following data with respect to a particular firm:

Inventory, start of period	$60,000
Net purchases, first month	50,000
Net sales, first month	90,000
Normal gross margin as a percentage of sales	40%

---

[1] Recent rulings of the Financial Accounting Standards Board and the Securities and Exchange Commission are causing the Internal Revenue Service to relax or remove this prohibition in many cases.

The estimated cost of goods sold during the month and the estimated merchandise inventory at the end of the month would be determined as follows:

(1) Estimated cost of goods sold:

Net sales...	$90,000	100%
Gross margin	36,000	40
Cost of goods sold	$54,000	60%

(2) Cost of goods available for sale:

Inventory, start of period	$ 60,000
Net purchases, first month	50,000
Cost of goods available for sale.....................	$110,000

(3) Estimated inventory at end of month:

Cost of goods available for sale.....................	$110,000
Less estimated cost of goods sold	54,000
Estimated end-of-month inventory.................	$ 56,000

The above computation is applicable only if the normal gross margin on sales has prevailed during the immediate past period and is expected to prevail during the following periods when the goods in the inventory will be sold. This type of calculation can be used to check the general reasonableness of the amount of an inventory that was computed on the basis of a physical count. Any sizable difference in the two calculations might serve to call attention to a possible mistake in the count, in costing the items, or a marked change in the realized rate of gross margin. The gross margin procedure can also be used to estimate the cost of an inventory that may have been destroyed by fire or other casualty. Such a calculation might be useful in negotiating an insurance settlement.

THE RETAIL METHOD OF INVENTORY ESTIMATION

Many retail merchants use a variation of the gross margin method to calculate cost of goods sold and ending inventory for interim-statement purposes. The procedure employed, called the retail method of inventory, requires keeping records of the prices at which purchased goods are marked to sell. This information, together with the record of the cost of goods purchased, makes it possible to compute the ratio between cost and retail prices. When the amount of retail sales is subtracted from the retail value of all goods available for sale, the result is the estimated retail value of the ending inventory. Multiplying this amount by the ratio of cost to selling price gives the estimated cost of the ending inventory.

Following is an example of the calculation of the estimated cost of an ending inventory of merchandise by the retail method:

	Cost	Retail
Inventory, start of period	$ 46,000	$ 65,000
Net purchases during period	96,500	125,000
Merchandise available for sale	$142,500	$190,000
Less sales for period		140,000
Inventory, end of period, at retail		$ 50,000
Ratio of cost to retail prices of merchandise available for sale ($142,500 ÷ $190,000)		75%
Estimated inventory, end of period, at cost (75% of $50,000)	$ 37,500	

The foregoing example was simplified by assuming that there were no changes in the prices at which the goods were marked to sell. In practice, such changes as additional markups, markup cancellations, and markdowns are commonplace and the calculation must take such adjustments into consideration.

In addition to using the retail method in estimating the cost of inventory for interim-statement purposes, the cost-retail ratio that is developed can be used to convert the amount of a physical inventory which originally has been priced at retail to its approximate cost.

PERPETUAL INVENTORY RECORDS

Firms that deal in certain types of merchandise sometimes find it feasible to keep up-to-date records of the quantities and costs of goods on hand at all times, known as perpetual inventory records. The general ledger account for Merchandise Inventory under such a system is somewhat like the account for Cash in Bank; a chronological record of each addition (purchase) and subtraction (sale) is maintained. The balance of the account at any time shows the cost of goods that should be on hand.

When perpetual inventory records are kept, the merchandise inventory account in the general ledger is usually a control account. A subsidiary ledger with an account for each type of goods is maintained. These accounts are often in the form of cards which provide spaces to show additions, subtractions, and the balance after each change. Goods sold can be assigned cost on either a specific identification, fifo, weighted average, or lifo basis.

Assume that 1,000 units of FAZDA were acquired by a firm on August 10 for a total of $1,500, and that the entire quantity was sold on September 7 for $2,000. The necessary entries would appear in a general journal as follows:

(1) At time of purchase:

Aug. 10 Inventory	1,500	
Accounts Payable or Cash..............................		1,500
Bought 1,000 units of FAZDA @ $1.50.		

(2) At time of sale:

Sept. 7 Accounts Receivable or Cash	2,000	
Sales		2,000
Sold 1,000 units of FAZDA @ $2.00.		
7 Cost of Goods Sold...	1,500	
Inventory		1,500
Cost of 1,000 units of FAZDA sold today.		

Perpetual inventories do not eliminate the need for taking peri-odic physical inventories. The records must be examined from time to time to discover and correct any errors. However, it is not always necessary to count everything at the same time. The stock can be counted and the records verified by groups of items, by depart-ments, or by sections as time permits, so long as the inventory is completely verified within a single accounting period.

A business that sells a wide selection of comparatively low-cost goods (such as a limited-price variety store) may not find it practical to keep a perpetual inventory. In contrast, a business that sells a relatively few high-cost items (an automobile dealer, for example) can maintain such a record without incurring excessive processing cost.

Many types of businesses often keep supplementary or auxiliary records of inventory items in terms of quantities only, called stock records. Stock records serve as a guide in purchasing operations, may help to reveal any shortages, and may provide information as to the goods on hand as a basis for assigning merchandise cost for in-terim-statement purposes.

BUILDING YOUR ACCOUNTING KNOWLEDGE

1. What are the fundamental differences between the periodic system of accounting for inventory and the perpetual system of accounting for in-ventory?
2. What is the first step in attempting to apportion merchandise costs be-tween sold and unsold goods?
3. If it is assumed that the first units purchased were the first ones sold, what is assumed about the source of the units left at the end of the accounting period?

4. What two factors are taken into account by the weighted average cost-ing method of merchandise cost allocation?

5. If it is assumed that all sales in the accounting period were of the goods most recently purchased, what is assumed about the source of the units left at the end of the accounting period?

6. When "lower of cost or market" is assigned to the items that comprise the ending merchandise inventory, what does "cost" mean? What does "market" mean?

7. For what two major purposes is the gross margin method of inventory estimation utilized?

8. For what two major purposes is the retail method of inventory estima-tion utilized?

Report No. 12-1

> Complete Report No. 12-1 in the study assignments and submit your working papers to the instructor for approval. Then continue with the following textbook discussion until Re-port No. 12-2 is required.

PREPAID EXPENSES

Office supplies, store supplies, advertising supplies, and other supplies purchased may not be wholly consumed in the period in which they are acquired. The premiums on insurance policies cover-ing merchandise, equipment, and buildings are often prepaid, but the terms of the policies may extend beyond the current accounting period. Rent and interest may be paid in advance, but the expenses may not be wholly incurred in the same accounting period. The cost of unused supplies on hand at the close of the accounting period and the portion of prepayments such as insurance, rent and interest that will benefit future periods are known as prepaid expenses. Prepaid expenses should be treated as current assets because the benefits will be realized within a comparatively short time.

When accounts are kept on the accrual basis, it is necessary to adjust certain of them at the close of each accounting period for the following:

(1) Supplies or services purchased during the period that were re-corded as **assets** at time of purchase and a portion of which was consumed or used during the period.

(2) Supplies or services purchased during the period that were re-corded as **expenses** at time of purchase and a portion of which was not consumed or used during the period.

ASSET METHOD OF ACCOUNTING FOR PREPAID EXPENSES

Supplies and services that may not be wholly consumed in the period in which they are purchased may be recorded as assets at the time of purchase. Under this method of accounting, it is necessary to adjust the accounts at the end of each accounting period in order that the used portions may be recorded as expenses.

Supplies. Supplies such as office supplies, store supplies, advertising supplies, fuel, and postage, which may not be wholly consumed in the accounting period in which they are acquired, are usually recorded as assets at the time of purchase. Office supplies include letterheads, envelopes, pencils, adding machine and computer tape, notebooks, punched cards, typewriter ribbons, and other miscellaneous supplies that are normally consumed in the operation of an office. Transactions arising from the purchase of supplies on account are entered in a multi-column purchases journal with one debit column for recording merchandise purchases and a second debit column for recording purchases of supplies. When supplies are purchased for cash, the transactions are entered in the combination journal (or other cash journal). In either case, the purchases are posted to the office supplies account in the general ledger.

At the end of each accounting period, an inventory of the office supplies on hand is taken, and an adjusting entry is made to record the amount of the office supplies consumed during the period. For example, if at the end of the accounting period, the office supplies account shows a debit balance of $924.68 and a physical inventory count reveals that the cost of supplies on hand amounts to $450, it is assumed that the supplies expense during the period is $474.68 ($924.68 − $450). The adjusting entry is as follows:

Office Supplies Expense..	474.68	
Office Supplies..		474.68
Office supplies consumed during period.		

After this entry is posted, the office supplies account will have a debit balance of $450, which is reported in the balance sheet as a current asset. The office supplies expense account will have a debit balance of $474.68, which is reported in the income statement as an operating expense. To illustrate, using T accounts:

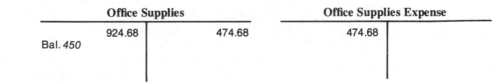

Office Supplies		Office Supplies Expense	
924.68	474.68	474.68	
Bal. *450*			

Store supplies include wrapping paper, twine, cellophane tape, corrugated board, paper bags, containers, cleaning supplies, and other miscellaneous supplies that are normally consumed in the operation of a store. Transactions arising from the purchase of such supplies should be recorded in the same manner as transactions arising from the purchase of office supplies. The end-of-period adjusting process and resulting treatment of asset and expense elements on the financial statements are similar.

Advertising supplies include catalogs, circulars, price lists, order blanks, and other miscellaneous supplies that are normally consumed in an advertising program. Transactions arising from the purchase of such supplies should be recorded in the same manner as transactions arising from the purchase of other types of supplies. The end-of-period adjusting process and resulting treatment of asset and expense elements on the financial statements are similar.

Postage. The cost of postage purchased is usually treated as a current asset and recorded by debiting Postage and by crediting the bank account. Some of the postage may be used on packages, and some on ordinary mail. If postage used on packages is billed to the customer, the entry to record the sale will include a credit to the postage account. Usually no entry is made when postage is used on ordinary mail each day, but periodically the postage on hand is counted (or valued, if a postage meter is used). The difference between the amount of the unused postage on hand and the debit balance of the postage account represents the amount of postage used and not billed to customers. This requires an adjusting entry to the postage account.

If the account for postage is debited (1) for the amount of postage on hand at the beginning of the month, $67, and (2) for the amount of postage purchased during the month, $218.60, and is credited (3) for the amount of postage used on packages during the month, $90, the account will have a debit balance of $195.60 at the end of the month. If at that time, the actual amount of postage on hand is found to be $64.20, the difference of $131.40 represents the amount of postage that appears to have been used and not billed to customers during the month. The following adjusting entry will be made:

Postage Expense	131.40	
Postage		131.40
Amount of postage used on ordinary mail.		

After this is posted, the postage account will have a debit balance of $64.20, which is reported in the balance sheet as a current asset. The postage expense account will have a debit balance of $131.40, which is reported as an operating expense in the income statement. To illustrate, using T accounts:

Postage			Postage Expense	
Bal √	67.00	90.00	131.40	
	218.60	131.40		
Bal. *64.20*				

A business may meet its postage requirements by (1) buying postage stamps, (2) making a deposit under the postal permit system for a certain amount of postage, or (3) using a postage meter. In the latter case, a certain amount of postage is paid for, and the meter is set so that the postage may be used as needed. Regardless of how postage is purchased, the accounting procedure can be the same. The prepaid postage is charged to the postage account and the amount of stamps used or postage consumed is charged to the proper expense account.

Insurance. A variety of risks are entailed in the operation of a business. Property such as buildings, furniture, machinery, supplies, and merchandise inventory may be damaged or destroyed by fire, water, earthquake, windstorm, or other natural disaster. Many types of property, especially money, may be stolen by burglars and sometimes by employees. State laws impose liability on the part of an employer to employees for injury or death arising out of the employees' work. The hazards connected with the ownership and operation of motor vehicles are well known. Accidents to persons unconnected with the business but occurring on business premises pose the threat of lawsuits and possibly large settlements. Loss of income as a result of the interruption of business operations because of a fire or a flood is a possibility.

It is possible to obtain insurance against the types of losses enumerated above and certain others not mentioned. A separate insurance policy relating to each type of risk can be obtained, but in recent years, the practice of obtaining one policy covering most or all of the risks has become commonplace. Such contracts are described as "package," "blanket," or "multiperil" policies. In total, the cost of such types of insurance is lower than a collection of policies for separate individual risks.

A contract under which an insurance company (the insurer) agrees to protect the business (the insured) from loss is known as an insurance policy. The amount that the insured is required to pay for insurance protection is known as the premium. The premium is usually stated as a specified rate per $1,000 of insurance for one or more years. Rates for workers' compensation insurance and automobile insurance are subject to change each year even though the coverage is part of a policy that includes other matters. The rate for the other features may be for a three-year period. The premium for a three-year coverage is usually 2.7 times the one-year rate, which is a type of quantity discount. Since insurance is usually purchased for a period of one or more years and the premium is paid in advance by the insured, the amount paid is usually charged to a prepaid insurance account. This account is classified as a current asset.

Expired Insurance. The prepaid insurance account gradually decreases in value as the life of the insurance policy grows shorter. It is customary to record at the close of each accounting period the total amount of prepayment that expired during the period just ended. The expired amount is recorded as an expense. If the management of the business does not see a need for any breakdown of the insurance expense, an end-of-year adjusting entry such as the following would suffice:

```
Insurance Expense.................................................................. xxx
    Prepaid Insurance ............................................................       xxx
        Insurance expired during the year.
```

The amount in the above entry may be determined by referring to the policy (or policies) and calculating the portion of the premium that relates to the year just ended. The amount of the premium for each major type of coverage is shown on the face of the policy. If more detail about the insurance expense is wanted, it would be possible to analyze the total and to classify it into, perhaps, delivery equipment insurance expense, fire insurance expense (with subclassifications relating to building, to furniture and fixtures, and to merchandise), workers' compensation insurance expense, and public liability insurance expense. Separate accounts can be established to provide as much detail as needed.

If a business has several insurance policies, it may be useful to maintain an auxiliary record known as an Insurance Policy Register. This record provides spaces to show the date and number of each policy, name of the insurer, type and amount of coverage, total term, expiration date, total premium, and columns to show the premium applicable to each month. Usually, a separate page is used for each year.

Canceled Insurance. The insurance company or the insured may cancel an insurance policy at any time before the expiration of the policy. If a policy is canceled, the insured is entitled to receive a refund of that part of the premium applicable to the unexpired period. The amount of the refund will depend upon whether the policy is canceled by direct action of the insurance company or at the request of the insured. When the policy is canceled directly by the insurance company, the premium for the expired period is computed on a pro rata basis. When the policy is canceled at the request of the insured, the premium for the expired period is usually computed on a short-term rate basis, which means that the insurance company's refund to the insured is less than the amount of the unexpired premium. The amount refunded is recorded by debiting the bank account and by crediting the prepaid insurance account. The remaining unexpired premium, if any, is then debited to Insurance Expense and credited to Prepaid Insurance.

Prepaid Rent. When business property is rented for more than one accounting period on the basis of a lease agreement, and the lease payment is made in advance, it is usual to regard the amount of the lease payment as prepaid rent. Prepaid rent is classified as a current asset.

At the end of the accounting period, the amount of rent expense relating to the period just ended should be determined, and an adjusting entry made to transfer that portion of the lease payment from the prepaid rent account to the rent expense account. For example, assume that on July 1, an office building was leased by the business for a three-year period, and a lease payment of $36,000 was made in advance. The entry to record the lease payment is as follows:

July 1	Prepaid Rent...	36,000	
	Cash..		36,000
	Three-year lease of office building.		

On December 31, it was determined that one-sixth of the lease had expired; therefore, the following adjusting entry was made:

Dec. 31	Rent Expense	6,000	
	Prepaid Rent		6,000
	Prepaid rent transferred to rent expense.		

After the foregoing entry is posted, the prepaid rent account will have a debit balance of $30,000, which represents 2½ years that the lease will remain active. The $30,000 of prepaid rent is reported in the balance sheet as a current asset. The $6,000 debit balance of the rent expense account is reported in the income statement under the heading of "Operating expenses" (and the subheading of "Administrative expenses" if operating expenses are subclassified).

One advantage of using the asset method of accounting for prepaid expenses is that the adjusting entries required at the end of the period are of the write-off type. Such adjustments do not need to be reversed at the start of the new period.

EXPENSE METHOD OF ACCOUNTING FOR PREPAID EXPENSES

Supplies and services that may not be wholly consumed in the period in which they are purchased may be recorded as expenses at the time of purchase. Under this method of accounting, it is necessary to adjust the accounts at the end of each accounting period in order that the unused portions may be recorded as assets. For example, if office supplies purchased during an accounting period are charged to the office supplies expense account, it will be necessary to adjust the account at the end of the period for the cost of the supplies on hand. To illustrate, assume that Office Supplies Expense had been charged for a total of $375 during the period and an inventory taken at the end of the period shows that supplies on hand amount to $125. The following adjusting entry is recorded:

Office Supplies	125	
Office Supplies Expense		125
Office supplies on hand.		

After this entry is posted, the office supplies expense account will have a debit balance of $250, which is reported in the income statement as an operating expense. The office supplies account will have a debit balance of $125, which is reported in the balance sheet as a current asset. To illustrate, using T accounts:

Office Supplies		Office Supplies Expense	
125		375	125
		Bal. *250*	

When the expense method of accounting is followed, the adjustments made at the end of the period are called deferral adjustments, because they defer expenses to the next period. Adjustments of this type should be reversed at the start of the new period. In the above example relating to office supplies, the reversing entry would be:

Office Supplies Expense	125	
Office Supplies		125

The effect of the adjusting, closing, and reversing procedure is (1) to remove the unused or unexpired amount from an expense account at the end of the period, (2) to transfer the remaining amount to the expense and revenue summary account, and (3) at the start of the new period, to transfer back to the expense account the amount of expense that had been previously deferred.

The asset and expense methods of accounting for prepaid expenses give the same final result. In the asset method, an amount that will eventually become the expenses of current and future periods is first put into an asset account, and at the end of each period, a proper portion is transferred to an expense account. In the expense method, the original amount is first put into an expense account. At the end of each accounting period, the portion that will be an expense of future periods is moved into an asset account and subsequently brought back into the related expense account by a reversing entry at the start of the new period.

BUILDING YOUR ACCOUNTING KNOWLEDGE

1. What are the two methods of recording the amounts of supplies or services purchased when accounts are kept on the accrual basis?
2. How is the value of office supplies, store supplies, advertising supplies, or postage on hand at the end of the accounting period determined?
3. Under what heading should supplies or postage on hand be reported in the balance sheet?
4. Under what heading should supplies or postage expense be reported in the income statement?
5. Why has the practice of obtaining a single "multi-peril" insurance policy become commonplace in recent years?
6. Under what heading should prepaid insurance be reported in the balance sheet? Prepaid rent?
7. What type of end-of-period adjusting entries are required when the asset method of accounting for prepaid expenses is used? Do such adjustments need to be reversed?
8. What type of end-of-period adjusting entries are required when the expense method of accounting for prepaid expenses is used? Do such adjustments need to be reversed?

Report No. 12-2

> *Complete Report No. 12-2 in the study assignments and submit your working papers to the instructor for approval. Then continue with the textbook discussion in Chapter 13 until Report No. 13-1 is required.*

EXPANDING YOUR BUSINESS VOCABULARY

What is the meaning of each of the following terms?

average cost (p. 337)

consignee (p. 335)

consignment (p. 334)

consignor (p. 335)

cost (p. 340)

cost apportionment (p. 339)

deferral adjustments (p. 351)

first-in, first-out (fifo) (p. 336)

gross margin method (p. 341)

insurance policy (p. 348)

in transit (p. 335)

inventory sheet (p. 334)

last-in, first-out (lifo) (p. 337)

lower of cost or cost to replace (p. 340)

lower of cost or market (p. 340)

market (p. 340)

natural business year (p. 333)

periodic system (p. 332)

perpetual inventory records (p. 343)

perpetual system (p. 333)

premium (p. 348)

prepaid expenses (p. 345)

retail method (p. 342)

rule of conservatism (p. 339)

short-term rate basis (p. 350)

specific identification (p. 335)

stock records (p. 344)

taking a physical inventory (p. 333)

weighted average cost (p. 337)

CHAPTER 13

ACCOUNTING FOR PROPERTY, PLANT, AND EQUIPMENT

CHAPTER OBJECTIVES

The objectives of this chapter are to enable you:

▶ To determine the cost of property, plant, and equipment.

▶ To explain the nature and purpose of depreciation, the different acceptable depreciation methods and their possible effects on net income.

▶ To account for the acquisition, disposition, and depreciation of property, plant, and equipment.

▶ To prepare a form of property, plant, and equipment record.

▶ To describe the reporting of depreciation in financial statements.

▶ To explain the nature of wasting assets and the two different methods of accounting for their depletion.

Many types of business assets, acquired with the expectation that they will remain in service for a number of accounting periods, are called property, plant, and equipment assets or long-term assets. The descriptions fixed assets and capital assets are used sometimes. Such assets can be classified in various ways. From a legal standpoint, all property is either real property or personal property. Real property (realty or real estate) includes land and anything attached to the land. In nearly all cases, any real property owned by a business is considered to be a long-term asset. Real estate acquired as a short-term investment is an exception. Personal property includes everything else that can be owned other than real property. Many kinds of personal property also are classified as property, plant, and equipment assets. Furniture, equipment, motor vehicles, machinery, patents, and copyrights are common examples of personal property that is owned and used by a business for a number of accounting periods.

Another way of classifying long-term assets is on the basis of tangibility. All real property is tangible (has physical substance). The same is true of such personal property as furniture, equipment, and machinery. Major examples of intangible (no physical substance) assets are patents, copyrights, leases, franchises, trademarks, and goodwill. These are considered long-term assets because they are expected to bring future economic benefit and, except for goodwill, have a legal status that allows them to be classified as property. The subject of goodwill will be considered in Chapter 16.

Sometimes businesses own interests in other incorporated businesses in the form of capital stock, bonds, or long-term notes. Government bonds or notes are also commonly owned. If these investments are temporary in nature, they are considered as marketable securities and should be classified as current assets. If these assets are expected to be owned for a long time, they are considered long-term investments and should be shown in the balance sheet under the heading Investments.

For accounting purposes, a common classification of property, plant, and equipment is on the basis of how the original cost of the property is handled in the process of determining net income. The cost of land used only as a site for a store, a factory, a warehouse, or a parking lot is normally left undisturbed in the accounts as long as the land is owned. Because land does not lose its capability to serve these purposes, it does not depreciate. Tangible assets such as buildings, furniture, and equipment are usually called depreciable assets, because they wear out or are used up as time passes. In determining net income, a portion of the cost of such assets is charged off as depreciation expense. In a similar fashion, the cost of such intangible properties as patents, copyrights, and leaseholds is gradually charged off as expense to the periods benefited by the ownership of the assets. As applied to intangible assets, however, the periodic write-off is termed amortization in contrast to depreciation of certain tangible assets. Actually, the meaning of the word amortization is broad enough to include depreciation, but customarily the write-off of the cost of most tangible long-term assets is called depreciation, while the write-off of the cost of intangible long-term assets is called amortization.

Certain long-term assets whose physical substance is consumed in the operation of a business are called wasting assets. Common examples include mines, stands of timber, and oil and gas wells. The cost of such property is allocated to the periods in which its removal or exhaustion occurs. This periodic write-off is called depletion.

For the sake of brevity, land, buildings, and various types of equipment will often be referred to in the following sections simply as long-term assets. It should be understood that these assets are all in the tangible category.

LAND, BUILDINGS, AND EQUIPMENT

In accounting for tangible long-term assets, two major issues need to be addressed: (1) what elements should be included in the cost of a particular asset or group of assets and (2) how the cost should be allocated or apportioned to those future accounting periods that will benefit from the use of such an asset or group of assets.

COST OF LONG-TERM ASSETS

Long-term assets may be purchased for cash or on account. The amount at which long-term assets should be recorded initially is the total of all outlays needed to put them in use. This total may include the purchase price, transportation charges, installation costs, and any other costs that are incurred up to the point of placing the asset in service. In some cases, interest may be included in the cost. For example, if money is borrowed for the purpose of constructing a building or other facility, it is considered sound accounting to add the interest incurred during the period of construction to the cost of such building or facility. It is important that the total cost of a depreciable asset be properly accounted for, because this cost becomes the basis for the periodic depreciation write-off.

Transactions involving the purchase of property, plant, and equipment may be recorded in the appropriate book of original entry by debiting the proper asset account and by crediting the bank account for the amount paid, or by crediting the proper liability account, such as Accounts Payable, Notes Payable, or Mortgage Payable, for the obligation incurred.

Additions or improvements represent an increase in the value of long-term assets and should be recorded by debiting the proper asset account and by crediting the bank account or the proper liability account. For example, if an addition to a building is constructed, the total cost incurred should be debited to the building account. In the same manner, the cost of improvements, such as the installation of partitions, shelving, hardwood or tile floors, sprinkler systems, air conditioning systems, or any other improvements that increase the usefulness of the property, should be recorded by debiting the building or building improvement account. The costs of landscaping grounds surrounding an office or factory building represent improvements in the land which enhance its value. Assessments for street improvements, sidewalks, sewers, flood prevention, or parks also represent improvements in, or enhancement of the value of the land. Such costs and assessments should be recorded by debiting the land account.

DEPRECIATION OF LONG-TERM ASSETS

The central task in attempting to determine net income or loss on a periodic basis is to allocate revenue to the period in which it is earned and to assign expenses to the periods that are benefited from the outlays. Long-term assets frequently last for many years and, accordingly, benefit a number of periods. The process of determining and recording the depreciation of most long-term assets is carried on in an effort to assign their cost to the periods that they benefit or serve.

It should be emphasized that depreciation is a process of cost allocation, not a process of valuation. Many factors cause the values of long-term assets to change over time, and the assignment of long-term costs to future accounting periods is very unlikely to produce net amounts in the asset accounts that represent current values. These net amounts (cost less accumulated depreciation) are merely the portions of the original costs which have not yet been allocated to expense.

Causes of Depreciation. Most long-term assets lose their usefulness over time. The allocation of the cost or other recorded value of a long-term asset over those future periods expected to benefit from its use is called depreciation. There are two major types of depreciation: (1) physical and (2) functional.

Physical depreciation refers to the loss of usefulness because of deterioration from age and from wear. It is generally continuous, though not necessarily uniform from period to period. Assets exposed to the elements may wear out at a fairly regular rate. Assets not exposed to the elements may slowly deteriorate whether in use or not, but the speed at which they deteriorate often is related to the extent to which they are used.

Functional depreciation refers to the loss of usefulness because of inadequacy or obsolescence. The growth of a business may result in some of its long-term assets becoming inadequate. The assets remain capable of doing the job for which they were acquired, but the job has become too big for them. Assets may become obsolete because of a change in the demand for products or services, or because of the development of new methods, equipment, or processes which either reduce costs, or increase quality, or both.

Calculating the Amount of Depreciation for a Period. The net cost of an asset should be apportioned over the periods the asset is expected to serve. Net cost means original cost less scrap or salvage value. Scrap or salvage value is quite difficult to predict in most cases. Unless such value is expected to be a significant fraction of original cost, it usually is ignored (considered to be zero). Scrap or salvage value normally is a significant amount in the case of automobiles and trucks. Although the estimation of salvage value can be difficult, the major challenge in depreciation accounting is to attempt to foretell either how many periods the assets will serve or how many units of service the asset will provide. If it were possible to know that a machine could operate a total of 100,000 hours, it would be easy to decide that 5 percent of its net cost should be charged to the first year if during that year the machine operated 5,000 hours. Likewise, a certain knowledge that an asset would last 10 years and equally serve each of those years would solve the problem of how to apportion its cost. Unfortunately, there is no way of knowing exactly how long an asset will last or exactly what its output will be. All that can be done is to make estimates based upon past experience. In attempting to make such estimates, the accountant may be assisted by information relating to assets previously owned by the business or be guided by the experience of others.

Statistics supplied by trade associations and government agencies (such as the Internal Revenue Service) may help. Opinions of engineers or appraisal companies may be sought. Past experience with respect to physical depreciation may be a very good guide for the future. Past events, however, are not much help in attempting to predict depreciation caused by inadequacy or obsolescence. Uncertainty surrounds all depreciation calculations.

Methods of Calculating Depreciation. There are several different ways of calculating the amount of depreciation to be recorded each period. The most commonly used methods are the following:

(1) Straight-line method.
(2) Declining-balance method.
(3) Sum-of-the-years-digits method.
(4) Units-of-output method.

Depreciation may be taken into consideration in calculating income subject to federal and state income taxes. A business is not required to calculate depreciation in the same way for both income tax and business accounting purposes. However, because depreciation is only an estimate, many firms adopt depreciation practices for business accounting purposes that are also acceptable for income tax determination purposes. This does not impose severe limitations, since the tax laws generally allow any method that is reasonable and consistently followed, although the first three methods named above are specifically mentioned in the law.

Straight-Line Method. The depreciation method in which the net cost of an asset is apportioned equally over its estimated useful life in terms of months or years is called the straight-line method. For example, assume that a frame building costs $52,500 and is expected to be used for 25 years. At the end of that time, the building will have to be torn down. It is hoped that proceeds from the sale of used building materials, such as lumber, plumbing fixtures, and electrical fixtures, will be as much as the cost of demolition. These considerations lead to the conclusion that the scrap or salvage value should be considered as zero. The amount of depreciation each year would be $2,100, computed as follows:

$$\frac{\$52,500 \text{ (cost)} - 0 \text{ (scrap value)}}{25 \text{ years}} = \$2,100 \text{ annual depreciation}$$

The annual rate of depreciation would be 4 percent (100% ÷ 25 years).

A month is usually the shortest period that is considered in depreciation accounting. An asset purchased on or before the fifteenth of the month is considered to have been owned for the full month. An asset purchased after the fifteenth of the month is considered to have been acquired the first of the next month.

The difference between the cost of an asset and the total amount charged off as depreciation as of a certain date is its **undepreciated cost** (sometimes called **book value**). In the foregoing illustration, the undepreciated cost of the building after the first year, assuming it was in use for 12 months, would be $50,400 [$52,500 (cost) − $2,100 (depreciation)]. When the straight-line method is used, the undepreciated cost of the asset decreases uniformly period by period. As shown on the graph below, the undepreciated cost over a number of periods is a downward-sloping, but perfectly straight line. That is how the method got its name.

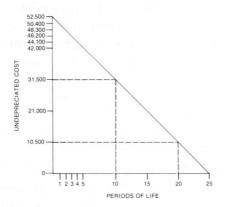

The straight-line method's outstanding advantage is its simplicity. Since depreciation is based upon estimates, many business people and accountants believe that the use of more complicated procedures is not warranted. The calculation of depreciation on a straight-line basis is still the most widely followed practice.

Declining-Balance Method. Many long-term assets require repairs and replacement of parts to keep them in service. Such expenses usually increase as the assets grow older. Some accountants believe that depreciation expense should be higher in early years to offset the higher repair and maintenance expenses of the later years. Another reason advanced in support of an accelerated depreciation method is the contention that assets contribute proportionately more to the business during the years that the assets are comparatively new. For these reasons, it may be desirable to calculate depreciation in a way that will give larger write-offs in the early years of the life of the unit. One way to accomplish this result is to apply a fixed or uniform rate to the undepreciated cost of the property each year. The depreciation method using a fixed or uniform rate applied to the undepreciated cost, resulting in successively smaller depreciation charges as the undepreciated cost diminishes year by year is called the declining-balance method.

A formula to calculate a rate which will leave a predetermined amount at the end of a predetermined number of years is as follows:

$$\text{Rate} = 1 - \sqrt[n]{s \div c}$$

Where n = number of years of estimated life
s = estimated salvage value
c = original cost

This rate is applied each year to the undepreciated cost of the asset to determine the depreciation for the year. There must always be some salvage or scrap value involved, and any rate less than 100 percent will never reduce the original amount to zero.

In practice, however, the rate used is rarely calculated by a formula. Instead, a rate equal to the maximum allowed for federal income tax purposes is used. Upon meeting certain conditions, the maximum allowed is either twice the straight-line rate, 1½ times the straight-line rate, or 1¼ times the straight-line rate. In the discussion that follows, twice the straight-line rate is used. Because a rate is used that is double the straight-line rate, the method is sometimes referred to as the double-declining-balance method.

Assume that a new asset with a cost of $1,000, an expected life of 4 years, and a $100 estimated salvage value at the end of its useful life, is to be depreciated on the declining-balance basis. The company wishes to handle depreciation in the same way for both income tax and business accounting purposes. Accordingly, since the straight-line rate is 25 percent (100% ÷ 4 years), the declining-balance rate would be 50 percent (2 × 25%). The undepreciated cost at the end of each year would be as shown below:

Year	Undepreciated Cost Beginning of Year	Rate	Annual Depreciation	Accumulated Depreciation End of Year	Undepreciated Cost End of Year
1	$1,000.00	50%	$500.00	$500.00	$500.00
2	500.00	50	250.00	750.00	250.00
3	250.00	50	125.00	875.00	125.00
4	125.00	50	25.00	900.00	100.00

Note in the illustration above that although salvage value is not considered directly in the determination of the depreciation amount, the asset should not be depreciated below its estimated salvage value. Thus the amount of depreciation actually recorded in the final year (Year 4) is limited to $25 ($125 − $100).

For income tax purposes, the declining-balance rate can be abandoned at any time without permission, and the undepreciated cost at that date, less any estimated salvage value, can be written off in equal installments over the estimated remaining life. For example, in the foregoing illustration, suppose that at the end of the second year when the asset had an undepreciated cost of $250, it appeared likely that the salvage value would be zero. Accordingly, $125 ($250 ÷ 2) depreciation could be taken for each of the two remaining years.

Sum-of-the-Years-Digits Method. The depreciation method using a steadily decreasing rate applied to net cost (original cost less salvage value), resulting in successively smaller depreciation charges is known as the sum-of-the-years-digits method. This method is similar in effect to the declining-balance method. However, with the years-digits method, a write-down to the exact amount of estimated salvage value (which might be zero) is possible. The write-off each year is based on a schedule of fractions obtained by listing the digits that represent the years of the estimated life of the asset and adding these digits to get a denominator for all of the fractions. The largest digit is used as the numerator for the first year, the next largest digit as the numerator for the second year, etc. For example, suppose that the estimated life of an asset is 4 years. The sum of the digits (4 + 3 + 2 + 1) equals 10 (the denominator). A formula can also be used to determine the denominator, as follows:

$$S = N \left(\frac{N + 1}{2} \right)$$

S = sum of the digits
N = number of years of estimated life

If the life of the asset is 4 years:

$$S = 4 \left(\frac{4 + 1}{2} \right) = 4(2\frac{1}{2}) = 10$$

The denominator equals 10.

Therefore, write off 4/10 of the net cost (original cost less estimated salvage value) the first year, 3/10 the second year, 2/10 the third year, etc. As applied to an asset costing $1,000, with an estimated salvage value of $100, the results would be as follows:

Year	Net Cost	Rate	Annual Depreciation	Accumulated Depreciation End of Year	Undepreciated Cost End of Year
1	$900	4/10	$360	$360	$640
2	900	3/10	270	630	370
3	900	2/10	180	810	190
4	900	1/10	90	900	100

This method has been popular since 1954 when the last major revision of the Internal Revenue Code was adopted.

Units-of-Output Method. The depreciation method that estimates the number of units of service or output that can be secured from an asset and allocates the net cost of the asset to the periods it serves on the basis of the use or output during each period is called the units-of-output or units-of-production method. This measure of service does not exist in many assets.

The units-of-output method may be used for certain types of machinery, equipment, and vehicles. For example, assume that a company finds from experience that it can obtain 75,000 miles of service from certain types of trucks before they become so worn out that the need for extensive repairs and replacements makes it advisable for the company to dispose of them. The company purchases a new truck of this type at a cost (apart from tires, which are separately depreciated) of $8,000. The company expects that the truck can be traded in for $2,000 after 75,000 miles of service. The estimated net cost to be charged to operations during the life of the truck is, therefore, $6,000. The estimated depreciation per mile is 8 cents ($6,000 ÷ 75,000 miles). If the truck is driven 24,000 miles the first year, the depreciation charge for that year would be $1,920 (24,000 × $.08).

COMPARISON OF METHODS

The results of the different depreciation methods are experienced in two ways: (1) through the pattern of depreciation charges and the resultant periodic undepreciated cost amount on the balance sheet, and (2) through the periodic determination of net income on the income statement.

Depreciation Pattern and Undepreciated Costs. The following tabulation contrasts the results of using straight-line, declining-balance, and sum-of-the-years digits depreciation methods for an asset costing $1,000, with a ten-year estimated life and an estimated salvage value of $100:

	Straight-Line Method		Declining-Balance Method		Sum-of-the Years-Digits Method	
Year	Depre-ciation Charge	Undepre-ciated Cost End of Year	Depre-ciation Charge	Undepre-ciated Cost End of Year	Depre-ciation Charge	Undepre-ciated Cost End of Year
1	$90.00	$910.00	$200.00	$800.00	$163.64	$836.36
2	90.00	820.00	160.00	640.00	147.27	689.09
3	90.00	730.00	128.00	512.00	130.91	558.18
4	90.00	640.00	102.40	409.60	114.55	443.63
5	90.00	550.00	81.92	327.68	98.18	345.45
6	90.00	460.00	65.54	262.14	81.82	263.63
7	90.00	370.00	52.43	209.71	65.45	198.18
8	90.00	280.00	41.94	167.77	49.09	149.09
9	90.00	190.00	33.55	134.22	32.73	116.36
10	90.00	100.00	26.84	107.38	16.36	100.00

Under the straight-line method, the annual depreciation charge was determined by dividing the net cost of $900 ($1,000 cost − $100 salvage value) by 10 years.

Under the declining-balance method, salvage value was ignored since it is a built-in factor, and twice the straight-line rate was applied to the undepreciated cost at the start of each year. With a 10-year life, the straight-line rate is 10 percent, so twice this is 20 percent. The undepreciated cost at the end of 10 years ($107.38) is very close to the estimated salvage value of $100. If this were not the case, the declining-balance procedure could have been dropped at some point and in the years remaining, equal charges could have been made to write off all but the estimated salvage value.

Under the sum-of-the-years digits method, salvage value was taken into consideration. The sum of the digits, 1 through 10, is $55 \left[10\left(\frac{10 + 1}{2} \right) \right]$. Therefore, the charge for the first year was 10/55 of the net cost, 9/55 in the second year, and so on.

Effect on Net Income Calculation. Over a number of years, the total of the amounts of the calculated annual net income will be about the same regardless of the method of depreciation used. For any one year, however, the method of depreciation used may make a significant difference in the amount of the calculated net income. For example, assume that a business acquired a number of new depreciable assets at a cost of $50,000, with an estimated life of 10 years and an estimated scrap value of $5,000. For the first year of operation, revenue was $125,000 and all costs and expenses except depreciation amounted to $100,000. Following is a comparison of three very condensed income statements of the new business showing the net income for the first year after applying the three depreciation methods:

	Straight-Line Depreciation Method Used		Declining-Balance Depreciation Method Used		Sum-of-the-Years-Digits Depreciation Method Used	
Revenue..................		$125,000		$125,000		$125,000
Costs and expenses other than depreciation.........	$100,000		$100,000		$100,000	
Depreciation............	4,500	104,500	10,000	110,000	8,182	108,182
Net income...........		$ 20,500		$ 15,000		$ 16,818

To verify the depreciation calculation, refer to Year 1 of the example at the top of page 364 and multiply by 50, since that example was based on a $1,000 asset, and this illustration assumes that the depreciable assets cost $50,000.

Note that the calculated amount of net income in the first case is over one third greater than the amount in the second case. Clearly significant differences in net income may result from the choice of depreciation methods. In the preceding chapter, the effects of the choice of inventory method on net income were noted. It is apparent that periodic business income calculation is not an exact science, but rather an art involving careful judgment based on an understanding of acceptable alternatives and the consequences of their use.

BUILDING YOUR ACCOUNTING KNOWLEDGE

1. Describe five different ways of classifying long-term assets.
2. What may be included in the total amount at which a long-term asset is recorded initially?
3. How should additions or improvements representing an increase in the value of long-term assets be recorded?
4. How should the cost of such activities as landscaping grounds be recorded?
5. What are the two major causes of depreciation?
6. What is meant by the "net cost" of a long-term asset?
7. What are the four most commonly used methods of calculating depreciation, and how do they differ in their application?
8. Why cannot the units-of-output method of depreciation be applied to all depreciable long-term assets?

Report No. 13-1

> Complete Report No. 13-1 in the study assignments and submit your working papers to the instructor for approval. Then continue with the textbook discussion until Report No. 13-2 is required.

ACCOUNTING PROCEDURE

The number of accounts for tangible long-term assets that will be recorded in the general ledger will depend upon the number of depreciable assets, the type of information required by the management, and in the case of all but land, the sort of depreciation procedure that is to be followed. Land is not subject to depreciation in business accounting. If there are very few long-term assets, a separate account for each one with a related depreciation account can be kept in the general ledger. In such a case, the periodic depreciation for each asset should be calculated and recorded separately.

If the business has a considerable number of depreciable long-term assets, it is likely that a summary general ledger account will be kept for each major class of assets, such as one account for buildings, one for machinery and equipment, one for office furniture and equipment, and one for delivery trucks. Each of these summary accounts will have a related accumulated depreciation account. It is highly desirable that such summary accounts be supported by some sort of supplementary or subsidiary records. If depreciation is calculated on a unit basis (meaning a separate calculation and record of depreciation for each unit), it is common practice to maintain a subsidiary record of each unit. Such records commonly take the form of cards. Space is provided on each card to show the details about the asset, including the cost of the unit (which supports the debit in the general ledger asset account), and the amount of depreciation taken each period (which supports the credits in the general ledger accumulated depreciation account). Space is also provided to record matters relating to the disposition of the asset. A typical property, plant, and equipment record card of this type is shown below. Note that salvage value was considered in arriving at the amount of annual depreciation, $120 [($700 original cost − $100 estimated salvage value) ÷ 5 years]. Also note that the 20% rate (100% ÷ 5 years) is applied to the original cost of $700, less the $100 estimated salvage value.

PROPERTY, PLANT, AND EQUIPMENT RECORD

Description Typewriter

Age when acquired New

Estimated life 5 years

Account Office Equipment

Estimated salvage value $100

Rate of annual depreciation based on cost less salvage value 20%

COST					DEPRECIATION RECORD			
Date Purchased		Description	Amount		Year	Rate	Amount	Total To Date
1980					1980	20%	120 00	120 00
Jan.	7	IBM Selectric II typewriter	700	00	1981	20%	120 00	240 00
		# 7340836			1982	20%	60 00	300 00
		Von Brocken Office Equipment			19			
		Company, City			19			
		Less estimated salvage value	100	00	19			
		Net cost	600	00	19			
					19			
					19			

SOLD, EXCHANGED, OR DISCARDED						
Date	Explanation	Amount Realized	More than Less than	√ Undepr. Cost	Accum. Depr.	
1982						
July 1	Sold	450 00		50 00	300 00	

Property, Plant, and Equipment Record

Following is a narrative of the transactions that were recorded on the card:

January 7, 1980. Purchased IBM Selectric II typewriter, No. 7340836, from the Von Brocken Office Equipment Company, City, for $700.

December 31, 1980. Depreciation of typewriter at annual rate of $120 [($700 cost − $100 salvage value) × .20].

December 31, 1981. Depreciation of typewriter at annual rate of $120.

July 1, 1982. Sold typewriter for $450 cash.

Before the sale of the typewriter on July 1, 1982, was recorded, depreciation for the half year, amounting to $60, was recorded by debiting Depreciation Expense — Office Equipment and by crediting Accumulated Depreciation — Office Equipment. The sale was then recorded as indicated by the following two-column journal entry:

Bank	450	
Accumulated Depreciation — Office Equipment	300	
Office Equipment..		700
Gain on Sale of Office Equipment		50
Sold IBM Selectric II typewriter #7340836.		

The $60 depreciation for the half year was entered on the record card. The sale was also entered on the record card, after which the card was transferred from a file of assets owned to a file of assets sold, exchanged, or discarded. Such an asset record, when properly kept, will provide all the information needed in claiming the proper amount of depreciation of long-term assets as a deduction from gross income in the annual income tax returns. The gain resulting from the sale of the typewriter for $50 more than its undepreciated cost represents taxable income, which must be reported in the income tax return for the year in which the sale was made.

In some accounting systems, no effort is made to calculate the periodic depreciation on each unit separately. Instead, depreciation is calculated for groups of assets. The grouping is usually by similar types of assets and similarity of average length of life. A depreciation rate involving the use of an average life which is applied to a number of assets that may include various types of related property is called a group or composite rate. If this procedure is followed, there may be relatively few summary asset and related accumulated depreciation accounts in the general ledger, and there are not likely to be very extensive subsidiary records. No record is kept of the periodic depreciation on each unit since depreciation is calculated for each group as a whole. Even if the group procedure is followed, however, it is desirable to have an individual record for each asset that will show its acquisition date, cost, location, and date and nature of disposition.

RECORDING DEPRECIATION

Depreciation usually is recorded at the end of the period, along with other necessary adjusting entries. One or more depreciation expense accounts may be debited, and one or more accumulated depreciation accounts may be credited. The number of each of these accounts depends upon the degree of detail that is desired in the general ledger accounts and for the periodic statements. Often there is one depreciation expense account for each major type of asset, such as Depreciation Expense — Buildings, Depreciation Expense — Furniture and Fixtures, and Depreciation Expense — Delivery Equipment. A business that classifies expenses on a departmental basis may use a considerable number of depreciation expense accounts.

In the normal course of events, the only entries in the accumulated depreciation accounts are those made at the end of each period to record the depreciation for the period then ended. When some disposition is made of a depreciable asset (such as its sale, exchange, retirement, or destruction by fire), depreciation should be recorded for the interval between the date of the last regular adjustment of the accounts and the date of the disposition of the asset. Usually, the depreciation is calculated to the nearest full month.

DISPOSITION OF LONG-TERM ASSETS

A long-term asset may be disposed of in any one of the following ways:

(1) It may be discarded or retired.
(2) It may be sold.
(3) It may be exchanged or traded in for property of like kind or for other property.

If the asset being removed has been depreciated on a group basis, no gain or loss will be recognized when the asset is removed. The cost of the item must be credited to the proper group asset account. The cost less any amount received for the item is charged to the proper group accumulated depreciation account. The discussion in the paragraphs that follow relates to assets that have been depreciated on an individual basis.

Discarding or Retiring Long-Term Assets. A long-term asset may be discarded or retired whether or not it has been fully depreciated. If it has been fully depreciated, no gain or loss will be realized. If it has not been fully depreciated, the undepreciated cost of the discarded asset will represent a loss. Such a loss may be the result of underestimating the depreciation of the asset for the period of time that it has been in use, or it may be the result of obsolescence. Often, it is better to scrap an obsolete machine and buy a new one even though a loss is realized on the old machine.

To illustrate, on July 16, postal scales that had no exchange or sale value were discarded. The property, plant, and equipment record indicated that the scales originally had cost $100 and that depreciation amounting to a total of $75 had been recorded as a credit to the accumulated depreciation — store equipment account.

This event involved a loss of $25 ($100 − $75) that was the undepreciated cost of the discarded asset. The transaction was recorded as indicated by the following two-column journal entry:

Loss on Discarded Store Equipment..	25	
Accumulated Depreciation — Store Equipment	75	
Store Equipment..		100
Discarded postal scales.		

When this entry is posted, the debit of $75 to the accumulated depreciation account and the credit of $100 to the store equipment account will remove the amounts relating to the postal scales from the balances of these accounts. The debit of $25 to Loss on Discarded Store Equipment records the realized loss that will be reflected on the income statement.

When a long-term asset is discarded after it has been fully depreciated, even though no gain or loss results from the transaction, the amounts relating to the discarded asset should be eliminated from the account balances by debiting the accumulated depreciation account and by crediting the asset account with the amount of the original cost of the asset.

Selling Long-Term Assets. If a long-term asset is sold, it is necessary to know its undepreciated cost before the proper amount of any gain or loss resulting from the transaction can be determined. The undepreciated cost of an asset is the difference between its cost and the total amount of accumulated depreciation recorded. When a long-term asset is sold at its undepreciated cost, no gain or loss results from the transaction; when it is sold for more than its undepreciated cost, the difference represents a gain; when it is sold for less than its undepreciated cost, the difference represents a loss.

Assume that an adding machine costs $300 and depreciates at the rate of 10 percent a year. The annual depreciation is recorded by the following two-column journal entry:

Depreciation Expense — Office Equipment	30	
Accumulated Depreciation — Office Equipment.............................		30

At the end of the 3 years, the undepreciated cost of the adding machine will be $210, the difference between the cost price ($300) and the accumulated depreciation ($90).

If the adding machine was sold at the end of 3 years for $225 cash, the transaction should be recorded by the following two-column journal entry:

Bank	225	
Accumulated Depreciation — Office Equipment	90	
Office Equipment..		300
Gain on Sale of Office Equipment		15
Sold adding machine.		

When this entry is posted, the debit of $90 to the accumulated depreciation account will offset the amounts recorded previously as credits to the accumulated depreciation account over a period of 3 years. The amount credited to Office Equipment will offset the purchase price of $300 previously recorded as a debit to Office Equipment. These entries have the effect of completely eliminating the amounts relating to the old adding machine from the office equipment and accumulated depreciation accounts. The gain of $15 ($225 sales price — $210 undepreciated cost) realized from the sale of the adding machine is reported as a Gain on Sale of Office Equipment. This gain should be listed under the heading of "Other revenue" in the income statement.

If the adding machine referred to was sold at the end of 3 years for $175 instead of $225, there would be a loss of $35 ($210 undepreciated cost − $175 sales price), instead of a gain of $15. The transaction should be recorded by the following two-column journal entry:

Bank	175	
Accumulated Depreciation — Office Equipment	90	
Loss on Sale of Office Equipment	35	
Office Equipment		300
Sold adding machine.		

When this entry is posted, the debit of $90 to the accumulated depreciation account and the credit of $300 to the office equipment account will eliminate the amounts relating to the old adding machine from these accounts. The loss resulting from the sale of the old adding machine for $35 less than its undepreciated cost will be reported as a Loss on Sale of Office Equipment. This loss should be listed under the heading of "Other expense" in the income statement.

Exchange or Trade-In of Long-Term Assets. A long-term asset may be exchanged or traded in for other property. Accepted financial accounting treatment, in most cases, is based on the fair market values of the asset exchanged. A value that is agreed upon in a current sales transaction by a willing buyer and a willing seller is known as a fair market value. On the other hand, tax regulations often allow the asset acquired to be assigned a cost equal to the undepreciated cost of the asset given up.

If one asset is traded in on the purchase of another, a trade-in allowance frequently is granted which may be equal to, greater than, or less than the undepreciated cost of the asset traded in. Trade-in allowances frequently do not reflect fair market values, so that any gain or loss calculated based on a trade-in allowance may not be an accurate measurement of the situation.

In financial accounting, long-term assets are classified into two categories for purposes of exchange or trade-in: similar (the tax laws refer to these as ''of like kind'') and dissimilar (the tax laws refer to these as ''not of like kind''). Financial accounting follows the rule of conservatism in accounting for exchanges of similar assets, recognizing all losses but no gains.

To illustrate the exchange or trade in of similar assets (like kind), assume that a delivery truck that cost $5,600 and has been owned for 3 years is traded in for another delivery truck which is to be used for a similar purpose. Depreciation in the amount of $1,600 has been taken each year — a total of $4,800. Thus, the undepreciated cost of the truck is $800 ($5,600 − $4,800). If the trade-in value of the old truck is $1,200 and the new truck has a fair market value of $7,000, $5,800 would be paid in cash ($7,000 − $1,200), and the transaction should be recorded in two-column journal entry form as follows:

Delivery Equipment (new truck)	6,600	
Accumulated Depreciation — Delivery Equipment	4,800	
Delivery Equipment (old truck)		5,600
Bank		5,800
Purchased a new truck.		

The new truck's cost ($6,600) is the sum of the undepreciated cost of the old truck ($800) and the cash paid ($5,800). This cost becomes the basis for future depreciation charges. Note that this journal entry ignores the $400 gain, which is the difference between the undepreciated cost of $800 and the trade-in value of the old truck of $1,200. When the above entry is posted, the cost of the old truck will be eliminated from the delivery equipment account and that account will be charged with the cost of the new truck. The accumulated depreciation on the old truck will also be eliminated from the accumulated depreciation account, and no gain will be recognized in recording the transaction. This method of accounting also conforms to the tax laws.

If the fair market value of the new truck had been only $6,500, and the trade in value of the old truck only $700, cash of $5,800 would still be paid. Proper financial accounting would require the following two-column journal entry:

Delivery Equipment (new truck)	6,500	
Accumulated Depreciation — Delivery Equipment	4,800	
Loss on Exchange of Delivery Equipment	100	
Delivery Equipment (old truck)		5,600
Bank		5,800
Purchased a new truck.		

Note that in this situation the new truck is recorded at its fair market value and that a $100 loss (the excess of the undepreciated cost over the trade-in allowance) on the exchange is charged to a special loss account. This method of accounting does not conform to the tax laws, because losses for tax purposes (like gains for tax purposes) are not recognized in connection with a like kind exchange. The proper journal entry for tax purposes would be the same as the entry previously illustrated on page 372 where a gain on the exchange was involved but not recorded.

In transactions involving an exchange of dissimilar property (not of like kind), any gain or loss resulting from the transaction should be recognized and recorded, both for financial accounting purposes and for income tax purposes.

To illustrate, assume that the $250 cost of a typewriter was charged to the office equipment account and its depreciation amounting to $50 had been credited to the accumulated depreciation account each year for two years. At the end of two years, the typewriter was traded in on a new cash register having a fair market value of $575. The trade-in allowance was $170, and the balance, $405, was paid in cash. Since this transaction did not involve an exchange of property of like kind, any gain or loss should be recognized. Because $170 was allowed for an asset that had an undepreciated cost of $150 ($250 cost of asset − $100 accumulated depreciation), the transaction involved a gain of $20. The transaction should be recorded in the following two-column journal entry:

Office Equipment	575	
Accumulated Depreciation — Office Equipment	100	
Office Equipment		250
Bank		405
Gain on Exchange of Office Equipment		20
Purchased a new cash register.		

When this entry is posted, the debit of $100 to the accumulated depreciation account will offset the amounts recorded previously as credits to that account over a period of two years. The amount credited to Office Equipment will offset the purchase price of the typewriter previously recorded as a debit to that account. These entries have the effect of completely eliminating the amounts relating to the old typewriter from the office equipment account and the accumulated depreciation account. The gain realized on the old typewriter is reported as a Gain on Exchange of Office Equipment. Had the trade-in allowance been less than the undepreciated cost of the typewriter, the difference would have represented a loss to be reported as a Loss on Exchange of Office Equipment.

FULLY DEPRECIATED LONG-TERM ASSETS

A long-term asset is said to be fully depreciated when the recorded depreciation is equal to the cost of the asset. When an asset is fully depreciated, no further depreciation should be recorded. Since the rate of depreciation is based on its estimated useful life, an asset may still be used after it is fully depreciated. In this case, the cost of the asset and an equal amount of accumulated depreciation are usually retained in the accounts. When a fully depreciated asset is scrapped, the cost of the asset and the total amount of depreciation should be removed from the accounts. Such an adjustment involves a debit to the proper accumulated depreciation account and a credit to the proper long-term asset account for the cost of the asset.

In some states a taxable value is placed on a fully depreciated long-term asset if the asset is in continued use. Under such circumstances, the taxable value of the fully depreciated asset should be stated in the property, plant, and equipment record as a guide in preparing the property tax schedule. The taxable values of fully depreciated long-term assets and the undepreciated costs of other long-term assets should be listed so that the total taxable value of the long-term assets may be determined.

DEPRECIATION IN THE FINANCIAL STATEMENTS

Most accountants and business people consider depreciation to be an operating expense and so classify it in the income statement. There may be as much subclassification as the management desires. Depreciation of delivery equipment, for example, may be classed as a selling expense, while depreciation of office furniture and equipment may be classed as an office or general administrative expense.

In view of the close relationship between long-term asset accounts and their accumulated depreciation accounts, the accepted practice in the preparation of balance sheets is to show the amount of the accumulated depreciation as a deduction from the cost of the asset. The difference, representing undepreciated cost, is extended to be included in the asset total.

Accumulated depreciation accounts, like allowances for doubtful accounts, are sometimes called asset valuation accounts. An accumulated depreciation account, however, only values the asset in a very limited and remote sense. The difference between the cost of the asset and the balance of the accumulated depreciation account is not expected to have any relation to the market value of the asset.

Such assets are not intended for sale. What they might bring, if sold, is usually of small consequence. The difference between the gross amount of the long-term assets and the related accumulated depreciation accounts simply represents costs not yet charged to operations. Some companies so describe this difference in their balance sheets.

WASTING ASSETS

A wasting asset is any real property which is acquired for the purpose of removing or extracting the valuable natural resource on or in the property. Stands of timber, mines, oil wells, gas wells, or land acquired in the belief that the property contains minerals, oil, or gas that can be extracted, are examples of wasting assets because, in most cases, it is expected that the valuable product eventually will be removed or exhausted so as to leave the property relatively valueless. In the case of many types of mines and wells, only the valuable materials below the surface are owned. The land, as such, may not be owned by the mining, oil, or gas company.

Depletion. The consumption or exhaustion of wasting assets is called depletion. Apart from income tax considerations, the accounting problem is to apportion the cost of such assets to the periods in which they are consumed. The procedure called cost depletion is very similar to that involved in computing depreciation on a units-of-output basis. The cost of the property is reduced by estimated salvage or residual value, if any, and the difference is divided by the estimated number of units that the property contains. The result is the depletion expense per unit. This amount times the number of units removed and sold during the period will give the depletion expense for the period.

To illustrate the computation of and proper accounting for depletion, consider the following example. A coal mine is acquired at a cost of $500,000. No salvage value is expected. The estimated number of units available for production is 1,000,000 tons. During the current year, 160,000 tons of coal are mined and sold. The computation of the amount of depletion expense is as follows:

$500,000 ÷ 1,000,000 tons = 50¢ per ton
160,000 tons × 50¢ per ton = $80,000 depletion expense

The depletion is recorded by means of the following two-column journal entry:

Depletion Expense	80,000	
Accumulated Depletion — Coal Mine		80,000
Depletion based on 160,000 tons of coal @ 50¢ a ton.		

The difference between the cost of the mine and the amount of the accumulated depletion is the undepleted cost of the property:

Cost of coal mine	$500,000
Less accumulated depletion	80,000
Undepleted cost of mine	$420,000

It is customary to show the accumulated depletion as a deduction from the property account in the balance sheet in order to indicate the undepleted cost of the property. Depletion Expense is a temporary account that is closed into Expense and Revenue Summary at the end of the accounting period. It should be reported as an operating expense in the income statement. It is an expense that may be deducted in calculating taxable income.

From time to time the estimate of the quantity of the resource that remains in the property has to be changed. The usual practice is to make a new calculation of the depletion per unit, starting with the most recently determined undepleted cost of the property and dividing that amount (less estimated salvage value, if any) by the number of units extracted during the current year plus the current estimate of the number of units remaining. For example, the mine mentioned in the previous illustration had an undepleted cost of $420,000 at the start of the second year. Assume that during that year, 250,000 tons were extracted, and at the end of the year the engineers estimate that 950,000 tons remain. The calculation of the revised depletion expense per unit and depletion expense for the second year would be as follows:

$$\frac{\$420,000}{250,000 \text{ tons} + 950,000 \text{ tons}} = 35¢ \text{ per ton}$$

$$250,000 \text{ tons} \times 35¢ = \$87,500 \text{ depletion expense}$$

Depletion Expense for Federal Income Tax Purposes. Special rules govern the amount of the deduction for depletion expense that can be taken for federal income tax purposes. The taxpayer may compute the amount in the cost depletion manner explained in the preceding paragraphs. However, certain taxpayers who own and operate oil and gas wells (basically where the resource is regulated or sold under a fixed contract) and certain types of mines may use percentage depletion. Under this method, depletion is equal to certain specified percentages (which vary from 5 percent to 22 percent) of the amount of the sales of the period subject to stated maximum and minimum limits. The dollar amount deductible is limited to 50 percent of the taxable income exclusive of any depletion deduction.

BUILDING YOUR ACCOUNTING KNOWLEDGE

1. What details about a particular long-term asset are provided by a property, plant, and equipment record? What details should be provided even if the group procedure is followed?
2. For what time interval should depreciation be recorded when a depreciable asset is disposed of?
3. What are the three major ways in which a long-term asset may be disposed of?
4. From what two major causes may a loss result when a long-term asset is discarded or retired? Will a gain or loss result if a discarded or retired asset has been fully depreciated?
5. When a long-term asset is sold, what must be known about the asset in order to determine the proper amount of gain or loss on the sale?
6. Describe the major differences between accounting for a "similar" (or "like kind") exchange of long-term assets, and accounting for a "dissimilar" (or "not of like kind") exchange. Indicate the ways in which financial accounting and income tax procedures differ in dealing with long-term asset exchanges.
7. What does the difference between the gross amount of long-term assets and the related accumulated depreciation accounts represent to accountants?
8. What depreciation method is very similar to cost depletion? How does percentage depletion differ from cost depletion?

Report No. 13-2

> *Complete Report No. 13-2 in the study assignments and submit your working papers for approval. Then continue with the textbook discussion in Chapter 14 until Report No. 14-1 is required.*

EXPANDING YOUR BUSINESS VOCABULARY

What is the meaning of each of the following terms?

amortization (p. 356)
book value (p. 360)
capital assets (p. 355)
cost allocation (p. 357)
cost depletion (p. 375)
declining-balance method
  (p. 361)
depletion (pp. 356, 375)
depreciable assets (p. 355)
depreciation (pp. 356, 358)
fair market value (p. 371)
fixed assets (p. 355)
group or composite rate (p. 368)
intangible (p. 355)
Investments (p. 355)
long-term assets (p. 355)

marketable securities (p. 355)
percentage depletion (p. 376)
personal property (p. 355)
property, plant, and equipment
  assets (p. 355)
real property (p. 355)
straight-line method (p. 359)
sum-of-the-years-digits method
  (p. 362)
tangible (p. 355)
trade-in allowance (p. 371)
undepreciated cost (p. 360)
unit basis (p. 366)
units-of-output (production)
  method (p. 363)
wasting assets (pp. 356, 375)

CHAPTER 14

INTERNAL ACCOUNTING CONTROL

CHAPTER OBJECTIVES

The objectives of this chapter are to enable you:

▶ To define internal accounting control and to explain its importance in operating a business.

▶ To identify the basic elements of good internal accounting control.

▶ To explain the application of internal accounting control concepts in the two major operating cycles of every business: (1) the revenue cycle and (2) the expenditure cycle.

There are enormous variations in size, type of operation, and product lines of companies. Each of these factors affects the type of control system appropriate for a particular company. For example, a very small business often uses only a limited number of formal control procedures and has little segregation of duties because there are few people to perform the duties in the first place. The key internal control element in this situation is the owner-manager who personally supervises the activities of the business. On the other hand, as the size and nature of a business become larger and more complex, it becomes impossible for the owner to maintain such close contact with all the activities of the business. Consequently, the owner must rely more on a formal internal accounting control system to ensure that the activities of the business are being conducted properly and errors or fraud are prevented or promptly detected. It is important to recognize that it is impossible to define the "correct" system of internal accounting control for all businesses.

In this chapter, certain fundamental internal accounting control concepts are explained and many dimensions of the application of these concepts are illustrated. Some of the internal accounting controls, such as the use of prenumbered documents, are relevant for virtually every business. Other controls, such as an ideal segregation of duties, are not feasible for very small firms. Clearly, the exact system of internal accounting control for a given firm should be developed based on that firm's needs and business environment.

INTERNAL ACCOUNTING CONTROL CONCEPTS

In order to appreciate why many documents, records and procedures exist and are used in particular ways in accounting, an understanding of the concept of internal accounting control and the key elements of internal accounting control is needed.

MEANING AND IMPORTANCE OF INTERNAL CONTROL

An internal accounting control system is defined as all the procedures, documents, and records used by a business to protect its assets and to ensure that the activities of the business are properly performed and documented. The system should provide assurance that (1) all transactions are properly authorized and accounted for, (2) access to assets is permitted only to authorized parties for authorized purposes, and (3) records of assets are verified periodically by examining the related physical properties.

Internal accounting control is essential to the functioning of a business. There is hardly an aspect of a business that is not affected by it. For example, when shipments are made to customers, the system must ensure that the customers are billed and the related amounts collected. Then, the system must ensure that cash receipts from sales are received and recorded by the business and not kept by an employee. Similarly, the system must ensure that purchases are made only of goods to be used in the business and that bills are paid only for goods and services actually purchased and received by the business. In addition, management decisions often are based on accounting information; the control system must ensure that this information is accurate and up to date.

Internal accounting control systems can take many different forms in different businesses; they can be quite simple or very complex. Regardless of their form, however, internal accounting controls are critical to the efficient functioning of a business.

KEY ELEMENTS OF INTERNAL CONTROL

Before looking at specific applications of internal accounting control in individual areas of a business, it will help to examine the basic elements or principles underlying the entire concept. Four key elements of internal accounting control can be identified:

(1) Segregation of duties.
(2) Authorization procedures and related responsibilities.
(3) Record-keeping procedures.
(4) Independent checks on performance.

Segregation of Duties. Segregation of duties involves assigning duties in such a way that (1) different employees are responsible for different parts of a transaction, and (2) employees who maintain accounting records do not have custody of the firm's assets. Appropriate segregation of duties helps to detect errors promptly and reduces the possibility of employee fraud. For example, assume that one employee is responsible for ordering goods, a second employee for receiving goods, a third employee for paying for goods based on proper evidence of purchase, and a fourth employee for accounting for the purchase of and payment for the goods. Such a segregation of duties provides a built-in check of one employee on another in that the amounts ordered, received, paid for, and recorded in the accounting records must agree; otherwise some error has occurred. Similarly, no one of these four employees can obtain goods for personal use or make improper payments for goods without being caught.

The duties of record keeping and asset custody should be segregated in order to prevent employees from stealing business assets and concealing their theft by modifying the accounting records. For example, assume that one employee is responsible for receiving customer remittances on account, and a second employee is responsible for recording sales and customer remittances in the accounting records. This segregation of duties prevents the first employee from keeping the customers' remittances because the customer would complain if billed by the second employee for amounts that already had been remitted. Similarly, the second employee has no incentive to make improper entries in the accounting records because of lack of access to cash receipts.

Authorization Procedures and Related Responsibility. Sound authorization procedures involve assigning responsibilities so that only properly authorized activities take place in the business and the persons responsible for such activities and the related assets are identified at every step in the process. Basically, this element of internal accounting control should ensure that transactions do not occur without sufficient authorization. For some transactions this authorization can be general. For example, a sales clerk in a department store has general authorization to make sales of particular goods using a particular cash register and perhaps keying in a specific clerk number. For other transactions, the authorization is likely to be specific. For example, major production equipment of a business normally is bought or sold only if specific written authorization is obtained from management at a relatively high level. Whether the authorization is general or specific, the control concept remains the same; someone should be responsible for every activity in which a business engages. Unless someone has authorized and assumed responsibility for an action, that action should not be taken by the business. Correspondingly, after some activity has occurred, it should be possible to determine who authorized it and therefore is held responsible.

Record-Keeping Procedures. Proper record-keeping procedures include use of accounting records and documents in such a way that whenever business activities occur, the accounting system reacts. A major dimension of this internal accounting control element is the use of prenumbered documents that must be generated promptly when an activity occurs and then subsequently accounted for. Subsequent accounting for prenumbered documents can be simplified by recording and filing the documents in numerical order. This element of internal accounting control helps ensure that all valid activities of the business are recorded and that only valid activities are recorded. For example, assume that prenumbered sales receipts are used, that one copy of the receipt is issued to a customer whenever a sale occurs and the other copy is retained in the firm's files. In this situation, if the numerical sequence of receipts is complete and there are no duplicate receipts recorded, it is reasonable to assume that all sales transactions are accounted for and only valid sales transactions are recorded.

Independent Checks on Performance. This last key element of internal accounting control includes the various methods used by a business to ensure that management's accounting rules and regulations are being followed. Perhaps the most easily recognized type of independent check on performance is that provided by the internal audit department of a business. The internal audit department has broad responsibility to see that the internal accounting control system is effective. This includes responsibilities for determining (1) that the system is properly designed and (2) that there is compliance with the segregation of duties, with authorization, and with record-keeping procedures dictated by the system. The first responsibility is fulfilled primarily by making sure that the system is characterized by the key elements of internal control that are described in this section. The second responsibility is fulfilled by testing and analyzing the business activities that occur during the year. For example, the numerical sequence of sales invoices or checks can be accounted for by maintaining numerical order. The sum of the balances in the accounts receivable ledger can be verified with the general ledger accounts receivable balance. A bank reconciliation can be prepared. Canceled checks can be traced to appropriate supporting documents.

In addition to the specific performance checks provided by the internal audit department, a system of independent checks is built into many phases of the business. For example, if the accounts receivable records, sales journal, and general ledger are maintained by three different people in the accounting department, each of these employees provides an automatic independent check on a part of the work of the other two employees. If any one of these employees does not perform the prescribed procedures correctly, the accounting records will not agree. Another type of independent check built into the system literally involves some duplication of work. This happens whenever an employee is responsible for verifying the work of a fellow employee, such as when the price, quantity, and total dollar amount of a sales invoice must be verified by a second employee before it is mailed to a customer. Many of these built-in checks can exist throughout a company's accounting system and can help provide assurance that various procedures are being properly performed.

BUILDING YOUR ACCOUNTING KNOWLEDGE

1. Why is it impossible to define the "correct" system of internal accounting control for all businesses?
2. What assurance should be provided by an internal accounting control system?
3. How would appropriate segregation of duties prevent an employee responsible for receiving customer remittances on account from keeping the customers' remittances?
4. How do sound authorization procedures contribute to internal accounting control?
5. Why should documents be prenumbered and subsequently accounted for?
6. What are the responsibilities of an internal audit department?

Report No. 14-1

> *Complete Report No. 14-1 in the study assignments and submit your working papers to the instructor for approval. Then continue with the textbook discussion until Report No. 14-2 is required.*

APPLICATION IN THE REVENUE CYCLE

The revenue cycle includes all the functions involved in receiving customer orders, providing goods and services, billing customers, and collecting payments — either on account or for cash sales. Diagramming and briefly explaining the revenue cycle will assist in understanding internal accounting control in the revenue cycle. A flowchart of the basic elements of the revenue cycle appears on the following page. Many variations of the revenue cycle are possible for different businesses. The flowchart shown here assumes a medium-sized business that deals in a tangible product.

The Credit Sales portion of the flowchart shows that a customer who purchases merchandise on account usually sends a purchase order to a particular business. In response to this order, a sales order would be generated by the business. This sales order is the basis for preparing a shipping order which causes goods to be shipped to the customer. One copy of the shipping order is sent to the customer with the goods and a second copy is sent to the Billing section so that a bill, the sales invoice, will be sent to the customer. A second copy of the sales invoice is sent to the Accounts Receivable and General Ledger sections for recording in the accounting records.

The Collections and Cash Sales portion of the flowchart depicts the processing of both collections on account and collections from cash sales. Collections on account are generally received by mail from customers. Normally included with the check is a remittance advice, which is a document indicating the purpose of the payment, that is, the bill that is being paid. Remittance advices are sent to the Accounts Receivable and General Ledger sections for recording and the checks are sent to the cashier, who prepares a deposit slip and sends it with the checks to the bank. The bank returns a validated deposit slip to the Accounting Department.

Sales clerks normally use cash registers to handle cash sales. Customer remittances of cash or checks are forwarded to the cashier, who prepares a deposit slip and sends the deposit to the bank. The cash register tape is sent to the Accounting Department for recording. A validated deposit slip is returned to the Accounting Department by the bank.

The Internal Audit Department has responsibility to oversee or monitor the entire system of internal accounting control depicted in the flowchart. Its functions might include making sure that goods are shipped only on the basis of authorized shipping orders or that all collections on account are properly posted.

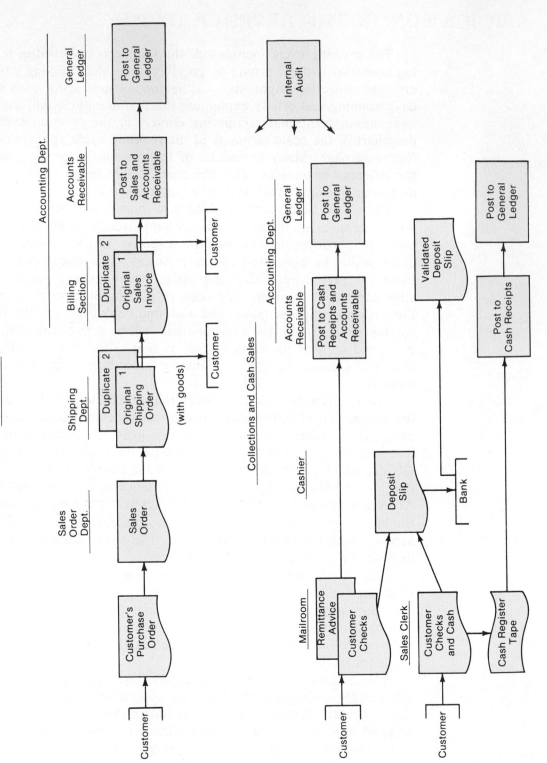

Flowchart of Revenue Cycle

Credit Sales

Internal accounting control over the revenue cycle will now be discussed in some detail. The partial records illustrated are those of Fishler & Marvon, a partnership engaged in the bakery business. The merchandise accounts are kept on a departmental basis — Dept. A handles pastries and cakes, Dept. B handles bread and rolls. Since internal accounting controls relevant for credit sales differ significantly from those relevant for cash sales, cash sales and credit sales are discussed separately here.

CASH SALES

Most businesses make at least a portion of their sales for cash rather than on account. Regardless of the percentage of sales made for cash, certain basic internal accounting control procedures should be employed.

Cash Register Tapes and Sales Tickets. Receipts from cash sales are generally controlled by the use of a cash register that generates a cash register tape in duplicate; one copy for the customer and one copy to be retained for the firm's records. At the end of each day, the cash and any checks received from customers are sent to the cashier for preparation of the bank deposit, and the cash register tapes are either picked up by or sent to the accounting department for entry in the accounting records.

An alternative system for handling cash sales that is used by many businesses is the preparation of a separate sales ticket for each transaction. A salesclerk prepares a sales ticket in duplicate for each sale, and these tickets and the related cash receipts are then handled in a manner similar to that used for cash register tapes and related cash receipts. The only additional control necessary when sales tickets are used is that the tickets should be prenumbered and subsequently accounted for by number.

Deposit Slip. The cashier prepares a deposit slip in duplicate for the cash and checks received from the salesclerks and sends both copies with the deposit to the bank. The validated deposit slip should be returned by the bank to the firm's accounting department.

Accounting Procedures for Cash Sales. The first accounting record affected by cash sales is the record of cash receipts. The cash register tapes, the sales tickets, or a listing of the tickets are the basis for the postings to the record of cash receipts. Examples of postings of cash sales can be seen in the portion of the record of cash receipts of Fishler & Marvon illustrated on page 395.

The second accounting record affected by cash sales is the general ledger. At the end of each month, a summary posting is made from the record of cash receipts to the general ledger cash and sales accounts for the appropriate amounts.

When each validated deposit slip is returned by the bank to the firm's accounting department, the amount deposited is compared with the amount posted to the record of cash receipts based on the cash register tapes or sales tickets. This procedure ensures that all cash sales collected by the salesclerks and forwarded to the cashier were in fact properly deposited.

This system appears to control adequately what happens to cash once a proper cash register or sales ticket record is made of each cash sale. A question might be raised, however, as to the control that exists over the salesclerks to see that a valid cash register entry or sales ticket is prepared in the first place. The answer essentially is the customer. Any customer purchasing merchandise expects to receive some kind of receipt for the amount remitted. In order to provide such a receipt, the salesclerk must generate either a cash register entry or a sales ticket. It would still be possible for the salesclerk to alter a sales ticket subsequently, but if these documents are reviewed by the accounting department or internal audit staff, frequent alterations in sales tickets would be questioned.

CREDIT SALES

Internal accounting control procedures for credit sales typically are more complicated than those for cash sales. By their nature, credit sales involve more documents, more people, and more accounting records.

Customer Purchase Order. The customer's purchase order initiates a sales transaction. Since the customer intends to purchase goods from another business, clearly one firm's purchase is another firm's sale. Customer orders can be received either by mail or by telephone. If an order is received by telephone, the customer order document usually is generated internally by the seller. Based on the customer order, a sales order is prepared.

Sales Order. The sales order is a document prepared by the sales order department which authorizes sales of merchandise to a customer. It would be possible to use the customer order as a sales order, but control and handling efficiency are improved if a separate sales order is generated. A sales order prepared by Fishler & Marvon's Bakery for a sale to Heritage House is illustrated below. Sales orders should be prenumbered and subsequently all numbers should be accounted for. If any numbers are missing, this would suggest that some orders have been lost and not properly processed. Sales orders are often prepared in duplicate so that the sales order department can retain one copy for its files. Many companies also have a separate credit department. If a credit department exists, the sales order is sent to the credit department to obtain approval of a sale to any charge customer. Note the credit approval that appears on the Fishler & Marvon sales order reproduced below. After credit is approved, the sales order is sent to the shipping department.

	SALES ORDER		No. 403	
Fishler & Marvon's Bakery 1604 N. Milburn Indianapolis, IN 46202-9001				
Customer:	Heritage House 4990 US Highway 31S Indianapolis, IN 46227-5123		Date	May 6, 19--

Quantity	Description	Amount	Total
50 dz.	assorted danish	217	
20	assorted coffee cakes	45	
26	assorted cakes	90	
225 dz.	assorted buns and rolls	252	
115	assorted breads	87	691

Credit approval: *CD*

Sales Order

Shipping Order. The shipping order is the document that provides authorization to ship merchandise. It is an important control document in a firm's information system. An example of a shipping order for a shipment from Fishler & Marvon to Heritage House appears on page 390. This shipping order was prepared based on the sales order that appears above. Shipping orders should be prenumbered and subsequently accounted for by number in order to ensure that all shipments are properly recorded and that all goods shipped are billed to the purchasers. One copy of the shipping order is sent to the customer with the goods and the other copy is sent to the billing section so that a sales invoice can be prepared.

SHIPPING ORDER		No. 395

Fishler & Marvon's Bakery
1604 N. Milburn
Indianapolis, IN 46202-9001

Customer:
    Heritage House
    4990 US Highway 31S
    Indianapolis, IN 46227-5123

Date   May 6, 19--
Shipping instructions our truck
To be delivered   May 7, 19--

Quantity	Description	Amount	Total
50 dz.	assorted danish	217	
20	assorted coffee cakes	45	
26	assorted cakes	90	
225 dz.	assorted buns and rolls	252	
115	assorted breads	87	691

Shipping Order

Sales Invoice. A multiple-copy sales invoice, which is the company's bill to the customer, is prepared in the billing section of the accounting department as soon as the copy of the shipping order has been received, indicating that the goods have been shipped. A copy of a summary sales invoice that was generated based on the shipping order appearing above is reproduced on page 391. In Fishler & Marvon's system, this invoice showing sales summarized in terms of pastries and breads is supported by a detailed sales invoice (not shown) listing items purchased, unit prices, and extended amounts. This document is extremely important from a control standpoint. In conjunction with the shipping order, the sales invoice provides assurance that all goods shipped are also billed. Sales invoices should be prenumbered and subsequently accounted for by number in order to provide this assurance of proper billing. If any sales invoice number is missing from the sequence, it would suggest that some shipment was not billed or perhaps that the billing was not posted to the accounting records. In addition, each sales invoice should be supported by a shipping order to make certain that sales are recorded only for goods actually shipped to customers. One copy of the sales invoice is sent to the customer and a second copy is sent to accounting. Other copies of the sales invoice might also be used in an accounting information system but the two copies described above are the minimum necessary. In many accounting information systems, the sales invoices must be verified as to price, quantity, and extended amounts before they are mailed to customers.

SUMMARY SALES INVOICE		No. 391

Fishler & Marvon's Bakery
1604 N. Milburn
Indianapolis, IN 46202-9001

Customer: Date   May 7, 19--

    Heritage House
    4990 US Highway 31S
    Indianapolis, IN 46227-5123

Description	Amount	Total
Pastries	352	
Breads	339	691

Summary Sales Invoice

Accounting Procedures for Credit Sales. Accounting procedures for recording sales were explained to a great extent in Chapter 7. That discussion is extended here in order to emphasize the internal accounting control aspects of the recording process.

The first accounting record affected by sales transactions is a firm's sales register or journal. A portion of the sales register for Fishler & Marvon is illustrated on page 392. The individual sales invoices represent the basis for entries in the sales register. In most accounting information systems, entries to such a register represent the first point at which sales activities are reflected in the accounting records. Neither the customer order, nor the sales order, nor the shipping order, nor the preparation of the sales invoice directly affects any accounting record. This makes the sales register particularly important from a control standpoint. Note that the sales invoices are entered in the sales register not only in chronological

	DEBIT								CREDIT				
GENERAL LEDGER				DAY	NAME	SALE NO.		SALES		GENERAL LEDGER			
ACCT. NO.	AMOUNT	√	ACCOUNTS RECEIVABLE	√				DEPT. A	DEPT. B	ACCT. NO.	AMOUNT	√	
			1089 00	√ 4	Ayres Dept. Stores	387		685 00	404 00				1
			896 00	√ 4	Bakemeier's Bakery	388		560 00	336 00				2
			665 00	√ 4	Methodist Hospital	389		231 00	434 00				3
			584 00	√ 7	Brother Juniper's	390		423 00	161 00				4
			691 00	√ 7	Heritage House	391		352 00	339 00				5
			537 00	√ 7	Houlihan's Place	392		364 00	173 00				6
			22356 00					12403 00	9953 00				8
			22356 00					12403 00	9953 00				8
			(131)					(611)	(621)				9

SALES REGISTER FOR MONTH OF *May* **19 - -** **PAGE** *9*

Fishler & Marvon's Sales Register (*Partial*)

order but also in numerical order. This feature of the recording process makes the sales register a convenient place to account for the numerical sequence of sales invoices.

A second accounting record affected by sales transactions is the accounts receivable ledger. A portion of the accounts receivable ledger for Fishler & Marvon is reproduced at the top of page 393. For good internal accounting control, the individual sales invoices should be the basis for posting to the individual customer accounts in the accounts receivable ledger. Note that the individual postings for sales invoices Nos. 387, 388, and 389 appear in these customer accounts, just as they appeared in the sales register shown above. Posting to the individual customer accounts from the sales invoices rather than from the sales register provides an independent check on the posting process. If the postings of customer accounts were made from the sales register, any error in posting the sales register would automatically be carried forward to the accounts receivable ledger. On the other hand, if both the sales register and the customer accounts are posted from individual sales invoices by different accounting department employees, a posting error by either employee would cause the records to disagree, unless of course, both employees made exactly the same error. The posting error would be discovered at the end of the month because at that time, the individual customer account balances in the accounts receivable ledger would be scheduled, totaled, and compared with the general ledger accounts receivable control, which is posted from the total of the sales register entries.

The third accounting record affected by sales transactions is the general ledger. As explained in Chapter 7, at the end of the month a summary posting would be made from the sales register to the appropriate general ledger accounts. The accounts and amounts posted for May are indicated at the bottom of the columns in the sales reg-

NAME *Ayres Department Stores*   TERMS *Net*
ADDRESS *1 W. Washington St., Indianapolis, IN 46204-5174*

DATE	ITEM	POST. REF.	DEBIT	CREDIT	BALANCE
19-- May 1	Balance	✓			81300
4		S387	108900		190200

NAME *Bakemeier's Bakery*   TERMS *Net*
ADDRESS *2039 N. Capitol Ave., Indianapolis, IN 46202-4240*

DATE	ITEM	POST. REF.	DEBIT	CREDIT	BALANCE
19-- May 1	Balance	✓			40900
4		S388	89600		130500

NAME *Methodist Hospital*   TERMS *Net*
ADDRESS *1604 N. Capitol Ave., Indianapolis, IN 46202-5126*

DATE	ITEM	POST. REF.	DEBIT	CREDIT	BALANCE
19-- May 1	Balance	✓			54200
4		S389	66500		120700

Fishler & Marvon's Accounts Receivable Ledger *(Partial)*

ister on page 392. The posting that is of particular interest for purposes of the present discussion is the one to accounts receivable for $22,356. The general ledger accounts receivable control account is reproduced below. After posting from the sales register, the account has a balance of $28,044. This represents the total balances in all accounts receivable as of the end of May, after posting all charge sales made during May.

ACCOUNT *Accounts Receivable*   ACCOUNT NO. *131*

DATE	ITEM	POST. REF.	DEBIT	CREDIT	BALANCE DEBIT	BALANCE CREDIT
19-- May 1	Balance	✓			568800	
31		SR9	2235600		2804400	

Accounts Receivable Account in General Ledger

Remittance Advice and Check. When a customer makes a remittance by mail, it is customary for the customer to include a remittance advice with the check. The remittance advice is a form showing the customer's name and address and the amount of the remittance. A good example of a remittance advice appears below. For good internal accounting control, the checks and remittance advices should be separated in the mailroom; the checks should be sent to the cashier and the remittance advices to the accounting department. If a customer remittance arrives without a remittance advice, a remittance advice should be prepared in the mailroom for forwarding to the accounting department.

MH **Methodist Hospital**
1604 N. Capitol Ave.
Indianapolis, IN 46202-4492

Date   May 4, 19--

Enclosed is our payment of the following:

Invoice Date	No.	Description	Amount
4/27	379	Assorted pastries, rolls, and breads	542.00
		Deductions	-0-
		Net	542.00

Remittance Advice

The processing of the checks and remittance advices is designed to ensure that customer remittances on account are properly received, deposited, and recorded in the firm's records. If employees in the mailroom attempt to retain any customer remittances for their own use, the fraud will be discovered because mailroom employees do not have access to the accounting records. Consequently, the customer will undoubtedly be billed again for the amount previously remitted but intercepted by the mailroom employees. When the customer complains about the billing, the theft will be discovered. The actions of the cashier who receives the remittances from the mailroom are similarly controlled. The accounting department employees have access to the accounting records and can fraudulently alter them, but these employees have no access to the remittances and therefore, no incentive to modify the accounting records.

Deposit Slip. The cashier prepares a deposit slip in duplicate for the checks and cash received from the mailroom, and sends both copies along with the checks and cash to the bank. A common form of deposit slip is reproduced below. These deposit slips are often prenumbered. The bank validates the deposit slip and returns it to the depositing firm.

DEPOSIT SLIP		$\frac{3\text{-}4}{740}$

Fishler & Marvon's Bakery
1604 N. Milburn
Indianapolis, IN 46202-9001

Date _____ May 2 _____ 19 __

**FEDERAL
NATIONAL
BANK**
Indianapolis, Indiana

Currency	2,043	50
Coin	116	50
Checks		
Total from other side		
Total	2,160	00

⑆ 074000009⑆   92 641 8 ⑈

Deposit Slip

Accounting Procedures for Collections. The first accounting record affected by collections on account is the record of cash receipts, a special journal used to record all cash receipts. The individual remittance advices are the basis for entries in this record. A portion of the record of cash receipts for Fishler & Marvon is illustrated below.

RECORD OF CASH RECEIPTS FOR MONTH OF *May*   19 --   PAGE *12*

	DEBIT						CREDIT						
	GENERAL LEDGER							CASH SALES		GENERAL LEDGER			
ACCT. NO.	AMOUNT	√	BANK NET AMOUNT	DAY	RECEIVED FROM DESCRIPTION		ACCOUNTS RECEIVABLE	√	DEPT. A	DEPT. B	ACCT. NO.	AMOUNT	√
					AMOUNTS FORWARDED								
			2807 00	1	Cash Sales				1580 00	1227 00			
			2160 00	2	Cash Sales				1195 00	965 00			
			2451 00	4	Cash Sales				1309 00	1142 00			
			2717 00	5	Cash Sales				1498 00	1219 00			
			1027 00	5	Ayres Dept. Stores		1027 00	√					
			814 00	5	Bakemeier's Bakery		814 00	√					
			542 00	5	Methodist Hospital		542 00	√					
			92267 00 92267 00				25417 00 25417 00		35376 00 35376 00	30988 00 30988 00		486 00 486 00	
			(111)				(131)		(611)	(621)		(√)	

Fishler & Marvon's Record of Cash Receipts *(Partial)*

A second accounting record affected by the collections is the accounts receivable ledger. The receipts are posted to the accounts receivable ledger in chronological order and the source of each receipt is indicated. For good internal accounting control, the individual remittance advices should be used to post to the individual customer accounts in the accounts receivable ledger. The portion of the accounts receivable ledger illustrated on page 393 is reproduced below, with three additional items, the remittances on account by the three customers during May. Note that having different accounting department employees use the remittance advices to post separately to the accounts receivable ledger provides the same type of control over the cash receipts posting process that separate posting to the accounts receivable ledger from the individual sales invoices provided over the sales posting process. If an error was made in posting either to the general ledger or to the accounts receivable ledger, the error would be discovered at the end of the month when the total of the balances in the accounts receivable ledger is compared with the general ledger accounts receivable control account balance.

NAME *Ayres Department Stores*   TERMS *Net*
ADDRESS *1 W. Washington St., Indianapolis, IN 46204-5174*

DATE	ITEM	POST. REF.	DEBIT	CREDIT	BALANCE
19-- May 1	Balance	✓			81300
4		S387	108900		190200
5		C		102700	87500

NAME *Bakemeier's Bakery*   TERMS *Net*
ADDRESS *2039 N. Capitol Ave., Indianapolis, IN 46202-4240*

DATE	ITEM	POST. REF.	DEBIT	CREDIT	BALANCE
19-- May 1	Balance	✓			40900
4		S388	89600		130500
5		C		81400	49100

NAME *Methodist Hospital*   TERMS *Net*
ADDRESS *1604 N. Capitol Ave., Indianapolis, IN 46202-5126*

DATE	ITEM	POST. REF.	DEBIT	CREDIT	BALANCE
19-- May 1	Balance	✓			54200
4		S389	66500		120700
5		C		54200	66500

Fishler & Marvon's Accounts Receivable Ledger (*Partial*)

Another accounting record affected by the collections is the general ledger. At the end of each month, a summary posting would be made from the record of cash receipts to the appropriate general ledger accounts. The accounts and amounts posted for May are indicated at the bottom of the columns in the record of cash receipts on page 395. The general ledger accounts receivable control account shown on page 393 is reproduced below, with one additional item, the credit total of $25,417 from the May record of cash receipts. After this posting, the account has a balance of $2,627. This represents the total of the balances in all individual customer accounts receivable as of the end of May, after crediting the customer accounts for all remittances received.

In the previous discussion of deposit slips, it was noted that validated deposit slips are returned by the bank to the firm. Internal control is strengthened if these deposit slips are returned to the accounting department of the firm rather than to the cashier. An accounting department employee should compare the amount shown on the validated deposit slip with the amounts recorded in the record of cash receipts as remittances on account. This procedure ensures that customer remittances on account as indicated on the remittance advices and recorded in the record of cash receipts were in fact deposited by the cashier.

ACCOUNT *Accounts Receivable*					ACCOUNT NO. *131*	
DATE	ITEM	POST. REF.	DEBIT	CREDIT	BALANCE DEBIT	BALANCE CREDIT
19-- May 1	Balance	✓			568800	
31		SR9	2235600		2804400	
31		CR12		2541700	262700	

Accounts Receivable Account in General Ledger

BUILDING YOUR ACCOUNTING KNOWLEDGE

1. What functions are included in the revenue cycle?
2. What purposes are served by the shipping order?
3. Why should postings to individual customer accounts receivable be made from the sales invoices rather than from the sales register?
4. Why are checks and remittance advices separated in the mailroom, with the checks being sent to the cashier, and the remittance advices to the accounting department?
5. What control exists over salesclerks to see that a valid cash register entry is made or a sales ticket is prepared when a sale occurs?
6. What three accounting records are affected by collections on account?

7. Why should validated deposit slips be returned by the bank to the accounting department of the firm rather than to the cashier?

Report No. 14-2

> Complete Report No. 14-2 in the study assignments and submit your working papers to the instructor for approval. Then continue with the textbook discussion until Report No. 14-3 is required.

APPLICATION IN THE EXPENDITURE CYCLE

The expenditure cycle includes all of the functions involved in acquiring and receiving goods from suppliers and in making payments for the goods purchased. Diagramming and briefly explaining the expenditure cycle will assist in understanding internal accounting control in the expenditure cycle. A flowchart of the basic elements of the expenditure cycle appears on the following page. Many variations of the expenditure cycle are possible for different businesses. For example, in a small business, all the purchasing and payment activities might be performed by a single owner/manager. Purchases might be made directly from sales representatives who visit the store, perhaps with the goods ready for delivery. At the other extreme, in very large firms two or three different levels of authorization might be required in order to make expenditures above a specified dollar amount. The flowchart presented here assumes a medium-sized business that purchases tangible products.

The Purchases portion of the flowchart shows that any department or person in the firm wanting to purchase goods must prepare an authorized purchase requisition and forward it to the purchasing department. The purchasing department examines the purchase requisition and prepares a purchase order and sends it to the appropriate supplier. When the goods arrive from the supplier, a receiving report is prepared in the receiving department. This receiving report and a copy of the purchase order are sent to the accounting department where eventually they are matched with the purchase invoice received from the supplier. The purchase order, receiving report, and purchase invoice provide the basis for preparing a voucher, which is a document used to authorize payments for goods and services. The voucher is posted to the voucher register, an accounting record similar to an accounts payable journal.

The Payments portion of the flowchart indicates that the voucher and supporting documents are used by the cashier as a basis for

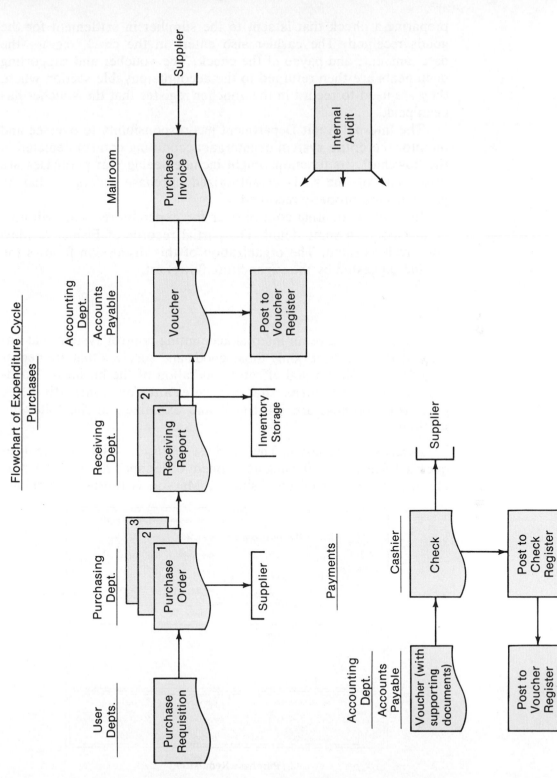

Flowchart of Expenditure Cycle
Purchases

preparing a check that is sent to the supplier in settlement for the goods received. The cashier also enters in the check register the date, amount, and payee of the check. The voucher and supporting documents are then returned to the accounts payable section where they are used to record in the voucher register that the voucher has been paid.

The Internal Audit Department has responsibility to oversee and monitor the entire system of internal accounting control depicted in the flowchart. Its functions might include seeing that purchases are made only on the basis of authorized purchase orders or that all payments are properly recorded.

Internal accounting control over the expenditure cycle will now be discussed in some detail. The partial records of Fishler & Marvon are illustrated. The organization of this discussion follows the outline suggested by the expenditure flowchart.

ACQUISITION OF GOODS

A firm must have an internal accounting control system that ensures that it purchases only those goods and services that are necessary for the efficient and effective operation of the business. Documents and procedures that are relevant for controlling the purchasing process are illustrated and explained in the following sections.

Purchase Requisition. The purchase requisition is a document requesting that the purchasing department order specific goods. A purchase requisition used by Fishler & Marvon is reproduced below.

	Purchase Requisition No. 318
Fishler & Marvon's Bakery 1604 N. Milburn Indianapolis, IN 46202-9001	Date issued May 1, 19-- Date required May 6, 19--
Order From Capital City Products 1021 E. 54 St. Indianapolis, IN 46220-1693	Dept. A Deliver to J. Marvon

Quantity	Description
20	Large bakery trays

Purchasing Dept. Memorandum
Date May 1, 19--
Issued To Capital City Products
1021 E. 54 St.
Indianapolis, IN 462201693

Placed by *J. Marvon*
Approved by *J. Fishler*
Purchase Order No.   402

Purchase Requisition

Purchase requisitions should be prenumbered and subsequently accounted for by number. This is to ensure that all requisitions are properly handled by the purchasing department and that the individual responsible for requesting that any merchandise be purchased can be subsequently identified if necessary.

The purchase requisition itself does not authorize a purchase. The requisition must first be approved. For a minor purchase, the approval might come from a department supervisor, whereas a major purchase should be approved at a higher level of management. When approved, the purchase requisition authorizes the purchasing department to generate a purchase order.

Purchase Order. The purchase order is an explicit request by the firm to buy goods from a supplier. A purchase order used by Fishler & Marvon is reproduced below. This purchase order was prepared based on the purchase requisition illustrated on page 400. Purchase orders should be prenumbered and subsequently accounted for by number, in order to ensure either that all of the goods on an order are received or that the order is canceled, and that only goods that have been ordered are received and paid for subsequently. The number of copies of the purchase order that are prepared depends on the particular accounting information system. There are likely to be at least three copies. One copy is sent to the supplier, a second copy goes to the accounting department, and the third copy is retained by the purchasing department for its files. A fourth copy could be sent to the individual who requisitioned the goods, and a fifth copy could be sent to the receiving department for use as a receiving report.

			Purchase Order No. 402
Fishler & Marvon's Bakery 1604 N. Milburn Indianapolis, IN 46202-9001	Date	May 1, 19--	
	Delivery by	May 6, 19--	
To	Terms	Net	
Capital City Products 1021 E. 54 St. Indianapolis, IN 46220-1693			

Quantity	Description	Unit Price
20	Large bakery trays	4.45

J. Fishler

Purchase Order

Receiving Report. Whether or not a copy of the purchase order is used for this purpose, a document called a receiving report should be prepared promptly by the receiving department for all goods received by the firm. Receiving reports should be prenumbered and subsequently accounted for by number to ensure that all goods received are properly recorded. There are normally two copies of the receiving report. One copy is sent to the accounting department, and the other remains with the goods for forwarding to the inventory storage area.

PAYMENT FOR GOODS USING THE VOUCHER SYSTEM

Much of the material covered thus far in this chapter was addressed previously in other sections of the text. For example, basic features of accounting for sales were explained in Chapter 7, and accounting for purchases was addressed in Chapter 6. For this reason, recording procedures in these areas generally have not been explained and illustrated in detail in this chapter. In contrast, the accounting system used to control payments for items purchased by the business has received rather limited attention previously. Therefore, the recording aspects of internal accounting control over payments will be explained in greater detail in this section.

A system for controlling expenditures that is used by many businesses is known as a voucher system. Such a system is very useful for controlling cash disbursements, because written authorization is required for each disbursement. A voucher system usually involves the use of vouchers, a voucher register, a vouchers payable account in the general ledger, voucher checks, and a check register. There are several alternative accounting procedures applicable to the voucher system. For instance, ordinary checks may be used and recorded in a simple cashbook or in a cash payments journal. Like most bookkeeping and accounting processes, the voucher system is flexible and readily adaptable to various situations.

The use of the voucher system of accounting is not advisable under all conditions, but it usually may be used to advantage when one or more of the following circumstances exist:

(1) When the volume of transactions is large enough to require a system of control over expenditures.
(2) When the nature of the business is such that it is desirable to record invoices at the time that they are received rather than when payment is made.
(3) When it is the custom of the firm to pay all invoices in full at maturity instead of making partial or installment payments.

There are generally five key documents in a voucher system: a purchase order, a receiving report, a purchase invoice, a voucher, and a check. Purchase orders and receiving reports were described previously. The purchase invoice and voucher will now be explained.

Purchase Invoice. A purchase invoice is the supplier's bill for goods, materials, or other assets purchased or for services rendered. A purchase invoice received by Fishler & Marvon for the purchase of bakery trays from Capital City Products is reproduced below. When the purchase invoice is received by the accounts (or vouchers) payable section of the accounting department, it should be compared with the purchase order and receiving report on file in that department to determine that the invoice is for the quantity ordered and received and for the proper price. In addition, mathematical accuracy of the invoice should be verified and the account to be charged for the purchase should be determined.

An alternative approach to purchase invoice verification used by some firms is to have the different employees responsible for ordering and receiving goods participate in the verification process. The receiving clerk would verify receipt of the assets purchased and the purchasing agent would verify the quantities, prices, and terms of the order. The accounting department would then verify the mathematical accuracy of the invoice and determine the account distribution.

		Invoice No. **263**
CAPITAL CITY PRODUCTS 1021 E. 54 ST. INDIANAPOLIS, IN 46220-1693		

Sold to	Date	May 6, 19--
Fishler & Marvon's Bakery 1064 N. Milburn Indianapolis, IN 46202-9001	Terms	Net

Quantity	Description	Unit Price	Total
20	Large bakery trays	4.45	89.00

Received by   S. Sutton
Date   5/7

Purchase Invoice

Voucher. Based on the verified purchase invoice, receiving report, and purchase order, a voucher is prepared by the vouchers payable section. The voucher is a key internal accounting control document which provides authorization for payment for goods or services. The voucher normally provides space to record the invoice date, the goods or services purchased, accounts to be charged, authorization for payment, date of payment, and number of the check issued. There is no standard form of voucher; it varies depending on the nature of the business, the classification of accounts, and the distribution desired. Regardless of its form, however, for good internal accounting control the voucher should be prenumbered and subsequently accounted for by number in order to ensure that all disbursements are properly recorded and that disbursements are made only for authorized purchases.

A voucher that was prepared by the voucher clerk for Fishler & Marvon is shown on the following page. The information recorded on this voucher was obtained from the invoice shown on page 403. All of the information on the front and the account distribution on the back of this voucher would be recorded when the voucher is prepared. The payment information would be recorded when the voucher is paid.

Recording Vouchers. There are two accounting records involved in recording vouchers: the voucher register and the general ledger. All vouchers should be recorded in the voucher register. The voucher register is basically an expanded purchases journal that is used to record purchases of all types of assets and services. It is similar in many respects to the invoice register described in Chapter 6. The voucher register represents the first point at which purchases activities are reflected in the accounting records. In addition, each entry in the voucher register is a key step leading to the payment of a specific amount. This makes the voucher register particularly important from a control standpoint. To the extent feasible, vouchers should be recorded in the voucher register in numerical order to facilitate accounting for the numerical sequence of the vouchers.

The ruling and the columnar headings of a voucher register depend upon the nature of the business and the desired classification of purchases and expenses. One form of voucher register is shown on page 406. Reference to that illustration will show that Voucher No. 264, which is reproduced on page 405, was recorded by debiting Store Equipment, Account No. 211, and by crediting Vouchers Payable, Account No. 317, for $89.

Fishler & Marvon's Bakery
1604 N. Milburn
Indianapolis, IN 46202-9001

VOUCHER

No. 264   Date Issued May 7 19 --   Terms Net   Due May 7 19 --
To   Capital City Products
Address   1021 E. 54 St., Indianapolis, IN 46220-1693

Invoice Date	Description	Amount
May 6	20 Large bakery trays	89 00

Authorized by
J. Fishler

Prepared by
S. Sutton
Voucher Clerk

Voucher *(front)*

DISTRIBUTION

Purchases		Operating Expenses		Sundry Accounts	
Dept. A	Dept. B	Acct. No.	Amount	Acct. No.	Amount
				211	89 00

PAYMENT

Date of Payment May 7 19 --   Check No. 619   Amount $ 89.00

CERTIFICATION

This voucher has been audited carefully and is correct in every respect.

C. O'Donnell
Accountant

Voucher *(back)*

Following is a description of the vouchers that are shown recorded in the voucher register:

May 1 No. 258, Tucker Leasing Co.; store and office rent, Account No. 8117, $1,200, and Account No. 8131, $800.

    4 No. 259, Flowers Baking Co.; merchandise, Account No. 711, $2,440, and Account No. 721, $1,076.

    4 No. 260, Heileman Baking Co.; merchandise, Account No. 711, $1,005, and Account No. 721, $2,206.

VOUCHER REGISTER FOR MONTH OF *May* 19 __ PAGE *13*

PURCHASES DR.		OPERATING EXPENSES DR.			SUNDRY ACCOUNTS DR.			DAY	VOU. NO.	TO WHOM ISSUED	SUNDRY ACCOUNTS CR.			VOUCHERS PAYABLE CR.	DISPOSITION	
DEPT. A	DEPT. B	ACCT. NO.	AMOUNT	√	ACCT. NO.	AMOUNT	√				ACCT. NO.	AMOUNT	√		DATE	CK. NO.
										AMOUNTS FORWARDED						
		8117	120000	√				1	253	Tucker Leasing Co.				200000	5/1	611
		8131	80000	√												
244000	107600							4	259	Flowers Baking Co				351600	5/7	614
100500	220600							4	260	Heileman Baking Co.				321100	5/7	615
169400	169500							4	261	International Bakers				338900	5/7	616
342800								4	262	Omar Bakeries				342800	5/7	617
121700	230300							4	263	Tri-Baking Co				352000	5/7	618
					211	8900	√	7	264	Capital City Products				8900	5/7	619
		8111	15500	√				8	265	Indianapolis Star				15500	5/8	622
		8112	74900	√				15	266	Payroll	311	22400	√	417900	5/15	620
		8113	82800	√							314	48000	√			
		8132	130600	√												
		8133	100000	√												
		8114	100000	√												
4411700	3261900		1235300			409800						144000		9174700		
4411700	3261900		1235300			409800						144000		9174700		
(711)	(721)		(811)			(√)						(√)		(317)		

Fishler & Marvon's Voucher Register (*Partial*)

May 4   No. 261, International Bakers; merchandise, Account No. 711, $1,694, and Account No. 721, $1,695.

4   No. 262, Omar Bakeries; merchandise, Account No. 711, $3,428.

4   No. 263, Tri-Baking Co.; merchandise, Account No. 711, $1,217, and Account No. 721, $2,303.

7   No. 264, Capital City Products; bakery trays, Account No. 211, $89.

8   No. 265, Indianapolis Star; advertising, Account No. 8111, $155.

15   No. 266, Payroll, May 1–15, $4,179. Distribution: Store Clerks Wage Expense, Account No. 8112, $749; Truck Drivers Wage Expense, Account No. 8113, $828; Office Salaries Expense, Account No. 8132, $1,306; Jane Fishler, Salary Expense, Account No. 8133, $1,000; Joel Marvon, Salary Expense, Account No. 8114, $1,000. Taxes withheld: FICA Tax Payable, Account No. 311, $224; Employees Income Tax Payable, Account No. 314, $480.

Voucher No. 266 was based on a report of the payroll clerk. The amount payable is the net amount of the payroll after deducting the taxes withheld. The total wages and salaries earned during the pay period ended May 15 amounted to $4,883 represented by:

Store clerks wage expense	$ 749.00
Truck drivers wage expense	828.00
Office salaries expense	1,306.00
Jane Fishler, salary expense	1,000.00
Joel Marvon, salary expense	1,000.00
Total	$4,883.00

Note that five lines were required to record this transaction in the voucher register. This was because of the five entries in the Operating Expenses Dr. column.

To prove the voucher register, it is only necessary to determine that the sum of the debit footings is equal to the sum of the credit footings. The footings should be proved before the totals are forwarded and before the summary posting is completed.

Both individual posting and summary posting from the voucher register to the general ledger are required. In addition, individual posting from the voucher register to the operating expense ledger is required. The individual posting involves posting each item entered in the Sundry Accounts Dr. and Cr. Amount columns to the proper account in the general ledger, and posting each item in the Operating Expense Dr. Amount column to the proper account in the operating expense subsidiary ledger. As each item is posted, a check mark should be placed beside it in the check ($\sqrt{}$) column of the voucher register. The page number of the voucher register should also be entered in the Posting Reference column of the ledger account to which the amount is posted.

The summary posting of the voucher register required each month involves the following procedures:

(1) The total of the column headed Purchases — Dept. A should be posted as a debit to the purchases — Dept. A account in the general ledger.

(2) The total of the column headed Purchases — Dept. B should be posted as a debit to the purchases — Dept. B account in the general ledger.

(3) The total of the column headed Operating Expenses Dr. should be posted as a debit to the operating expenses account in the general ledger, which is the control account for the operating expenses subsidiary ledger.

(4) The total of the column headed Vouchers Payable Cr. should be posted as a credit to the vouchers payable account in the general ledger.

As the total of each column is posted from the voucher register, the account number should be written in parentheses immediately below the total. The page number of the voucher register should also be written in the Posting Reference column of the ledger account to which it is posted. Check marks should be placed in parentheses below the totals of the Sundry Accounts Dr. and Cr. amount columns in the voucher register to indicate that these totals should not be posted.

Paying Vouchers. After the vouchers are recorded in the voucher register, they may be filed according to due date or alphabetically by supplier name in an unpaid vouchers file. Regardless of the way in which the vouchers are filed, they should be paid according to the terms stated in the invoice. Delay in payment may result in discounts being lost or in the loss of credit standing.

When they become due, the vouchers and supporting documents should be presented to the cashier or other proper disbursing officer for payment. The disbursing officer should review each voucher and supporting documents for propriety of the expenditure, prepare and sign the check, and mail it directly the supplier. In no case should a check be written without a supporting voucher and documentation. Ordinary checks may be used. In some cases, however, a voucher check is used, which is a check with space for copying data from the invoice or other sources of information concerning the voucher to which the check relates. In the illustration below, a voucher check

Voucher Check

issued to Capital City Products in payment of its invoice of May 6 is reproduced. The statement attached to it provides space for details of the invoice, including its date, number, description, amount, deductions, if any, and net amount. The information given on the statement attached to the check is for identification purposes and serves as a remittance advice to the payee of the check. Whether an ordinary check or a voucher check is used, the checks should be prenumbered and subsequently accounted for by number to ensure that no unauthorized disbursements occur.

After the voucher has been paid, the disbursing officer should cancel the voucher and supporting documents to indicate payment. This ensures that a voucher will not be processed again to generate a duplicate payment. The canceled voucher and supporting documents are then returned to the vouchers payable section for filing either numerically or alphabetically in a paid vouchers file. In either case, the numerical sequence should be strictly controlled for possible missing or duplicate vouchers.

Recording Checks. Three accounting records are affected by the check-recording process: the check register, voucher register, and general ledger. All checks issued in payment of vouchers may be recorded in a check register. A check register is an accounting record of all checks written by a firm. When the charges pertaining to each voucher have been recorded in the voucher register, it is not

CHECK REGISTER FOR MONTH OF *May*						
VOUCHERS PAYABLE DR.		DAY	DRAWN TO THE ORDER OF		BANK CR.	
NO.	AMOUNT			CK. NO.	AMOUNT	
			AMOUNTS FORWARDED			1
258	2000 00	1	*Tucker Leasing Co.*	611	2000 00	2
249	217 00	2	*Acorn Paper*	612	217 00	3
254	62 00	4	*Stansifer's Garage*	613	62 00	4
259	3516 00	7	*Flowers Baking Co.*	614	3516 00	5
	8265 00				8265 00	20
	8265 500				8265 500	21
	(317)				(111)	22

Fishler's & Marvon's Check Register (*Partial*)

necessary to make provision for distribution of charges in the check register. It is not unusual, however, to find that columns are provided in the check register to record deductions that may be made at the time of payment, such as purchases discounts. The form of check register shown above does not have such a column. After checks are recorded in the check register, an entry should also be made in the Disposition columns of the voucher register to show that the voucher has been paid, as illustrated in the disposition columns of the voucher register on page 406. This entry, which would be made by the vouchers payable clerk based on a canceled voucher, serves the same purpose as a debit entry in a supplier's ledger account.

Following is a description of the checks that are shown recorded in the check register reproduced on page 409.

> May 1 No. 611, Tucker Leasing Co., $2,000, in payment of Voucher No. 258.
>   2 No. 612, Acorn Paper, $217, in payment of Voucher No. 249.
>   4 No. 613, Stansifer's Garage, $62, in payment of Voucher No. 254.
>   7 No. 614, Flowers Baking Co., $3,516, in payment of Voucher No. 259.

To prove the check register, it is only necessary to determine that the footing of the Bank Cr. column is equal to the footing of the Vouchers Payable Dr. column. The footings should be proved before the totals are forwarded and before the summary posting is completed.

No individual posting from the check register is required. It is only necessary to complete the summary posting at the end of each month.

The summary posting procedure is as follows:

> (1) The total of the column headed Vouchers Payable Dr. should be posted as a debit to the vouchers payable account in the general ledger.
> (2) The total of the column headed Bank Cr. Amount should be posted as a credit to the bank account in the general ledger.

As the total of each column is posted from the check register, the account number should be written in parentheses immediately below the total. The page number of the check register should also be written in the Posting Reference column of the ledger account to which the amount is posted.

Proving Vouchers Payable. When the voucher system is used, it is possible to dispense with a subsidiary accounts payable ledger. The file of unpaid vouchers serves as the detail to support the balance of the vouchers payable account after all posting has been completed. The voucher register itself partially performs this function. Every blank in the Disposition columns of the register shows that the indicated voucher is unpaid. The unpaid vouchers file can be consulted if more detail about any item is needed.

When a trial balance is prepared at the end of a period, the balance of the vouchers payable account should be verified by preparing a list of the vouchers contained in the unpaid vouchers file. The total amount of this list should be equal to the balance of the account.

If a subsidiary accounts payable ledger is not maintained and if unpaid vouchers are filed according to due date, there is no way of quickly finding out how much is owed to a particular supplier. This may not be considered important. Businesspeople using the voucher system tend to think in terms of unpaid invoices rather than being primarily concerned with the total amount owed to each of their suppliers. However, if the latter information is needed, copies of the vouchers may be filed according to the names of the suppliers. A subsidiary accounts payable ledger may be maintained if one is desired.

Purchases Returns and Allowances. When a voucher system of accounting is used, purchases returns and allowances must be recorded in such a way that the accounts currently reflect such transactions, that the voucher register shows the proper amounts payable, and that the amount of the affected unpaid voucher is reduced. A commonly used procedure involves three steps:

(1) A notation of the return or allowance is made on the affected voucher and the credit memo is attached to it.
(2) A notation of the reduction is made in the voucher register beside the amount of the affected voucher.
(3) The transaction is formally recorded by means of a general journal entry.

A return or allowance relating to a merchandise purchase would require a debit to Vouchers Payable and a credit to Purchases Returns and Allowances. If the return or allowance is related to a purchase of a long-term asset or to some expense, the credit in the entry would be to the asset or expense account.

Partial Payments. When a business using the voucher system makes partial payments on invoices, special handling is required. If it is known at the outset that an invoice will be paid in installments, a separate voucher for each installment should be prepared in the first place. If it is decided to make a partial payment on an invoice already vouchered and recorded, the original voucher should be canceled and two or more new ones issued. The total amount of the new vouchers should be equal to that of the old voucher. The vouchers would be recorded in the voucher register by a debit to Vouchers Payable in the Sundry Accounts — Dr. column for the amount of the old voucher, and by a credit to Vouchers Payable in the Vouchers Payable Cr. column for the amounts of the new vouchers. A note should be made in the Disposition columns of the voucher register indicating that the old voucher has been canceled and showing the numbers of the new vouchers issued. Payments of the vouchers should then be recorded in the usual manner.

BUILDING YOUR ACCOUNTING KNOWLEDGE

1. What functions are included in the expenditure cycle?
2. Purchase orders are typically prepared in multiple-copy form. What is done with the different copies of the purchase order?
3. Why is a voucher system very useful for controlling cash disbursements?
4. Under what circumstances is there usually an advantage in using a voucher system?
5. What two accounting records are involved in recording vouchers?
6. What are the appropriate procedures for paying vouchers?
7. Why should the disbursing officer cancel a voucher and supporting documents to indicate payment after the voucher is paid?
8. When a voucher system is used, how is the vouchers payable account balance verified at the end of a period?

Report No. 14-3

> *Complete Report No. 14-3 in the study assignments and submit your working papers for approval. Then continue with the textbook discussion in Chapter 15 until Report No. 15-1 is required.*

EXPANDING YOUR BUSINESS VOCABULARY

What is the meaning of each of the following terms:

authorization procedures (p. 382)

check register (pp. 400, 409)

customer's purchase order (p. 388)

independent check (p. 383)

internal accounting control system (p. 380)

internal audit department (p. 383)

purchase invoice (p. 403)

purchase order (p. 401)

purchase requisition (p. 400)

receiving report (p. 402)

record-keeping procedures (p. 382)

record of cash receipts (p. 395)

remittance advice (p. 394)

sales invoice (p. 390)

sales order (p. 388)

sales register (p. 391)

segregation of duties (p. 381)

shipping order (p. 389)

voucher (pp. 398, 404)

voucher check (p. 408)

voucher register (pp. 398, 404)

voucher system (p. 402)

CHAPTER 15

ACCOUNTING CONCEPTS AND ACCEPTED PRACTICES

CHAPTER OBJECTIVES

The objectives of this chapter are to enable you:

▶ To describe and explain the basic accounting concepts of:

(1) The Business Entity
(2) The Monetary Unit
(3) Periodicity, Realization, and Matching
(4) Transaction-Based Records and Historical Cost
(5) The Going Concern
(6) The Accrual Basis

▶ To describe and explain the widely accepted accounting practices of:

(1) Conservatism
(2) Consistency and Comparability
(3) Adequate Disclosure
(4) Materiality and Practicality
(5) Objectivity and Verifiability
(6) Legality

The framework that underlies modern business accounting is a blend of various assumptions, conventions, requirements, practical compromises, and restraints. Because these factors are so interrelated, it is not possible to list them in an unquestioned order of importance. The student should remember this in the discussion that follows. In the organization of this chapter, the various matters are grouped according to (1) those that can be regarded as concepts and (2) those that may be classed as accepted practices. However, it will soon become apparent that there is some overlap between the categories.

BASIC CONCEPTS IN FINANCIAL ACCOUNTING

The basic concepts in financial accounting include: (1) the business entity, (2) the monetary unit, (3) periodicity and the related concepts of realization and matching, (4) transaction-based records and the related concept of historical cost, (5) the going concern, and (6) the accrual basis.

THE BUSINESS ENTITY

As applied to business accounting, the entity concept means that the business to which the records (or financial statements) relate is treated as a separately identifiable economic unit. This economic unit can be defined in various ways without regard to legal considerations of who actually owns the property and who is liable for the debts. In connection with the discussions and illustrations of the accounts of a single-owner business (a sole proprietorship), it was stressed that while the owner might possess various properties, only the property used in the business was taken into account. Likewise, the record of liabilities excluded any of the proprietor's debts of a nonbusiness or personal nature. Consequently, there was no accounting for any type of revenue and expense not connected with business operations. Of course, a business could be considered to include other, perhaps wholly unrelated, profit-seeking activities if the owner so desires. Or, the accounting entity could consist of the assets used by the business and the liabilities incurred on behalf of the business, even though, legally, the property belonged to the owner who was personally liable for the debts.

In the case of business partnerships (discussed in the next chapter), the separate entity is almost a legal reality. Property can be owned by a partnership. However, with limited exceptions, the debts of the firm may become personal liabilities of each of the partners. In the case of business corporations (also discussed in the next chapter), the business entity is a legal reality. Corporations can own property, incur debt, sue, and be sued. The debts of a corporation are debts of the corporate entity, not personal debts of its owners (stockholders). This is one of the reasons for the wide popularity of the corporate form of business organization.

Probably the greatest extension of the entity concept occurs when one corporation owns most or all of another (or perhaps several others). While each corporation is a legal entity and each has a separate set of records, their individual financial statements are combined to present what is known as a consolidated income statement and a consolidated balance sheet. From the viewpoint of the stockholders of the parent corporation (the corporation that controls the other corporations in the consolidated group), there is, in effect, just one entity. (Because of various factors such as intercorporate transactions and situations in which a parent corporation owns less than 100 percent of another corporation, the process of preparing consolidated statements may be complicated. A simplified version of the process will be discussed in Chapter 26.)

THE MONETARY UNIT

The monetary unit used by American accountants (United States and Canada) to measure financial transactions is the dollar. In Great Britain, the unit is the pound, and in West Germany, the unit is the mark. Whatever form of monetary unit is used, it is not as reliable a measuring unit as is a physical measure, such as the meter or kilogram, because the value of money fluctuates. This can cause the monetary unit to have different values at different points in time.

For several decades, the question of whether changes in the value of the dollar should be recognized in the accounting process has been discussed and debated. It is well known that the purchasing power of the dollar is constantly changing — nearly always declining. The impact of this on the financial statements is greatest in the case of long-term assets. Quite apart from the question of whether the amounts reported on a balance sheet should approximate current market values of the assets as opposed to historical cost, is the problem that the amounts shown as the costs of long-term assets may be a mixture of some dollars spent perhaps 25 years ago, some 20 years ago, some 10 years ago, and some more recently. Almost certainly, the value of the dollar was not the same at those different times. The amount charged to depreciation expense would be, in consequence, a mixture of different-valued dollars. To a lesser extent, all this may apply to shorter-term assets whose costs become expenses within a shorter period of time; for example, inventories. Another point is that the dollars of revenue for a single period generally represent similar purchasing power, while the dollars of expense deducted may be a diverse mixture.

In spite of these difficulties, accountants continue to accept the monetary unit concept, which means that business transactions are measured in terms of money and the purchasing power of money is assumed to be stable. This continued acceptance of the concept is explained by the fact that money is still a common ingredient of all business transactions and does provide a practical measurement unit capable of lending objectivity and uniformity to financial data.

Awareness of the limitations of the monetary unit as a measuring device is not lacking. Accounting reports necessarily are limited in scope by the use of the monetary measure. Such matters as competitive advantage or disadvantage, employee attitudes, management talents, and working conditions often cannot be stated adequately in dollar terms. Accountants simply feel that the interpretation of the effects of any changes in the value of money should be made by the users of the accounting reports rather than by the accountants.

The effects of the instability of the dollar on accounting reports may be illustrated as follows. Assume that a business bought equipment for $50,000 ten years ago and it now costs $100,000 to replace the equipment because inflation has cut the value of the dollar in half during the ten-year period. If the old equipment is fully depreciated and the net income of the business over the ten-year period was equal to $50,000, this implies that the cost of the old equipment has been recovered and the firm has had a profit of $50,000. However, the firm has not really had a profit at all, because it will require both the recovered cost of the old equipment ($50,000) and the $50,000 of reported net income to purchase the new equipment for $100,000. Thus, the reported net income might be viewed as a mirage.

The growing interest in reporting accounting information either adjusted for general price-level changes or in terms of replacement costs will be discussed in Chapter 30.

PERIODICITY, REALIZATION, AND MATCHING

Central to business accounting is the concept that income determination may be made on a periodic basis, known as the periodicity concept. This means that income should always be determined annually, and in addition, sometimes for shorter periods, such as quarterly or monthly. Any period shorter than a year is described as an interim period. The periodic determination requirement causes most of the problems associated with income measurement.

In order to determine income on a periodic basis, the accountant must decide when to recognize revenue and expenses. Revenue is recognized in accordance with the realization concept. Revenue generally is considered to be realized when there is a receipt of cash or a claim to cash in exchange for goods or services. For example, a car is taken to a service station for a tankful of gasoline (goods) and a car wash (services). The dealer may either receive cash or allow the use of a credit card (a claim to cash) in settlement. In either event, the dealer is considered to have realized revenue, even though the use of the credit card would create an account receivable on the dealer's books.

Once a decision is made regarding when to recognize revenue (using the realization concept), the expenses must next be recognized in accordance with the matching concept. The matching concept is that expenses incurred to generate particular revenues should be matched with those revenues that they helped to generate. For example, if the dealer in the previous example recorded the sale of gasoline, the cost of the gasoline sold should be matched against the revenue realized from the sale. Uncollectible accounts receivable represent a potential problem if revenue is considered realized when a claim to cash is created. The usual solution is the periodic estimation of uncollectible accounts expense, which then becomes part of the income calculation for the same period in which the receivables were recorded. This estimation process was discussed in Chapter 8.

It is in attempting to perform the matching process that the periodic-income-determination requirement poses the largest problem. Two outstanding examples of expense-matching problems are: (1) the apportionment of merchandise cost between cost of goods sold and end-of-period inventory, where specific identification of the units sold is not possible (discussed in Chapter 12), and (2) the allocation of the cost of most long-term assets by means of depreciation, depletion, or amortization (discussed in Chapter 13). Considerable judgment and estimation are necessary in each of these cases. Nonetheless, the matching of revenues and expenses is a fundamental part of the accrual accounting process.

TRANSACTION-BASED RECORDS AND HISTORICAL COST

Fundamental to business accounting is the idea that there is nothing to account for until a transaction occurs. Closely allied to this notion is the requirement that the amount to be recorded when the transaction involves the acquisition of an asset is the acquisition cost, or historical cost, of that asset. The historical cost concept holds that, generally, no adjustment will be made to this amount in later periods, except to allocate the original cost of the asset to periodic expense as the asset is consumed.

Accountants do not deny that changes in the values of assets occur over time. Rather, accountants generally insist on objective, verifiable evidence before they are willing to record information in the accounts. (Objective, verifiable evidence is discussed in a later section of this chapter.) Differences between the historical cost of a business's assets and the various market values of those assets that may exist at some later date may be difficult to measure and may never materialize. Consequently, accountants are reluctant to record such value changes in the accounts. In contrast, when a transaction occurs, the objective, verifiable evidence that the accountant seeks becomes available. Add to this the application of the realization concept discussed in the previous section and the case for transaction-based historical cost accounting gains strength.

THE GOING-CONCERN

A well-established tradition in business accounting is that in the absence of strong reason to believe otherwise, a business should be assumed to have a continuing, indefinite life. This is called the going-concern concept, or concept of continuity. Several arguments are offered in support of this concept. Corporations can have virtually perpetual existence. In the other two forms of business organizations, proprietors and partners will die, but the businesses involved can be continued by others — perhaps by those who inherit the business, by remaining partners, or by those to whom the business may be sold. It is argued that, in most cases, the owners and managers of a business intend and hope that the business will continue indefinitely. They usually make decisions with a view to maintaining the existence of the business, often in the hope of expanding it.

The reality of the economic world does not give full support to the going-concern concept. Business failures are commonplace. The mortality rate among new businesses is especially high. However, the alternative to assuming that a business will continue indefinitely would be to make an estimate of its probable life. What is a reasonable estimate? Two years? Five years? Ten years? Whatever the estimated life, it would mean that the acquisition of a depreciable asset with a potential useful life greater than the expected life of the business might seem inadvisable. Whenever long-term assets were acquired, the nature of depreciation calculations could be affected. The estimated life of the business rather than the estimated useful life of the asset might become the controlling element. In addition, the longer a business were to survive, the greater would be the chance for its continued existence; thus some depreciation rates might have to be revised and rerevised. Since this alternative option to a continuity concept is so unattractive (perhaps unworkable), the going-concern concept seems the more sensible alternative.

THE ACCRUAL BASIS

As discussed in Chapter 8, according to the accrual basis concept, revenue is recognized in the accounting period in which it is earned, and expenses are recognized in the accounting period in which they are incurred, regardless of whether the receipt or disbursement of cash takes place in the same period. Revenue is recognized when money or a legal claim to money is obtained in exchange for something of value. Revenue accrues when an inflow of assets causes an increase in owner's equity other than from an investment of assets in the business by the owner. Expense accrues when an asset outflow or an additional liability causes owner's equity to decrease other than from a withdrawal of assets by the owner or owners.

The accrual basis of accounting involves the periodic matching of revenue with the expenses related to its realization. Revenue from sales must be matched with the cost of goods sold and the various other expenses incidental to conducting a business. The simple matching of cash receipts for a particular period with the cash paid for goods or services acquired in that period is meaningless for the most part. Collections may relate to sales of the current period and payments may relate to purchases during a previous period or vice versa. The expenses related to most long-term assets occur as the property loses its usefulness. The accrual basis recognizes changes in a variety of assets and liabilities in determining periodic net income — not just cash changes.

It is the combined effect of the realization and matching concepts coupled with the accrual basis concept, that provides some assurance that income is accurately measured and reported each period.

BUILDING YOUR ACCOUNTING KNOWLEDGE

1. Does the business entity concept identify only the legal property and legal debts of the business enterprise or may it be broader than this? Discuss.

2. How do accountants justify the use of the monetary unit as a measuring device?

3. How do the realization and matching concepts relate to the periodicity concept? Give two examples of this relationship.
4. How is the historical cost concept related to transaction-based records?
5. What attribute of corporations supports the going-concern concept? What experiences of proprietors and partners support it?
6. Since the realities of the economic world do not fully support the going-concern concept, how is it justified by accountants? Discuss.
7. When is revenue considered to be earned on the accrual basis? When is expense considered to be incurred on this basis?
8. What problems are created by a simple matching of cash received from customers during an accounting period with the cash paid for goods or services purchased in that same period?

Report No. 15-1

Complete Report No. 15-1 in the study assignments and submit your working papers to the instructor for approval. Then continue with the textbook discussion until Report No. 15-2 is required.

ACCEPTED ACCOUNTING PRACTICES

In an attempt to serve the interests of various groups of people concerned with business affairs as reported in periodic financial statements, several practices have become widely accepted in the accounting process. Some of these practices have grown out of the concepts that have been discussed. Others are intended to help make accounting reports easier to understand. Many involve a compromise between partially-conflicting objectives. Six of the most important of these practices are discussed in the paragraphs that follow.

CONSERVATISM

The customs, concepts, and conventions of modern business accounting involve a tendency (some say a bias) toward conservatism. Generally, this means that when two or more acceptable ways of allocating the cost of an asset between benefiting periods can be used, the one that causes reported assets and periodic income to be smaller usually is chosen. The widely-used "cost or market, whichever is lower" method for assigning a value to the end-of-period merchandise inventory will cause both the inventory and the income for the period just ended to be smaller than otherwise. As applied to depreciation, if equally good reasons exist to use either a ten-year or a twelve-year estimated life for a depreciable asset, most accountants would use the shorter life. For the years the asset is used, both the income of each of the periods and the undepreciated cost of the asset at the end of each period will be smaller than if the longer life were used. When the question arises whether to charge the total cost of an item to expense immediately or to treat it as an asset to be amortized, the "expense-it-now" option usually is followed.

Probably the most all-encompassing example of the practice of conservatism stems from the historical-cost and realization concepts, which do not permit "writing up" assets even if they are thought at a later date to be worth more than the accounts show. Some accountants contend that refusing to show current or present values for all assets causes many balance sheets to be almost worthless. However, if such write-ups were to become accepted practice, either accountants would have to be trained as appraisers or appraisers would have to be employed. It is questionable whether the values thus determined would qualify as objective, verifiable evidence. Historical costs, generally, do meet this test. Further, either the amount of the write-up would have to be considered as revenue even though there were no inflows of cash or receivables (or other assets), or provision would have to be made in the accounts to record unrealized revenue. In the opinion of many accountants and business executives, so-called unrealized revenue is not revenue at all.

The conservatism practice is thought to have become deeply imbedded in accounting for two major reasons: (1) If unquestioned absolute accuracy in accounting is not possible, there is probably less danger of damaging the interests of existing and prospective owners and creditors by following conservative practices. (2) Conservative accounting practices lead to lower reported income for tax purposes and therefore lower taxes. Income tax laws do not require that most items be handled in the same way for tax purposes as they are in the accounts, but businesses typically find it easier to account for their activities in the same way for financial reporting purposes as for tax purposes. Further, a tax approach is easier to defend if it corresponds to what is done in the accounts.

CONSISTENCY AND COMPARABILITY

It has already been noted that the problems posed by the periodicity and matching concepts (which are fundamental to business accounting) preclude the attainment of absolute accuracy in the calculation of periodic income. Nevertheless, the users of financial statements invariably want to make comparisons between current and past results. This combination of circumstances makes it necessary to have a degree of consistency in accounting methods which makes comparability from period to period possible. One example of this need is found in the choice of an accounting method for merchandise inventory. Regardless of whether fifo or lifo is considered best, it is not difficult to imagine the possible consequence of switching from one to the other each year. This switching might make any comparison of the results of operations for several years almost meaningless. Frequent changes of the depreciation method could produce a similar undesirable result. Stated loosely, the rule is: "If you cannot be completely certain of your choice of method, at least use it consistently."

The consistency practice must not be carried to such an extreme that it is taken to mean that a method of accounting once adopted must never be changed. Changing circumstances may require a change in accounting method, but it is not expected that numerous and substantial changes will be needed each year. When important changes are made, it is essential that the financial statements clearly indicate (by footnote or otherwise) the changes made and the reasons therefor. Sometimes data are included in the explanation to show what the result might have been if the change had not been made. The act of providing an explanation of what was done, and why, is an example of compliance with the practice of adequate disclosure.

ADEQUATE DISCLOSURE

For at least the following three reasons, the practice of adequate disclosure must be followed in the preparation of accounting reports:

(1) Financial statement users want to know which of the various generally accepted accounting principles and practices have been used.
(2) There is a danger that significant facts about what has taken place during the period under review will somehow get "buried" among all the other information that the report contains or else remain undisclosed.
(3) There has been an increasing demand from users of financial reports for more information about the business.

To meet the adequate disclosure requirement, a number of procedures have evolved. The use of explanatory notes, either in the body of financial statements or as footnotes, has become widespread. (Mention was made in the previous section of the importance of disclosing any important changes in the use of an accounting method.) What is termed the "all inclusive" type of income statement has become widely used. Such a statement not only shows the composition of the income (loss) from regular operations for the period, but, in addition, any unusual gains or losses that have occurred.

The annual reports of large corporations often include an assortment of tables and graphs intended to emphasize significant trends in their corporate business affairs. Often statistical data of a nonfinancial nature are included, such as the number of employees or the number of units produced. Annual reports of this type always include a message from the company president or board chairperson that draws attention to important things that happened during the year, including any major changes in management personnel and a general forecast for the year or years ahead.

In the interest of adequate disclosure, multiproduct-line companies are now required to provide information about major segments or product lines of the business by both the Securities and Exchange Commission and the Federal Trade Commission. It has also been proposed that annual reports should include a financial budget (forecast) so that interested parties can have an idea of "what's coming." Professional ethics rules prohibit auditors from vouching for the achievability of forecast data, although there is no rule against vouching for the basic assumptions and calculations involved. However, a published forecast might reveal information useful to competitors, and since the reported plans may not work out, many business managers and accountants fear that such a procedure might do more harm than good. Just how far adequate disclosure should go is an unsettled issue. Nevertheless, the inclusion of forecast data in published annual reports is increasing.

MATERIALITY AND PRACTICALITY

In the field of law, there is a maxim of *de minimis non curat lex*, which means that the law is not concerned with trifles. The same can be said of accounting. In accounting, what is called the practice of materiality and practicality means that the concepts of accrual accounting need not be followed in the case of amounts that are too small to make any real difference. For example, even though a waste basket that cost $5 may be expected to be useful for many years, it is not necessary to account for it as an asset to be depreciated. Simply treat the expenditure as, perhaps, miscellaneous expense. It is an almost universal practice for each business to establish some "cut-off point" that the accountant should follow in recording such expenditures. In the case of a small business, the point might be $25 or $50; larger businesses may have a higher limit. Consistency of treatment is, of course, necessary.

In the handling of certain year-end adjustments, the amount involved may dictate whether an adjustment should be made. For example, it may be unnecessary to bother with accrued interest payable or receivable in the amount of $2.65 or to record the fact that $15 of the supplies expense account balance (amounting to more than $400) actually relates to supplies that are still on hand.

Probably the most important application of the practice of materiality is in connection with the financial statements. Adequate disclosure does not require that a petty cash fund of $100 be shown by itself rather than being lumped together with cash in bank, or that the detail be shown for prepaid expenses whose total is equal to one percent of total assets. In fact, the interests of adequate disclosure are best served by preparing financial statements and schedules that are not so filled with detail that the significant matters may be obscured.

Another widespread practice that is followed in the interest of eliminating the immaterial aspects of financial statements is to eliminate cents; instead, each amount is rounded to the nearest dollar. In fact, the financial statements of very large companies frequently show amounts rounded to the nearest $1,000.

OBJECTIVITY AND VERIFIABILITY

Data that are entered in the accounting records and later reported in the financial statements of a business generally should be supported by source documents or other records that are both objective and verifiable forms of evidence that certain transactions occurred. This is the practice of objectivity and verifiability. When evidence is not completely objective, as in the case of doubtful accounts receivable or long-term asset depreciation, the most objective evidence available should be used. Sales tickets, purchase invoices, and employee paychecks are examples of source documents that provide evidential matter. Records of past experience in collecting accounts receivable are an example of objective evidence for recording doubtful accounts expense.

The notion of objectivity is that such source documents or records of past experience provide unbiased, factual evidence of real transactions and events that have occurred. The notion of verifiability is that any two accountants looking independently at the same evidence probably would record the related entry in the same way.

LEGALITY

Accounting records and reports must conform with certain legal requirements, such as tax regulations, contract provisions, and state incorporation laws, that relate to specific business transactions. This is the practice of legality. For example, it is illegal to evade taxes or reduce the required tax payments by ignoring or flaunting the law. It is also illegal to fail or refuse to record payroll tax deductions when keeping employee payroll records. The structure of the equity section of a corporation balance sheet often is affected by the laws of the state in which the firm is incorporated. In addition, the ability of a corporation to pay dividends can be determined by state incorporation laws. The accounting records must be kept in such a way that compliance with applicable laws can be determined.

BUILDING YOUR ACCOUNTING KNOWLEDGE

1. Give three examples of the application of the practice of conservatism.
2. Why are consistency and comparability closely associated in business accounting?
3. If an important change in accounting method takes place, how should it be indicated to users of financial statements?
4. Give three reasons for observing the practice of adequate disclosure.
5. Explain why materiality is closely associated with practicality.
6. What is the relationship between materiality and adequate disclosure?
7. What attributes make source documents both objective and verifiable?
8. Give two examples of legal requirements to which accounting records and reports must conform.

Report No. 15-2

> *Complete Report No. 15-2 in the study assignments and submit your working papers for approval. Then continue with the textbook discussion in Chapter 16 until Report No. 16-1 is required.*

EXPANDING YOUR BUSINESS VOCABULARY

What is the meaning of each of the following terms?

accrual basis (p. 420)

adequate disclosure (p. 423)

concept of continuity (p. 419)

conservatism (p. 421)

consistency and comparability
   (p. 423)

consolidated balance sheet
   (p. 416)

consolidated income statement
   (p. 416)

entity concept (p. 415)

going-concern concept (p. 419)

historical cost concept (p. 418)

interim period (p. 417)

legality (p. 426)

matching concept (p. 418)

materiality and practicality
   (p. 424)

monetary unit concept (p. 416)

objectivity (p. 425)

periodicity concept (p. 417)

realization concept (p. 417)

unrealized revenue (p. 422)

verifiability (p. 426)

CHAPTERS 11–15

SUPPLEMENTARY PRACTICAL ACCOUNTING PROBLEMS

Problem 11-A Notes receivable register

Cheryl Knight is a dealer in paintings and framing materials. In accounting for notes received from customers in return for extensions of time in paying their obligations, Knight uses a notes receivable register similar to the one reproduced on pages 320 and 321. Following is a narrative of transactions involving notes received from customers during the current year.

Mar. 5 Received from Earl Woolman a 60-day, 9% note (No. 1) for $900 dated March 4, and payable at First National Bank, Willow Brook.

Apr. 28 Received from Keith Kovacik a 90-day, 8% note (No. 2) for $700 dated April 27, and payable at Second National Bank, Mayfield.

May 3 Received a check for $913.50 in payment for Earl Woolman's note due today plus interest.

18 Received from Gerald Scasny a 60-day, 8% note (No. 3) for $850 dated May 17, and payable at Northern Trust Company, Park Ridge.

July 16 Received a check for $861.33 in payment for Gerald Scasny's note due today plus interest.

26 Received a check for $714 in payment for Keith Kovacik's note due today plus interest.

Sept. 3 Received from Ann Bagnall a 90-day, 9% note (No. 4) for $950 dated September 2, and payable at Monroe State Bank, Monroe.

Dec. 2 Received a check from Monroe State Bank for $961.38 in payment of the note due yesterday plus interest less a $10 collection charge.

Required: (1) Prepare entries in two-column journal form to record the transactions. Foot the amount columns as a means of proof. (2) Make the required entries in a notes receivable register to provide a detailed auxiliary record of the notes received by Knight.

Problem 11-B   Notes payable

D. L. Bennett operates a department store. Sometimes, Bennett finds it necessary to issue notes to suppliers to obtain extensions of time for payment of accounts. Unless otherwise stated, all notes are made payable at the Brown County Bank, Newburg. Following is a narrative of transactions involving notes issued by Bennett during the current year:

Feb. 1 Borrowed $1,200 from the bank on a 90-day, 9% note (No. 1).

Mar. 8 Issued a 60-day, 8% note (No. 2) for $725 to Black & Decker Co.

Apr. 20 Issued a 60-day, 7% note (No. 3) for $920 to R. W. Hess & Co.

May 2 Issued a check for $1,227 to the bank in payment of note due today plus interest.

7 Gave Black & Decker Co. a check for $9.67 in payment of the interest due today and a new note (No. 4), for $725, due in 60 days, with interest at 8%, in settlement of the note due today.

June 19 Issued a check for $930.73 to R. W. Hess & Co. in payment of note due today plus interest.

July 2 Borrowed $4,000 from the bank on a 90-day, 9% note (No. 5).

6 Issued a check for $734.67 to Black & Decker Co. in payment of note due today plus interest.

Sept. 30 Gave Brown County Bank a check for $90 in payment of the interest due today and a new note (No. 6) for $4,000, due in 60 days with interest at 9%, in settlement of the note due today.

Nov. 29 Issued a check for $4,060 to the bank in payment of note due today plus interest.

Required: (1) Prepare entries in two-column journal form to record the transactions. Foot the amount columns as a means of proof. (2) Make the required entries in a notes payable register similar to the one reproduced on pages 326 and 327, to provide a detailed auxiliary record of the notes issued.

Problem 12-A   Application of fifo, weighted average, and lifo methods

The Novus Company is in the wholesale hardware business. Stock record cards are kept of all merchandise handled. The data with respect to Article X were assembled from the stock record cards and appeared as shown at the top of page 430.

On hand at beginning of period......................... 700 units
First purchase during period .... 800 units @ $35
Second purchase during period .... 700 units @ $37
Last purchase during period............................. 650 units @ $38
In stock at end of period .... 540 units

Novus Company had sales of $127,000 during the period.

Assume that the units in stock at the beginning of the period were assigned a cost of $34 each under the fifo method, $33 each under the weighted average method, and $31 each under the lifo method.

Required: Compute ending inventory, cost of goods sold, and gross margin under (1) the fifo method, (2) the weighted average method, and (3) the lifo method of cost assignment. (Carry the weighted average unit cost to four decimal places.)

Problem 12-B   Application of the lower of cost or market rule

Rockland Distributors has four items in its ending inventory: Products W, X, Y, and Z. The quantities, costs, and market values of these items are given below:

Product	Quantity	Cost	Market
W	300	$10	$11
X	400	12	11
Y	260	15	14
Z	450	13	15

Assume that Rockland uses the fifo lower of cost or market method of cost assignment.

Required: Calculate the dollar amount of ending inventory by applying the lower of cost or market rule to: (1) the total inventory, and (2) each item in the inventory.

Problem 12-C   Postage account

Wattley & Wise is a mail-order house. Metered postage is used on parcel post packages. Deposits are made for postage under the postal permit system. Postage stamps are purchased for other purposes. All prepaid postage is charged to Postage, Account No. 154, and periodically the postage used is charged to the following expense accounts:

819   Freight Out (Parcel Post)
824   Advertising Postage Expense
839   General Postage Expense

During the month of June, the postage used on parcel post packages amounted to $911, and on advertising matter, $714. On June 30, the unused stamps on hand amounted to $293, and the unused metered postage amounted to $450.

Required: (1) Open the necessary accounts and enter the debit balance of the postage account before adjustment, $2,610. (2) Make the required adjusting entry in general journal form to record all postage expense for the month. (3) Post the entry to the appropriate accounts.

Problem 13-A   Depreciation of long-term assets; trade in

On February 1, 19A, Parry & Sterns, a partnership, began the wholesale distribution of heating equipment. In accounting for their long-term assets, the following accounts are used:

```
271    Office Equipment
271.1  Accumulated Depreciation — Office Equipment
281    Store Equipment
281.1  Accumulated Depreciation — Store Equipment
291    Delivery Equipment
291.1  Accumulated Depreciation — Delivery Equipment
331    Accounts Payable
817    Depreciation Expense — Office Equipment
818    Depreciation Expense — Store Equipment
819    Depreciation Expense — Delivery Equipment
```

The following is a narrative of transactions involving the purchase of long-term assets during the year ended December 31, 19A:

Feb. 12   Invoice No. 218 — Purchased cabinet file for office use on account from The Steelcase Co., $380; estimated useful life, 10 years; estimated trade-in value at end of 10 years, $50.

Mar. 7   Invoice No. 232 — Purchased a small truck for delivery purposes on account from Molding Motors, Inc., $5,600; estimated useful life, 4 years; estimated trade-in value at end of 4 years, $600.

Apr. 18   Invoice No. 239 — Purchased an office table on account from The National Furniture Co., $240; estimated useful life, 20 years; no salvage value.

July 2   Invoice No. 274 — Purchased showcases on account from S. C. Jones Co., $750; estimated useful life, 15 years; no salvage value.

Aug. 28   Invoice No. 291 — Purchased used double-pedestal desk for use in storeroom on account from Snyder Store Equipment Co., $260; estimated useful life, 20 years; no salvage value.

Sept. 9   Invoice No. 312 — Purchased used Olivetti Underwood typewriter, No. 5837852-11 on account from Olivetti Underwood

Corporation, $285; estimated useful life, 5 years; estimated trade-in value at end of 5 years, $25.

On February 7, 19C, after recording twenty-three months' depreciation, the delivery truck purchased on March 7, 19A, was traded in for a new truck with a market value of $6,600, and $3,600 in cash also was paid.

Required: (1) Record the foregoing transactions in proper two-column journal form. (2) Foot the amount columns. (3) Determine the annual rate of depreciation (straight-line method) applicable to the net cost of each of the long-term assets purchased, compute the amount of depreciation accumulated during the current year ended December 31, 19A, and prepare an entry in two-column journal form to record the depreciation. (4) Prepare a two column journal entry to record the transaction on February 7, 19C. Recognize the gain or loss, if appropriate, for financial accounting purposes.

Problem 13-B   Wasting asset — depletion and sale

Burns Enterprises, Inc., owns a gravel pit that was purchased a few years before for $90,000. Depletion has been calculated on the basis of 15 cents for every cubic yard of gravel excavated. At the beginning of the current year, the balance of the accumulated depletion account was $6,450. During the first four months of this year, 19A, 40,000 cubic yards of gravel were excavated, and on May 2, 19A, the pit was sold for $79,500 cash.

Required: Prepare entries in general journal form, to record (1) the depletion accumulated for the first four months of the year, and (2) the sale of the gravel pit, recognizing any gain or loss on the sale.

Problem 14-A   Cash sales and sales on account

Linda Broady is the owner of a radio, television, and stereo equipment store. Following is a list of the general ledger accounts that are affected by this problem with the September 1 balances indicated:

111   Cash, $4,191.80
131   Accounts Receivable, $3,927.20

341   Sales Tax Payable, $179.10
611   Sales, $31,095.60

As of September 1, the accounts receivable had debit balances as follows:

Sally Graham, 1512 Blackburn St., Wheaton; $681.20
Alan Hancock, 1586 Briarcliffe Blvd., Lombard; $932.00
Fred Jacobs, 122 Main St., Wheaton; $1,014.00
Ilsa Milburn, 655 Roosevelt Rd., Glen Ellyn; $717.60
James Orndorff, 542 Kenilworth, Batavia; $582.40

The narrative of September sales and collections transactions is as follows:

Sept. 1   (Wednesday) Charge sale No. 362, Ilsa Milburn, $397 plus $15.88 sales tax.
      3   Cash sales of $419 plus $16.76 sales tax.
      4   Collected $1,014 on account from Fred Jacobs.
      6   Charge sale No. 363, Sally Graham, $125 plus $5 sales tax.
      8   Collected $717.60 on account from Ilsa Milburn.
    10   Charge sale No. 364, Alan Hancock, $750 plus $30 sales tax.
    11   Cash sales of $229 plus $9.16 sales tax.
    14   Cash sales of $549 plus $21.96 sales tax.
    16   Collected $681.20 on account from Sally Graham.
    18   Charge sale No. 365, James Orndorff, $210 plus $8.40 sales tax.
    20   Collected $932 on account from Alan Hancock.
    22   Cash sales of $492 plus $19.68 sales tax.
    24   Charge sale No. 366, Fred Jacobs, $155 plus $6.20 sales tax.
    25   Cash sales of $785 plus $31.40 sales tax.
    27   Collected $582.40 on account from James Orndorff.
    29   Charge sale No. 367, Ilsa Milburn, $445 plus $17.80 sales tax.

Required: (1) Open the necessary general ledger accounts and enter the September 1 balances, using four-column ledger paper. (2) Open the accounts receivable ledger and enter the September 1 balances, using three-column ledger paper. (3) Enter the charge sales for September and post directly to the proper customers' accounts, using a sales register similar to the one reproduced on page 392. (4) Enter the cash sales and collections on account for September and post the collections directly to the proper customers' accounts, using a record of cash receipts similar to the one reproduced on page 395. (5) Foot, prove the footings, enter the totals, and rule the sales register and the record of cash receipts. Complete the summary posting and update the account balances. (6) Prove the balance of the accounts receivable account by preparing a schedule of the accounts receivable as of September 30.

Problem 14-B   Voucher register; check register; schedule of unpaid vouchers

Vibrawell Electronics, a business just organized, uses a voucher register and a check register similar to those shown on pages 406 and 409.

Checks were issued in payment of any invoices subject to discount on the day preceding the last day of the discount period.

The narrative of transactions of the month is as follows:

Oct. 3 Issued Voucher No. 1 for $150 to establish a petty cash fund and cashed Check No. 1 for that amount. (Petty Cash Fund, Account No. 112.)

3 Received an invoice for $300 from the Clark Real Estate Co. for rent. Issued Check No. 2 in payment of the invoice. (Rent Expense, Account No. 8115.)

4 Received an invoice for $1,928.75 from the Collins Radio-Stereo Manufacturers, Inc., for merchandise. Date of invoice, September 29; terms, 1/10, n/30.

5 Received an invoice for $275 from Swanson Equipment Co. for an office desk purchased. Date of invoice, October 3; terms, net 30 days. (Office Equipment, Account No. 231.)

6 Received a bill for telephone service from the Commonwealth Telephone Co. and issued Check No. 3 for $21.60 in payment. (General Office Expense, Account No. 8118.)

7 Received a bill for office supplies from W. J. Brown & Co. and issued Check No. 4 for $52.75 in payment. (Office Supplies, Account No. 182.)

8 Received an invoice for $932.75 from the Tandy Corporation for a shipment of merchandise. Date of invoice, October 6; terms, 2/15, n/60.

12 Received an invoice for $78.65 from the Carter Advertising Agency for advertising service. Issued Check No. 6 in payment. (Advertising Expense, Account No. 8117.)

13 Received an invoice for $62.90 from the Nationwide Insurance Co. for insurance. Issued Check No. 7 in payment. (Prepaid Insurance, Account No. 186.)

14 Received an invoice for $1,894.60 from the Lafayette Radio Manufacturing Co. for a shipment of radio parts. Date of invoice, October 11; terms, 1/10, n/30.

15 Issued Payroll Voucher No. 11 covering wages earned for the half month as follows:

> Warehouse salaries, $1,260.
> Delivery salaries, $165.75.
> Office salaries, $1,050.
> Sales salaries, $980.
>
> Taxes withheld:
> FICA tax, $241.90
> Employees' income tax, $622.25.

Issued Check No. 8 in payment of Payroll Voucher No. 11. The following accounts will be affected in recording the payroll:

111	Bank
311	FICA Tax Payable
314	Employees' Income Tax Payable
318	Vouchers Payable
8111	Warehouse Salaries Expense
8112	Delivery Salaries Expense
8113	Office Salaries Expense
8114	Sales Salaries Expense

17 Issued a voucher for $100 to be used in purchasing stamps for the office. Cashed Check No. 9 for this amount and obtained the stamps. (Charge to Office Supplies, Account No. 182.)

19 Received from the First National Bank a notice of the maturity of a $1,000 non-interest-bearing note dated September 30 due them. Issued Check No. 10 for that amount. (Notes Payable, Account No. 315.)

20 Received an invoice from Mechanicraft for $75.21, the cost of repairs on warehouse machinery. Issued Check No. 11 in payment. (Repairs, Account No. 8116.)

21 Received an invoice for $2,985.20 from Zenith Radio & TV for a shipment of merchandise. Date of invoice, October 20; terms, 1/10, n/30.

24 Received an invoice for $283.52 for warehouse supplies purchased from the Midland Container Co.; terms, on account. (Warehouse Supplies, Account No. 181.)

26 Received an invoice from Cridland Lifts for $9,875, the cost of a lift truck for use in the warehouse. Terms, net 30 days. (Warehouse Equipment, Account No. 232.)

28 Received an invoice for $1,045.60 from the General Electric Co. for a shipment of merchandise. Date of invoice, October 27; terms, 2/10, n/30.

31 Issued Payroll Voucher No. 19 covering wages earned for the half month as follows:

Warehouse Salaries, $1,200
Delivery Salaries, $190
Office Salaries, $1,050
Sales Salaries, $980

Taxes withheld:
  FICA Tax, $239.40
  Employees' Income Tax, $615.60

Issued Check No. 15 in payment of Payroll Voucher No. 19.

Required: (1) Record the foregoing transactions in the voucher register and check register. (2) Foot and prove the footings of both the voucher register and the check register. (3) Open an account for vouchers payable and post to it the footings of the Vouchers Payable columns in the voucher register and the check register. Use a T form of account. (4) Prove the balance of the vouchers payable account by preparing a schedule of the unpaid vouchers from the voucher register.

Problem 15-A   The business entity

Livingston's Bakery, owned and operated by James A. Livingston, is in the process of separating the assets and liabilities of the business enterprise from Livingston's personal assets and liabilities as of December 31, 19––. Livingston has solicited your help.

The list of assets, liabilities, income, and withdrawals is given below and on the next page:

Cash in bank (First National Bank) for business affairs..	$15,200
Cash in bank (Lincoln Bank) for personal affairs..	34,260
Accounts receivable owed to Livingston's Bakery..	16,273
Allowance for doubtful accounts on Livingston's Bakery accounts receivable..............	625
Merchandise inventory of Livingston's Bakery	62,175
Prepaid insurance:	
James A. Livingston...............................	325
Livingston's Bakery	450
Supplies:	
Livingston's Bakery	75
James A. Livingston...............................	50
Store equipment.......................................	4,320
Accumulated depreciation on store equipment.	1,750
Delivery truck used by the business..............	5,200
Accumulated depreciation on delivery truck....	2,875
Automobile for personal use........................	7,500
Store building owned as a personal asset (net)..	10,500
Real estate investment owned by Livingston ...	5,500
Notes payable to outsiders by Livingston........	3,500
Notes payable to outsiders by Livingston's Bakery..	4,750
Accrued interest payable on notes:	
Livingston's Bakery	51
James A. Livingston...............................	24
Accounts payable to outsiders by:	
James A. Livingston...............................	2,750
Livingston's Bakery	6,780
Sales tax owed by bakery	1,577

Taxes payable withheld — Livingston's Bakery	$ 740
Notes receivable owed to Livingston	2,500
Mortgage due on Livingston's home	15,875
Net income of Livingston's Bakery for 19––	25,250
James A. Livingston's withdrawals for 19––	20,200

Required: From the above list (1) separate those items that clearly relate to Livingston's Bakery, and prepare a balance sheet as of December 31, 19––, in report form. (2) The separation of business assets and liabilities from personal assets and liabilities is an adaptation of what accounting concept?

CHAPTER 16

ACCOUNTING FOR OWNER'S EQUITY

CHAPTER OBJECTIVES

The objectives of this chapter are to enable you:

▶ To explain the characteristics, advantages, and disadvantages of the single proprietorship form of business operation, and to account for proprietary transactions.

▶ To explain the nature of a business partnership and its advantages and disadvantages.

▶ To explain the manner in which a partnership is formed, and to recognize a partnership agreement.

▶ To explain and prepare the accounting entries needed to record:

(1) The formation of a partnership.
(2) The admission of a new partner, including the possible accounting for goodwill.
(3) The compensation of partners.
(4) The allocation of partnership profits and losses.
(5) The dissolution of a partnership.

▶ To prepare the owners' equity section of a partnership balance sheet.

▶ To explain the nature of business corporations and the accounting for corporate owners' (stockholders') equity, including:

(1) The advantages and major disadvantage of a private business corporation.
(2) The manner in which a corporation is organized.
(3) The nature of the ownership interest in a corporation and the nature of its operation.
(4) The preparation of the accounting entries peculiar to a business corporation.
(5) The preparation of the entries required to record the incorporation of a single proprietorship and of a partnership.
(6) The preparation of the owners' equity section of a corporation balance sheet.

The accounting equation — ASSETS = LIABILITIES + OWNER's EQUITY — reflects the fact that both outsiders and insiders have interests in the assets of a business. The claims of the outsiders are known as the liabilities of the business, while the interests of the insiders are known as the owners' or stockholders' equity in the assets of the business. Proper accounting for owners' equity in three types of business organizations will be discussed in this chapter: (1) the single proprietorship, (2) the partnership, and (3) the corporation. Whether an enterprise is operated by an individual as a single proprietorship, by two or more individuals as a partnership, or by stockholders through directors and officers as a corporation has little or no bearing on proper accounting procedure for recording routine transactions. However, there are significant differences in the owners' equity structures of these three types of businesses, and therefore differences in the accounting for and reporting of owners' or stockholders' equity transactions.

THE SINGLE PROPRIETORSHIP

A business that is owned and operated by one person is known as a single proprietorship. When there is only one owner, the amount of the owner's interest in the business is called owner's equity. Sometimes the designations net worth or capital are used. The word "Capital" commonly follows the name of the owner as a part of the title of the account that shows the amount of the owner's equity element in the business.

In small merchandising enterprises and in personal service enterprises the single proprietorship form of organization predominates. The medical and dental professions, for example, are composed largely of individuals who are engaged in practice as sole owners. One reason for the popularity of the single proprietorship form of operation is that it is easily organized and does not involve formal or legal agreement with others as to ownership or conduct. Anyone may engage in a lawful enterprise merely by complying with state and local laws.

ORGANIZATION OF A SINGLE PROPRIETORSHIP

When operating an enterprise as a sole owner, an individual decides the amount and the nature of the property that will be invested in the business. The original investment may consist of cash only, or of cash and any other property, such as merchandise, office equipment, store equipment, or delivery equipment. The property invested usually is segregated and accounted for separately from other property that may be owned by the proprietor, in accordance with the business entity concept. An individual may engage in more than one enterprise and may operate each enterprise separately as a single proprietorship. In such cases, it may be desirable to keep separate records of the activities of each enterprise.

In comparison with other forms of business organization, the single proprietorship offers certain advantages, such as:

(1) Simplicity of organization.
(2) Freedom of initiative and industry.
(3) Reduction of government reporting requirements.
(4) Strengthening of incentive to individual effort.

The single proprietorship form of organization has some disadvantages, of which the following are the most significant:

(1) The amount of available capital may be limited.
(2) The amount of available credit may be restricted.
(3) The proprietor has sole responsibility for all debts incurred.
(4) The proprietor is legally obligated to assume all debts of the business as personal debts.

ACCOUNTING PROCEDURE

The accounting procedure for handling the transactions uniquely related to a single proprietorship can be classified into six topics as follows:

(1) Owner's equity accounts.
(2) Opening entries.
(3) Current period proprietary transactions.
(4) Closing revenue, expense, and summary accounts.
(5) Closing the owner's drawing account.
(6) Owner's equity section of a single proprietorship balance sheet.

Each of these topics is discussed below.

Owner's Equity Accounts. There are two types of owner's equity accounts: (1) permanent and (2) temporary.

In a single proprietorship, the owner's capital account is the only permanent owner's equity account. The account is usually given the name of the owner of the enterprise followed by "Capital" or "Proprietor."

The temporary owner's equity accounts are those in which increases and decreases in owner's equity arising from the transactions completed during an accounting period are recorded, such as the owner's drawing or personal account and all of the revenue and expense accounts. At the end of each year, it is customary to close the temporary revenue and expense accounts by transferring their balances to one or more summary accounts. These summary accounts are then closed to the permanent owner's equity account. The owner's drawing account is also closed to the permanent owner's equity account.

Opening Entries. An individual may invest cash and other property in a single proprietorship enterprise. If the investment consists solely of cash, the opening entry will involve a debit to Cash or Bank and a credit to the owner's capital account for the amount invested.

If cash and other property, such as office equipment or store equipment, are invested, the opening entry will involve a debit to Cash or Bank for the amount of the cash invested, debits to appropriate equipment accounts for the amounts of the other property invested, and a credit to the owner's capital account for the total amount of the investment.

If, at the time of organizing an enterprise, there are any liabilities applicable to the property invested, such as accounts payable, notes payable, or mortgages payable, the amounts of the liabilities should be credited to appropriate liability accounts and the owner's capital account should be credited only for the excess of the amount of the assets invested over the total amount of the liabilities.

For example: Linda Sullivan starts a merchandising business by investing cash, $6,000, office equipment, $1,500, and store equipment, $1,000. Sullivan owes $400 on the office equipment. The opening entry in two-column general journal form to record the investment is:

Bank[1]	6,000	
Office Equipment	1,500	
Store Equipment	1,000	
Accounts Payable		400
Linda Sullivan, Capital		8,100
Investment in business.		

Some small business enterprises start and operate with very few records. No journals or ledgers are used. Cash receipts and disbursements are kept on check stubs. The amounts of accounts receivable and payable can be found only by consulting files of uncollected charge-sale slips and unpaid bills. At the end of a period, various calculations relating to inventory, doubtful accounts, expired insurance, depreciation, and accruals are made in informal fashion and the several bits of information are pieced together to prepare an income statement and a balance sheet. These statements are often incorrect. Conditions and facts may have been overlooked. Business papers may have been lost. The absence of double-entry records means that one method of checking the mathematical accuracy of the assembled figures is not available.

While such informal accounting practices may barely suffice when the enterprise is small and transactions are few, the time will come when a formal accounting system is needed. To start such a system, it is necessary to prepare a balance sheet from the information at hand and to use this as a basis for an opening journal entry to record the assets, liabilities, and owner's equity of the enterprise.

For example, assume that J. T. Gannon has been operating a business without any formal, double-entry accounting records. After several months, Gannon decides that proper records are necessary. With the help of an accountant, a balance sheet for the business is constructed which is reproduced on the next page. The information

---

[1]The bank account is debited for the amount of cash invested because it is the usual custom of business firms to deposit all cash receipts in the bank and to make all disbursements by check. Under this plan, a cash account need not be kept in the general ledger. Instead, all receipts may be debited to the bank account and all disbursements may be credited to the bank account. It should be understood, however, that a cash account and one or more bank accounts may be kept in the general ledger, if desired.

supplied by the balance sheet is used in preparing the two-column general journal entry shown below the statement.

J. T. GANNON
Balance Sheet
December 31, 1982

Assets			Liabilities		
Cash		$ 2,275	Notes payable	$2,000	
Accounts receivable	$3,600		Accounts payable	2,900	
Less allowance for doubtful accounts	400	3,200	Total liabilities		$ 4,900
Merchandise inventory		8,670			
Store equipment	$5,000		Owner's Equity		
Less accumulated depreciation	500	4,500	J. T. Gannon, capital		13,745
Total assets		$18,645	Total liabilities and owner's equity		$18,645

Jan. 2	Bank	2,275	
	Accounts Receivable	3,600	
	Merchandise Inventory	8,670	
	Store Equipment	5,000	
	Notes Payable		2,000
	Accounts Payable		2,900
	Allowance for Doubtful Accounts		400
	Accumulated Depreciation — Store Equipment		500
	J. T. Gannon, Capital		13,745

After the necessary accounts in the general ledger have been opened, the debits and the credits of the opening journal entry are posted in the usual manner. Each asset account is debited and each liability account, the allowance for doubtful accounts, and accumulated depreciation are credited for the respective amounts shown in the balance sheet. Gannon's capital account is credited for the equity in the business. In opening the accounts receivable ledger, the balances of the accounts with customers are entered directly from a schedule of accounts receivable. In opening the accounts payable ledger, the balances of the accounts with suppliers are entered directly from a schedule of accounts payable.

Current Period Proprietary Transactions. Certain types of transactions may be referred to as proprietary transactions because they affect either the owner's drawing account or the capital account. The following are typical proprietary transactions:

   (1) Periodic withdrawals of cash for personal use of owner.
   (2) Payment of owner's personal or family bills with business cash.
   (3) Withdrawal of cash or other assets by the owner intended as a partial liquidation of the business.
   (4) Investment of cash or other assets by owner intended as a permanent increase in assets and owner's equity.

Cash withdrawn periodically by the owner for personal use is charged to the owner's drawing or personal account on the assumption that such amounts represent withdrawals in anticipation of income. These withdrawals are sometimes regarded as salary or compensation for personal services rendered; however, they actually represent decreases in the owner's equity in the business and cannot be treated as an operating expense of the enterprise.

The payment of personal or family bills with business funds should be recorded as a withdrawal of cash by the owner. It is quite common for a sole owner of a business or professional enterprise to pay all personal, family or household bills by issuing checks against the same bank account that is used for business expenditures of the enterprise. However, care should be used in recording all checks issued. Those representing personal or family expenditures should be charged to the owner's drawing or personal account. Those representing business expenditures should be charged to the proper expense, asset, or liability accounts.

An owner may, at any time, permanently withdraw a portion of the cash or other assets invested in the business, or make additional investments in the business in the form of cash or other property. Withdrawals are considered to be decreases in the permanent invested capital and should be charged to the capital account. Additional investments are considered to be increases in the capital and should be credited to the capital account.

Closing Revenue, Expense, and Summary Accounts. At the end of each year, it is customary to close the temporary owner's equity accounts. As the temporary accounts are closed, their balances usually are transferred to an account entitled Expense and Revenue Summary.

In a merchandising enterprise, however, there also may be a summary account called Cost of Goods Sold. In the closing process, the cost of goods sold account is debited for (1) the amount of the merchandise inventory at the beginning of the year and (2) the amount of the purchases for the year; it is credited for (1) the amount of purchases returns and allowances for the year, (2) the amount of purchases discounts for the year, and (3) the amount of the merchandise inventory at the end of the year. After transferring these amounts, the balance of the account represents the cost of goods sold during the year, and it is in turn transferred to Expense and Revenue Summary. Note that this is a more indirect closing procedure than the approach using only the Expense and Revenue Summary that was discussed in Chapter 10.

The difference between the amount of debits and the amount of credits to the Expense and Revenue Summary represents the amount of the net income or the net loss for the year. If the summary account has a credit balance, it represents net income; if the account has a debit balance, it represents net loss. The balance of the expense and revenue summary account at the end of the accounting period is then transferred to the owner's capital account by means of a journal entry. If the expense and revenue summary account has a credit balance, the journal entry will involve a debit to Expense and Revenue Summary and a credit to the owner's capital account for the amount of the net income. If the summary account has a debit balance, the journal entry will involve a debit to the owner's capital account and a credit to Expense and Revenue Summary for the amount of the net loss.

Closing the Owner's Drawing Account. The owner's drawing account usually is closed at the end of each year by transferring its balance directly to the owner's capital account. The drawing account usually has a debit balance, and it may be closed by means of a journal entry debiting the owner's capital account and crediting the drawing account for the amount of its balance.

After transferring the balances of the expense and revenue summary account and the owner's drawing account to the owner's capital account, the balance of the owner's capital account represents the owner's equity in the enterprise at the end of the year.

Owner's Equity Section of a Single Proprietorship Balance Sheet. The method of exhibiting the owner's equity of a single proprietorship in the balance sheet is shown on pages 11, 137, and 275. There may be some variation in the account titles used by different enterprises. However, the final results should be the same since the balance sheet is an exhibit of the accounting elements: (1) the assets, (2) the liabilities, and (3) the owner's equity. The owner's equity section of the balance sheet should be arranged to show the owner's equity in the business at the beginning of the accounting period, the net increase or the net decrease in the equity during the period, and the amount of equity at the end of the period.

BUILDING YOUR ACCOUNTING KNOWLEDGE

1. Identify four advantages of a single proprietorship in comparison with other forms of business organization.
2. Identify four disadvantages of a single proprietorship form of business organization.
3. What are the two types of owner's equity accounts? Give examples of each in a single proprietorship.
4. When a set of formal, double-entry accounting records is started by a single proprietor for the first time, what is the source of information for preparing the opening entry?
5. How should the payment of personal or family bills using business funds be recorded by the single proprietorship?
6. Describe the use of a summary cost of goods sold account in the closing process of a merchandising type of enterprise.
7. How is the owner's drawing account usually closed at the end of each year?
8. How should the owner's equity section of a single proprietorship balance sheet be arranged?

Report No. 16-1

> Complete Report No. 16-1 in the study assignments and submit your working papers to the instructor for approval. Then continue with the following textbook discussion until Report No. 16-2 is required.

THE PARTNERSHIP

When two or more individuals engage in an enterprise as co-owners, the organization is known as a partnership. This form of organization is common to practically all types of enterprises. However, it is more popular among personal service enterprises than among merchandise enterprises. For example, the partnership form of organization is quite common in the legal and public accounting professions.

ORGANIZATION OF A PARTNERSHIP

The Uniform Partnership Act states that "a partnership is an association of two or more persons who carry on, as co-owners, a business for profit." The partners may, by agreement, unite their capital, labor, skill, or experience in the conduct of a business for their mutual benefit. While under certain circumstances a partnership may be formed by means of an oral or implied agreement, it is desirable that a partnership agreement be evidenced by a written contract. A written agreement containing the various provisions under which a partnership is to operate is known as a partnership agreement. There is no standard form of partnership agreement, but there are certain provisions that are essential, such as:

(1) Date of agreement.
(2) Names of the partners.
(3) Kind of business to be conducted.
(4) Length of time the partnership is to run.
(5) Name and location of the business.
(6) Investment of each partner.
(7) Basis on which profits or losses are to be shared by the partners.
(8) Limitation of partners' rights and activities.
(9) Salary allowances to partners.
(10) Division of assets upon dissolution of the partnership.
(11) Signatures of the partners.

The conventional form of partnership agreement is reproduced on the following page.

In comparison with the single proprietorship form of organization, the partnership form offers certain advantages, such as the following:

(1) The ability and the experience of the partners are combined in one enterprise.
(2) More capital may be raised because the resources of the partners are combined.
(3) Credit may be improved because each general partner is personally liable for partnership debts.

There are some disadvantages that are peculiar to the partnership form of organization, such as the following:

PARTNERSHIP AGREEMENT

THIS CONTRACT, made and entered into on the first day of July 1, 19--, by and between Jane Fishler of Indianapolis, Indiana, and Joel Marvon of the same city and state.

WITNESSETH: That the said parties have this day formed a partnership for the purpose of engaging in and conducting a wholesale and retail business in the city of Indianapolis under the following stipulations which are a part of this contract:

FIRST: The said partnership is to continue for a term of twenty-five years from July 1, 19--.

SECOND: The business is to be conducted under the firm name of Fishler & Marvon, at 1604 N. Milburn, Indianapolis, Indiana.

THIRD: The investments are as follows: Jane Fishler, cash, $30,000; Joel Marvon, cash, $15,000. These invested assets are partnership property.

FOURTH: Each partner is to devote her/his entire time and attention to the business and to engage in no other business enterprise without the written consent of the other partner.

FIFTH: During the operation of this partnership, neither partner is to become surety or bonding agent for anyone without the written consent of the other partner.

SIXTH: Each partner is to receive a salary of $24,000 a year, payable $1,000 in cash on the fifteenth day and last business day of each month. At the end of each annual fiscal period, the net income or the net loss shown by the income statement, after the salaries of the two partners have been allowed, is to be shared as follows: Jane Fishler, 60 percent; Joel Marvon, 40 percent.

SEVENTH: Neither partner is to withdraw assets in excess of her/his salary, any part of the assets invested, or assets in anticipation of net income to be earned, without the written consent of the other partner.

EIGHTH: In the case of the death or the legal disability of either partner, the other partner is to continue the operations of the business until the close of the annual fiscal period on the following June 30. At that time the continuing partner is to be given an option to buy the interest of the deceased or incapacitated partner at not more than 10 percent above the value of the deceased or incapacitated partner's proprietary interest as shown by the balance of her/his capital account after the books are closed on June 30. It is agreed that this purchase price is to be paid one half in cash and the balance in four equal installments payable quarterly.

NINTH: At the conclusion of this contract, unless it is mutually agreed to continue the operation of the business under a new contract, the assets of the partnership, after the liabilities are paid, are to be divided in proportion to the net credit of each partner's capital account on that date.

IN WITNESS WHEREOF, the parties aforesaid have hereunto set their hands and affixed their seals on the day and year above written.

Jane Fishler   (Seal)

Joel Marvon   (Seal)

Partnership Agreement

(1) Each partner is individually liable for all of the debts of the partnership. The liability of each partner is not limited to a pro rata share of the partnership debts. Each partner is personally liable for all of the debts of the business to the same extent as if the business were a sole proprietorship. Under the laws of some states, certain partners may limit their liability. At least one partner, however, must be a general partner who is responsible for all of the debts of the partnership.

(2) The interest of a partner in the partnership cannot be transferred without the consent of the other partners.

(3) Termination of the partnership agreement, bankruptcy of the firm, or death of one of the partners dissolves the partnership.

ACCOUNTING PROCEDURE

In accounting for the operations of a partnership, it is necessary to keep a separate capital account for each partner. It is also customary to keep a separate drawing or personal account for each partner. While no new principles are involved in keeping these accounts, care should be used in preparing the opening entry and in recording any transactions thereafter that affect the respective interests of the partners.

Opening Entries. Partners may invest cash and other property in the partnership. Certain liabilities may be assumed by the partnership, such as accounts payable, notes payable, and mortgages payable. In opening the books for a partnership, it is customary to prepare a separate journal entry to record the investment of each partner. The proper asset accounts should be debited for the amounts invested, the proper liability accounts should be credited for the amounts of obligations assumed, and each partner's capital account should be credited for the residual equity in the assets. The opening entries for Fishler & Marvon based on the partnership agreement reproduced on page 448 may be made in general journal form, as follows:

Bank...	30,000	
Jane Fishler, Capital		30,000
J. Fishler invested $30,000 in cash.		

Bank...	15,000	
Joel Marvon, Capital		15,000
J. Marvon invested $15,000 in cash.		

If, instead of investing $30,000 in cash, Fishler invested office equipment valued at $3,400 on which is owed $850, delivery equipment valued at $3,800 on which is owed $750 represented by a mortgage, and $24,400 in cash, the proper opening entry in two-column general journal form to record the investment should be as follows:

Bank..	24,400	
Office Equipment..	3,400	
Delivery Equipment	3,800	
Vouchers Payable		850
Mortgage Payable		750
Jane Fishler, Capital		30,000
J. Fishler's investment in partnership.		

Two or more individuals who have been engaged in business as sole owners may form a partnership for the purpose of combining their businesses. Their respective balance sheets may be the basis for the opening entries to record the investments of such partners. For example, assume that on April 1, R. M. Trump and J. W. Towle form a partnership under the firm name of Trump & Towle to continue the conduct of the businesses which they have been operating as sole owners. The balance sheets reproduced on page 451 are made a part of the partnership agreement. They agree to invest their assets and also that the partnership shall assume the liabilities shown in their respective balance sheets. Each partner is to receive credit for the equity in the assets invested, and the profits and losses are to be shared on a 50-50 basis. In case of dissolution, the assets are to be distributed between the partners in the ratio of their capital interests at the time of dissolution.

When two single proprietors decide to combine their businesses, generally accepted accounting principles usually require that non-cash assets (primarily inventories and long-term assets) be taken over at their fair market values as of the date of formation of the partnership. Since it probably cannot be determined as of March 31, 1982, which of the accounts receivable may later prove to be uncollectible in whole or in part, the amount of each accounts receivable balance cannot be adjusted for the currently accumulated allowance for doubtful accounts. It is, therefore, usual practice to record the full amount of the accounts receivable as a debit and the amount of the allowance for doubtful accounts as a credit in journalizing each partner's investment in the books of the partnership. In this way, the accounts receivable are recorded at their approximate fair market value. Subsequent end-of-period adjustments of the allowance for doubtful accounts on the books of the partnership will reflect future collection experience with respect to the combined accounts

R. M. TRUMP
Balance Sheet
March 31, 1982

Assets			Liabilities		
Cash		$ 2,643	Notes payable	$1,500	
Accounts receivable......	$2,302		Accounts payable..........	4,201	
Less allowance for			Total liabilities		$ 5,701
doubtful accounts	179	2,123			
Merchandise inventory .		10,239			
Store equipment............	$1,600		Owner's Equity		
Less accumulated			R. M. Trump, capital......		10,489
depreciation	415	1,185	Total liabilities and		
Total assets....................		$16,190	owner's equity............		$16,190

J. W. TOWLE
Balance Sheet
March 31, 1982

Assets			Liabilities		
Cash		$ 1,477	Notes payable	$2,500	
Accounts receivable......	$2,200		Accounts payable..........	5,516	
Less allowance for			Total liabilities		$ 8,016
doubtful accounts	300	1,900			
Merchandise inventory .		12,372			
Supplies		119			
Office equipment............	$1,800		Owner's Equity		
Less accumulated			J. W. Towle, capital		10,702
depreciation	450	1,350			
Store equipment............	$2,000				
Less accumulated					
depreciation	500	1,500	Total liabilities and		
Total assets....................		$18,718	owner's equity............		$18,718

receivable of Trump & Towle. Any accounts receivable on either set of books considered to be uncollectible as of March 31, 1982, should be written off by a debit to the Allowance for Doubtful Accounts and a credit to Accounts Receivable. None was so considered in this case.

Because both Trump & Towle had been using the fifo method of inventory costing, the values shown for merchandise inventories on their respective balance sheets are mutually acceptable as approximations of fair market value as of March 31, 1982. This is because of the lish (last-in still-here) aspect of the fifo method. If Trump or Towle had been using some other inventory costing method, the merchandise inventory amounts might require restatement to reflect the appropriate fair market value, with effects on the partner's capital accounts similar to those for long-term assets discussed below.

It is determined that the fair market value of Trump's store equipment as of March 31, 1982, is $1,500, so this amount should be recorded on the books of the new partnership, rather than the undepreciated cost of $1,185 ($1,600 − $415) shown on Trump's balance sheet as of that date. In like manner, it is determined that the fair market values of Towle's office equipment and store equipment as of March 31, 1982, are $1,625 and $1,800 respectively, so these amounts should be recorded on the books of the new partnership, rather than the respective undepreciated costs of $1,350 ($1,800 − $450) and $1,500 ($2,000 − $500) shown on Towle's balance sheet as of that date. The differences between the fair market values and the undepreciated costs of the long-term assets contributed by each partner are reflected in the respective credits to the partners' capital accounts of $10,804 and $11,277 shown in the opening entries at the top of the following page.

For tax purposes, R. M. Trump must use the undepreciated cost of $1,185 to value the store equipment investment, and J. W. Towle must use the undepreciated costs of $1,350 and $1,500 to value the office equipment and store equipment respectively. Their net capital investments for tax purposes would thus be $10,489 and $10,702 respectively, which are the amounts shown as owner's equity on their March 31, 1982, balance sheets.

Observe that the ratio of the partners' investments in the partnership ($10,804 to $11,277) is not exactly the same as their profit-and-loss sharing ratio (50% each). The basis on which profits and losses are to be shared is a matter of agreement between the partners, and not necessarily the same as their investment ratio. There are factors other than the assets invested that may enter into a profit-and-loss sharing agreement. For example, one partner may contribute most of the assets but render no services, while the other partner may contribute less in assets but devote full time to the activities of the partnership.

Admitting a New Partner. A new partner may be admitted to a partnership by agreement among the existing partners. The admission of a new partner calls for the dissolution of the old partnership and the creation of a new partnership. A new partnership agreement that includes all of the necessary provisions should be prepared. For

April 1	Bank	2,643	
	Accounts Receivable......................................	2,302	
	Merchandise Inventory	10,239	
	Store Equipment	1,500	
	Notes Payable		1,500
	Accounts Payable..		4,201
	Allowance for Doubtful Accounts		179
	R. M. Trump, Capital......................................		10,804*
	R. M. Trump's investment in partnership.		

*R. M. Trump, Capital (before partnership)		$10,489
Add: Fair market value of store equipment	$1,500	
Undepreciated cost..	1,185	315
		$10,804

April 1	Bank	1,477	
	Accounts Receivable......................................	2,200	
	Merchandise Inventory	12,372	
	Supplies	119	
	Office Equipment	1,625	
	Store Equipment	1,800	
	Notes Payable		2,500
	Accounts Payable..		5,516
	Allowance for Doubtful Accounts		300
	J. W. Towle, Capital		11,277*
	J. W. Towle's investment in partnership.		

*J. W. Towle, Capital (before partnership)..................			$10,702
Add: Fair market value of office equipment	$1,625		
Undepreciated cost..	1,350	$275	
Fair market value of store equipment	$1,800		
Undepreciated cost..	1,500	300	575
			$11,277

example, assume that Trump and Towle admit R. L. Hilgert as a new partner as of July 1, and agree to share profits and losses on the basis of their capital interests. If Hilgert's investment consisted of cash only, the proper entry to admit Hilgert to the partnership would involve a debit to the bank account and a credit to Hilgert's capital account for the amount invested. If Hilgert has been operating a business as a sole owner and the business is taken over by the partnership, Hilgert's balance sheet reproduced on page 454 will serve as a basis for preparing the opening entry. Assume that, as of July 1, Hilgert was admitted to the partnership. The assets listed in the balance sheet are taken over, the liabilities are assumed, and Hilgert is given credit for the equity in the assets of the business.

R. L. HILGERT
Balance Sheet
June 30, 1982

Assets			Liabilities		
Cash		$ 2,493	Notes payable	$3,770	
Accounts receivable	$5,954		Accounts payable	3,146	
Less allowance for			Total liabilities		$ 6,916
doubtful accounts	449	5,505			
Merchandise inventory		11,371	Owner's Equity		
			R. L. Hilgert, capital		12,453
			Total liabilities and		
Total assets		$19,369	owner's equity		$19,369

The proper entry in two-column general journal form to admit Hilgert as a partner is shown below:

July 1	Bank	2,493	
	Accounts Receivable	5,954	
	Merchandise Inventory	11,371	
	Notes Payable		3,770
	Accounts Payable		3,146
	Allowance for Doubtful Accounts		449
	R. L. Hilgert, Capital		12,453
	R. L. Hilgert admitted to partnership.		

Because Hilgert has no knowledge of any uncollectible accounts receivable as of June 30, 1982, and has been using the fifo method of inventory costing, no fair market value adjustments of the noncash asset account balances were made for purposes of this entry.

Goodwill. Some business organizations earn profits that are very large in relation to the amount of the recorded assets. The unique earning power of a business, which may be due to exceptional management, good location, or other factors, is called goodwill. Since goodwill is difficult to measure and may not prove to be permanent, accountants do not permit its formal recognition as an asset unless it has been purchased.

For example, assume that Trump & Towle purchased the business of R. L. Hilgert for $17,000 cash, acquiring all of the business assets except cash and assuming the business liabilities. If the net book values of Hilgert's net accounts receivable and merchandise inventory were considered to be reasonable approximations of their fair market values ($5,505 + $11,371 = $16,876), and Hilgert's total liabilities of $6,916 were assumed, Trump & Towle paid $17,000 for assets with net values of $9,960 ($16,876 − $6,916). The $7,040 difference between the $17,000 paid and the $9,960 of specific assets acquired may be considered to be the price paid for the goodwill of Hilgert's business. The transaction may be recorded as follows:

July 1	Accounts Receivable	5,954	
	Merchandise Inventory	11,371	
	Goodwill	7,040	
	Notes Payable		3,770
	Accounts Payable		3,146
	Allowance for Doubtful Accounts		449
	Bank		17,000
	Purchased R. L. Hilgert's business.		

It is also permissible to record goodwill if a new partner is taken into a firm and is allowed a capital interest in excess of the net assets that were invested. For example, suppose that instead of purchasing Hilgert's business, Trump & Towle had agreed to give Hilgert a capital interest of $19,493 in exchange for Hilgert's business assets and liabilities (including the business cash). Also assume that, as in the previous case, the net book values of Hilgert's noncash assets were considered to be reasonable approximations of their fair market values. Hilgert's investment may be recorded as follows:

July 1	Bank	2,493	
	Accounts Receivable	5,954	
	Merchandise Inventory	11,371	
	Goodwill	7,040	
	Notes Payable		3,770
	Accounts Payable		3,146
	Allowance for Doubtful Accounts		449
	R. L. Hilgert, Capital		19,493
	R. L. Hilgert admitted to partnership.		

Goodwill is considered to be an intangible long-term asset. When goodwill is recorded in the accounts, it is usually reported in the balance sheet as the last item in the asset section.

Compensation of Partners. The compensation of partners (other than their shares of profits) may be in the nature of salaries, royalties, commissions, bonuses, or other compensation. The amount of each partner's compensation and the method of accounting for it should be stated in the partnership agreement. For example, the partnership agreement between Fishler & Marvon shown on page 448 states that each partner is to receive a salary of $2,000 a month. When all partners receive the same salaries and when profits and losses are shared equally, it is immaterial whether the salaries are treated as an expense of the partnership or as withdrawals of anticipated profits. Under the federal income tax law, salaries or other compensation paid to partners for services rendered may not be claimed as a deduction from gross income in the income tax information return of the partnership unless such salaries are guaranteed. In this latter event, the amounts may be treated as deductions. (The partners, of course, must report such income in their individual returns.) However, apart from income tax considerations, the partnership agreement may provide that partners' salaries are to be treated as operating expenses in computing the net income or the net loss to be shared by the partners.

If partners' salaries are treated as operating expenses, it is usually advisable to keep a separate salary account for each partner. For example, the salaries specified in the partnership agreement between Jane Fishler and Joel Marvon are to be treated as operating expenses. If the salaries are paid regularly, such as monthly or semimonthly, it will be necessary only to debit each partner's salary account and to credit the bank account. Instead of paying partners' salaries regularly in cash, they may be credited to the partners' drawing accounts. The partners may then draw against such salaries at will. Under this plan, the proper entry to record each partner's salary on each payday is to debit the salary account and to credit the drawing account for the proper amount. If partners' salaries are not treated as an expense of the partnership, it is not necessary to keep a salary account for each partner. Thus, amounts withdrawn by the partners as compensation for services may simply be charged to their respective drawing accounts.

Allocation of Partnership Profits and Losses. The partnership agreement should specify the basis on which profits and losses are to be shared by the partners. In the absence of any agreement between the partners, profits and losses must be shared equally regardless of the ratio of the partners' investments. If the partnership agreement specifies how profits are to be shared but does not specify how losses are to be shared, the losses must be shared on the same basis as that indicated for the profits.

After closing the temporary accounts into Expense and Revenue Summary at the end of the accounting period, the balance of the summary account represents either net income or net loss. If the account has a credit balance, it represents net income; if the account has a debit balance, it represents net loss.

The balance of the expense and revenue summary account should be allocated in accordance with the partnership agreement. If the account has a credit balance, the entry to close the account requires a debit to Expense and Revenue Summary and credits to the partners' drawing or capital accounts for the proper share of the net income in each case. Because the partners may formally or informally agree that they will not withdraw any of their permanent investments without mutual consent, it may be preferable to credit their drawing accounts with their respective shares of net income. Any credit balances in partners' drawing or personal accounts can then be reduced by withdrawals without restriction.

Dissolution of a Partnership. Dissolution of a partnership may be brought about through bankruptcy or the death of one of the partners. No partner can retire from the partnership without the consent of the remaining partners. To do so would constitute a violation of the partnership agreement and would make the retiring partner liable to the remaining partners for any loss resulting from the retirement.

By agreement, a partner may retire and be permitted to withdraw assets equal to, less than, or greater than the amount of the retiring partner's interest in the partnership. The book value of a partner's interest is shown by the credit balance of the partner's capital account after all profits or losses have been allocated in accordance with the agreement and the books are closed. If upon retirement cash or other assets equal to the credit balance of the retiring partner's capital account are withdrawn, the transaction will have no effect upon the capital of the remaining partners.

Suppose, for example, that sometime after R. L. Hilgert had been taken into the partnership of Trump & Towle, Hilgert expressed a desire to retire and the partners agreed to the withdrawal of cash equal to the amount of Hilgert's equity in the assets of the partnership. After closing the temporary owner's equity accounts into Expense and Revenue Summary, and after allocating the net income and closing the partners' drawing accounts, assume that the partners' capital accounts had credit balances as follows:

R. M. Trump	$ 9,000
J. W. Towle	12,000
R. L. Hilgert	16,000

This indicates that the book value of Hilgert's interest in the partnership amounts to $16,000. If this amount is withdrawn in cash, the entry in two-column general journal form to record the transaction on the books of the partnership is as follows:

```
R. L. Hilgert, Capital ..................................................................... 16,000
    Bank ...................................................................................              16,000
        R. L. Hilgert retired, withdrawing $16,000 in equity settle-
    ment.
```

While the transaction involves a decrease in cash with a corresponding decrease in the total capital of the partnership, it does not affect the equity of the remaining partners. Trump still has an equity of $9,000 and Towle an equity of $12,000 in the partnership assets.

If a retiring partner agrees to withdraw less than the book value of the interest, the effect of the transaction will increase the capital accounts of the remaining partners. To record such a transaction it is necessary to debit the retiring partner's account for the amount of its credit balance, to credit the assets withdrawn, and to credit the difference to the capital accounts of the remaining partners. Thus, if Hilgert agreed to withdraw only $12,000 in settlement of the interest, the transaction should be recorded in the books of the partnership as follows:

```
R. L. Hilgert, Capital ..................................................................... 16,000
    Bank ...................................................................................              12,000
    R. M. Trump, Capital............................................................              1,714
    J. W. Towle, Capital..............................................................              2,286
        R. L. Hilgert retired, withdrawing $12,000 in equity settle-
    ment.
```

The difference between Hilgert's equity in the assets of the partnership and the amount of cash withdrawn is $4,000 ($16,000 − $12,000). This difference is divided between the remaining partners on the basis stipulated in the partnership agreement; i.e., the ratio of their capital interests after allocating net income and closing their drawing accounts. On this basis, Trump is credited for 9/21 of $4,000, or $1,714, while Towle is credited for 12/21 of $4,000, or $2,286.

If a partner is permitted to withdraw more than the book value of the interest, the effect of the transaction will decrease the capital accounts of the remaining partners. Thus, if Trump and Towle agreed to the withdrawal of $20,000 in settlement of Hilgert's interest, the transaction should be recorded in the books of the partnership as shown at the top of page 459.

R. L. Hilgert, Capital	16,000	
R. M. Trump, Capital	1,714	
J. W. Towle, Capital	2,286	
Bank		20,000
R. L. Hilgert retired, withdrawing $20,000 in equity settlement.		

The excess of the amount of cash ($4,000) withdrawn over Hilgert's equity in the partnership is divided between the remaining partners on the basis stipulated in the partnership agreement. Thus, Trump is debited for 9/21 of $4,000, or $1,714, while Towle is debited for 12/21 of $4,000, or $2,286.

When a partner retires from the business, the partner's interest may be purchased by one or more of the remaining partners or by an outside party. If the retiring partner's interest is sold to one of the remaining partners, the retiring partner's equity is merely transferred to the other partner. Thus, if instead of withdrawing cash in settlement of the equity in the partnership, Hilgert's equity is sold to Trump, the entry to record the transaction on the books of the partnership is as follows:

R. L. Hilgert, Capital	16,000	
R. M. Trump, Capital		16,000
R. M. Trump purchased R. L. Hilgert's interest in the partnership.		

The amount paid to Hilgert by Trump is a personal transaction not recorded on the books of the partnership and is immaterial to the firm. Any gain or loss resulting from the transaction is a personal gain or loss of the withdrawing partner and not of the firm. Thus, whatever amount is involved, the credit in Hilgert's account is to be transferred to Trump's account.

Owners' Equity Section of a Partnership Balance Sheet. The method of showing the equity of the partners in the balance sheet of a partnership is similar to that of a single proprietorship, except that the equity of each partner should be shown separately. An illustration of the owners' equity section of a balance sheet for the partnership of Trump & Towle whose accounts are kept on a calendar year basis is shown on page 460, assuming the following:

Net income for the year	$20,000
Profit and loss ratio	50-50
Withdrawals during the year:	
Trump	$4,000
Towle	5,000

Owners' Equity

R. M. Trump:			
Capital, April 1, 1982..		$10,804	
Net income (50% of $20,000)	$10,000		
Less withdrawals	4,000	6,000	
Capital, April 1, 1983..			$16,804
J. W. Towle:			
Capital, April 1, 1982..		$11,277	
Net income (50% of $20,000)	$10,000		
Less withdrawals	5,000	5,000	
Capital, April 1, 1983..			16,277
Total owners' equity..			$33,081

BUILDING YOUR ACCOUNTING KNOWLEDGE

1. Identify eleven essential provisions of a partnership agreement.

2. Identify three advantages of a partnership in comparison with a single proprietorship.

3. Identify three disadvantages of a partnership form of business organization.

4. When two single proprietors decide to combine their businesses, at what values do generally accepted accounting principles usually require that noncash assets be taken over by the partnership?

5. When a new partner who has been the sole owner of a business is admitted to a partnership by having the partnership take over the old business, what usually serves as the basis for preparing the opening entry?

6. Why do accountants not permit the formal recognition of goodwill as an asset unless it has been purchased?

7. In the absence of any agreement between the partners, how must profits and losses be shared? If the partnership agreement specifies how profits are to be shared, in the absence of any agreement between the partners as to how losses are to be shared, what must be true with respect to losses?

8. Identify two ways in which a partnership may be dissolved without the consent of the remaining partners. What form of partnership dissolution requires the consent of the remaining partners?

Report No. 16-2

> *Complete Report No. 16-2 in the study assignments and submit your working papers to the instructor for approval. Then continue with the textbook discussion until Report No. 16-3 is required.*

THE CORPORATION

A private corporation is an artificial person created by law for a specific purpose. A corporation differs from a single proprietorship or a partnership with respect to organization, ownership, and distribution of net income or net loss.

In contrast to a partnership, the corporate form of organization has several advantages. The most important of these are:

(1) Except in very unusual cases, the owners (stockholders) have no personal liability for the debts of the corporation.

(2) The shares of ownership are easily transferred from one person to another.

(3) The corporation has a perpetual life that is independent of the lives of its owners.

(4) More capital may be raised because the resources of numerous stockholders are combined.

A major disadvantage of the corporate form of organization is that the net income of a corporation is taxed and any cash dividends resulting from that income are also taxable to the stockholders, resulting in so-called double taxation.

ORGANIZATION OF A CORPORATION

In order to incorporate an enterprise, a charter must be obtained from the state in which the corporation is to be formed. The persons who file articles of incorporation are known as the incorporators. Such persons must be competent to contract, some or all of them must be citizens of the state in which the articles are to be filed, and usually each incorporator is required to be a subscriber for one or more shares of the capital stock. All of the incorporators must sign the articles of incorporation.

The procedure in incorporating an enterprise must conform to the laws of the state in which it is desired to incorporate. The laws of the different states vary considerably in their provisions relating to the organization of corporations. Persons desiring to incorporate a business should acquaint themselves with the laws of the particular state in which they wish to incorporate, as it will be necessary to comply with the laws of that state. The following excerpts from the laws of one of the states will illustrate a typical procedure to be observed in forming a corporation:

Private corporations may be created by the voluntary association of three or more persons for the purposes authorized by law and in the manner hereinafter mentioned.

A charter must be prepared, setting forth:
(1) The name of the corporation;
(2) The purpose for which it is formed;
(3) The place or places where the business is to be transacted;
(4) The term for which it is to exist;
(5) The number of directors or trustees, and the names and residences of those who are appointees for the first year; and
(6) The amount of the capital stock, if any, and the number of shares into which it is divided.

It must be subscribed by three or more persons, two of whom must be citizens of this State, and must be acknowledged by them, before an officer duly authorized to take acknowledgments of deeds.

The articles of incorporation shall also set forth the minimum amount of capital with which the corporation will commence business, which shall not be less than $1,000. The articles of incorporation may also contain any provision which the incorporators may choose to insert for the management of the business and for the conduct of the affairs of the corporation, and any provisions creating, defining, limiting, and regulating the powers of the corporation, the directors and the stockholders, or any class of the stockholders.

The affidavit of those who executed the charter shall be furnished to the Secretary of State, showing:
(1) The name, residence, and post office address of each subscriber to the capital stock of such company;
(2) The amount subscribed by each, and the amount paid by each;
(3) The cash value of any property received, with its description, location, and from whom and the price at which it was received; and
(4) The amount, character, and value of labor done, and from whom and the price at which it was received.

The Charter. After the articles of incorporation have been filed, and other conditions, such as the payment of incorporation fees, have been fulfilled, the document is examined by a court or an administrative officer. If the instrument is satisfactory and all requirements have been met, a license, a certificate of incorporation, or a charter is issued and recorded or filed as required by the particular statute of the state concerned. While, as previously stated, the provisions of law governing corporate organizations vary in different states, in general they require that the charter include such matters as the name, purpose, duration, location, and capitalization of the corporation.

Ownership of a Corporation. The owner's equity in a corporation is called capital stock. To make it possible to have many owners — often with different ownership interests — the capital stock is divided into units called shares. The persons forming a corporation (the incorporators) and those who wish to become owners subscribe for shares. Each subscriber agrees to buy a certain number of shares for a certain amount per share. Typically, payment is made in cash, although assets other than cash are used sometimes.

Subscriptions to the capital stock of a corporation may be made before or after incorporation. A subscription made before incorporation is a contract entered into between the subscriber and the incorporator or promoter and not between the subscriber and the corporation. The corporation, as such, does not exist until after the articles of incorporation have been filed with the proper state official and approved. A subscription for capital stock after incorporation is a contract between the subscriber and the corporation.

Stockholders. All parties owning shares of stock in a corporation are known as stockholders (sometimes called shareholders). In order to possess all of the rights of a stockholder of record, the party owning stock must have the ownership properly recorded on the books of the corporation. If stock is acquired from a previous stockholder, the transfer is not complete until it is recorded on the appropriate record of the corporation. Until this takes place, the new shareholder cannot be issued a certificate of stock (a document that is evidence of ownership), cannot vote at a stockholders' meeting, nor share in any dividends declared by the board of directors.

Directors. It would be impractical for all of the stockholders of a large corporation to meet periodically or at special times to decide upon questions in connection with the direction and management of company affairs. For this reason, the stockholders elect a board of directors — a group that is charged with the management and direction of corporate affairs. The board of directors is responsible to the stockholders for the proper management of corporate affairs. The directors are the legal agents of the corporation.

A board of directors usually consists of three or more stockholders. When the board is unusually large in number, it is customary to appoint an executive committee, consisting of from three to five members of the board, which is given authority to administer the affairs of the corporation.

Officers. The board of directors elects the officers of the corporation. Usually a president, vice-president, secretary, and treasurer are elected as executive officers. One person may hold two positions; for instance, the same person may serve both as secretary and treasurer or as vice-president and treasurer. All of the officers are responsible to the board of directors and receive their instructions from the board. The officers have no authority other than to perform the duties required by the bylaws of the corporation and the statutes of the state. Generally, they are liable for any fraud or misrepresentation, or for exceeding the rights and powers conferred upon them by the bylaws of the company or the statutes of the state.

Capital Stock. The charter obtained by a business corporation specifies the amount of capital stock that it is authorized to issue. The state of incorporation authorizes a corporation to issue a certain number of shares of stock, and it is illegal for a company to issue more shares than is authorized in its charter. A certificate of stock representing 250 shares issued to Clare B. Harris by The Weaver Company, Inc., is reproduced on page 465. The fact that the certificate illustrated has such a low number ("2") means that it is part of the original issue of these shares. One certificate is prepared for each block of shares issued, not for each share issued, unless the issue consists of a single share. (Procedures for handling a transfer of shares by the cancellation of a certificate and the issuance of another to a new owner will be discussed later in the chapter.)

Capital stock may or may not have par value. Par value is a technical legal matter. In general, par value represents the smallest amount that the corporation can accept in exchange for a share of stock at the time it is originally issued without the buyer of the stock incurring some liability to the corporation. In many states, par-value stock cannot be sold originally by the corporation for less than par value. In most states, it is possible for corporations to issue stock that has no par value.

If the corporation issues only one type of capital stock, it is called common stock. The stockholders own the corporation "in common." Among other things, the stockholders have the right to vote for directors and upon certain other matters, and the right to share in dividends. Dividends are distributions to stockholders resulting either from profitable operations or from the fact that the corporation is being dissolved. In all cases, these rights are in direct proportion to the number of shares of stock owned.

Some corporations have more than one class or type of stock. The classes differ with respect to the rights which go with the own-

NUMBER 2

SHARES 250

THE WEAVER COMPANY, INC.

This Certifies that ___Clare B. Harris___ is the owner of

Two hundred fifty - - - - - - - - - - - - - fully paid and non-assessable shares

of the par value of $100 each, of

the Common Stock of the Weaver Company, Inc.

transferable only on the books of the Corporation by the holder hereof in person or by duly authorized Attorney upon surrender of this Certificate properly endorsed.

Witness the seal of the Corporation and the signatures of its duly authorized officers.

Dated ___July 1, 19--___

Esther Anderson
Secretary

J. A. Weaver
President

Certificate of Stock

ership of the stock. In addition to common stock, a corporation may have one or more types of preferred stock, which may entitle the owner to receive a limited share of the earnings before the common stockholders receive any dividends or may involve a prior claim upon assets in the event that the corporation is dissolved. Sometimes preferred stock has a preference as to both dividends and assets. Frequently, preferred stockholders do not have voting rights.

If a corporation has only one class of capital stock outstanding, the book value per share of such stock is equal to the total owners' equity of the corporation (assets less liabilities) divided by the number of shares outstanding. If the corporation also has preferred stock outstanding, the book value per share of common stock will be the total owners' equity less the portion that is allocated to the preferred stock divided by the number of shares of common stock outstanding.

The market value per share of a stock is the price at which the share is traded in the market, the price that is quoted by a stock broker or the price reported in the financial pages of a daily newspaper. The market value per share and the book value per share are usually not the same. The market value is influenced by a number of factors, particularly the corporation's chances for success in the future. Market value is easy to determine if the corporation's stock is listed and actively traded on an organized stock exchange. Otherwise, market value can only be estimated. It would be most improbable that the par value (if any), the book value, and the market value of a stock of a corporation were the same amounts at any one point in time.

TRANSACTIONS AND ACCOUNTS UNIQUE TO A CORPORATION

The day-to-day operating transactions of a corporation are similar to those of a single proprietorship or of a partnership of a like nature. Certain transactions involving the owners' equity of a business are unique if the enterprise is incorporated. Examples of such transactions include:

(1) Capital stock subscriptions.
(2) Amounts received to apply on capital stock subscriptions.
(3) Issuance of capital stock to subscribers.
(4) Transfer of capital stock from one stockholder to another stockholder.
(5) Declaration and payment of dividends.

In order to account for these types of transactions, certain accounts are required by a corporation. A list of the major accounts and related classifications that are unique to the corporate form of organization is shown below:

Account	Classification
Capital Stock	Owners' equity
Subscriptions Receivable	Asset
Capital Stock Subscribed	Owners' equity
Retained Earnings (sometimes called Earnings Retained in the Business)	Owners' equity
Dividends Payable	Liability

ACCOUNTING PROCEDURE

In accounting for the operations of a corporation, two major stockholders' equity or owners' equity accounts are kept — Capital

Stock and Retained Earnings. In addition, an asset account — Subscriptions Receivable — and an owners' equity account — Capital Stock Subscribed — are kept to record unpaid subscriptions to capital stock. A liability account — Dividends Payable — is kept to record the corporation's liability for any dividends declared but not yet paid. The use of these accounts will be discussed fully in the remainder of this chapter.

Owners' Equity Accounts. One of the features of accounting for corporate owners' equity is the distinction that is maintained in the records between owners' equity that results from investments by stockholders — referred to as paid-in capital; and owners' equity that results from profitable operations — referred to as retained earnings. In the case of certain types of corporate transactions, this distinction as to the source of the owners' equity is not evident, but in most cases the difference is reflected in the accounts. For example, when the corporation exchanges its stock for cash or other property equal in amount to the par value of the shares issued, the transaction is recorded by debiting the proper asset account and by crediting Capital Stock. If there is more than one type of capital stock, there should be an account for each type.

Starting a Business Corporation. A business corporation may be started in a variety of ways. A corporation may sell its stock directly to new stockholders for cash or may obtain subscriptions to its stock. A subscription is an agreement to buy a certain number of shares at an agreed price (possibly at par, if the stock has par value) and to pay for them at or within a specified time, either in full at one time or in installments over a period of time. For example, a subscription is received for 100 shares at a price of $50 each (assumed to be the par value of each share in this case). The transaction is recorded by debiting Subscriptions Receivable and by crediting Capital Stock Subscribed for $5,000. Collections on the subscription are debited to Cash (or whatever is accepted in lieu of cash) and credited to Subscriptions Receivable. When the subscription is paid in full, the stock is issued and an entry is made debiting Capital Stock Subscribed and crediting Capital Stock for $5,000. As long as the subscriptions receivable account has a balance representing an amount that is expected to be collected, the account is treated as an asset and is shown on the balance sheet. Capital Stock Subscribed is a stockholders' equity account, the balance of which indicates the amount that eventually will be added to Capital Stock.

Following is a narrative of selected corporate common stock transactions with illustrative two-column general journal entries:

(1) The Weaver Company, Inc., was incorporated with an authorized issue of 1,000 shares of common stock, par value $100 per share. At the time of incorporation, subscriptions had been received as follows:

J. A. Weaver	500 shares
Clare B. Harris	250 shares
Esther Anderson	250 shares

The stock was subscribed for at par value and one half of the subscription price was paid in cash, the balance to be paid on demand.

To record this transaction it is necessary (a) to record the stock subscriptions received, and (b) to record the cash received to apply on the subscription price. These entries may be made in two-column general journal form as illustrated below:

(a)

Subscriptions Receivable	100,000	
Capital Stock Subscribed		100,000
Received subscriptions to capital stock at par, as follows:		
J. A. Weaver, 500 shares		
Clare B. Harris, 250 shares		
Esther Anderson, 250 shares		

(b)

Bank	50,000	
Subscriptions Receivable		50,000
Received cash on account for subscriptions to capital stock, as follows:		
J. A. Weaver, $25,000		
Clare B. Harris, $12,500		
Esther Anderson, $12,500		

(2) Received cash from subscribers to capital stock in settlement of balances due, as follows:

J. A. Weaver	$25,000
Clare B. Harris	12,500
Esther Anderson	12,500

This transaction involves an increase in the asset Cash and a decrease in the asset Subscriptions Receivable. The transaction may be recorded in two-column general journal form, as follows:

Bank	50,000	
Subscriptions Receivable		50,000

Received cash in settlement of the balance due from
subscribers to capital stock, as follows:
J. A. Weaver, $25,000
Clare B. Harris, $12,500
Esther Anderson, $12,500

(3) Issued certificates of stock to the following subscribers who had remitted their subscriptions in full:

J. A. Weaver .... 500 shares
Clare B. Harris .... 250 shares
Esther Anderson... 250 shares

Usually, certificates of stock are not issued until subscriptions are remitted in full. In this case, the subscribers remitted their subscriptions in full and the stock certificates are issued. The transactions are recorded in two-column general journal form, as follows:

Capital Stock Subscribed	100,000	
Capital Stock[2]		100,000

Capital stock issued to subscribers as follows:
J. A. Weaver, 500 shares
Clare B. Harris, 250 shares
Esther Anderson, 250 shares

After posting the above entry, the capital stock account will have a credit balance of $100,000, which is the par value of the capital stock outstanding.

(4) J. A. Weaver's stock certificate for 500 shares was returned and Weaver requested that 100 shares be transferred to R. F. Pudlowski. A new certificate for 400 shares is to be issued to Weaver.

This transaction indicates that out of 500 shares owned by Weaver, 100 shares were sold to Pudlowski. Transferring capital stock from one stockholder to another involves the cancellation of the old certificate and the issuance of new certificates for the proper numbers of shares. In this case, it is necessary to cancel the original

---

[2]When both common stock and preferred stock are authorized in the charter of a corporation, separate accounts should be kept for each class of stock. A memorandum entry of the number of shares authorized should be entered in the Item column of each capital stock account.

certificate for 500 shares issued to Weaver and to issue two new certificates, one to Pudlowski for 100 shares and the other to Weaver for 400 shares. This transaction has no effect upon the assets, liabilities, or capital of the corporation. It is merely a transfer of stock between stockholders and the only entry required is a transfer entry in the capital stock records kept by the corporation.

Corporation Profits, Losses, and Dividends. At the end of each accounting period, the balance of the expense and revenue summary account is transferred to the retained earnings account. If a corporation is operated at a loss, the amount of the net loss which is transferred from the expense and revenue summary account to the retained earnings account might result in the retained earnings account having a debit balance. This balance is termed a deficit and will appear as a deduction in the stockholders' equity section of the corporation's balance sheet.

A decision on the part of the directors of a corporation to pay a dividend is commonly referred to as a declaration of dividends. The directors usually specify that the dividends shall be paid to the stockholders of record as of a certain date, which means that only stockholders whose stock is recorded in their names on that date are entitled to receive dividends. Any stockholder who acquires stock after that date is not entitled to share in the dividend previously declared.

Dividends may be paid immediately upon being declared or at some later date. Large corporations usually do not pay dividends until some time after the date of declaration. When dividends are declared and such dividends are payable in cash at a later date, the dividends declared represent a liability of the corporation. It is customary to record the declaration by debiting Retained Earnings and by crediting Dividends Payable.

To illustrate, assume that the board of directors at its annual meeting held on June 15 voted to pay a cash dividend of $6 per share to be paid on July 1 to stockholders of record June 15. As of the date of declaration, there are 1,000 shares issued and outstanding. The transaction may be recorded in two-column general journal form, as follows:

June 15	Retained Earnings...	6,000	
	Dividends Payable...		6,000
	Dividend declared by board of directors.		

The dividends payable account will have a credit balance until all dividends declared are paid in full. When dividends are paid immediately upon being declared, there is no need for setting up a dividends payable account.

To record the payment of the dividend declared in the foregoing transaction, it is necessary to debit Dividends Payable and to credit the bank account, as follows:

```
July 1   Dividends Payable..............................................................   6,000
              Bank.......................................................................             6,000
                 Paid dividend declared June 15.
```

This transaction has the effect of decreasing the liability, Dividends Payable, by $6,000 with a similar decrease in the asset Cash. After the transaction is posted, the dividends payable account will have no balance.

Incorporating a Single Proprietorship. The legal steps involved in incorporating a single proprietorship are the same as in organizaing a new corporation. Usually, the sole proprietor becomes the principal stockholder in the corporation and transfers the assets of the proprietorship business to the corporation in exchange for capital stock. The business liabilities may also be assumed by the corporation. The same books of account may be continued or an entirely new set of records may be installed.

Assume that The Fialka Company, Inc., was organized to take over the business formerly conducted by W. F. Fialka as sole owner. Fialka subscribes for 400 shares of the capital stock of The Fialka Company, Inc., at $100 per share and transfers the equity in the proprietorship (on a fair market value basis, as usually required by generally accepted accounting principles) to apply on the subscription. Just before the transfer at the end of the year, the balance sheet of the business appeared as reproduced on page 472.

Fialka's net accounts receivable are believed to be collectible and the merchandise inventory is costed on a fifo basis. However, the fair market values of the long-term assets as of December 31, 1982, are considered to be: office equipment, $1,800; store equipment, $1,400; and delivery equipment, $2,000. A comparison of these values with the undepreciated cost amounts shown in the balance sheet reveals that the fair market values are larger by a total of $700 ($5,200 fair market value − $4,500 undepreciated costs). Thus, Fialka's equity in the business is considered to be $20,500, or $700 more than the amount of $19,800 that is shown on the balance sheet dated December 31, 1982.

W. F. FIALKA
Balance Sheet
December 31, 1982

Assets			Liabilities		
Cash		$ 6,200	Notes payable	$1,500	
Accounts receivable	$4,940		Accounts payable	4,160	
Less allowance for			Total liabilities		$ 5,660
doubtful accounts	520	4,420			
Merchandise inventory		10,340			
Office equipment	$2,000				
Less accumulated					
depreciation	500	1,500	Owner's Equity		
Store equipment	$1,600		W. F. Fialka, capital		19,800
Less accumulated					
depreciation	400	1,200			
Delivery equipment	$3,800				
Less accumulated					
depreciation	2,000	1,800	Total liabilities and		
Total assets		$25,460	owner's equity		$25,460

The following entry is made on Fialka's books to recognize the fair market values of the long-term assets:

Office Equipment	300	
Store Equipment	200	
Delivery Equipment	200	
W. F. Fialka, Capital		700
Adjustment of long-term assets to fair market values.		

If Fialka intends to continue to use the same set of books with only those modifications needed because of the change to the corporate form of enterprise, the entries to record the subscription and its partial payment by the transfer of the business assets and liabilities to the corporation should be as follows:

Subscriptions Receivable	40,000	
Capital Stock Subscribed		40,000
W. F. Fialka subscribed for 400 shares of stock at par.		

W. F. Fialka, Capital	20,500	
Subscriptions Receivable		20,500
Assets and liabilities of W. F. Fialka transferred to corporation at fair market value.		

After the foregoing entries are posted, Fialka's capital account will have no balance. The corporate accounts listed at the top of page 473 will take the place of Fialka's capital account in the general ledger:

Capital Stock   Capital Stock Subscribed
Subscriptions Receivable

As in the case of the Trump & Towle partnership, for tax purposes, Fialka must use the undepreciated costs of the three long-term assets as shown by the December 31, 1982, balance sheet on page 472, and the net capital investment for tax purposes would be considered to be $19,800, as shown also by the balance sheet.

If, instead of using the same books of account that were used by Fialka, a new set of books is installed by the corporation, a two-column general journal entry should be made to record the transfer of the accounts of the single proprietorship to the corporation. Since the long-term assets are being taken over at their fair market values, they should be recorded on the books of the corporation at these values, which represent the costs of the assets to the corporation. The accounts of Fialka are then transferred to The Fialka Company, Inc., by means of a two-column general journal entry on the books of the corporation, as follows:

Bank	6,200	
Accounts Receivable	4,940	
Merchandise Inventory	10,340	
Office Equipment	1,800	
Store Equipment	1,400	
Delivery Equipment	2,000	
Notes Payable		1,500
Accounts Payable		4,160
Allowance for Doubtful Accounts		520
Subscriptions Receivable		20,500
Assets and liabilities of W. F. Fialka transferred to corporation at fair market value.		

Assuming that the balance due on the subscription was paid, a stock certificate for 400 shares is issued to Fialka and the transactions are recorded on the books of the corporation, as follows:

Bank	19,500*	
Subscriptions Receivable		19,500
Cash received from W. F. Fialka in settlement of balance due on subscription to capital stock.		
*$40,000 Subscriptions Receivable Dr.		
less $20,500 Subscriptions Receivable Cr.		

Capital Stock Subscribed	40,000	
Capital Stock		40,000
Issued 400 shares of capital stock to W. F. Fialka.		

Incorporating a Partnership. When a partnership is incorporated, the partners may become stockholders of the corporation.

The same books of account may be continued or a new set of books may be installed by the corporation. Assume that The Detrick Company, Inc., is organized with an authorized capital of $100,000 to take over the business formerly conducted by Detrick & Detrick, a partnership. The partners subscribe for capital stock of the corporation, as follows:

> Glenn Detrick, 600 shares @ $50 .... $30,000
> Trudy Detrick, 400 shares @ $50.......................... 20,000

Detrick and Detrick, as individuals, are to receive credit toward their subscriptions for their respective equities in the assets of the partnership.

The subscriptions to the capital stock should be recorded as indicated in the following two-column general journal entry:

Subscriptions Receivable	50,000	
Capital Stock Subscribed..		50,000
Received subscriptions to capital stock as follows:		
Glenn Detrick, 600 shares		
Trudy Detrick, 400 shares		

The following balance sheet for the partnership was prepared just prior to the time of incorporating the business on April 1, 1982. It has already been adjusted to recognize the fair market values of the inventory and long-term assets as of that date, and the Detricks had no knowledge of any specific uncollectible accounts receivable at the date of incorporation.

DETRICK & DETRICK
Balance Sheet
March 31, 1982

Assets			Liabilities		
Cash		$ 8,500	Notes payable	$3,000	
Notes receivable............	$1,000		Accounts payable..........	4,860	
Accounts receivable......	4,950		Total liabilities............		$ 7,860
	$5,950				
Less allowance for					
doubtful accounts	400	5,550			
Merchandise inventory .		12,750			
Office equipment...........	$2,000				
Less accumulated			Owners' Equity		
depreciation	600	1,400	Glenn Detrick, capital ...	$12,684	
Delivery equipment	$1,600		Trudy Detrick, capital....	8,456	
Less accumulated			Total owners' equity ..		21,140
depreciation	800	800	Total liabilities and		
Total assets...................		$29,000	owners' equity...........		$29,000

If the books of the partnership are to be continued in use by the corporation, the transfer of the partners' equities to the corporation may be made by means of the following two-column general journal entry:

Glenn Detrick, Capital	12,684	
Trudy Detrick, Capital	8,456	
Subscriptions Receivable		21,140
Assets and liabilities of Detrick & Detrick transferred to corporation at fair market value.		

After this entry is posted, the partners' accounts will have no balances.

As in the previous cases, for tax purposes, Detrick & Detrick must use the undepreciated costs of their long-term assets and the book value of their inventory as of March 31, 1982, prior to any fair market value adjustments, and value their net capital investments accordingly.

If instead of using the same books of account that were used by Detrick & Detrick, a new set of books is installed by the corporation, a two-column general journal entry on the books of the corporation is required to transfer the accounts of the partnership to the corporation. This journal entry is:

Bank	8,500	
Notes Receivable	1,000	
Accounts Receivable	4,950	
Merchandise Inventory	12,750	
Office Equipment	1,400	
Delivery Equipment	800	
Notes Payable		3,000
Accounts Payable		4,860
Allowance for Doubtful Accounts		400
Subscriptions Receivable		21,140
Assets and liabilities of Detrick & Detrick transferred to corporation at fair market value.		

Assuming that Detrick & Detrick paid the balance due on their subscriptions and that stock certificates were issued to them, the transactions should be recorded on the books of the corporation, as follows:

Bank	28,860	
Subscriptions Receivable		28,860
Received cash from subscribers as follows:		
Glenn Detrick, $17,316		
Trudy Detrick, $11,544		

Capital Stock Subscribed	50,000	
Capital Stock		50,000
Issued capital stock to subscribers.		

Owners' Equity Section of a Corporation Balance Sheet. The difference between the amounts of the assets and of the liabilities of a corporation is called either ''Capital'' or ''Stockholders' Equity'' and is so described in the balance sheet of the corporation. Generally, the amount resulting from the issuance of capital stock and the amount resulting from undistributed earnings are shown. At the end of the first year of operations, the owners' equity section of the balance sheet of The Detrick Company, Inc., appeared as follows:

Stockholders' Equity

Capital stock (2,000 shares authorized;	
500 shares issued and outstanding)........	$50,000
Retained earnings...	16,000
Total stockholders' equity........................	$66,000

Because of differences in capital structure, there may be considerable variation in the capital sections of balance sheets prepared for different corporations. If more than one kind of capital stock is issued, each kind should be listed separately. There may be retained earnings (accumulated income) or a deficit (accumulated losses) at the end of the year. A deficit should be shown as a deduction from the amount resulting from the issuance of the capital stock in arriving at the total stockholders' equity of a corporation.

BUILDING YOUR ACCOUNTING KNOWLEDGE

1. Identify four advantages of the corporate form of business organization in contrast to a partnership. Identify a major disadvantage of the corporate form.

2. What qualifications are necessary to be one of the incorporators of a corporation?

3. What is the nature of a subscription to capital stock made before a business is incorporated?

4. What generally are the legal liabilities of the officers of a corporation?

5. What are the usual rights of common stockholders?

6. Identify the five major accounts unique to the corporate form of business organization and give their balance sheet classifications.

7. Describe the accounting effect and the necessary entry or entries for the transfer of shares from one corporate stockholder to another.

8. When do dividends become a liability of the corporation?

9. When an existing single proprietorship or partnership is incorporated, at what values do generally accepted accounting principles usually require that noncash assets be taken over by the corporation?

10. Identify the two major divisions of the stockholders' equity section of a corporate balance sheet.

Report No. 16-3

> Complete Report No. 16-3 in the study assignments and submit your working papers to the instructor for approval. Then continue with the textbook discussion in Chapter 17 until Report No. 17-1 is required.

EXPANDING YOUR BUSINESS VOCABULARY

What is the meaning of each of the following terms?

board of directors (p. 463)   capital (p. 439)
book value per share (p. 465)   capital stock (p. 463)

certificate of stock (p. 463)
charter (p. 462)
common stock (p. 464)
corporation (p. 461)
declaration of dividends (p. 470)
deficit (p. 470)
dividends (p. 464)
double taxation (p. 461)
executive committee (p. 463)
goodwill (p. 454)
incorporators (p. 461)
market value per share (p. 465)
net worth (p. 439)

owner's equity (p. 439)
paid-in capital (p. 467)
par value (p. 464)
partnership (p. 446)
partnership agreement (p. 447)
preferred stock (p. 465)
retained earnings (p. 467)
shares (p. 463)
single proprietorship (p. 439)
stockholders (or shareholders)
   (p. 463)
stockholders of record (p. 470)
subscription (pp. 463, 467)

CHAPTER 17

ACCRUAL ACCOUNTING APPLIED TO A MEDIUM-SCALE WHOLESALE-RETAIL BUSINESS

CHAPTER OBJECTIVES

The objectives of this chapter are to enable you:

▶ To describe how accrual accounting is applied to a medium-size wholesale-retail business with two departments operated as a partnership.

▶ To explain for such a business the record-keeping phases of the accounting cycle (source documents, books of original entry, ledgers, and auxiliary records).

▶ To prepare the following new books of original entry:

    (1) Sales register
    (2) Record of cash receipts
    (3) General journal with special columns

▶ To prepare a subsidiary operating expense ledger with its own chart of accounts.

▶ To describe the accounting for temporary investments, using the account for government notes as an example.

▶ To describe the use of departmental cost of goods sold accounts.

In the wholesale portion of a wholesale-retail merchandising enterprise, the merchandise handled is usually purchased directly from manufacturers, importers, or producers. The merchandise is sold to retailers and distributors, who in turn sell to consumers at retail prices. The wholesaler usually buys in sizable quantities and has storage facilities that make it possible to carry a large stock of merchandise. Goods may be purchased for cash or on account and, likewise, the goods may be sold for cash or on account. A large percentage of the wholesale business involves the use of credit. The retail portion of such a business is handled in a manner similar to that explained and illustrated in Chapters 8, 9, and 10.

FACTORS AFFECTING ACCOUNTING RECORDS USED

The books of account and the auxiliary records of a wholesale-retail business will vary depending upon a number of factors, such as the following:

(1) Type of business organization.
(2) Volume of business.
(3) Office equipment used.
(4) Information desired by the management and others concerned with the operation of the business.

Type of Business Organization. A wholesale-retail merchandising enterprise may be conducted as a single proprietorship, a partnership, or a corporation. In the single proprietorship and the partnership forms of organization, there are no distinctive records to be kept. As explained in Chapter 16, however, in the corporate form of organization, certain corporate records, such as a minute book, a stock certificate record, and a stockholders ledger, usually are kept. The type of organization will also affect the accounts that are kept. In a single proprietorship, it may be necessary to keep two accounts for the proprietor — one for recording capital and the other for recording personal transactions. In a partnership, it is necessary to keep separate accounts for each partner. In the case of a corporation, however, it is necessary to keep separate accounts for capital stock, retained earnings, and dividends payable.

Volume of Business. The volume of business is an important factor in determining the types of records and the number of accounts to be maintained. Obviously, the records and the accounts of a firm with annual sales of a million dollars or more will differ considerably from one with annual sales of only $50,000 a year. In a business with numerous departments, management may demand more financial statistical information and have a greater need for adequate control.

When manual methods are used, there is a fairly direct relationship between the size of a business and the number of persons engaged in keeping its records. When several persons are required, the work must be divided in some logical fashion. This means that a separate record or book of original entry will be kept for each major type of business transaction. For example, one journal may be provided to record purchases, another to record sales, another to record cash receipts, another to record checks written, and a general journal to record transactions that cannot be recorded in the special journals. The books of final entry (the ledgers) also will be subdivided. It is likely that there will be one or more subsidiary ledgers to record the details about some of the elements that are shown in summary in some of the general ledger accounts. For example, one subsidiary ledger may be for individual customers' accounts (accounts receivable) and another may be for individual operating expense accounts. (A subsidiary ledger for individual accounts payable would not be used if a voucher system is maintained.) Each employee engaged in an accounting activity may specialize in keeping one of these records.

A functional division of the accounting activity may have, among others, the following advantages — it:

(1) Becomes an integral part of the internal control system, as discussed in Chapter 14.
(2) Makes possible a more equitable distribution of the work load among several employees.
(3) Provides for a more detailed classification of transactions in the books of original entry.
(4) Makes possible periodic summary posting to the general ledger.

Office Equipment. The accounting system is certain to be affected by the use of various types of office equipment. In recent years there has been a great expansion in the use of electronic accounting, calculators, and other office machines. In the modern office of a big business enterprise, a large share of the bookkeeping work is done with the aid of electronic posting machines, accounting machines, and photographic equipment. Many large companies utilize computers and other associated data processing equipment.

Regardless of the extent to which equipment is used in performing the accounting function, the fundamental principles involved in keeping the accounts continue to apply. A knowledge of accounting theory and practice on the part of those employed in accounting positions is just as essential as if no machines were used.

Information Desired. The accounting system must be designed to provide the desired information for management and others concerned with the operation of a business. Management would like to know where the business stands financially from time to time, as well as the results of operations for given periods of time. Accounting may be required to supply such information of a statistical nature as well as the usual accounting reports. For example, the accounts must be kept so as to provide all the information needed for all of the various tax reports required by the federal, state, and local governments. In recent years there has been a tremendous increase in the number of tax reports and in the amount of tax information that must be furnished. Many large firms have found it necessary to organize a tax accounting department separate from the general accounting department.

ACCOUNTING PROCEDURE

Jane Fishler and Joel Marvon are partners who conduct a whole-sale-retail bakery business. Pastries and cakes are handled in Department A, breads and rolls in Department B. Such merchandise is purchased on account from various bakery suppliers. The bakery products are sold primarily for cash to retail customers. A small number of sales on account also are made to restaurants and wholesale customers. In the following sections, the books of account and accounting procedures for Fishler & Marvon are explained and illustrated.

BOOKS OF ACCOUNT

The records maintained by Fishler & Marvon consist of the following:

    (1) Books of original entry
        (a) Voucher register
        (b) Sales register
        (c) Record of cash receipts
        (d) Check register
        (e) General journal
    (2) Books of final entry
        (a) General ledger
        (b) Subsidiary ledgers:
            Accounts receivable ledger
            Operating expense ledger
    (3) Auxiliary records
        (a) Petty cash disbursements record
        (b) Long-term asset record

Voucher Register. A comparison of the format of Fishler & Marvon's voucher register shown on pages 498–499 with that of the voucher register reproduced on page 406 reveals that they are identical. This form of voucher register was described in detail in Chapter 14.

Sales Register. Fishler & Marvon keeps a multicolumn sales register as illustrated on page 500. Since there is no sales tax on food sales in the state in which Fishler & Marvon operates, no sales tax collections are necessary. Note that General Ledger Debit amount, Credit amount, and Account No. columns are provided. In addition, a special debit amount column is provided for Accounts Receivable, and special credit columns are provided for (1) Sales, Department A, and (2) Sales, Department B. A Sale No. column is provided to tie in the entry for each sale with the related source document.

Proving the Sales Register. The sales register may be footed and the footings proved daily or periodically by comparing the sum of the debit footings with the sum of the credit footings. When a page is filled and the amount columns footed, the footings should be proved, and the totals carried forward to the top of the next page. It is customary to start a month at the top of a new page.

Posting from the Sales Register. Completing the posting from the sales register involves both individual and summary posting. Individual posting is required from the General Ledger Debit and Credit columns, and may be required from the Accounts Receivable Debit column in some accounting systems. In Fishler & Marvon's system, however, individual posting to the accounts receivable ledger is done directly from the sales invoices. This posting usually is done daily. As each item is posted, a check mark is entered in the Check (√) column following the General Ledger Debit, Accounts Receivable Debit, or General Ledger Credit Amount column of the sales register.

The summary posting usually is completed at the end of each month and involves the following procedure (Account Nos. relate to the chart of accounts shown on page 487).

(1) The total of the column headed Accounts Receivable should be posted as a debit to Accounts Receivable, Account No. 131, in the general ledger.
(2) The total of the column headed Sales, Dept. A, should be posted as a credit to Sales — Department A, Account No. 611, in the general ledger.
(3) The total of the column headed Sales, Dept. B, should be posted as a credit to Sales — Department B, Account No. 621, in the general ledger.

As the total of each column is posted, the account number should be written in parentheses immediately below the total in the sales register. The final step in both individual and summary posting to the general ledger is to enter the initials "SR" and the page number of the sales register in the Posting Reference column of the proper general ledger account to the left of the amount posted. The final step in individual posting to the accounts receivable ledger is to enter the letter "S" and the sale number in the Posting Reference column of the proper customer's account to the left of the amount posted. A check mark should be placed in parentheses below the totals of the General Ledger Debit and Credit columns to indicate that these totals are not posted.

Record of Cash Receipts. Fishler & Marvon keeps a multicolumn record of cash receipts. Reference to the record of cash receipts reproduced on page 501 reveals that General Ledger Debit amount, Credit amount, and Account No. columns are provided. In addition, a special debit amount column is provided for Bank. All cash and cash items are recorded by debiting the bank account immediately. This practice usually is followed when a business deposits all its cash receipts in a bank on the day they are received and makes all its disbursements (other than petty cash) by check. On the credit side, special amount columns are provided for Accounts Receivable, Cash Sales — Department A, and Cash Sales — Department B.

Proving the Record of Cash Receipts. The record of cash receipts may be footed and the footings proved daily or periodically by comparing the sum of the debit footings with the sum of the credit footings. When a page is filled, the amount columns should be footed, the footings proved, and the totals carried forward to the top of the next page. It is customary to start a month at the top of a new page.

Posting from the Record of Cash Receipts. Completing the posting from the record of cash receipts involves both individual posting and summary posting. Individual posting is required from the General Ledger Debit and Credit columns. Individual posting to the accounts receivable ledger is done directly from the remittance advices. This posting usually is done daily. As each item is posted, a check mark is entered in the Check ($\sqrt{}$) column following the General Ledger Debit, Accounts Receivable Credit, or General Ledger Credit Amount column of the record of cash receipts.

The summary posting usually is completed at the end of each month and involves the following procedure:

(1) The total of the column headed Bank should be posted as a

debit to Federal National Bank, Account No. 111, in the general ledger.

(2) The total of the column headed Accounts Receivable should be posted as a credit to Accounts Receivable, Account No. 131, in the general ledger.

(3) The total of the column headed Cash Sales, Dept. A, should be posted as a credit to Sales — Department A, Account No. 611, in the general ledger.

(4) The total of the column headed Cash Sales, Dept. B, should be posted as a credit to Sales — Department B, Account No. 621, in the general ledger.

As the total of each column is posted, the account number should be written in parentheses immediately below the total in the record of cash receipts. The final step in both individual and summary posting to the general ledger is to enter the initials "CR" and the page number of the record of cash receipts in the Posting Reference column of the proper general ledger account to the left of the amount posted. The final step in individual posting to the accounts receivable ledger is to enter the letter "C" (for collection) in the Posting Reference column of the proper customer's account to the left of the amount posted. A check mark should be placed in parentheses below the totals of the General Ledger Debit and Credit columns to indicate that these totals are not posted.

Check Register. A comparison of the format of Fishler & Marvon's check register reproduced on page 502 with that of the check register reproduced on page 409 will reveal that the formats are identical. This form of check register was described in detail in Chapter 14.

General Journal. The general journal is used for recording all transactions that cannot be recorded in the special journals. Fishler & Marvon uses a general journal (reproduced on page 503) with three amount columns — Detail, Debit, and Credit — as well as an Account No. column. The Detail column is used to record debits to specific operating expense ledger accounts to support each of the debits to the control account, Operating Expenses, Account No. 811 in the general ledger. Adjusting, closing, and reversing entries also are recorded in the general journal.

Proving the General Journal. The general journal may be footed and the footings proved daily or periodically by comparing the Debit footing with the Credit footing. When a page is filled, the three amount columns should be footed, the Debit and Credit footings proved, and the totals carried forward to the top of the next page. It is customary to start a month at the top of a new page.

Posting from the General Journal. Completing the posting from the general journal involves only individual posting from the Detail, Debit and Credit columns. This posting usually is done daily. Since the account numbers normally are entered in the Acct. No. column when the entries are recorded, posting is indicated by entering a check mark in the Check ($\sqrt{\ }$) column following each of the amount columns as each item is posted. The initial "G" and the page number of the general journal then should be entered in the Posting Reference column of the proper general ledger (or operating expense ledger) account to the left of the amount posted.

Although no summary posting is required, a check mark should be placed in parentheses below the Detail, Debit, and Credit column totals at the end of each month to indicate that these totals are not posted. Check marks should also be placed in parentheses below the proving totals of the adjusting and closing entries in the general journal after each of these sets of entries has been posted.

General Ledger. Fishler & Marvon uses a general ledger with four-column ledger account ruling. The accounts are arranged in this ledger in numerical order according to the chart of accounts reproduced on page 487. Note that the chart includes some accounts not used in previous presentations. A brief discussion of these new accounts follows.

Government Notes, Account No. 121. This account is used to record the cost of the United States government notes owned by Fishler & Marvon. From time to time, the partners find that the firm's bank balance is larger than necessary. To supplement earnings from regular operations, the excess cash is temporarily invested in certain types of government notes which earn a relatively high rate of return. The notes can be sold or redeemed with little risk of loss. Because there is no intention to hold the notes for a long period of time, they are regarded as temporary investment and classified as a current asset of the firm. In the end-of-period adjustment process, any interest accrued on the notes is recorded as a debit to Accrued Interest Receivable, Account No. 122 and a credit to Interest Earned, Account No. 911.

Cost of Goods Sold – Department A and Cost of Goods Sold – Department B, Account Nos. 751 and 761. These two accounts are similar to Expense and Revenue Summary in that they are used only at the end of the accounting period in the closing process. Each of these accounts is used to summarize the elements that enter into the calculation of the cost of goods sold by each department. The debit balances of the merchandise inventory account (representing the be-

FISHLER & MARVON
CHART OF GENERAL LEDGER ACCOUNTS

Current Assets*

Cash
111 Federal National Bank
112 Petty Cash Fund

Temporary Investments
121 Government Notes

Receivables
122 Accrued Interest Receivable
131 Accounts Receivable
    131.1 Allowance for Doubtful
        Accounts

Inventories
141 Merchandise Inventory —
    Department A
151 Merchandise Inventory —
    Department B

Supplies and Prepayments
181 Store Supplies
182 Office Supplies
186 Prepaid Insurance

Long-Term Assets
211 Store Equipment
    211.1 Accumulated Depreciation
        — Store Equipment
221 Delivery Equipment
    221.1 Accumulated Depreciation
        — Delivery Equipment
231 Office Equipment
    231.1 Accumulated Depreciation
        — Office Equipment

Current Liabilities
311 FICA Tax Payable
312 FUTA Tax Payable
313 State Unemployment Tax Payable
314 Employees Income Tax Payable
315 Notes Payable
316 Accrued Interest Payable
317 Vouchers Payable

Owners' Equity
511 Jane Fishler, Capital
    511.1 Jane Fishler, Drawing
521 Joel Marvon, Capital
    521.1 Joel Marvon, Drawing
531 Expense and Revenue Summary

Revenue from Sales
611 Sales — Department A
    611.1 Sales Returns and
        Allowances — Department A
621 Sales — Department B
    621.1 Sales Returns and
        Allowances — Department B

Cost of Goods Sold
711 Purchases — Department A
    711.1 Purchases Returns and
        Allowances — Department A
721 Purchases — Department B
    721.1 Purchases Returns and
        Allowances — Department B
751 Cost of Goods Sold — Department A
761 Cost of Goods Sold — Department B

Operating Expenses
811 Operating Expenses

Other Revenue
911 Interest Earned

Other Expense
921 Interest Expense

*Words in bold type represent headings and not account titles.

ginning inventory) and the purchases account, together with the credit balance of the purchases returns and allowances account, are closed to the cost of goods sold account. When the amount of the ending inventory is recorded, the cost of goods sold account is credited. The balance of this account then represents the cost of goods sold for the indicated department. These balances then are closed to the expense and revenue summary account.

Accounts Receivable Ledger. Fishler & Marvon uses an accounts receivable ledger with balance-column account ruling. The accounts are arranged in this ledger in alphabetic order. A control account, Accounts Receivable (Account No. 131), is kept in the general ledger. At the end of each month, it is customary to prepare a schedule of the accounts receivable, the total of which should be the same as the balance of the accounts receivable control account.

Posting to the customers' accounts in the accounts receivable ledger may be done either from the books of original entry or directly from the documents that represent the transactions. The accountant for Fishler & Marvon follows the latter practice, using copies of sales invoices, remittance advices, and credit memorandums. A check mark is placed in the Check ($\sqrt{}$) column next to the Accounts Receivable amount column either in the sales register or record of cash receipts, or next to the credit column in the general journal, each time an entry is made. This reminds the bookkeeper that posting is done directly from source documents.

Operating Expense Ledger. Fishler & Marvon uses an operating expense ledger with balance-column account ruling. The accounts are arranged in numerical order. A chart of the accounts for Fishler & Marvon appears on the following page. A control account, Operating Expenses (Account No. 811), is kept in the general ledger. At the end of each month, it is customary to prepare a schedule of the operating expenses, the totals of which should be the same as the balance of the operating expenses control account.

All posting to the operating expense accounts is done from the books of original entry. As each item is posted, the initials and the page of the journal from which it is posted are entered in the Posting Reference column of the account.

As each entry involving an operating expense account is made in either the voucher register or general journal, the appropriate subsidiary ledger account number is written in the Acct. No. column to the left of the proper amount column. Then, when each of these amounts is posted to the operating expense ledger, a check mark is placed in the Check ($\sqrt{}$) column just to the right of the proper amount column.

Auxiliary Records. Fishler & Marvon keeps certain auxiliary records such as a petty cash disbursements record, a long-term asset record, voucher check stubs, and vouchers.

FISHLER & MARVON
CHART OF OPERATING EXPENSE LEDGER ACCOUNTS

Selling Expenses

8111 Advertising Expense
8112 Store Clerks Salary Expense
8113 Truck Drivers Wage Expense
8114 Joel Marvon, Salary Expense
8115 Truck Gas and Oil Expense
8116 Truck Repairs & Maintenance Expense
8117 Store Rent
8118 Delivery Equipment Insurance Expense
8119 Store Equipment Insurance Expense
8121 Store Supplies Expense
8123 Depreciation of Store Equipment
8124 Depreciation of Delivery Equipment
8125 Miscellaneous Selling Expense

Administrative Expenses

8131 Office Rent Expense
8132 Office Salaries Expense
8133 Jane Fishler, Salary Expense
8134 Heat, Light and Water Expense
8135 Telephone Expense
8136 Uncollectible Accounts Expense
8137 Office Supplies Expense
8138 Postage Expense
8139 Office Equipment Insurance Expense
8141 Depreciation of Office Equipment
8142 Payroll Taxes Expense
8143 Miscellaneous General Expense

The format of the petty cash disbursements record is similar to that of the petty cash disbursements record illustrated on pages 240 and 241 of Chapter 8. The format of the long-term asset record is similar to the format of the long-term asset record illustrated on page 367 of Chapter 13. The voucher check and voucher formats were illustrated on pages 408 and 405 of Chapter 14. To conserve space, Fishler & Marvon's auxiliary records are not illustrated in this chapter.

ACCOUNTING PROCEDURE ILLUSTRATED

The accounts of Fishler & Marvon are kept on the basis of a fiscal year ending June 30. The books of original entry (voucher register, sales register, record of cash receipts, check register, and general journal) are shown on pages 498–499, 500, 501, 502 and 503. The general ledger and subsidiary ledgers are not reproduced in this illustration. Following is a narrative of the June transactions that were shown recorded in the illustrations.

FISHLER & MARVON
NARRATIVE OF TRANSACTIONS

Monday, June 1

Issued Voucher No. 296 to Tucker Leasing Co., Indianapolis,

for $2,000, of which $1,200 represents store rent expense and $800 represents office rent expense.

Since the type of voucher used by Fishler & Marvon was illustrated in Chapter 14, it will not be illustrated in this chapter. Instead, sufficient detail will be given to explain each entry in the voucher register illustrated on pages 498–499. The voucher register illustration also begins with three unpaid vouchers from the previous month, May.

Issued Check No. 701 in payment of Voucher No. 271, and Check No. 702 in payment of Voucher No. 296.

Reference to the voucher register illustration on page 498 will reveal the payees and amounts of these two checks. Note that, in addition to the check register entries, the date and number of each check are written in the Disposition columns of the voucher register.

Cash sales for the day were $1,568 for Dept. A and $1,432 for Dept. B.

Cash sales are recorded in the record of cash receipts illustrated on page 501. Note that the cash sales of Dept. A bakery goods are carefully separated from the cash sales of Dept. B bakery goods.

Tuesday, June 2

Received checks from customers on account as follows:

Brother Juniper's, $674, for merchandise sold on May 28.
Houlihan's Place, $428, for merchandise sold on May 28.
The Tin Star, $652, for merchandise sold on May 28.

Checks sent in by customers are accompanied by remittance advices, which are used to enter the transactions in the record of cash receipts illustrated on page 501 and to post to the individual customer accounts receivable ledger (not shown).

Cash sales for the day were $1,485 for Dept. A and $1,396 for Dept. B.

Wednesday, June 3

Issued Checks Nos. 703 and 704 in payment of Vouchers Nos. 294 and 295.

Issued Voucher No. 297 to Acorn Paper, Indianapolis, for store paper supplies, $167. (Charged to Account No. 181.)

Made charge sales as follows:

Bakemeier's Bakery, Indianapolis, pastries, $612; breads, $224; Sale No. 397.

Heritage House, Indianapolis, pastries, $327; breads, $295; Sale No. 398.

Sam's Deli, Indianapolis, pastries, $195; breads, $420; Sale No. 399.

Entries in the sales register and postings to individual customer accounts receivable (not shown) are made from carbon copies of the sales invoices. The sales register is illustrated on page 500. Note that pastries are Dept. A sales and breads are Dept. B sales. All sales are numbered consecutively.

Cash sales for the day were $1,401 for Dept. A and $1,270 for Dept. B.

Thursday, June 4

Issued Voucher No. 298 to Indiana Bell, Indianapolis, for June telephone service, $84.

Received checks from customers on account as follows:

Ayres Department Stores, $984, for merchandise sold to them on May 30.

Bakemeier's Bakery, $819, for merchandise sold to them on May 30.

Methodist Hospital, $504, for merchandise sold to them on May 30.

Cash sales for the day were $1,507 for Dept. A and $1,168 for Dept. B.

Friday, June 5

Issued vouchers as follows:

Voucher No. 299 to Flowers Baking Co., Indianapolis, $3,805; pastries, $2,467; breads, $1,338.

Voucher No. 300 to International Bakers, Anderson, $3,644; pastries, $1,780; breads, $1,864.

Voucher No. 301 to Omar Bakeries, Indianapolis, pastries, $3,717.

Invoices for the previous week's purchases are received from suppliers on Friday and on the last day of the month for any other purchases through that date.

Made charge sales as follows:

Ayres Department Stores, Indianapolis, pastries, $639; breads, $351; Sale No. 400.

Brother Juniper's, Indianapolis, pastries, $375; breads, $127; Sale No. 401.

Houlihan's Place, Indianapolis, pastries, $277; breads, $123; Sale No. 402.

Cash sales for the day were $1,318 for Dept. A and $1,113 for Dept. B.

Saturday, June 6

Cash sales for the day were $1,305 for Dept. A and $1,134 for Dept. B.

END-OF-THE-WEEK WORK

(1) Footed the amount columns in the books of original entry, entered the footings in small figures immediately below the line on which the last entry appeared, and proved the footings. (2) Proved the bank balance in the following manner:

Bank balance, June 1	$21,768*
Add receipts June 1–6 per record of cash receipts	20,158
Total	$41,926
Subtract checks issued June 1–6 per check register	10,072
Bank balance, June 6	$31,854

*From General Ledger Account No. 111 not shown in this illustration.

(3) Completed the individual posting from the books of original entry to the general ledger and operating expenses ledger accounts. (Accounts receivable ledger accounts were posted directly from the sales invoices and remittance advices.)

Monday, June 8

Issued Credit Memorandum No. 7 to Brother Juniper's, $6, as an allowance for having delivered the wrong pastry order.

The pastry had been billed as a part of Sale No. 401. The allowance transaction was recorded in the general journal illustrated on page 503, after which the credit memorandum was posted immediately as a credit to the account of Brother Juniper's in the accounts receivable ledger. ("CM" stands for credit memorandum in the journal entry explanation.)

Cash sales for the day were $1,429 for Dept. A and $1,194 for Dept. B.

Tuesday, June 9

Received checks from customers on account as follows:

Bakemeier's Bakery, $836, for merchandise sold on June 3.
Heritage House, $622, for merchandise sold on June 3.
Sam's Deli, $615, for merchandise sold on June 3.

Cash sales for the day were $1,481 for Dept. A and $1,237 for Dept. B.

Wednesday, June 10

Issued Checks Nos. 705, 706, 707, and 708 in payment of Vouchers Nos. 297, 299, 300, and 301.

Made charge sales as follows:

Bakemeier's Bakery, Indianapolis, pastries, $526; breads, $257; Sale No. 403.

Methodist Hospital, Indianapolis, pastries, $197; breads, $422; Sale No. 404.

The Tin Star, Indianapolis, pastries, $260; breads, $179; Sale No. 405.

Cash sales for the day were $1,448 for Dept. A and $1,205 for Dept. B.

Thursday, June 11

Issued Voucher No. 302 to Indianapolis Power & Light, Indianapolis, for May electricity bill, $199.

Received checks from customers on account as follows:

Ayres Department Store, $990, for merchandise sold on June 5.

Brother Juniper's, $496, for merchandise sold on June 5, less the $6 allowance for having delivered the wrong pastry order.

Houlihan's Place, $400, for merchandise sold on June 5.

Cash sales for the day were $1,510 for Dept. A and $1,277 for Dept. B.

Friday, June 12

Issued Vouchers as follows:

Voucher No. 303 to Heileman Baking Co., Fort Wayne, $3,217; pastries, $1,047; breads, $2,170.

Voucher No. 304 to Omar Bakeries, Indianapolis, pastries, $3,675.

Voucher No. 305 to Tri-Baking Co., Indianapolis, $3,530; pastries, $1,216; breads, $2,314.

Made charge sales as follows:

Ayres Department Stores, Indianapolis, pastries, $636; breads, $402, Sale No. 406.

Brother Juniper's, Indianapolis, pastries, $363; breads, $121, Sale No. 407.

Houlihan's Place, Indianapolis, pastries, $285; breads, $189, Sale No. 408.

Cash sales for the day were $1,270 for Dept. A and $1,001 for Dept. B.

Saturday, June 13

Issued Voucher No. 306 to Indianapolis Water Co., Indianapolis, for May water bill, $143.

Cash sales for the day were $1,186 for Dept. A and $933 for Dept. B.

END-OF-THE-WEEK WORK

(1) Footed the amount columns in the books of original entry, entered the footings in small figures immediately below the line on which the last entry appeared, and proved the footings. (2) Proved the bank balance in the following manner.

Bank balance, June 1	$21,768
Add receipts, June 1–13 per record of cash receipts	39,288
Total	$61,056
Subtract checks issued June 1–13 per check register	21,405
Bank balance, June 13	$39,651

(3) Completed the individual posting from the books of original entry to the general ledger and operating expense ledger accounts.

Monday, June 15

Issued Voucher No. 307 to the Federal National Bank for the payment of the following taxes:

Employees' income tax (withheld during May)		$ 980
FICA tax imposed —		
on employees (withheld during May)	$445	
on the employer	445	890
Total		$1,870

Issued Voucher No. 308 to Payroll for the semimonthly wages, $4,496.

Fishler & Marvon follows the policy of paying their employees on the 15th and the last day of each month. The business is subject to the taxes imposed under the Federal Insurance Contributions Act (for old-age benefits and hospital insurance), and the Federal Unemployment Tax Act (for unemployment insurance purposes), and is required to make contributions to the state unemployment compensation fund. They are also required to withhold a percentage of their employees' wages both for FICA and for income tax purposes. In addition to the wages paid to employees, the Fishler & Marvon partnership agreement provides that each partner is to receive a salary of $2,000 a month, payable semimonthly. The salaries of the partners constitute an operating expense of the business and do not represent "wages" as defined in the social security and income tax laws; hence, their salaries are not subject to the FICA tax imposed upon employers and employees. Neither are such salaries subject to withholding for employee's income tax.

Each payday the bookkeeper is supplied with a report prepared by the payroll clerk showing the total amount of wages and salaries earned during the pay period, the amount of payroll deductions, and the net amount of cash needed for payroll purposes. The report for June 15 appears below.

PAYROLL STATEMENT Period Beginning June 1 and Ending June 15				
		DEDUCTIONS		Net
Classification	Total Earnings	FICA Tax	Employees' Income Tax	Amount Payable
Store Clerks Wages................................	833.00	58.31	114.95	659.74
Truck Drivers Wages..............................	920.00	64.40	148.00	707.60
Office Salaries..	1,447.00	101.29	217.05	1,128.66
Partners' Salaries:				
J. Fishler	1,000.00	None	None	1,000.00
J. Marvon	1,000.00	None	None	1,000.00
	5,200.00	224.00	480.00	4,496.00

Employer's payroll taxes:
(a) FICA tax, 7% of $3,200.00 .... $224.00
(b) Unemployment compensation taxes —
    State unemployment compensation tax, 2.7% of $1,000 ..... $27.00
    FUTA tax, 0.7% of $1,000 .... 7.00   34.00
    Total... $258.00

A check made payable to Payroll is issued for the net amount payable. This check is then cashed at the Federal National Bank to obtain currency in the denominations necessary to pay each employee. The bookkeeper is instructed to deposit Fishler's and Marvon's salaries in their individual bank accounts and to furnish them with duplicate copies of the deposit tickets.

The payroll voucher was entered in the voucher register by debiting the proper salary accounts for the earnings, by crediting the proper liability accounts for the taxes withheld, and by crediting the vouchers payable account for the amount of the check to be subsequently issued. The payroll taxes imposed on the employer were recorded in the general journal by debiting Operating Expenses in the Debit column, by debiting Payroll Taxes Expense in the Detail column, and by crediting the proper liability accounts for the taxes imposed.

Issued Checks Nos. 709 and 710 in payment of Vouchers Nos. 307 and 308.

Fishler reported that interest coupons amounting to $540 from government notes were deposited in the Federal National Bank. This transaction was recorded in the record of cash receipts.

Cash sales for the day were $1,438 for Dept. A and $1,230 for Dept. B.

The white space appearing at this point in the illustrated records indicates omission of the transactions completed on the days between June 15 and 30.

Tuesday, June 30

Issued vouchers as follows:

Voucher No. 319 to Flowers Baking Co., Indianapolis, $3,370; pastries, $1,009; breads, $2,361.

Voucher No. 320 to Omar Bakeries, Indianapolis, pastries, $2,083.

Voucher No. 321 to U.S. Post Office for postage, $49.

Voucher No. 322 to Petty Cash to replenish the petty cash fund. The following report was submitted by the clerk responsible for the fund.

Statement of Petty Cash Disbursements
for June

Acct. No.	Description	Amount
8111	Advertising Expense	$ 11.00
8115	Truck Gas & Oil Expense	10.00
8125	Miscellaneous Selling Expense	25.00
8135	Telephone Expense	2.00
8143	Miscellaneous General Expense	66.00
	Total Disbursements	$114.00

Voucher No. 323 to Payroll for the semimonthly wages, $4,496, in accordance with the payroll statement for the period June 16–30, shown on page 497.

Issued Checks Nos. 738, 739, and 740 in payment of Vouchers Nos. 321, 322, 323.

Received checks from customers on account as follows:

Heritage House, $691, for merchandise sold on June 24.
The Tin Star, $595, for merchandise sold on June 24.

Cash sales for the day were $1,542 for Dept. A and $1,346 for Dept. B.

END-OF-THE-MONTH WORK

(1) Footed the amount columns, proved the footings, entered the totals, and ruled each of the books of original entry. (2) Proved the bank balance in the following manner:

Bank balance, June 1	$ 21,768
Total receipts for June per record of cash receipts	86,492
Total	$108,260
Less total checks issued during June per check register	79,564
Bank balance, June 30	$ 28,696

PAYROLL STATEMENT Period Beginning June 16 and Ending June 30		DEDUCTIONS		Net Amount Payable
Classification	Total Earnings	FICA Tax	Employees' Income Tax	
Store Clerks Wages..............................	814.00	56.98	112.10	644.92
Truck Drivers Wages	938.00	65.66	150.70	721.64
Office Salaries......................................	1,448.00	101.36	217.20	1,129.44
Partners' Salaries:				
J. Fishler	1,000.00	None	None	1,000.00
J. Marvon	1,000.00	None	None	1,000.00
	5,200.00	224.00	480.00	4,496.00

Employer's payroll taxes:

(a) FICA tax, 7% of $3,200.00 .... $224.00

(b) Unemployment compensation taxes —

    State unemployment compensation tax, 2.7% of $1,000 ..... $27.00

    FUTA tax, 0.7% of $1,000 .... 7.00   34.00

       Total... $258.00

(The accounting procedure used is similar to that shown on pages 494–495 relating to payroll.)

(3) Completed the individual posting from the books of original entry to the general ledger and to the operating expense ledger accounts. (4) Completed the summary posting of the totals of the special columns of each of the books of original entry to the general ledger accounts. (5) Prepared a trial balance and schedules of accounts receivable, vouchers payable, and operating expenses.

Step (5) would be completed as a part of the normal routine at the end of each month. However, since the end of June is also the end of the fiscal year for Fishler & Marvon, the procedure is varied slightly. The preparation of the general ledger trial balance and the schedule of operating expenses is combined with the preparation of the end-of-year work sheets used to assist in producing the income statement for the year and the balance sheet as of June 30. This process is described and illustrated in the following chapter. (The schedule of accounts receivable is shown on page 536.)

VOUCHER REGISTER FOR MONTH OF June 19 —   PAGE 25

	PURCHASES DR.		OPERATING EXPENSES DR.			SUNDRY ACCOUNTS DR.		DAY	VOU. NO.	TO WHOM ISSUED	SUNDRY ACCOUNTS CR.			VOUCHERS PAYABLE CR.	DISPOSITION	
	DEPT. A	DEPT. B	ACCT. NO.	AMOUNT	✓	ACCT. NO.	AMOUNT				ACCT. NO.	AMOUNT	✓		DATE	CK. NO.
										AMOUNTS FORWARDED						
1								5/26	271	Acorn Paper				235 00	6/1	701
2								5/31	294	Flowers Baking Co.				4275 00	6/3	703
3								5/31	295	Omar Bakeries				3562 00	6/3	704
4														8072 00		
5			811.7	1200 00 ✓				1	296	Tucker Leasing Co.				2000 00	6/1	702
6			811.31	800 00 ✓												
7						181	167 00 ✓	3	297	Acorn Paper				167 00	6/10	705
8			811.35	840 00 ✓				4	298	Indiana Bell				840 00	6/19	719
9	2467 00	1338 00						5	299	Flowers Baking Co.				3805 00	6/10	706
10	1780 00	1864 00						5	300	International Bakeries				3644 00	6/10	707
11	3717 00							5	301	Omar Bakeries				3717 00	6/10	708
12			811.34	199 00 ✓				11	302	Indianapolis Power + Light				199 00	4/25	727
13	1047 00	2170 00						12	303	Heileman Baking Co.				3217 00	6/16	712
14	3675 00							12	304	Omar Bakeries				3675 00	6/16	713
15	1216 00	2314 00						12	305	Tri- Baking Co.				3530 00	6/16	714
16			811.34	143 00 ✓		311	143 00	13	306	Indianapolis Water Co.				143 00	6/27	773
17						314	89 00 ✓	13	307	Federal National Bank				1870 00	6/15	709
18			811.12	833 00 ✓			98 00 ✓	15	308	Payroll	311	224 00 ✓		4496 00	6/15	710
19			811.13	920 00 ✓							314	480 00 ✓				
20			811.32	1447 00 ✓												
21			811.33	1000 00 ✓												
22			811.14	1000 00 ✓												
48	1009 00	2361 00						30	319	Flowers Baking Co.				3370 00		
49	2083 00							30	320	Omar Bakeries				2083 00		
50			811.38	49 00 ✓				30	321	U.S. Post Office		704 00		49 00	6/30	738
51	5226 00	3438 00		5047 00			4537 00	30		Carried forward		704 00		9552 00		

Voucher Register — Fishler & Marvon *(continued)*

VOUCHER REGISTER FOR MONTH OF *June* 19 —   PAGE 26

	PURCHASES DR.		OPERATING EXPENSES DR.			SUNDRY ACCOUNTS DR.			DAY	VOU. NO.	TO WHOM ISSUED	SUNDRY ACCOUNTS CR.			VOUCHERS PAYABLE CR.	DISPOSITION		
	DEPT. A	DEPT. B	ACCT. NO.	AMOUNT	√	ACCT. NO.	AMOUNT	√				ACCT. NO.	AMOUNT	√		DATE	CK. NO.	
1	5226700	3438000		504700			453700				AMOUNTS FORWARDED		70400		9552700			1
2			8111	1100	√				30	322	*Petty Cash*				11400			2
3			8115	1000	√													3
4			8125	2500	√													4
5			8135	200	√													5
6			8143	6600	√													6
7			8112	81400	√				30	323	*Payroll*	311	22400	√	449600			7
8			8113	93800	√							314	48000	√				8
9			8132	144800	√													9
10			8133	100000	√													10
11			8114	100000	√													11
12	5226700	3438000		1036100			453700						140800		10013700			12
12	5226700	3438000		1036100			453700						140800		10013700			12
13	(711)	(721)		(811)			(√)						(√)		(317)			13

Voucher Register — Fishler & Marvon (*concluded*)

SALES REGISTER FOR MONTH OF June, 19 —   PAGE 27

			DEBIT		CREDIT		
			General Ledger / Accounts Receivable		SALES		General Ledger
DAY	NAME	SALE NO.	ACCT. NO. / AMOUNT	ACCOUNTS RECEIVABLE	DEPT. A	DEPT. B	ACCT. NO. / AMOUNT
3	Bakemeier's Bakery	397		83600	61200	22400	
3	Heritage House	398		62200	32700	29500	
3	Sam's Deli	399		61500	19500	42000	
5	Ayres Department Stores	400		99000	63900	35100	
5	Brother Juniper's	401		50200	37500	12700	
5	Houlihan's Place	402		40000	27700	12300	
10	Bakemeier's Bakery	403		78300	52600	25700	
10	Methodist Hospital	404		61900	19700	42200	
10	The Tin Star	405		43900	26000	17900	
12	Ayres Department Stores	406		103800	63600	40200	
12	Brother Juniper's	407		48400	36300	12100	
12	Houlihan's Place	408		47400	28500	18900	

Totals:

Accounts Receivable: 1693600 / 1693600   (131)

Dept. A: 9544400   (611)   Dept. B: 7392000   (621)

Sales Register — Fishler & Marvon

RECORD OF CASH RECEIPTS FOR MONTH OF *June*   19 —   PAGE *35*

DEBIT GENERAL LEDGER ACCT. NO.	AMOUNT	✓	DAY	BANK NET AMOUNT	RECEIVED FROM — DESCRIPTION	ACCOUNTS RECEIVABLE	✓	CASH SALES DEPT. A	DEPT. B	GENERAL LEDGER ACCT. NO.	AMOUNT	✓
					AMOUNTS FORWARDED							
			1	300000	Cash sales			156800	143200			
			2	67400	Brother Juniper's	67400	✓					
			2	42800	Hamilton's Place	42800	✓					
			2	65200	The Tin Star	65200	✓					
			2	298100	Cash sales			148500	139600			
			3	267100	Cash sales			140100	127000			
			4	98400	Ayres Department Stores	98400	✓					
			4	81900	Bahemier's Bakery	81900	✓					
			4	50400	Methodist Hospital	50400	✓					
			4	267500	Cash sales			150700	116800			
			5	243100	Cash sales			131800	111300			
			6	243900	Cash sales			130500	113400			
			8	262300	Cash sales	404100		142900	119400			
			9	83600	Bahemier's Bakery	83600	✓					
			9	62200	Heritage House	62200	✓					
			9	61500	Sam's Deli	61500	✓					
			9	271800	Cash sales			148100	123700			
			10	265300	Cash sales			144800	120500			
			11	99000	Ayres Department Stores	99000	✓					
			11	49600	Brother Juniper's	49600	✓					
			11	40000	Hamilton's Place	40000	✓					
			11	278700	Cash sales			151000	127700			
			12	227100	Cash sales			127000	100100			
			13	341900	Cash sales	802000		118600	93300		1495800 1490800	
			15	54000	Interest on Gov't Notes					911	54000	✓
			15	266800	Cash sales			143800	123000			

			30	69100	Heritage House	69100	✓					
			30	59500	The Tin Star	59500	✓					
			30	288800	Cash sales			154200	134600			
				288800 1649200		1527300		1537300 3739600	1346100 3328300		54000 54000	
				(111)		(131)		(311)	(421)		(✓)	

Record of Cash Receipts — Fishler & Marvon

CHECK REGISTER FOR MONTH OF *June* 19 — PAGE 24

VOUCHERS PAYABLE DR. NO.	AMOUNT	DAY	DRAWN TO THE ORDER OF	CK. NO.	BANK CR. AMOUNT	
			AMOUNTS FORWARDED			1
271	235 00	1	Acorn Paper	701	235 00	2
296	2000 00	1	Tucker Leasing Co.	702	2000 00	3
294	4275 00	3	Flowers Baking Co.	703	4275 00	4
295	3562 00	3	Omar Bakeries	704	3562 00	5
297	167 00	10	Acorn Paper	705	167 00	6
299	3805 00	10	Flowers Baking Co.	706	3805 00	7
300	3644 00	10	International Bakers	707	3644 00	8
301	3717 00	10	Omar Bakeries	708	3717 00	9
307	1870 00	15	Federal National Bank	709	1870 00	10
308	4496 00	15	Payroll	710	4496 00	11
321	49 00	30	U.S. Post Office	738	49 00	46
322	114 00	30	Petty Cash	739	114 00	47
323	4496 00	30	Payroll	740	4496 00	48
	79564 00				79564 00	49
	(3/7)				(111)	50

Check Register — Fishler & Marvon

GENERAL JOURNAL   PAGE 41

	DATE	DESCRIPTION	ACCT. NO.	DETAIL	✓	DEBIT	✓	CREDIT	✓	
1	19— June 8	Sales Returns and Allowances – Dept. A	611.1			600	✓			1
2		Accounts Receivable	131					600	✓	2
3		Brother Juniper's, CM 7.								3
4	15	Operating Expenses	811			25800	✓			4
5		Payroll Taxes Expense	8142	258 00	✓					5
6		FICA Tax Payable	311					224000	✓	6
7		FUTA Tax Payable	312					700	✓	7
8		State Unemployment Tax Payable	313					2700	✓	8
9		Payroll Taxes – June 15 payroll.								9

	DATE	DESCRIPTION	ACCT. NO.	DETAIL	✓	DEBIT	✓	CREDIT	✓	
38	30	Operating Expenses	811			25800	✓			38
39		Payroll Taxes Expense	8142	25800	✓					39
40		FICA Tax Payable	311					224000	✓	40
41		FUTA Tax Payable	312					700	✓	41
42		State Unemployment Tax Payable	313					2700	✓	42
43		Payroll Taxes – June 30 payroll.		51600		62800		62800		43
44				51600	(✓)	62800	(✓)	62800	(✓)	44
45										45
46										46
47										47
48										48

General Journal — Fishler & Marvon

BUILDING YOUR ACCOUNTING KNOWLEDGE

1. What are the differences in the owner's equity accounts that are kept in a single proprietorship, a partnership, and a corporation?
2. Name five separate books of original entry and indicate the type of business transaction normally recorded in each.
3. Give four advantages of a functional division of the accounting activity.
4. What kinds of equipment often are used to aid the bookkeeping work in the modern office of a big business enterprise?
5. What special information requirement has led to the organization of specialized accounting departments in large firms?
6. Describe the function of each of the five books of original entry kept by Fishler & Marvon.
7. Describe the function of each of the two subsidiary ledgers kept by Fishler & Marvon.
8. What are the two major auxiliary records that Fishler & Marvon maintain? Name two other auxiliary records that are kept in files by Fishler & Marvon.

Report No. 17-1

> *The study assignments contain an analysis test that should be completed at this time. Before beginning work on the test, this chapter should be reviewed thoroughly. The narrative of transactions for June should be checked with the illustrations to see how each transaction is recorded and to note the effect of each transaction on the accounts involved. Special attention should be given to the analyses following certain transactions. Unless the procedure involved in recording the transactions completed by Fishler & Marvon during the month of June is thoroughly understood, you cannot hope to make a satisfactory grade on the test.*

EXPANDING YOUR BUSINESS VOCABULARY

What is the meaning of each of the following terms:

Detail column (p. 485)   record of cash receipts (p. 484)
operating expense ledger   sales register (p. 483)
  (p. 488)

CHAPTER 18

ACCOUNTING PROCEDURE
AT YEAR END

CHAPTER OBJECTIVES

The objectives of this chapter are to enable you:

▶ To prepare a ten-column, end-of-year summary work sheet supplemented by a three-column end-of-year operating expenses work sheet.

▶ To prepare end-of-year departmental summary accounts for cost of goods sold.

▶ To prepare adjustments that involve debits to accounts on the operating expenses work sheet (with a summary debit to the general ledger account, Operating Expenses) and credits to various general ledger accounts on the summary work sheet.

▶ To prepare the adjusting entries and the closing entries in the general journal (using the summary work sheet as a guide) and post to the general ledger end-of-period summary accounts (Expense and Revenue Summary, and the two departmental accounts for cost of goods sold).

▶ To prepare the post-closing trial balance.

▶ To prepare any reversing entries required in the general journal as of the first day of the new accounting period.

One of the several reasons for maintaining a set of accounting records is to make it possible to prepare periodic financial reports, including an income statement for the fiscal year and a balance sheet as of the close of that year. Long experience has shown that one of the fastest ways to produce these financial statements is (1) to use the information provided by the accounts — as reflected by the year-end trial balance taken after the regular posting has been completed, (2) to determine the needed adjustments, and (3) to bring these amounts together in a manner that facilitates statement preparation. The device most commonly used for these purposes is the work sheet. A work sheet is an effective means of processing data.

SUMMARY AND SUPPLEMENTARY YEAR-END WORK SHEETS

A simple eight-column work sheet for a personal service enterprise was discussed and illustrated in Chapter 5. A ten-column work sheet for a retail merchandising business was introduced in Chapter 9. Following is a discussion and illustration of Fishler & Marvon's ten-column summary work sheet supplemented by a three-column operating expenses work sheet. In the preceding chapter, a partial narrative of transactions for this firm for the month of June, 19—— (the last month of the fiscal year) was given. These transactions were recorded in the books of original entry. The books of original entry were reproduced as they would appear after both the individual and the summary posting had been completed. The general ledger accounts and the accounts in each of the two subsidiary ledgers (accounts receivable and operating expenses) were not reproduced. However, it may be assumed that trial balances of these ledgers were taken. The general ledger was found to be in balance and the total of the account balances in each subsidiary ledger was found to agree with the balance of the related control account in the general ledger.

SUMMARY YEAR-END WORK SHEET

The Fishler & Marvon work sheet is shown on pages 508 and 509. It is identical to that used for Boyd's Clothiers on pages 260 and 261. The first step in its preparation was to write the proper

Fishler & Marion
Work Sheet
For the Year Ended June 30, 19—

Account	Acct. No.	Trial Balance Debit	Trial Balance Credit	Adjustments Debit	Adjustments Credit	Adj. Trial Balance Debit	Adj. Trial Balance Credit	Income Statement Debit	Income Statement Credit	Balance Sheet Debit	Balance Sheet Credit
1 Federal National Bank	111	2869600				2869600				2869600	
2 Petty Cash Fund	112	15000				15000				15000	
3 Government Notes	121	1000000				1000000				1000000	
4 Accrued Interest Receivable	122			(i) 4500		4500				4500	
5 Accounts Receivable	131	914800				914800				914800	
6 Allowance for Doubtful Accts.	131.1		5000		(p) 15000		20000				20000
7 Merchandise Inventory—Dept. A	141	142800		(a) 140000	(a) 142800	140000				140000	
8 Merchandise Inventory—Dept. B	151	117500		(b) 125000	(b) 117500	125000				125000	
9 Store Supplies	181	747800			(m) 643800	104000				104000	
10 Office Supplies	182	658000			(n) 595100	62900				62900	
11 Prepaid Insurance	186	461000			(o) 386000	75000				75000	
12 Store Equipment	211	1648000				1648000				1648000	
13 Accumulated Depr.—Store Eq.	211.1		140600		(q) 164800		305400				305400
14 Delivery Equipment	221	4760000				4760000				4760000	
15 Accumulated Depr.—Del. Eq.	221.1		3569900		(r) 595000		4164900				4164900
16 Office Equipment	231	1586000				1586000				1586000	
17 Accumulated Depr.—Off. Eq.	231.1		117800		(s) 154000		271800				271800
18 FICA Tax Payable	311		89500				89500				89500
19 FUTA Tax Payable	312		4100				4100				4100
20 State Unemployment Tax Pay.	313		12200				12200				12200
21 Employees Income Tax Pay.	314		97600				97600				97600
22 Notes Payable	315		-0-				-0-				-0-
23 Accrued Interest Payable	314		-0-				-0-				-0-
24 Vouchers Payable	317		2864500				2864500				2864500
25 Jane Fishler, Capital	511		3382200				3382200				3382200
26 Jane Fishler, Drawing	511.1	860000				860000				860000	
27 Joel Marion, Capital	521		1407300				1407300				1407300
28 Joel Marion, Drawing	521.1	650000				650000				650000	

Fishler & Marvon — Ten-Column Work Sheet

Line	Account Title	Acct. No.	Trial Balance Dr	Trial Balance Cr	Adjustments Dr	Adjustments Cr	Income Statement Dr	Income Statement Cr
29	Sales – Department A	611		6129100				6129100
30	Sales Ret. & Allow. – Dept. A	611.1	31300				31300	
31	Sales – Department B	621		5174900				5174900
32	Sales Ret. & Allow. – Dept. B	621.1	28200				28200	
33	Purchases – Department A	711	52398800			(c) 52398800		
34	Purchases Ret. & Allow. – Dept. A	711.1		68200	(e) 68200			
35	Purchases – Department B	721	38842000			(d) 38842000		
36	Purchases Ret. & Allow. – Dept. B	721.1		38500	(f) 38500			
37	Cost of Goods Sold – Dept. A	751			(a) 142800 (c) 52398800 (g) 140000	(e) 68200 (g) 140000	52333400	
38						52333400		
40	Cost of Goods Sold – Dept. B	761			(b) 117500 (d) 38842000	(f) 38500 (h) 125000	38796000	
43	Operating Expenses	811	17114270 0		(j-p) 2553700		19696400	
44	Interest Earned	911		108000		112500		112500
45	Interest Expense	921	–0–		(i) 4500		–0–	
46			124873500	124873500	94431000	94431000	125700100	110853000
47	Net Income						2195300	
48							113080600	113080600

509

heading at the top, to insert the proper heading in the space provided at the top of each of the five pairs of amount columns, and to list the general ledger account titles and numbers in the spaces provided at the left. Note that with one exception (refer to the chart of accounts given on page 487 for the complete list) the title and number of each general ledger account was listed even though some of the accounts had no balances at the time the trial balance was taken. The one exception is Expense and Revenue Summary, Account No. 531. This account is used in the formal process of closing the books but is not needed on the work sheet. Expense and Revenue Summary was included in the Boyd's Clothiers work sheet on pages 260–261 because the account was used to adjust the beginning and ending inventories. These inventory adjustments in the Fishler & Marvon work sheet are made using two cost of goods sold accounts that Boyd's Clothiers did not maintain. Note also that for Cost of Goods Sold — Department A, Account No. 751, and Cost of Goods Sold — Department B, Account No. 761, three lines were allowed in each case to accommodate the several debits and credits that will be involved. (The purpose of the cost of goods sold account is to provide a means of bringing together all the elements that are involved in calculating the amount of this cost: (1) beginning inventory, (2) purchases, (3) purchases returns and allowances, and (4) ending inventory.) The account balances were entered in the first pair of columns (trial balance) and these columns were totaled to prove their equality.

Adjustment of the Merchandise Accounts. Eight entries (a–h), were made in the adjustments columns of the work sheet to show the calculation of the cost of goods sold for each department and to adjust the merchandise inventory accounts.

Entry (a): The amount of the beginning inventory for Department A, $1,428, was transferred to Cost of Goods Sold — Department A by a debit to that account (No. 751) and by a credit to Merchandise Inventory — Department A, Account No. 141.

Entry (b): The amount of the beginning inventory for Department B, $1,175, was transferred to Cost of Goods Sold — Department B by a debit to that account (No. 761) and by a credit to Merchandise Inventory — Department B, Account No. 151.

Entry (c): The amount of the purchases for the year by Department A, $523,988, was transferred to Cost of Goods Sold — Department A by a debit to that account (No. 751) and by a credit to Purchases — Department A, Account No. 711.

Entry (d): The amount of the purchases for the year by Department B, $388,420, was transferred to Cost of Goods Sold — Department B by a debit to that account (No. 761) and by a credit to Purchases — Department B, Account No. 721.

Entry (e): The amount of the purchases returns and allowances for the year for Department A, $682, was transferred to the proper cost of goods sold account by a debit to Purchases Returns and Allowances — Department A, Account No. 711.1, and by a credit to Cost of Goods Sold — Department A, Account No. 751.

Entry (f): The amount of the purchases returns and allowances for the year for Department B, $385, was transferred to the proper cost of goods sold account by a debit to Purchases Returns and Allowances — Department B, Account No. 721.1, and by a credit to Cost of Goods Sold — Department B, Account No. 761.

Entry (g): The cost assigned to the June 30 merchandise inventory for Department A, $1,400, was debited to that account (No. 141) with an offsetting credit to Cost of Goods Sold — Department A, Account No. 751. Fishler & Marvon uses the periodic method of accounting for inventory. A physical count of the goods on hand at the year's end had been made. Reference to recent purchase invoices provided unit costs for the various items. Each time a physical inventory is taken, the quantities found to be on hand are recorded on detailed physical inventory summary sheets, showing the quantity, unit price, and extension for each pastry and cake item in Department A, and the total extensions.

Entry (h): The cost assigned to the June 30 merchandise inventory of Department B, $1,250, was debited to that account (No. 151) with an offsetting credit to Cost of Goods Sold — Department B, Account No. 761. The procedure followed in determining the inventory cost in Department B was the same as that described above for Department A.

The amount of the cost of goods sold for each department was determined by subtracting the sum of the two credits from the sum of the two debits to each of the cost of goods sold accounts. The amounts, $523,334 for Department A and $387,960 for Department B, were extended to the Adjusted Trial Balance Debit column.

Adjustment of the Interest Accounts. On June 30, Fishler & Marvon owned $10,000 face value, 10.8 percent United States government notes. Semiannual interest totaling $540 had been collected on June 15. Since that date, interest for 15 days amounting to $45 had accrued. In order to have the calculation of the net income for the year reflect the correct amount of interest earned, this type of accrual had to be taken into consideration.

Entry (i): The interest receivable on June 30, $45, was recorded on the work sheet by debiting Accrued Interest Receivable, Account No. 122, and by crediting Interest Earned, Account No. 911. (Because Fishler & Marvon has no notes payable outstanding on June 30, no adjustment for accrued interest expense or payable is required at this time.)

At this point, work on the summary end-of-year work sheet was suspended temporarily until certain information needed from the supplementary work sheet for operating expenses was determined.

SUPPLEMENTARY WORK SHEET FOR OPERATING EXPENSES

To provide the desired information, the income statement that was prepared had to be supplemented by a schedule of operating expenses. The accounting records of Fishler & Marvon include a subsidiary operating expenses ledger which is controlled by the account Operating Expenses (No. 811) in the general ledger. A considerable number of the operating expense accounts required end-of-year debit adjustments (with, of course, a summary debit to the general ledger control account). These adjustments involved offsetting credits to various general ledger accounts.

To assemble all the information needed both for the income statement and for the supporting schedule of operating expenses, and to facilitate the recording of adjustments in the general ledger and subsidiary ledger accounts (which must be done later), a supplementary operating expenses work sheet was used. As will be seen, it is very closely tied in with the summary work sheet. The Fishler & Marvon operating expenses work sheet is reproduced on page 513. Note that it was given an appropriate heading that included the period involved. This work sheet needed only three amount columns: (1) to show the account balances when the trial balance was taken, (2) to provide space for certain adjustments, and (3) to show the adjusted amounts. In every case only debits were involved. The titles and numbers of all the accounts in the subsidiary operating expenses ledger were placed in the columns provided at the left. (Refer to the chart of accounts given on page 487 for the complete list.) Observe that a considerable number of the accounts had no balance when the trial balance was taken. The balance of each account was entered in the Trial Balance Debit column. That column was totaled. If the total, $171,427, did not agree with the balance shown on the summary work sheet for Operating Expenses, Account No. 811 (the control account), it would have been necessary to discover and correct the discrepancy before the preparation of either work sheet could proceed.

Fishler & Marvon
Supplementary Operating Expenses Work Sheet
For the Year Ended June 30, 19—

Account	Acct. No.	Trial Balance Debit	Adjustments Debit	Adj. Trial Balance Debit
Advertising Expense	8111	208500		208500
Store Clerks' Wage Expense	8112	2034800		2034800
Truck Drivers' Wage Expense	8113	2198000		2198000
Joel Marvon, Salary Expense	8114	2400000		2400000
Truck Gas & Oil Expense	8115	519000		519000
Truck Repairs & Maint. Expense	8116	58000		58000
Store Rent Expense	8117	1440000		1440000
Delivery Eq. Insur. Expense	8118		(o) 190000	190000
Store Eq. Insur. Expense	8119		(o) 96000	96000
Store Supplies Expense	8121		(m) 643800	643800
Depreciation of Store Eq.	8123		(j) 164800	164800
Depreciation of Deliv. Eq.	8124		(k) 595000	595000
Misc. Selling Expense	8125	29500		29500
Office Rent Expense	8131	960000		960000
Office Salaries Expense	8132	3466000		3466000
Jane Fishler, Salary Expense	8133	2400000		2400000
Heat, Light & Water Expense	8134	464500		464500
Telephone Expense	8135	103400		103400
Uncollectible Accts. Expense	8136		(p) 15000	15000
Office Supplies Expense	8137		(n) 595100	595100
Postage Expense	8138	54600		54600
Office Eq. Insur. Expense	8139		(o) 100000	100000
Depreciation of Office Eq.	8141		(l) 154000	154000
Payroll Taxes Expense	8142	729300		729300
Misc. General Expense	8143	77100		77100
		17142700	2553700	19696400

Fishler & Marvon — Operating Expenses Work Sheet

All the adjustments that follow (for depreciation, supplies used, insurance expired, and the doubtful accounts provision) involved both the summary work sheet and the supplementary work sheet. One or more operating expense accounts were debited on the operating expenses work sheet, and one or more general ledger accounts were credited on the summary work sheet.

Depreciation Expense. In the general ledger of Fishler & Marvon, there are three long-term asset accounts with related accumulated depreciation accounts: Store Equipment, Delivery Equipment, and Office Equipment. In the operating expenses ledger, there are three depreciation expense accounts that correspond to the asset classifications. The firm's policy is that no depreciation is taken on assets owned for less than six months. The following schedule was prepared to determine the estimated depreciation expense for the year.

SCHEDULE OF DEPRECIATION EXPENSE
For the Year Ended June 30, 19--

Asset	Cost	Annual (Straight-Line) Rate of Depreciation	Depreciation For the Year
Store Equipment	$16,480	10%	$1,648
Delivery Equipment	47,600	12½	5,950
Office Equipment	15,400*	10	1,540

*Note that the balance of the office equipment account shown on the work sheet on page 508 is $15,860. That is because the cost of an electronic desk calculator ($460) purchased on June 18 is included. Since this asset has been owned for less than six months, no depreciation is taken on it.

Based on the calculations shown on the schedule, the following adjustments were made on the work sheets — the debits on the operating expenses work sheet and the credits on the summary work sheet:

Entry (j): Depreciation of Store Equipment, Account No. 8123, was debited and Accumulated Depreciation — Store Equipment, Account No. 211.1, was credited for $1,648.

Entry (k): Depreciation of Delivery Equipment, Account No. 8124, was debited and Accumulated Depreciation — Delivery Equipment, Account No. 221.1, was credited for $5,950.

Entry (l): Depreciation of Office Equipment, Account No. 8141, was debited and Accumulated Depreciation — Office Equipment, Account No. 231.1, was credited for $1,540.

Supplies Expense. The general ledger of Fishler & Marvon includes two asset accounts for supplies — Store Supplies and Office Supplies. When purchased, the supplies are recorded as assets by debiting the accounts, Store Supplies, Account No. 181, and Office Supplies, Account No. 182. An inventory of unused supplies is taken at the end of the year so that the cost of the supplies used can be calculated and charged to the proper operating expense accounts. The following schedule was prepared to determine the needed adjustments. Note that the amount shown for each type of supplies was determined by a count of the unopened packages and boxes, which were assigned approximate costs of recent purchases.

SCHEDULE OF SUPPLIES USED
For the Year Ended June 30, 19--

Asset	Account Balance June 30, 19--	Amount on Hand June 30, 19--	Expense For Year
Store Supplies	$7,478	$1,040	$6,438
Office Supplies	6,580	629	5,951

Based upon the calculation, the following adjustments were made on the work sheets:

Entry (m): Store Supplies Expense, Account No. 8121, was debited and Store Supplies, Account No. 181, was credited for $6,438.

Entry (n): Office Supplies Expense, Account No. 8137, was debited and Office Supplies, Account No. 182, was credited for $5,951.

Insurance Expense. Prepaid insurance premiums are recorded by Fishler & Marvon in the same manner as supplies. At the time of payment of a premium, the amount paid is recorded as an asset by debiting Prepaid Insurance, Account No. 186. At the end of the fiscal year, June 30, calculations are made to determine the fraction of the total term of each policy that elapsed during the year. Each amount thus determined is classified according to the type of asset insured and charged to the proper insurance expense account. The operating expenses ledger of Fishler & Marvon includes insurance expense accounts for the insurance on delivery equipment, store equipment, and office equipment.

The following schedule of insurance expense was prepared from a file of information relating to insurance policies.

SCHEDULE OF INSURANCE EXPENSE
For the Year Ended June 30, 19--

Type of Property Insured	Expense for Year
Delivery Equipment	$1,900
Store Equipment	960
Office Equipment	1,000
Total	$3,860

Based upon this schedule, the following adjustment was made on the work sheets:

Entry (o): Delivery Equipment Insurance Expense, Account No. 8118, was debited for $1,900; Store Equipment Insurance Expense, Account No. 8119, was debited for $960; Office Equipment Insurance Expense, Account No. 8139, was debited for $1,000; and Prepaid Insurance, Account No. 186, was credited for $3,860.

Doubtful Accounts. Fishler & Marvon uses the allowance method of accounting for doubtful accounts. On the basis of "aging" the accounts receivable, it was estimated that $200 of such accounts will not be collected. Since there already is a $50 balance in the allowance for doubtful accounts, $150 more is needed to make the required $200. The following entry was made on the work sheets:

Entry (p): Uncollectible Accounts Expense, Account No. 8136, was debited and Allowance for Doubtful Accounts, Account No. 131.1, was credited for $150.

COMPLETING THE OPERATING EXPENSES WORK SHEET

In order to complete this work sheet, the amount for each operating expense account was extended into the Adjusted Trial Balance column. Note that in every case, the extended amount was either the unadjusted amount or the amount of the adjustment. The Adjustments and Adjusted Trial Balance columns were then totaled. Since only debits were involved in this work sheet, the total of the Adjusted Trial Balance column, $196,964, had to be equal to the sum of the totals of the Trial Balance and Adjustments columns ($171,427 + $25,537). A double rule was made below the three totals.

COMPLETING THE SUMMARY WORK SHEET

To complete the adjustments on the summary work sheet, the balance of the control account, Operating Expenses, had to be increased to reflect the total of all of the debits to the operating expenses that had been made on the supplementary work sheet. Accordingly, that total, $25,537, was entered on the line for Operating Expenses, Account No. 811, in the Adjustments Debit column. Note that the debit was identified as "(j–p)," since it was offset by credits to seven general ledger accounts made when adjustments (j) through (p) were entered on the work sheets to adjust the operating expense accounts.

The Adjustments columns were totaled to prove the equality of the debits and credits. The amounts in the Trial Balance columns, adjusted where indicated by amounts in the Adjustments columns, were extended to the Adjusted Trial Balance columns. The latter also were totaled to prove the equality of the debits and credits. Each amount in the Adjusted Trial Balance columns was extended to the proper Income Statement or Balance Sheet column. The last four columns were then totaled.

Note that the Income Statement Credit column exceeded the Debit column by $21,953, and that the Balance Sheet Debit column exceeded the Credit column by the same amount. This means that Fishler & Marvon had a profitable year. "Net Income" was written on the next line at the left, and the amount, $21,953, was placed in the two proper places (debit Income Statement column and credit Balance Sheet column). The Income Statement and Balance Sheet columns were then totaled to prove that each pair was in balance. Double rules were made below the final totals in all ten columns.

The summary work sheet then can be used to prepare the income statement for the fiscal year (shown on page 531) and the balance sheet as of the last day of that year (shown on page 535). The supplementary work sheet provided the information for the schedule of operating expenses (shown on page 533).

BUILDING YOUR ACCOUNTING KNOWLEDGE

1. What three functions does a work sheet perform in processing data for the preparation of year-end (or other period-end) financial reports?

2. What was the first step in the preparation of the Fishler & Marvon summary work sheet?

3. Why was the Expense and Revenue Summary account omitted from the Fishler & Marvon work sheet when it was included in the Boyd's Clothiers work sheet?

4. What is the purpose of each of the cost of goods sold accounts maintained by Fishler & Marvon?

5. How many entries were made in the adjustments columns of the Fishler & Marvon summary work sheet to show the calculation of the cost of goods sold for each department and to adjust the departmental merchandise inventory accounts? Briefly explain the purpose of each of these adjustments.

6. What was the purpose of the only other adjustment made entirely in the summary work sheet?

7. What is the purpose of the supplementary work sheet for operating expenses? How many columns does it have and what is the purpose of each column?

8. How many entries were made both in the adjustments columns of the Fishler & Marvon summary work sheet and in the adjustments column of the supplementary operating expenses work sheet? Briefly explain the purpose of each of these adjustments.

Report No. 18-1

> *Complete Report No. 18-1 in the study assignments. Do not submit the report at this time. Since Reports Nos. 18-1 and 18-2 are related, you should retain the working papers until you have completed both reports. Continue with the textbook discussion until Report No. 18-2 is required.*

ADJUSTING, CLOSING, AND REVERSING ENTRIES

The most important function of the year-end work sheet is to facilitate the preparation of the income statement and the balance sheet as soon as possible after the end of the accounting period. Having completed the work sheets illustrated and discussed in the preceding pages, the accountant for Fishler & Marvon would next prepare the financial statements. A secondary function of the work sheets is to aid in the process of formally recording the adjusting and closing entries in the books. For the purpose of organization of subject matter in this textbook, adjusting, closing, and reversing entries will be considered next. The financial statements will be illustrated and discussed in Chapter 19.

JOURNALIZING THE ADJUSTING ENTRIES

Adjusting entries as of June 30 were recorded in the general journal reproduced on pages 520–521. The form of general journal used by Fishler & Marvon provided a special Detail column for charges to the accounts in the operating expenses subsidiary ledger. Journalizing the adjusting entries involved the use of this column as well as the Debit and Credit columns. Several features of these entries should be noted:

(1) The general ledger accounts are debited or credited in the conventional form; each subsidiary ledger account and its detail are also recorded. However, the account numbers were entered when the journalizing was done, *not* as a step in the posting.

(2) The entries were made in the same order as shown alphabetically (a) through (p), on the work sheets (pages 508–509, and 513). While this order is not essential, the danger of omitting an entry is slightly reduced by using the work sheets as a guide in journalizing the entries.

(3) To be sure that the total of the debits equaled the total of the credits, the Debit and Credit columns were footed. The Detail column was footed and found to agree with the total of the Adjustments Debit column on the operating expenses work sheet. Finally, the totals were entered, and the usual rulings were made.

POSTING THE ADJUSTING ENTRIES

As the individual amounts in the Debit and Credit columns were posted to the accounts (indicated by the account numbers), a check mark ($\sqrt{}$) was made to the right of each amount in the column provided. A check mark also was made in parentheses below the total of each of these two columns to indicate that the amount was *not* posted to any ledger. In the case of the entries in the Detail column, a check mark was placed to the right of each amount as it was posted. A check mark was also made in parentheses below the total

GENERAL JOURNAL PAGE 42

DATE	DESCRIPTION	ACCT. NO.	✓	DETAIL	✓	DEBIT	✓	CREDIT	✓	
19-- June 30	*Adjusting Entries*									1
	Cost of Goods Sold - Dept. A	751			✓	142800				2
	Merchandise Inventory - Dept. A	141					✓	142800	✓	3
	Cost of Goods Sold - Dept. B	761			✓	117500				4
	Merchandise Inventory - Dept. B	151					✓	117500	✓	5
	Cost of Goods Sold - Dept. A	751			✓	52398800				6
	Purchases - Dept. A	711					✓	52398800	✓	7
	Cost of Goods Sold - Dept. B	761			✓	38842000				8
	Purchases - Dept. B	721					✓	38842000	✓	9
	Purchases Returns & Allow. - Dept. A	711.1			✓	68200				10
	Cost of Goods Sold - Dept. A	751					✓	68200	✓	11
	Purchases Returns & Allow. - Dept. B	721.1			✓	38500				12
	Cost of Goods Sold - Dept. B	761					✓	38500	✓	13
	Merchandise Inventory - Dept. A	141			✓	140000				14
	Cost of Goods Sold - Dept. A	751					✓	140000	✓	15
	Merchandise Inventory - Dept. B	151			✓	125000				16
	Cost of Goods Sold - Dept. B	761					✓	125000	✓	17
	Accrued Interest Receivable	122			✓	4500				18
	Interest Earned	911					✓	4500	✓	19

Account Title	Acct. No.				
Operating Expenses	811		2553700 ✓		
Depreciation of Store Equipment	8123	164800 ✓			164800 ✓
Accumulated Depr.- Store Equip.	211.1				164800 ✓
Depreciation of Delivery Equipment	8124	595000 ✓			595000 ✓
Accumulated Depr.- Delivery Equip.	221.1				
Depreciation of Office Equipment	8141	154000 ✓			154000 ✓
Accumulated Depr.- Office Equip.	231.1				
Store Supplies Expense	8121	643800 ✓			643800 ✓
Store Supplies	181				
Office Supplies Expense	8137	595100 ✓			595100 ✓
Office Supplies	182				
Delivery Equipment Insurance Expense	8118	190000 ✓			
Store Equipment Insurance Expense	8119	96000 ✓			
Office Equipment Insurance Expense	8139	100000 ✓			
Prepaid Insurance	186				386000 ✓
Uncollectible Accounts Expense	8136	15000 ✓			
Allowance for Doubtful Accounts	131.1				15000 ✓
		2553700 (✓)	2553700 (✓)	9443000 (✓)	9443000 (✓)

Fishler & Marvon — Adjusting Entries

of that column to indicate that the amount was also *not* posted to any ledger. In both the general ledger and the operating expenses ledger, the page of the general journal (G42) was placed in the Posting Reference column as each posting was made.

JOURNALIZING THE CLOSING ENTRIES

The page of the general journal showing the closing entries as of June 30, 19––, is reproduced on page 523. Certain features of these entries should be noted:

(1) Each closing entry was made in conventional form — the names of the accounts to be debited or credited were given. The names of the accounts to be credited were slightly indented. As in the case of the adjusting entries, however, the numbers of the accounts were entered at the time of journalizing. The check marks were made later as the posting was completed.

(2) The order of the closing entries follows a logical sequence. The revenue accounts are closed first, followed by the expense accounts. The third entry closes the expense and revenue summary account by dividing the income ($21,953) between Fishler and Marvon in a 60-40 ratio as their partnership agreement specifies. The last two closing entries transfer the amount of each partner's withdrawals to the related capital account. The amount columns were footed to prove the equality of the debits and credits.

Note that, while there was a credit of $196,964 to close Operating Expenses, Account No. 811, the individual credits to close the twenty-five accounts in the operating expenses subsidiary ledger were not shown. One reason is that the form of the journal page does not accommodate credits to the operating expenses accounts, because these accounts rarely are credited (except when they are closed). The occasional transaction that requires a credit to an operating expense account can be handled by noting *both* the number of the control account (No. 811) and the number of the subsidiary ledger account in the account number column provided just to the left of the Detail column. The amount of the credit will then be posted as a credit to both accounts.

The operating expense accounts in the subsidiary ledger *must be closed* at the end of the fiscal year. The manner of doing so is illustrated by the reproduction of the account for Advertising Expense, Account No. 8111, shown on page 524. When a general ledger control account is closed, all accounts in a ledger that is subsidiary to that control account also must be closed. The space and time re-

GENERAL JOURNAL   PAGE 43

DATE	DESCRIPTION	ACCT. NO.	✓	DETAIL	✓	DEBIT	✓	CREDIT	
19-- June 30	Closing Entries								1
	Sales—Dept. A	611				612191 00	✓		2
	Sales—Dept. B	621				517490 00	✓		3
	Interest Earned	911				1125 00	✓		4
	Expense and Revenue Summary	531						1130806 00	✓	5
	Expense and Revenue Summary	531				1088533 00	✓		6
	Sales Returns & Allowances—Dept. A	611.1						3133 00	✓	7
	Sales Returns & Allowances—Dept. B	621.1						2820 00	✓	8
	Cost of Goods Sold—Dept. A	751						523334 00	✓	9
	Cost of Goods Sold—Dept. B	761						387960 00	✓	10
	Operating Expenses	811						196964 00	✓	11
	Expense and Revenue Summary	531				21953 00	✓		12
	Jane Fishler, Capital	511						13172 00	✓	13
	Joel Marvon, Capital	521						8781 00	✓	14
	Jane Fishler, Capital	511				8600 00	✓		15
	Jane Fishler, Drawing	511.1						8600 00	✓	16
	Joel Marvon, Capital	521				6500 00	✓		17
	Joel Marvon, Drawing	521.1						6500 00	✓	18
						2276712 00		2276712 00		19
						(✓)		(✓)	

Fishler & Marvon — Closing Entries

quired to list all of the subsidiary ledger accounts, numbers, and balances (twenty-five in the present case) can be saved if all subsidiary ledger expense accounts are closed at the same time that the operating expenses account is closed.

POSTING THE CLOSING ENTRIES

The postings were made to the general ledger accounts indicated. A check mark was placed in the column provided in the general journal as each posting was made. The page of the general journal (G43) was noted in the Posting Reference column of the account involved. As mentioned in the preceding paragraph, the balance of each account in the subsidiary operating expenses ledger was closed in the manner indicated by the entry on the last line of the illustration of the account for Advertising Expense shown below. (Note that "G43" was entered in the Posting Reference column, since that is the page of the general journal on which the closing entry for the operating expenses control account was made.) The other twenty-four operating expense accounts were closed in a similar fashion.

ACCOUNT *Advertising Expense*					ACCOUNT NO. 8111
DATE	ITEM	POST. REF.	DEBIT	CREDIT	BALANCE
19-- June 1	Dr. Balance	✓			2074 00
30		VR26	11 00		2085 00
30		G43		2085 00	-0-

Closed Subsidiary Operating Expense Ledger Account

The expense and revenue summary account and the two cost of goods sold accounts after the adjusting and closing entries had been posted are reproduced on page 525. Note that these accounts are summarizing accounts that are used only at the end of the accounting period. In some accounting systems, cost of goods sold accounts are used throughout the year if such cost is known at the time of sale. This is possible if perpetual inventories are maintained. In the periodic inventory method of Fishler & Marvon, the cost of goods sold accounts are used only at the end of the fiscal year.

ACCOUNT	Expense and Revenue Summary				ACCOUNT NO. 531	
DATE	ITEM	POST. REF.	DEBIT	CREDIT	BALANCE DEBIT	BALANCE CREDIT
19-- June 30		J43		113080600		
30		J43	110885300			2195300
30	To Close	J43	2195300		–0–	–0–

ACCOUNT	Cost of Goods Sold – Department A				ACCOUNT NO. 751	
DATE	ITEM	POST. REF.	DEBIT	CREDIT	BALANCE DEBIT	BALANCE CREDIT
19-- June 30	Beg. Inventory	J42	142800			
30	Purchases	J42	52398800			
30	Purchases R + A	J42		68200		
30	End. Inventory	J42		140000	52333400	
30	Exp. & Rev. Summary	J43		52333400	–0–	–0–

ACCOUNT	Cost of Goods Sold – Department B				ACCOUNT NO. 761	
DATE	ITEM	POST. REF.	DEBIT	CREDIT	BALANCE DEBIT	BALANCE CREDIT
19-- June 30	Beg. Inventory	J42	117500			
30	Purchases	J42	38842000			
30	Purchases R + A	J42		38500		
30	End. Inventory	J42		125000	38796000	
30	Exp. & Rev. Summary	J43		38796000	–0–	–0–

Closed General Ledger Summary Accounts

POST-CLOSING TRIAL BALANCE

After the closing entries were posted, a trial balance of the general ledger accounts that remained open was taken to prove the equality of the debit and credit balances. The post-closing trial balance of the general ledger of Fishler & Marvon is reproduced on page 526.

Some accountants feel that it is necessary to prepare a post-closing trial balance in the form illustrated and file it with various other records. Others think that it is sufficient merely to use an adding machine tape to list and total (1) the amounts of the debit balances and (2) the amounts of the credit balances to be sure that the totals are the same. In the latter case, if the ledger was found not to be in

Account	Acct. No.	Dr. Balance	Cr. Balance
Fishler & Marvon			
Post Closing Trial Balance			
June 30, 19 - -			
Federal National Bank	111	28 696 00	
Petty Cash Fund	112	150 00	
Government Notes	121	10 000 00	
Accrued Interest Receivable	122	45 00	
Accounts Receivable	131	9 148 00	
Allowance for Doubtful Accounts	131.1		200 00
Merchandise Inventory – Department A	141	1 400 00	
Merchandise Inventory – Department B	151	1 250 00	
Store Supplies	181	1 040 00	
Office Supplies	182	629 00	
Prepaid Insurance	186	750 00	
Store Equipment	211	1 648 00	
Accumulated Depreciation – Store Equip.	211.1		3 054 00
Delivery Equipment	221	47 600 00	
Accumulated Depreciation – Delivery Equip.	221.1		4 649 00
Office Equipment	231	1 586 00	
Accumulated Depreciation – Office Equip.	231.1		2 718 00
FICA Tax Payable	311		895 00
FUTA Tax Payable	312		41 00
State Unemployment Tax Payable	313		122 00
Employees Income Tax Payable	314		976 00
Vouchers Payable	317		28 645 00
Jane Fishler, Capital	511		38 394 00
Joel Marvon, Capital	521		16 354 00
		133 048 00	133 048 00

Fishler & Marvon — Post Closing Trial Balance

balance, the cause of the discrepancy would have to be located and remedied. Then the tapes would be discarded.

REVERSING ENTRIES

One adjusting entry of the accrual type, Accrued Interest Receivable, was made as of June 30 in the amount of $45. In order that interest collections may be recorded in routine fashion in the new period, Fishler & Marvon follows the practice of reversing accrual adjustments. The first entries for the new period are the reversals of the previous accrual adjustments. The reversing entry made on July 1, 19--, is shown below.

	DATE	DESCRIPTION	ACCT. NO.	DETAIL	√	DEBIT	√	CREDIT	
21	July 1	Reversing Entry							21
22		Interest Earned	911			4500 √			22
23		Accrued Interest Receivable	122					4500 √	23

Fishler & Marvon — Reversing Entry

BUILDING YOUR ACCOUNTING KNOWLEDGE

1. What is the purpose of the Detail column in Fishler & Marvon's general journal?
2. In what two ways are the accounts identified in entering the adjusting entries in the general journal?
3. Why are the Debit and Credit columns of the general journal footed? Why is the Detail column footed?
4. In what two ways are the accounts identified in entering the closing entries in the general journal?
5. What is the purpose of each of the five closing entries made by Fishler & Marvon?
6. How is the posting of the individual amounts in the adjusting and closing entries indicated in the general journal? In the general and operating expenses ledgers?
7. What is the purpose of the post-closing trial balance? What do some accountants use as a substitute?
8. Why does the accountant for Fishler & Marvon reverse accrual adjustments?

Report No. 18-2

> *Complete Report No. 18-2 in the study assignments and submit Reports Nos. 18-1 and 18-2 for approval. Continue with the textbook discussion in Chapter 19 until Report No. 19-1 is required.*

EXPANDING YOUR BUSINESS VOCABULARY

What is the meaning of each of the following terms:

adjusting entries (p. 519)

closing entries (p. 522)

post-closing trial balance (p. 525)

reversing entries (p. 526)

summary year-end work sheet (p. 507)

supplementary work sheet for operating expenses (p. 512)

CHAPTER 19

THE ANNUAL REPORT

CHAPTER OBJECTIVES

The objectives of this chapter are to enable you:

▶ To describe and explain the nature of an annual report.

▶ To prepare a summarized income statement that shows the components and amounts of gross margin on sales by departments and in total, supplemented by schedules of cost of goods sold and of operating expenses.

▶ To analyze the income statement using percentage analysis, merchandise turnover analysis, and comparative analysis.

▶ To prepare a balance sheet for a partnership supplemented by a schedule of accounts receivable.

▶ To analyze the balance sheet using ratio analysis and comparative analysis.

▶ To perform an analysis of profitability of a business.

▶ To describe and prepare a statement of changes in financial position, including a supporting schedule of changes in working capital.

The term annual report as applied to a business usually refers to the financial statements and schedules relating to the accounting (fiscal) year of the enterprise. The report generally includes an income statement, a balance sheet, and a statement of changes in financial position. In business corporations with many stockholders (thousands, even hundreds of thousands, in some cases), the annual report may be a thirty- to sixty-page printed publication — sometimes in full color with numerous pictures of the company's products, plants, officers, and various graphs and statistics in addition to the financial statements. Reports of this type usually include a letter addressed to the stockholders signed by the president of the corporation or by the chairman of the board of directors and sometimes by both. The letter is printed in the report booklet and is often described as "highlights" of the year. Such annual reports invariably include a reproduction of the opinion (sometimes referred to as the Auditor's Report) of the CPA firm that performed the audit of the company's financial statements.

Annual reports of the elaborate type just mentioned are not used if the business has few owners. In a partnership, it is probable that only the partners and, possibly, one or two of the officials at their bank see the reports. The annual report of Fishler & Marvon consists of the following statements and schedules:

> Income Statement for the Year
> > Schedule of Cost of Goods Sold
> > Schedule of Operating Expenses
>
> Balance Sheet as of June 30
> > Schedule of Accounts Receivable
>
> Statement of Changes in Financial Position for the Year
> > Schedule of Changes in Working Capital

THE INCOME STATEMENT

The income statement and schedule of cost of goods sold for the year ended June 30, 19--, for Fishler & Marvon are reproduced on page 531. They were prepared from information provided by the Income Statement columns of the work sheet reproduced on pages 508 and 509. The income statement is arranged to show the sales, cost of goods sold, and the gross margin on sales for each department as well as in total. The schedule of cost of goods sold shows the components that made up the cost of goods sold for each department and the total.

The schedule of operating expenses reproduced on page 533 was prepared from information provided by the operating expenses work sheet shown on page 513. The schedule provides the detail of what makes up the total amount of operating expenses ($196,964) shown on the income statement. If there were only five or ten accounts for operating expenses, it is probable that (1) there would have been no subsidiary ledger for such expenses and (2) the accounts would have been included in the income statement, in which case no schedule would have been needed. There is wide variation in the form and content of financial statements. Some accountants, for example, may present the components of cost of goods sold in the income statement instead of in the "supporting" schedule as illustrated below.

FISHLER & MARVON
Income Statement
For the Year Ended June 30, 19--

	Dept. A	Dept. B	Total
Sales...	$612,191	$517,490	$1,129,681
Less sales returns and allowances........	313	282	595
Net sales	$611,878	$517,208	$1,129,086
Cost of goods sold....................................	523,334	387,960	911,294
Gross margin on sales............................	$ 88,544	$129,248	$ 217,792
Operating expenses.................................			196,964
Operating income................................			$ 20,828
Other revenue:			
Interest earned.....................................			1,125
Net income			$ 21,953

Fishler & Marvon — Income Statement

FISHLER & MARVON
Schedule of Cost of Goods Sold
For the Year Ended June 30, 19--

	Dept. A	Dept. B	Total
Merchandise inventory, July 1, 19--.........................	$ 1,428	$ 1,175	$ 2,603
Purchases	$523,988	$388,420	$912,408
Less purchases returns and allowances...................	682	385	1,067
Net purchases..	$523,306	$388,035	$911,341
Merchandise available for sale	$524,734	$389,210	$913,944
Less merchandise inventory, June 30, 19--..............	1,400	1,250	2,650
Cost of goods sold...	$523,334	$387,960	$911,294

Fishler & Marvon — Schedule of Cost of Goods Sold

INTERPRETING THE INCOME STATEMENT

There are numerous ways to analyze an income statement. Three types of analysis will be dealt with in this chapter: (1) percentage analysis, (2) merchandise turnover, and (3) comparative analysis.

Percentage Analysis. In order of importance, the most significant items shown by the annual income statement are the total amounts of (1) net income, (2) sales, (3) cost of goods sold and gross margin (considered together because of the interrelationship), and (4) operating expenses. The dollar amounts of these items take on added meaning if their proportionate relationship to each other is computed and compared. Using Fishler & Marvon's income statement as an example, the customary way of studying these relationships is by percentage analysis, using net sales as the base, 100 percent.

Net sales	$1,129,086	100 %
Cost of goods sold	911,294	80.7
Gross margin	$ 217,792	19.3%
Operating expenses	196,964	17.4
Operating income	$ 20,828	1.9%
Other revenue	1,125	——
Net income	$ 21,953	1.9%

When the relatively minor amount of other revenue is considered, net income is slightly less than 2 percent of net sales. In other words, each dollar of net sales resulted in about two cents of net profit.

Fishler & Marvon may then compare these percentages with the same percentages for other similar wholesale/retail bakery businesses, or with their own percentages of operating results for prior years, to determine the relative profitability of their bakery operation.

The same type of analysis can be applied to the data for the net sales, cost of goods sold, and gross margin of each department, as shown below.

	Dept. A		Dept. B	
Net sales	$611,878	100 %	$517,208	100%
Cost of goods sold	523,334	85.5	387,960	75
Gross margin	$ 88,544	14.5%	$129,248	25%

Fishler & Marvon might find this analysis useful in the determination of the relative emphasis to place on the output of each department, the possible expansion or contraction of either department, or the need for a review of the pricing policies in either department.

Merchandise Turnover. The data reported in the income statement and in the schedule of cost of goods sold make it possible to compute the merchandise turnover during the year. For the business

FISHLER & MARVON
Schedule of Operating Expenses
For the Year Ended June 30, 19--

Selling expenses:

Advertising expense	$ 2,085
Store clerks wage expense	20,348
Truck drivers wage expense	21,980
Joel Marvon, salary expense	24,000
Truck, gas, and oil expense	5,190
Truck repairs and maintenance expense	580
Store rent expense	14,400
Delivery equipment insurance expense	1,900
Store equipment insurance expense	960
Store supplies expense	6,438
Depreciation of store equipment	1,648
Depreciation of delivery equipment	5,950
Miscellaneous selling expense	295
Total selling expenses	$105,774

Administrative expenses:

Office rent expense	$ 9,600
Office salaries expense	34,660
Jane Fishler, salary expense	24,000
Heat, light, and water expense	4,645
Telephone expense	1,034
Uncollectible accounts expense	150
Office supplies expense	5,951
Postage expense	546
Office equipment insurance expense	1,000
Depreciation of office equipment	1,540
Payroll taxes expense	7,293
Miscellaneous general expense	771
Total administrative expenses	$ 91,190
Total operating expenses	$196,964

Fishler & Maryon — Schedule of Operating Expenses

as a whole, the average inventory was $2,626.50 ($2,603 beginning inventory plus $2,650 ending inventory, divided by two). Since the total cost of goods sold was $911,294, the turnover was almost 347 times ($911,294 ÷ $2,626.50). This means that, on the average, goods remained in stock for about a day, an obviously desirable condition for a bakery. Using the same calculation for each department reveals that the turnover in Department A was 370.1, and in Department B, 320.0. The turnover ratio can help Fishler & Marvon determine whether they are carrying significant amounts of slow-moving bakery products. Based on the departmental turnover ratios, Fishler & Marvon might want to examine in detail the turnover of selected products carried in Department B.

Comparative Analysis. Added meaning is given to the information supplied by an income statement if it is compared with statements for past periods. By using such comparative analysis, answers will be provided to such vital questions as: Are sales growing or shrinking? How much has net income increased or decreased (both absolutely and relatively)? Has the gross margin percentage become larger or smaller? It may be assumed that the first thing each partner did after looking at the income statement for the year just ended was to compare it with the statement for the preceding year — probably for several preceding years. Often, income statements and other financial statements are prepared in comparative form to aid in their interpretation.

BUILDING YOUR ACCOUNTING KNOWLEDGE

1. What three financial statements generally are included in the annual report of a business?
2. Who are likely to be the only users of the annual report of a partnership?
3. What three major items are shown for each department and in total on the Fishler & Marvon income statement?
4. What is the source of the information contained in the schedule of operating expenses?
5. What is the customary way of relating cost of goods sold, gross margin, operating expenses, and net income to net sales using percentage analysis? What use is made of such analysis?
6. How is the merchandise turnover for the year computed? What use is made of the turnover ratio?
7. How is the technique of comparative analysis applied to the information supplied by an income statement? What vital questions does comparative analysis help to answer?
8. What are the two major categories of expenses shown on the schedule of operating expenses of Fishler & Marvon?

Report No. 19-1

> *Complete Report No. 19-1 in the study assignments. Do not submit the report at this time. Since Reports 19-1, 19-2, and 19-3 are related, you should retain the working papers until you have completed all three reports. Continue with the textbook discussion until Report No. 19-2 is required.*

THE BALANCE SHEET

The balance sheet of Fishler & Marvon as of June 30, 19--, arranged in report form, is reproduced on page 535. It was prepared

FISHLER & MARVON
Balance Sheet
June 30, 19--

Assets

Current assets:

Cash..		$28,846
Government notes...........................		10,000
Accrued interest receivable............		45
Accounts receivable........................	$ 9,148	
Less allowance for doubtful accounts...	200	8,948

Merchandise inventories:

Department A................................	$ 1,400	
Department B................................	1,250	2,650
Supplies and prepayments.............		2,419
Total current assets.....................		$52,908

Long-term assets:

	Cost	Accum. Depr.	Undepr. Cost	
Store equipment..............................	$16,480	$ 3,054	$13,426	
Delivery equipment..........................	47,600	41,649	5,951	
Office equipment.............................	15,860	2,718	13,142	
Total long-term assets.................	$79,940	$47,421		32,519
Total assets..				$85,427

Liabilities

Current liabilities:

Accounts payable............................		$28,645
Accrued and withheld payroll taxes...		2,034
Total current liabilities.................		$30,679

Owners' Equity

	Jane Fishler	Joel Marvon	
Capital, July 1, 19--............................	$33,822	$14,073	
Net income ($21,953, divided 60% – 40%)..	13,172	8,781	
Less withdrawals.............................	(8,600)	(6,500)	
Capital, June 30, 19--	$38,394	$16,354	54,748
Total liabilities and owners' equity....			$85,427

Fishler & Marvon — Balance Sheet

from information provided by the Balance Sheet columns of the work sheet reproduced on pages 508 and 509. Note that the current assets were presented first and arrayed in their probable order of liquidity. Cash was shown first followed by government notes. These notes are regarded as temporary investments since they can be liquidated with relative ease if a shortage of cash should occur.

Accrued interest receivable, accounts receivable (less the allowance for doubtful accounts) and merchandise inventories were shown next, and lastly supplies and prepayments. These latter items are included as current assets because their present ownership means that less money will have to be spent for such purposes in the near future. It is not expected that these items will be directly converted into cash. Long-term assets of Fishler & Marvon are the last assets listed. They are shown in columnar form, an approach not previously illustrated, for the purpose of condensing the report.

All of the liabilities of the firm are current liabilities. The owners' equity section is arranged to show the nature and amount of the change in each partner's equity during the year.

The balance sheet is supported by a schedule of accounts receivable as of June 30, 19--. This schedule is just a list of the subsidiary accounts receivable ledger accounts as of the close of the year. It is not an integral part of the balance sheet.

FISHLER & MARVON
Schedule of Accounts Receivable
June 30, 19--

Ayres Department Stores	$1,596
Bakemeier's Bakery	1,342
Brother Juniper's	1,016
Heritage House	1,065
Houlihan's Place	958
Methodist Hospital	1,078
Sam's Deli	1,041
The Tin Star	1,052
	$9,148

Fishler & Marvon — Schedule of Accounts Receivable

INTERPRETING THE BALANCE SHEET

In interpreting the balance sheet, it is important to remember that the amounts of certain assets as shown on a conventional balance sheet do not necessarily reflect their current values. For example, even though most of Fishler & Marvon's inventory is sold each day, there may be unsalable items in the inventory that remain on hand for another day or more. Also, the **undepreciated cost** of the long-term assets (the difference between the original cost of these assets and the depreciation so far charged off as expense) does not indicate what these assets would bring if they were to be sold nor does it indicate what it would cost to buy these assets. The difference ($32,519 in total) merely represents the amount, less any expected scrap or salvage value, that is to be charged against future revenues. With these considerations in mind, there are ways to analyze the balance sheet. Two commonly used types of analysis are discussed below: (1) ratio analysis and (2) comparative analysis.

Ratio Analysis. One use of the balance sheet is to aid in judging the liquidity of a business, that is, the ability of the enterprise to meet its current debt obligations. Besides the relative amounts of current assets and current liabilities, the composition of these resources and obligations must also be considered in judging liquidity. Two commonly used measures of liquidity are the current ratio and the quick ratio. The ratio of the current assets ($52,908) to current liabilities ($30,679) of Fishler & Marvon is 1.7 to 1. This is adequate, but of equal or greater significance is the fact that the "quick" assets (cash, temporary investments, and current receivables) total $47,839 — 1.56 times the current liabilities. This indicates that the firm more than passes the acid test (a ratio of quick assets to total current liabilities of at least 1 to 1).

Comparative Analysis. As in the case of income statements, a comparison of current and past balance sheets may be informative. Comparative balance sheets are often presented in stockholders' reports. In some cases, an analysis that involves expressing one amount as a percent of another may be helpful. In other cases, comparisons of ratios may be more meaningful.

This type of analysis can be illustrated by using the comparative balance sheet summary of Fishler & Marvon on page 544. Note that the current ratio has improved from 1.2 to 1 ($36,588 ÷ $29,890) to 1.7 to 1 ($52,908 ÷ $30,679) from the beginning to the end of the year. In addition, current assets amounted to 62% of total assets at the end of the year, compared with only 47% at the beginning of the year.

These ratios and percentages indicate that Fishler & Marvon have strengthened their financial control of the business during the year. The percentages also suggest that Fishler & Marvon probably could afford to increase their investment in long-term assets.

ANALYSIS OF PROFITABILITY

Analysis of profitability involves the use of both income statement and balance sheet data. The amount of annual net income does not mean too much by itself. However, when this amount is contrasted with the volume of sales, the average total amount of the assets, or the average total of the owners' equity element of the business, a better indication of profitability is provided. It was noted on page 532 that Fishler & Marvon had net income equal to almost 2 percent of net sales. The relationship between Fishler & Marvon's net income and their assets and owners' equity will now be considered.

According to the comparative balance sheet summary on page 544, Fishler & Marvon had average total assets for the fiscal year of $81,606 [($77,785 + $85,427) ÷ 2]. The ratio of net income to average total assets, which is known as **return on assets**, was therefore almost 27 percent (net income of $21,953 ÷ average total assets of $81,606).

Fishler & Marvon's average total owners' equity for the fiscal year was $51,322 [($47,895 + $54,748) ÷ 2]. The ratio of net income to average owners' equity, which is known as **return on equity**, was therefore nearly 43 percent (net income of $21,953 ÷ average owners' equity of $51,322).

Both the return on assets and the return on equity of Fishler & Marvon appear to be very favorable. In judging these relationships, however, it must be remembered that no income tax has been taken into consideration, since partnerships, as such, do not pay income taxes. In their individual income tax returns, Fishler & Marvon must include their shares of the partnership net income along with any "salary" payments or allowances. The amount of any cash or other assets received from the firm is not relevant to the calculation of each partner's taxable income. The amount of income tax that each partner must pay depends upon the total amount of income from various sources, the amount of various deductions that may be taken, and the number of exemptions to which the partner is entitled.

BUILDING YOUR ACCOUNTING KNOWLEDGE

1. In what order are the current assets arrayed on the balance sheet of Fishler & Marvon?
2. Why are supplies and prepayments included among the current assets?
3. What group of assets is listed after the current assets?
4. What is the owner's equity section of the balance sheet arranged to show?
5. Give two examples of balance sheet assets that do not necessarily reflect their current values.
6. What are the current ratio and the quick ratio used to judge or measure?
7. What are the percentage of net income to sales, the return on assets, and the return on owner's equity, used to measure?

Report No. 19-2

> *Complete Report No. 19-2 in the study assignments. Do not submit the report at this time. Since Reports 19-1, 19-2, and 19-3 are related, you should retain the working papers until you have completed all three reports. Continue with the textbook discussion until Report No. 19-3 is required.*

THE STATEMENT OF CHANGES IN FINANCIAL POSITION

The annual report of Fishler & Marvon includes a statement of changes in financial position for the year. Since this type of statement has not been discussed or illustrated in earlier chapters, its nature and purpose will be explained before the one for Fishler & Marvon is considered.

NATURE AND PURPOSE OF THE STATEMENT

The managers of a business have the dual objective of generating net income (profitability) and of keeping the enterprise solvent (liquidity). It would seem that success in achievement of the first objective would automatically assure achievement of the second objective. Net income brings in cash — either at once, or as soon as receivables are collected. To assure solvency or liquidity is not that simple, however, The cash inflow resulting from profitable operations may be used to acquire long-term assets, to discharge long-term indebtedness, or it may be withdrawn by the owners. Many profitable and growing businesses suffer from a continual shortage of working capital (current assets minus current liabilities). Sometimes the reverse is the case. There may be little or no net income, and yet by occasional sales of long-term assets, by borrowing on a long-term basis, or by additional investments by the owners, the business maintains ample working capital. The increase or decrease in working capital is the result of the interplay of various management actions and outside influences.

In analyzing the affairs of a business, it is helpful to know the reasons for an increase or a decrease in working capital during the period under review. To provide this information, a special type of financial statement that explains the change in working capital has been developed. The preferred title for this financial statement is the statement of changes in financial position. However, it is sometimes called the fund-change statement, the statement of sources and appli-cations of funds, or the statement of changes in working capital.

In ordinary usage, "funds" often is used as a synonym for cash. The term "fund" is used to describe cash or other assets set aside for a specified purpose such as a petty cash fund. In government finance and accounting, a fund is a segregated collection of cash and other assets (and, sometimes, related liabilities) held or used for a certain purpose, such as a highway construction fund. In connection with the Statement of Changes in Financial Position, the word "funds" generally means working capital. A statement of changes in financial position is a statement explaining the increase or decrease in the working capital of a business during a specified period of time.

An alternative approach used by a minority of companies is to express the changes in financial position in terms of cash. Some ac-countants argue that a statement of sources and applications of cash can better explain what is happening to the business. For certain purposes, periodic statements of cash receipts and disbursements are needed. However, in judging the current position and the changes that have occurred, it can be very misleading to look only at what has happened to cash. To illustrate, consider the following comparative statement of the current assets and current liabilities of a business at the beginning and end of a year:

	Beginning of Year	End of Year
Current Assets		
Cash	$ 20,000	$100,000
Temporary investments	40,000	10,000
Receivables (net)	80,000	60,000
Inventories and prepayments	60,000	70,000
Total	$200,000	$240,000
Current Liabilities		
Notes, accounts, and taxes payable	50,000	160,000
Working capital	$150,000	$ 80,000

Cash increased 400 percent but the current position of the com-pany deteriorated seriously. The current ratio changed from 4 to 1 ($200,000:$50,000) to only 1.5 to 1 ($240,000:$160,000), and the quick (acid-test) ratio from 2.8 to 1 ($140,000:$50,000) to 1.06 to 1 ($170,000:$160,000). In analyzing what has happened in the busi-ness, the $70,000 decrease in working capital is of far more concern than the increase in cash of $80,000. A statement of changes in fi-nancial position based on working capital is much more informative than a statement based on cash receipts and disbursements. For this reason, the statement of changes in financial position expressed in terms of working capital is the dominant practice today. The working capital approach is explained and illustrated in this chapter.

SOURCES OF FUNDS

Funds may be secured or obtained in four ways:

Investments by Owners. When the owners invest cash or other current assets in the business, working capital is increased.

Profitable Operations. When there has been net income for an accounting period, the increase in cash and receivables due to sales and other revenue must have been more than the total of the decrease in inventory (because of goods sold) and either the decrease in cash or the increase in current payables that took place when expenses were incurred. (The special problem of depreciation and a few other expenses that do not reduce working capital when incurred will be discussed at a later point.)

Long-Term Borrowing. When money is borrowed and the promised date of repayment is two or more years in the future, working capital is increased as a result of a current asset increasing and a long-term liability increasing. (Short-term borrowing does not affect working capital because the increase in cash is exactly offset by the increase in a current liability — usually notes payable.)

Sale of Long-Term Assets. When long-term assets, such as land, buildings, equipment, or trucks are sold, usually either cash or current receivables is increased. In either case, working capital is increased.

APPLICATIONS OF FUNDS

Funds may be applied or used in four ways:

Withdrawals of Owners. When the owners of a business take money out either because there has been a profit, or as a withdrawal of their capital investment, working capital is reduced. In corporations, the payment of cash dividends is an example of this type of application of funds.

Unprofitable Operations. Working capital is reduced if the decrease in inventory (because of goods sold) and either the decrease in cash or the increase in current payables that took place when expenses were incurred must have been more than the increase in cash and receivables due to sales and other revenue.

Repayment of Long-Term Borrowing. When long-term liabilities, such as mortgages payable, are paid, cash and thus working capital are reduced. The discharge of short-term obligations does not affect working capital because the decrease in cash is offset by an equal decrease in a current liability.

Purchase of Long-Term Assets. When a long-term asset (land, building, equipment, etc.) is purchased, either cash is reduced or accounts payable is increased. In either case, working capital is diminished.

SIMPLIFIED EXAMPLE OF STATEMENT OF CHANGES IN FINANCIAL POSITION

The statement of changes in financial position is prepared from information supplied by the balance sheets at the beginning and end of the accounting period involved, plus certain other data found in the income statement. To illustrate, the balance sheets of Weisberg & Woodward at the beginning and end of the year 19–– are shown below.

	Beginning of Year	End of Year
Assets		
Cash	$ 60,000	$ 80,000
Receivables	180,000	160,000
Inventory	200,000	180,000
Total current assets	$440,000	$420,000
Land	40,000	40,000
Building and equipment		220,000
	$480,000	$680,000
Liabilities and Owners' Equity		
Notes payable	$ 40,000	$ 60,000
Accounts payable	180,000	120,000
Total current liabilities	$220,000	$180,000
Mortgage payable		120,000
Weisberg, capital	140,000	200,000
Woodward, capital	120,000	180,000
	$480,000	$680,000

During the year, Weisberg and Woodward each invested an additional $20,000 and there were no withdrawals. The net income for the year was $80,000.

The amount of working capital at the start of the year was $220,000 ($440,000 − $220,000). At the end of the year, the amount of working capital was $240,000 ($420,000 − $180,000). The change, then, was an increase of $20,000. The objective of the statement of changes in financial position is to explain how this happened.

Comparison of the two balance sheets reveals that building and equipment increased from zero to $220,000. A building was constructed during the year and completed just before the year ended. At that time the equipment also was purchased. Acquisition of these assets was a $220,000 application of funds. Mortgage payable increased from zero to $120,000 — a source of funds. (The money was borrowed on a long-term basis by giving a note secured by a mortgage on the land and building.) The owners' equity in the business increased from $260,000 ($140,000 + $120,000) to $380,000 ($200,000 + $180,000). This $120,000 increase in funds came from two sources: (1) the net income for the year, $80,000, and (2) the partners' additional investment of $40,000 in total. These findings can be classified to produce the statement shown below.

WEISBERG & WOODWARD
Statement of Changes in Financial Position
For the Year Ended December 31, 19––

Sources of funds:		
Net income for the year..	$ 80,000	
Investment by partners...	40,000	
Long-term borrowing...	120,000	$240,000
Application of funds:		
Purchase of building and equipment		220,000
Increase in working capital		$ 20,000

Weisberg & Woodward — Statement of Changes in Financial Position

ASSEMBLING THE DATA FOR STATEMENT OF CHANGES IN FINANCIAL POSITION

There are various techniques for assembling and organizing data to produce a statement of changes in financial position. If the calculations are likely to be complicated, it may be advisable to use a special work sheet, otherwise the use of a work sheet is not warranted. The first step is to summarize, in comparative form, the balance sheets at the beginning and end of the period. Fishler & Marvon used the balance sheet at the close of the preceding year (not reproduced in this textbook) and the balance sheet at the close of the year just ended (reproduced on page 535). The statements were summarized and the changes in each element were noted, as follows:

	Beginning of Year	End of Year	Increase (Decrease)
Cash	$25,502	$28,846	$ 3,344
Government notes		10,000	10,000
Receivables (net)	6,456	8,993	2,537
Merchandise inventories	2,603	2,650	47
Supplies and prepayments	2,027	2,419	392
Total current assets	$36,588	$52,908	$16,320
Long-term assets (less accumulated depreciation)	41,197	32,519	(8,678)
Total assets	$77,785	$85,427	$ 7,642
Notes and interest payable	$ 2,643	—0—	$ (2,643)
Accounts payable	25,219	$28,645	3,426
Accrued and withheld payroll taxes	2,028	2,034	6
Total current liabilities	$29,890	$30,679	$ 789
Owners' equity	47,895	54,748	6,853
Total liabilities and owners' equity	$77,785	$85,427	$ 7,642

The foregoing summary shows that working capital increased $15,531 (current assets increased $16,320 while current liabilities increased only $789). The purpose of the statement of changes in financial position is to explain this increase. Note that cash only increased $3,344. This was overshadowed by the increase in temporary investments, coupled with the increase in net receivables and the modest increase in the current liabilities. It was mentioned earlier that the change in the amount of cash is not as significant as the change in working capital, especially when surplus cash is temporarily invested in high-return, relatively liquid securities.

The list of sources and applications of funds was enumerated on pages 541 and 542. The possible sources are: (1) investment by owners, (2) profitable operations, (3) long-term borrowing, and (4) sales of long-term assets. Fishler and Marvon made no investments during the year; there was no long-term borrowing or sale of long-term assets; hence, the only source of funds for the year under review was profitable operations.

The possible applications of funds are: (1) withdrawals by owners, (2) unprofitable operations, (3) repayment of long-term borrowing, and (4) purchase of long-term assets. Items (2) and (3) do not apply since the year had been profitable and there were no long-term debts to repay during the year. Since both partners made withdrawals during the year and a piece of equipment had been purchased, items (1) and (4) are to be considered as applications of funds.

The sources of funds and applications of funds for the Fishler & Marvon business will be explained in the following sections.

SOURCES OF FUNDS: OPERATIONS

The income statement of Fishler & Marvon for the year ended June 30, 19--, revealed a net income of $21,953. This amount represented a source of working capital for the business, which can be explained as follows. There were two types of revenue: sales and interest earned. In both cases, either cash was collected or a current receivable (accounts receivable or accrued interest receivable) was increased, and accordingly, working capital was increased. Almost all expenses that were incurred caused working capital to be reduced. Cost of goods sold reduced the merchandise inventory — an important current asset. Prepaid Insurance, a current asset, was reduced by an amount equal to the cost of the insurance that expired during the period. The allowance for doubtful accounts was, in effect, a reduction of current receivables. Most of the expenses incurred caused either an immediate reduction in cash or an increase in a current payable of some sort. If the current assets are reduced or the current liabilities are increased, working capital is reduced.

The single exception to the foregoing analysis of the effect of expenses upon working capital is depreciation expense. When the depreciation of the three types of long-term assets was recorded (refer to adjustments (j), (k), and (l) in the work sheets on pages 508 and 509), the offset to the depreciation expense debit was a credit to the proper accumulated depreciation account. Accumulated depreciation represents the total amount of asset cost charged to operations. An addition to accumulated depreciation is a reduction in the undepreciated cost of the long-term asset — not a reduction in a current asset.

The total amount of Fishler & Marvon's depreciation expense for the year was $9,138 ($1,648 + $5,950 + $1,540). Since this expense did not reduce working capital (funds), for purposes of the statement of changes in financial position, the amount of the net income for the year, $21,953, was increased by the amount of the depreciation expense for the year and reported as follows:

Funds provided by current operations:
Net income (per income statement) $21,953
Add expenses not requiring funds:
Depreciation 9,138
Total funds provided by current operations $31,091

Another method of showing "funds provided by current operations" would be to deduct expenses that reduced working capital from total revenue that increased working capital (sales and interest earned). The difference would be $31,091, the same amount as shown on page 545. Depreciation expense is not mentioned in the statement if this method is used. In the Fishler & Marvon statement, the operating expenses excluding depreciation would total $187,826, and funds provided by current operations would be shown as follows:

Funds provided by current operations:		
Net sales	$1,129,086	
Other revenue	1,125	$1,130,211
Less expenses that reduced working capital:		
Cost of goods sold	$ 911,294	
Operating expense (excluding $9,138 of depreciation expense)	187,826	1,099,120
Funds provided by current operations		$ 31,091

The above method is not commonly followed because it is considered desirable to have the statement of changes in financial position start with the amount shown as the net income in the income statement. This treatment serves to tie the financial statements together in a more professional manner.

A great deal of misunderstanding has arisen about depreciation in the statement of changes in financial position. The idea that "depreciation is a source of funds" is entirely incorrect. Depreciation, while difficult to measure on a periodic basis, is a very real expense. It differs from other expenses only in that most expenses reduce working capital, while depreciation expense is a reduction in certain long-term assets. With most other expenses, the disbursement of cash and recognition of the expense are closely related — money is disbursed in the same period that the expense is incurred. In a few cases, money was spent in the preceding period, such as payments for inventory and supplies that were not sold or used until the next period; and in some cases, money will not be disbursed until the next period, such as employer's payroll taxes that relate to one year but are not paid until the next year. Depreciation is considered an expense because cash was disbursed when the assets that are being depreciated were bought. Depreciation is too often misunderstood because the point in time that the money was spent for the depreciable asset and the point in time when the outlay becomes an expense may be far apart.

Another argument that may be used to show that depreciation is not a source of funds is as follows: Suppose that depreciation expense had been overlooked in calculating the net income for a period. Would the funds provided by current operations be any less? The answer clearly is "no." If Fishler & Marvon had failed to record the depreciation expense totalling $9,138, the net income for the year would have been incorrectly calculated to be $31,091. In the statement of changes in financial position, that amount would be shown as funds provided by current operations, just as when the net income calculation includes the depreciation expense.

There are some other expenses that have the same characteristics as depreciation. These expenses arise whenever an asset is purchased and gradually written off as an expense over a number of succeeding years. A good example is a patent. Patents have a legal life of 17 years. A company may have purchased a patent soon after it was issued. The management of the acquiring company may not think that the patent will be valuable for 16 to 17 years, but may expect that ownership of the patent will be of benefit, perhaps, for 10 years. Accordingly, one tenth of the cost may be charged to an expense for each of the ten years, which is described as amortizing the cost. The portion written off each year is described as **amortization expense**. A patent is classified as a long-term asset. As portions of its cost are taken into expense, no decrease in working capital is involved. Accordingly, amortization expense, like depreciation expense, must be "added back" to determine the amount of funds provided by current operations.

Occasions may arise when the net income figure must be further modified to arrive at funds provided by current operations. If, for example, a piece of land that cost $15,000 some years before was sold for $18,000 and the $3,000 profit was reported in the income statement, that amount, $3,000, would have to be excluded from funds provided by current operations. Unless the business was engaged in buying and selling land, such a transaction would not be considered a part of regular operations. The $18,000 received from the sale of the land would be reported separately as a source of funds from the sale of long-term assets in the statement of changes in financial position.

Current operations were the only source of funds for Fishler & Marvon during the year ended June 30, 19--. The two types of applications of funds during that year will be considered next.

APPLICATION OF FUNDS: OWNERS' WITHDRAWALS

The owners' equity section of the balance sheet for the year ended June 30, 19--, shown on page 535 indicates that during the year, Fishler withdrew $8,600 and Marvon, $6,500. These amounts are shown in the application section of the statement of changes in financial position.

APPLICATION OF FUNDS: PURCHASE OF LONG-TERM ASSETS

The analysis of the changes in the balance sheets of Fishler & Marvon, shown on page 544, shows a decrease in the total undepreciated cost (cost less accumulated depreciation) of the long-term assets in the amount of $8,678. There was a decrease in the total undepreciated cost amounting to $9,138 caused by depreciation expense for the year. This amount of depreciation, $9,138, was taken into consideration in preparing the income statement. If the decrease in undepreciated cost due to depreciation for the year was $9,138, but the total decrease was only $8,678, there must have been an application of funds in the amount of $460 ($9,138 − $8,678) to purchase some new long-term assets. An examination of the long-term asset accounts revealed that on June 18, an electronic desk calculator was purchased at a cost of $460. Since the bill had been paid, the decrease in cash reduced working capital; hence the purchase of office equipment is an application of funds for the year. This acquisition was so reported in the statement of changes in financial position.

STATEMENT OF CHANGES IN FINANCIAL POSITION WITH SUPPORTING SCHEDULE OF CHANGES IN WORKING CAPITAL

The annual report of Fishler & Marvon includes a statement of changes in financial position with a supporting schedule of changes in working capital. These are reproduced on page 549. The statement of changes in financial position explains the net change in working capital that occurred between the start and the close of the fiscal year. The supporting schedule shows the amounts of the changes in the elements that comprise working capital (current assets and current liabilities). The balance sheets as of the beginning and end of the year provided the data for the schedule. Such a schedule is customarily provided when the working capital approach is used in preparing the statement of changes in financial position. It is important to note that the increase in working capital in the statement itself must agree with the increase in working capital shown in the schedule — $15,531 in this case.

Statements of changes in financial position are not always presented in the form illustrated. One form sometimes used begins with the amount of working capital at the beginning of the period (usually a year). To this are added the sources of funds, appropriately classified. The applications of funds are then shown and their total is subtracted to show the amount of working capital at the end of the

FISHLER & MARVON
Statement of Changes in Financial Position
For the Year Ended June 30, 19--

Sources of funds:		
Funds provided by current operations:		
Net income (per income statement)...		$21,953
Add expenses not requiring funds:		
Depreciation		9,138
Total funds provided by operations		$31,091
Applications of funds:		
Partners' withdrawals:		
Jane Fishler..	$8,600	
Joel Marvon	6,500	
Purchase of office equipment..	460	
Total funds applied		15,560
Increase in working capital		$15,531

Fishler & Marvon — **Statement of Changes in Financial Position**

FISHLER & MARVON
Schedule of Changes in Working Capital
For the Year Ended June 30, 19--

	Beginning of Year	End of Year	Working Capital	
			Increase	Decrease
Cash	$25,502	$28,846	$ 3,344	
Government notes.............................	—0—	10,000	10,000	
Receivables (net)..............................	6,456	8,993	2,537	
Merchandise inventories	2,603	2,650	47	
Supplies and prepayments..............	2,027	2,419	392	
Notes and interest payable..............	2,643	—0—	2,643	
Accounts payable.............................	25,219	28,645		$ 3,426
Accrued and withheld payroll taxes	2,028	2,034		6
			$18,963	$ 3,432
Increase in working capital				15,531
			$18,963	$18,963

Fishler & Marvon — **Schedule of Changes in Working Capital**

period. As was noted earlier, titles other than "statement of changes in financial position" sometimes are used. By whatever name it is called, the inclusion of the statement in the annual report has now become standard practice.

BUILDING YOUR ACCOUNTING KNOWLEDGE

1. Why is solvency or liquidity not assured merely because a business is profitable?

2. Give three alternate titles for the statement of changes in financial position.

3. What does the term "funds" generally mean as used in connection with the statement of changes in financial position?

4. What alternative approach is used by a minority of companies to express changes in financial position? Why is the working capital approach explained and illustrated in this chapter?

5. List four potential sources of funds. List four potential applications of funds.

6. What is the first step in assembling the data for the statement of changes in financial position.

7. What misconception about depreciation in the statement of changes in financial position has arisen? What is too often the reason for this misunderstanding? Why is the alternative method of showing "funds provided by current operations" discussed on pages 545 and 546 not commonly used in practice?

8. What two types of applications of funds are shown on the Fishler & Marvon statement of changes in financial position?

Report No. 19-3

Complete Report No. 19-3 in the study assignments and submit your working papers for Reports Nos. 19-1, 19-2 and 19-3 for approval. Continue with the textbook discussion in Chapter 20 until Report No. 20-1 is required.

EXPANDING YOUR BUSINESS VOCABULARY

What is the meaning of each of the following terms?

acid test (p. 537)   Auditor's report (p. 530)
amortization expense (p. 547)   comparative analysis (p. 533)
annual report (p. 529)   fund (p. 540)
application of funds (p. 541)   fund-change statement (p. 540)

CHAPTER 20

INTERIM FINANCIAL STATEMENTS

CHAPTER OBJECTIVES

The objectives of this chapter are to enable you:

▶ To define and describe interim financial statements.

▶ To explain the reason for preparing interim statements.

▶ To explain the tentative nature and the limitations of interim financial statements.

▶ To prepare interim financial statements using the summary-work-sheet technique supplemented by the technique of deriving an interim income statement by the use of successive year-to-date income statements.

▶ To describe the special problem of accounting for property taxes on an interim basis.

In accounting for business operations, it is general practice to determine income or loss on an annual basis and to prepare balance sheets at annual intervals. While the calendar year is widely used as the fiscal year, many firms adopt the natural business year, which is a year that starts and ends at the time when business activity is at its lowest. In any case, twelve months is the basic time interval. Interested parties, notably owners and managers, need more frequent reports of the affairs of a business. For this reason, it is common to prepare interim financial statements. Interim means "between." An income statement for a period of time shorter than, and within the limits of, the fiscal year is an **interim income statement**. A balance sheet as of a date other than the close of the fiscal year is an **interim balance sheet**.

INTERIM STATEMENTS

Interim statements may be prepared for any segment of a year. However, it is impractical to use a very short period such as a day or a week because of (1) the considerable amount of work involved in producing the statements, and (2) the fact that the shorter the period, the more unreliable the determination of income. Many of the problems of accounting (in contrast to pure data gathering, recording, and storing) arise because numerous items of value are acquired in one period, but are not sold or used entirely within that period. Two important examples are (1) the problem of allocating cost between goods sold (or used) and goods unsold (or unused) at the end of the period, and (2) in the case of most long-term assets, the problem of cost allocation by means of depreciation. The need to allocate inventory costs is a particularly good example of the difficulty of preparing interim statements. At the end of the fiscal year, physical inventories may be taken to determine (or, in some cases, to verify) the quantities of merchandise inventory and various supplies on hand. The procedure is likely to be time consuming and, thus, expensive. It cannot be done at the end of every interim period. Estimates generally have to be used for interim-statement purposes. The shorter the period, the greater the problem.

Because of constraints just mentioned, the month is considered to be the smallest time segment generally used for interim-statement purposes. Monthly time segments have the advantage of being universally understood.

Interim statements may be prepared on a quarterly (three months) basis. Quarterly statements tend to be somewhat more reliable than monthly statements. This is because the estimation and allocation methods used for items such as uncollectible accounts, depreciation, and inventories do not have as significant an effect in determining income for a quarter as they do for a period as short as a month. In addition, quarters are more comparable in length. Quarterly statements in a very condensed form commonly are furnished to the stockholders of large business corporations.

In the majority of cases, interim statements must be regarded as very provisional or tentative in nature. Despite their imperfections, these statements can be useful if they are carefully interpreted.

USING WORK SHEETS TO PRODUCE INTERIM FINANCIAL STATEMENTS

It has been demonstrated in previous chapters that the end-of-year work sheet is a useful device to (1) assist in the production of the annual income statement and the year-end balance sheet, and (2) aid in the year-end process of formally adjusting and closing the accounts. The same type of work sheet can materially assist in the production of interim statements. Adjustments are recorded on the work sheet, but no formal adjusting or closing of the accounts is done at the end of interim periods.

The use of interim period work sheets is illustrated in this chapter for the preparation of interim financial statements of the Reidenbach & Reidenbach Wholesale Hardware Company owned and operated as a partnership by Richard C. Reidenbach and his daughter, Erica A. Reidenbach. For purposes of this illustration, the business is not departmentalized and the general ledger contains comparatively few accounts. Assume that appropriate books of original entry and auxiliary records are used, and there is no subsidiary operating expenses ledger. The firm uses the calendar year as its fiscal year.

The partners share profits and losses in a 50-50 ratio. The determination of net income takes partners' salaries into account. The accountant for the company prepares monthly income statements and year-to-date income statements, as well as balance sheets, as of the last day of each month. A year-to-date income statement is one that covers a variable time period from the beginning of the fiscal year up to and including the last day of the most current month.

WORK SHEET FOR THE FIRST MONTH OF A FISCAL YEAR

An eight-column work sheet for the first month is reproduced on pages 556 and 557. To conserve space, the Adjusted Trial Balance columns are not shown. For purposes of simplicity, the amounts are rounded to the nearest dollar. The amounts in the Trial Balance columns were taken from the general ledger after the posting for the month of January had been completed. The reasons why some accounts have no balances will become apparent in the discussion that follows.

The following entries were made in the Adjustments amount columns.

Entry (a): The amount of the beginning inventory of merchandise, $2,562,297, was debited to Cost of Goods Sold, Account No. 761, and was credited to Merchandise Inventory, Account No. 161.

Entry (b): The amount of the purchases for the month, $1,568,974, was debited to Cost of Goods Sold, Account No. 761, and was credited to Purchases, Account No. 711.

Entry (c): The amount of the purchases returns and allowances for the month, $19,521, was debited to Purchases Returns and Allowances, Account No. 711.1, and was credited to Cost of Goods Sold, Account No. 761.

Entry (d): The amount of the purchases discount for the month, $34,038, was debited to Purchases Discount, Account No. 711.2, and was credited to Cost of Goods Sold, Account No. 761.

Entry (e): The amount assigned to the merchandise inventory at January 31, $2,555,000, was debited to Merchandise Inventory, Account No. 161, and was credited to Cost of Goods Sold, Account No. 761. The firm uses the perpetual method of inventory accounting and maintains a stock record of certain high value items. The stock records indicate the quantities of these items that were presumed to be on hand at January 31. Since very little discrepancy had been found in prior years between these records and the physical counts, the records were considered reliable. Quantities of various low value items were estimated. All quantities were costed by reference to recent purchase invoices.

Entry (f): The interest accrued, $18,229, since January 1, on the $2,500,000 mortgage payable was debited to Interest Expense, Account No. 911, and was credited to Accrued Interest Payable, Account No. 317. Interest at 8¾ percent per annum is payable semiannually each January 1 and July 1. Interest for the six months ended last December 31 ($109,374) was paid on January 2 since January 1 was a holiday. The determination of net income or loss for January must take into account the interest that has accrued during the month.

Entry (g): The amount of the insurance expense for January, $4,605, was debited to Insurance Expense, Account No. 815, and was credited to Prepaid Insurance, Account No. 185. The insurance policy file provides the information needed to calculate the amount.

Entry (h): The estimated cost of store supplies used during the month, $4,012, was debited to Supplies Expense, Account No. 821, and was credited to Store Supplies, Account No. 181. This amount was determined by subtracting the estimated cost of the store supplies on hand, January 31, $9,360, from the balance of the store supplies account, $13,372. Note that the firm uses the asset method of accounting for supplies.

Entry (i): The depreciation for the month, $14,082, was debited to Depreciation Expense, Account No. 814, with credits to Accumu-

Account	Acct. No.	Trial Balance	
		Debit	Credit
First National Bank	111	61,380	
Accounts Receivable	131	332,691	
Allowance for Doubtful Accounts	131.1	3,210	
Merchandise Inventory	161	2,562,297	
Store Supplies	181	13,372	
Prepaid Insurance	185	18,693	
Land	211	975,000	
Building	221	4,061,616	
Accumulated Depreciation — Building	221.1		2,043,738
Furniture and Equipment	241	451,776	
Accumulated Depreciation - Furniture and Equipment	241.1		150,465
Delivery Equipment	251	156,811	
Accumulated Depreciation — Delivery Equipment	251.1		77,113
FICA Tax Payable	311		15,777
FUTA Tax Payable	312		658
State Unemployment Tax Payable	313		3,550
Employees Income Tax Payable	314		18,613
Accrued Interest Payable	317		
Accounts Payable	318		391,490
Mortgage Payable	411		2,500,000
Richard C. Reidenbach, Capital	511		1,770,014
Richard C. Reidenbach, Drawing	511.1	9,987	
Erica A. Reidenbach, Capital	521		1,457,720
Erica A. Reidenbach, Drawing	521.1	7,558	
Sales	611		1,971,510
Sales Returns and Allowances	611.1	19,555	
Sales Discount	611.2	42,052	
Purchases	711	1,568,974	
Purchases Returns and Allowances	711.1		19,521
Purchases Discount	711.2		34,038
Cost of Goods Sold	761		
Salaries and Commissions Expense	811	131,479	
Payroll Taxes Expense	812	12,096	
Partners' Salaries Expense	813	8,000	
Depreciation Expense	814		
Insurance Expense	815		
Property Tax Expense	816		
Utilities Expense	817	3,606	
Telephone Expense	818	1,067	
Delivery Expense	819	4,739	
Supplies Expense	821		
Uncollectible Accounts Expense	822		
Miscellaneous Expense	823	8,248	
Interest Expense	911		
		10,454,207	10,454,207
Accrued Property Tax Payable			
Net Income			

WHOLESALE HARDWARE COMPANY
Sheet
January 31, 19--

Adjustments		Income Statement		Balance Sheet	
Debit	Credit	Debit	Credit	Debit	Credit
				61,380	
				332,691	
	(j) 9,550				6,340
(e) 2,555,000	(a) 2,562,297			2,555,000	
	(h) 4,012			9,360	
	(g) 4,605			14,088	
				975,000	
				4,061,616	
	(i) 8,462				2,052,200
				451,776	
	(i) 2,353				152,818
				156,811	
	(i) 3,267				80,380
					15,777
					658
					3,550
					18,613
	(f) 18,229				18,229
					391,490
					2,500,000
					1,770,014
				9,987	1,457,720
				7,558	
			1,971,510		
		19,555			
		42,052			
	(b) 1,568,974				
(c) 19,521					
(d) 34,038					
(a) 2,562,297	(c) 19,521	1,522,712			
(b) 1,568,974	(d) 34,038				
	(e) 2,555,000				
		131,479			
		12,096			
		8,000			
(i) 14,082		14,082			
(g) 4,605		4,605			
(k) 9,775		9,775			
		3,606			
		1,067			
		4,739			
(h) 4,012		4,012			
(j) 9,550		9,550			
		8,248			
(f) 18,229		18,229			
	(k) 9,775				9,775
6,800,083	6,800,083	1,813,807	1,971,510	8,635,267	8,477,564
		157,703			157,703
		1,971,510	1,971,510	8,635,267	8,635,267

Work Sheet for One-Month Period

lated Depreciation — Building, Account No. 221.1, $8,462, Accumulated Depreciation — Furniture and Equipment, Account No. 241.1, $2,353, and Accumulated Depreciation — Delivery Equipment, Account No. 251.1, $3,267. The firm uses straight line depreciation calculated at the following annual rates; building 2½ percent; furniture and equipment, 6¼ percent; and delivery equipment, 25 percent. These rates were applied to the cost of the assets as shown in the trial balance, and 1/12 of each resulting amount was taken as the depreciation for January. No long-term assets were purchased during January.

Entry (j): The amount of the doubtful accounts provision for the month, $9,550, was debited to Uncollectible Accounts Expense, Account No. 822, and was credited to Allowance for Doubtful Accounts, Account No. 131.1. Experience has indicated that uncollectible account losses average ½ of 1 percent of net sales. Net sales for January amounted to $1,909,903 [$1,971,510 (gross sales) − $19,555 (sales returns and allowances) − $42,052 (sales discount)]. One half of one percent of $1,909,903, is $9,550. While it is assumed that the allowance account has a credit balance on January 1, it should be noted that the January 31 trial balance shows the account to have a debit balance of $3,210. Evidently the write-offs of uncollectible accounts receivable were larger than the January 1 balance. It is possible that the January 1 balance of the allowance for doubtful accounts was insufficient, but if the algebraic sum of the January 1 balance and the $9,550 provision proves to be adequate to take care of losses relating to sales on account to January 31, no additional allowance need be set up at this time.

Entry (k): The property tax assignable to January, $9,775, was debited to Property Tax Expense, Account No. 816, and was credited to Accrued Property Tax Payable. Note that the latter title had to be added to the list and that no account number is shown. The reason is that there is no need for such an account in the general ledger. The account is used solely to produce interim financial statements.

Property taxes pose a special accounting problem. Such taxes do not accrue in the conventional sense. Usually the amount of the tax is not known until the tax bill is received several months after the assessment date. The tax may be paid in two installments: one half by a specified day late in the calendar year and the other half by a specified day in the following spring. Property tax expense commonly is accounted for on a cash basis, that is, no record is made until a payment occurs. By the end of the year, the property tax expense account shows the amount of tax actually paid during the year. Reidenbach & Reidenbach accounts for property taxes in their interim report in the following manner: In the year just ended they paid $56,310 in April, and $58,650 in December. Since another $58,650 must be paid in April of the current year, it seems reasonable to allocate one sixth of the amount to each of the first six months. This is accomplished by a debit to the expense account and a credit to the liability. The purpose of the entry is to give the month of January a reasonable share of the year's property tax expense. Not all accountants treat property tax expense in precisely this manner, but some procedure has to be followed to cause a reasonable amount to be included in the income determination for each interim period.

The work sheet was completed by (1) totaling the Adjustments columns to prove their equality, (2) extending the amounts as adjusted to the proper Income Statement or Balance Sheet columns, (3) footing the last four columns to determine the net income for the month and entering this amount, $157,703, in the Income Statement Debit and the Balance Sheet Credit columns, and (4) entering the totals and making the rulings.

THE INTERIM STATEMENTS FOR JANUARY

The income statement for the month of January, 19––, for Reidenbach & Reidenbach Wholesale Hardware Company is reproduced on page 560. The balance sheet as of January 31, 19–– is shown on page 561. Note that, in the owners' equity section, the net income for the month is apportioned between the partners in the agreed ratio: 50%–50%. (The $1 difference is due to rounding.)

The procedure of preparing a work sheet and the interim financial statements is almost identical to the steps that normally are followed at the end of the year. At year-end, however, the work of the accountant will not cease with statement preparation. The adjusting entries have to be journalized and posted, followed by the journalizing and posting of the needed closing entries. It is likely that a post-closing trial balance will have to be taken. In many cases, certain reversing entries will have been journalized and posted. At the end of each interim period, however, none of these bookkeeping steps is involved.

WORK SHEET FOR THE FIRST TWO MONTHS OF A FISCAL YEAR

The work sheet for the first two months is reproduced on pages 564 and 565. The amounts in the Trial Balance columns were the

REIDENBACH & REIDENBACH WHOLESALE HARDWARE COMPANY
Income Statement
For the Month of January, 19—

Sales		$1,971,510
Less: Returns and allowances		(19,555)
Sales discounts		(42,052)
Net sales		$1,909,903
Cost of goods sold:		
Merchandise inventory, January 1	$2,562,297	
Purchases	1,568,974	
Less: Returns and allowances	(19,521)	
Purchases discounts	(34,038)	
Cost of merchandise available for sale	$4,077,712	
Less merchandise inventory, January 31	2,555,000	1,522,712
Gross margin on sales		$ 387,191
Operating expenses:		
Salaries and commissions expense	$ 131,479	
Payroll taxes expense	12,096	
Partners' salaries expense	8,000	
Depreciation expense	14,082	
Insurance expense	4,605	
Property tax expense	9,775	
Utilities expense	3,606	
Telephone expense	1,067	
Delivery expense	4,739	
Supplies expense	4,012	
Uncollectible accounts expense	9,550	
Miscellaneous expense	8,248	
Total operating expenses		211,259
Operating income		$ 175,932
Interest expense		18,229
Net income		$ 157,703

Reidenbach & Reidenbach Wholesale Hardware Company — Income Statement

balances of all of the general ledger accounts after the posting for the month of February had been completed. A comparison of the January 31 trial balance on page 556 with the trial balance for February 28 on page 564 reveals that there are no changes in the balances of several accounts. As explained previously, this is because the adjustments made in the work sheet for January were solely to produce interim financial statements for January, and are not made a formal part of the accounting records.

The balance of the merchandise inventory account (No. 161) remains unchanged until the accounts are adjusted at the end of the year. There are no changes in the balances of the land and delivery equipment accounts (Nos. 211 and 251) because no assets of these

REIDENBACH & REIDENBACH WHOLESALE HARDWARE COMPANY
Balance Sheet
January 31, 19--

Assets

Current assets:

Cash		$ 61,380
Accounts receivable	$ 332,691	
Less allowance for doubtful accounts.	6,340	326,351
Merchandise inventory		2,555,000
Store supplies		9,360
Prepaid insurance		14,088
Total current assets		$2,966,179

Long-term assets:

Land		$ 975,000
Building	$4,061,616	
Less accumulated depreciation	2,052,200	2,009,416
Furniture and equipment	$ 451,776	
Less accumulated depreciation	152,818	298,958
Delivery equipment	$ 156,811	
Less accumulated depreciation	80,380	76,431
Total long-term assets		3,359,805
Total assets		$6,325,984

Liabilities

Current liabilities:

FICA tax payable	$ 15,777
FUTA tax payable	658
State unemployment tax payable	3,550
Employees income tax payable	18,613
Accrued interest payable	18,229
Accrued property tax payable	9,775
Accounts payable	391,490
Total current liabilities	$ 458,092

Long-term liability:

Mortgage payable	2,500,000
Total liabilities	$2,958,092

Owners' Equity

Richard C. Reidenbach, capital:

Capital, January 1	$1,770,014	
Add net income (50% of $157,703)	78,852	
Less withdrawals	(9,987)	
Capital, January 31		$1,838,879

Erica A. Reidenbach, capital:

Capital, January 1	$1,457,720	
Add net income (50% of $157,703)	78,851	
Less withdrawals	(7,558)	
Capital, January 31,		1,529,013
Total owners' equity		3,367,892
Total liabilities and owners' equity		$6,325,984

Reidenbach & Reidenbach Wholesale Hardware Company — Balance Sheet

types were acquired or disposed of during February. None of the accumulated depreciation accounts (No. 221.1, 241.1, and 251.1) received any debits, since none of the related assets was retired or sold during February, and the accumulated depreciation accounts will receive no credits until the year-end adjustments are recorded.

Accrued Interest Payable, Account No. 317, has no balance at the end of either month since the accrual is not recorded on a monthly basis. There was no transaction during February that affected the balance of Mortgage Payable, Account No. 411. The partners' capital accounts (Nos. 511 and 521)) are unchanged, since neither partner made any additional investment in February. The accounts will be unaffected by withdrawals and net income or loss until the annual closing entries are posted at the end of the year. The accounts for Depreciation Expense (No. 814), Insurance Expense (No. 815), Supplies Expense, (No. 821), and Uncollectible Accounts Expense (No. 822), have no balances at the end of either month, since they normally are not debited until the year-end adjustments are recorded. Property Tax Expense, Account No. 816, and Interest Expense, Account No. 911, have no balances at the end of either month, since no payments of property taxes were made during either month, and the payment of mortgage interest on January 2 discharged the liability recorded at the end of the previous year. Cost of Goods Sold, Account No. 761, and Expense and Revenue Summary, Account No. 531 (not shown), have no balances at either date, since these accounts are used solely in the end-of-year process of formally adjusting and closing the accounts.

The entries in the Adjustments columns of the work sheet for the two months ended February 28 involve exactly the same accounts as the entries on the work sheet for the month ended January 31.

Entry (a): Cost of Goods Sold, Account No. 761, was debited and Merchandise Inventory, Account No. 161, was credited for exactly the same amount, $2,562,297, as on the earlier work sheet, since the January 1 inventory was involved in the calculations of cost of goods sold both for January alone and for the two-month period ended February 28.

Entries (b), (c), and (d): The balances of Purchases, Account No. 711, $2,798,627, Purchases Returns and Allowances, Account No. 711.1, $37,089, and Purchases Discount, Account No. 711.2, $64,676, were transferred to Cost of Goods Sold, Account No. 761. In each case, the balance represents the amount for the two months.

Entry (e): Merchandise Inventory, Account No. 161, was debited and Cost of Goods Sold, Account No. 761, was credited for $2,365,000, the estimated amount of the inventory on February 28.

Entry (f): Interest Expense, Account No. 911, was debited and Accrued Interest Payable, Account No. 317, was credited for $36,548, the mortgage interest accrued for the two months.

Entry (g): Insurance Expense, Account No. 815, was debited and Prepaid Insurance, Account No. 185, was credited for $9,138, the share of insurance premiums applicable to the two months. (The amount is not exactly twice the amount for January because one policy expired early in February and was renewed at a slightly lower rate.)

Entry (h): Supplies Expense, Account No. 821, was debited and Store Supplies, Account No. 181, was credited for $7,703, which was the calculated cost of supplies used during the two months. This amount was determined by subtracting the estimated cost of supplies on hand February 28, $8,840, from the amount of the balance of the store supplies account on February 28, $16,543.

Entry (i): Depreciation Expense, Account No. 814, was debited for $28,164, and Accumulated Depreciation — Building, Account No. 221.1 was credited for $16,924, Accumulated Depreciation — Furniture and Equipment, Account No. 241.1, was credited for $4,706, and Accumulated Depreciation — Delivery Equipment, Account No. 251.1, was credited for $6,534. In each case, the amount is exactly twice that for January. During February, $55,449 was added to the furniture and equipment account and $2,691 to the building account. Since the partnership does not compute depreciation on assets owned for less than one month, no depreciation was taken on these newly acquired assets.

Entry (j): Uncollectible Accounts Expense, Account No. 822, was debited and Allowance for Doubtful Accounts, Account No. 131.1, was credited for $18,142. This amount was determined by taking ½ of 1 percent of the net sales for the two months, $3,628,436 ($3,745,495 − $37,153 − $79,906).

Entry (k): Property Tax Expense, Account No. 816, was debited and Accrued Property Tax Payable was credited for $19,550. This amount represents the share of property tax expense for the two months. It is exactly twice the amount of the adjustment for January.

Note that in calculating the amounts of insurance expense, depreciation expense, interest expense and property tax expense, the fact that January had more days than February was ignored. The month — not the number of days — was the unit of time used.

REINDENBACH & REIDENBACH
Work
For the Two-Month Period

Account	Acct. No.	Trial Balance Debit	Trial Balance Credit
First National Bank	111	85,860	
Accounts Receivable	131	421,947	
Allowance for Doubtful Accounts	131.1	8,039	
Merchandise Inventory	161	2,562,297	
Store Supplies	181	16,543	
Prepaid Insurance	185	19,444	
Land	211	975,000	
Building	221	4,064,307	
Accumulated Depreciation — Building	221.1		2,043,738
Furniture and Equipment	241	507,225	
Accumulated Depreciation — Furniture and Equipment	241.1		150,465
Delivery Equipment	251	156,811	
Accumulated Depreciation — Delivery Equipment	251.1		77,113
FICA Tax Payable	311		15,146
FUTA Tax Payable	312		1,288
State Unemployment Tax Payable	313		6,958
Employees Income Tax Payable	314		17,048
Accrued Interest Payable	317		
Accounts Payable	318		245,059
Mortgage Payable	411		2,500,000
Richard C. Reidenbach, Capital	511		1,770,014
Richard C. Reidenbach, Drawing	511.1	36,302	
Erica A. Reidenbach, Capital	521		1,457,720
Erica A. Reidenbach, Drawing	521.1	30,863	
Sales	611		3,745,495
Sales Returns and Allowances	611.1	37,153	
Sales Discount	611.2	79,906	
Purchases	711	2,798,627	
Purchases Returns and Allowances	711.1		37,089
Purchases Discount	711.2		64,676
Cost of Goods Sold	761		
Salaries and Commissions Expense	811	257,699	
Payroll Taxes Expense	812	23,708	
Partners' Salaries Expense	813	16,000	
Depreciation Expense	814		
Insurance Expense	815		
Property Tax Expense	816		
Utilities Expense	817	7,032	
Telephone Expense	818	2,086	
Delivery Expense	819	9,287	
Supplies Expense	821		
Uncollectible Accounts Expense	822		
Miscellaneous Expense	823	15,673	
Interest Expense	911		
		12,131,809	12,131,809
Accrued Property Tax Payable			
Net Income			

WHOLESALE HARDWARE COMPANY
Sheet
Ended February 28, 19--

Adjustments		Income Statement		Balance Sheet	
Debit	Credit	Debit	Credit	Debit	Credit
				85,860	
				421,947	10,103
	(j) 18,142				
(e) 2,365,000	(a) 2,562,297			2,365,000	
	(h) 7,703			8,840	
	(g) 9,138			10,306	
				975,000	
				4,064,307	2,060,662
	(i) 16,924				
				507,225	
	(i) 4,706				155,171
				156,811	
	(i) 6,534				83,647
					15,146
					1,288
					6,958
					17,048
	(f) 36,458				36,458
					245,059
					2,500,000
					1,770,014
				36,302	
					1,457,720
				30,863	
			3,745,495		
		37,153			
		79,906			
	(b) 2,798,627				
(c) 37,089					
(d) 64,676					
(a) 2,562,297	(c) 37,089	2,894,159			
(b) 2,798,627	(d) 64,676				
	(e) 2,365,000				
		257,699			
		23,708			
		16,000			
(i) 28,164		28,164			
(g) 9,138		9,138			
(k) 19,550		19,550			
		7,032			
		2,086			
		9,287			
(h) 7,703		7,703			
(j) 18,142		18,142			
		15,673			
(f) 36,458		36,458			
	(k) 19,550				19,550
7,946,844	7,946,844	3,461,858	3,745,495	8,662,461	8,378,824
		283,637			283,637
		3,745,495	3,745,495	8,662,461	8,662,461

Work Sheet for Two-Month Period

The work sheet was completed in the usual manner. Net income for the two-month period ended February 28, 19––, in the amount of $283,637 was calculated.

INTERIM STATEMENTS — SUCCESSIVE PERIODS

The work sheet reproduced on pages 564 and 565 assembled the data needed for an income statement covering the two-month period ended February 28, 19––, and a balance sheet as of the same date. The accountant for the partnership uses the same procedure to develop a succession of year-to-date income statements and month-end balance sheets. Income statements of this type are valuable for comparative purposes. Owners and managers are interested in learning how the progress in the current year compares with that of the preceding years.

In addition to the cumulative, year-to-date-income statement, an interim income statement is needed for each month by itself. Little effort is required to produce such statements using the year-to-date information. The technique is illustrated on page 567. At the left is the income statement of the company for the two-month period ended February 28, 19––. This was prepared from the Income Statement columns of the work sheet reproduced on pages 564 and 565. Next shown is the income statement for January, 19––. This statement is exactly the same as the one shown on page 560 developed from the Income Statement columns of the January work sheet on pages 556 and 557. At the right is the income statement for February, 19––, which was derived by subtracting the amounts in the January statement from those in the January–February statement, with the exception of the February merchandise inventory.

Since the income statements show the calculation of cost of goods sold, the amounts of the beginning and ending merchandise inventories shown in the February statement were not derived by subtraction. The beginning inventory for February, $2,555,000, was the ending inventory for January. The ending inventory for February, $2,365,000, is also the ending inventory for the two-month period.

The balance sheet as of February 28, 19––, is reproduced on page 568. This was prepared from the Balance Sheet columns of the work sheet on pages 564 and 565. Note that the owners' equity section shows each partner's equity as of January 1, plus the share of the net income for the two-month period less the withdrawals during the two-month period, to arrive at the amount of each partner's eq-

REIDENBACH & REIDENBACH WHOLESALE HARDWARE COMPANY
Income Statements

	For Two Months Ended February 28, 19—	For January, 19—	For February, 19—
Sales	$3,745,495	$1,971,510	$1,773,985
Less: Returns and allowances	(37,153)	(19,555)	(17,598)
Sales discounts	(79,906)	(42,052)	(37,854)
Net sales	$3,628,436	$1,909,903	$1,718,533
Cost of goods sold:			
Merchandise inventory, beginning of period	$2,562,297	$2,562,297	$2,555,000
Purchases	2,798,627	1,568,974	1,229,653
Less: Returns and allowances	(37,089)	(19,521)	(17,568)
Purchases discounts	(64,676)	(34,038)	(30,638)
Cost of merchandise available for sale	$5,259,159	$4,077,712	$3,736,447
Less merchandise inventory, end of period	2,365,000	2,555,000	2,365,000
	2,894,159	1,522,712	1,371,447
Gross margin on sales	$734,277	$387,191	$347,086
Operating expenses:			
Salaries and commissions expense	$257,699	$131,479	$126,220
Payroll taxes expense	23,708	12,096	11,612
Partners' salaries expense	16,000	8,000	8,000
Depreciation expense	28,164	14,082	14,082
Insurance expense	9,138	4,605	4,533
Property tax expense	19,550	9,775	9,775
Utilities expense	7,032	3,606	3,426
Telephone expense	2,086	1,067	1,019
Delivery expense	9,287	4,739	4,548
Supplies expense	7,703	4,012	3,691
Uncollectible accounts expense	18,142	9,550	8,592
Miscellaneous expense	15,673	8,248	7,425
Total operating expenses	414,182	211,259	202,923
Operating income	$320,095	$175,932	$144,163
Interest expense	36,458	18,229	18,229
Net income	$283,637	$157,703	$125,934

Reidenbach & Reidenbach Wholesale Hardware Company — Income Statements

REIDENBACH & REIDENBACH WHOLESALE HARDWARE COMPANY
Balance Sheet
February 28, 19—

Assets

Current assets:
Cash .... $ 85,860
Accounts receivable .... $ 421,947
Less allowance for doubtful accounts.. 10,103   411,844

Merchandise inventory................................ 2,365,000
Store supplies 8,840
Prepaid insurance..................................... 10,306

    Total current assets.................................. $2,881,850

Long-term assets:
Land .... $ 975,000
Building $4,064,307
Less accumulated depreciation............. 2,060,662   2,003,645

Furniture and equipment .... $ 507,225
Less accumulated depreciation............ 155,171   352,054

Delivery equipment................................. $ 156,811
Less accumulated depreciation............ 83,647   73,164

    Total long-term assets 3,403,863

Total assets $6,285,713

Liabilities

Current liabilities:
FICA tax payable..................................... $ 15,146
FUTA tax payable..................................... 1,288
State unemployment tax payable 6,958
Employees income tax payable 17,048
Accrued interest payable......................... 36,458
Accrued property tax payable.................. 19,550
Accounts payable...................................... 245,059

    Total current liabilities............................ $ 341,507

Long-term liability:
Mortgage payable 2,500,000

    Total liabilities $2,841,507

Owners' Equity

Richard C. Reidenbach, capital:
Capital, January 1 .... $1,770,014
Add net income (50% of $283,637)........ 141,819
Less withdrawals..................... (36,302)

Capital, February 28.................................. $1,875,531

Erica A. Reidenbach, capital:
Capital, January 1 .... $1,457,720
Add net income (50% of $283,637)........ 141,818
Less withdrawals..................... (30,863)

Capital, February 28.................................. 1,568,675

    Total owners' equity............................... 3,444,206

Total liabilities and owners' equity $6,285,713

Reidenbach & Reidenbach Wholesale Hardware Company — Balance Sheet

uity on February 28. An alternative would be: Partners' equity on January 31 (as shown in the balance sheet on page 561), plus the share of the February net income less the February withdrawals. The result would have been the same.

It should be evident that a similar procedure would have been employed if quarterly, rather than monthly, interim statements had been prepared.

BUILDING YOUR ACCOUNTING KNOWLEDGE

1. What two circumstances make it impractical to use a very short period for the preparation of interim statements (such as a day or a week)?
2. What advantage do monthly time segments have for interim statement preparation?
3. Why are interim statements which are prepared on a quarterly basis generally more reliable than interim statements prepared on a monthly basis?
4. Why is it unnecessary for an interim-statement work sheet to provide aid in formally adjusting and closing the accounts?
5. Describe how Reidenbach & Reidenbach determines its ending merchandise inventory for interim statement purposes.
6. Briefly describe the special accounting problem posed by the assessment and collection of property taxes.
7. How did the firm of Reidenbach & Reidenbach derive the amounts for its February, 19–– income statements?

Report No. 20-1

> *Complete Report No. 20-1 in the study assignments and submit your working papers to the instructor for approval. The instructor will then give directions as to the work to be done next.*

EXPANDING YOUR BUSINESS VOCABULARY

What is the meaning of each of the following terms?

interim balance sheet (p. 553)

interim income statement
  (p. 553)

natural business year (p. 552)

year-to-date income statement
  (p. 554)

SUPPLEMENTARY PRACTICAL ACCOUNTING PROBLEMS

Problem 16-A Opening entry — Proprietorship

On September 1, Carla A. Jenson organized a photographic equipment and supplies enterprise and opened a new set of books. Following is a list of the assets that were invested in the business.

Cash	$16,563
Office equipment	7,245
Store equipment	6,763
Delivery truck	4,346
Total	$34,917

Jenson owed $3,624 on the delivery truck that was purchased on account.

Required: Prepare the opening entry in general journal form.

Problem 16-B Opening entry — proprietorship

William Hedges, who has been conducting a wholesale wallpaper and paint enterprise, decides to install a formal set of books as of January 2. The balance sheet is shown at the top of page 572.

WILLIAM HEDGES
Balance Sheet
December 31, 19––

Assets			Liabilities		
Cash		$ 5,434	FICA tax payable..............	$ 164	
Accounts receivable	$8,724		Employees income tax		
Less allowance for			payable..........................	125	
doubtful accounts	826	7,898	Accounts payable.............	5,376	
Merchandise inventory....		19,273	Total liabilities..................		$ 5,665
Prepaid insurance............		429			
Store equipment	$8,000		**Owner's Equity**		
Less accumulated			William Hedges, capital...		34,609
depreciation..................	760	7,240	Total liabilities and		
Total assets......................		$40,274	owner's equity		$40,274

Required: Prepare the opening entry in general journal form.

Problem 16-C Capital account — proprietorship

K. Vankirk is engaged in the wholesale leather goods business. After closing the revenue and expense accounts for the calendar year ended December 31, the expense and revenue summary account, No. 521, had a credit balance of $24,608. At the same time Vankirk's capital account, No. 511, had a credit balance of $72,363, and the drawing account, No. 511.1, had a debit balance of $20,000.

Required: (1) Open Vankirk's capital account, drawing account, and expense and revenue summary account, using the four-column account form of ledger paper. Enter the December 31 balances. (2) Assuming that Vankirk wishes to have the balances of both the expense and revenue summary and drawing accounts transferred to the capital account, journalize and post the required entries. After posting, account Nos. 521 and 511.1 should show "zero" balances, and account No. 511 should show Vankirk's present equity.

Problem 16-D Opening entries — partnership

M. A. McIntosh has been operating a wholesale hardware business as a single proprietor. The balance sheet prepared as of September 30 is shown at the top of page 573:

The fair market value of the equipment on September 30 is $6,200. The book values of the other assets are equal to their approximate fair market values. On October 1 of the current year, J. R. McIntosh is admitted as a partner with a 40 percent interest in the business to be conducted under the firm name of McIntosh &

M. A. MCINTOSH
Balance Sheet
September 30, 19--

Assets			Liabilities		
Cash		$ 8,420	FICA tax payable	$ 180	
Accounts receivable	$10,280		Employees income tax		
Less allowance for			payable	120	
doubtful accounts	920	9,360	Notes payable	7,000	
Merchandise inventory.		16,354	Accounts payable	6,540	
Store equipment	$ 6,200		Total liabilities		$13,840
Less accumulated					
depreciation	1,200	5,000	**Owner's Equity**		
			M. A. McIntosh, capital .		25,294
			Total liabilities and		
Total assets		$39,134	owner's equity		$39,134

McIntosh Hardware. Under the partnership agreement, J. R. McIntosh invests $17,663 in cash. The assets of M. A. McIntosh become the property of the partnership and the liabilities are assumed by the partnership.

Required: Prepare the necessary opening entries in general journal form to record the investments of the partners, assuming that a new set of books is installed by the partnership.

Problem 16-E   Opening entries — partnership

Marsha D. Howard and Susan M. Mello are competitors in the wholesale drug business. On July 1 of the current year, they form a partnership to be operated under the firm name of Howard & Mello. Their balance sheets as of June 30 are reproduced below and on page 574.

MARSHA D. HOWARD
Balance Sheet
June 30, 19--

Assets			Liabilities		
Cash		$ 7,635	FICA tax payable	$ 267	
Accounts receivable	$6,732		Employees income tax		
Less allowance for			payable	210	
doubtful accounts	305	6,427	Notes payable	4,200	
Merchandise inventory.		12,636	Accounts payable	5,475	
Delivery equipment	$7,200		Total liabilities		$10,152
Less accumulated					
depreciation	1,400	5,800	**Owner's Equity**		
Office equipment	$3,400		Marsha D. Howard,		
Less accumulated			capital		24,746
depreciation	1,000	2,400	Total liabilities and		
Total assets		$34,898	owner's equity		$34,898

SUSAN M. MELLO
Balance Sheet
June 30, 19--

Assets			Liabilities		
Cash		$11,743	FICA tax payable	$ 235	
Accounts receivable......	$4,899		Employees income tax		
Less allowance for			payable	197	
doubtful accounts	186	4,713	Accounts payable..........	10,776	
Merchandise inventory.		10,255	Total liabilities		$11,208
Delivery equipment	$7,400				
Less accumulated					
depreciation	1,800	5,600			
Office equipment...........	$3,200		**Owner's Equity**		
Less accumulated			Susan M. Mello, capital.		23,703
depreciation	600	2,600	Total liabilities and		
Total assets...................		$34,911	owner's equity...........		$34,911

The partnership agreement provides that the assets are to be taken over at their fair market values and that the liabilities are to be assumed by the partnership. Mello's balance sheet has already been adjusted to recognize fair market values. The fair market values of Howard's delivery equipment and office equipment are $6,100 and $2,900, respectively. The agreement also provides that to equal Howard's investment, Mello is to contribute a sufficient amount of additional cash. It is also agreed that the partners will share profits and losses equally.

Required: Prepare the necessary opening entries in general journal form to record the investments of the partners, assuming that a new set of books is installed by the partnership.

Problem 16-F   Distribution of partner's share

The Baldus Upholstering Co., a partnership, is engaged in the wholesale upholstering business. Ownership of the firm is vested in G. E. Baldus, D. J. Smith, C. L. Richardson, and J. M. Hanson. Profits and losses are shared equally.

Richardson died on July 5. In the distribution of the partnership assets, the remaining partners agreed to buy Richardson's widow's interest at 105% of its book value. When the books were closed on July 5, Richardson's capital account had a credit balance of $22,560. On August 15, a partnership check was issued to the widow in final settlement.

Required: Compute the amount to be paid to Richardson's widow under the agreement, and prepare the general journal entry required to record the check on the books of the partnership.

Problem 16-G   Subscriptions Receivable; Capital Stock

On January 2, The Mohawk Carpet Co. was incorporated with an authorized issue of 4,000 shares of common capital stock, par value $100 per share. Subscriptions were received from the following:

C. B. Nagel	1,000 shares, $100,000
J. A. Nagel	1,000 shares, $100,000
J. M. Hale	1,200 shares, $120,000
J. A. Carstens	800 shares, $ 80,000

On January 6, all subscribers paid the amounts due. The stock certificates were issued on January 10.

Following is a list of the corporate accounts to be kept:

Capital Stock	Capital Stock Subscribed
Subscriptions Receivable	

Required: Prepare the general journal entries required to record (1) the stock subscriptions received, (2) the cash received to apply on subscriptions, and (3) the capital stock issued.

Problem 16-H   Cash dividend

The following transactions relate to payment of cash dividends by The Royce Rolling Mill Co.:

Mar. 28   The board of directors declared a cash dividend of $5 per share, payable May 16, to holders of record April 15. There were 44,610 shares of stock outstanding.

May 16   The company mailed dividend checks amounting to $223,050 to stockholders.

Required: Record (1) the dividend declaration on March 28 and (2) the dividend payment on May 16, using standard two-column general journal paper.

Problem 16-I   New set of books for a corporation

C. Feldman, S. White, and D. Owen are partners under the firm name of Feldman, White & Owen. On January 2, The Gateway City Distributing Co., with an authorized capital of $125,000, consisting of 5,000 shares of common stock, par value $25 per share, was organized to take over the business formerly conducted by the partnership. The following balance sheet of the partnership was prepared at the time of incorporating the business. It has already been adjusted to reflect the fair market values of the inventory and long-term assets as of December 31.

FELDMAN, WHITE & OWEN
Balance Sheet
December 31, 19––

Assets			Liabilities		
Cash		$21,445	FICA tax payable	$ 275	
Accounts receivable......	$18,875		Employees income tax		
Less allowance for			payable	254	
doubtful accounts	2,060	16,815	Accounts payable..........	10,229	
Merchandise inventory.		29,663	Total liabilities...............		$10,758
Office equipment...........	$ 6,400				
Less accumulated			**Owners' Equity**		
depreciation...............	2,150	4,250	C. Feldman, capital	$24,561	
Delivery equipment	$ 8,800		S. White, capital	22,776	
Less accumulated			D. Owen, capital	18,078	65,415
depreciation...............	4,800	4,000	Total liabilities and		
Total assets...................		$76,173	owners' equity...........		$76,173

The partners subscribed for capital stock of the corporation as follows:

C. Feldman ....2,000 shares @ $25, $50,000
S. White...2,000 shares @ $25, $50,000
D. Owen ....1,000 shares @ $25, $25,000

The partners, as individuals, received credit toward their subscriptions for their respective equities in the assets of the partnership, and gave their personal checks for the balance of their respective subscriptions. A new set of books is to be installed by the corporation.

Required: Prepare entries in general journal form on the corporation books to record the following: (1) the subscriptions to the capital stock of the corporation, (2) the transfer of the assets and liabilities of the partnership to the corporation, (3) the receipt of cash in settlement of the balances due on the respective subscriptions, and (4) the issuance of stock certificates.

There are no Supplementary Practical Accounting Problems for Chapter 17.

Problem 18-A   Summary work sheet; supplementary work sheet

Montich & Fouss are partners in a wholesale mercantile business. Their accounts are kept on a fiscal year basis, with the year ending on May 31. The accounts with customers and operating expenses are kept in subsidiary ledgers with control accounts in the general ledger. Any necessary adjustments in the operating expense accounts are made at the end of each year after a trial balance is taken. Since annual financial statements must be prepared, the accountant prepares a ten-column summary work sheet and a three-column supplementary operating expenses work sheet at the end of each year as a means of compiling and classifying the information needed in financial statement preparation.

The following accounts in the operating expense ledger require adjustment as of May 31:

Insurance Expense	8121	
Store Supplies Expense	8123	
Postage Expense	8124	
Depreciation of Store Equipment	8125	
Depreciation of Delivery Equipment	8126	
Fuel Expense	8134	$ 1,214.65
Uncollectible Accounts Expense	8136	
Office Supplies Expense	8138	
Depreciation of Office Equipment	8141	
All others (to balance)		197,643.22
		$198,857.87

The data to provide the information needed in adjusting the general ledger accounts and the operating expenses ledger accounts are shown below:

Merchandise inventory, May 31	$173,425.63
Insurance expense	973.50
Store supplies inventory, May 31	263.00
Postage inventory, May 31	171.25
Depreciation of store equipment	472.27
Depreciation of delivery equipment	1,681.10
Fuel inventory, May 31	85.00
Estimated uncollectible accounts expense	113.79
Office supplies inventory, May 31	204.00
Depreciation of office equipment	693.97
Interest accrued on government notes, May 31	72.25
Interest accrued on notes payable, May 31	87.00

The trial balance of the general ledger taken as of May 31 is shown on page 578. To conserve space, the accounts primarily involved in the adjusting and closing process are given. To make it possible to complete the work sheet, in two cases the balances of several accounts are shown as one amount.

Required: Prepare a ten-column summary work sheet for the year ended May 31, 19––, and a supplementary work sheet for operating expenses. Use as a guide the work sheets reproduced on pages 508–509 and 513. Allow 3 lines for Cost of Goods Sold on the summary work sheet.

MONTICH & FOUSS
Trial Balance
May 31, 19––

First National Bank	111	10,437.45	
Government Notes	121	10,000.00	
Accrued Interest Receivable	122		
Accounts Receivable	131	17,234.90	
Allowance for Doubtful Accounts	131.1		403.26
Merchandise Inventory	151	166,471.11	
Store Supplies	161	1,563.20	
Office Supplies	163	1,321.16	
Fuel	164	673.75	
Postage Stamps	165	973.10	
Prepaid Insurance	166	1,429.90	
Long-Term Assets (cost)		19,711.60	
Accumulated Depreciation — Store Equipment	271.1		1,165.63
Accumulated Depreciation — Delivery Equipment	281.1		1,988.73
Accumulated Depreciation — Office Equipment	291.1		1,068.55
Accrued Interest Payable	316		
Other Current Liabilities			15,571.67
J. E. Montich, Capital	511		87,422.47
J. E. Montich, Drawing	511.1	15,110.60	
D. J. Fouss, Capital	521		85,271.16
D. J. Fouss, Drawing	521.1	13,279.10	
Sales	611		1,284,156.33
Sales Returns and Allowances	611.1	10,714.15	
Sales Discount	611.2	9,673.11	
Purchases	711	1,013,647.15	
Purchases Returns and Allowances	711.1		7,216.30
Purchases Discount	711.2		6,905.05
Cost of Goods Sold	751		
Operating Expenses	811	198,857.87	
Interest Earned	911		256.75
Interest Expense	921	327.75	
		1,491,425.90	1,491,425.90

Retain the solution to this problem for use in Problems 18-B, 19A, and 19B.

Problem 18-B   Adjusting entries; closing entries; and reversing entries

The work sheets for Montich & Fouss for the year ended May 31, 19––, completed in Problem 18-A, will be used to solve this problem.

Required: (1) Prepare the entries necessary to adjust the general ledger accounts and the operating expense ledger accounts as of May 31, 19––. Use the general journal illustration reproduced on pages 520–521 as a guide. (2) After making the required entries, foot the amount columns of each general journal page to prove the footings. (3) Prepare the entries required to close the following types of accounts in the general ledger: revenue accounts, expense accounts, the expense and revenue summary account, No. 531, and the partners' drawing accounts. Distribute the balance of the expense and revenue summary account equally between the two partners. Use the general journal illustration reproduced on page 523 as a guide. (4) Prepare the necessary entries to reverse the accrual adjustments as of June 1, 19––. Use the general journal illustration reproduced on page 527 as a guide. (5) After making the required entries, foot the amount columns of each general journal page to prove the footings. (6) Assuming that the individual posting to the general ledger accounts and the operating expense ledger accounts has been completed, insert the necessary check marks in the general journal. Enter the totals of the amount columns on each page and rule each page of the general journal. Assuming that the summary posting has been completed, make the necessary notations in the general journal.

Problem 19-A   Income statement; balance sheet

The summary work sheet for Montich & Fouss for the year ended May 31, 19––, completed in Problem 18-A, will be used to solve this problem. Presented below is some detail regarding the summary amounts that were shown on the work sheet:

Long-term assets (cost):	
Store equipment	$ 4,825.60
Delivery equipment	6,777.90
Office equipment	8,108.10
	$19,711.60

Other current liabilities:	
Notes payable	$ 7,000.00
Accounts payable	7,624.96
Accrued and withheld payroll taxes	946.71
	$15,571.67

Required: (1) Prepare an income statement for the year ended May 31, 19––. Since the business is not departmentalized, a separate schedule of cost of goods sold is not needed. Use as a guide the statement for Boyd's Clothiers illustrated on page 271. However, insufficient data are available either to itemize the operating expenses or to prepare a separate schedule of them. Round all amounts to the nearest dollar. (2) Prepare a balance sheet as of May 31, 19––. Use as a guide the balance sheet illustrated on page 535. While the firm maintains subsidiary ledgers of accounts receivable and accounts payable, trial balances of these are not provided and, thus, the preparation of schedules is not possible. Round all amounts to the nearest dollar.

Retain the solution to this problem for use in Problem 19-B.

Problem 19-B   Statement of changes in financial position; schedule of changes in working capital

Use the work sheets of Montich & Fouss from Problem 18-A or the balance sheet from 19-A. Additional information is given below:

Beginning of Year Balance Sheet Information

Cash	$ 5,976
Government notes and accrued interest....................................	—
Accounts receivable (net)..	12,583
Merchandise inventory	160,515
Supplies and prepayments..	1,169
Total current assets..	$180,243
Long-term assets (less accumulated depreciation)	15,488
Total assets..	$195,731
Notes and accrued interest payable	$ 11,533
Accounts payable...	10,841
Accrued and withheld payroll taxes	664
Total current liabilities	$ 23,038
Owners' equity..	172,693
Total liabilities and owners' equity	$195,731

Required: Prepare (1) a statement of changes in financial position for the year ended May 31, 19--, supplemented by (2) a schedule of changes in working capital for that year. Use as a guide the statement and schedule illustrated on page 549.

Problem 20-A   Completing the work sheet

The Fowlers are partners in the wholesale grocery business. They share profits and losses in the following ratio: J. Fowler, senior partner, 60%; M. Fowler, junior partner, 40%. Salaries are included in the profit shares. The calendar year is used as a fiscal year.

The partnership's accountant prepares quarterly and year-to-date income statements, as well as balance sheets, as of the last day of each quarter. The completed trial balance for Fowler & Fowler for the quarter ended March 31, 19--, is shown on the next page.

Required: (1) Prepare a ten-column work sheet for the quarter ended

FOWLER & FOWLER
Trial Balance
For the Quarter Ended March 31, 19--

First Commercial Bank	111	42,924	
Accounts Receivable	131	87,594	
Allowance for Doubtful Accounts	131.1	487	
Merchandise Inventory	161	677,812	
Store Supplies	181	4,855	
Prepaid Insurance	185	7,625	
Land	211	237,600	
Building	221	674,526	
Accum. Depreciation — Building	221.1		384,937
Delivery Equipment	231	41,896	
Accum. Depreciation — Delivery Equipment	231.1		18,418
Furniture and Equipment	251	118,208	
Accum. Depreciation—Furniture and Equipment	251.1		43,189
FICA Tax Payable	311		2,570
FUTA Tax Payable	312		114
State Unemployment Tax payable	313		770
Employees' Income Tax Payable	314		4,283
Accrued Interest Payable	317		——
Accounts Payable	318		107,501
Mortgage Payable	411		432,000
J. Fowler, Capital	511		503,762
J. Fowler, Drawing	511.1	3,372	
M. Fowler, Capital	521		368,836
M. Fowler, Drawing	521.1	2,552	
Sales	611		418,384
Sales Returns and Allowances	611.1	3,907	
Sales Discount	611.2	7,973	
Purchases	711	337,868	
Purchases Returns and Allowances	711.1		3,329
Purchases Discount	711.2		6,721
Cost of Goods Sold (allow 3 lines)	761		
Salaries and Commissions Expense	811	28,558	
Payroll Taxes Expense	812	2,170	
Partners' Salaries Expense	813	10,692	
Depreciation Expense	814	——	
Insurance Expense	815	——	
Property Tax Expense	816	——	
Utilities Expense	817	860	
Telephone Expense	818	355	
Delivery Expense	819	1,114	
Supplies Expense	821	——	
Uncollectible Accounts Expense	822	——	
Miscellaneous Expense	823	1,866	
Interest Expense	911	——	
		2,294,814	2,294,814
Accrued Property Tax Payable			——

March 31, 19--. Use as your guide the sample work sheet on pages
508 and 509 except that in the ten-column work sheet, you will have
the Adjusted Trial Balance columns. Enter the above trial balance in

the trial balance columns of the work sheet. From the following data and information, enter the necessary adjustments in the adjustments columns of the ten-column work sheet:

(a) Transfer the beginning merchandise inventory to Cost of Goods Sold.
(b) Transfer the purchases for the quarter to Cost of Goods Sold.
(c) Transfer the purchases returns and allowances for the quarter to Cost of Goods Sold.
(d) Transfer the purchases discounts for the quarter to Cost of Goods Sold.
(e) Amount of ending merchandise inventory, $669,834.
(f) Interest accrued on mortgage since January 1, $8,400.
(g) Insurance expense for quarter, $1,157.
(h) Store supplies used during quarter, $1,508.
(i) Depreciation of building, $2,155.
   Depreciation of delivery equipment, $872.
   Depreciation of furniture and equipment, $656.
(j) Estimated uncollectible accounts expense for quarter, $1,982.
(k) Property tax assignable to quarter, $2,635.

(2) Extend the adjusted amounts to the adjusted trial balance columns and foot the columns as a means of proof. (3) Complete the work sheet, determine the amount of net income or net loss, and foot the income statement and balance sheet columns as a means of proof.

The solution to this problem will be needed in solving Problem 20-C.

Problem 20-B   Completing the work sheet

This is a continuation of Problem 20-A. The completed trial balance for Fowler & Fowler for the six-month period ended June 30, 19––, is shown on page 583.

Required: (1) Prepare a ten-column work sheet for the six-month period ended June 30, 19––. Use as your guide the sample work sheet on pages 508 and 509, except that in the ten-column work sheet, you will have the Adjusted Trial Balance columns. Enter the trial balance on page 583 in the trial balance columns of the work sheet. From the data and information given below and on pages 583–584, enter the necessary adjustments in the adjustments columns of the ten-column work sheet:

(a) Transfer the beginning merchandise inventory to Cost of Goods Sold.
(b) Transfer the purchases for the six-month period to Cost of Goods Sold.

FOWLER & FOWLER
Trial Balance
For the Six-Month Period Ended June 30, 19––

First Commercial Bank	111	48,686	
Accounts Receivable	131	99,854	
Allowance for Doubtful Accounts	131.1	1,319	
Merchandise Inventory	161	677,812	
Store Supplies	181	6,005	
Prepaid Insurance	185	8,299	
Land	211	237,600	
Building	221	674,526	
Accum. Depreciation — Building	221.1		384,937
Delivery Equipment	231	41,896	
Accum. Depreciation — Delivery Equipment	231.1		18,418
Furniture and Equipment	251	133,877	
Accum. Depreciation—Furniture and Equipment.	251.1		43,189
FICA Tax Payable	311		2,527
FUTA Tax Payable	312		227
State Unemployment Tax Payable	313		1,530
Employees' Income Tax Payable	314		4,213
Accrued Interest Payable	317		——
Accounts Payable	318		114,215
Mortgage Payable	411		432,000
J. Fowler, Capital	511		503,762
J. Fowler, Drawing	511.1	7,186	
M. Fowler, Capital	521		368,836
M. Fowler, Drawing	521.1	5,473	
Sales	611		804,605
Sales Returns and Allowances	611.1	7,434	
Sales Discount	611.2	15,282	
Purchases	711	641,950	
Purchases Returns and Allowances	711.1		6,361
Purchases Discount	711.2		12,809
Cost of Goods Sold (allow 3 lines)	761		
Salaries and Commissions Expense	811	56,647	
Payroll Taxes Expense	812	4,306	
Partners' Salaries Expense	813	21,384	
Depreciation Expense	814	——	
Insurance Expense	815	——	
Property Tax Expense	816	——	
Utilities Expense	817	1,846	
Telephone Expense	818	668	
Delivery Expense	819	2,077	
Supplies Expense	821	——	
Uncollectible Accounts Expense	822	——	
Miscellaneous Expense	823	3,502	
Interest Expense	911	——	
		2,697,629	2,697,629
Accrued Property Tax Payable			——

(c) Transfer the purchases returns and allowances for the six-month period to Cost of Goods Sold.

(d) Transfer the purchases discounts for the six-month period to Cost of Goods Sold.

   (e) Amount of ending merchandise inventory, $664,488.
   (f) Interest accrued on mortgage since January 1, $16,800.
   (g) Insurance expense for six-month period, $2,305.
   (h) Store supplies used during period, $2,789.
   (i) Depreciation of building, $4,310.
      Depreciation of delivery equipment, $1,744.
      Depreciation of furniture and equipment, $1,312.
   (j) Estimated uncollectible accounts expense for period, $3,850.
   (k) Property tax assignable to period, $5,270.

(2) Extend the adjusted amounts to the adjusted trial balance columns and foot the columns as a means of proof. (3) Complete the work sheet, determine the amount of net income or net loss, and foot the income statement and balance sheet columns as a means of proof.

The solution to this problem will be needed in solving Problem 20-C.

Problem 20-C   Interim statements

This is a continuation of Problems 20-A and 20-B. The ten-column work sheets completed in these two previous problems will be used here.

Required: (1) Prepare a year-to-date income statement for the six-month period ended June 30, 19––, an income statement for the quarter ended March 31, 19––, and an income statement for the quarter ended June 30, 19––. Use as your guide the sample comparative income statements on page 567. (2) Prepare a balance sheet in report form as of June 30, 19––, using as your guide the sample balance sheet on page 568.

CHAPTER 21

THE CORPORATE ORGANIZATION

CHAPTER OBJECTIVES

The objectives of this chapter are to enable you:

▶ To define a corporation and describe its characteristics, including the difference between **domestic** and **foreign** corporations.

▶ To explain the nature of state incorporation laws, including the features of certain state laws that make them popular states in which to incorporate.

▶ To describe the process of forming a business corporation, and to prepare **articles of incorporation** and **corporation bylaws**.

▶ To describe and explain the rights that go with the ownership of capital stock.

▶ To describe and prepare a **proxy** form.

▶ To explain the duties and responsibilities of directors and officers.

▶ To describe and prepare certain records peculiar to a corporation:

(1) Corporation minute book	**(4)** Stockholders ledger
(2) Subscription records	**(5)** Stock transfer record
(3) Stock payment record	

More than a century and a half ago, John Marshall, then Chief Justice of the United States Supreme Court, described a **corporation** as follows:

> "A corporation is an artificial being, invisible, intangible, and existing only in contemplation of law."

The definition draws attention to the fact that a corporation is a **legal entity**: entity means oneness — something set apart, separate and distinct — a unit. Thus, a corporation is a unit which, by law, is separate and distinct from its owners. A corporation can own property, enter into contracts, and incur debt in its own name. A corporation can sue and be sued.

Businesses organized as sole proprietorships are not legal entities. Partnerships are legal entities to a limited extent. The assets of businesses organized as sole proprietorships or partnerships legally belong to the proprietors or to the partners, and the debts of such businesses are legally the personal debts of the owners. However, the assets and the liabilities of a corporation are those of the business.

In accounting, every business is assumed to be a separate entity regardless of whether the enterprise is a sole proprietorship, a partnership, or a corporation. In each case, the assets and the liabilities are assumed to be those of the business itself. In the case of corporations, however, such an assumption is not needed. Legally, it is a fact.

ORGANIZATION AND MANAGEMENT

There are more businesses organized as sole proprietorships and partnerships than as corporations in the United States. However, corporations do more dollar volume of business in the aggregate than the other two types of business organizations combined.

CHARACTERISTICS OF THE CORPORATION

Some of the characteristics of the corporate form of organization are described in the following paragraphs.

Limited Liability of Owners. Ownership in a corporation is divided into shares of capital stock. The owners of a corporation cannot be compelled to contribute additional capital to the company if their stock is fully paid for at the time of issuance. This usually is the case and often is required by law. These stockholders have no personal liability for the debts of the corporation. In comparison, sole proprietors and general partners have unlimited personal liability for the debts of their businesses. The limited-liability feature is a major reason for the popularity of the corporate form of organization.

Transferable Ownership Units. Usually, any stockholder can transfer stock to another person without the knowledge or the consent of the other stockholders and without disturbing the normal activities of the corporation. In a partnership, a partner's interest cannot be transferred without the consent of the other partner or partners, and if a partner withdraws, the partnership is automatically dissolved.

Unlimited Life. Corporations are chartered either with perpetual life or with provision for renewal if the charter specifies a limit, irrespective of the deaths of any stockholders or disposal of their stock. A sole proprietorship ends with the death of the proprietor and a partnership ends with the death or withdrawal of any partner.

Suitability for Large-Scale Operations. While there are many small corporations, certain types of businesses must be operated on a relatively large scale. There are various economies with large-scale operations. Furthermore, the corporate form of organization makes it possible to secure substantial amounts of capital with which to operate. Large numbers of investors in the stock of corporations provide most of the capital required for their operation.

Taxation of Corporate Earnings. A major disadvantage of the corporate form of organization is the fact that corporations must pay income taxes. Sole proprietorships and partnerships, as such, do not have to pay income taxes. The net income or the net loss from a proprietorship is reported as a part of the owner's personal income tax return. Partnerships file information tax returns but they are not required as such to pay income taxes. Each partner's distributive share of the firm's net income or net loss is reported as a part of a personal income tax return.

Corporations are subject to a special corporation income tax, and the individual stockholders of corporations are subject to personal income tax on certain distributions that they receive from their companies. Distributions of corporate earnings such as cash or other property by a corporation to its stockholders are called dividends. Such dividends represent taxable income to the stockholders.

The process of taxing corporate income both to the company that earns it and to the stockholders of the company who receive it — known as double taxation — is considered by many to be unfair.

This practice has hindered widespread adoption of the corporate form of organization by smaller businesses.

Government Regulation. A further disadvantage of the corporate form of organization is the restriction of freedom to act. Federal, state, and local governments may restrict the corporation's ownership of real property, the purchase of its own stock, and the excessive retention of its earnings. If a corporation does business in several states, each state may impose its own financial reporting and tax return filing requirements. This leads to extensive duplication of some accounting work, and requires great breadth of knowledge about various federal, state and local laws and regulations.

DOMESTIC CORPORATIONS AND FOREIGN CORPORATIONS

All states have general laws authorizing the creation of corporations by specified numbers of persons who comply with their requirements. Such laws are known as statutes. It is not necessary that a company be incorporated in the state in which it expects to do all or some portion of its business. A company may be incorporated under the laws of one state and operate exclusively in another state. However, a corporation must obtain a license from any state other than the one in which it is incorporated before it can do business in that other state.

A corporation organized under the laws of any one state takes a serious risk when it transacts business within the borders of any other state without first obtaining a license to do business in that other state. A corporation that does not have a license to do business in a particular state may not have the right to take action in the courts of that state to enforce its contracts or to collect its receivables. In some states specific penalties are provided, imposing fines or imprisonment (or both) on the agents of corporations doing business without such a license.

Corporations are classified as (1) domestic corporations or (2) foreign corporations. A company incorporated under the laws of the state in which its business is conducted is called a domestic corporation. A company incorporated under the laws of any state other than the one in which it is doing business is called a foreign corporation by the latter state. It usually is necessary for a corporation to maintain an office in the state in which its certificate of incorporation was obtained. It is not necessary, however, to conduct the regular business operations of the company from that office. The maintenance of an office with an authorized agent in charge usually is sufficient.

It also may be necessary to keep certain corporate records in that office.

STATE INCORPORATION LAWS

The organizers of a company should be familiar with the general corporation laws of the state in which they desire to incorporate. The formation of a private corporation for the purpose of conducting a business enterprise is not as simple as the formation of a sole proprietorship or a partnership for business purposes. A corporation may be formed only with the expressed or the implied permission of a government body. In the United States, the power to create corporations rests largely with the various state legislatures. All of the states have general laws authorizing the creation of corporations. Persons desiring to incorporate must comply with the laws of the state in which incorporation is desired. These provisions vary in the different states. Under the Model Business Corporation Act, in effect in the majority of states, the incorporators may consist of "three or more natural persons of full age."

Variations in the corporation laws of the different states make some states more attractive than others for the purpose of incorporation. Delaware and New Jersey are noted for the great number of companies incorporated under their laws. Following are some of the reasons often given for the popularity of the more liberal state incorporation laws:

(1) Capital stock may be issued for cash, for services performed, for personal property such as a patent or contract, or for real estate or real estate leases. In the absence of actual fraud, the judgment of the directors of the corporation as to the value of the property for which the stock was issued is conclusive, and stock so issued is considered fully paid.

(2) Voting power may be vested in one or more classes of stock, to the exclusion of other classes. This makes it possible for an individual or a group of individuals with an idea for a patent, or possessing a going business, to obtain capital through the sale of stock without losing control of the corporation.

(3) The directors need not be stockholders. Less than a majority of the whole board of directors may constitute a quorum. When vacancies occur in the board of directors, they may be filled by a vote of a majority of the remaining directors. The right to elect all or a majority of the directors may be confined to one class of stock. The board of directors may appoint an executive committee consisting of two or more of its members who may exercise the powers of the board of directors in the management of the business.

(4) Shares of capital stock owned by persons or by corporations outside of the state are not subject to taxation. Cash and securities of the corporation may be kept on deposit in the state without the payment of any personal property taxes.

(5) The stock and transfer books are open for inspection only to stockholders and there is no state tax on the issue or transfer of stock.

(6) There may be no corporation income tax in a particular state for companies incorporated in, but not doing business in that state.

Many of the provisions just stated and others that are considered attractive will be found in the corporation laws of a number of states. In view of the many variations of the corporation laws of the several states, it is advisable for organizers to consult a competent attorney before taking steps to obtain a certificate of incorporation from a particular state.

INCORPORATORS

Individuals who unite in filing an application for incorporating are known as incorporators. The incorporators must be legally competent to contract, and usually each incorporator is required to be a subscriber for one or more shares of the capital stock of the corporation.

The incorporators direct the affairs of the corporation and may take such steps as are proper to improve the organization of the corporation. After the articles of incorporation have been filed and recorded, the incorporators may hold the so-called "first meeting of the incorporators" for the purpose of adopting bylaws, electing directors, and transacting any other business that may properly be brought before the meeting.

ARTICLES OF INCORPORATION

Incorporators must file articles of incorporation or articles of association that comply with the requirements of the state statutes. When the incorporators have complied with the legal requirements, including the payment of required fees, a legal document known as the articles of incorporation (sometimes known as a certificate of incorporation) is approved by the Secretary of State or other official whose duty it is to approve articles of incorporation that meet the requirements of the state law.

The articles of incorporation are frequently referred to as a charter. Usually the incorporators must sign the articles of incorporation and acknowledge the document before a notary public or other officer authorized by law. When the articles of incorporation have been signed and acknowledged by the incorporators, the original must be filed in the proper state office and a copy thereof, certified by the proper state official, should be filed with the recorder of the county in which the principal office of the corporation is located. A third copy of the articles should be retained by the corporation. The procedure for incorporation under the laws of the different states varies as to details, but in most states it follows substantially the procedure described above. An illustration of articles of incorporation is shown on page 592.

CORPORATION BYLAWS

The internal rules and regulations adopted by the stockholders of a corporation are known as bylaws. The bylaws of a corporation usually are adopted at the first meeting of the incorporators after the filing and recording of the articles of incorporation. After that, the power to make, alter, or repeal bylaws rests with the stockholders, unless in the articles of incorporation that power is conferred upon the directors. Typical bylaws of a corporation are illustrated on pages 593 and 594.

The bylaws are for the government and regulation of persons connected with the corporation and usually are not binding upon other persons. Reasonable bylaws, legally adopted, that are neither contrary to public policy nor inconsistent with the general law of the land, are binding upon all stockholders regardless of their knowledge or consent. Any bylaws that are not contrary to the laws of the state under which the company is incorporated may be adopted for the purpose of controlling the operations of a corporation. The bylaws usually provide for the time and place of holding stockholders' and directors' meetings, the number of days' notice for meetings, requirements for a quorum, the number of directors, names of committees, titles of officers, transfers of stock, signing of checks, reporting period, annual statements; and such other matters covering the duties and the removal of officers, agents, and employees as may be decided upon from time to time.

STOCKHOLDERS

The owner of the stock of a corporation is called a stockholder or shareholder. The form issued by a corporation to show the name of

C-101 Prescribed by Secretary of State

Articles of Incorporation

— OF —

THE WOOD MANUFACTURING CO., INC.

(Name of Corporation)

The undersigned, a majority of whom are citizens of the United States, desiring to form a corporation, for profit, under Sections 1701.01 et seq. of the Revised Code of Ohio, do hereby certify:

FIRST. The name of said corporation shall be ....

The Wood Manufacturing Co., Inc.

SECOND. The place in Ohio where its principal office is to be located is ....

Cincinnati ...., Hamilton ....County.

(City, Village or Township)

THIRD. The purposes for which it is formed are:

To manufacture, purchase or otherwise acquire, own, mortgage, pledge, sell, assign, and transfer, or otherwise dispose of, to invest, trade, deal in and deal with goods, wares, and merchandise and real and personal property of every class and description.

FOURTH. The number of shares which the corporation is authorized to have outstanding is one thousand (1,000) and the par value of each such share is One Hundred Dollars ($100), amounting in the aggregate to One Hundred Thousand Dollars ($100,000).

FIFTH. The amount of stated capital with which the corporation shall begin business is

.........................Fifty Thousand..........................Dollars ($50,000.00).

IN WITNESS WHEREOF, We have hereunto subscribed our names, this...........1st.......day

of.......September........, 19 82.

THE WOOD MANUFACTURING CO., INC.

(Name of Corporation)

James H. Wood

James H. Wood

Tina A. Rabat

Tina A. Rabat

G. R. Heslep

G. R. Heslep

(INCORPORATORS' NAMES SHOULD BE TYPED OR PRINTED BENEATH SIGNATURES)

N. B. Articles will be returned unless accompanied by form designating statutory agent. See Section 1701.07, Revised Code of Ohio.

Form C-101

Articles of Incorporation

BYLAWS
OF
THE WOOD MANUFACTURING CO., INC.

ARTICLE I — OFFICES

1. The principal office of the company shall be in the City of Cincinnati, County of Hamilton, Ohio.

2. The corporation may also have offices at such other places as the board of directors may from time to time see fit to establish in accord with the requirements of the business of the corporation.

ARTICLE II — SEAL

1. The corporate seal shall have inscribed thereon the name of the corporation, the year of its organization, and the words "Corporate Seal, Ohio." Said seal may be used by causing it or a facsimile thereof to be impressed or affixed or reproduced or otherwise.

ARTICLE III — STOCK

1. Certificates of stock shall be issued in numerical order, be signed by the president and secretary, and be sealed with the corporation seal.

2. Transfers of stock shall be made in the books of the corporation only by the person named in the certificate, or his/her duly authorized attorney, and upon surrender of the certificate therefor.

ARTICLE IV — STOCKHOLDERS

1. The annual meeting of the stockholders shall be held in the principal office of the company in Cincinnati, Ohio, sometime during the second week of January.

2. Special meetings of the stockholders may be called at the principal office of the company at any time, by resolution of the board of directors, or upon written request of the stockholders holding one fourth of the outstanding stock.

3. Notice of regular and special meetings of the stockholders shall be prepared by the secretary and mailed to the last known post office address of each stockholder not less than ten days before such meeting and in the case of a special meeting, such notice shall state the object or objects thereof.

4. A quorum at any meeting of the stockholders shall consist of a majority of the stock of the company represented in person or by proxy.

5. The election of directors shall take place at the time of the annual meeting of the stockholders. The election shall be by ballot and each stockholder of record shall be entitled to cast one vote for each share of stock held by him/her.

ARTICLE V — DIRECTORS

1. A board of five directors shall be elected annually by the stockholders for a term of one year and they shall serve until the election and acceptance of duly qualified successors. Vacancies may be filled by the board for the unexpired term.

2. Regular meetings of the board of directors shall be held in the principal office of the company in Cincinnati, Ohio on the last Saturday of each month at 9 a.m., if not a legal holiday; but if a legal holiday then on the following Monday.

3. Special meetings of the board of directors to be held in the principal office of the company in Cincinnati, Ohio, may be called at any time by the president or by request of a majority of the directors.

4. Notice of regular and special meetings of the board of directors shall be prepared by the secretary and mailed to each member of the board not less than five days before such meeting. Notices of special meetings shall state the purposes thereof.

5. A quorum at any meeting of the board of directors shall consist of a majority of the entire membership of the board.

6. At the first regular meeting of the board of directors after the election of directors each year, the officers of the company shall be elected for a period of one year. The board shall fix the compensation of the officers.

Corporation Bylaws *(Continued)*

ARTICLE VI — OFFICERS

1. The officers of the company shall consist of a president, a vice-president, a secretary, and a treasurer, who shall be elected for a term of one year and shall hold office until their successors are duly elected and qualified.

2. The president shall preside at all meetings and have general supervision of the affairs of the company; shall sign all certificates, contracts, and other instruments of the company as authorized by the board of directors; shall make reports to the directors and stockholders; and shall perform all such duties as are incident to his office and are properly required of him by the board of directors. In the absence or disability of the president, the vice-president shall exercise all his functions.

3. The secretary shall issue notices for all meetings of the board of directors and stockholders; shall keep minutes of such meetings; shall have charge of the seal and the corporate records; shall sign, with the president, such instruments as will require such signature; and shall make such reports and perform such other duties as are incident to her office, or are properly required of her by the board of directors.

4. The treasurer shall have the custody of all moneys and securities of the company, and shall keep regular books of account. He/she shall sign such instruments as require his/her signature, and shall perform all duties incident to his/her office or that are properly required of him/her by the board of directors. He/she shall give bond for the faithful performance of his/her duties in such sum and with such sureties as are required by the board of directors.

ARTICLE VII — AMENDMENTS

These bylaws may be amended, repealed, or altered, in whole or in part by a three-fourths vote of the entire outstanding stock of the company, at any regular meeting of the stockholders or at any special meeting duly called for such purpose.

CERTIFICATION OF BYLAWS

We, the undersigned, James H. Wood and Tina A. Rabat, respectively, the duly elected president and secretary of The Wood Manufacturing Co., Inc., do hereby certify that the foregoing bylaws were duly adopted by the stockholders of said corporation at the first meeting held on the 15th day of September, 1982, in the principal office of the said corporation at 534 Broadway, Cincinnati, Ohio.

In Testimony Whereof, we have hereunto signed our signatures and affixed the seal of said corporation this 15th day of September, 1982.

JAMES H. WOOD, *President*
TINA A. RABAT, *Secretary*

CORPORATE SEAL

Corporation Bylaws (*Concluded*)

the stockholder and the number of shares owned is called a stock certificate. An illustration of a stock certificate appears on page 465.

A certificate of stock may indicate ownership of any number of shares of stock. It is not necessary for a corporation to issue a separate certificate for each share of capital stock sold; instead, one certificate may be issued to each purchaser for the total number of shares purchased.

The Model Business Corporation Act requires that capital stock certificates state the following:

(1) The state of incorporation.
(2) The name of the person to whom issued.
(3) The number and the class of shares represented and the designation of the series, if any.
(4) The par value of each share or a statement that there is no par value.
(5) If there is more than one class of shares, a summary of the rights or restrictions of each class.

Stockholders usually have the right to:

(1) Vote at stockholders' meetings.
(2) Share in corporate earnings.
(3) Purchase new shares in proportion to existing holdings.
(4) Share in any distribution of corporate assets.

These rights are discussed in the paragraphs that follow.

Unless stockholders own shares of a class of stock that carries no voting rights, they have a right to attend stockholders' meetings, to vote in the election of officers or directors who establish corporate policies, and to vote upon any other matters that properly may come before the stockholders' meetings. Each share of stock usually carries one vote. A stockholder who cannot be present at a stockholders' meeting may authorize another stockholder to vote the shares. This is known as voting by proxy. A typical proxy is shown below.

PROXY

THE WOOD MANUFACTURING CO., INC.

The undersigned hereby appoints James H. Wood and Tina A. Rabat, and each of them attorneys and proxies, with power of substitution, to vote at the annual meeting of stockholders of The Wood Manufacturing Co., Inc., to be held at Cincinnati, Ohio, on January 12, 19--, or at any adjournment thereof, according to the number of votes that the undersigned would be entitled to vote if personally present. Such proxies, and each of them, may vote for the directors named in the Proxy Statement received by the undersigned and on all other matters that may legally come before the meeting.

Date. . . . . .19. .   . . .
Signature of Stockholder

152

Proxy

Each share of stock of a class on which a dividend may be declared entitles its owner to receive a proportionate amount of any dividends distributed by the corporation. Certain classes of stock usually give the holder the right, known as the preemptive right, to purchase a proportionate number of any new shares that the corporation might issue. The preemptive right gives each stockholder a chance to maintain a proportionate equity in the corporation. However, the stockholder is not obliged to take advantage of this right.

In the event that the corporation goes out of business — liquidates — each stockholder has the right to share in the distribution of the assets. The distribution is on a proportional, share-for-share basis, although there may be a rank or order of claims if the corporation has more than one class of stock outstanding.

In order to enjoy any of the rights that have been mentioned, stockholders' stock must be properly recorded on the books of the corporation. When the stockholder acquires shares directly from the corporation as part of an original issue, the capital stock certificate will be recorded on the books of the corporation. When shares of capital stock are acquired by purchase from other stockholders rather than directly from the corporation, it is necessary to have the stock transferred on the books of the corporation before the new stockholders will be entitled to vote or to share in any dividends declared.

DIRECTORS

A group of persons elected by the stockholders to determine corporate policies and select the officers who manage a corporation is known as the board of directors. The board of directors possesses the power of general control of the corporation. Directors are not allowed to vote by proxy and must personally attend meetings of the board in order to be entitled to vote. Usually it may appoint an executive committee to act for it between regular board meetings. The active management of a corporation usually is entrusted to the corporate officers who are elected by the board and are responsible to the board. Unless otherwise provided in the bylaws of the corporation, the board of directors has sole authority to declare dividends. As long as the directors act in good faith, they are not liable for losses resulting from their policy-making decisions.

The number of directors to be elected and eligibility for membership on a board of directors are determined by state statute, by the articles of incorporation, or by the bylaws of the corporation. In the election of directors, as in other matters, each stockholder usually is entitled to one vote for each share of stock owned.

OFFICERS

While stockholders are actually the owners of the corporation, they do not have the right to bind the company by a contract. This right usually belongs to the officers of the corporation. The officers may be, and often are, stockholders; but it is in their capacity as officers, not as stockholders, that they can contract in the name of the corporation.

The officers usually are selected by the board of directors. Unless restricted by the bylaws, however, the officers need not be members of the board of directors nor even stockholders. The officers usually consist of a president, one or more vice-presidents, a secretary, and a treasurer. One person may hold more than one office. For example, the same person may be elected secretary-treasurer. When two or more vice-presidents are elected, each may be assigned special duties. One vice-president may be put in charge of production, one in charge of sales, one in charge of finance and/or accounting, and a fourth in charge of public relations. The officers of a corporation are merely agents who are responsible to the board of directors. The duties of the officers may be prescribed by the board of directors subject to the provisions of the certificate of incorporation and the bylaws.

BUILDING YOUR ACCOUNTING KNOWLEDGE

1. Explain whether or not and the extent to which sole proprietorships, partnerships, and corporations are legal entities.
2. Briefly describe six major characteristics of the corporate form of business organization.
3. What risks does a corporation organized under the laws of any one state run when it transacts business within the borders of any other state without a license?
4. Briefly describe six reasons often given for the popularity of the more liberal state incorporation laws.
5. What usually is required of individuals who wish to become the incorporators of a new corporate entity?
6. What legal action must the incorporators usually take before filing the articles of incorporation in the proper state office?

7. When are the bylaws of a corporation usually adopted?
8. List five items of information that are required to be stated on capital stock certificates by the Model Business Corporation Act.
9. What group of individuals usually has the right to bind a corporation to a contract?

Report No. 21-1

> Complete Report No. 21-1 in the study assignments and submit your working papers for approval. Continue with the following textbook discussion until Report No. 21-2 is required.

CORPORATE RECORDS

In recording the operating transactions of a corporation, records or books of account similar to those used by a sole proprietorship and by a partnership may be used. The only records peculiar to the corporate form of organization are those required for recording:

(1) Minutes of the meetings of —
    (a) the incorporators
    (b) the stockholders
    (c) the board of directors
(2) Subscriptions to capital stock
(3) Issuance, ownership, and transfer of capital stock

State laws vary with respect to what corporate records must be kept. Usually a corporation is required by law to keep a minute book and a stockholders ledger. Other corporate records may be prescribed by the bylaws. Under the laws of most states stockholders have the right to examine the corporate records, but usually such inspection is limited to the original or duplicate stock records containing the names and the addresses of the stockholders and the number of shares held by each.

CORPORATION MINUTE BOOK

A corporation minute book is used to record the proceedings of the meetings of the stockholders and of the directors. Sometimes the provisions of the articles of incorporation are copied into the minute book or a copy of the articles may be bound in the minute book. Following the articles of incorporation, it is customary to keep a record of the bylaws adopted by the incorporators at their first meeting after the articles are approved or adopted by the stockholders in subsequent meetings. The minutes of the stockholders' meetings may be kept in one book and the minutes of the directors' meetings may be kept in another book. If all the minutes are recorded in a single book, it is customary to allot a portion of the book to the stockholders' meetings and another portion to the directors' meetings so that the minutes of each may be recorded consecutively. While the stockholders usually meet but once a year, the directors may meet more often.

In recording the minutes of a meeting of the stockholders or of the directors, it is important that the following information be recorded;

(1) The character of the meeting, that is, whether it is a stockholders' meeting or a directors' meeting.

(2) The date and the place of the meeting and whether it is a regular or a special meeting.

(3) If it is a board of directors' meeting, the names of those present, indicating whether or not a quorum was present. If it is a stockholders' meeting, the name of the presiding officer, names of other officers, and either the names of the stockholders present or the number of shares represented at the meeting.

(4) A complete record of the proceedings of the meeting, which may include decisions to purchase or sell property, declare dividends, issue bonds, or adopt or amend bylaws. Should any act of the board of directors or of the stockholders affect the accounting records, information concerning the action taken must be communicated to the accountant. For instance, the declaration of a dividend must be reported to the accountant in order that the required entry may be made in the books of account.

The minute book is one of the most important of the corporate records and should be kept with the utmost care. It should be considered a permanent record of the corporation. Usually it is the duty of the secretary of a corporation to keep the minutes of all regular and special meetings of both the board of directors and the stockholders. Typical minutes of a meeting of stockholders are illustrated at the top of page 600.

SUBSCRIPTION RECORDS

Subscriptions to capital stock may be made before or after incorporation. Since a corporation does not exist until after the articles of incorporation have been approved, any subscription to capital stock made before incorporation is merely an agreement to subscribe for

---

MINUTES OF FIRST MEETING OF STOCKHOLDERS
THE WOOD MANUFACTURING CO., INC.

Held September 15, 1982

Pursuant to written call and waiver of notice signed by all the incorporators, the first meeting of The Wood Manufacturing Co., Inc., was held in its principal office at 534 Broadway, Cincinnati, Ohio, at 1 p.m., September 15, 1982.

Mr. James H. Wood called the meeting to order and was elected chairman by motion unanimously carried. Tina A. Rabat was elected secretary. There were present in person: James H. Wood, Tina A. Rabat, Anna M. Wong, Tony F. Cruz, and Laura R. Porter.

The chairman reported that the articles of incorporation had been filed with the Secretary of State on September 9, 1982, and that a certified copy had been filed with the County Recorder on September 10, 1982. Upon motion duly made and carried, said articles of incorporation were accepted, the directors named therein approved, and the secretary instructed to cause a copy of such articles to be inserted in the minute book of the company.

The secretary presented bylaws prepared by counsel, which were read, article by article. Upon motion, duly made, seconded and carried, it was resolved that the bylaws submitted be, and the same hereby are, adopted as the bylaws of this corporation, and that the secretary be, and she hereby is, instructed to cause the same to be inserted in the minute book immediately following the copy of the articles of incorporation.

There being no further business, the meeting was declared adjourned.

> *JAMES H. WOOD, Chairman*
> *TINA A. RABAT, Secretary*

Corporation Minutes

---

stock. Such an agreement is a contract between the subscriber and the promoter of the corporation or its incorporators. A subscription to capital stock made after incorporation is a contract between the subscriber and the corporation.

One who agrees to purchase capital stock of a corporation is known as a subscriber. A list of subscribers is known as a subscription list. A subscription list usually consists of one or more sheets of paper with suitable headings on which subscribers may acknowledge their subscriptions for a specified number of shares of capital stock. One or more subscription lists may be circulated simultaneously. An example of a subscription list is illustrated at the top of page 601.

At the time of accepting subscriptions, a record should be made in the books of the corporation. If there are only a few subscribers, their subscriptions may be recorded in an ordinary journal. When there are many subscribers, a subscription register may serve a useful purpose. A subscription register may be either a bound book or a loose-leaf book. Usually it is designed to provide approximately the same information as the subscription list, that is, the names and the addresses of the subscribers, the number of shares subscribed, and the amount of the subscriptions. Even when a subscription register

---

SUBSCRIPTION LIST
THE WOOD MANUFACTURING CO., INC.

To Be Incorporated Under the Laws of Ohio

Capital Stock $100,000   Par Value $100 a share

We, the undersigned, hereby severally subscribe for and agree to take at par value, the number of shares of the capital stock of The Wood Manufacturing Co., Inc. set opposite our respective signatures, said subscriptions to become due upon completion of the organization of said company, and to be then payable in cash on demand of the treasurer of the company.

Cincinnati, Ohio

August 2, 1982

NAME ADDRESSES	SHARES	AMOUNT
James H. Wood, 7850 Camargo Rd., Cincinnati, OH 45243-1152	300	$30,000
Tina A. Rabat, 5720 Winton Rd., Cincinnati, OH 45232-2425	100	10,000
Anna M. Wong, 5307 Eastknoll Ct., Cincinnati, OH 45239-3654	75	7,500
Tony F. Cruz, 6705 Hampton Dr., Cincinnati, OH 45236-4977	15	1,500
Laura R. Porter, 1466 Deerwood Ct., Cincinnati, OH 45239-3866	10	1,000

Subscription List

---

is used, subscriptions should be recorded in summary form in the regular books of the corporation. The subscription list or any complete record of subscriptions accepted will provide the information needed in making the proper entry in the regular books of account. The amount due a corporation from subscribers to its capital stock represents an asset that is usually recorded in the books of account as Subscriptions Receivable.

The accounts with subscribers may be kept in the general ledger or in a subsidiary ledger known as a subscription ledger or a stock payment record. A subscription ledger usually is used when the stock is to be paid for in installments. A subscriber may pay for capital stock with cash or other property. A standard form of account ruling for a subscription ledger or stock payment record is illustrated at the top of page 602.

A narrative of the transactions recorded in the account reproduced in the illustration is given below:

Sept. 1   Ira K. Davis subscribed for 20 shares of common stock at par value, making a down payment of $200 and agreeing to make additional payments of $200 a month until the stock is paid for in full, at which time a certificate is to be issued to him.

Oct. 1   Received $200 to apply on stock subscription.

Nov. 1   Received $200 to apply on stock subscription.

Dec. 1   Received $200 to apply on stock subscription.

| | | | STOCK PAYMENT RECORD | | | | SHEET NO. 1 |

NAME *Ira K. Davis*
ADDRESS *P.O. Box 32, Cleveland, Ohio 44101-6921*

DATE	NO. SHARES PUR-CHASED	AMOUNT PER SHARE	SUB-SCRIPT. NO.	TOTAL DEBIT	DATE OF CREDIT	PAYMENTS WEEKLY — SEMIMONTHLY — MONTHLY	AMOUNTS OF CREDIT
1932 Sept. 1	20	100 00	1	2000 00	*1932 Sept. 1*	*Down Payment*	200 00
					Oct. 1	*First Installment*	200 00
					Nov. 1	*Second Installment*	200 00
					Dec. 1	*Third Installment*	200 00
						TOTAL $	

NAME OF SALESPERSON	COMMISSION	% PAID	19
PAID $	IN FULL AND CERTIFICATE NO.	ISSUED	19
		SIGNATURE	AUDITOR

Stock Payment Record

If a subsidiary subscription ledger is used, a control account must be kept in the general ledger. The title of such a control account usually is Subscriptions Receivable. The function of the subscriptions receivable control account and of the subscription ledger is practically the same as the function of an accounts receivable control account and an accounts receivable ledger. The balance of the subscriptions receivable control account may be proved at any time by preparing a list of the balances of the subscribers' accounts kept in the subsidiary subscription ledger. The total amount due from subscribers as shown by this list should be the same as the balance of the control account.

STOCK CERTIFICATE BOOK

When a subscriber has paid for a subscription in full, the corporation issues a certificate for the number of shares subscribed for and fully paid. The blank certificates sometimes are bound in a book known as a **stock certificate book**. A stock certificate and its stub represent one page of a stock certificate book.

Both the certificates and the stubs should be numbered consecutively. The certificate should show the name of the stockholder, the number of shares represented, and the date of issue as shown in the illustration on page 465. It should also be signed by the president and the secretary of the corporation. The stub, when properly filled in, should show the number of shares issued, the name of the stockholder, and the date of issue. Sometimes, in the case of relatively small corporations, the stockholder is required to sign the stub as a receipt for the certificate. In the case of large corporations this procedure is impractical. Sometimes when a stock certificate is canceled it is attached to the stub to which it was originally connected.

STOCKHOLDERS' LEDGER

The general ledger of a sole proprietorship contains the capital account of the proprietor. The general ledger of a partnership contains a capital account for each partner. In the general ledger of a corporation, however, the stockholders' equity in the company shows the total amounts of each of the various types of owners' equity and not the name and the share of each owner. Since it is essential to have a record of the number of shares owned by each stockholder, it is common practice to maintain a ledger which contains an account for each stockholder. Such a stockholders' ledger is not a subsidiary ledger in the usual sense because its accounts contain information relating only to the number of shares; dollar amounts usually are not shown. If, as is sometimes the case, the general ledger capital stock accounts show number of shares as well as dollar amounts, there is a special sort of control account-subsidiary ledger relationship.

The information recorded in each stockholder's account should include the following:

(1) The date, the certificate number, and the number of shares issued to the stockholder by the corporation.
(2) The date, the certificate number, and the number of shares issued to the stockholder from other stockholders.
(3) The date, the certificate number, and the number of shares transferred from the stockholder to other stockholders.
(4) The balance, representing the number of shares held by the stockholder.

The stockholders ledger is an important corporate record. This ledger and the corporation minute book are two records that most corporations are required by law to keep.

A standard form of account ruling for a stockholders ledger is illustrated at the top of page 604.

Following is a narrative of transactions recorded in the account reproduced in the illustration:

STOCKHOLDERS LEDGER						
STOCKHOLDER *R. J. Koepke*						
ADDRESS *114 Cambridge Drive, Wilmington, Delaware 19803-4157*						

DATE	CERTIFICATE NOS.		RECEIVED FROM	TRANSFERRED TO	NO. OF SHARES	BALANCE
	OLD	NEW				
1952 *July 5*		*23*	*Original Issue*		*50*	*50*
Aug. 25	*23*	*36*		*D. H. Price*	*10*	*40*
Sept. 1	*18*	*46*	*D. G. Fischer*		*12*	*52*

Stockholders Ledger Account

July 5 Issued Certificate No. 23 for 50 shares of common
stock to R. J. Koepke who has paid the related subscription in full.

Aug. 25 Koepke surrendered Certificate No. 23 for 50 shares
and requested that 10 shares be transferred to D. H.
Price. Issued a new certificate, No. 36, for 40 shares
to Koepke.

Sept. 1 D. G. Fischer surrendered Certificate No. 18 for 12
shares with a request that the stock be transferred to
R. J. Koepke. Issued Certificate No. 46 for 12 shares
to Koepke.

STOCK TRANSFER RECORD

Since stockholders have the right to transfer stock owned in a
corporation and the corporation is required to keep a record of its
outstanding stock, it is advisable for the corporation to keep some
sort of a stock transfer record. A standard form of transfer record is
illustrated below.

DATE OF TRANSFER ON BOOKS	SURRENDERED		NAMES OF STOCKHOLDERS INVOLVED IN THE TRANSFER AND SIGNATURES OF ATTORNEYS MAKING THE TRANSFERS	REISSUED	
	CERT. NOS.	NO. OF SHARES		CERT. NOS.	NO. OF SHARES
1952 *Aug. 25*	*23*	*50*	BY *R. J. Koepke*	*36*	*40*
			TO *D. H. Price*	*37*	*10*
			SIGNED *S. L. Wells* (ATTORNEY)		

Stock Transfer Record

A stock transfer record is designed to record transfers of capital
stock from one stockholder to another and to provide the informa-

tion needed in keeping the stockholders ledger. The following transaction is recorded in the illustration:

> Aug. 25 R. J. Koepke surrendered Certificate No. 23 for 50 shares and requested that 10 shares be transferred to D. H. Price. Issued Certificate No. 36 for 40 shares to Koepke and Certificate No. 37 for 10 shares to Price.

When stock is transferred, the transferrer must endorse the certificate and the signature must be witnessed.

A person who has access to the corporate records should be designated to record the transfer of the stock. This may be the corporation secretary or a transfer agent. The person who is authorized to transfer the stock is known as the attorney, but is not necessarily a lawyer.

It is customary for corporations to close the transfer record a specified number of days before the annual meeting or before the payment of dividends. Stockholders must have their stock transferred and duly registered in the books of the corporation prior to the closing of the transfer records to be eligible to vote or to receive dividends, as the case may be. For instance, a corporation in notifying stockholders of the annual meeting to be held on June 21, 1982, advised that:

> "In accordance with Section 40 of the corporation's bylaws, the board of directors has fixed May 31, 1982, as the record date of the stockholders entitled to notice of and to vote at said meeting and only stockholders of record at the close of business on May 31, 1982, may be entitled to vote thereat."

In declaring a dividend, it is customary for the board of directors to specify not only the date of payment but also the date of record in the following manner:

> "A dividend of one dollar a share is declared, payable July 1 to stockholders of record June 24."

A stockholder who acquired stock too late to have it recorded by June 24 would not be entitled to share in this dividend.

BUILDING YOUR ACCOUNTING KNOWLEDGE

1. Briefly describe four types of information that should be recorded in the minutes of a stockholders' or directors' meeting.
2. What is the nature of an agreement to subscribe for capital stock before incorporation? After incorporation?

3. What basic information about the subscribers usually is contained in a subscription register?
4. How may the balance of the subscriptions receivable control account be proved?
5. What three items of information should be shown on a stock certificate and also on its stub?
6. Why is a stockholders' ledger maintained to supplement the accounts that relate to the stockholders' equity in the general ledger of a corporation?
7. Briefly describe the information that should be recorded in an individual stockholder's ledger account.
8. What are the consequences of a stockholder acquiring a stock too late to have it recorded by the date of record?

Report No. 21-2

> *Complete Report No. 21-2 in the study assignments and submit your working papers for approval. Continue with the textbook discussion in Chapter 22 until the next report is required.*

EXPANDING YOUR BUSINESS VOCABULARY

What is the meaning of each of the following terms?

articles (certificate) of
   incorporation (p. 590)
board of directors (p. 596)
bylaws (p. 591)
charter (p. 590)
corporation (p. 586)
corporation minute book
   (p. 598)
directors (p. 596)
dividends (p. 587)
domestic corporation (p. 588)
double taxation (p. 587)
foreign corporation (p. 588)
incorporators (p. 590)
legal entity (p. 586)
liquidates (p. 596)

officers (p. 597)
preemptive right (p. 596)
statutes (p. 588)
stock certificate (p. 594)
stock certificate book (p. 602)
stock transfer record (p. 604)
stockholder (shareholder)
   (p. 591)
stockholders' ledger (p. 603)
subscriber (p. 600)
subscription ledger (stock
   payment record) (p. 601)
subscription (p. 599)
subscription list (p. 600)
subscription register (p. 600)
voting by proxy (p. 595)

CHAPTER 22

ACCOUNTING FOR CAPITAL STOCK

CHAPTER OBJECTIVES

The objectives of this chapter are to enable you:

▶ To define and describe the various uses of the term "value" in connection with capital stock:

par value	book value
no-par value	market value

▶ To describe and define the two major classes of capital stock:

(1) Common stock
(2) Preferred stock
    (a) participating and nonparticipating
    (b) cumulative and noncumulative
    (c) convertible
    (d) callable

▶ To explain the difference between issued and unissued capital stock.

▶ To define and explain treasury stock.

▶ To describe and explain the use of accounts for:

Capital Stock
Subscriptions Receivable
Capital Stock Subscribed
Premium on Capital Stock
Discount on Capital Stock

Donated Capital
Paid-In Capital from Sale of Treasury Stock
Organization Costs

▶ To prepare various forms of the stockholders' equity section of corporate balance sheets.

It has been noted that, unless specifically denied, each share of capital stock of a business corporation gives its owner certain rights: (1) the right to vote upon various corporate matters, (2) the right to share in any distribution of earnings, (3) the right to subscribe for any additional shares that may be later authorized, and (4) the right to share in the distribution of assets if the corporation is liquidated. For a variety of reasons, some of these rights are modified or denied in connection with certain types of capital stock. The purpose of the first part of this chapter is to consider the nature and purpose of these modifications, and the several ways in which the term "value" is used in connection with capital stock.

TYPES AND VALUES OF CAPITAL STOCK

The type of stock, the number of shares authorized and the par value, if any, are specified in the articles of incorporation. The laws of the state usually specify the minimum amount of capital that must be paid in before the corporation can begin business. This does not necessarily mean that all of the authorized stock must be issued immediately. It is necessary only to issue the number of shares needed to provide the minimum amount of paid-in capital specified by law. Additional authorized shares may be issued from time to time if the corporation finds it desirable to increase its capital. After all of the authorized shares have been issued and are outstanding, no more shares may be issued without securing an amendment to the articles of incorporation.

PAR-VALUE STOCK

The **par value** (sometimes called the **face value**) of a share of stock represents the minimum amount of cash or other property that the corporation may accept in exchange for the share when it is issued originally. The incorporators may designate any amount as the par value of shares of a class of capital stock. It is unusual to have shares with a par value of less than 10 cents or more than $100.

Par values of $1, $10, $25, $50, and $100 are frequently used. The par value of each share times the number of shares authorized is known as the authorized capital of the corporation. The articles of incorporation of The Wood Manufacturing Co., Inc., reproduced on page 592, specify an authorized capital of $100,000 divided into 1,000 shares with a par value of $100 each.

Capital stock usually is not issued until it is paid for in full. Ordinarily, stock may be paid for with cash, with other property, with labor performed, or with services rendered. When stock has been fully paid for, neither the corporation nor its creditors have any further financial claim on the stockholders. If stock is issued without having been fully paid for and the corporation later becomes insolvent, its creditors may force the original purchasers to pay the difference between the purchase price and the par value of the stock.

Generally, the various state laws make it illegal for a corporation to pay any dividends that would reduce its total stockholders equity below the par value of the shares outstanding. Thus, any losses up to the amount of the total par value of outstanding shares will reduce the equity or interest of the stockholders but will not impair the claims of the creditors.

Par value is strictly a legal matter. It does not have any direct relationship to the market value of the shares, though unfortunately, uninformed investors sometimes have been misled into thinking that par value represents what the stock is worth. Each share of stock, with or without par value, represents a proportionate interest in the owners' equity element of a corporation. If there are 10,000 shares of only one class of stock issued (and outstanding), the holder of 100 shares has a 1 percent ownership interest. This means that the holder has votes which count 1 percent, gets 1 percent of any earnings that are distributed as dividends, and if the corporation were to liquidate, would get 1 percent of anything remaining after all creditors were paid in full.

NO-PAR-VALUE STOCK

Capital stock that does not designate any par value is called no-par-value stock (or, simply, no-par stock). The articles of incorporation specify the number of such shares of no-par stock that may be issued. Most states allow corporations to issue such stock. Shares of this type can be sold for whatever they will bring. There cannot be shareholder liability for any amount by which the original issue price may have been less than the par or stated value of the stock. Such a liability is called a discount liability.

Laws permitting the use of no-par shares came to pass because of certain abuses that arose in connection with par-value stock. Unscrupulous promoters and stock salespersons took advantage of the fact that some people did not understand the meaning of par value. Property accepted in exchange for stock sometimes was overvalued so that the shares issued would be fully paid. This overvaluation could occur because directors, acting for the corporation in purchasing property from themselves as individuals, have the power to place a value upon property accepted in exchange for stock. Sometimes they exchanged their property at a greatly exaggerated value for shares of stock that, technically, were issued as being fully paid. When no-par shares are used, there is less temptation to overvalue property received in exchange for shares. Actual and potential stockholders are less likely to be misled if the shares do not have par value. Corporations formed in recent years have shown some tendency to favor no-par stock, although the use of par-value shares still is popular.

Long established customs and legal precedent die hard, however. The laws permitting no-par stock frequently provide that each share of such stock shall be assigned a stated value, a nominal amount determined by the corporate directors. A stated value of $1 may be established for each share. In such cases, the legal capital of the corporation is equal to the number of shares outstanding times the stated value per share. Stated value and par value have essentially the same effect for accounting purposes.

In accounting for the sale of no-par shares with a stated value, some accountants credit an amount equal to the stated value to the capital stock account and the amount of any excess to an account entitled Paid-In Capital in Excess of Stated Value. The recommended procedure, however, is to credit the entire amount received to the capital stock account. The stated value of the shares can be noted parenthetically in the balance sheet.

BOOK VALUE

The book value of a share of capital stock is the total dollar amount of stockholder equity represented by each share. If there is only one class of capital stock, the book value per share is calculated by dividing the total stockholders' equity by the number of shares outstanding. Calculations of book value per share are made for purposes of analysis and comparison. The subject is considered further in Chapter 29.

MARKET VALUE

The price at which a share of capital stock may be purchased or sold at a given time is described as its market value. Many factors affect the market value of capital stock. Some of these factors are as follows:

(1) The effectiveness of the company management.
(2) The business outlook for the company.
(3) The current rate of dividends and the past dividend record of the company.
(4) The financial position of the company as indicated by its balance sheet.
(5) The earnings of the most recent period as indicated by its income statement.
(6) The stability of the earnings of the company over a period of years.
(7) The general economic conditions.

In the case of stocks which are listed (their prices are quoted in financial publications) for trading on a stock exchange, the most recent price at which the shares were traded is regarded as the market value. Most big cities have stock exchanges — the New York Stock Exchange being the best known.

In the case of stocks not listed on any exchange (often called over-the-counter stocks), it may be more difficult to estimate their market value. If there has been a recent sale of an unlisted stock, its selling price may be considered the present market value. Bid and asked prices for shares not listed on major exchanges are tabulated and reported in many newspapers. These listings are also considered to be an indication of market value. Certain brokers make a specialty of dealing in unlisted stock. They operate a so-called over-the-counter market. Through such brokers, information may usually be obtained as to the bid and asked prices of unlisted stocks. Any information that will aid in forecasting the price at which stock may be bought or sold will be helpful in estimating the market value of such stock.

CLASSES OF CAPITAL STOCK

There are two major classes of stock: (1) Common stock and (2) Preferred stock. Basically, all capital stock represents an ownership equity or interest in a corporation. Unless specifically restricted by the articles of incorporation, each share carries the same rights with respect to voting privileges, dividends, and participation in the division of assets in the event of dissolution.

COMMON STOCK

If there is only one class of stock outstanding, all corporate shares will have all of the rights previously mentioned. Such an issue of stock would be classed as common stock.

Some corporations have more than one class of common stock outstanding. The different issues often are designated as "Class A Common" or "Class B Common." The differences usually relate either to dividend preferences (even though the several issues are called common stock) or voting rights. Certain classes of stock may entitle the holder to vote for only a limited number of directors. Such a device is used to enable the holders of one class of stock to maintain control of the corporation.

PREFERRED STOCK

Stocks that carry certain specified preferences, or first claims, are called preferred stock. Usually these preferences relate to either or both of the following:

(1) **Preference as to Dividends.** Shares with a dividend preference entitle their owners to receive dividends of a certain amount (often expressed as a percent of the par value of the shares) before shares of an issue with secondary preferences or without preferences receive anything.

(2) **Preference as to Assets.** Shares with a liquidating preference entitle the holders to receive, in the event the corporation liquidates, a certain amount before shares with secondary preference or no preference receive anything. If there is a liquidation preference, it is never less than the par value of the shares and is often a few dollars more.

There is no promise or guarantee that there will be either any dividends or anything to distribute if the corporation liquidates, but preferred stockholders have a prior or first claim (up to a specified limit) upon whatever is available. Preferred stock usually does not have voting rights.

Corporations sometimes have more than one class of preferred stock outstanding. The issues are usually differentiated with such names as "First Preferred" or "Second Preferred." If the first preferred has a specified dividend rate of 6 percent and the second preferred 8 percent, it means that dividends of 6 percent per share will have to be paid on the first preferred shares before the holders of the second preferred shares can receive any dividends. After the first preferred shares have been paid, then a dividend of 8 percent per share will have to be paid on the second preferred shares before the common stockholders can receive any dividends. The dividend rate per share can also be expressed as so many dollars or cents per share such as "$4 preferred." For shares with a par value of $50, a $4 dividend would be the equivalent of 8 percent.

Participating and Nonparticipating Preferred Stock. If preferred dividends are limited to the stated dividend rate, the stock is said to be nonparticipating. Preferred stock that is given a right to share with the common stock in dividends in excess of a stated dividend rate is said to be participating. There are many possible participation arrangements. In all cases, the preferred stock receives its regular dividend first if there are any dividends paid during the year. Usually the participation does not begin until the holders of the common stock have received a specified amount. Beyond that amount, the preferred stock and the common stock may share according to some specified plan or ratio in any further dividends that are to be paid.

If there is an equal division of any excess dividends between the preferred shares and the common shares, without any limit as to the amount the preferred shares may receive, the preferred stock is said to be fully participating. Often the extent of participation is limited. The preferred stock might have a 7 percent stated dividend rate with participation up to 9 percent. In that case the owners of the preferred shares would never receive dividends in any year in excess of 9 percent of the par value of the stock held. Participating preferred stock is not very prevalent.

Cumulative and Noncumulative Preferred Stock. Preferred stock on which the claims for dividends may be accumulated from year to year is called cumulative preferred stock. The holder of such stock is entitled to a specified rate of dividend and, if the directors do not declare the dividend in any year (whether because of insufficient earnings or otherwise), the unpaid amount will accumulate until it is paid out of the earnings of subsequent years. The accumulating amounts are not a liability of the corporation, except that they must be paid before the preferred stockholders can receive current dividends and before the common stockholders can receive any dividends.

Preferred stock on which the claims for dividends do not accumulate from year to year is called noncumulative preferred stock. If the earnings of a particular year do not warrant the declaration of dividends, there is no carry-over of dividends to succeeding years. The holder of noncumulative preferred stock is only entitled to receive dividends if the earnings for the year are sufficient to pay such dividends and if the board of directors declares them.

Convertible Stock. If a class of stock is issued that is exchangeable for some other class of stock, it is called convertible stock. Thus, a corporation may issue a class of preferred stock that may be converted into common stock at a specified time and in a specified ratio as to the number of common shares (or a fraction thereof) that may be obtained in exchange for each preferred share. This offers the stockholders the advantage of being able to convert preferred stock into common stock should they so desire. Such action might be desirable if the market value of the common stock becomes greater than the market value of the preferred stock.

Callable Preferred Stock. Preferred shares which can be redeemed (repurchased) at the option of the corporation are known as callable preferred stock. The price at which these shares are callable is usually slightly above their par value, and the difference is known as a call premium. For example, an issue of $100 par-value preferred stock may be callable at the option of the corporation on and after a specified date at $105 per share plus any unpaid dividends.

ISSUED AND UNISSUED STOCK

Authorized capital stock that has not been issued is known as unissued stock. It has no asset value and should not be listed in the balance sheet of the company as an asset. Such stock may be considered to have potential value in that it may be issued at any time for the purpose of acquiring additional assets. When a corporation sells its capital stock, certificates are issued to the stockholders and the stock is said to be issued and outstanding. The total amount relating to each class of stock which has been issued should be shown separately in the balance sheet.

TREASURY STOCK

Corporations may reacquire their own shares of capital stock either by purchase or by donation. The stock may be retired or held for resale. Stock that is held for resale is considered to be treasury stock. Treasury stock may not be voted at the stockholders' meetings and does not share in dividends declared. The total number of shares of capital stock outstanding at any time is the total number of shares issued less the total number of any treasury shares.

When a corporation reacquires its own stock by purchase, it is usually recorded at cost and is reported in the balance sheet as a final deduction in the owners' equity section. When a corporation reacquires its own stock by donation, or at no cost, all that is needed is a notation in the Item column on the debit side of the capital stock account to show the number of shares reacquired. In preparing a balance sheet the number of donated shares held in the treasury should be noted. Since a corporation cannot own itself either in whole or in part, treasury stock should not be listed in the balance sheet as an asset.

BUILDING YOUR ACCOUNTING KNOWLEDGE

1. List four rights that each share of capital stock of a business corporation gives its owner.
2. If an insolvent corporation has issued par value stock without it having been fully paid for, for what amount are the original holders of the stock liable to creditors?
3. Under what circumstances do various state laws generally make it illegal for a corporation to pay dividends?
4. What determines a stockholder's proportionate interest in the owner's equity element of a corporation?
5. Briefly describe why laws permitting the use of no-par-value stock came to pass.
6. List seven factors that may affect the market value of capital stock.
7. Briefly describe the two major preferences that preferred stockholders may claim.
8. What is a corporation's obligation with respect to accumulating amounts of unpaid cumulative preferred stock dividends?
9. At what value is treasury stock usually recorded, and how is such stock usually reported on the balance sheet?

Report No. 22-1

> *Complete Report No. 22-1 in the study assignments and submit your working papers for approval. Continue with the following textbook discussion until the next report is required.*

RECORDING CAPITAL STOCK TRANSACTIONS

The practices followed in accounting for assets, liabilities, revenue, and expenses of corporations are generally the same as those for single proprietorships and partnerships. The peculiarities of corporate accounting relate to owners' equity. Accounting for capital stock transactions will be considered in this section. Accounting for corporate earnings and distributions to stockholders will be explained in the following chapter.

CORPORATE ACCOUNTS — PAR-VALUE STOCK

In recording corporate transactions relating to capital stock with par value, accounts of the following types may be needed.

Capital Stock	Discount on Capital Stock
Subscriptions Receivable	Treasury Stock
Capital Stock Subscribed	Donated Capital
Premium on Capital Stock, or	Paid-In Capital from Sale of
Paid-In Capital in Excess of Par	Treasury Stock
or Stated Value	Organization Costs

If a corporation has more than one class of par-value stock, the number of accounts needed will be greater in order to provide for proper identification of the results of transactions involving each class.

ACCOUNTING FOR AUTHORIZATION AND ISSUANCE OF CAPITAL STOCK

The articles of incorporation specify the amount of the authorized capital stock of a corporation. The dollar amount of the stock and the number of shares authorized may be recorded by means of a memorandum entry in the corporation journal. Usually a memorandum entry is also made in the capital stock account to show the dollar amount and the number of shares authorized. When more than one class of stock is authorized, there should be a separate account kept for each class. For example, the Landmark Corporation is formed with the authority to issue 2,000 shares of 7 percent preferred stock, par value $100 per share, and 5,000 shares of common stock, par value $50 per share. Separate accounts should be kept for Preferred Stock and for Common Stock, and a notation of the number of shares of each class of stock authorized should be made in the Item column of the accounts. If 1,600 shares of the preferred stock are sold at par for cash and 1,000 shares of the common stock are issued in exchange for land valued at $50,000, the transactions are recorded as follows:

(1)	Bank	160,000	
	Preferred Stock..		160,000
	Sold 1,600 shares of preferred stock at par for cash.		
(2)	Land	50,000	
	Common Stock		50,000
	Issued 1,000 shares of common stock at par in exchange for land valued at $50,000.		

The stockholders' equity section of the balance sheet of the Landmark Corporation prepared just after the preceding transactions had been recorded should appear as follows:

Paid-in capital:
  Preferred stock, 7%, par $100
    (2,000 shares authorized; 1,600 shares issued)... $160,000
  Common stock, par $50
    (5,000 shares authorized; 1,000 shares issued)...   50,000
Total paid-in capital $210,000

If at some later date the charter is amended to permit the issuance of additional shares or to reduce the number of shares authorized, it is only necessary to make a memorandum entry in the corporation journal of the action taken and to make a similar entry in the capital stock accounts.

ACCOUNTING FOR CAPITAL STOCK SUBSCRIPTIONS

Corporations sometimes accept subscriptions for their capital stock. The conditions of the subscription contract may call for the subscribers to make payment of the agreed amount in full at a specified date or in several installments over a period of time. Subscriptions for capital stock are usually recorded by debiting Subscriptions Receivable and by crediting Capital Stock Subscribed. If the Landmark Corporation obtained subscriptions for 2,000 shares of its common stock at par value, the journal entry to record these subscriptions would be as follows:

(3)	Common Stock Subscriptions Receivable	100,000	
	Common Stock Subscribed..		100,000
	Received subscriptions for 2,000 shares of common stock at par.		

It should be noted that the word "Common" appears in each of the account titles. Since the corporation has two classes of stock that may be subscribed for, separate accounts for each class are kept.

If there are a number of subscribers and the conditions of the subscription contract involve installment payments of the purchase price, it is probable that a subsidiary subscription ledger (see page 602) will be used. This ledger is controlled by the subscriptions receivable account in the general ledger.

Assume that subscribers for 1,000 shares pay their subscriptions in full ($50,000), while subscribers for the other 1,000 shares pay 20 percent, or $10,000, on their subscriptions. The journal entry to record these payments is as follows:

(4)	Bank	60,000	
	Common Stock Subscriptions Receivable....................		60,000
	Received cash in full settlement of subscription for 1,000 shares of common stock at $50 per share and $10,000 to apply on subscriptions for 1,000 shares of common stock.		

The amounts received would be credited to the proper accounts in the subscription ledger. At this point the subscriptions receivable account has a debit balance of $40,000. The sum of all of the balances in the subsidiary ledger should equal this amount. If the amounts due from subscribers for capital stock represent bona fide, collectible claims, it is acceptable accounting practice to show the debit balance of the subscriptions receivable account as an asset in the balance sheet. If it is likely that the amount will be collected soon, the account may be classified as a current asset.

Because the subscriptions for 1,000 shares have been paid in full, the certificates will be issued. The issuance would be recorded as follows:

(5)	Common Stock Subscribed	50,000	
	Common Stock..		50,000
	Capital stock certificates for 1,000 shares of common stock issued to subscribers who have paid in full.		

At this point, the corporation's equity accounts would appear in T account form as follows:

Common Stock Subscriptions Receivable				**Common Stock Subscribed**			
(3)	100,000	(4)	60,000	(5)	50,000	(3)	100,000
Bal.	40,000					Bal.	50,000

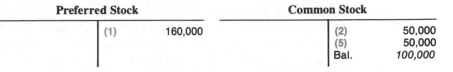

Preferred Stock				Common Stock		
	(1)	160,000			(2)	50,000
					(5)	50,000
					Bal.	*100,000*

The common stock subscribed account has a credit balance of $50,000, which represents the par value of the 1,000 shares for which the full price has not yet been received. This account will be closed upon the issuance of the shares, once the full subscription price has been received.

The balance sheet of the Landmark Corporation, after all of the foregoing transactions have been recorded, should appear as shown below:

LANDMARK CORPORATION
Balance Sheet

Assets			Stockholders' Equity		
Current assets:			Paid-in capital:		
Cash	$220,000		Preferred stock, 7%, par $100 (2,000 shares authorized; 1,600 shares issued)		$160,000
Common stock subscriptions receivable	40,000				
Total current assets		$260,000	Common stock, par $50 (5,000 shares authorized; 2,000 shares issued)	$100,000	
Property, plant, and equipment:					
Land		50,000	Common stock subscribed (1,000 shares)	50,000	150,000
			Total stockholders'		
Total assets		$310,000	equity		$310,000

The common stock subscriptions receivable, instead of being shown as an asset, may be shown in the stockholders' equity section of the balance sheet as a deduction from common stock subscribed. The resulting difference represents the amount actually paid in by the subscribers to common stock to the date of the balance sheet. If there is any question of the collectibility of subscriptions receivable, this procedure must be followed. Some accountants prefer this treatment in any event.

ACCOUNTING FOR PREMIUM OR DISCOUNT ON CAPITAL STOCK

Original issues of par-value capital stock often are sold either at par or more than par. If the state law permits, they also may be sold for less than par. When shares of stock are sold or exchanged for more than par value, the excess is termed a premium and it should be credited to Premium on Capital Stock. An alternative title for this account is Paid-In Capital in Excess of Par Value. If shares are sold for less than their par value, the difference is termed a discount and it should be debited to Discount on Capital Stock. Issuance at a discount is illegal in many states and it is seldom encountered. When the corporation has issues of both preferred and common stock outstanding, the word "Preferred" or "Common" should be substituted for "Capital" in the appropriate account title.

To illustrate, suppose that the Landmark Corporation sells 200 shares of preferred stock at $103 per share (a $3 premium) and 400 shares of common stock at $48 per share (a $2 discount). The journal entries to record these sales are as follows:

Bank...	20,600	
Preferred Stock		20,000
Premium on Preferred Stock		600
Sold 200 shares of preferred stock at $103 per share.		
Bank...	19,200	
Discount on Common Stock...	800	
Common Stock...		20,000
Sold 400 shares of common stock at $48 per share.		

Premium on capital stock is treated as an addition to stockholders' equity and the credit balance should be so reported in the stockholders' equity section of the balance sheet. Discount on capital stock is treated as a deduction from stockholders' equity and the debit balance should be so reported in the same section of the balance sheet. If desired, the discount account debit balance may be written off against an accumulated credit balance in the premium account. In a state where the law permits, discount on capital stock may be written off against an accumulated credit balance in the retained earnings account.

It has been mentioned that the laws pertaining to par value and stock discount have invited such subterfuges as overvaluing assets accepted in exchange for shares so that the existence of a discount is hidden. When assets are overvalued for this or any other reason, the capital stock is said to be watered.

Under the federal income tax law, no gain or loss arises from the original sale of capital stock by a corporation. It is immaterial whether the stock is sold at a premium or at a discount. The sale of an original issue of stock represents only a capital transaction. It involves neither a taxable gain nor a deductible loss regardless of the selling price.

ACCOUNTING FOR TREASURY STOCK

Treasury stock refers to the shares of stock that have been reacquired by the issuing corporation and that have not been formally canceled. Treasury stock may be acquired either by donation or by purchase. On rare occasions, stockholders may agree to donate some of their shares on a pro rata basis. These shares then can be sold to provide cash. Accountants are not in universal agreement as to how treasury stock transactions should be recorded. The recommended procedure is to record treasury stock at its cost irrespective of any par value. If this practice is followed, only a memorandum entry is needed if the treasury stock is acquired by donation. When the donated shares are sold, an account entitled Donated Capital may be credited. For example, suppose that 400 shares of treasury stock that had been donated by the stockholders are sold for $40 per share. The journal entry to record this transaction is as follows:

Bank..	16,000	
Donated Capital..		16,000
Sold 400 shares of donated treasury stock at $40 per share.		

A corporation sometimes purchases its own capital stock for one of the following reasons:

(1) The corporation may wish to reduce the amount of capital stock outstanding, thereby reducing the capitalization of the corporation. This may be desirable at a time when the stock can be purchased at a discount. When the shares are formally canceled, the stock ceases to be treasury stock and reverts to the status of unissued stock.

(2) A corporation may have sold capital stock to its employees under an agreement to repurchase the shares if the workers leave the employment of the company. The price at which the shares will be repurchased usually is covered by the agreement.

(3) A corporation may purchase some of its shares to stabilize the market price of the stock.

(4) A corporation may want to obtain some of its shares to give to officers or employees as a bonus or to sell to officers or employees under a stock option agreement.

When a corporation purchases its own stock, Treasury Stock should be debited for the cost. When treasury stock is sold for more than its cost, Treasury Stock should be credited for the original cost of the stock and Paid-In Capital from Sale of Treasury Stock should be credited for the amount of the excess over cost. When treasury stock is sold for less than its cost, Treasury Stock should be credited for the original cost of the shares and Paid-In Capital from Sale of Treasury Stock should be debited for the amount of the excess of cost over selling price.

For example, suppose a corporation purchases 3,000 shares of its common stock for $16 per share. The journal entry to record the transaction would be as follows.

Common Treasury Stock	48,000	
Bank		48,000
Purchased 3,000 shares of common stock at $16 per share.		

If 1,000 shares of the treasury stock later were sold for $21 per share, the journal entry to record the transaction would be as follows:

Bank	21,000	
Common Treasury Stock		16,000
Paid-In Capital from Sale of Treasury Stock		5,000
Sold 1,000 treasury shares at $21 per share.		

If the other 2,000 treasury shares were sold for $14 per share, the journal entry to record the transaction would be as follows:

Bank	28,000	
Paid-In Capital from Sale of Treasury Stock	4,000	
Common Treasury Stock		32,000
Sold 2,000 treasury shares at $14 per share.		

If there was no paid-in capital account from previous sales of treasury stock, the $4,000 difference between the cost and the reissuance price of the treasury shares could be charged to some other paid-in capital account of this type. If there were no other paid-in capital accounts, the $4,000 difference would be charged to Retained Earnings.

There should be a separate treasury stock account for each class of treasury stock in the possession of the corporation. The balance of each of these accounts, representing the cost of the treasury shares on hand, is shown in the balance sheet as a deduction from the total amount of stockholders' equity of all types. This treatment is illustrated in the stockholders' equity section of a balance sheet shown on page 627.

Accountants do not accept the notion that a corporation can realize a gain or sustain a loss by dealing in its own shares. Paid-In Capital from Sale of Treasury Stock is, as its name indicates, a paid-in (invested) capital account. The amount of the balance of the account is shown in the balance sheet in the paid-in capital portion of the stockholders' equity section.

ACCOUNTING FOR NO-PAR VALUE STOCK

Accounting for transactions involving capital stock without par value may be simpler than with par-value stock. If the shares have a stated value, and this value is treated in the accounts as though it were par, the accounting is virtually the same as for par value stock. However, when no-par value stock with no stated value is sold, shares are issued and the capital stock account is credited for the amount of money or the value of property received. There is no premium or discount to record. The number of shares issued should be noted in the account.

Subscriptions for no-par stock are recorded in a manner similar to that followed in the case of par-value stock. The subscriptions receivable account is debited and the capital stock subscribed account is credited for the full amount of the subscriptions. If there are numerous subscribers, a subsidiary subscription ledger should be used. When the stock certificates are issued, after the full price has been received, the capital stock subscribed account should be debited and the capital stock account should be credited for the full amount received for the stock.

The accounting for no-par treasury stock transactions does not differ from the accounting for par-value treasury stock transactions, assuming that the cost basis is used.

ACCOUNTING FOR ORGANIZATION COSTS

In the organization of a corporation, certain costs are incurred, such as incorporation fees, attorneys' fees, and promotion expense, which are known as organization costs (sometimes called organization expenses). Organization costs differ from operating expenses in that they apply to the entire life of a corporation rather than to one accounting period. It is, therefore, customary to treat organization costs as an intangible asset. In the interest of conservatism, it is common practice to amortize (write off) the cost over a period of years. If it is decided to amortize organization costs over a period of five years, one fifth of the original amount should be written off each year by an end-of-period adjusting entry debiting Amortization of Organization Costs and crediting Organization Costs. The amount of the Amortization of Organization Costs can be treated as a non-operating expense in the income statement. For federal income tax purposes, organization costs may be amortized over any period of time except that the period may not be less than sixty months. This approach also is generally accepted in accounting practice, because such costs are not ordinarily material in relation to total assets or net income.

CAPITAL STOCK TRANSACTIONS

To illustrate the application of some of the principles of accounting for capital stock that have been discussed to this point, a narrative of transactions and the entries pertaining to capital stock of The Payne Manufacturing Company Inc. are presented below.

It is assumed that a subsidiary subscription ledger and a subsidiary stockholders ledger are maintained. A stock transfer record, similar to the one illustrated on page 604, is used to record such transactions as those occurring on August 9, October 4 and 19, and December 6.

TRANSACTIONS

July 1 The Payne Manufacturing Company, Inc., was incorporated with the authority to issue 2,000 shares of 7% preferred capital stock, par value $100, and 4,000 shares of common stock without par value.

Incorporated The Payne Manufacturing Company, Inc., with an authorized issue of 2,000 shares of 7% preferred stock, par value $100, and 4,000 shares of common stock without par value.

1 At the first meeting of the incorporators, the following subscriptions for the capital stock were accepted:

Acuff — 1,000 shares of preferred stock at $104 per share
Berra — 600 shares of preferred stock at $104 per share
Cooke — 1,000 shares of common stock at $40 per share
Dowd — 600 shares of common stock at $40 per share
Eder — 400 shares of common stock at $40 per share

Preferred Stock Subscriptions Receivable	166,400	
Common Stock Subscriptions Receivable	80,000	
Preferred Stock Subscribed		160,000
Common Stock Subscribed		80,000
Premium on Preferred Stock		6,400

Received subscriptions for capital stock as follows:
Preferred stock subscribed at $104 per share — Acuff, 1,000 shares, Berra, 600 shares.
Common stock subscribed at $40 per share — Cooke, 1,000 shares, Dowd, 600 shares, Eder, 400 shares.

19 The following was received from subscribers to apply on their subscriptions for capital stock:

Acuff — Cash, $104,000
Berra — Cash, $31,200
Cooke— Cash, $4,000; Land, $36,000
Dowd — Machinery and equipment, $24,000
Eder   — Cash, $4,000

Bank	143,200	
Land..	36,000	
Machinery and Equipment	24,000	
Preferred Stock Subscriptions Receivable...........................		135,200
Common Stock Subscriptions Receivable...........................		68,000

Received cash and other property in settlement of sub-
scriptions for capital stock as follows:
   To apply on preferred stock subscriptions:
   Acuff — Cash, $104,000 (in full)
   Berra — Cash, $31,200
   To apply on common stock subscriptions:
   Cooke — Cash, $4,000; Land, $36,000 (in full)
   Dowd — Machinery and equipment, $24,000 (in full)
   Eder — Cash, $4,000

19 Issued stock certificates to the following subscribers, who
had paid their subscriptions in full:

Acuff — 1,000 shares of preferred stock
Cooke— 1,000 shares of common stock
Dowd — 600 shares of common stock

Preferred Stock Subscribed...	100,000	
Common Stock Subscribed	64,000	
Preferred Stock...		100,000
Common Stock		64,000

Stock certificates issued to subscribers as follows:
   Acuff — 1,000 shares preferred stock
   Cooke — 1,000 shares common stock
   Dowd — 600 shares common stock

Aug. 9 Stockholder Acuff returned the certificate for 1,000 shares
of preferred stock and requested that 300 shares of this
stock be transferred to Fein. (These shares had been sold
to Fien by Acuff.) Issued a new certificate to Acuff for 700
shares and a certificate to Fein for 300 shares.

No general journal entry required.

23 Sold 400 shares of preferred stock to Gellner at a price of
$103 per share. Received cash in full settlement and issued
the certificate.

Bank	41,200	
Preferred Stock...		40,000
Premium on Preferred Stock..		1,200
Sold 400 shares of preferred stock to Gellner at $103 per share.		

26   Sold 20 shares of common stock to Haley at a price of $35 per share. Received cash in full settlement and issued the certificate.

Bank	700	
Common Stock		700
Sold 20 shares of common stock to Haley at $35 per share.		

Oct. 4   Purchased 200 shares of the preferred stock owned by Acuff for a total of $19,600. Acuff returned the certificate for 700 shares and was issued a new certificate for 500 shares. The shares purchased are to be held as treasury stock; accordingly, a certificate for 200 shares was made out in the name of the company.

Preferred Treasury Stock..	19,600	
Bank...		19,600
Purchased 200 shares of preferred stock from Acuff at $98 per share.		

19   Purchased 20 shares of common stock owned by Haley for a total of $600. The stock is to be held in the treasury.

Common Treasury Stock.,..	600	
Bank...		600
Purchased 20 shares of common stock from Haley at $30 per share.		

Dec. 6   Sold the 20 shares of common treasury stock to Jacobs for $640.

Bank	640	
Common Treasury Stock		600
Paid-In Capital from Sale of Treasury Stock		40
Sold 20 shares of common treasury stock to Jacobs at $32 per share.		

Assume that The Payne Manufacturing Company, Inc., earned a net income of $30,000 for the six months ended December 31. Further assume that no dividends have been declared to that date. The T accounts at the top of page 627 reflect the corporation's equity accounts.

Preferred Stock Subscribed			
July 19	100,000	July 1	160,000
		Bal.	*60,000*

Common Stock Subscribed			
July 19	64,000	July 1	80,000
		Bal.	*16,000*

Preferred Stock		
	July 19	100,000
	Aug. 23	40,000
	Bal.	*140,000*

Common Stock		
	July 19	64,000
	Aug. 26	700
	Bal.	*64,700*

Premium on Preferred Stock		
	July 1	6,400
	Aug. 23	1,200
	Bal.	*7,600*

Paid-In Capital From Sale of Treasury Stock		
	Dec. 6	40

Preferred Treasury Stock	
Oct. 4	19,600

Common Treasury Stock			
Oct. 19	600	Dec. 6	600
Bal.	*—0—*		

Accordingly, the capital section of the balance sheet of the company as of December 31, should appear as reproduced below.

Stockholders' Equity

Paid-in capital:		
Preferred stock, 7%, par $100		
(2,000 shares authorized; 1,400 shares issued)	$140,000	
Preferred stock subscribed, (600 shares)...................	60,000	$200,000
Common stock, no par		
(4,000 shares authorized; 1,620 shares issued)	$ 64,700	
Common stock subscribed, (400 shares)...................	16,000	80,700
Premium on preferred stock	$ 7,600	
Paid-in capital from sale of treasury stock................	40	7,640
Total paid-in capital...		$288,340
Retained earnings...		30,000
		$318,340
Less preferred treasury stock, (2,000 shares at cost) ...		19,600
Total stockholders' equity...		$298,740

After completing the posting from the journal of The Payne Manufacturing Company, Inc., Preferred Stock Subscriptions Receivable will have a debit balance of $31,200 and Common Stock Subscriptions Receivable will have a debit balance of $12,000. The sum of these balances may be listed among the assets in the balance sheet. If it is expected that the amounts due on subscriptions will be collected in the near future, they may be listed as current assets. Otherwise, most accountants would probably prefer to treat Preferred Stock Subscriptions Receivable as a deduction from Preferred Stock Subscribed, and Common Stock Subscriptions Receivable as a deduction from Common Stock Subscribed in the stockholders' equity section of the balance sheet.

BUILDING YOUR ACCOUNTING KNOWLEDGE

1. What information about the authorized capital stock of a corporation usually is entered in the corporation journal and in the capital stock account by means of memorandum entries?
2. In what two ways may the conditions of a capital stock subscription contract require subscribers to make payment for their shares?
3. Under what circumstances is it probable that a subsidiary subscription ledger will be kept?
4. What is the alternative to treating common stock subscriptions receivable as an asset on the balance sheet? Under what circumstances must the alternative procedure be followed?
5. How is a premium on capital stock usually reported on the balance sheet? A discount on capital stock?
6. Briefly describe the nature of treasury stock.
7. Give four reasons why a corporation sometimes purchases its own capital stock.
8. How is paid-in capital from the sale of treasury stock usually shown in the balance sheet?
9. Give some examples of organization costs and briefly describe the nature of such costs in contrast to operating expenses.

Report No. 22-2

> *Complete Report No. 22-2 in the study assignments and submit your working papers for approval. Continue with the textbook discussion in Chapter 23 until the next report is required.*

EXPANDING YOUR BUSINESS VOCABULARY

What is the meaning of each of the following terms?

authorized capital (p. 609)
book value (p. 610)
callable preferred stock (p. 614)
call premium (p. 614)
common stock (p. 612)
convertible stock (p. 614)
cumulative preferred stock
 (p. 613)
discount (p. 620)
discount liability (p. 609)
fully participating (p. 613)
liquidating preference (p. 612)
listed (p. 611)
market value (p. 611)
no-par-value stock (p. 609)

noncumulative preferred stock
 (p. 613)
nonparticipating (p. 613)
organization costs (expenses)
 (p. 623)
outstanding (pp. 609, 614)
over-the-counter stocks (p. 611)
par (face) value (p. 608)
participating (p. 613)
preferred stock (p. 612)
premium (p. 620)
stated value (p. 610)
treasury stock (pp. 614, 621)
unissued stock (p. 614)
watered (p. 620)

CHAPTER 23

ACCOUNTING FOR CORPORATE EARNINGS

CHAPTER OBJECTIVES

The objectives of this chapter are to enable you:

▶ To describe how the term "earnings" is used in a corporation.

▶ To explain the distinction between stockholders' equity resulting from investments in the corporation and equity resulting from profitable operations and moderate dividend policy.

▶ To explain the use of the retained earnings account, including the accounting for **appropriations** of retained earnings.

▶ To explain and prepare a **statement of retained earnings** and a combined **income and retained earnings statement**.

▶ To describe and explain the accounting for a **recapitalization**.

▶ To describe how **cash dividends**, **stock dividends**, and **liquidating dividends** affect stockholders' equity.

In accounting for all types of businesses it is common practice to use the term capital to describe the excess of the dollar amount of the assets over the dollar amount of the liabilities. The designation stockholders' equity for a corporation is superior to the term "capital" because the word "capital" has a variety of meanings in economics, law, and business. However, long-standing custom sanctions the use of the word capital as a synonym for stockholders' equity. In the discussion that follows, the terms capital and stockholders' equity are used interchangeably.

The term earnings has two different, though not unrelated, meanings. The word is a synonym for net income — the excess of revenue over expenses. Revenue and expense are reasons for increases and decreases in assets and stockholders' equity (capital). (See page 17.) Accordingly, "earnings" is a reason for an increase in capital. In addition, the term is used to describe asset inflows — often cash and short-term receivables — that resulted from having had net income (the results of profitable operations). The expression "earnings retained in the business" means net asset inflows that resulted from having had profitable operations, in excess of the amount of assets that have been distributed as dividends. The way in which the term earnings is used may cause it to mean either (1) a reason why one or more assets were obtained, or (2) the asset or assets that were obtained.

EARNINGS RETAINED IN THE BUSINESS

There are two major sources of capital for every type of business: (1) capital that results from the investment of cash or other property by the owner or owners, and (2) capital that results from earnings retained in the business. In the case of single proprietorships and partnerships, little or no effort is made to distinguish between these two types of capital. In the accounts of a single proprietorship, all of the owner's equity usually is recorded in the capital account of the proprietor. The balances in the capital accounts of a partnership usually represent each member's share of the owners' equity in the partnership. In corporation accounting, more attention is paid to the source of the capital, that is, to the distinction between paid-in or invested capital and capital resulting from retained earnings.

PAID-IN CAPITAL

The original capital of a corporation is usually derived from the sale of capital stock. The amount received from the sale of capital stock is called the paid-in (or invested) capital of the stockholders. Subsequently, the capital of a corporation may be increased by the sale of additional capital stock, additional contributions by the original stockholders or by the retention of earnings for use in the business.

Paid-in capital, sometimes referred to as invested capital, should be recorded in the proper capital stock accounts to the extent of the par value or stated value of the stock. This amount usually constitutes the legal capital of a corporation. If the stock is sold for more than par, the excess is credited to an account entitled Premium on Capital Stock (or other similar designation). The result is that if (1) only common stock has been issued and (2) there have been no stock dividends, the total amount of paid-in capital is the sum of the amount credited to the capital stock account plus the amount credited to the premium account.

The foregoing remarks about the sale of stock above par value apply only to the original sale of the shares by the corporation. After that, some or all of a shareholder's shares may be sold for whatever they may bring. The records of the corporation are affected by such transfers only to the extent that an accurate and up-to-date record of share ownership must be maintained.

RETENTION OF EARNINGS

Capital resulting from the retention of earnings should be recorded in an account with an appropriate title, such as Retained Earnings or Earnings Retained in the Business A corporation seldom distributes all of its net earnings to stockholders. Usually only a portion of the earnings is distributed, and the balance is retained as additional capital to help finance the growth of the business. It is not uncommon to find that a major portion of the capital of a corporation has resulted from earnings retained in the business. Many of today's large corporations started originally as small companies, and their growth was financed primarily from retained earnings. This was particularly true prior to the time of high corporate income taxes. As income tax rates have increased, it has become more difficult for corporations to finance their growth or expansion with capital derived from earnings retained in the business. If the retention of earnings takes place in an amount considered excessive by the taxing authorities, an additional "penalty" tax may be imposed. The result is that under current conditions an increasing amount of the financial need of corporations must be met by the sale of additional stock or by issuing bonds or other evidences of indebtedness.

THE RETAINED EARNINGS ACCOUNT

The net income of corporations is calculated in much the same manner as that of sole proprietorships and partnerships. At the end of the accounting period, the accounts are adjusted and the revenue and expense accounts are closed into the expense and revenue summary account. A credit balance in this account represents net income; a debit balance signifies a net loss. Beyond this point the accounting procedures for corporations differ from those of sole proprietorships and partnerships. The balance of the expense and revenue summary account of a corporation is transferred to the retained earnings account.

With rare exceptions, every transaction and event that involves a gain or loss to the business must be entered into the calculation of net income or loss for the period and be reported in the income statement. The accepted approach is to arrange the income statement to show Income Before Extraordinary Gains (Losses) followed by any such items to produce the final Net Income (or Net Loss). This means that generally there are very few debits and credits to the retained earnings account. Typically the only credit to the account is for the net income of a period. The account is debited if there has been a net loss. Other debits to the account result from declarations of dividends by the board of directors and appropriations of retained earnings.

APPROPRIATIONS OF RETAINED EARNINGS

As applied to a business corporation and the accounting for its retained earnings, the term appropriation means a resolution by the board of directors to set aside a part of the credit balance of the retained earnings account for a specific use. The amount involved should be transferred to another stockholders' equity account with a suitable title. The purpose of this procedure is to inform readers of the balance sheet, especially stockholders (1) that the appropriated amount is unavailable for dividends or (2) that such an appropriation is required as part of a borrowing agreement or (3) that an appropriation is made because the corporation makes, or is planning to make, large investments in long-term assets. Appropriating the earnings in this way precludes paying them out as cash dividends. Sometimes the directors think that it is prudent to reduce the balance of the retained earnings account especially if it is large and steadily growing. In any case, the accountant is directed to debit a specified amount to Retained Earnings and credit an account with an appropriate title, such as Appropriation for Bond Interest. It should be apparent that such an entry merely transfers funds from one equity account to another. The entry amounts to no more than the renaming of some of the owners' equity that resulted from profitable operations which previously had been designated as retained earnings.

The practice of appropriating retained earnings is disappearing. Corporate stockholders generally do not regard the figure shown as retained earnings as the total amount that will soon or sometime be distributed as cash dividends. The need no longer exists to make one or more appropriations to advise balance-sheet readers that retained earnings is not all available for cash dividends. Any restriction on dividends that is a part of a loan agreement can be mentioned in a footnote.

STATEMENT OF RETAINED EARNINGS

In order to explain the change in the amount of retained earnings between two successive balance sheet dates, it is customary to prepare a statement of retained earnings. To illustrate the relationship between such a statement and the balance sheet of a corporation, a condensed balance sheet followed by a statement of retained earnings of The Marsh Machinery Company, Inc., are reproduced below:

THE MARSH MACHINERY COMPANY, INC.
Balance Sheet
December 31, 1982
(in thousands)

Total assets $104,390	Total liabilities		$ 18,494
	Stockholders' Equity		
	Common stock, $50 par value, (authorized 1,000,000 shares; outstanding 682,720 shares)	$34,136	
	Premium on capital stock	4,730	
	Earnings retained for use in the business....	47,030	85,896
Total assets $104,390	Total liabilities and stockholders' equity.		$104,390

THE MARSH MACHINERY COMPANY, INC.
Statement of Retained Earnings
For the Year Ended December 31, 1982
(in thousands)

Balance, January 1	$44,346
Net income for the year..	6,098
	$ 50,444
Cash dividends — $5 per share...	3,414
Balance, December 31...	$47,030

The balance sheet shows that the capital paid in by the stock-holders amounts to $38,866,000 ($34,136,000 + $4,730,000), while the capital resulting from the retained earnings amounts to $47,030,000. The statement of retained earnings provides an explanation of the changes in the retained earnings account during the year. The balance of the account ($44,346,000) was increased by the amount of net income for the year ($6,098,000), and was reduced by the payment of cash dividends ($3,414,000).

Note that over half of the capital of the business has been provided by retained earnings. As a result, the stockholders' equity has grown until their stock has a book value of $125.81 a share ($85,896,000 ÷ 682,720) though its average issue price since the company began operations was only $56.93 a share ($38,866,000 ÷ 682,720).

COMBINED INCOME AND RETAINED EARNINGS STATEMENT

The statement of retained earnings can be combined with the income statement. Such a statement, called an income and retained earnings statement, for The Marsh Machinery Company, Inc., with the detail of the income statement omitted, is shown below. This combined statement serves to account for the change in the balance of the retained earnings account during the year. Opinion is divided as to whether such a combined statement is superior to presenting the income statement separate from the statement of retained earnings.

THE MARSH MACHINERY COMPANY, INC.
Income and Retained Earnings Statement
For the Year Ended December 31, 1982
(in thousands)

Net income	$ 6,098
Retained earnings, January 1	44,346
	$50,444
Less cash dividends — $5 per share	3,414
Retained earnings, December 31	$47,030

An alternative arrangement that is often used is shown below:

Net income	$ 6,098
Less cash dividends — $5 per share	3,414
Net increase in retained earnings	$ 2,684
Retained earnings, January 1	44,346
Retained earnings, December 31	$47,030

RECAPITALIZATION

With the knowledge and consent of its stockholders, a corporation may secure an amendment to its articles of incorporation to permit it to change the legal value of its stock. Usually the change is to a lower par value or to no-par value. Generally this involves calling in the old stock certificates and issuing new certificates. A major reason for reducing either the par value or the stated value of capital stock without increasing the number of shares outstanding is to eliminate an accumulated deficit. If a corporation operates at a loss for a prolonged period of time, the sum of the assets will become less than the total liabilities plus paid-in capital, and the retained earnings account will have a debit balance, which is called a deficit. Officers, directors, and stockholders of a corporation dislike having to show a deficit. As long as there is a deficit, the corporation may not declare or pay dividends. This causes the corporation's stock to have a low market value. One way to eliminate a deficit is to recapitalize the corporation and reduce the par or stated value of the capital stock. Such a recapitalization is illustrated in the following paragraphs.

Assume that The Knapp Corporation had a deficit of $600,000 as shown by the condensed balance sheet below.

THE KNAPP CORPORATION
Balance Sheet

Total assets	$5,200,000	Total liabilities	$1,800,000
		Stockholders' Equity	
		Capital stock................... $4,000,000	
		Less deficit..................... 600,000	3,400,000
		Total liabilities and	
Total assets	$5,200,000	stockholders' equity.	$5,200,000

There were 40,000 shares of capital stock outstanding with a par value of $100 per share. In order to eliminate the deficit of $600,000, it was decided to obtain an amendment to the articles of incorporation to permit an exchange of the old shares of capital stock for an equal number of new shares with a par value of $50 per share. The exchange of stock certificates was recorded by the following journal entry:

Capital Stock (old)	4,000,000	
Capital Stock (new)		2,000,000
Premium on Capital Stock..		2,000,000

Premium on Capital Stock was credited for $2,000,000 because the new stock was, in effect, issued at a premium. The par value of the old stock was $4,000,000, whereas the par value of the new stock was only $2,000,000. The debit balance in the retained earnings account would then be eliminated by the following journal entry:

Premium on Capital Stock	600,000	
Retained Earnings		600,000

After the exchange of shares and the elimination of the Retained Earnings deficit were recorded in the manner suggested, the capital section of the balance sheet of the company would appear as follows:

Stockholders' Equity

Capital stock	$2,000,000	
Premium on capital stock	1,400,000	$3,400,000

The exchange of shares had no effect upon the assets or the liabilities. It should also be noted that the total capital after exchanging the stock and writing off the deficit is the same as before. The book value per share of stock was not affected. There are still 40,000 shares of stock outstanding and the total capital of the company is still $3,400,000; hence, the book value of each share of stock is still $85 a share. A reduction of the legal capital and the elimination of the deficit in the accounts were the only results of these events.

Corporate recapitalizations have various purposes and take a variety of forms. Frequently, there is a revaluation of assets, as well as a reduction in the par or stated value of the capital stock. This approach is known as a quasi-reorganization. Recapitalizations also may involve the elimination of one or more classes of stock and, sometimes, bonds. These alternate forms of recapitalization are subjects for a more advanced course.

BUILDING YOUR ACCOUNTING KNOWLEDGE

1. What are the two major sources of capital for every type of business?
2. To what extent should paid-in or invested capital be recorded in the proper capital stock accounts?
3. From what source does a major portion of the capital of a corporation frequently come?

4. On what financial statement must almost every transaction and event that involved a gain or loss to the business be reported?
5. What is the purpose of showing an appropriation amount in the owners' equity section of a corporate balance sheet?
6. What alternative procedure is available to advise balance-sheet readers of a restriction on dividends?
7. For what change does a combined income and retained earnings statement serve to account?
8. What is a major purpose of reducing the par or stated value of capital stock without increasing the number of shares outstanding?
9. What additional result took place in the exchange of shares of the Knapp Corporation?

Report No. 23-1

> *Complete Report No. 23-1 in the study assignments and submit your working papers for approval. Continue with the following textbook discussion until Report No. 23-2 is required.*

EARNINGS DISTRIBUTED TO STOCKHOLDERS

A distribution of earnings in either cash or other assets by a corporation to its stockholders is known as a dividend. When the dividend is paid in cash, it is known as a cash dividend. If a corporation issues additional shares of its own stock to the stockholders on a proportional ownership basis, these are known as stock dividends. When a corporation is being dissolved and any assets are distributed to the stockholders, the distribution is known as a liquidating dividend.

CASH DIVIDENDS

Most corporation dividends are paid in cash and represent the distribution of corporate earnings. Some corporations are able to pay dividends regularly; that is, annually, semiannually, or quarterly. Other corporations pay dividends irregularly. It has been noted that the size and the frequency of dividend distributions depend upon earnings, the amount of cash available, and the plans and policies of the directors.

Three dates are involved in the declaration and the payment of dividends: (1) the date of declaration, (2) the date of record, and (3) the date of payment. For example, a board of directors might meet on January 25 and declare a dividend of $5 a share on common stock, payable on February 15 to stockholders of record on February 5.

The result of such a declaration is to make the corporation liable for the dividend on the date of declaration, January 25. The date of record, February 5, is the day on which the names of stockholders entitled to receive the dividend are determined. However, the dividend will not be paid until February 15. To be eligible to receive the dividend, a stockholder's ownership of stock must be recorded in the books of the corporation not later than February 5. Thereafter any stock of the corporation that may be transferred is said to be transferred ex-dividend. This means that anyone acquiring the stock after February 5 will not be entitled to share in the dividend declared on January 25, even though the dividend may be paid after the stock is acquired.

Sometimes each dividend declared is given a number to distinguish it from those that have been declared in the past. Dividends on different classes of capital stock should be accounted for separately. To illustrate, assume that the board of directors declares a semiannual dividend of $6 per share on 4,000 shares of preferred stock outstanding and a semiannual dividend of $4 per share on 10,000 shares of common stock outstanding. Assume that this is the 37th dividend on the preferred stock and the 28th on the common stock. These declarations should be recorded, in general journal form, as follows:

Retained Earnings	24,000	
Preferred Dividends Payable, No. 37		24,000
Declared a dividend of $6 per share on 4,000 shares of preferred stock outstanding.		
Retained Earnings	40,000	
Common Dividends Payable, No. 28		40,000
Declared a dividend of $4 per share on 10,000 shares of common stock outstanding.		

When the dividends are paid, each of the dividends payable accounts should be debited and Bank should be credited. If a balance sheet were prepared on some date between the time the dividends were declared and the time they were paid, the balances of the two dividends payable accounts would be included among the current liabilities.

Sometimes large corporations with many stockholders draw a single check to cover a particular dividend and deposit the check in a special bank account. Such a transaction should be recorded by a debit to the special dividend checking account and a credit to the general checking account. Special check forms are used in paying such a dividend. The individual dividend checks may be recorded in a special dividend check register or in a dividend record similar to the one shown below. No other record need be made until the canceled checks are received from the bank together with a statement covering the special dividend deposit account. At that time the sum of the checks paid and canceled by the bank may be recorded by debiting Dividends Payable and by crediting the special dividend checking account. After all the dividend checks have been paid by the bank and the proper entries have been made in the books of the corporation, the dividends payable account and the special dividend checking account will have zero balances.

DIVIDEND RECORD

DIVIDEND NO.	DATE DECLARED	RATE	NO. OF SHARES	AMOUNT	NAME OF STOCKHOLDER	HOW PAID	DATE PAID
1	1982 Jan. 15	$2.50	300	750 00	Donald L. Pettigrew	Check	1982 Jan. 30
1	15	$2.50	100	250 00	Patricia A. Champion	"	- 30
1	15	$2.50	75	187 50	K. W. Risley	"	30
1	15	$2.50	15	37 50	G. S. Stewart	"	30
1	15	$2.50	10	25 00	Donald Blair	"	30

Dividend Record

In some instances, dividend checks are returned unclaimed or are never presented for payment to the bank on which they are drawn. Checks that are unclaimed may be canceled when they are returned. Payment may be stopped on any checks not returned and not presented to the bank for payment within a reasonable length of time. The total of such unclaimed and uncashed checks may be recorded by debiting Dividends Payable and by crediting Unclaimed Dividends. At the same time the unused portion of the dividend checking account should be transferred back to the general checking account. The account with Unclaimed Dividends will have a credit balance as long as any dividend checks remain unpaid. This balance should be reported in the balance sheet as a current liability.

STOCK DIVIDENDS AND STOCK SPLITS

A proportionate distribution of shares of a corporation's own stock to its stockholders is termed a stock dividend. Corporations may distribute this type of dividend for one or more of several reasons:

(1) The company may be short of cash and may be unable or unwilling to borrow to pay a cash dividend.

(2) It may be in the stockholders' interest to have more shares with a lower market price, as low-priced shares usually are more readily marketable. A greater number of shares outstanding makes wider ownership possible, and wider ownership may be desired in some cases.

(3) The corporation may have a large credit balance in Retained Earnings and the directors may consider it advisable to transfer a portion of this balance to a paid-in capital category for purposes of subsequent balance sheet presentation.

When a stock dividend is declared, an amount equal to the market value of the shares to be distributed should be charged to the retained earnings account. If the stock has a par or stated value, Stock Dividends Distributable should be credited for the par or stated value of the shares, and the excess of market value over par or stated value should be credited to Premium on Capital Stock. If the stock in question has neither par nor stated value, the market value of the dividend shares should be debited to Retained Earnings and credited to Stock Dividends Distributable. Stock Dividends Distributable is not a liability since no money is owed. If a balance sheet is prepared as of a date between the declaration and distribution of the stock dividend, the balance of the account should be reported in the stockholders' equity section of the statement. When the dividend shares are distributed, an entry should be made debiting Stock Dividends Distributable and crediting Capital Stock.

A stock dividend does not affect the assets, the liabilities, or the total capital of the corporation. The transaction merely transfers part of the balance of the retained earnings account to one or more paid-in capital accounts. Note that such a transfer weakens the distinction between invested capital and earned capital.

The proportionate amount of a common stockholder's interest in a corporation is not affected by a stock dividend of the same class of shares. The stockholders will have more shares, but the book value of each one will be proportionately reduced. For example, the owner of 100 shares of common stock of a corporation with 1,000 shares of common stock outstanding has a 10 percent interest in the total equity that belongs to the common shareholders. If a 20 percent common stock dividend were distributed, that stockholder would own 120 of 1,200 shares. There would still be a 10 percent interest in the equity — neither more nor less than before the dividend.

An exchange of one share of an old issue of stock for a multiple or fractional number of shares of a new issue of essentially the same class of stock is known as a stock split. The usual purpose of a stock split is to improve the marketability of the shares by reducing the market price per share. Note that increasing the market price per share of low-priced shares may accomplish the same purpose. Having a greater number of shares outstanding also makes it possible to have a wide ownership of the stock. The accounting for a stock split differs from that for a stock dividend in that none of the capital accounts is affected by a stock split. A stock split requires no formal journal entry and may be recorded simply by a memorandum entry in the general journal and in the appropriate capital stock accounts.

The distinction between a stock dividend and a stock split is largely a matter of degree. If the stock distribution is less than 20–25% of the outstanding shares, it is normally accounted for as a stock dividend. If the distribution is more than 20–25% of the outstanding shares, it is normally accounted for as a stock split. Generally, stock dividends and stock splits are not regarded as income to the recipient and are not subject to income tax.

LIQUIDATING DIVIDENDS

A liquidating dividend is very different from an ordinary cash dividend. An ordinary cash dividend is a distribution of earnings — a return on the stockholders' investment. A liquidating dividend represents a return of the stockholders' investment. The liquidation of the firm need not be completed before liquidating dividends are paid. As assets are converted into cash, the money may be distributed to the stockholders. Mining companies sometimes pay partial liquidating dividends as their ore reserves are depleted. They may pay dividends that represent partly earnings and partly a return of capital.

When a corporation is being completely dissolved or liquidated, first the liabilities must be paid in full. Next, if there are outstanding preferred shares that have a preference as to assets, the holders of such shares must receive the full amount to which they are entitled, including unpaid dividends if the stock is cumulative, before the common stockholders receive anything. Whatever is left is distributed proportionately to the common stockholders. Usually all such distributions are made in cash. Sometimes, however, property other than cash is distributed to the stockholders. Upon receiving the final distribution, the stockholders will return their stock certificates.

When articles of dissolution are filed with the proper state official, the corporation ceases to exist.

APPLICATION OF PRINCIPLES

A narrative of selected transactions completed by The Oliver Manufacturing Company, Inc., illustrates the principles involved in recording dividends declared and paid. The general journal entries necessary to record each event follow the transaction.

NARRATIVE OF TRANSACTIONS

Jan. 11   The board of directors declared dividends as follows:

On preferred stock: quarterly dividend No. 21, of $3 a share on 3,000 shares.

On common stock: dividend No. 11, of 50 cents a share on 30,000 shares.

Both dividends are payable in cash on February 1, to stockholders of record on January 20.

Retained Earnings..	9,000	
Preferred Dividends Payable, No. 21.....................................		9,000
Declared $3 per share dividend on 3,000 shares of preferred stock outstanding.		
Retained Earnings..	15,000	
Common Dividends Payable, No. 11.....................................		15,000
Declared a dividend of 50 cents a share on 30,000 shares of common stock outstanding.		

28   The shares of preferred stock are held by a very few people. Checks in payment of such dividends are drawn on the regular checking account. The shares of common stock are held by a large number of people. Special checks drawn on a dividend checking account are used to pay common stock dividends. Accordingly, the treasurer drew a check for $15,000 on the regular bank account and deposited it in the dividend checking account for the common stock dividend.

First National Bank, Dividend Account	15,000	
First National Bank, General Account		15,000
Transferred $15,000 to special dividend account.		

30   Checks drawn on the regular bank account in payment of the preferred dividend were prepared and mailed. Special

checks drawn on the dividend checking account in payment of the common dividend were also prepared and mailed.

Preferred Dividends Payable, No. 21	9,000	
First National Bank, General Account		9,000
Paid preferred dividend, No. 21.		

Feb. 27   A statement covering the dividend checking account for the common stock was received from the bank together with the canceled checks. It was noted that all checks issued had been paid.

Common Dividends Payable, No. 11..	15,000	
First National Bank, Dividend Account...................................		15,000
Dividend checks issued January 30, in payment of common dividend No. 11, paid by bank per statement of this date.		

Mar. 15   The board of directors declared a stock dividend of one share of common stock for every ten shares of common held. The market value of the common shares is $28 each. The par value of each share is $25. The stock will be distributed on April 5 to stockholders of record on March 25.

Retained Earnings..	84,000	
Common Stock Dividends Distributable...............................		75,000
Premium on Common Stock		9,000
Declared a dividend to common stockholders distributable in common stock on the basis of one share for every ten held (3,000 shares).		

Apr. 5   Certificates for the 3,000 shares of dividend stock were issued to the common stockholders.

Common Stock Dividends Distributable	75,000	
Common Stock		75,000
Issued 3,000 shares of common stock in settlement of stock dividend declared March 15.		

BUILDING YOUR ACCOUNTING KNOWLEDGE

1. What are the names of the three dates involved in the declaration and payment of dividends?
2. Why might each dividend that is declared be given a number?
3. Briefly describe how a large corporation may use a special bank account for the payment of dividends.

4. How does a corporation handle dividend checks that are returned unclaimed? That are never presented for payment to the bank on which they are drawn?
5. Give three reasons why a corporation may elect to distribute a stock dividend.
6. What effect does a stock dividend have on the accounts of the corporation? A stock split?
7. How does a liquidating dividend differ from an ordinary cash dividend?
8. What is the first step in the complete liquidation of a corporation?
9. What is the final step in the complete liquidation of a corporation?

Report No. 23-2

Complete Report No. 23-2 in the study assignments and submit your working papers for approval. Continue with the textbook discussion in Chapter 24 until Report No. 24-1 is required.

EXPANDING YOUR BUSINESS VOCABULARY

What is the meaning of each of the following terms?

appropriation (p. 633)
cash dividend (p. 638)
capital (p. 630)
date of record (p. 639)
deficit (p. 636)
dividend (p. 638)
earnings (p. 631)
Earnings Retained in the Business (p. 632)
ex-dividend (p. 639)
income and retained earnings statement (p. 635)

liquidating dividend (pp. 638, 642)
net income (p. 631)
paid-in capital (p. 631)
quasi-reorganization (p. 637)
Retained Earnings (p. 632)
statement of retained earnings (p. 634)
stock dividend (pp. 638, 640)
stock split (p. 642)
stockholders' equity (p. 630)

CHAPTER 24

ACCOUNTING FOR CORPORATE BONDS

CHAPTER OBJECTIVES

The objectives of this chapter are to enable you:

▶ To define and describe a corporate bond.

▶ To describe several ways in which corporation bonds may be classified.

▶ To describe the two streams of payment that must be accounted for with every bond issue and to define the concept of present value.

▶ To describe and prepare the entries to record the issuance of bonds under various circumstances, and describe accounts for:

    (1) Bonds payable
    (2) Premium on bonds payable
    (3) Discount on bonds payable

▶ To describe the nature of bond interest rates and prepare entries to record bond interest, its accrual, and the amortization of bond premium or discount, and describe accounts for:

    (1) Bond interest expense
    (2) Accrued bond interest payable

▶ To describe and prepare entries to record retirement of bonds under various circumstances, and describe accounts for:

    (1) Gain on bonds redeemed
    (2) Loss on bonds redeemed
    (3) Bond sinking funds

To supplement the funds provided by the stockholders of a corporation, additional funds may be obtained by issuing bonds. A bond is similar to a long-term note in that it is an interest-bearing, negotiable instrument in which the maker promises to pay a certain amount of money at a definite or determinable future date. Bonds usually are secured with respect to either principal or interest, or both, by a pledge of certain corporate property assets.

CORPORATE BONDS

The right to borrow money is implied in the charter of a corporation. The board of directors usually decides when and how much to borrow. If only a small amount of money is needed or if the money will be repaid in a short time, notes usually will be issued. The notes may be secured or unsecured. If the corporation has a good credit standing, it may be able to borrow on its unsecured notes. If this is the case, the liability that arises is recorded as Notes Payable. If the notes are secured by a mortgage, the liability is recorded as Mortgage Payable.

When a corporation borrows a large sum of money (commonly, several million dollars) for a long period of time (five to thirty years or more), it is customary to issue bonds instead of notes. A bond issue usually consists of a number of bonds. All of the bonds comprising the issue need not have the same denomination. They may be for $1,000, $5,000, $10,000, or more.

If bonds are secured, all of the bonds in a particular issue usually will be secured under one deed of trust. A deed of trust is a mortgage on certain specified properties. The deed is placed in the hands of a trustee who represents the bondholders. The deed of trust states the terms and the conditions under which the bonds are issued and under which the property is held for their security. Reference is made in the bonds to the deed of trust by which they are secured. Both the deed of trust and the bonds issued refer to each other in such a manner that all of the terms and conditions are clearly stated in both. The trustee has the right to act in behalf of the bondholders and may begin foreclosure proceedings if it becomes necessary to do so in order to safeguard their interests.

CLASSIFICATION OF BONDS

Bonds may be classified as to (1) the purpose of the issue, (2) the security of the bonds, or (3) the payment of the principal.

As to the Purpose of the Issue. When bonds are issued to acquire funds for a specific purpose, the bonds may be classified as:

(1) Improvement bonds
(2) Purchase-money bonds
(3) Refunding bonds
(4) Adjustment bonds

Improvement bonds are bonds issued to acquire funds for the construction of new buildings, such as an office building, a warehouse, a power plant, or some other type of permanent structure.

Purchase-money bonds are issued in exchange for assets or as part payment of the purchase price of an asset that has already been constructed.

Refunding bonds are a new series of bonds issued for the purpose of raising funds to be used either to pay off an old series of bonds that is soon to mature, or to retire outstanding bonds prior to maturity.

Adjustment bonds are new types of securities issued to the holders of securities already outstanding when companies that are in financial difficulties are being reorganized. For instance, bondholders may be given new bonds bearing a lower rate of interest in exchange for their old bonds. If a corporation is unable to pay the interest on its outstanding bonds because of reduced earnings, the bondholders may agree to take a new issue of bonds bearing a lower rate of interest in exchange for the old bonds.

As to Security. Bonds are often classified on the basis of the security offered. Such bonds may be classified as follows:

(1) Mortgage bonds
(2) Collateral-trust bonds
(3) Guaranteed bonds
(4) Debenture bonds

Mortgage bonds are bonds secured by a mortgage on corporate property assets, such as real estate, equipment, or leaseholds. Such bonds are sometimes designated as first mortgage bonds, second mortgage bonds, etc., according to the lien or claim by which they are secured. Thus, a first mortgage bond is a first lien or claim on the property covered by the mortgage.

Collateral-trust bonds are bonds secured by a deposit of stocks, bonds, mortgages, or other intangible collateral with a trustee under a trust agreement.

Guaranteed bonds are bonds of subsidiary or affiliated corporations that are guaranteed as to the payment of principal or interest, or both, by the parent company or another affiliated company. To be effective, the guarantee must be in writing and must either be stated on the bond or attached to it.

Debenture bonds are bonds secured solely by the general credit of the corporation issuing the bonds, rather than by any specific assets of the corporation.

As to Payment of Principal. Bonds are sometimes classified in accordance with the provisions made as to the payment of the principal, such as:

(1) Term bonds
(2) Serial bonds
(3) Convertible bonds
(4) Callable bonds

Term bonds are bonds issued together so that they all have the same maturity date. There may be a provision for a sinking fund which will cause a portion of the bonds to be retired before they become due, but the legal date of maturity is the same for the entire issue. Bond sinking funds will be discussed in the third section of this chapter.

Serial bonds are bonds issued in a series so that a specified amount of the principal matures each year. This is a means of providing for paying off a bond issue on the installment basis. Serial bonds may be secured or unsecured. If secured by a mortgage on certain property assets covering the entire issue, provision may be made for the relinquishment of portions of the security after the redemption of each series. Otherwise, all of the mortgaged property may be tied up until the last series of bonds is redeemed. If unsecured, serial bonds are similar to debenture bonds.

Convertible bonds are bonds issued giving the holder the option of exchanging the bonds for other bonds or capital stock of the corporation. Such a privilege may become valuable should the market value of these other securities of the corporation increase substantially. The basis upon which the conversion may be made is usually specified and the time within which the conversion must be made is often limited.

Callable bonds are bonds issued with a provision that they may be called for redemption before the date of maturity. Many bond issues have such a provision. Thus, twenty-year bonds may be issued with a provision that they are subject to call for payoff by the issuing corporation at any time after ten years from date of issue.

Bonds and stock often are mentioned in the same breath, but basically they are very different. A bond is an obligation of the issuing corporation — a promise to pay a certain amount of money on a certain date. Stock represents corporate ownership or equity; there is no promise to pay any definite amount at any stated time. Bondholders are creditors of a corporation; stockholders are owners.

ACCOUNTING FOR BONDS ISSUED

The discussion of accounting for the issuance of bonds will be more readily understood by the use of an example. The following facts are assumed regarding the issue of first mortgage bonds sold to the public by the Walworth Corporation.

> Date of issue: April 1, 1982
> Date of sale: April 1, 1982
> Principal amount: $200,000
> Denomination of each bond: $1,000
> Maturity date: March 31, 1997
> Contract interest rate: 8 percent, payable semiannually each April 1 and October 1

The Walworth Corporation issue of first mortgage bonds will also be used in the discussions of accounting for bond interest expense, and the retirement of bonds later in the chapter.

Factors that Determine Sales Price. There are numerous factors that determine the price at which bonds will sell. Two of the more important of these are (1) the rate of interest (contract or coupon rate) that the bond carries and (2) the current market or effective rate of interest on similar investment opportunites.

If the interest rate on the Walworth bonds is the same as the current market rate, the bonds will sell for their face value, $200,000. If the rate on the Walworth bonds is lower than the current market rate, the bonds will sell at a discount, or at a price less than their face value. Alternatively, if the rate on the Walworth bonds is higher than the current market rate, the bonds will sell at a premium, or at a price in excess of their face value.

In order to appreciate why the bonds sell at these different prices depending on the relationship between the interest rate on the bond and the current market rate, it is important to recognize the different cash flows related to the bond, and to understand the concept of present value.

Two Streams of Payment. Every bond issue requires the accounting for two cash flows, or streams of payment. In the Walworth Corporation case, the cash payments are: (1) the thirty semi-annual interest payments of $8,000 each to bondholders, beginning October 1, 1982, and (2) the repayment of the $200,000 principal amount to bondholders on March 31, 1997. The time-chart below illustrates how these two streams of payment affect the Walworth Corporation:

```
MONEY                                                    MATURITY
RECEIVED                                                   DATE
FROM CREDITORS
ON APRIL 1, 1982                                      MAR. 31, 1997

      ┌──── SEMIANNUAL INTEREST PAYMENTS OF $8,000 EACH ────┐
      ↓ ↓ ↓ ↓ ↓ ↓ ↓ ↓ ↓ ↓ ↓ ↓ ↓ ↓ ↓ ↓ ↓ ↓ ↓ ↓ ↓ ↓ ↓ ↓ ↓ ↓ ↓ ↓ ↓ ↓
        1   2   3   4   5   6   7   8   9  10  11  12  13  14
      ↓──── REPAYMENT OF THE $200,000 PRINCIPAL ──────────────→
      0                                                      15
                            YEARS
```

In effect, Walworth Corporation must repay its bondholders a total of $440,000 during the 15-year period, consisting of $240,000 interest that is made up of 30 equal payments of $8,000 each, and the $200,000 of borrowed principal due March 31, 1997.

Present Value. To understand the accounting for bonds issued and the related interest expense, it is necessary to be acquainted with the concept of present value. The price that a bond buyer is willing to pay now for future benefits is called the present value of the bonds. In the case of the Walworth Corporation, the amount received for the $200,000, 8 percent bonds issued on April 1, 1982, will be the sum of (1) the present value of the 30 semiannual interest payments of $8,000 each plus (2) the present value of $200,000 to be repaid in 15 years. Three possible relationships exist between the interest rate on the bond and the market rate, one of which will determine the price of the bonds as computed in the paragraphs that follow.

Present Value of Bonds Issued at Face Value. Assume that the market rate of interest for the Walworth Corporation bonds on April 1, 1982, was exactly the same as the contract rate, or 8%. In this case, the bonds would have sold at their face value. The present value of the two streams of payment would then be as follows:

Present value of 30 semiannual interest payments of $8,000 each, at 8% compounded semiannually............	$138,340
Present value of $200,000 due in 15 years, at 8% compounded semiannually	61,660
Total present value of bond issue............................	$200,000

The two present values shown above were calculated using the two mathematical tables contained in the Appendix: Table 1 — Present Value of Annuity of $1 at compound interest, and Table 2 — Present Value of $1 at compound interest. An annuity is a series of identical amounts. Two items of information are needed to use these tables: (1) the number of interest payment periods over the life of the bond issue, and (2) the effective annual interest rate for this same life. The rule is: Use a period number twice the size of the life of the bond issue in years, and an interest rate half the size of the effective annual rate to enter the tables. The two present values shown above were calculated as follows:

Step 1. Entering Table 1 for *30* periods and *4* percent, the interest annuity present value factor is 17.2920.

Step 2. Entering Table 2 for *30* periods and *4* percent, the principal present value factor is .3083. These factors are then used as follows:

Step 3. The approximate present value of the interest is $138,336 ($8,000 × 17.2920).

Step 4. The approximate present value of the principal amount due in 15 years is $61,660 ($200,000 × .3083).

Step 5. These two present values add to $199,996 ($138,336 + $61,660), which is $4 short of the $200,000 face value of the bond issue. This difference is a rounding error caused by the fact that the present value factors in Tables 1 and 2 of the Appendix are rounded values. The difference of $4 is therefore arbitrarily added to the present value of the interest payments, because the error effect on that amount probably was greater. There are 30 contracted interest payments and only one contracted principal payment.

Issuance of Bonds at Face Value. The sale and issuance of the Walworth Corporation 8% bonds on April 1, 1982, at a market rate of 8%, would be recorded as follows:

1982		
April 1 Bank...	200,000	
First Mortgage Bonds Payable...............................		200,000
Sold 8% mortgage bonds at face value.		

Present Value of Bonds Issued at a Premium. Assume that the market rate of interest for the Walworth Corporation 8% bonds on April 1, 1982, was 7%. In this case, the bonds would sell at a premium, or a price in excess of their face value. The present value of the two streams of payment would then be as follows:

Present value of 30 semiannual interest payments of $8,000 each at 7% compounded semiannually............	$147,137
Present value of $200,000 due in 15 years, at 7% compounded semiannually	71,260
Total present value of bond issue as of April 1, 1982......	$218,397

The two present values shown above were calculated as follows:

Step 1. Entering Table 1 for *30* periods and *3½* percent, the interest annuity present value factor is 18.3921.

Step 2. Entering Table 2 for *30* periods and *3½* percent, the principal present value factor is .3563. These factors are then used as follows:

Step 3. The approximate present value of the interest annuity is $147,137 ($8,000 × 18.3921).

Step 4. The approximate present value of the principal amount due in 15 years is $71,260 ($200,000 × .3563).

Step 5. These two present values add to $218,397, which becomes the price at which the bonds are sold on April 1, 1982.

Note that the market rate, not the contract rate, is used in these calculations. The market rate also was used in the calculation of the present value of the bonds issued at their face value. In that case, the rate was the same as the contract rate.

Issuance of Bonds at Premium. The sale and issuance of the Walworth Corporation 8% bonds on April 1, 1982, at a market rate of 7%, would be recorded as follows:

1982			
April 1	Bank	218,397	
	First Mortgage Bonds Payable..............................		200,000
	Premium on Bonds Payable..................................		18,397
	Sold 8% first mortgage bonds at a market rate of 7%.		

Present Value of Bonds Issued at a Discount. Assume that the market rate of interest for the Walworth Corporation 8% bonds was 9%. In this case, the bonds would sell at a discount, or a price lower than their face value. The present value of the two streams of payment would then be as follows:

Present value of 30 semiannual interest payments of $8,000 each at 9% compounded semiannually............	$130,311
Present value of $200,000 due in 15 years, at 9% compounded semiannually	53,400
Total present value of bond issue as of April 1, 1982......	$183,711

The two present values were calculated as follows:

Step 1. Entering Table 1 for *30* periods and *4½* percent, the interest annuity present value factor is 16.2889.

Step 2. Entering Table 2 for *30* periods and *4½* percent, the principal present value factor is .2670. These factors are then used as follows:

Step 3. The approximate present value of the interest annuity is $130,311 ($8,000 × 16.2889).

Step 4. The approximate present value of the principal amount due in 15 years is $53,400 ($200,000 × .2670).

Step 5. These two present values add to $183,711, which becomes the price at which the bonds were sold on April 1, 1982.

Once again, note that the market rate, not the contract rate, is used in these calculations.

Issuance of Bonds at Discount. The sale and issuance of the Walworth Corporation 8% bonds on April 1, 1982, at a market rate of 9%, would be recorded as follows:

```
1982
April  1   Bank........................................................................  183,711
           Discount on Bonds Payable.......................................   16,289
              First Mortgage Bonds Payable.............................              200,000
              Sold 8% first mortgage bonds at a market rate
              of 9%.
```

Sale of Bonds Between Interest Dates. All of the preceding examples involve the sale of bonds on the very day interest began. The entries would be equally correct if the bonds were sold on any interest date. When bonds are sold between interest dates, however, the buyer must pay for the amount of interest that had accrued since the last interest date. Bond prices are quoted at certain amounts plus accrued interest. On the first regular interest date following the purchase, the amount of interest paid at time of purchase will be returned to the buyer.

For example, suppose that the Walworth Corporation experiences delays so that the bonds are not sold until May 1 following the issue date of April 1. Five months later on October 1, the purchasers will receive checks for the full six months interest (April 1 to October 1). For this reason, the buyers will have to pay the corporation $1,333 ($200,000 × 8% ÷ 12) for one month's interest that is accrued when the bonds are purchased. The sale would be recorded as shown at the top of page 655.

The additional amount received on May 1 because of the interest accrued since April 1 is recorded as a credit to Bond Interest Expense. By crediting this accrued interest to Bond Interest Expense,

1982		
May 1	Bank	201,333
	First Mortgage Bonds Payable	200,000
	Bond Interest Expense	1,333
	Sold first mortgage bonds at 100 plus accrued interest, April 1–May 1.	

that account will show the amount of interest expense actually incurred, $6,667, when it is debited for the interest paid on the bonds on October 1 amounting to $8,000 ($8,000 − $1,333 = $6,667).

RECORDS OF BONDHOLDERS AND BOND TRANSFERS

In order that corporate bondholders can receive periodic payments of interest, it is generally necessary that an accurate and up-to-date record of bond ownership be maintained. Because corporate bonds can be bought and sold, just as in the case of shares of stock, appropriate bond transfer records must be used. When a bond is sold to a new owner, a new certificate in the name of the new owner must be prepared and the old certificate canceled. If there are few bondholders and infrequent changes of ownership, a bondholders ledger and bond transfer record generally similar in form to those records for stockholders illustrated on page 604 may suffice. If there are hundreds or even thousands of bondholders and a large volume of ownership transfers, the necessary records undoubtedly will involve the use of electronic computers. Very frequently such records are maintained by the fiscal agent for the bonds who may also be the trustee.

COUPON BONDS

An exception to the requirement that a record of bond ownership be maintained exists in the case of coupon bonds. Although coupon bonds are no longer issued by business corporations, it was once common practice to issue these "bearer" instruments, meaning that the bonds would be payable at maturity to whomever had them. Such bonds were issued with a number of small interest coupons attached. Each coupon had a maturity or due date. Since bond interest is usually payable semiannually, a twenty-five year bond would have 50 coupons, the first coupon due six months from the issue date of the bonds, the next one six months later, and so on. The last coupon is due on the maturity date of the bond. Each coupon is for six months' interest. To illustrate, each coupon of a 25-year, 9%, $10,000 bond, is for $450 (½ of 9% × $10,000). When the bond was originally issued, it actually had fifty-one promises to pay specified amounts: fifty promises to pay $450 on the interest dates and one promise to pay $10,000 on the maturity date. As each coupon comes due, the holder of the bond removes — usually cuts off or clips — the coupon and presents it for payment. In many cases, the bondholder's bank accepts matured coupons for deposit.

Business corporations no longer issue coupon bonds because now they must report annually to the Internal Revenue Service the name of everyone to whom $10 or more interest was paid. However, there probably are billions of dollars of coupon bonds still outstanding that were issued before the reporting requirement became effective. Furthermore, governments (federal, state, and local) still use coupon bonds in their borrowings.

Five facts about coupon bonds should be noted:

(1) The issuer of the bonds cannot keep a record of who owns the bonds, which makes the accounting task easier. This statement is not true if the ownership of a bond is "registered," a practice sometimes followed to protect the bondholder.

(2) The corporation issuing a coupon bond does not have to prepare and mail interest checks every six months. Just before each interest date the total amount due can be given to the bank that acts as the fiscal agent in paying the coupons.

(3) Since unregistered coupon bonds are bearer instruments, the owners must take care that the bonds do not get lost, destroyed, or stolen.

(4) When a coupon bond is sold, it is literally that specific bond that changes hands. Because such bonds may be handled by many people over a number of years, the bonds usually are printed or engraved on sturdy, parchment-type paper.

(5) The bondholder is put to the trouble of having to remove matured coupons every six months and present them in order to obtain the interest payment.

BUILDING YOUR ACCOUNTING KNOWLEDGE

1. Explain the manner in which a deed of trust and a bond issue refer to each other.

2. Explain the difference between a corporate bond and a corporate stock from the standpoint of the corporation that issues either one.

3. Describe the two cash flows, or streams of payment that must be accounted for in connection with every bond issue.

4. What rule must be followed with respect to the period number and the interest rate when entering a present value table to obtain factors for the calculation of the present value of a bond issue?

5. Is the contract rate or the market rate used to calculate the present value of the interest annuity arising from a bond issue? To calculate the present value of the principal amount due when the bond issue matures?

6. When bonds are sold between interest dates, what must the buyer pay besides the agreed upon value of the bonds themselves?

7. What action is taken with reference to the bond certificate when a bond is sold to a new owner?

8. List five basic facts about coupon bonds.

Report No. 24-1

> *Complete Report No. 24-1 in the study assignments and submit your working papers for approval. Continue with the textbook discussion until Report No. 24-2 is required.*

ACCOUNTING FOR BOND INTEREST EXPENSE

The interest rate specified in the bond contract, known as the contract or coupon rate, may differ from the market or effective rate at the time the bonds are sold. As previously illustrated, if the market rate of interest is higher than the contract rate at the time of sale, the bonds will be sold at a discount, or for less than their face value. On the other hand, as previously illustrated, if the market rate of interest is lower than the contract rate at the time of sale, the bonds will be sold at a premium, or for more than their face value.

INTEREST EXPENSE ON BONDS ISSUED AT FACE VALUE

Bond interest usually is paid every six months, and is customarily recorded separately from other types of interest expense. The first semiannual interest payment on October 1 on the Walworth Corporation's $200,000 face value issue of 8%, first mortgage bonds, dated April 1, 1982, may be recorded in the general journal as follows:

1982			
Oct. 1	Bond Interest Expense	8,000	
	Bank		8,000
	Made semiannual payment of interest on 8% bonds outstanding.		

At the close of each accounting period, an adjusting entry should be made to record any interest accrued on bonds payable since the last interest payment date. If the accounting period closed as of December 31, three months' interest has accrued (October 1 to December 31) which amounts to $4,000. It is therefore necessary to adjust the accounts as follows:

```
1982
Dec. 31   Bond Interest Expense...................................................... 4,000
              Accrued Bond Interest Payable ..................................          4,000
              Accrued bond interest.
```

After the posting is completed, the bond interest expense account will have a debit balance of $12,000 and the accrued bond interest payable account will have a credit balance of $4,000. In T account form, the two accounts would appear as follows:

Bond Interest Expense		**Accrued Bond Interest Payable**	
1982		1982	
Oct. 1 8,000		Dec. 31 4,000	
Dec. 31 4,000			
_12,000_			

The balance of the bond interest expense account represents the total interest expense incurred from April 1 to December 31. The balance of the accrued bond interest payable account represents the amount of the accrued liability on December 31.

The December 31, 1982, adjusting entry normally would be reversed as of January 1, 1983. The next semiannual interest payment on April 1, 1983, would then be made exactly like the entry made on October 1, 1982.

INTEREST EXPENSE AND PREMIUM AMORTIZATION

Assume that the Walworth Corporation 8% bonds were sold when the market rate was 7%, as illustrated on pages 652–653. Because the bonds were sold at a premium, the amount of semiannual interest that actually is paid is not the true interest expense for the period. The bond interest expense account must be adjusted to recognize the effect of the original premium. The process of adjusting the bond interest expense account for any premium or discount is called amortization of the premium or discount.

There are two commonly used methods of amortizing premium (or discount) over the life of a bond: (1) interest and (2) straight-line. The interest method is the recommended method, but the straight-line method is acceptable if the results are not significantly different from those obtained using the interest method. Each of these methods is illustrated in the following sections.

Interest Method. Under the interest method, the interest expense each period is equal to the effective rate multiplied by the beginning-of-period carrying value of the bonds.

For the Walworth Corporation bonds, the market rate of interest, 3½% for six months, multiplied by the issue price (which is also the carrying value in the first period) of $218,397 is equal to $7,644, which is considered to be the effective interest expense. The amount of premium to be amortized is the difference between the effective interest expense and the semiannual contract interest of $8,000, or $356 ($8,000 − $7,644).

The entry to record the first semiannual interest payment and the amortization of bond premium on October 1, 1982, would appear as follows:

1982			
Oct. 1	Bond Interest Expense	7,644	
	Premium on Bonds Payable	356	
	Bank		8,000
	Made semiannual payment of interest on 8% bonds outstanding and amortized six months' premium on effective interest basis.		

The adjusting entry for accrued interest on the bonds as of December 31, 1982, would require a new effective interest calculation. The carrying value of the bond issue as of October 1, 1982, would be $218,041 ($218,397 issue price less $356 of premium amortized on October 1, 1982). The accrued interest on December 31 would be $218,041 × 1¾% (7% × $3/_{12}$ = 1¾%), the effective interest rate for three months, or $3,816. The contractual interest accrued as of that date would still be $4,000 (2% contract interest for three months × $200,000 face value of bonds). The difference of $184 ($4,000 − $3,816) would be the amount of premium to be amortized. The necessary adjusting entry would then appear as follows:

1982			
Dec. 31	Bond Interest Expense	3,816	
	Premium on Bonds Payable	184	
	Accrued Bond Interest Payable		4,000
	Accrued bond interest.		

After the posting is completed, the bond interest expense, accrued bond interest payable, and premium on bonds payable accounts would appear in T account form as follows:

Bond Interest Expense			
1982			
Oct. 1	7,644		
Dec. 31	3,816		
	11,460		

Accrued Bond Interest Payable	
	1982
	Dec. 31 4,000

Premium on Bonds Payable			
1982		1982	
Oct. 1	356	Apr. 1	18,397
Dec. 31	184		
	540		17,857

The balance of the bond interest expense account ($11,460) represents the total effective interest expense from April 1, 1982, to December 31, 1982. The balance of the accrued bond interest payable account represents the amount of the accrued liability on December 31. The balance of the premium on bonds payable account ($17,857) represents the premium still to be amortized during the remaining 14¼ years of life of the bond issue.

The December 31, 1982, adjusting entry normally would be reversed as of January 1, 1983. The next semiannual interest and premium amortization entry on April 1, 1983, would take the same form as the entry of October 1, 1982, illustrated on page 659. However, the effective interest (debit to Bond Interest Expense) would be calculated as $218,041 (the carrying value of the bond issue on October 1, 1982) × 3½%, or $7,631, and the bond premium amortization would thus amount to $369 ($8,000 − $7,631). The entry would appear as follows:

1983			
Apr. 1	Bond Interest Expense	7,631	
	Premium on Bonds Payable	369	
	Bank		8,000
	Made semiannual payment of interest on 8% bonds outstanding and amortized six months' premium on effective interest basis.		

Premium on Bonds Payable should be classified as an adjunct (addition to) liability account. It would appear on the December 31, 1982, balance sheet of the Walworth Corporation under the Long-Term Liabilities heading as follows:

Long-term liabilities:		
Bonds payable	200,000	
Premium on bonds payable	17,857	217,857

Straight-Line Method. The straight-line method of amortization, which is simpler to apply than the interest method, provides for amortizing an equal amount of the premium each time period. To calculate the amount of premium to be amortized, the total original premium ($18,397) is divided by the life of the bond, typically expressed in terms of half years. The quotient is the amount of premium to be written off each half year. Application of this method to the Walworth Corporation bonds would yield amortization of 1/30 of $18,397, or $613 each half year. The entry to record the first semiannual interest payment and the amortization of bond premium on October 1, 1982, would appear as follows:

```
1982
Oct.  1    Bond Interest Expense..................................................    7,387
           Premium on Bonds Payable ..........................................      613
              Bank..........................................................................              8,000
              Made  semiannual  payment  of  interest  on  8%
              bonds  outstanding  and  amortized  six  months'
              premium on straight-line basis.
```

The adjusting entry for accrued interest on the bonds as of December 31, 1982, would include $4,000 for the contractual interest accrued as of that date, plus amortization of an appropriate portion of the premium on the bonds. The amount of premium to be amortized for 3 months (October 1 — December 31) would be $307 (½ × $613). The necessary adjusting entry would then appear as follows:

```
1982
Dec. 31    Bond Interest Expense..................................................    3,693
           Premium on Bonds Payable ..........................................      307
              Accrued Bond Interest Payable ...................................              4,000
              Accrued bond interest.
```

INTEREST EXPENSE AND DISCOUNT AMORTIZATION

Assume that the Walworth Corporation 8% bonds were sold at a market rate of 9%, as illustrated on pages 653–654. As in the case of bonds sold at a premium, the actual semiannual interest payment is not the true periodic interest expense. Once again, the bond interest expense account must be adjusted to amortize a portion of the original discount.

Interest Method. The market rate of interest, 4½% for six months, multiplied by the issue price of $183,711 is equal to $8,267, which is considered to be the effective interest expense. The amount of discount to be amortized is the difference between this amount and the $8,000 semiannual contract interest, or $267 ($8,267 − $8,000).

The entry to record the first semiannual interest payment and the amortization of bond discount on October 1, 1982, would appear as follows:

```
1982
Oct.  1   Bond Interest Expense.......................................................   8,267
              Discount on Bonds Payable.........................................              267
              Bank.............................................................................            8,000
              Made semiannual payment of interest on 8%
              bonds outstanding and amortized six months'
              discount on effective interest basis.
```

The adjusting entry for accrued interest on the bonds as of December 31, 1982, would require a new effective interest calculation. The carrying value of the bond issue as of October 1, 1982, would be $183,978 ($183,711 issue price plus $267 of discount amortized on October 1, 1982). The accrued interest on December 31 would be $183,978 × 2¼% (effective interest rate for three months) or $4,140. The difference between this amount and the accrued contractual interest of $4,000 as of that date, or $140 ($4,140 − $4,000) would be the amount of discount to be amortized. The necessary adjusting entry would then appear as follows:

```
1982
Dec. 31   Bond Interest Expense.......................................................   4,140
              Accrued Bond Interest Payable ..................................            4,000
              Discount on Bonds Payable.........................................              140
              Accrued bond interest.
```

After the posting is completed, the bond interest expense, accrued bond interest payable, and discount on bonds payable accounts would appear in T account form as follows:

Bond Interest Expense		Accrued Bond Interest Payable	
1982			1982
Oct. 1	8,267		Dec. 31	4,000
Dec. 31	4,140		
	12,407		

Discount on Bonds Payable			
1982		1982	
Apr. 1	16,289	Oct. 1	267
		Dec. 31	140
	15,882		407

The balance of the bond interest expense account ($12,407) represents the total effective interest expense from April 1, 1982, to December 31, 1982. The balance of the accrued bond interest payable account represents the accrued interest liability on December

31. The balance of the discount on bonds payable account ($15,882) represents the discount still to be amortized during the remaining 14¼ years of life of the bond issue.

The December 31, 1982, adjusting entry normally would be reversed as of January 1, 1983. The next semiannual interest and discount amortization entry on April 1, 1983, would take the same form as the October 1, 1982 entry illustrated on page 662. However, the effective interest (debit to Bond Interest Expense) would be calculated as $183,978 (the carrying value of the bond issue on October 1, 1982) × 4½%, or $8,279, and the bond discount amortization would amount to $279. The entry would appear as follows:

```
1983
Apr.  1   Bond Interest Expense.......................................................   8,279
              Discount on Bonds Payable..........................................                279
              Bank..............................................................................              8,000
              Made semiannual payment of interest on 8%
              bonds outstanding and amortized six months'
              discount on effective interest basis.
```

Discount on Bonds Payable should be classified as a contra (subtraction from) liability account. It would appear on the December 31, 1982, balance sheet of the Walworth Corporation under the Long-Term Liabilities heading as follows:

```
Long-term liabilities:
   Bonds payable ...........................................................   200,000
   Discount on bonds payable ......................................    15,882   184,118
```

Straight-Line Method. Application of the straight-line method to the Walworth Corporation bonds would yield discount amortization of 1/30 of $16,289 or $543 each half year. The entry to record the first semiannual interest payment and the amortization of bond discount on October 1, 1982, would appear as follows:

```
1982
Oct.  1   Bond Interest Expense.......................................................   8,543
              Discount on Bonds Payable..........................................                543
              Bank..............................................................................              8,000
              Made semiannual payment of interest on 8%
              bonds outstanding and amortized six months'
              discount on straight-line basis.
```

The adjusting entry for accrued interest on the bonds as of December 31, 1982, would include $4,000 for the contractual interest accrued as of that date, plus amortization of an appropriate portion of the discount on the bonds. The amount of discount to be amortized for 3 months (October 1–December 31) would be $272 (½ × $543). The necessary adjusting entry would then appear as follows:

```
1982
Dec. 31   Bond Interest Expense........................................   4,272
          Discount on Bonds Payable...........................                272
          Accrued Bond Interest Payable ..................              4,000
          Accrued bond interest.
```

DEFERRED CHARGES

Certain prepaid items, such as supplies, prepaid insurance, and prepaid interest, which will ordinarily be used up within the current operating cycle of a business, are generally treated as current assets. On the other hand, long-term prepayments such as expenditures for services or benefits, that are properly chargeable to a number of accounting periods should be grouped together or itemized under the heading of deferred charges in the asset section of the balance sheet. At one time, discount on bonds payable was classified as a deferred charge, and listed last among the assets, but this treatment is no longer acceptable.

DEFERRED CREDITS

It sometimes happens that the demands of reasonable matching of revenue and expense result in adjustment credits that cannot be considered liabilities in the usual sense, nor can they be regarded as a part of owner's equity. One example is the case of certain amounts of income tax that may become payable in the distant future, but are considered as current expense in the process of calculating periodic income. Another example arises when customers remit in advance for goods or services still to be provided. These circumstances give rise to what are called deferred credits. Deferred credits should be classified as liabilities on the balance sheet. At one time premium on bonds payable was classified as a deferred credit, but this treatment is no longer acceptable.

BUILDING YOUR ACCOUNTING KNOWLEDGE

1. What relationship between the market rate of interest and the contractual rate of interest determines that bonds will be sold at a discount? At a premium?

2. What is the purpose of the adjusting entry involving bond interest at the close of each accounting period?
3. How is the periodic interest expense on a bond issue determined using the interest method of amortization? Using the straight-line method?
4. How is the premium on bonds payable usually classified on the balance sheet? How is discount on bonds payable usually classified?
5. How do deferred charges differ from ordinary prepaid items?
6. How do deferred credits differ from ordinary liabilities?

Report No. 24-2

> *Complete Report No. 24-2 in the study assignments and submit your working papers for approval. Continue with the textbook discussion until Report No. 24-3 is required.*

ACCOUNTING FOR BONDS RETIRED

Usually, bonds issued by a corporation are redeemed at face value at their maturity. By that date, the entire amount of any issuance premium or discount should have been written off. To record the redemption, Bonds Payable is debited and Bank is credited. The retired bonds usually are marked "Canceled" and are stored until they are reviewed by the company auditors. After that, the bonds are destroyed.

Corporations may redeem part or all of a bond issue before maturity. In some cases, a corporation may compel the bondholders to surrender their bonds by taking advantage of an option to call the bonds before they mature. Unless the terms of the issue include such an option, however, this procedure is not possible. Without such an option, a corporation can purchase its bonds only if it has the money and if the holders of the bonds are willing to sell.

REDEMPTION OF BONDS ORIGINALLY SOLD AT FACE VALUE

Usually, there is either a gain or a loss involved in the redemption of bonds before their maturity date. If the bonds were originally sold at face value and the corporation pays more than the face amount when the bonds are redeemed, there is a loss. For example, the Walworth Corporation $200,000, 8% bond issue was sold at face value. If $20,000 of the issue is redeemed at 103 percent of face value, $20,600 ($20,000 × 103%) is paid to the bondholders and the corporation sustains a loss of $600. The journal entry to record this transaction would be as follows:

First Mortgage Bonds Payable..	20,000	
Loss on Bonds Redeemed..	600	
Bank...		20,600
Redeemed bonds with face value of $20,000 at 103.		

If bonds that originally were sold at face value are redeemed for a lesser amount, a gain results. If, in the preceding case, the price paid had been 97 percent of face value instead of 103 percent, there would have been a gain of $600. In this case, the journal entry to record the transaction would be as follows:

First Mortgage Bonds Payable..	20,000	
Gain on Bonds Redeemed		600
Bank...		19,400
Redeemed bonds with face value of $20,000 at 97.		

REDEMPTION OF BONDS ORIGINALLY SOLD AT A PREMIUM

If a corporation redeems part or all of its bonds that originally were sold at a premium, the calculation of the gain or the loss involved must take into account the premium amortization from the date of issue to the date of redemption. If the redemption is made at the end of the accounting period or on an interest payment date, the amortization of the premium on the bonds will be up-to-date. If the redemption is made at some other time, it will be necessary to record the amortization of the premium on the bonds for the time elapsed since the last regular premium amortization entry was made. The proper amounts should be debited to the bond interest expense and premium on bonds payable accounts and credited to the accrued bond interest payable account — the same accounts that are involved in the regular periodic interest expense and premium-amortization entry. These procedures are necessary under both the interest and the straight-line amortization methods.

Refer to the Walworth Corporation bonds which were sold at a premium for $218,397 (see pages 652–653). Assume that six years later the corporation redeems $20,000 of this issue at 108 percent. If the April 1, 1988, interest payment and premium amortization have been recorded, the carrying value of the $20,000 of bonds on April 1, 1988, according to the interest method of amortization, would be $21,320 ($20,000 plus $1,320 unamortized premium).

The journal entry to record the redemption of the bonds would be as follows:

```
1988
April  1   First Mortgage Bonds Payable ....................................... 20,000
           Premium on Bonds Payable ...........................................  1,320
           Loss on Bonds Redeemed .............................................    280
             Bank ..................................................................................       21,600
               Redeemed bonds with face value of $20,000 at
               108.
```

Note that this entry removes the portion of the premium account balance that relates to the bonds being redeemed. Bonds that are retired are removed from the liability account and any related unamortized premium must also be removed. The remaining balance of the premium account is the unamortized premium on the $180,000 face value of bonds still outstanding.

If the bonds had been redeemed at 103 percent, there would have been a gain rather than a loss on the redemption. The journal entry to record this redemption would be as follows:

```
1988
April  1   First Mortgage Bonds Payable ....................................... 20,000
           Premium on Bonds Payable ...........................................  1,320
             Gain on Bonds Redeemed ...........................................          720
             Bank ..................................................................................       20,600
               Redeemed bonds with face value of $20,000 at
               103.
```

Note that this entry does not reflect any change in the treatment of the premium account. The only difference is that a gain of $720 results instead of a loss of $280 as in the previous case, because the market price of the bonds redeemed is lower than their carrying value.

REDEMPTION OF BONDS ORIGINALLY SOLD AT A DISCOUNT

If a corporation redeems part or all of its bonds that originally were sold at a discount, the calculation of the gain or the loss involved must take into account the discount amortization from the date of issue to date of redemption. Before recording the redemption, the amortization of the discount on the bonds must be brought up-to-date. If the date of redemption is at the end of the accounting period or on an interest payment date, the amortization will be up-to-date. If this is not the case, the amount of discount amortization since the last regular discount write-off will have to be calculated and recorded. This amount would be debited to the bond interest expense account and credited to the accrued bond interest payable and bond discount accounts — the same accounts that are involved in the regular periodic interest expense and discount-amortization entry.

Refer to the Walworth Corporation bonds which were sold at a discount for $183,711 (see pages 653–654). Assume that 10 years later the corporation redeems $20,000 of this issue at 99. If the April 1, 1992, interest payment and discount amortization have been recorded, the carrying value of the $20,000 bonds on April 1, 1992, according to the interest method of amortization, would be $19,209 ($20,000 less $791 unamortized discount).

The journal entry to record this redemption would be as follows:

```
1992
April  1   First Mortgage Bonds Payable.........................................   20,000
           Loss on Bonds Redeemed...............................................      591
              Discount on Bonds Payable.........................................                791
              Bank..............................................................             19,800
                 Redeemed bonds with face value of $20,000 at
                 99.
```

Note that this entry removes the portion of the discount account balance that relates to the bonds being redeemed. Bonds that are retired are removed from the liability account and any unrelated unamortized discount must also be removed. The remaining balance of the discount account is the unamortized discount on the $180,000 face value of bonds still outstanding.

If the bonds had been redeemed at 95 percent, there would have been a gain rather than a loss on the redemption. The journal entry to record this redemption would be as follows:

```
1992
April  1   First Mortgage Bonds Payable.........................................  20,000
              Discount on Bonds Payable.........................................                791
              Gain on Bonds Redeemed ...........................................                209
              Bank..............................................................             19,000
                 Redeemed bonds with face value of $20,000 at
                 95.
```

Note that this entry does not reflect any change in the treatment of the discount account. The only difference is that a gain of $209 results instead of a loss of $591 as in the previous case, because the market price of the bonds redeemed is lower than their carrying value.

BOND SINKING FUNDS

In years past a variety of practices have been followed in connection with the accumulation of money to redeem corporation term bonds. In some instances, money has been set aside and invested over a period of years to provide the amount needed to redeem an issue of bonds at its maturity, in accumulations described as sinking funds or bond retirement funds. Sometimes the funds were established voluntarily; more often they were the result of requirements in the bond agreements (which are called indentures). Such requirements usually have provided that the trustee for a bond issue shall receive the necessary money and administer the fund. Sometimes, the issuing corporation was required to make appropriations of retained earnings equal to the specified additions to the fund.

Current practices in regard to bond sinking funds differ in purpose and operation from those described in the preceding paragraph. At the present time, the usual purpose of sinking funds is to provide what is termed "price support" for the bond issue. The bond indenture may require the corporation to pay to the trustee each year a stated percentage (often 1 or 2 percent) of the largest amount of bonds of the issue outstanding. The trustee, in turn, must use the money either to purchase some of the bonds in the market or, if necessary, to acquire them by the exercise of a special "sinking fund call provision" of the indenture. In some cases, a corporation can meet the fund requirements by purchasing the necessary amounts of bonds and delivering them (rather than money) to the trustee. The fact that either the trustee or the corporation periodically is buying a few bonds will both "support the market" and give greater security to the bonds that remain outstanding. These results are advantageous to the holders of the outstanding bonds.

The entries to record sinking fund transactions of this type can be very simple. If cash is paid to the trustee, all that is required is a debit to Bond Sinking Fund and a credit to Bank. When the trustee subsequently reports the amount of bonds redeemed and the price paid, an entry to record the redemption is made. This entry will be the same as one of those described previously in this section, except that the credit for the amount spent will be to Bond Sinking Fund rather than to Bank. If the corporation itself redeems the bonds, the entry needed will be identical with one of those already described.

When cash is paid to the trustee, the amount remitted by the corporation and the amount subsequently expended may not be exactly the same. The corporation might be obligated to pay $30,000 a year, but the trustee may be able to purchase bonds with a face value of $30,000 at a lower price. Any balance in the sinking fund account represents an asset and should be so reported in the corporation's balance sheet at the end of the asset section.

By the maturity date of the issue, some of the bonds already will have been redeemed. Little or no money may be in the sinking fund at this time, but probably no accumulation was intended in connection with the ultimate retirement of the bond issue. The money to redeem the remaining bonds will have to be provided by other means — possibly by the sale of a new issue of bonds, by the sale of stock, or by using cash accumulated for this purpose.

APPLICATION OF PRINCIPLES

To illustrate further the accounting for bonds issued, bond interest expense (including premium amortization), and the redemption of bonds at maturity, as well as the operation of a sinking fund of the type described, the following example is presented: The Hobbs Manufacturing Corporation issued first mortgage, 10-year, 8½ percent bonds, principal amount $600,000. Interest is payable January 1 and July 1. The bond indenture provides that the corporation is to pay to the trustee (a bank), $20,000 by December 15 of each year (except the tenth year), the money to constitute a sinking fund to be used to purchase bonds which subsequently will be canceled. The entries to record the transactions and events are recorded in general journal form below each transaction.

NARRATIVE OF TRANSACTIONS AND EVENTS

First Year

Jan. 2   The entire issue of 10-year, 8½% bonds, principal amount of $600,000, was sold when the market rate of interest was 8%. The corporation received a net amount of $620,393.

2	Bank..	620,393	
	First Mortgage Bonds Payable		600,000
	Premium on Bonds Payable...		20,393
	Sold 10-year, 8½% bonds, with face value of $600,000.		

July 1   Semiannual interest of $25,500 was paid and $684 of premium was amortized, using the interest method.

1	Bond Interest Expense...	24,816	
	Premium on Bonds Payable	684	
	Bank..		25,500
	Paid semiannual interest on bonds and amortized premium.		

Dec. 14   Payment to trustee, $20,000.

14	Bond Sinking Fund	20,000	
	Bank..		20,000
	Payment to trustee for sinking fund.		

31 Accrued interest on bonds, $25,500, and amortized $712 of premium, netting $24,788 of interest expense.

31	Bond Interest Expense...	24,788	
	Premium on Bonds Payable	712	
	Accrued Bond Interest Payable		25,500
	Accrued semiannual interest on bonds and amortized premium.		

Second Year

Jan. 2 Semiannual interest of $25,500 was paid (no reversing entry was made).

2	Accrued Bond Interest Payable......................................	25,500	
	Bank..		25,500
	Paid semiannual interest on bonds.		

23 Trustee reported that on January 16, bonds with a value of $20,000 were purchased for $19,800 plus $71 accrued interest for 15 days (January 1–16). Premium of $633 was amortized, resulting in a gain on redemption of $833.

23	First Mortgage Bonds Payable..	20,000	
	Premium on Bonds Payable	633	
	Bond Interest Expense..	71	
	Bond Sinking Fund...		19,871
	Gain on Bonds Redeemed		833
	Bonds redeemed by sinking fund trustee.		

Note: As of January 1 of the second year, the bonds redeemed had a carrying value of $20,633 ($20,000 + $633 of the original premium of approximately $680). The amortization of the premium on these bonds for the few days to January 16 was ignored since the amount was so small. Accordingly, the gain on the redemption was $833 ($20,633 − $19,800).

July 1 Semiannual interest of $24,650 was paid and $715 of premium was amortized.

1	Bond Interest Expense..	23,935	
	Premium on Bonds Payable	715	
	Bank..		24,650
	Paid semiannual interest on bonds and amortized premium.		

Note: The interest for this six months period relates to bonds with a face value of $580,000.

Dec. 13   Payment to trustee, $20,000.

13	Bond Sinking Fund	20,000	
	Bank...		20,000
	Payment to trustee for sinking fund.		

31   Accrued interest on bonds, $24,650, and amortized $744 of premium, netting $23,906 of interest expense.

31	Bond Interest Expense..	23,906	
	Premium on Bonds Payable	744	
	Accrued Bond Interest Payable		24,650
	Six months' interest accrued on bonds payable and premium amortized.		

Tenth Year

Note: No bonds were retired during the first year; bonds in the principal amount of $20,000 were retired each year for the next eight years. As of January 1 of this (tenth) year, the balance of the bonds payable account was $440,000; of the premium on bonds payable account, $2,076; of the accrued bond interest payable account, $18,700; and of the sinking fund account, $20,941.

Jan. 2   Semiannual interest of $18,700 was paid (no reversing entry was made).

2	Accrued Bond Interest Payable.......................................	18,700	
	Bank...		18,700
	Paid semiannual interest on bonds.		

8   Trustee reported that on January 6, bonds with a value of $20,000 were purchased for $20,150 plus $24 interest for five days (January 1–6).

8	First Mortgage Bonds Payable..	20,000	
	Premium on Bonds Payable	94	
	Bond Interest Expense..	24	
	Loss on Bonds Redeemed..	56	
	Bond Sinking Fund...		20,174
	Bonds redeemed by sinking fund trustee.		

Note: The bonds redeemed had a carrying value of $20,094 as of January 1 of the tenth year ($20,000 + $94 of the original premium of approximately $680). The amortization of premium on these bonds for the few days to January 6 was ignored since the amount was so small. Accordingly, the loss on redemption was $56 ($20,150 − $20,094).

July 1 Semiannual interest of $17,850 was paid and $971 of premium was amortized, netting $16,879 of interest expense.

1	Bond Interest Expense..	16,879	
	Premium on Bonds Payable	971	
	Bank..		17,850
	Paid semiannual interest on bonds and amortized premium.		

Note: The interest for this six months period relates to bonds with a face value of $420,000.

Dec. 28 A check for $419,683 was given to the trustee. (This, together with the $317 left in the sinking fund — January 1 balance, $20,491 less January 8 credit of $20,174 — provides the amount needed to redeem the bonds at maturity a few days later.)

28	Bond Sinking Fund	419,683	
	Bank..		419,683
	Payment to trustee for bond redemption.		

31 Accrued interest on bonds, $17,850, and amortized $1,010 of premium, netting $16,840 of interest expense.

31	Bond Interest Expense..	16,840	
	Premium on Bonds Payable	1,010	
	Accrued Bond Interest Payable		17,850
	Six months' interest accrued on bonds payable and premium amortized.		

Eleventh Year

Jan. 2 Semiannual interest of $17,850 was paid (no reversing entry was made).

2	Accrued Bond Interest Payable.....................................	17,850	
	Bank..		17,850
	Paid semiannual interest on bonds.		

20 Trustee reported that all bonds had been redeemed.

20	First Mortgage Bonds Payable.......................................	420,000	
	Bond Sinking Fund...		420,000
	Payment of first mortgage bonds at maturity by trustee.		

BUILDING YOUR ACCOUNTING KNOWLEDGE

1. Under what circumstances may a corporation compel its bondholders to surrender all or part of their bonds before their maturity?
2. Under what circumstances will there be a loss on redemption if the corporation originally sold its bonds at face value? A gain on redemption?
3. What must be taken into account if a corporation redeems a part or all of its bonds that were originally sold at a premium?
4. What must also be removed from the accounts when any bonds that are retired are removed from the liability account?
5. What must be taken into account in calculating the gain or loss on the redemption of bonds originally sold at a discount?
6. In connection with bond sinking funds, what has usually been required of the trustee for the bond issue by the bond indenture?
7. What is meant by "price support" for a bond issue in connection with bond sinking funds?

Report No. 24-3

> *Complete Report No. 24-3 in the study assignment and submit your working papers for approval. Continue with the textbook discussion in Chapter 25 until Report No. 25-1 is required.*

EXPANDING YOUR BUSINESS VOCABULARY

What is the meaning of each of the following terms?

adjunct liability (p. 660)
adjustment bonds (p. 648)
amortization (p. 658)
annuity (p. 652)
bond (p. 647)
bond retirement funds (p. 669)
callable bonds (p. 650)
collateral-trust bonds (p. 649)

contra liability (p. 663)
contract (coupon) rate (pp. 650, 657)
convertible bonds (p. 649)
coupon bonds (p. 655)
debenture bonds (p. 649)
deed of trust (p. 647)
deferred charges (p. 664)

deferred credits (p. 664)
discount (pp. 650, 653)
effective interest expense
  (p. 661)
guaranteed bonds (p. 649)
improvement bonds (p. 648)
indentures (p. 669)
interest annuity (pp. 653, 654)
interest method (p. 659)
market (effective) rate (pp. 650, 657)

mortgage bonds (p. 648)
premium (pp. 650, 652)
present value (p. 651)
principal (pp. 653, 654)
purchase-money bonds (p. 648)
refunding bonds (p. 648)
serial bonds (p. 649)
sinking funds (p. 669)
straight-line method (p. 660)
term bonds (p. 649)

APPENDIX

Compound Interest Tables

Table 1

PRESENT VALUE OF ANNUITY OF $1 AT COMPOUND INTEREST

Periods	Interest Rate							
n	1%	2%	3%	3½%	4%	4½%	5%	6%
1	0.9901	0.9804	0.9709	0.9662	0.9615	0.9569	0.9524	0.9434
2	1.9704	1.9416	1.9135	1.8997	1.8861	1.8727	1.8594	1.8334
3	2.9410	2.8839	2.8286	2.8016	2.7751	2.7490	2.7232	2.6730
4	3.9020	3.8077	3.7171	3.6731	3.6299	3.5875	3.5460	3.4651
5	4.8534	4.7135	4.5797	4.5151	4.4518	4.3900	4.3295	4.2124
6	5.7955	5.6014	5.4172	5.3286	5.2421	5.1579	5.0757	4.9173
7	6.7282	6.4720	6.2303	6.1145	6.0021	5.8927	5.7864	5.5824
8	7.6517	7.3255	7.0197	6.8740	6.7327	6.5959	6.4632	6.2098
9	8.5660	8.1622	7.7861	7.6077	7.4353	7.2688	7.1078	6.8017
10	9.4713	8.9826	8.5302	8.3166	8.1109	7.9127	7.7217	7.3601
11	10.3676	9.7868	9.2526	9.0016	8.7605	8.5289	8.3064	7.8869
12	11.2551	10.5753	9.9540	9.6633	9.3851	9.1186	8.8633	8.3838
13	12.1337	11.3484	10.6350	10.3027	9.9856	9.6829	9.3936	8.8527
14	13.0037	12.1062	11.2961	10.9205	10.5631	10.2228	9.8986	9.2950
15	13.8651	12.8493	11.9379	11.5174	11.1184	10.7395	10.3797	9.7122
16	14.7179	13.5777	12.5611	12.0941	11.6523	11.2340	10.8378	10.1059
17	15.5623	14.2919	13.1661	12.6513	12.1657	11.7072	11.2741	10.4773
18	16.3983	14.9920	13.7535	13.1897	12.6593	12.1600	11.6896	10.8276
19	17.2260	15.6785	14.3238	13.7098	13.1339	12.5933	12.0853	11.1581
20	18.0456	16.3514	14.8775	14.2124	13.5903	13.0079	12.4622	11.4699
21	18.8570	17.0112	15.4150	14.6980	14.0292	13.4047	12.8212	11.7641
22	19.6604	17.6580	15.9369	15.1671	14.4511	13.7844	13.1630	12.0416
23	20.4558	18.2922	16.4436	15.6204	14.8568	14.1478	13.4886	12.3034
24	21.2434	18.9139	16.9355	16.0584	15.2470	14.4955	13.7986	12.5504
25	22.0232	19.5235	17.4131	16.4815	15.6221	14.8282	14.0939	12.7834
26	22.7952	20.1210	17.8768	16.8904	15.9828	15.1466	14.3752	13.0032
27	23.5596	20.7069	18.3270	17.2854	16.3296	15.4513	14.6430	13.2105
28	24.3164	21.2813	18.7641	17.6670	16.6631	15.7429	14.8981	13.4062
29	25.0658	21.8444	19.1885	18.0358	16.9837	16.0219	15.1411	13.5907
30	25.8077	22.3964	19.6004	18.3921	17.2920	16.2889	15.3725	13.7648
31	26.5423	22.9377	20.0004	18.7363	17.5885	16.5444	15.5928	13.9291
32	27.2696	23.4683	20.3888	19.0689	17.8736	16.7889	15.8027	14.0840
33	27.9897	23.9886	20.7658	19.3902	18.1476	17.0229	16.0025	14.2302
34	28.7027	24.4986	21.1318	19.7007	18.4112	17.2468	16.1929	14.3681
35	29.4086	24.9986	21.4872	20.0007	18.6646	17.4610	16.3742	14.4982
36	30.1075	25.4888	21.8323	20.2905	18.9083	17.6660	16.5469	14.6210
37	30.7995	25.9695	22.1672	20.5705	19.1426	17.8622	16.7113	14.7368
38	31.4847	26.4406	22.4925	20.8411	19.3679	18.0500	16.8679	14.8460
39	32.1630	26.9026	22.8082	21.1025	19.5845	18.2297	17.0170	14.9491
40	32.8347	27.3555	23.1148	21.3551	19.7928	18.4016	17.1591	15.0463
41	33.4997	27.7995	23.4124	21.5991	19.9931	18.5661	17.2944	15.1380
42	34.1581	28.2348	23.7014	21.8349	20.1856	18.7235	17.4232	15.2245
43	34.8100	28.6616	23.9819	22.0627	20.3708	18.8742	17.5459	15.3062
44	35.4555	29.0800	24.2543	22.2828	20.5488	19.0184	17.6628	15.3832
45	36.0945	29.4902	24.5187	22.4955	20.7200	19.1563	17.7741	15.4558
46	36.7272	29.8923	24.7754	22.7009	20.8847	19.2884	17.8801	15.5244
47	37.3537	30.2866	25.0247	22.8994	21.0429	19.4147	17.9810	15.5890
48	37.9740	30.6731	25.2667	23.0912	21.1951	19.5356	18.0772	15.6500
49	38.5881	31.0521	25.5017	23.2766	21.3415	19.6513	18.1687	15.7076
50	39.1961	31.4236	25.7298	23.4556	21.4822	19.7620	18.2559	15.7619

Table 2

PRESENT VALUE OF $1 AT COMPOUND INTEREST

Periods	Interest Rate							
n	1%	2%	3%	3½%	4%	4½%	5%	6%
1	.9901	.9804	.9709	.9662	.9615	.9569	.9524	.9434
2	.9803	.9612	.9426	.9335	.9246	.9157	.9070	.8900
3	.9706	.9423	.9151	.9019	.8890	.8763	.8638	.8396
4	.9610	.9238	.8885	.8714	.8548	.8386	.8227	.7921
5	.9515	.9057	.8626	.8420	.8219	.8025	.7835	.7473
6	.9420	.8880	.8375	.8135	.7903	.7679	.7462	.7050
7	.9327	.8706	.8131	.7860	.7599	.7348	.7107	.6651
8	.9235	.8535	.7894	.7594	.7307	.7032	.6768	.6274
9	.9143	.8368	.7664	.7337	.7026	.6729	.6446	.5919
10	.9053	.8203	.7441	.7089	.6756	.6439	.6139	.5584
11	.8963	.8043	.7224	.6849	.6496	.6162	.5847	.5268
12	.8874	.7885	.7014	.6618	.6246	.5897	.5568	.4970
13	.8787	.7730	.6810	.6394	.6006	.5643	.5303	.4688
14	.8700	.7579	.6611	.6178	.5777	.5400	.5051	.4423
15	.8613	.7430	.6419	.5969	.5553	.5167	.4810	.4173
16	.8528	.7284	.6232	.5767	.5339	.4945	.4581	.3936
17	.8444	.7142	.6050	.5572	.5134	.4732	.4363	.3714
18	.8360	.7002	.5874	.5384	.4936	.4528	.4155	.3503
19	.8277	.6864	.5703	.5202	.4746	.4333	.3957	.3305
20	.8195	.6730	.5537	.5026	.4564	.4146	.3769	.3118
21	.8114	.6598	.5375	.4856	.4388	.3968	.3589	.2942
22	.8034	.6468	.5219	.4692	.4220	.3797	.3418	.2775
23	.7954	.6342	.5067	.4533	.4057	.3634	.3256	.2618
24	.7876	.6217	.4919	.4380	.3901	.3477	.3101	.2470
25	.7798	.6095	.4776	.4231	.3751	.3327	.2953	.2330
26	.7720	.5976	.4637	.4088	.3607	.3184	.2812	.2198
27	.7644	.5859	.4502	.3950	.3468	.3047	.2678	.2074
28	.7568	.5744	.4371	.3817	.3335	.2916	.2551	.1956
29	.7493	.5631	.4243	.3687	.3207	.2790	.2429	.1846
30	.7419	.5521	.4120	.3563	.3083	.2670	.2314	.1741
31	.7346	.5412	.4000	.3442	.2965	.2555	.2204	.1643
32	.7273	.5306	.3883	.3326	.2851	.2445	.2099	.1550
33	.7201	.5202	.3770	.3213	.2741	.2340	.1999	.1462
34	.7130	.5100	.3660	.3105	.2636	.2239	.1904	.1379
35	.7059	.5000	.3554	.3000	.2534	.2143	.1813	.1301
36	.6989	.4902	.3450	.2898	.2437	.2050	.1727	.1227
37	.6920	.4806	.3350	.2800	.2343	.1962	.1644	.1158
38	.6852	.4712	.3252	.2706	.2253	.1878	.1566	.1092
39	.6784	.4619	.3158	.2614	.2166	.1797	.1491	.1031
40	.6717	.4529	.3066	.2526	.2083	.1719	.1420	.0972
41	.6650	.4440	.2976	.2440	.2003	.1645	.1353	.0917
42	.6584	.4353	.2890	.2358	.1926	.1574	.1288	.0865
43	.6519	.4268	.2805	.2278	.1852	.1507	.1227	.0816
44	.6454	.4184	.2724	.2201	.1780	.1442	.1167	.0770
45	.6391	.4102	.2644	.2127	.1712	.1380	.1113	.0727
46	.6327	.4022	.2567	.2055	.1646	.1320	.1060	.0685
47	.6265	.3943	.2493	.1985	.1583	.1263	.1009	.0647
48	.6203	.3865	.2420	.1918	.1522	.1209	.0961	.0610
49	.6141	.3790	.2350	.1853	.1463	.1157	.0916	.0575
50	.6080	.3715	.2281	.1791	.1407	.1107	.0872	.0543

CHAPTER 25

ACCOUNTING FOR INVESTMENTS AND INTANGIBLE LONG-TERM ASSETS

CHAPTER OBJECTIVES

The objectives of this chapter are to enable you:

▶ To explain accounting for corporate stock investments and dividends received, and describe accounts for **investment in corporation stocks** and **dividend income**.

▶ To explain accounting for bond investments and bond interest earned, including amortization of premium and discount on bond investments, and describe the **investment in bonds** account.

▶ To prepare a record of stocks and bonds.

▶ To explain the difference between temporary and long-term investments.

▶ To explain the treatment of investment earnings in the income statement.

▶ To explain the nature of and the accounting for the major types of intangible assets.

In a general sense, every asset acquired and every expense incurred by a business is an investment, since the business is being operated for gain or profit. However, as used in this chapter, the term investment refers to the asset acquired (rather than to the act of acquiring it), and is taken to mean a revenue-producing asset of a type unrelated to the major activity of the business. Just as an individual may own stocks, bonds, and savings accounts which are unrelated to an occupation or profession, so business partnerships and corporations may own such properties. While under certain circumstances a wide variety of assets would merit consideration as investments, corporate stocks and various types of bonds (corporate and government) are major examples. The following discussion is limited to the accounting for these latter types of investments.

CORPORATE STOCK INVESTMENTS

If a corporation purchases shares of capital stock in another corporation, the transaction may be recorded by debiting an investment account entitled Investment in Corporation Stocks and by crediting Bank for the amount paid for the stock. If desired, a separate account may be kept for each company's stock purchased. For example, assume that a corporation purchased common stock of the International Business Machines Corporation and the Eastman Kodak Company. The accountant may open separate accounts for the investments, under the titles of Investment in IBM Corporation Common Stock and Investment in Eastman Kodak Company Common Stock. The usual plan, however, is to keep only a summary account entitled Investment in Corporation Stocks for all capital stocks purchased for investment purposes. Such a summary account should be debited at the time of purchase for the cost of any capital stock bought, which includes any brokers' fees incurred in the purchase.

If the Mercer Company, Inc., purchased 100 shares of the common stock of the Parker Chemical Co. for $60 per share and the broker's fee amounted to $310, the total cost would amount to $6,310. The transaction would be recorded by the following journal entry:

Investment in Corporation Stocks...	6,310	
Bank...		6,310
Purchased 100 shares of Parker Chemical Co. common stock.		

Corporation stocks for which market prices are readily available are known as marketable equity securities. If investments in marketable equity securities are temporary, current accounting practice requires that they be shown in the balance sheet at their cost or current market value, whichever is lower. This determination is based on the total costs and the total market values of such securities that are held by the corporation. The amount by which the market value of the securities has declined below their cost during a period is to be treated as a loss in determining net income. If the market value of the stocks rises in a subsequent period, the recovery of the previously recognized loss is to be treated as a gain in determining net income in that period.

Dividends on Corporate Stocks. Corporations may declare through their boards of directors two kinds of dividends, cash dividends and stock dividends. If a cash dividend amounting to $2 per share on the 100 shares of Parker Chemical Co. stock described above was received while the stock was owned, the transaction would have been recorded as follows:

Bank...	200	
Dividend Income		200
Dividend received on 100 shares of Parker Chemical Co.		
common stock.		

The receipt of a stock dividend ordinarily is not considered to be revenue and no entry other than a notation in the stock investment account is required. For example, some months after the Parker Chemical Co. stock was purchased, Parker distributed a 20 percent common stock dividend. When the certificate for 20 additional shares was received by Mercer Co. Inc., a notation of the receipt was made in the account for the Parker Chemical Co. investment. The acquisition of the additional shares did affect the basic cost of each share of stock. After this acquisition the $6,310 that had applied to the original 100 shares was reassigned to the 120 shares. Each share was thus assigned a cost of $52.58 ($6,310 ÷ 120 shares). In the event that some of the 120 shares are sold at a later date, any gain or loss will be determined by comparing the amount received with the basic cost of $52.58 per share times the number of shares sold.

Sale of Corporation Stock. The investment in corporation stocks account should be credited at the time of sale for the cost of any capital stock sold. If the stock is sold at a gain, the gain may be recorded by crediting a separate account entitled Gain on Sale of Corporation Stocks. If the stock is sold at a loss, the loss may be recorded by debiting an account entitled Loss on Sale of Corporation Stocks.

If the stock purchased by the Mercer Company, Inc., in Parker Chemical Co. for $6,310 was subsequently sold and the net proceeds of the sale amounted to $6,540, a gain of $230 would be realized and the transaction would have been recorded as follows:

Bank..	6,540	
Investment in Corporation Stocks...		6,310
Gain on Sale of Corporation Stocks..		230
Sold 120 shares of Parker Chemical Co. common stock.		

On the other hand, if the same stock had been subsequently sold for $6,270, a loss of $40 would be realized and the transaction would have been recorded as follows:

Bank..	6,270	
Loss on Sale of Corporation Stocks...	40	
Investment in Corporation Stocks...		6,310
Sold 120 shares of Parker Chemical Co. common stock.		

BOND INVESTMENTS

The borrowing of money through the issuance of bonds by governments of all types (federal, state, and local) and by business corporations is a widespread practice. Bonds are a popular form of investment because (1) nearly all bonds promise to pay interest periodically as well as the principal amount at maturity, (2) many bonds are secured by the mortgage of certain property or, in the case of government bonds, by taxing power, and (3) a bondholder is a creditor, not an owner. When a bond is purchased, the nature of the entry made to record the purchase depends upon whether the price includes any payment for accrued interest. For example, assume that a particular bond has a maturity value of $1,000, and promises interest at 9 percent payable semiannually on January 1 and July 1. If the price paid on January 1 (including a broker's commission of $20) was $1,020, the purchase would be recorded as indicated by the following journal entry:

Investment in Bonds..	1,020	
Bank		1,020
Purchased a $1,000 bond plus commission.		

Suppose, instead, that the same bond was purchased on April 1. In such event, interest amounting to $22.50 would have accrued since the last interest date, January 1. The cost of the bond would be $22.50 more to include accrued interest. The total amount paid (including broker's commission plus interest) would be $1,042.50, and the purchase would be recorded as indicated by the following journal entry:

Investment in Bonds	1,020.00	
Interest Earned	22.50	
Bank		1,042.50
Purchased a $1,000 bond plus commission and interest.		

The $22.50 was charged to Interest Earned to facilitate the recording of the regular $45 interest collection three months later (6 months' interest on $1,000 at 9 percent per year). This $45 interest is recorded by a debit to Bank and a credit to Interest Earned. The difference between the $22.50 debit to Interest Earned when the bond was purchased and the $45 credit to the account when six months' interest was collected is $22.50, the amount of interest earned for the three months that the bond has been owned. The effects of the two transactions on the interest earned account can be illustrated in T account form as follows:

Interest Earned

Bond purchase	22.50	Collection of interest	45.00
		Bal. 22.50	

Bond Interest Earned. Nearly all bonds promise to pay interest at a specified rate. The interest is usually paid semiannually, generally on either the first or fifteenth day of each of two months that are six months apart (January and July, March and September, etc.). As was mentioned in Chapter 24, bond interest is either (1) paid by check or (2) paid by the redemption of coupons that are attached to the bonds, as such coupons come due. Whatever the mechanics of payment, the receipt of bond interest should be recorded by a debit to Bank and a credit to Interest Earned.

If the bondholder's records are kept on a full accrual basis, an adjusting entry should be made at the end of the fiscal period to record any accrued bond interest earned. Assume for example, that the Leshen Corp. owns a $10,000, 9½ percent bond of the A. O. Smith Corp. which pays interest on April 15 and October 15. Interest at the rate of 9½ percent for 2½ months (October 15 to December 31) on $10,000 amounts to $197.92. The following journal entry on the books of Leshen Corp. should be made as of December 31:

Accrued Interest Receivable	197.92	
Interest Earned		197.92
Bond interest accrued to December 31.		

This entry should be reversed as of January 1 of the next year.

Premium and Discount on Bond Investments. An original issue of corporate bonds may sell for more or less than face value at prices that involve a premium or a discount. For example, the original purchaser of a bond may have paid a price of 98 percent of face value. Some months or years later, the market or going rate for this class of bonds may have fallen below the contractual rate for that bond so that the original purchaser can sell it for 102 percent of face value. Still later (but well before the bond matures), the market rate may have risen to such a point that the second owner cannot sell it for more than 96 percent of face value. In organized stock exchanges (where there also is trading in bonds), the prices for certain bond issues may change from day to day — or even from hour to hour.

When a bond is purchased, either as a temporary or a long-term investment, its cost — whether more or less than face value — should be debited to the investment in bonds account. If the purchaser of a bond regards it as a temporary investment the bond usually is carried in the accounts at its original cost until sold or otherwise disposed of. If the purchaser of a bond regards it as a long-term investment and expects to hold it to maturity, it is good accounting practice to periodically write off or amortize any premium or discount over the life of the bond. The periodic amortization of any premium is treated as a reduction of bond interest earned; the periodic amortization of any discount is regarded as additional bond interest earned.

For example, suppose that a $1,000, 8 percent, 8-year bond is purchased on January 1, 1982, for $1,096, a premium of $96. Interest is to be paid semiannually on July 1 and January 1. The purchase was recorded by debiting Investment in Bonds and by crediting Bank for $1,096. On July 1, the collection of $40 interest was recorded by a debit to Cash and a credit to Interest Earned. On December 31, an entry was made to record the $40 interest that had accrued since July 1. At this point, Interest Earned has a credit balance of $80 ($40 + $40).

If the bond is held until maturity, the owner will get $96 less than the bond cost. It is reasonable, therefore, to amortize (write off) the $96 premium over the eight-year life of the bond. This can be done on an effective interest rate basis, as was used and illustrated in Chapter 24. However, the simpler, straight-line method is satisfactory in many cases; $96 divided by 8 years is $12 per year. Accordingly, the following adjusting entry should be made as of the end of each of the eight years:

Interest Earned	12	
Investment in Bonds		12
Amortization of bond premium.		

When this entry is posted, the balance of the interest earned account is reduced to $68 ($80 − $12). The book value of the bond investment is reduced $12 each year. By the end of the eighth year, the book value will be $1,000, which is the amount that will be received when the bond is redeemed.

The logic of considering that the interest earned each year is $68, rather than $80, is explained by the following calculation.

Total amount to be received from ownership of bonds:	
Interest ($80 a year for 8 years)	$ 640
Upon redemption	1,000
Total	$1,640
Cost of bond	1,096
Excess of receipts over cost	$ 544

$544 divided by 8 years = $68 per year.

For federal income tax purposes, a taxpayer may elect to amortize premiums on bonds owned. If interest on the bonds is tax exempt, any premium must be amortized.

Assume that the bond in the foregoing example ($1,000, 8 percent, due 8 years from purchase date of January 1, 1982) was bought for $936, a discount of $64 ($1,000 − $936). The amortization of the discount at the end of each year should be $8 ($64 ÷ 8 years). The following adjusting entry should be made as of the end of each year.

Investment in Bonds	8	
Interest Earned		8
Amortization of bond discount.		

This entry adds $8 to the $80 already in the interest earned account ($40 interest receipt on July 1 and the $40 accrual as of December 31). If $8 is added each year to the bond investments account, by the end of the eighth year the book value of the bond will be $1,000, which is the amount that will be received when the bond is redeemed.

The logic of considering that the interest earned each year is $88, rather than $80, is explained by the calculation shown at the top of page 685.

For federal income tax purposes, discount need not be amortized. Upon redemption, the difference between cost and maturity value is treated either as a capital gain or as ordinary income, depending on how long the bonds have been held.

Total amount to be received from ownership of bond:	
Interest ($80 a year for 8 years)	$ 640
Upon redemption	1,000
Total	$1,640
Cost of bond	936
Excess of receipts over cost	$ 704

$704 divided by 8 years = $88 per year.

Sale or Redemption of Bonds. When a bond is sold before maturity, it is probable that a gain or loss will be realized. Suppose that a bond purchased a few months before at a cost of $5,320 is sold on an interest date for $5,439 (net after broker's commission). The journal entry to record the sale should be as follows:

Bank	5,439	
Investment in Bonds		5,320
Gain on Sale of Bonds		119
Sold bond.		

If the bond had been sold sometime later and the amount received was $67 more because of interest accrued, the journal entry to record the sale should be as follows:

Bank	5,506	
Investment in Bonds		5,320
Interest Earned		67
Gain on Sale of Bonds		119
Sold bond.		

When a bond is sold, its book value must be removed from the bond investments account. Book value may be (1) the original cost (as in the foregoing illustration) or (2) the original cost plus the total amount of discount amortized, or (3) the original cost minus the total amount of premium amortized. For example, suppose that a $20,000 bond was purchased three years ago for $20,230. At the date of purchase, the bond had 11½ years to go until maturity. Since the buyer originally intended to hold the bond until maturity, the accountant had amortized the premium of $230 ($20,230 − $20,000) at the rate of $20 ($230 ÷ 11½ years) for each full year. After three years, the bond investment account was reduced by a total of $60 (3 × $20) making the book value of the bond $20,170 ($20,230 − $60). If the bond is sold for a net of $19,829, including $19 interest accrued, the loss on the sale of the bond will be $360. The journal entry to record the sale is shown at the top of page 686.

If a bond is held to maturity and the premium or discount has been fully amortized, the entry to record the bond redemption is a debit to Bank and a credit to Investment in Bonds for the maturity

Bank	19,829	
Loss on Sale of Bonds..	360	
Investment in Bonds...		20,170
Interest Earned...		19
Sold bond.		

value (which will be the book value). No gain or loss will be involved.

If a bond is purchased at a premium and the premium is not amortized, the redemption at maturity will involve a loss equal to the amount of the premium. If a bond is purchased at a discount and the discount is not amortized, the redemption at maturity will involve a gain equal to the amount of the discount.

RECORD OF STOCKS AND BONDS

When investments in securities, such as bonds and capital stock, are sufficiently numerous to justify keeping a detailed record of them, special forms similar to the one reproduced below may be used for this purpose. The forms are so designed that all necessary information may be recorded on them conveniently. A separate sheet should be used for keeping a record of each bond and of each stock certficate owned. A description of the bond or stock certificate, together with information regarding its purchase and sale, may be recorded on the front of the form as shown in the illustration. The back of the form is ruled to provide for recording interest or dividends received during the period of ownership. This type of record usually is regarded as an auxiliary or memorandum record, and the information recorded on it is supplementary to the information recorded in the regular books of account.

RECORD OF STOCKS AND BONDS

NAME *U. S. Treasury Bond*

DESCRIPTION *# 80014 K*

DATE OF ISSUE *Aug. 15, 1977* DATE OF MATURITY *Aug. 15, 1989* INTEREST OR DIVIDEND *6 3/8* % PAYABLE *F & A* SEMI-ANNUALLY ✓

DENOMINATION

DATE	OF WHOM PURCHASED	DATE	SOLD TO	CERT. NO. OR BOND NO.	MATU-RITY	PAR VALUE	PRICE PAID	TOTAL COST	SOLD FOR	INTEREST OR DIVS. EARNED	LOSS OR GAIN
1977 Aug. 15	Subscription			80014 K	8/15/89	5,000	5,000	5,000.00			

Record of Stocks and Bonds

TEMPORARY INVESTMENTS VS. LONG-TERM INVESTMENTS

It is not unusual for businesses to find that they have accumulated more cash than is needed for the financing of current operations. Often this surplus of cash is temporary. In a few weeks or months, the money will be needed again for regular operations. Rather than allowing the money to accumulate in a bank account, it is desirable to use the money to produce some revenue — even if only a comparatively small amount. The otherwise-idle money may be invested in something likely to yield a return and also likely to be salable with little risk of loss whenever the money is needed. Investments in the form of "high grade" stocks or bonds (including notes or bills of the federal government) often are favored. Generally, securities that are actively traded on an organized exchange are preferred. If it is intended that the investment will be held for only a short time, it is called a temporary investment. Temporary investments are regarded as current assets and are so reported in the balance sheet — usually immediately following cash.

If there is no immediate prospect of liquidating an investment, it is considered to be a long-term investment. It was mentioned earlier that if long-term investments include bonds, it is customary to amortize any premium or discount that was involved when the bonds were purchased. Long-term investments are reported in the balance sheet following the current assets — often under the caption "Investments." Corporations sometimes maintain special funds such as bond sinking funds (for the retirement of their own bonds) and pension funds. The amounts in these funds usually are included in the investments category.

INVESTMENT EARNINGS IN THE INCOME STATEMENT

Investment (temporary or long-term) earnings should be reported near the bottom of the income statement following income (or loss) from operations. Such non-operating earnings are usually captioned "Other Revenue." Gains arising from the disposition of investments are similarly captioned; losses are shown as "Other Expenses."

ACCOUNTING FOR INTANGIBLE LONG-TERM ASSETS

In an accounting sense, the term "intangible" has come to have a very restricted meaning. The word itself is broad enough to include all types of assets that lack physical substance. Amounts on deposit in a bank, receivables of all types, prepaid insurance, and securities are all assets that have no physical substance. The fact that some of these assets are evidenced by documents or certificates of various types does not make the properties tangible. However, none of these assets is included in the category of intangibles as the term is used in accounting. Instead, the term intangible assets is used to refer to a limited group of certain valuable legal or economic rights that a firm may acquire. All of the items classified as intangibles are usually considered to be long-term assets and have the common characteristic of being of comparatively long duration. Major examples of intangibles include patents, copyrights, leases, leasehold improvements, franchises, trademarks, and goodwill.

Patents. A patent is a grant by the federal government to an inventor giving the exclusive right to produce, use, and sell an invention for a period of seventeen years. A firm may acquire a patent by original grant or by purchase from a prior patent owner. If a patentable invention is developed in the operation of a business, the cost associated with the patent may be either very nominal or quite considerable depending upon various circumstances. A manufacturing company that carries on regular research and development activities should treat the costs of such activities as current expenses. If patents are secured on any resulting inventions, the cost of such patents is considered to include only the fees paid to the government and probably also certain fees paid to patent attorneys for their services. In some cases, even these fees are considered to be ordinary expenses of the period in which they are incurred. Although the patents may become very valuable, under these circumstances they are not treated as assets in the records.

In many cases, patents are acquired by purchase and their cost is debited to Patents. If numerous patents are owned, a subsidiary or supplementary record showing the nature, life, and cost of each one may be maintained.

Since the life of a patent is specifically limited, any cost assigned to it should be allocated over no more than the number of years that the patent right will exist. The greatest number of years would be seventeen if the firm had acquired the patent at the time of its original issuance. If a patent that has already run five years is acquired, its cost should be apportioned over a period not exceeding twelve years. If the expected useful or economic life of a patent is something less than its legal life, the cost should be allocated over the shorter period.

If the cost of the patent is to be written off on a straight-line basis, the charge-off each year is determined by dividing the cost of the patent right by its expected life. Suppose, for example, that a patent with thirteen years to run is purchased at a cost of $8,000, and that the buyer expects the useful life of the patent to be only ten years. In that event, $800 ($8,000 ÷ 10 years) would be charged as expense for each of the ten years. The $800 is called the periodic amortization of the cost. The adjusting journal entry to record the amortization for a year would be as follows:

Patent Amortization	800	
Patents		800
Amortization of patent.		

Sometimes an account entitled Patent Expense is debited for the amount written off. On rare occasions the credit is to an account entitled Accumulated Amortization — Patents. The latter account is identical in nature to an accumulated depreciation account. In most cases, however, the credit is made directly to the asset account rather than to a contra account.

Patent amortization is usually treated as a manufacturing expense. Since patents are assets, their unamortized cost should be reported in the balance sheet as an intangible long-term asset.

Copyrights. A copyright is similar in many respects to a patent. It consists of a federal grant of the exclusive right to the reproduction and sale of a literary, artistic, or musical composition. A copyright is granted for life plus 50 years after the death of the holder. The cost of obtaining a copyright in the first place is very nominal and usually is treated as an ordinary and incidental expense by the one who secures it. However, if an existing copyright is purchased, the cost may be large enough and the expected future value sufficient to warrant charging the cost to an asset account titled Copyrights. If a number of copyrights are owned, a suitable subsidiary or supplementary record may be maintained.

It is a rare case in which a copyright would have an economic life as long as its legal life. In most cases the cost of a copyright is written off in a very few years. The write-off can be on a straight-line basis or in the proportion of the actual sales of the copyrighted article during the period to the total expected sales of the article. The amount of the write-off for each period is debited to Copyright Amortization (or Copyright Expense) and credited to Copyrights. The expense usually should be reported in the non-operating expense section of the income statement, because normally it is not an essential expense of regular corporate operations. Any unamortized portion of the cost of copyrights should be reported in the balance sheet as an intangible long-term asset.

Long-Term Leases. A long-term lease is a contract in which the owner, or lessor, of certain property (commonly real estate) agrees to let another person or firm, called the lessee, use it for a certain length of time in return for specified regular payments, usually monthly rental payments. In most cases, the original lessee (the person or firm that will use the property) acquires a lease at no cost apart from the monthly rental payments that must be made as the property is used.

There are two major types of leases: capital leases and operating leases. Capital leases are leases in which the lessee is viewed as effectively acquiring ownership of the leased asset, even though legal title remains with the lessor. There are complex rules for determining when a lease should be treated as a capital lease, but this is a subject for a more advanced course. A capital lease must be recorded both as an intangible long-term asset and as a long-term liability, using the present value of all future lease payments. (In order to calculate the present value, the life of the lease would be determined and an interest rate assumed, then an appropriate factor from Table 1 of the Appendix could be multiplied by the amount of the periodic lease payments.) The asset would be depreciated over its useful life and the liability would be reduced as lease payments were made over the life of the lease agreement.

Operating leases are leases in which the lessor is viewed as retaining ownership of the leased property. The lease payments in this case are treated as operating expenses when paid.

Most leases are transferable. Any one of several circumstances may cause a long-term lease to become valuable. For example, the long-term rental rate may be lower than currently existing market rental rates. Thus, the original lessee can sell the rights under a lease to another person or firm. The buyer then acquires an asset with a life that can be measured exactly. For example, suppose that a company buys what is left of a twenty-year lease on a certain store ten years after the lease started. The lease calls for monthly rental payments of $400. However, the company considers the location to be so desirable that it is willing to pay more than that. Therefore, it buys the lease (which has 10 years to run) for $24,000. The purchase is recorded by a debit of $24,000 to the account Leasehold and a credit to Bank.

If the lease has exactly 10 years, or 120 months to run, the cost ($24,000) will be allocated over this length of time. An adjustment of $200 ($24,000 ÷ 120 months) would be made monthly or $2,400 annually to amortize the proper amount. If the adjustment is to be made at the end of each month, the entry would be as follows:

Rent Expense	200	
Leasehold...		200
Amortization of leasehold.		

The debit is made to the rent expense account since the cost to obtain the lease is really the same thing as prepaid rent. The rent expense account already has been debited for the $400 cash rent paid to the owner of the property at the start of the month. Thus, the real rent expense to the tenant is $600 each month — $400 cash rent plus 1/120 of the $24,000 cost of the 120-month lease. The unamortized portion of the cost of the lease should be reported in the balance sheet as an intangible long-term asset.

Leasehold Improvements. A person or firm using property under a long-term lease may decide to incur costs to improve such property. These costs are known as leasehold improvements. In most cases whatever is left of any improvements or additions at the termination of the lease will belong to the owner of the property. In the records of the lessee, the cost of any long-term improvements is charged to an account titled Leasehold Improvements. This cost will be written off as expense over the number of years that such improvements are expected to benefit the lessee. If the benefit from these improvements is expected to be exhausted before the lease expires, the cost will be amortized over the expected economic life of the improvements. If, however, the benefit from the improvements is expected to extend beyond the life of the lease, then the cost of the improvements will be written off over the remaining period of the lease.

Suppose, for example, that three years after taking over the lease on the store mentioned previously, the lessee spends $4,900 restyling the front of the store and installing various modern features. The entry to record these improvements would be as follows:

Leasehold Improvements...	4,900	
Cash		4,900

These improvements will become a permanent part of the store and are expected to benefit the property for fifteen to twenty years. However, the lessee's right to use the property will end in seven years. Thus, the cost of the improvements would be amortized over a seven-year period. The adjusting journal entry at the end of each year would be as follows:

Amortization of Leasehold Improvements	700	
Leasehold Improvements...		700
Annual amortization of leasehold improvements.		

Amortization of Leasehold Improvements is an expense similar to depreciation and should be so reported in the operating section of the income statement. The unamortized portion of the cost of leasehold improvements should be reported in the balance sheet as an intangible long-term asset. Note that leasehold improvements usually have physical substance but, since they become a part of property owned by someone else, they are not considered to be a tangible asset of the lessee.

The original lessee of property might have leasehold improvement cost to account for, in addition to the present value of the future lease payments in the case of a capital lease. Such cost would be accounted for in the same manner as indicated above for the purchaser of an existing lease.

Franchises. A franchise is a grant of certain geographical rights or privileges for a specified time, an indefinite time, or forever. In many cases, franchises are granted to businesses by governments. Examples of governmental franchises included the right to operate buses or other public vehicles on city streets and the monopoly right to operate a power company or a telephone company. Business organizations sometimes enter into contracts that are called franchises. A manufacturer, for example, may give a franchise called a dealership to a certain person that gives the latter the exclusive right to sell the manufacturer's product in a specified geographic area.

Quite often there is little or no cost to the person or firm who originally secures a franchise right. However, if the right becomes valuable and its terms allow it to be transferred, a subsequent buyer of the franchise will have some accountable cost. The cost of a purchased franchise should be debited to a franchise account. Whether this cost should be written off and, if so, how fast, depends upon various circumstances. If the franchise has a specified term with no renewal option, the cost should be written off over a period no longer than the specified term. The period of the write-off may be less than the legal life if there is reason to think that the economic value will disappear before the right legally ends. Even if there is no reason to think that the value of an indefinite or perpetual franchise is diminishing, many accountants on grounds of conservatism favor amortizing the cost.

The amortization adjustment at the end of each period is similar to that made for other intangibles. In this case, the debit would be to an expense account titled Amortization of Franchise and the credit would be to the franchise account. The amount of the expense should be reported in the operating section of the income statement and the unamortized portion of the franchise cost should be reported in the balance sheet as an intangible long-term asset.

Trademarks. The manufacturer or seller of a product frequently wishes to identify the firm's merchandise in some unique fashion. The practice of using trademarks or registered trade names is widespread. The federal government offers legal protection to such designations by permitting them to be registered with the United States Patent Office. As long as the trademark or trade name is continuously used, the courts will protect the owner of a registered trademark by preventing others from using it, or by assessing damages against those who infringe upon such rights.

The person or firm who originally registers a trademark may have incurred little or no cost in its creation or, by contrast, may have incurred a sizable cost in its development. Such costs should be expensed when incurred. Since trademarks and trade names can be sold, however, a buyer will have some accountable cost. Inasmuch as a trademark or a trade name does not expire as long as it is used, the question arises as to whether any of the cost of such an asset should be amortized and, if so, over what period of time. The future value of a trademark or a trade name is highly uncertain. Conservatism suggests that any cost incurred in purchasing a trademark should be written off within a few years of its incurrence.

The periodic adjusting entry to record the amortization involves a debit to Amortization of Trademarks (or Trade Names) and a credit to Trademarks (or Trade Names). The amount written off should be reported as a non-operating expense in the income statement, because it is not an essential expense of regular corporate operations. The federal income tax law does not permit a tax deduction for the amortization of trademarks and trade names. Any unamortized portion of the cost of trademarks or trade names should be reported in the balance sheet as an intangible long-term asset.

Goodwill. Goodwill is usually defined as the present value of a firm's earnings in excess of the normal earnings for other firms in the same type of business. Exactly what is meant by "excess" and how to calculate such value is not generally agreed upon. Goodwill should not be recorded as an asset unless it has been purchased. In that case, its amount is known or can be determined.

Goodwill cannot be purchased by itself. It may arise in connection with transactions such as the admission of a new partner into a partnership (see Chapter 16) or the purchase of all of the assets of one business by another. If the price paid for the assets of the business that is "selling out" is larger than the sum of the agreed upon values of the identifiable assets being purchased, the excess is regarded as the amount paid for the goodwill of the acquired business.

For example, suppose that Casey Page, who owns and has been successfully operating the Page Supply Company, decides to sell the business. The officers of the Witte Corporation want to buy Page's business and merge it with their own business. The corporation's officers had the assets of the Page Supply Company appraised and it is decided that the property has the following values:

Accounts receivable	$32,500
Merchandise inventory	21,700
Furniture and fixtures	18,800
Land	15,000
Building	60,000
Total	$148,000

Page is to pay all the liabilities of the business and withdraw any cash that is left. Page agrees that the values placed on the assets are fair, but refuses to sell unless $175,000 is received. If the Witte Corporation decides to buy at this price, it will be paying $27,000 ($175,000 − $148,000) for the goodwill that relates to Page's business. Obviously the buyer would not pay the price asked unless it was believed that something of value was to be obtained. In this example, the directors of the Witte Corporation may feel that $27,000 is a reasonable price for the business contacts, patronage, and prestige developed by Page. If the offer is accepted and the price of $175,000 is paid in cash, the entry to record the transaction in the Witte Corporation's general journal would be as follows:

Accounts Receivable	32,500	
Merchandise Inventory	21,700	
Furniture and Fixtures	18,800	
Land	15,000	
Building	60,000	
Goodwill	27,000	
Bank		175,000
Purchased the assets of the Page Supply Co.		

One possible application of the present value approach would determine the $27,000 of goodwill as follows:

(1) If 8 percent is a normal rate of return for businesses like Page Supply Co., the net income should be about $11,840 ($148,000 × .08).

(2) Page's actual net income for the last year of operation was $14,000.

(3) Page's excess earnings over the normal amount for this type of business were $2,160 ($14,000 actual earnings minus $11,840 normal earnings).

(4) The capitalized present value of Page's excess earnings is $27,000 ($2,160 ÷ .08) and this is the value of the goodwill. In other words, the $27,000 of goodwill accounts for the $2,160 of excess earnings at the normal 8 percent rate of return.

If goodwill has been purchased and charged to an asset account, the question arises as to whether it should be written off and, if so, how fast. Goodwill has no legal life; its economic life is uncertain. Since a logical basis for amortizing the cost of goodwill is lacking, conservatism dictates that it should be written off in a very few years. Current accounting practice requires that goodwill be written off over its estimated life or forty years, whichever is shorter. If it were decided that the goodwill purchased by the Witte Corporation was to be written off over five years, the adjusting journal entry at the end of each of these years would be as follows:

Amortization of Goodwill	5,400	
Goodwill		5,400
Amortization of goodwill.		

If the write-off is made in this form, the amortized portion should be reported in the income statement as a non-operating expense, for the same reason as indicated for copyrights and trademarks. Amortization of goodwill is not deductible for federal income tax purposes. The unamortized portion of goodwill should be reported in the balance sheet as an intangible long-term asset.

Other Intangibles. The intangible assets that have been discussed thus far are the major examples of such property rights. Other examples include organization costs (necessary costs incurred in launching an enterprise), secret processes, and subscription lists. The usual practice is to amortize the costs of such property within a few years after acquisition.

Under the federal income tax law, organization cost is allowed as a tax deduction provided it is charged off over a period of not less than sixty months, beginning with the month in which the corporation begins business. The amount written off each year is usually recorded by debiting Amortization of Organization Cost and by crediting Organization Cost.

A common practice in regard to many intangibles has been to write off all of their cost except for $1 as soon as possible. The $1 is carried in the accounts and reported in the balance sheet indefinitely. This serves to call the attention of the readers of the balance sheet to the existence of such assets and to the fact that the company has followed the conservative practice of amortizing their costs. To find "Patents, Trademarks, and Goodwill................$1" listed among the assets in the balance sheet of a million-dollar corporation is not unusual, although the accounting profession no longer encourages this practice.

BUILDING YOUR ACCOUNTING KNOWLEDGE

1. How is the receipt of a stock dividend accounted for? Is the basic cost of a share increased or decreased as a result of a stock dividend?
2. Give three reasons why bonds are a popular form of investment.
3. Under what circumstances will the redemption of a bond investment at maturity involve a loss? A gain?
4. Over what period of time should the cost of a patent be allocated if its economic life is expected to be something less than its legal life?
5. How should the unamortized portion of the cost of a copyright be reported in the balance sheet?
6. How does conservatism suggest that the cost of a trademark or trade name be accounted for subsequent to acquisition?
7. If one business buys out another business, how is the amount of goodwill involved in the purchase determined?
8. Why has it been common practice for businesses to write off all but $1 of the cost of many intangibles as soon as possible?

Report No. 25-1

Complete Report No. 25-1 in the study assignments and submit your working papers to the instructor for approval. Then continue with the textbook discussion in Chapter 26 until Report No. 26-1 is required.

EXPANDING YOUR BUSINESS VOCABULARY

What is the meaning of each of the following terms?

amortize (p. 683)   capital leases (p. 690)
cash dividends (p. 680)   copyright (p. 689)

dealership (p. 692)

franchise (p. 692)

goodwill (p. 693)

intangible assets (p. 688)

investment (p. 679)

investment earnings (p. 687)

leasehold improvements (p. 691)

lessee (p. 690)

lessor (p. 690)

long-term investment (p. 687)

long-term lease (p. 690)

marketable equity securities
    (p. 679)

operating leases (p. 690)

organization costs (p. 695)

patent (p. 688)

stock dividends (p. 680)

temporary investment (p. 687)

trademarks (p. 693)

CHAPTERS 21–25

SUPPLEMENTARY PRACTICAL ACCOUNTING PROBLEMS

Problem 21-A Stockholders' Ledger

The Hoosier Group is a corporation, organized under the laws of Indiana, with an authorized capital of $1,000,000 divided into 10,000 shares of common stock, par value $100 a share. The company uses a standard form of stockholders' ledger. Following is a list of selected stock transactions:

Mar. 4 Issued Stock Certificate No. 32 for 280 shares of common stock to Joanne Widolff, 3628 N. Meridian, Indianapolis, Indiana. This stock is fully paid and nonassessable.

Apr. 14 Issued Stock Certificate No. 36 for 220 shares of common stock to John Zdravich, Route 2, Seymour, Indiana.

June 10 Zdravich surrendered Certificate No. 36 for 220 shares of common stock and requested that 100 shares be transferred to Widolff. Issued Certificate No. 39 for 100 shares to Widolff and Certificate No. 40 for 120 shares to Zdravich.

Sept. 21 Widolff surrendered Certificate No. 32 for 280 shares and Certificate No. 39 for 100 shares and requested that 340 shares be transferred to Jill Craig, 1420 West 18th Street, Columbus, Indiana. Issued Certificate No. 41 for 340 shares to Craig and Certificate No. 42 for 40 shares to Widolff.

Required: Open accounts in the stockholders ledger for Widolff, Zdravich, and Craig, and record the foregoing transactions directly in the accounts.

Problem 21-B   Stock transfer record; stockholders ledger

The Hercule Co. uses a standard transfer record to enter all transfers of its capital stock. This record is kept by the secretary of the company. Following is a narrative of stock transfers for the month of December:

Dec.   2   W. John Copeland, 2531 Cypress Street, Ocala, Florida, surrendered Certificate No. 41 for 140 shares of common stock and requested that it be transferred to Thomas Kroll, 8642 Gulf, St. Petersburg, Florida. Issued Certificate No. 61 for 140 shares to Kroll.

       7   Carol Banogg, 1431 N. Butler, Indianapolis, Indiana, surrendered Certificate No. 46 for 95 shares and requested that 45 shares of the stock be transferred to O. Ben McBane, 2112 Ball Blvd., Muncie, Indiana. Issued Certificate No. 62 for 45 shares to McBane and Certificate No. 63 for 50 shares to Banogg.

     16   Thomas Kroll surrendered Certificate No. 61 for 140 shares and requested that it be transferred to his daughter, Karen Kroll, 8642 Gulf, St. Petersburg, Florida. Issued Certificate No. 64 for 140 shares to Karen Kroll.

     23   Judy Hassell, 1422 Main Street, Golden, Colorado, surrendered Certificate No. 47 for 250 shares and requested that 100 shares be transferred to the First National Bank, Golden, Colorado. Issued Certificate No. 65 for 100 shares to the First National Bank and Certificate No. 66 for 150 shares to Hassell.

Required: (1) Record the foregoing transactions in the stock transfer record of the Hercule Company. (2) Open the necessary accounts in the stockholders ledger and post the entries from the transfer record to the stockholders ledger. In opening the stockholders accounts, record the following balances as of December 1:

First National Bank	0 shares
Carol Banogg	95 shares
W. John Copeland	140 shares
Judy Hassell	250 shares
Karen Kroll	0 shares
Thomas Kroll	260 shares
O. Ben McBane	56 shares

(3) After posting the stock transfers for December, prepare a list of the stockholders showing the number of shares held by each as of December 31.

Problem 22-A   Incorporation of a partnership

H. B. Chance and B. S. Stucky are partners. They decide to incorporate their business. On January 4, the company was incorporated. The authorized capital was $5,000,000, divided into 500,000 shares of common stock, par value $10 each.

Chance and Stucky decided to transfer all of the assets except cash, and all of the liabilities of the partnership to the corporation in exchange for 410,000 shares of stock at par. The corporation was to accept the assets and the liabilities at their net book values in each case, which were assumed to be approximately equal to their market values. Chance and Stucky divided the cash of the partnership and the stock of the corporation in the ratio of their capital interests in the partnership.

The balance sheet of the partnership on December 31 appeared as follows:

CHANCE AND STUCKY
Balance Sheet
December 31, 19––

Assets			Liabilities		
Cash		$ 100,000	Notes payable		$ 400,000
Accounts receivable......		1,200,000	Accounts payable..................		240,000
Materials inventory........		900,000	Total liabilities		$ 640,000
Land		380,000			
Buildings........................	$1,800,000		**Owners' Equity**		
Less accumulated depr.	340,000	1,460,000	H. B. Chance, capital.............		2,520,000
Machinery & equipment.	$ 975,000		B. S. Stucky, capital..............		1,680,000
Less accumulated depr.	175,000	800,000	Total liabilities and		
Total assets...................		$4,840,000	owners' equity....................		$4,840,000

Required: (1) Prepare an entry in general journal form to record the acquisition of the partnership assets and liabilities in exchange for stock. (2) Calculate the number of shares of stock each partner received.

Problem 22-B   Capital stock transactions

The Cory Manufacturing Co. was organized under the laws of Indiana with authority to issue 20,000 shares of preferred stock, par value $100 a share, and 50,000 shares of common stock with no par value.

Following is a narrative of selected transactions that occurred during the year:

Feb.   1   Subscriptions for capital stock, collectible on demand, were accepted as follows:

> 9,000 shares of preferred stock at par
> 25,000 shares of common stock at $50 a share

Mar. 1 Cash was received from subscribers in full payment for their subscriptions on February 1 and stock certificates were issued to all subscribers.

July 6 Issued Certificate No. 52 for 800 shares of common stock to Adam C. Carstens in payment for land valued at $40,000 to be used as a site for a new factory.

Oct. 4 Carstens sold 400 shares of the common stock to John A. Edwards and requested that the transfer be made on the records of the company. Certificate No. 52 for 800 shares was canceled and Certificates Nos. 53 and 54 were issued to Carstens and Edwards respectively for 400 shares each.

Required: Record the foregoing corporate transactions in the general journal of The Cory Manufacturing Co.

Problem 22-C   Corporate transactions

The Crystal City Manufacturing Co. was incorporated on January 4 with the authority to issue 5,000 shares of preferred stock with a par value of $100 per share and 100,000 shares of common stock with a par value of $20 per share.

Following is a narrative of selected transactions that occurred during the year:

Jan.   4 Issued 50,000 shares of common stock to the founders of the corporation in exchange for $600,000 in cash and patents valued at $400,000.

 5 The common stockholders donated 16,000 shares to the corporation to be sold to raise working capital.

26 All of the donated shares were sold for cash at $21 per share.

Feb. 8 Exchanged 1,700 shares of the preferred stock for machinery and equipment valued at $181,000.

22 Purchased 200 shares of common stock for $21 per share. The stock is to be held in the treasury.

Apr. 13 Sold 150 shares of treasury stock for $23 per share.

Dec. 31 The expense and revenue summary account has a credit balance of $172,000 after the revenue and expense accounts are closed into it.

Required: Prepare the entries in general journal form to record the foregoing transactions and to close the expense and revenue summary account to Retained Earnings.

Problem 23-A   Statement of Retained Earnings

The following information was taken from an annual report, dated June 30, 19B, of Southern Press, Inc., a corporation engaged in business as a book publisher:

Balance of retained earnings at beginning of period, July 1, 19A, $16,915,400.
Net income for the year ended June 30, 19B, $7,440,641.
Appropriation for contingencies, $850,000.
Cash dividends paid during the year on common stock, $2,130,000.
Cash dividends paid during the year on preferred stock, $750,000.

Required: From the foregoing information, prepare a statement of retained earnings showing the balance of retained earnings at the end of the period.

Problem 23-B   Declaration and distribution of dividends

The Alberta Oil Co. was incorporated with an authorized issue of 2,000 shares of 9% preferred stock, par value $100 a share, and 5,000 shares of common stock with no par value. At the time of the annual meeting of the board of directors on July 1, all of the preferred stock had been issued and was outstanding, and 3,000 shares of the common stock had been issued at a price of $40 a share, the entire selling price having been credited to the common stock account. The balance sheet of the company showed that it had retained earnings amounting to $265,000.

Following is a narrative of selected transactions completed by Alberta Oil Co. during July and August of the current year.

July   1   The board of directors declared dividends as follows:

> On preferred stock: quarterly dividend (No. 21) of $2.25 a share on 2,000 shares, payable in cash on August 1 to stockholders of record on July 20.
> On common stock: dividend (No. 37) of $1.25 a share on 3,000 shares, payable in cash on August 1 to stockholders of record on July 15.

Aug.   1   Checks were drawn on the regular checking account at the Energy National Bank to pay the preferred dividends and the common dividends.

Aug. 20   The board of directors declared a stock dividend of one share of common stock for every ten shares of common held, distributable September 15 to stockholders of record on September 6. The market value of the common stock is $47 per share.

Sept. 15   The stock dividend was distributed.

Required: Record the transactions listed above in general journal form for the Alberta Oil Co.

Problem 24-A   Sale of bonds between interest dates

On October 11, the Tollhouse Corporation sold a $700,000 issue of debenture bonds (dated October 1, interest at 8% per annum payable semimonthly on April 1 and October 1) at 99 plus ten days accrued interest (calculated on a 360-days-per-year basis).

Required: Prepare the entry in general journal form to record the transaction.

Problem 24-B   Bond interest expense and discount amortization

July	1	Graft & Graft, Inc., received $932,061, representing proceeds from the sale of $1,000,000 of 7% first mortgage bonds. The issue matures 10 years from this date. Interest is payable semi-annually on January 1 and July 1. The market rate of interest at the time the bonds were issued was 8%.
Dec.	31	Bond interest accrued to December 31 is to be recorded.
	31	The proper amount of bond discount is to be amortized, using the interest method.
	31	The bond interest expense account is to be closed into Expense and Revenue Summary.
Jan.	1	Reverse the adjusting entry for bond interest expense accrued and discount amortization on December 31.

Required: Prepare the entries in general journal form to record the foregoing.

Problem 24-C   Redemption of bonds

On July 7, 6 days after an interest payment date, Amir Corporation redeems $40,000 of 8% bonds at 101 plus accrued interest of $53.33. The unamortized discount related to these bonds as of the date of redemption is $328.

Required: Prepare the entry in general journal form to record the redemption of these bonds.

Problem 24-D   Bond interest expense, premium amortization, and sinking fund

As of December 31, 19––, certain accounts in the general ledger of the Norris Manufacturing Corporation had the following balances:

Bonds Payable	$410,000
Premium on Bonds Payable	4,100
Accrued Interest on Bonds Payable	12,300
Bond Sinking Fund	10,000

The above accounts relate to an issue of bonds that has been outstanding for ten years (less one day). Originally, bonds with a face value of $500,000 were sold at a price of 102. Interest at the rate of 8% per year is payable semiannually on January 1 and July 1. The bonds mature 20 years after the date of original issue. Under the terms of the bond indenture, the corporation must pay to the trustee (a bank) $10,000 by December 15 of each year. The trustee must use the money to redeem, by purchase in the open market or by exercising a call provision, bonds with a face amount of $10,000. As this has been done for 9 years, $90,000 of the bonds have been redeemed and canceled. The trustee has not yet reported on the disposition of the $10,000 paid two weeks earlier.

The proper premium-amortization entry has been made in each of the ten years that the bonds have been outstanding, using the straight-line method. Early the next year, the following events occurred:

Jan.   1   Semiannual interest was paid, $16,400, and premium was amortized.

       10   The trustee reported that on January 5, four $2,500 bonds were purchased at a price of 98 plus accrued interest of $8.89 — a total of $9,808.89.

Required: Prepare the entries in general journal form to record (1) the reversal of the interest expense accrual and premium amortization as of January 1, (2) the payment of the semiannual interest expense and the premium amortization, and (3) the sinking fund transaction.

Problem 25-A   Investment in corporate bonds and stocks

Carmine Fur Co., a manufacturer of fur garments, occasionally invests surplus cash in corporate bonds and stocks. Following is a narrative of such transactions that were completed during the current year:

Feb.   1   Issued a check for $6,540 in payment of 100 shares of Phelps Dodge Copper Co. common stock purchased at $65 a share, plus a broker's commission of $40.

Mar.   4   Purchased a $1,000, 8% Westinghouse Electric Co. bond for $1,000 on the interest date, plus a broker's commission of $15.

May 16   Issued a check for $3,045 in payment of $3,000 of Emerson Electric Co. 8% bonds due in 1990, plus a broker's commission of $25 and accrued interest of $20.

June 20   Sold 40 shares of Phelps Dodge Copper Co. common stock for $69 a share less a broker's commission of $18.

July   2   Redeemed a $1,000, 7% General Electric Co. bond that matured July 1 (original cost $940). (Assume that it is a ten-year bond, and make the last discount amortization entry, as well as the entry for the cash receipt of one-half year's interest before making the entry for the redemption.)

Sept. 3   Received a check for $40 for the semiannual interest on a $1,000, 8% Westinghouse Electric Co. bond.

Nov. 15   Received a check for $120 for the semiannual interest on the 8% bonds of the Emerson Electric Co.

Dec. 15   Received a check for $180 as a dividend of $3 a share on 60 shares of common stock of the Phelps Dodge Copper Co.

Required: Record the foregoing transactions on a sheet of two-column general journal paper and foot the amount columns to prove the equality of the debits and credits.

Problem 25-B   Interest accrued on bonds and amortization of premium

Packer Meat Co. owns a $20,000 Conill Corporation bond which was purchased at a premium several years ago. The bond pays interest at the annual rate of 9% in semiannual installments on April 1 and October 1. If the premium is to be fully amortized by the date the bond matures, $79.65 must be written off each year. The Packer Meat Co. keeps its records on a calendar-year basis.

Required: Prepare the general journal entries as of December 31 to record: (1) the interest accrued on the bond at the end of the year and (2) the amortization of premium for the year.

Problem 25-C   Goodwill amortization

On July 1, Alice Bramson, who owns Bramson Hair Products, agrees to sell the business to Luker Co. for $80,000. According to the agreement, Bramson will pay all of the liabilities and retain any cash that remains. The rest of the assets will be transferred to Luker Co. The values of the assets being acquired by Luker Co. are as follows:

Accounts Receivable	$12,000
Merchandise Inventory	23,000
Furniture & Fixtures	27,500
	$62,500

Required: Prepare the general journal entries to record: (1) the purchase on Luker Co.'s books and (2) the amortization for 6 months of the goodwill, assuming the goodwill is being written off over 5 years.

CHAPTER 26

ACCOUNTING FOR BRANCH AND CONSOLIDATED OPERATIONS

CHAPTER OBJECTIVES

The objectives of this chapter are to enable you:

▶ To describe the various meanings of the term **branch**.
▶ To explain and perform the necessary accounting for branch operations when the branch maintains its own self-contained accounting records.
▶ To explain the nature and workings of the **branch office ledger** and the **home office ledger**, which are interconnected by the use of **reciprocal accounts**, and to describe accounts for:

    (1) Branch Office
    (2) Home Office
    (3) Shipments to Branch
    (4) Shipments from Home Office

▶ To describe three types of corporate combinations.
▶ To describe and illustrate proper accounting for intercompany investments representing different percentages of ownership.
▶ To describe consolidated financial statements.
▶ To explain and illustrate the use of a consolidation work sheet in preparing consolidated financial statements.
▶ To describe a pooling of interests.

In an effort to sell more goods or services and thus to increase its profits, a business organization sometimes establishes one or more branches. The term branch covers a variety of different arrangements. Sometimes such units have many of the characteristics of complete and independent businesses. A branch may have its own bank account, receivables, merchandise inventory, long-term assets, and various liabilities. The manager of a branch may have wide authority in the management of all phases of the unit's operations. In other cases, a branch may be nothing more than a sales office and confine its activities to soliciting orders for goods that will be shipped from the main plant or home office. The branch manager may have the authority to bind the company only in sales contracts.

ACCOUNTING FOR BRANCH OPERATIONS

The size of a branch, the nature of its operations, and various other factors will determine what type of accounting records it will keep. In some cases, the branch keeps no permanent formal records. Daily or weekly summaries of branch activities are sent to the home office where all formal records are maintained. A small branch may have a revolving cash fund to use in making disbursements that are not made by the home office. This fund may be accounted for and reimbursed periodically by the home office in a manner similar to the procedure followed for petty cash funds. A larger branch may maintain a complete set of records of its operations. From an accounting standpoint, the branch may be a separate entity, keeping its own books of original entry and at least a general ledger, and preparing its own periodic financial statements.

RECIPROCAL ACCOUNTS

When formal records are kept at a branch office, it is common practice to follow a procedure that causes the general ledger of the branch and the general ledger of the home office to be interlocking or reciprocal to each other. In the ledger of the home office, there is an account entitled Branch Office. This account has a debit balance and shows the amount for which the branch must account. In the ledger of the branch, there is an account entitled Home Office. This account has a credit balance that shows the amount for which the branch is accountable to the home office. The balances of these two accounts are equal, but opposite; the debit balance in the one account offsets the credit balance in the other account; thus the two accounts are reciprocal. The relationship is illustrated by the following diagram.

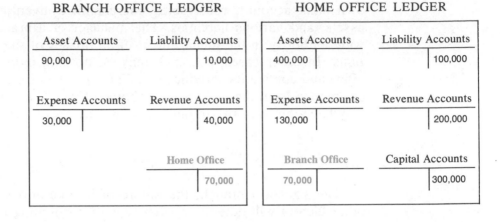

BRANCH OFFICE LEDGER   HOME OFFICE LEDGER

Asset Accounts	Liability Accounts		Asset Accounts	Liability Accounts
90,000	10,000		400,000	100,000
Expense Accounts	**Revenue Accounts**		**Expense Accounts**	**Revenue Accounts**
30,000	40,000		130,000	200,000
	Home Office		**Branch Office**	**Capital Accounts**
	70,000		70,000	300,000

Transactions between the home office and the branch require entries in both ledgers, and involve the reciprocal accounts. If, for example, the home office remits $10,000 to the branch, the entry in the home office ledger is a debit to Branch Office and a credit to Bank. In the branch ledger, Bank is debited and Home Office is credited. At the end of the period, the branch adjusts its accounts and closes the revenue and the expense accounts into Expense and Revenue Summary. The balance of Expense and Revenue Summary is closed to Home Office, a debit indicating a loss or a credit indicating a profit. When the branch income statement reaches the home office, the home office accountant makes an entry debiting Branch Office and crediting Branch Profit if there was a profit, or debiting Branch Loss and crediting Branch Office if there was a loss.

If the business is engaged in selling merchandise, there probably will be another pair of reciprocal accounts: Shipments to Branch in the home office ledger and Shipments from Home Office in the branch ledger. When the home office sends goods to the branch, the home office accountant debits Branch Office and credits Shipments to Branch. The branch accountant records the receipt of the goods by a debit to Shipments from Home Office and a credit to Home Office. If the branch gets all of its merchandise from the home office, the shipments from home office account replaces a purchases account in the branch records. If the branch purchases goods from outsiders, it may have a purchases account in addition to, or in place of, a shipments from home office account.

BRANCH ACCOUNTING PROCEDURE DURING THE FISCAL YEAR

In most respects, the usual accounting procedures are followed by both the home office and the branch. Each uses books of original entry, each has its general ledger, and each may have as many subsidiary ledgers as circumstances warrant. The peculiarities of branch accounting arise in connection with transactions or events that affect both home office and branch office accounts (the reciprocal accounts that have been described). The following example is presented to illustrate branch accounting procedure. In each instance, the transaction or event is given first, followed by the entries (all in general journal form) that should be made in the books of the branch and in the books of the home office. Note that each transaction is recorded simultaneously in the books of both the home office and the branch office without regard to dates; whereas in actual practice there usually would be some lapse of time between the dates on which the transactions are recorded in the books of each office.

On January 1, the general ledger accounts of the Hellwig Sales Co. had the balances as shown below:

Bank	$ 40,000	
Accounts Receivable	64,000	
Allowance for Doubtful Accounts		$ 1,400
Merchandise Inventory	56,000	
Prepaid Insurance	1,280	
Land	14,000	
Building	120,000	
Accumulated Depreciation — Building		56,000
Furniture and Fixtures	16,000	
Accumulated Depreciation — Furniture and Fixtures		6,800
Accounts Payable		62,000
Capital Stock		100,000
Retained Earnings		85,080
	$311,280	$311,280

(1) On January 2, the corporation established a branch in the town of Antigo and turned over to the manager of the branch, $16,000 in cash, furniture and fixtures that had just been purchased at a cost of $4,000, and merchandise that cost $14,000. The long-term assets used at a branch can be recorded either in the branch ledger or in the home office ledger. In this illustration, the long-term assets used at the branch are recorded in the branch ledger.

BRANCH OFFICE BOOKS:				HOME OFFICE BOOKS:		
Bank	16,000			Branch Office	34,000	
Furniture and Fixtures	4,000			Bank		16,000
Shipments from Home				Furniture and		
Office	14,000			Fixtures		4,000
Home Office		34,000		Shipments to Branch		14,000

(2) The branch manager purchased for cash additional furniture and fixtures for $10,000, paid $800 rent on the branch store, and paid a premium of $360 on a three-year fire insurance policy.

BRANCH OFFICE BOOKS: HOME OFFICE BOOKS:

Furniture and Fixtures..	10,000	
Operating Expenses[1]	800	
Prepaid Insurance	360	
Bank............................		11,160

No entry.

(3) The home office purchased goods on account for $190,000 and incurred operating expenses in the amount of $64,000.

BRANCH OFFICE BOOKS: HOME OFFICE BOOKS:

No entry.

Purchases	190,000	
Operating Expenses......	64,000	
Accounts Payable......		254,000

(4) The home office shipped goods costing $90,000 to the branch.

BRANCH OFFICE BOOKS: HOME OFFICE BOOKS:

Shipments from Home		
Office	90,000	
Home Office............		90,000

Branch Office	90,000	
Shipments to Branch.		90,000

(5) During the year, the branch had cash sales of $10,400 and sales on account of $96,000.

BRANCH OFFICE BOOKS: HOME OFFICE BOOKS:

Bank...............................	10,400	
Accounts Receivable	96,000	
Sales		106,400

No entry.

(6) During the year, the home office had cash sales of $44,000 and sales on account of $210,000.

BRANCH OFFICE BOOKS: HOME OFFICE BOOKS:

No entry.

Bank	44,000	
Accounts Receivable	210,000	
Sales		254,000

(7) The branch incurred additional operating expenses during the year (rent, wages, light, telephone, advertising, etc.) in the amount of $37,400. Total payments on account were $33,000.

---

[1] For the sake of brevity in this example, all expenses are charged to the single account, Operating Expenses.

BRANCH OFFICE BOOKS: HOME OFFICE BOOKS:

Operating Expenses...... 37,400
   Accounts Payable......   37,400   No entry.
Accounts Payable.......... 33,000
   Bank...........................   33,000

(8) Cash collections on the branch accounts receivable were $52,000.

BRANCH OFFICE BOOKS: HOME OFFICE BOOKS:

Bank............................. 52,000
   Accounts Receivable.   52,000   No entry.

(9) Cash collections on the home office accounts receivable were $172,000, and accounts having balances totaling $1,000 were determined to be worthless.

BRANCH OFFICE BOOKS: HOME OFFICE BOOKS:

                                            Bank 172,000
                                            Allowance for Doubtful
                                              Accounts   1,000
                                              Accounts
             No entry.   Receivable...........   173,000

(10) Home office payments to suppliers were $204,000.

BRANCH OFFICE BOOKS: HOME OFFICE BOOKS:

                                            Accounts Payable.......... 204,000
             No entry.   Bank...........................   204,000

(11) The branch returned to the home office for credit, goods costing $800.

BRANCH OFFICE BOOKS: HOME OFFICE BOOKS:

Home Office...................   800   Shipments to Branch   800
   Shipments from   Branch Office.............   800
      Home Office............   800

After posting the foregoing transactions, the branch office accounts appeared as shown in the following T accounts:

BRANCH OFFICE ACCOUNTS

	Bank				**Accounts Payable**		
(1)	16,000	(2)	11,160	(7)	33,000	(7)	37,400
(5)	10,400	(7)	33,000			*4,400*	
(8)	52,000		44,160				
34,240	78,400						

Accounts Receivable		
(5)	96,000	(8)	52,000
44,000		

Home Office		
(11)	800	(1)	34,000
		(4)	90,000
	123,200		124,000

Prepaid Insurance	
(2)	360

Sales	
	(5)	106,400

Furniture and Fixtures	
(1)	4,000
(2)	10,000
	14,000

Shipments from Home Office		
(1)	14,000	(11)	800
(4)	90,000		
103,200	104,000		

Operating Expenses	
(2)	800
(7)	37,400
	38,200

After posting the transactions, the home office accounts appeared as shown in the following T accounts:

HOME OFFICE ACCOUNTS

Bank		
Bal.	40,000	(1)	16,000
(6)	44,000	(10)	204,000
(9)	172,000		220,000
36,000	256,000		

Accounts Payable		
(10)	204,000	Bal.	62,000
		(3)	254,000
	112,000		316,000

Accounts Receivable		
Bal.	64,000	(9)	173,000
(6)	210,000		
101,000	274,000		

Allowance for Doubtful Accounts		
(9)	1,000	Bal.	1,400
		400	

Merchandise Inventory	
Bal.	56,000

Capital Stock	
	Bal.	100,000

Prepaid Insurance	
Bal.	1,280

Retained Earnings	
	Bal.	85,080

Page 723 of 856

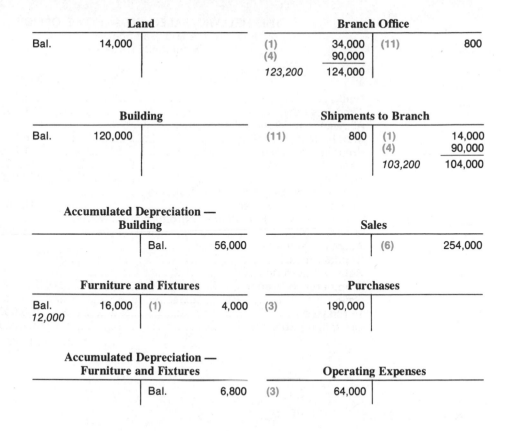

Land		
Bal.	14,000	

Branch Office			
(1)	34,000	(11)	800
(4)	90,000		
123,200	124,000		

Building		
Bal.	120,000	

Shipments to Branch			
(11)	800	(1)	14,000
		(4)	90,000
	103,200	104,000	

Accumulated Depreciation — Building		
	Bal.	56,000

Sales		
	(6)	254,000

Furniture and Fixtures			
Bal.	16,000	(1)	4,000
12,000			

Purchases		
(3)	190,000	

Accumulated Depreciation — Furniture and Fixtures		
	Bal.	6,800

Operating Expenses		
(3)	64,000	

The trial balance of the branch office accounts was taken at the end of the year as shown below.

THE HELLWIG SALES CO. — ANTIGO BRANCH
Trial Balance
December 31, 19--

Account	Dr. Balance	Cr. Balance
Bank	34,240	
Accounts Receivable	44,000	
Prepaid Insurance	360	
Furniture and Fixtures	14,000	
Accounts Payable		4,400
Home Office		123,200
Sales		106,400
Shipments from Home Office	103,200	
Operating Expenses	38,200	
	234,000	234,000

The following trial balance of the home office accounts was taken at the end of the year.

THE HELLWIG SALES CO. — HOME OFFICE
Trial Balance
December 31, 19--

Account	Dr. Balance	Cr. Balance
Bank	36,000	
Accounts Receivable	101,000	
Allowance for Doubtful Accounts		400
Merchandise Inventory	56,000	
Prepaid Insurance	1,280	
Land	14,000	
Building	120,000	
Accumulated Depreciation — Building		56,000
Furniture and Fixtures	12,000	
Accumulated Depreciation — Furniture and Fixtures..		6,800
Branch Office	123,200	
Accounts Payable		112,000
Capital Stock		100,000
Retained Earnings		85,080
Shipments to Branch		103,200
Sales		254,000
Purchases	190,000	
Operating Expenses	64,000	
	717,480	717,480

ACCOUNTING PROCEDURE FOR YEAR-END CLOSING OF BRANCH OFFICE AND HOME OFFICE BOOKS

The accounting procedure for closing the books of a branch office at the end of the year is similar to that discussed previously for a single-location business. The major difference is that the branch net income (or net loss) is transferred to the home office account, since the branch office has no retained earnings account.

The accounting procedure for closing the books of the home office at the end of the year is similar to that discussed previously for a single-location business. The major difference is that the branch net income (or net loss), taken up through the branch office account, is transferred to an account called Branch Profit prior to closing the home office books. Then, the branch profit account is closed to Expense and Revenue Summary in the usual manner for temporary accounts.

COMBINED FINANCIAL STATEMENTS OF HOME OFFICE AND BRANCH

Combined financial statements, in which the results of operations and the financial data of both entities are merged, frequently are prepared with the aid of special work sheets. Each work sheet would have columns for the home office account balances, columns for the branch account balances, a pair of Eliminations columns (Debit and Credit) and columns for the combined results. On the income statement work sheet, the shipments to branch account from the home office books would be eliminated against the shipments from home office account on the branch books. On the balance sheet work sheet, the Branch Office and Home Office reciprocal accounts would be eliminated. Similar account balances would be combined on both work sheets. Because of their similarity to the consolidated work sheets discussed in the next section, branch work sheets are not illustrated here.

BUILDING YOUR ACCOUNTING KNOWLEDGE

1. What kind of accounting procedure might be followed by a small branch operation? A larger branch operation?
2. What is the significance of the debit balance of the Branch Office account? The credit balance of the Home Office account?
3. What entry does the home office accountant make to record a profit realized by the branch? A loss realized by the branch?
4. How does the home office record the act of sending goods to the branch? How does the branch office respond on receipt of the shipment from the home office?
5. What kinds of transactions or events are responsible for the peculiarities of branch accounting?
6. What is the major difference between closing the books of a branch office and closing the books of a single-location business?
7. What is the major difference between closing the books of a home office and closing the books of a single-location business?
8. What accounts are eliminated against each other on a combined income statement work sheet? On a combined balance sheet work sheet?

Report No. 26-1

> *Complete Report No. 26-1 in the study assignments and submit your working papers for approval. Continue with the textbook discussion until Report No. 26-2 is required.*

ACCOUNTING FOR CONSOLIDATED OPERATIONS

The terms merger, consolidation, and acquisition are commonly used to describe different types of corporate combinations. These terms are difficult to define because they are sometimes used loosely in practice.

TYPES OF CORPORATE COMBINATIONS

In general, a merger is a combination of two corporations in such a way that one of the businesses ceases to exist as a legal entity. A consolidation is a combination of two corporations in which a new legal entity is formed and both of the combining companies cease to exist. An acquisition is a combination in which one company acquires control of another company but both companies continue to exist as legal entities.

Of the three types of business combinations, the one of primary interest here is the acquisition. In the following sections, proper accounting for the acquisition of part or all of one company by another will be described and illustrated. Accounting for the companies in periods subsequent to the acquisition also will be examined.

ACCOUNTING FOR INTERCOMPANY INVESTMENTS

Proper accounting for investments in other companies generally is determined by the percentage of ownership. The key percentages and related accounting rules are described in this section.

Less than 20 Percent Ownership. If a company acquires less than 20 percent of another company's stock, the investment should be accounted for according to the cost method. Under this method, the investment is recorded and maintained at its cost. Any dividends received from the other company are recorded and reported as current income.

To illustrate, assume that Tor Company acquired 1,000 shares of the common stock of Tee Company at a cost of $20,000. Tee Company had 10,000 shares of common stock outstanding at the time of this acquisition. Tor Company would record this 10 percent investment under the cost method by means of the following journal entry:

Investment in Tee Company	20,000	
Cash		20,000
To record purchase of 1,000 shares of Tee Co. stock.		

One year later, Tee Company reported a net income of $18,000, and distributed cash dividends to its common stockholders of $8,000 (80¢ per share). Under the cost method, Tor Company would make no record of Tee's net income for the year, but the dividends received would be recorded as follows:

Cash	800	
Dividend Income		800
To recognize dividends on Tee Co. stock (80¢ × 1,000 shares).		

From 20 to 50 Percent Ownership. If a company acquires 20 to 50 percent of another company's stock, the investment should be accounted for according to the equity method. Under this method, the investment is once again recorded at its cost. However, the investment account is subsequently increased (decreased) by the acquiring company's share of the acquired company's net income (loss), and is decreased by the acquiring company's share of any dividend distributions by the acquired company.

To illustrate, assume the same facts as the preceding example, except that in this case, Tor Company acquires 3,000 shares (30 percent) of the common stock of Tee Company at a cost of $60,000. Tor would record this investment by means of the following journal entry:

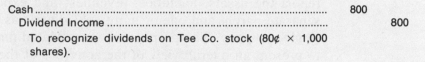

Investment in Tee Co.	60,000	
Cash		60,000
To record purchase of 3,000 shares of Tee Co. stock.		

One year later (under the equity method) Tor would record its share of Tee's net income of $18,000 as follows:

Investment in Tee Co.	5,400	
Income from Tee Co.		5,400
To recognize 30% (3,000 shares ÷ 10,000 shares) of the net income of Tee Co.		

In addition (under the equity method) the dividends received would be entered as follows:

Cash	2,400	
Investment in Tee Co.		2,400
To recognize dividends on Tee Co. stock (80¢ × 3,000 shares).		

Over 50 Percent Ownership. If a company acquires more than 50 percent of another company's voting stock, the acquiring company is said to hold a controlling interest in the acquired company. A company which controls the activities of another company through own-

ership of its voting stock is known as the parent company. The company which is controlled is known as the subsidiary.

When a company owns more than 50 percent of the voting stock of another company, the parent usually issues consolidated financial statements. Consolidated financial statements are statements which report the assets, liabilities, revenues, and expenses of the legally separate parent and one or more subsidiaries as though they were a single company. The purpose of consolidated financial statements is to present an overall view of the activities of the parent and subsidiaries as one economic entity.

PREPARATION OF CONSOLIDATED FINANCIAL STATEMENTS

To explain further the parent-subsidiary relationship and to illustrate the preparation of consolidated financial statements, two different possible investments by Paula Company in the stock of Stanley Company will be examined. In the first situation, Paula Company acquires 100 percent control of Stanley Company. In the second situation, Paula acquires only 80 percent control of Stanley.

Consolidations with 100 Percent Control. Assume that Paula Company purchased 100 percent of Stanley Company's stock for $630,000. The book value of Stanley's net assets (its capital stock plus its retained earnings), at the time of acquisition was $510,000.

Date of Acquisition. Paula would record the purchase of Stanley's stock in an investment account at its cost of $630,000. In order to prepare consolidated financial statements, Paula's investment account and Stanley's capital stock and retained earnings accounts must be eliminated to avoid double counting. A work sheet for the preparation of a consolidated balance sheet for Paula Company and Stanley Company, as of the date of acquisition, is shown on page 719. The first two columns show balance sheet data for the two companies as separate entities, including Paula's investment in Stanley of $630,000. A pair of columns is provided for eliminations, and the consolidated balance sheet data are shown in the right-hand column.

Since the book value of Stanley's net assets at the date of acquisition was only $510,000 (capital stock of $45,000 + retained earnings of $465,000), this means that Paula's cost of $630,000 exceeded the book value of the acquired assets by $120,000. In order to prepare a consolidated balance sheet, this excess of cost over book value must be assigned to specific assets based on their current market values, so that they are properly reflected at their current cost to Paula Company. Any remaining amount which cannot be assigned

PAULA COMPANY AND STANLEY COMPANY
Consolidation Work Sheet
Date of Acquisition

	Paula Co.	Stanley Co.	Eliminations		Consolidated Balance Sheet
			Debit	Credit	
Assets					
Cash...	765,000	105,000			870,000
Accounts receivable	502,500	120,000			622,500
Inventories......................................	622,500	360,000			982,500
Long-term assets (net)	2,520,000				2,520,000
Investment in Stanley Co.	630,000			(a) 630,000	
Goodwill			(a) 120,000		120,000
Total assets	5,040,000	585,000			5,115,000
Liabilities and Stockholders' Equity					
Accounts payable	225,000	75,000			300,000
Capital stock — Paula Co.	3,525,000				3,525,000
Capital stock — Stanley Co.		45,000	(a) 45,000		
Retained earnings — Paula Co........	1,290,000				1,290,000
Retained earnings — Stanley Co......		465,000	(a) 465,000		
Total liabilities and stockholders' equity.........	5,040,000	585,000	630,000	630,000	5,115,000

to specific assets should be treated as goodwill. To keep the illustration simple, it is assumed that the total current market value of Stanley's assets is equal to their total book value. Therefore, the entire $120,000 excess of cost over book value would be assigned to goodwill in this case.

To eliminate the investment account, a credit of $630,000 must be made on the work sheet. Debits necessary to eliminate the capital stock and retained earnings accounts of Stanley are $45,000 and $465,000, a total of $510,000. The remaining debit of $120,000 represents the goodwill, which is recorded as part of this elimination entry. The following entry summarizes the elimination process:

(a) Capital Stock — Stanley Co. 45,000
     Retained Earnings — Stanley Co.................................... 465,000
     Goodwill... 120,000
         Investment in Stanley Co.   630,000
         To eliminate stockholders' equity of Stanley Co. and investment in Stanley Co., and to recognize goodwill.

The above entry is *not* a part of the accounting records of either Paula or Stanley, but is merely a necessary work sheet elimination in the consolidation activity. The assets and liabilities of the parent and subsidiary companies are combined for the consolidated balance sheet, after making any necessary eliminations. The capital stock and retained earnings reported on the consolidated balance sheet are those of the parent company only.

One Year After Acquisition. In years following the acquisition, Paula and Stanley maintain separate accounting records as individual entities. In order to report the financial position and results of operations of Paula and Stanley together, both a consolidated balance sheet and a consolidated income statement must be prepared. A work sheet for the preparation of a consolidated balance sheet and a consolidated income statement for Paula Company and Stanley Company one year after acquisition is shown below reflecting the following eliminations:

PAULA COMPANY AND STANLEY COMPANY
Consolidation Work Sheet
One Year After Acquisition

	Paula Co.	Stanley Co.	Eliminations Debit	Eliminations Credit	Consolidated Statements
Sales	2,250,000	900,000	(a) 450,000		2,700,000
Cost of goods sold	1,230,000	570,000		(a) 450,000	1,350,000
Operating expenses	540,000	150,000	(d) 12,000		702,000
Total expenses	1,770,000	720,000			2,052,000
Net income (not extended)	480,000	180,000			
Consolidated net income					648,000
Assets					
Cash	1,027,500	45,000			1,072,500
Accounts receivable	682,500	210,000			892,500
Accounts receivable — Paula Co.		120,000		(b) 120,000	
Inventories	727,500	420,000			1,147,500
Long-term assets (net)	3,364,500				3,364,500
Investment in Stanley Co.	630,000			(c) 630,000	
Goodwill			(c) 120,000	(d) 12,000	108,000
Total assets	6,432,000	795,000			6,585,000
Liabilities and Stockholders' Equity					
Accounts payable	240,000	105,000			345,000
Accounts payable — Stanley Co.	120,000		(b) 120,000		
Capital stock — Paula Co.	4,302,000				4,302,000
Capital stock — Stanley Co.		45,000	(c) 45,000		
Retained earnings — Paula Co. (not extended)	1,770,000				
Retained earnings — Stanley Co. (not extended)		645,000	(c) 465,000		
Consolidated retained earnings					1,938,000
Total liabilities and stockholders' equity	6,432,000	795,000	1,212,000	1,212,000	6,585,000

Entry (a)

During the first year, Stanley sold merchandise costing $300,000 to Paula for $450,000, all of which was further sold for $610,000 by Paula to outside parties by year end. Elimination entry (a) which appears on the work sheet offsets the intercompany sales of

$450,000 against the intercompany cost of goods sold of $450,000. In this way, only the sales to outsiders by the two companies as a whole, $610,000, are included in consolidated sales, and only the cost of goods sold of the two companies as a whole, $300,000, is included in consolidated cost of goods sold. The elimination entry in general journal form is as follows:

(a)	Sales...	450,000	
	Cost of Goods Sold		450,000
	Elimination of intercompany sales and cost of goods sold.		

Entry (b)

At the end of the year, Paula owes Stanley $120,000 for the goods purchased during the year. Since this account payable on Paula's books does not represent an amount owed to outsiders, and this account receivable on Stanley's books does not represent an amount owed by outsiders, these related asset and liability accounts should be eliminated. Elimination entry (b) accomplishes this. In general journal form, it appears as follows:

(b)	Accounts Payable — Stanley Co......................................	120,000	
	Accounts Receivable — Paula Co................................		120,000
	Elimination of intercompany receivable and payable.		

Entry (c)

Elimination entry (c) is the same as entry (a) for consolidation at the date of acquisition, which is illustrated in general journal form on page 719. This entry eliminates the original investment amount against Stanley's capital stock and retained earnings balances at the date of acquisition and recognizes the goodwill of $120,000.

Entry (d)

One more entry is necessary to complete the consolidation process in years subsequent to the acquisition. The goodwill of $120,000 must be amortized as an expense over some reasonable time period. Paula elected to amortize the goodwill over a 10-year period, resulting in amortization expense of $12,000 per year. Entry (d), which classifies the $12,000 as an operating expense and as a reduction of goodwill, in general journal form is as follows:

(d)	Operating Expenses..	12,000	
	Goodwill		12,000
	Amortization of goodwill.		

After these entries are made on the work sheet, the account balances are extended to the Consolidated Statements column, with two exceptions. (1) The consolidated net income is *calculated* based on the individual extended revenue and expense amounts. (2) The consolidated retained earnings is *calculated* based on the individual extended asset and liability amounts. Note that the consolidated retained earnings is equal to the sum of Paula Company's retained earnings ($1,770,000) plus the retained earnings accumulated by Stanley Company since the date of acquisition ($180,000), less the amount of goodwill amortized ($12,000). The $180,000 amount is the difference between Stanley Company's retained earnings at acquisition of $465,000 (see page 719) and its current retained earnings of $645,000 (see page 720). The data necessary to prepare a consolidated income statement and a consolidated balance sheet now appear in the Consolidated Statement column.

Consolidations with Less than 100 Percent Control. Assume that Paula Company purchased only 80 percent of Stanley Company's stock rather than the 100 percent in the previous illustration. Further assume that the purchase price was $504,000, and that the book value of Stanley's net assets (capital stock + retained earnings) at the time of acquisition was once again $510,000. In this situation, an additional accounting problem arises — how to account for the minority interest. The minority interest is the portion of a partially owned subsidiary (20 percent in this case) that is owned by stockholders other than the parent company.

Date of Acquisition. Paula would record the purchase of Stanley's stock in an investment account at its cost of $504,000. As in the previous illustration, in order to prepare consolidated financial statements, Paula's investment account and Stanley's capital stock and retained earnings accounts must be eliminated. It will also be necessary in this case to recognize the minority interest in Stanley. A work sheet for the preparation of a consolidated balance sheet for Paula Company and Stanley Company as of the date of acquisition is shown on page 723.

Since the book value of Stanley's net assets at the date of acquisition was $510,000, Paula's 80 percent interest in these assets is $408,000 (80% × $510,000). This means that Paula's cost exceeded the book value of the acquired assets by $96,000 ($504,000 − $408,000). If it is assumed that the total current market value of

PAULA COMPANY AND STANLEY COMPANY
Consolidation Work Sheet
Date of Acquisition

	Paula Co.	Stanley Co.	Eliminations		Consolidated Balance Sheet
			Debit	Credit	
Assets					
Cash	891,000	105,000			996,000
Accounts receivable	502,500	120,000			622,500
Inventories	622,500	360,000			982,500
Long-term assets (net)	2,520,000				2,520,000
Investment in Stanley Co.	504,000			(a) 504,000	
Goodwill			(a) 96,000		96,000
Total assets	5,040,000	585,000			5,217,000
Liabilities and Stockholders' Equity					
Accounts payable	225,000	75,000			300,000
Capital stock — Paula Co.	3,525,000				3,525,000
Capital stock — Stanley Co.		45,000	(a) 45,000		
Retained earnings — Paula Co.	1,290,000				1,290,000
Retained earnings — Stanley Co.		465,000	(a) 465,000		
Minority interest				(a) 102,000	102,000
Total liabilities and stockholders' equity	5,040,000	585,000	606,000	606,000	5,217,000

Stanley's assets is equal to their total book value, this $96,000 would be assigned to goodwill in preparing the consolidated balance sheet.

The goodwill of $96,000 and the minority interest in Stanley are recognized as results of elimination entry (a) on the work sheet. The investment account is eliminated by means of the credit of $504,000. Debits of $45,000 and $465,000 are made to eliminate the capital stock and retained earnings accounts of Stanley. A debit of $96,000 recognizes the goodwill. A final credit of $102,000 is made to recognize the minority interest in Stanley. This minority interest can be calculated as follows:

Minority Interest %	×	Stanley Stockholders' Equity	=	Minority Interest in Dollars
20%	×	$510,000	=	$102,000

In general journal form, the entry is as follows:

(a) Capital Stock — Stanley Co.	45,000	
Retained Earnings — Stanley Co.	465,000	
Goodwill	96,000	
Investment in Stanley Co.		504,000
Minority Interest in Stanley Co.		102,000

Elimination of stockholders' equity of Stanley Co. and investment in Stanley Co., and recognition of goodwill and minority interest.

On the consolidated balance sheet, the minority interest often is shown as a separate category between the liabilities and stockholders' equity sections. An acceptable alternative is to classify the minority interest as part of stockholders' equity.

One Year After Acquisition. A work sheet for the preparation of a consolidated balance sheet and income statement for Paula Company and Stanley Company one year after acquisition is shown below reflecting the following eliminations:

PAULA COMPANY AND STANLEY COMPANY
Consolidation Work Sheet
One Year After Acquisition

	Paula Co.	Stanley Co.	Eliminations Debit	Eliminations Credit	Consolidated Statements
Sales	2,250,000	900,000	(a) 450,000		2,700,000
Cost of goods sold	1,230,000	570,000		(a) 450,000	1,350,000
Operating expenses	540,000	150,000	(d) 9,600		699,600
Total expenses	1,770,000	720,000			2,049,600
Net income (not extended)	480,000	180,000			650,400
Less minority interest in Stanley Co. net income			(e) 36,000		36,000
Consolidated net income					614,400
Assets					
Cash	1,153,500	45,000			1,198,500
Accounts receivable	682,500	210,000			892,500
Accounts receivable — Paula Co.		120,000		(b) 120,000	
Inventories	727,500	420,000			1,147,500
Long-term assets (net)	3,364,500				3,364,500
Investment in Stanley Co.	504,000			(c) 504,000	
Goodwill			(c) 96,000	(d) 9,600	86,400
Total assets	6,432,000	795,000			6,689,400
Liabilities and Stockholders' Equity					
Accounts payable	240,000	105,000			345,000
Accounts payable — Stanley Co.	120,000		(b) 120,000		
Capital stock — Paula Co.	4,302,000				4,302,000
Capital stock — Stanley Co.		45,000	(c) 45,000		
Retained earnings — Paula Co. (not extended)	1,770,000				
Retained earnings — Stanley Co. (not extended)		645,000	(c) 465,000		
Consolidated retained earnings					1,904,400
Minority interest in Stanley Co.				(c) 102,000	
				(e) 36,000	138,000
Total liabilities and stockholders' equity	6,432,000	795,000	1,221,600	1,221,600	6,689,400

Entries (a), (b), and (c)

Entries (a) to eliminate intercompany sales and cost of goods sold and (b) to eliminate intercompany receivables and payables, are the same as those which appear on the work sheet on page 720, and which are explained on pages 720–721. Entry (c) is the same as entry (a) for consolidation at the date of acquisition, which is illustrated in general journal form on page 719. This entry eliminates the original investment amount against Stanley's capital stock and retained earnings balances at the date of acquisition, and recognizes the goodwill of $96,000 and the minority interest of $102,000.

Entry (d)

Paula elects to amortize the goodwill of $96,000 over a 10-year period, resulting in amortization expense of $9,600 per year. Entry (d) records the $9,600 as an operating expense and as a reduction of goodwill. In general journal form, the entry would appear as follows:

(d)	Operating Expenses..	9,600	
	Goodwill		9,600
	Amortization of goodwill.		

Entry (e)

One additional entry is necessary in years subsequent to the date of acquisition to complete the consolidation process. The minority interest in Stanley's net income for the year must be recognized. The 20 percent minority interest in Stanley's net income of $180,000 is $36,000. This $36,000 should be recognized as a deduction from consolidated net income and as an increase in the minority interest in Stanley. Entry (e) accomplishes this. In general journal form, this entry is as follows:

(e)	Minority Interest in Stanley Co. Net Income	36,000	
	Minority Interest in Stanley Co.		36,000
	Recognition of minority share of Stanley Co. net income for the year.		

After these entries are made on the work sheet, the account balances are extended to the Consolidated Statements column, with the same two exceptions as in the work sheet on page 720. (1) The consolidated net income is *calculated* based on the individual extended revenue, expense, and minority interest amounts. (2) The consolidated retained earnings is *calculated* based on the individual extended asset, liability, and minority interest amounts. Note that in this case, the consolidated retained earnings is equal to the sum of Paula Company's retained earnings ($1,770,000) plus the retained earnings accumulated by Stanley since the date of acquisition ($180,000) less the amount of goodwill amortized ($9,600) and the minority interest's share of Stanley's net income ($36,000).

PURCHASE VERSUS POOLING OF INTERESTS

Throughout the illustrations in this chapter, it has been assumed that the parent company acquired the stock of the subsidiary company for cash. For accounting purposes, this is known as a **purchase**.

An alternative approach to the combining of two companies is for the parent to issue its stock in exchange for the subsidiary's stock. When two companies combine in such a way that substantially all of the voting stock of the subsidiary company is acquired by the parent company, and the voting shareholders of the two companies become the voting shareholders of the combined company, this is known as a **pooling of interests**.

Accounting for a pooling of interests differs from the accounting illustrated in previous sections of this chapter in that no purchase is considered to have taken place. Therefore there is no change in the book value of the assets or equities of the combined companies. There is no recognition of goodwill or recognition of current market values of assets when a pooling of interests occurs. The parent company carries its investment in the subsidiary at the book value of the subsidiary's stockholders' equity.

Detailed application of pooling of interests accounting procedures, and a complete discussion of the conditions that must be met in order to use the pooling of interests approach in accounting for a business combination, are subjects for a more advanced text.

BUILDING YOUR ACCOUNTING KNOWLEDGE

1. Identify and describe three types of business combinations.
2. When is it appropriate to account for intercompany investments according to the cost method?
3. Describe proper accounting under the equity method to record the acquiring company's share of the acquired company's net income and dividend distribution.
4. When is it appropriate to issue consolidated financial statements?
5. What is the purpose of consolidated financial statements?

6. If the acquiring company's cost exceeds the book value of the acquired company's net assets, how should this excess be accounted for in preparing a consolidated balance sheet?

7. If the subsidiary sells merchandise to the parent and the parent subsequently sells this merchandise to outsiders, how should the transaction between the subsidiary and the parent be accounted for in preparing a consolidated income statement?

8. In what two ways may the minority interest be shown on a consolidated balance sheet?

9. Describe a pooling of interests.

Report No. 26-2

> *Complete Report No. 26-2 in the study assignments and submit your working papers for approval. Continue with the textbook discussion until Report No. 27-1 is required.*

EXPANDING YOUR BUSINESS VOCABULARY

What is the meaning of each of the following terms?

acquisition (p. 716)
branch (p. 707)
Branch Office (p. 707)
consolidated financial statements
    (p. 718)
consolidation (p. 716)
controlling interest (p. 717)
cost method (p. 716)
equity method (p. 717)
Home Office (p. 707)
interlocking (p. 707)

merger (p. 716)
minority interest (p. 722)
net assets (p. 718)
parent (p. 718)
pooling of interests (p. 726)
purchase (p. 726)
reciprocal (p. 707)
Shipments to Branch (p. 708)
Shipments from Home Office
    (p. 708)
subsidiary (p. 718)

CHAPTER 27

ACCOUNTING FOR A JOB-ORDER MANUFACTURING BUSINESS

CHAPTER OBJECTIVES

The objectives of this chapter are to enable you:

▶ To describe **manufacturing cost** and the interrelated inventories of a manufacturing business, and to define the terms:

Direct materials	Materials inventory
Indirect materials	Cost of materials used
Direct labor	Work in process inventory
Indirect labor	Cost of goods manufactured
Factory overhead	Finished goods inventory

▶ To explain the various bases of assigning cost to inventories, the application of the lower-of-cost-or-market rule to the work in process and finished goods inventories of a manufacturing business, and the use of perpetual inventories in manufacturing businesses.

▶ To define, describe, and explain **job order cost accounting**, and to prepare a diagram illustrating the "flow" of costs through the general ledger accounts that are typical of a job-oriented cost accounting system.

▶ To recognize a **job cost sheet**, a **materials requisition**, and a **daily time sheet**, and explain their uses in a job order system.

▶ To describe the nature of factory overhead, to explain the use of a **predetermined factory overhead rate**, and to define **overabsorbed** and **underabsorbed factory overhead**, **service departments**, **average activity** and **direct costing**.

▶ To perform the record-keeping phases of the accounting cycle for a small job-order manufacturing corporation, including such phases of the cycle as source documents, journals, ledgers, and auxiliary records.

▶ To describe a subsidiary factory overhead ledger and its related chart of accounts.

A manufacturing business makes articles for sale, rather than purchasing them in finished form as is the case in a merchandising business. Because of this, the business operations of a manufacturing enterprise are more complex and its accounting processes are more elaborate. Records must be kept of the cost of materials acquired and used, labor costs incurred, and various other costs that arise in the operation of the factory. Normally, at the end of an accounting period, there are some unused materials, some unfinished goods, and some finished but unsold goods on hand. The various elements of manufacturing cost must be allocated in an equitable manner to the several types of inventory and to the goods that were sold.

MANUFACTURING COST; INVENTORIES OF A MANUFACTURING BUSINESS

The primary elements of manufacturing cost are (1) materials, (2) labor, and (3) factory overhead. The nature of each of these elements is discussed in the paragraphs that follow.

MATERIALS

Certain materials are needed in the manufacture of a product. A manufacturer of automobiles requires sheet metal, bar steel, fabric, tires, and scores of other articles. A manufacturer of dies and molds requires steel plates, steel bars, springs, bolts, nuts and screws. The only distinction between materials and finished goods, in many instances, is their relationship to a particular manufacturer. The finished goods of one manufacturer may be materials of another. Thus, flour is finished goods to a miller but materials to a baker; silver may be the finished product of a mining company but may constitute materials to a manufacturer of silverware. Materials used in manufacturing may be classified as:

(1) Direct materials.
(2) Indirect materials.

Direct materials normally include those that enter into and become a part of the finished product. Thus, the leather and the linings used in the manufacture of shoes are direct materials. Similarly, the sheet metal, bar steel, fabric, and many other materials used in the manufacture of an automobile are direct materials.

Indirect materials include those used in the manufacturing process that do not become a part of the finished product. Thus, oil and grease used in the operation of machinery are indirect materials. Such materials are often referred to as factory supplies. Indirect materials also may include inexpensive items that may become a part of the finished product, but whose small cost is most easily accounted for as a part of factory overhead. Nails, screws, washers, and glue sometimes are treated as indirect materials.

LABOR

Wages paid to factory workers constitute a part of the cost of the finished product. The employees of a factory may be divided into two classes:

(1) Those who devote their time to converting the materials into finished goods. Such workers may do assembly work or may operate factory machinery. The wages paid to such workers are directly chargeable to the cost of the products being manufactured. This type of labor usually is referred to as direct labor.

(2) Those who devote their time to supervision or to work of a general nature. Such workers may include superintendents, inspectors, timekeepers, engineers, repairpersons, receiving clerks, and janitors. The wages paid to such workers cannot be charged directly to the cost of the products being manufactured but must be included in the indirect costs of the factory operation. This type of labor usually is referred to as indirect labor.

While there are many different methods employed in the handling of payrolls, the final results are the same. The payroll should be classified to facilitate the distribution of labor charges. Separate ledger accounts should be used for direct factory labor, indirect factory labor, sales salaries, office salaries, and administrative salaries. When labor cost is properly analyzed and recorded so as to distinguish between direct and indirect labor, and between labor employed in the factory and in other departments, the accounts will provide better information for preparing the income statement.

FACTORY OVERHEAD

It is impossible to operate a factory without incurring a variety of additional costs, often called factory overhead. This group of costs is sometimes described as manufacturing expense, indirect manufacturing expense, or factory burden. Factory overhead may be classified as:

(1) Indirect materials.
(2) Indirect labor.
(3) Other factory overhead.

Indirect materials and indirect labor have already been discussed. Other factory overhead includes a variety of things, such as:

(1) Depreciation of factory buildings and equipment.
(2) Repairs to factory buildings and equipment.
(3) Insurance on factory buildings and equipment.
(4) Property taxes applicable to factory buildings and equipment.
(5) Heat, light, and power consumed.

The accounts kept to record the factory overhead of different firms vary extensively. The information desired in a separate schedule of factory overhead, or in such other reports as may be required, determines what accounts should be kept. Each distinct type of any cost sizable in amount should be recorded in a separate account.

As factory overhead costs are incurred, they should be recorded as debits to the proper accounts. Costs that are wholly chargeable to manufacturing should be recorded in separate accounts. Repairs to factory buildings and equipment is an example of this type of cost. There are certain other costs of a general overhead nature that cannot be charged either wholly to manufacturing or wholly to any other single department. These costs must be prorated or apportioned on some equitable basis. Power cost, for example, may be distributed on the basis of the amount of power consumed by various departments. Property taxes on land and buildings may be allocated in relation to the departmental space occupied in the buildings. Property taxes on furniture, fixtures, machinery, and equipment may be apportioned in relation to the value of the property in each department. A reasonable basis of distribution or allocation must be found for each cost of this type.

INVENTORIES OF A MANUFACTURING BUSINESS

The inventory of a merchant consists of finished goods only. In contrast to this, a manufacturer usually has three inventories: (1) finished goods, (2) work in process, and (3) materials. If perpetual inventories are not kept, it is necessary to determine the amounts of the inventories of materials and of work in process at the beginning and at the end of the period in order to determine the cost of goods manufactured. Similarly, the beginning and ending inventories of finished goods must be determined in order to calculate the cost of goods sold. The relationship between these elements is as follows:

COST OF
MATERIALS USED
{
Beginning inventory of materials
+ Materials purchases (plus freight in, less returns and discounts)
= Total cost of materials available for use
− Ending inventory of materials
= COST OF MATERIALS USED
}

COST OF GOODS
MANUFACTURED
{
Beginning inventory of work in process
+ Cost of materials used
+ Direct labor
+ Factory overhead
= Total factory costs
− Ending inventory of work in process
= COST OF GOODS MANUFACTURED
}

COST OF
GOODS SOLD
{
Beginning inventory of finished goods
+ Cost of goods manufactured
= Cost of finished goods available for sale
− Ending inventory of finished goods
= COST OF GOODS SOLD
}

ASSIGNING COST TO INVENTORIES

In assigning cost to goods on hand at a certain time, one of the bases listed below must be used:

(1) Cost basis
  (a) First-in, first-out (fifo) cost
  (b) Average cost
  (c) Last-in, first-out (lifo) cost
(2) The lower of cost (fifo or average) or market (cost to replace)

These methods of allocating cost between goods sold and goods on hand in a merchandising business were discussed and illustrated in Chapter 12. Any of these methods can be used by a manufacturing business in allocating the cost of materials purchased between the materials used and those which are still on hand at the end of the period. In the cases of inventories of work in process and of finished goods, cost includes (1) materials cost, (2) direct labor cost, and (3) factory overhead associated with the production of the goods.

In some cases, it may be difficult to determine the costs that relate to the work that is in process. The difficulty may be insurmountable if the company has a large number of different products in various stages of completion at the end of the period. There usually is little difficulty in determining the total cost of materials and direct labor used, as well as the total factory overhead incurred during the period. The problem is to allocate or apportion these costs between the goods completed during the period and the work in process at the end of the period. Often, the assignment of costs involves a considerable element of estimation, especially in the determination of the degree of completion of partly finished products.

Considerable accuracy is attainable in some cases, however. The nature of the product and the method of manufacture or processing may make it possible to compute the cost of the materials and the direct labor that have gone into the goods that have been finished and into those that are incomplete at the end of the period. The factory overhead may· be apportioned on some reasonable basis. Sometimes it is allocated in proportion to direct labor. To illustrate this allocation approach, assume that the accounts of a manufacturer disclose the following information:

Cost of work in process, first of year	$ 36,000
Cost of materials used during year	140,000
Direct labor for year	200,000
Factory overhead for year	160,000

It is determined that in the work in process at the end of the year, $28,000 is the cost of materials and $30,000 is the cost of direct labor in these incomplete goods. Factory overhead is to be allocated in proportion to direct labor. For the year, factory overhead amounts to 80 percent ($160,000 ÷ $200,000) of direct labor. Therefore, $136,000 (80% of $170,000) of factory overhead is allocated to finished goods and $24,000 (80% of $30,000) of factory overhead is allocated to work in process. The allocation of all material, direct labor, and overhead costs between finished and unfinished goods would be as follows:

	Total	Cost Apportioned to	
		Goods Finished During Year	Ending Inventory of Work in Process
Opening inventory of work in process	$ 36,000	$ 36,000	—
Materials used......................................	140,000	112,000	$28,000
Direct labor	200,000	170,000	30,000
Factory overhead.................................	160,000	136,000(1)	24,000(2)
	$536,000	$454,000	$82,000

(1) 80% of $170,000
(2) 80% of $30,000

INVENTORIES AT COST OR MARKET, WHICHEVER IS LOWER

As discussed previously in Chapter 12, the term "market," as used in relation to inventories, usually means the replacement cost as of the date of the inventory for the particular merchandise in the volume in which it is usually purchased. If the lower-of-cost-or-market procedure is used, the market value of each article on hand should be compared with the cost of the article, and the lower of the two should be taken as the inventory value of the article. In certain situations, it is proper to use the lower of either the total cost of all the items or the total market value of all the items in the inventory.

Because the "cost or market, whichever is lower" rule often is applied both to the work in process and to the finished goods inventories of a manufacturer, the term "market" has to be specially interpreted. Usually there is no market in which goods exactly like those manufactured can be purchased. The rule effectively becomes "cost or cost to replace, whichever is lower." Cost to replace may have to be estimated. Sometimes the cost of the latest lot of goods finished can be used as a measure. If there has been no change in any of the cost elements since such goods were completed, their unit cost may be considered as the unit cost to replace.

To illustrate the application of the rule, assume that a manufacturer has 6,000 units of Product A on hand at the end of the period. On the basis of first-in, first-out, the cost of this inventory is $11,280 (2,400 items at $2 each plus 3,600 items just completed at $1.80 each). Assuming that there has been no change in the prices of materials, rates of labor, or other cost elements since the last lot of goods was completed, the replacement cost would be $1.80 per unit or $10,800 for the 6,000 units. If the "cost or cost to replace, whichever is lower" rule is to be followed, the manufacturer will assign $10,800 as the amount of the inventory, because the cost to replace is lower than the cost. On the other hand, if replacement cost had been higher than the original production cost, the original cost of

$11,280 would have been used. If there had been changes in the prices of materials, rates of labor, or other items of factory overhead since the last items were produced, the latest incurred cost could not be used as a measure of replacement cost. The manufacturer would have to estimate what the cost to replace would be after giving effect to the new conditions.

PERPETUAL INVENTORIES

Merchants and manufacturers like to know the quantities and the costs of goods on hand at all times without taking the time to count the stock. For this reason, they maintain perpetual inventories. A perpetual inventory, sometimes called a book or running inventory, is a continuous record of the amount of materials or goods on hand. A perpetual inventory is a very natural application in a computer-based accounting system.

When a perpetual inventory of materials is kept, there is no materials purchases account in the ledger. Instead, all purchases are debited to the materials inventory account. Under this system, a record must be kept of the quantity and the cost of all materials used or returned, which amount is credited to the materials inventory account. After all posting has been completed, the balance of the account shows the cost of the materials that are presumed to be on hand.

Usually the materials inventory account controls a subsidiary ledger called a stores ledger. This ledger has an account (frequently in the form of a card) for each item in the inventory. The card shows the quantity and cost of materials received, the quantity and cost of materials issued, and the resulting balance. The postings to these accounts are kept up-to-date so that reference to each stores ledger card will show the quantity and the cost of the item on hand at any time. Often, the form of the stores ledger cards (accounts) includes a memorandum column in which to record the quantity of materials ordered but not yet received.

The use of perpetual inventories does not eliminate the necessity for periodically making a count of the materials or goods on hand. The perpetual inventory shows what should be on hand. The record may be wrong to the extent that errors may have been made or goods may have been lost, destroyed, or stolen. Some types of goods are subject to physical shrinkage. At least once a year a physical inventory should be taken. If the quantity of materials on hand is found to be more or less than the quantity shown by the inventory records, an adjustment of the accounts is needed. For example, if the balance of the materials inventory account showed the cost of materials on hand to be $16,000 but upon physical count the cost of the materials totaled only $15,000, an adjusting entry would be needed debiting Cost of Goods Sold and crediting Materials for $1,000. The shortage is charged to Cost of Goods Sold on the assumption that no portion of the missing materials is in Work in Process or Finished Goods Inventory. This assumption yields sufficiently accurate results in most cases. Similarly, the discovery of an overage or a shortage of work in process or finished goods would require an adjustment to the cost of goods sold account.

When perpetual inventories are maintained, it is not necessary to take an inventory of everything at the same time. One type of materials can be counted and the finding compared with the stores or stock card for that item. Another type can be inventoried at a different time. Adjustments can be made as shortages or overages are discovered. In such cases, inventory short and over accounts can be used that are closed at the end of the period. Some large companies are taking physical inventory of some type of materials each working day.

Unless a manufacturer has a suitable cost accounting system, it is unlikely that a perpetual inventory of work in process will be maintained. Also, without such a system it usually is difficult to keep an accurate perpetual inventory of finished goods. In some cases, however, records of materials, work in process, and finished goods are kept in terms of quantities alone. When the record is in this form, it is purely supplementary and there is no control account. Nevertheless, this type of record may be helpful in inventory control.

BUILDING YOUR ACCOUNTING KNOWLEDGE

1. Why are the business operations of a manufacturing business more complex and its accounting processes more elaborate than those of a merchandising business?
2. What are the three primary elements of manufacturing cost?
3. What are the two major types of materials and how do they differ?
4. What is the usual distinction between direct and indirect labor?
5. Give five examples of other factory overhead in addition to indirect materials and indirect labor.
6. What are the three inventories usually found in a manufacturing business?
7. In what two ways may the replacement cost of work in process and finished goods inventories be determined?

8. Why does the use of perpetual inventories not eliminate the necessity for periodically making a count of the materials or goods on hand?

Report No. 27-1

> *Complete Report No. 27-1 in the study assignments and submit your working papers for approval. Continue with the textbook discussion until Report No. 27-2 is required.*

JOB ORDER COST ACCOUNTING

The term cost accounting refers to those activities concerned with the assignment of incurred costs to various business operations, including the design and operation of systems that will generate information to help control costs. This section will be confined to a discussion of the major practices followed in order to assign factory costs to units produced. Product cost information is needed for two reasons:

(1) To assist in setting selling prices or, in many cases, to determine whether the prices that are being charged to customers are high enough to provide a gross margin that will help cover nonmanufacturing costs and expenses and contribute to net income. Even though the overall result seems to be satisfactory, the management of a multiproduct manufacturing business wants to know whether (and how much) each product or "product line" is adding to (or subtracting from) the net result.

(2) To assist in the determination of the net income (or net loss) of each period. When goods are manufactured rather than purchased, there must be some means of assigning a reasonable share of incurred costs to (a) products finished but unsold at the end of the accounting period — the finished goods inventory, and (b) products that are unfinished at the end of the period — the work in process inventory.

While many cost accounting systems may be described as somewhat "hybrid," there are two basic types: (1) job order and (2) process. Job order costing is discussed in this section. Process costing will be discussed in Chapter 28.

THE JOB COST SHEET

If the product is made to customers' orders or specifications, or if products are made in separately identifiable "lots" or "batches," a job order cost accounting system will be suitable. Such a system would be well suited to such enterprises as a printing shop, a cabinet shop, or a toolmaker. The core of this type of system is a record commonly called a job cost sheet or sometimes just job sheet or job card. On the job cost sheet are entered (1) the cost of materials that can be clearly identified with the job — direct materials, (2) the labor cost that can be clearly identified with the job — direct labor, and (3) a share of the factory overhead cost that may reasonably be assigned to the job. An illustration of one form of job cost sheet is reproduced below. This form is in common use, but the record may take a different form. Sometimes, an ordinary ledger account form is used. Whatever form the record takes and by whatever name it is called, its function is to serve as a place to bring together the three elements of the cost of each job — direct materials, direct labor, and a share of factory overhead.

Hartup Tool, Inc.

JOB COST SHEET

Job. No. __219__   Date __Jan. 15__

Item __Single cavity mold--15" back cover__

For __RCA__   Date Completed __Feb. 13__

DIRECT MATERIALS		DIRECT LABOR		FACTORY OVERHEAD	
Req. No.	Amount	Hours	Amount	Direct Labor	$35,033.40
				Overhead Rate	55%
393	$6,139.10	4,210	$34,119.80	Overhead Applied	$19,268.37
		112	913.60	SUMMARY	
				Direct Materials	$ 6,139.10
				Direct Labor	35,033.40
				Overhead	19,268.37
				Total Cost	$60,440.87

Job Cost Sheet

Collectively, the job cost sheets comprise the job cost ledger. This job cost ledger is subsidiary to the general ledger account Work in Process (sometimes called Goods in Process or Jobs in Process).

ACCOUNTING FOR MATERIALS

The subject of accounting for materials, including mention of the distinction between "direct" and "indirect" materials, was discussed in the previous section. In a cost accounting system, it is common practice to keep perpetual inventories. Except in cases where only a few different materials are used, it is quite likely that there will be a materials ledger or stores ledger. This materials ledger is subsidiary to the general ledger account Materials.

A form called a materials requisition or stores requisition usually is used in connection with the movement of and accounting for materials. This form serves both as an authorization (when properly approved) to the storekeeper to issue materials, and as a source document for recording the movement of materials. After the costs of the requisitioned materials have been entered on the form, it can be used as the basis for credits in the stores ledger and debits in the job cost ledger (for direct materials put into production) and for debits in the factory overhead ledger (for indirect materials used in the factory). A summary of the requisitions provides the amounts to be credited to the control account for materials, with debits to the control accounts for work in process and for factory overhead in the general ledger. One form of materials requisition is illustrated below.

Requested by: *Carol Moore* Date: *January 20, 19--* Charge to: *Job No. 228 — Materials*				Req. No.: *407* Approved: *J. L.*	
Item No.	Description	Quantity	Unit Cost	Total Cost	
SP10	*3" × 18" × 30" steel plate*	*1*	*1,137.52*	*1,137.52*	
Received by: *CM*			Date received: *January 20, 19--*		

Materials Requisition

ACCOUNTING FOR LABOR

The practices followed in accounting for the earnings, payroll deductions, and the payment of wages and salaries to employees have been described and illustrated at several earlier points in the textbook. Fundamentally the same procedures are involved in the case of a factory with a job order cost accounting system, except that more detail is involved in accounting for labor cost. The earnings of workers whose services are considered to be indirect labor must be charged to the proper factory overhead accounts. The earnings of workers whose services are considered to be **direct labor** must be charged to the jobs on which they worked. This requires that some procedure be followed for keeping a record of the time worked and labor cost incurred on each job. A wide variety of practices designed to provide this information are in use. One such practice is to require the direct labor employees to complete a **daily time sheet** or **time ticket** similar to the one reproduced below. This form may be prepared manually, or it may be completed as a printout from a computer-based timekeeping system. The tickets may be summarized by days, weeks, or months, to provide the direct labor cost of each of the jobs involved.

Hartup Tool, Inc.

DAILY TIME SHEET

Name Ophir Falk   Date 1/26

Job No.	Start	Stop	Hours Reg.	O.T.	Equiv. Hours	Rate	Amount Earned
229	8:00	12:00	4		4	8.00	32.00
223	1:00	6:00	4	1	$5\frac{1}{2}$	8.00	44.00
							76.00

Approved P.R.

Daily Time Sheet

A special problem may arise if overtime pay is involved. Under certain circumstances, the total labor cost — including overtime premium — is properly chargeable to the jobs on which the overtime was worked. In other cases, overtime may have been necessary because of a heavy production schedule, but it may not be reasonable to charge the particular jobs involved with the extra cost incurred because overtime hours were required. (Note that it is only the premium part of the pay that is at issue here. Each job normally would be charged for the total hours at the straight-time rate.) In such cases, the overtime premium portion of the labor cost may be charged to factory overhead.

It is rather common practice to charge factory overhead for the portion of the employer's payroll taxes that relates to all types of factory labor, since such taxes are considered to be an indirect labor cost. Also, factory overhead usually is charged for the cost of any "fringe benefits" (vacation pay, for example) that relate to factory workers.

ACCOUNTING FOR FACTORY OVERHEAD

The nature of factory overhead was discussed on pages 731–732. In connection with job order cost accounting systems, the major problem is the assignment of a reasonable amount of the factory overhead to each job. When more than one type of product is manufactured, a method of factory overhead apportionment that is sensible and equitable must be used. The assignment problem is complicated by the nature of many of the costs that comprise factory overhead. Most of these costs do not vary directly with the volume of production, such as depreciation of factory building and equipment, for example. Some types of factory overhead, such as vacation pay and repairs and maintenance of machinery, are incurred irregularly throughout the year, but their costs do not entirely apply to the months in which they are recorded.

The foregoing considerations have led to the practice of calculating a so-called predetermined factory overhead rate to be used in assigning factory overhead cost to the jobs worked on during a year. Suppose, for example, that the intention is to assign all of the factory overhead cost for each year to the jobs worked on during that year, and it is decided that a direct-labor-cost basis of assignment will give reasonable results. The rate to be used each year is calculated by using the following formula:

$$\frac{\text{Estimated Factory Overhead Cost for the Coming Year}}{\text{Estimated Direct Labor Cost for the Coming Year}} = \begin{array}{l}\text{Factory Overhead}\\\text{as a Percent of}\\\text{Direct Labor Cost}\end{array}$$

Suppose it is estimated that, during the coming year, factory overhead cost will be $540,000 and direct labor cost will be $600,000. The predetermined rate for that year would be 90 percent ($540,000 ÷ $600,000). As each job is completed during the year, an amount equal to 90 percent of the direct labor cost incurred on the job during that year would be added as the job's share of factory overhead cost. At the end of that year, 90 percent of the direct labor cost thus far incurred would be added as a part of the cost of the unfinished jobs (work in process).

It is likely that there will be a control account, Factory Overhead, in the general ledger and a related factory overhead subsidiary ledger. So as not to disturb this relationship, the total amount of factory overhead added to the job cost records may be recorded in the journal by a debit to Work in Process and a credit to Factory Overhead Applied (a contra account to the control account, Factory Overhead).

It is unlikely that both the estimate of factory overhead cost and the estimate of total direct labor cost will turn out to be exactly correct. Either estimate may be too high or too low. There will be some difference between the amount of factory overhead cost actually incurred and the total amount assigned to the jobs worked on during the year. The difference between the balance of Factory Overhead and the balance of Factory Overhead Applied is described as overabsorbed or underabsorbed factory overhead. Some times the terms overapplied and underapplied are used. If the difference is relatively small, it is common practice to close the amount of any over- or-underabsorption to Cost of Goods Sold, rather than recalculate the cost of each job. If there is a large difference, a number of recalculations may be required.

Throughout the foregoing discussion, it has been assumed that neither direct labor nor factory overhead is being accounted for on a departmental basis. If the accounting is departmentalized, the record keeping is more complicated. A direct-labor-cost basis of assigning departmental overhead may be suitable for certain departments, while a direct-labor-hour or machine-hour basis may be more suitable for other departments. If departmentalized cost accounting records are maintained, it will be necessary to allocate costs that are common to all departments (such as factory administration costs and occupancy costs). There may also be certain service departments (personnel and factory maintenance, for example) whose costs must be allocated to the producing departments prior to the assignment of factory overhead to jobs.

The policy of attempting to assign all of the factory overhead cost incurred during a given year to the production of that year is not always followed. Many manufacturing businesses use what is known as a normal capacity or average activity basis of assigning factory overhead. Normal capacity is an average annual measure based on several years' projection. The idea is to assign factory overhead in such a way that, on the average, over several years all factory overhead incurred will be assigned to jobs. However, in any single year it is unlikely that the amount incurred and the amount assigned will be substantially the same. This method is intended to avoid marked changes in unit costs because of fluctuation in the level of production. Another practice that is popular, though not yet an accepted method of accounting, is to assign only variable factory overhead (overhead which varies with the volume of output) to the units produced. Fixed factory overhead costs do not vary with the volume of output. They are described as period costs (in contrast to product costs which vary in relation to output), and are treated as expenses each year — not as a part of the total cost of units produced. This method of assigning only variable overhead costs to units of output is called direct costing. Some think that its numerous advantages will cause direct costing to become the most widely followed method of cost accounting in years to come.

FLOW OF COSTS THROUGH JOB ORDER COST ACCOUNTS

To illustrate the flow of costs through the accounts of a manufacturing company using job order cost accounting, a summary of the entries made to record costs incurred, jobs completed, and the cost of finished goods sold is presented. The illustration relates to the Bass Manufacturing Company for the month of January. The accounts of the company are kept on a calendar-year basis. Only transactions involving manufacturing costs are summarized and only six general ledger accounts are shown. Because of space limitations, each of the four subsidiary ledgers illustrated includes only a few accounts. The company uses a voucher system and maintains appropriate books of original entry and auxiliary records. As of January 1, the inventory accounts had the following balances:

General Ledger Accounts		Subsidiary Ledger Accounts	
		Stores ledger:	
Materials	$26,000	Material A	$12,000
		Material B	8,000
		Material C	6,000
		Job Cost ledger:	
Work in Process	16,000	Job No. 604	16,000
		Finished Goods ledger:	
Finished Goods	38,000	Product Y	24,000
		Product Z	14,000

The three-column general journal format illustrated on page 503 for Fishler & Marvon's Bakery will be used here. Postings to accounts in T form in both the general ledger and the subsidiary ledgers are shown on page 744. (The accounts are positioned to indicate the flow of costs.) Note that the ending balances in the general ledger control accounts agree with the totals of the subsidiary ledger account balances.

For purposes of illustration, all of the transactions summarized are presented in the form of general journal entries.

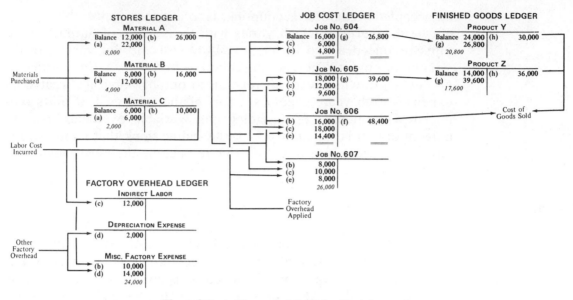

**Flow of Costs Through Job Order Cost Accounts
(Subsidiary Ledgers)**

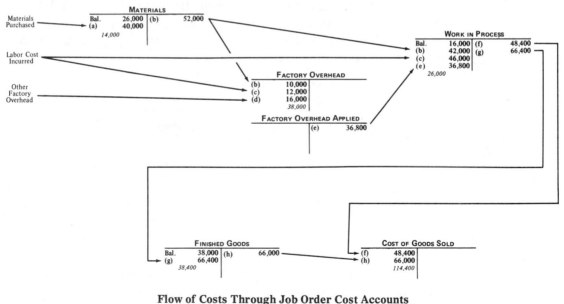

**Flow of Costs Through Job Order Cost Accounts
(General Ledger)**

(a) Materials (direct and indirect) purchased during month,
$40,000.

DESCRIPTION	DETAIL	DEBIT	CREDIT
Materials..		40,000	
In stores ledger:			
Material A...	22,000		
Material B...	12,000		
Material C...	6,000		
Vouchers Payable...............................			40,000

(b) Materials requisitioned from stores during month, $52,000 (direct materials, $42,000; indirect materials, $10,000).

DESCRIPTION	DETAIL	DEBIT	CREDIT
Work in Process......................................		42,000	
In job cost ledger:			
Job No. 605.....................................	18,000		
Job No. 606.....................................	16,000		
Job No. 607.....................................	8,000		
Factory Overhead...................................		10,000	
In factory overhead ledger:			
Miscellaneous Factory Expense.....	10,000		
Materials..			52,000
In stores ledger:			
Material A...	26,000		
Material B...	16,000		
Material C...	10,000		

(c) Factory labor cost for the month, $58,000 (direct labor, $46,000; indirect labor, $12,000).

DESCRIPTION	DETAIL	DEBIT	CREDIT
Work in Process......................................		46,000	
In job cost ledger:			
Job No. 604.....................................	6,000		
Job No. 605.....................................	12,000		
Job No. 606.....................................	18,000		
Job No. 607.....................................	10,000		
Factory Overhead...................................		12,000	
In factory overhead ledger:			
Indirect Labor...................................	12,000		
Vouchers Payable, FICA Tax Payable, etc.			58,000

(d) Other factory overhead cost incurred during month, $16,000.

DESCRIPTION	DETAIL	DEBIT	CREDIT
Factory Overhead......................................		16,000	
In factory overhead ledger:			
Depreciation Expense......................	2,000		
Miscellaneous Factory Expense.....	14,000		
Accumulated Depreciation — Factory Building and Equipment, Vouchers Payable, Prepaid Insurance, etc.			16,000

(e) Factory overhead applied during month, $36,800 (80 percent of direct labor on jobs).

DESCRIPTION	DETAIL	DEBIT	CREDIT
Work in Process..		36,800	
In job cost ledger:			
Job No. 604......................................	4,800		
Job No. 605......................................	9,600		
Job No. 606......................................	14,400		
Job No. 607......................................	8,000		
Factory Overhead Applied......................			36,800

(f) Job No. 606 completed and immediately shipped directly to customer (cost, $48,400).

DESCRIPTION	DETAIL	DEBIT	CREDIT
Cost of Goods Sold.....................................		48,400	
Work in Process			48,400
In job cost ledger:			
Job No. 606......................................	48,400		

(g) Jobs No. 604 and 605 completed and placed in stock, $66,400.

DESCRIPTION	DETAIL	DEBIT	CREDIT
Finished Goods		66,400	
In finished goods ledger:			
Product Y...	26,800		
Product Z...	39,600		
Work in Process			66,400
In job cost ledger:			
Job No. 604......................................	26,800		
Job No. 605......................................	39,600		

(h) Cost of Products Y and Z sold during month, $66,000.

DESCRIPTION	DETAIL	DEBIT	CREDIT
Cost of Goods Sold.....................................		66,000	
Finished Goods			66,000
In finished goods ledger:			
Product Y...	30,000		
Product Z...	36,000		

BUILDING YOUR ACCOUNTING KNOWLEDGE

1. What are the two major reasons that product cost information is needed by a manufacturing business?
2. What two purposes are served by a materials requisition?

3. A daily time sheet provides a record of what two items of information about each job?
4. Why is it common practice to charge factory overhead for the portion of the employer's payroll taxes that relates to all types of factory labor?
5. Name three bases used for assigning factory overhead to each job in connection with job order cost accounting systems.
6. State the formula for calculating a predetermined factory overhead rate for use in assigning factory overhead to jobs based on direct labor cost.
7. Why is Factory Overhead Applied, rather than Factory Overhead, credited for the total amount of factory overhead added to the job cost records?
8. Why do many manufacturing businesses use a normal capacity or average activity basis of assigning factory overhead to jobs?

Report No. 27-2

> *Complete Report No. 27-2 in the study assignments and submit your working papers for approval. Continue with the textbook discussion until Report No. 27-3 is required.*

THE CHARTS OF ACCOUNTS AND RECORDS OF A MANUFACTURING BUSINESS

To illustrate the accounting for a manufacturing business, the text will describe the case of Hartup Tool, Inc. The company is a small manufacturing concern whose operations are confined to manufacturing and selling two products — dies and molds. No merchandise is purchased for resale in its original form. The company uses a job order cost accounting system and keeps perpetual inventories. Thus, at year-end, the finished goods inventory, work in process inventory, materials inventory, and cost of goods sold accounts should properly reflect the manufacturing costs of the period applicable to each one of these accounts.

CHARTS OF ACCOUNTS

The charts of accounts of Hartup Tool, Inc., are reproduced on pages 748–749. There is a similarity in the titles of certain factory overhead, administrative expense, and selling expense accounts. For example, there are three depreciation accounts: Depreciation of Factory Building and Equipment, Account No. 7406, Depreciation of Office Equipment, Account No. 8204, and Depreciation of Deliv-

HARTUP TOOL, INC.

CHART OF GENERAL LEDGER ACCOUNTS

Current Assets

Cash
- 111 First National Bank
- 112 Petty Cash Fund

Temporary Investments
- 121 Government Notes

Receivables
- 122 Accrued Interest Receivable
- 131 Accounts Receivable
- 131.1 Allowance for Doubtful Accounts

Inventories
- 161 Finished Goods Inventory
- 162 Work in Process Inventory
- 163 Materials Inventory

Supplies and Prepayments
- 181 Office Supplies
- 183 Factory Supplies
- 185 Prepaid Insurance

Long-Term Assets
- 211 Land
- 221 Building
- 221.1 Accumulated Depreciation — Building
- 231 Factory Equipment
- 231.1 Accumulated Depreciation — Factory Equipment
- 241 Delivery Equipment
- 241.1 Accumulated Depreciation — Delivery Equipment
- 251 Office Equipment
- 251.1 Accumulated Depreciation — Office Equipment
- 261 Organization Costs

Current Liabilities
- 311 FICA Tax Payable
- 312 FUTA Tax Payable
- 313 State Unemployment Tax Payable
- 314 Employees Income Tax Payable
- 315 Corporation Income Tax Payable
- 316 Notes Payable
- 317 Accrued Interest Payable
- 318 Vouchers Payable
- 319 Accrued Payroll Payable
- 321 Dividends Payable

Long-Term Liabilities
- 421 Bonds Payable

Stockholders' Equity
- 511 Capital Stock
- 521 Retained Earnings
- 531 Expense and Revenue Summary

Revenue
- 611 Sales
- 631 Interest Income

Costs and Expenses
- 741 Factory Overhead
- 741.1 Factory Overhead Applied
- 811 Cost of Goods Sold
- 821 Operating Expenses
- 911 Interest Expense
- 921 Charitable Contributions Expense
- 931 Income Tax Expense

HARTUP TOOL, INC.

CHART OF FACTORY OVERHEAD LEDGER ACCOUNTS

- 7401 Indirect Labor
- 7402 Utilities Expense
- 7403 Drafting Supplies Expense
- 7404 Factory Supplies Expense
- 7405 Factory Building Maintenance
- 7406 Depreciation of Factory Building and Equipment
- 7407 Insurance Expense — Factory Building and Equipment
- 7408 Real Estate Taxes — Factory
- 7409 Payroll Taxes — Factory
- 7411 Miscellaneous Factory Overhead

HARTUP TOOL, INC.
CHART OF OPERATING EXPENSES LEDGER ACCOUNTS

Administrative Expenses
8201 Office Salaries Expense
8202 Officers' Salaries Expense
8203 Office Supplies Expense
8204 Depreciation of Office Equipment
8205 Office Equipment Insurance Expense
8206 Real Estate Taxes — Office
8207 Payroll Taxes — Administrative
8208 Officers Life Insurance Expense
8209 Organization Costs Amortization
8211 Miscellaneous Office Expense

Selling Expenses
8231 Sales Salaries Expense
8232 Travel Expense
8233 Advertising Expense
8235 Depreciation of Delivery Equipment
8236 Delivery Equipment Insurance Expense
8237 Uncollectible Accounts Expense
8238 Payroll Taxes — Selling
8239 Miscellaneous Selling Expense

ery Equipment, Account No. 8235. Depreciation of factory building and equipment is factory overhead, depreciation of office equipment is an administrative expense, and depreciation of delivery equipment is a selling expense. It is necessary to classify such charges by recording them in appropriate accounts so that the proper information may be set forth in the annual reports. Insurance also must be apportioned among the proper cost and expense accounts.

LEDGERS

While all the accounts shown in the charts of accounts of Hartup Tool, Inc., may be kept in one general ledger, it has been found advantageous to keep the accounts with customers, the materials inventory records, the accounts for factory overhead, the job cost sheets, the accounts for operating expenses, and the accounts with stockholders in subsidiary ledgers with control accounts in the general ledger. At the top of page 750 are the names of the subsidiary ledgers and the titles of the control accounts that are kept in the general ledger.

Hartup Tool, Inc., uses the four-column account form in the general ledger. The three-column account form (illustrated on page

Control Account	Subsidiary Ledger
131 Accounts Receivable	Accounts receivable ledger
161 Finished Goods Inventory	Finished goods ledger
162 Work in Process Inventory	Job cost ledger
163 Materials Inventory	Stores ledger
511 Capital Stock	Stockholders' ledger
741 Factory Overhead	Factory overhead ledger
821 Operating Expenses	Operating expense ledger

215) is used in the accounts receivable ledger, factory overhead ledger, and operating expense ledger. Inasmuch as the balances of these ledgers are normally debits, it is not necessary to provide columns for both debit and credit balance entries. It is customary to extend the balance following each entry in an accounts receivable ledger because of the need for credit information in handling current sales on account. In a factory overhead ledger or an operating expense ledger, the balance need be extended only at the end of each month or when taking a trial balance. The procedure is as follows:

(1) Foot the Debit and Credit amount columns.
(2) Compute the new balance.
(3) Enter the new balance in the Balance column.

After all posting has been completed, the balance of the control account for Accounts Receivable, Account No. 131, may be proved by preparing a schedule of accounts receivable from the data in the subsidiary ledger. The balances of the control accounts for Factory Overhead, Account No. 741, and Operating Expenses, Account No. 821, also may be proved by preparing schedules of their respective subsidiary ledgers.

The form of the account in the stockholders ledger used by Hartup Tool, Inc., is of the same design as the account illustrated on page 604. This account differs from other account forms in that it does not provide any information as to the dollar amount of the shares owned by each stockholder; instead, it provides information only as to the number of shares owned. The control account for the stockholders ledger is Capital Stock, Account No. 511. This control account shows the total par value or stated value of the stock issued. The balance of the control account may be proved by preparing a schedule of the shares issued to stockholders from the information provided in the stockholders ledger and multiplying the total number of shares issued by the par value or stated value of each share.

Since Hartup Tool, Inc., uses the voucher system of accounting, a subsidiary accounts payable ledger is not maintained. The voucher register not only serves as an invoice register but also provides information regarding vouchered liabilities. Further detail can be secured by reference to the files of unpaid and paid vouchers. The management of the company feels that the voucher register and these two files provide all of the information needed with respect to transactions with suppliers.

JOURNALS

The number, the nature, and the variety of the transactions of Hartup Tool, Inc., warrant the use of the following books of original entry:

(1) Voucher register
(2) Sales register
(3) Record of cash receipts
(4) Check register
(5) General journal

A voucher register with the following amount columns is used:

Materials Inventory Dr.
Factory Overhead Dr.
Operating Expenses Dr.
Sundry Accounts Dr.
Sundry Accounts Cr.
Vouchers Payable Cr.

A sales register with the following amount columns is used:

Accounts Receivable Dr./Sales Cr.
Cost of Goods Sold Dr./Finished Goods Cr.

A column for sales taxes is not provided since all the sales of Hartup Tool, Inc., are made to manufacturers for use as equipment in various manufacturing processes. There is no need to provide for a departmental distribution of sales.

A cash receipts record with the following amount columns is used:

General Ledger Dr.
Bank Dr.
Accounts Receivable Cr.
Cash Sales Cr.
General Ledger Cr.

A check register with the following amount columns is used:

Vouchers Payable Dr.
Materials Inventory Cr.
Bank Cr.

A general journal with three amount columns is used. The first column is used to record amounts to be posted to subsidiary ledger accounts. The second and third columns are used to record amounts to be debited and credited to general ledger accounts. This form of journal was discussed in connection with Fishler & Marvon's Bakery on pages 485 and 486 of Chapter 17 and illustrated on page 503 of Chapter 17.

AUXILIARY RECORDS

Various auxiliary records are usually kept by businesses to supplement the journals and ledgers. Such auxiliary records may include the following:

    (1) Petty cash disbursements record
    (2) Long-term asset record
    (3) Payroll records
    (4) Stock transfer record

The purpose of auxiliary records is to supply the detailed information needed in the operations of an enterprise. For example, the long-term assets record provides a detailed record of equipment and buildings owned, showing the date when acquired, cost, rate of depreciation, and total amount of accumulated depreciation. The preparation and maintenance of formal payroll registers and employees' earnings records is mandatory for companies subject to the requirements of the Federal Fair Labor Standards Act (the wages and hours law) and the social security acts. Hartup Tool, Inc., keeps all of the auxiliary records listed above.

BUILDING YOUR ACCOUNTING KNOWLEDGE

1. Why is it necessary for Hartup Tool, Inc., to classify its depreciation charges by recording them in three different expense accounts?
2. List the titles of the control accounts kept in the general ledger of Hartup Tool, Inc., and the subsidiary ledger that each such account controls.
3. For which of its ledgers does Hartup Tool, Inc., use the three-column account form? The four-column account form?
4. Why is it customary to extend the balance following each entry in the accounts receivable ledger? What is the procedure for extending the balance in a factory overhead account ledger or an operating expense account ledger?

5. What type of information is provided by the stockholders ledger account form used by Hartup Tool, Inc.?
6. What two functions does the voucher register of Hartup Tool, Inc., perform?
7. List the books of original entry used by Hartup Tool, Inc.
8. List the auxiliary records kept by Hartup Tool, Inc.

Report No. 27-3

Complete Report No. 27-3 in the study assignments and submit your working papers for approval. Continue with the textbook discussion until Report No. 28-1 is required.

EXPANDING YOUR BUSINESS VOCABULARY

What is the meaning of each of the following terms?

average activity (p. 742)
book inventory (p. 735)
cost accounting (p. 737)
daily time sheet (p. 740)
direct costing (p. 743)
direct labor (pp. 730, 738, 740)
direct materials (pp. 730, 738)
factory burden (p. 731)
factory overhead (pp. 731, 738)
Factory Overhead Applied (p. 742)
factory supplies (p. 730)
finished goods inventory (p. 737)
fixed factory overhead costs (p. 743)
Goods in Process (p. 738)
indirect labor (pp. 730, 739)
indirect manufacturing expense (p. 731)
indirect materials (p. 730)
job card (p. 738)
job cost ledger (p. 738)
job cost sheet (p. 738)
job order (p. 738)
Jobs in Process (p. 738)

manufacturing expense (p. 731)
materials ledger (p. 739)
materials requisition (p. 739)
normal capacity (p. 742)
overabsorbed factory overhead (p. 742)
overapplied (p. 742)
period costs (p. 743)
perpetual inventory (p. 735)
predetermined factory overhead rate (p. 741)
product costs (p. 743)
running inventory (p. 735)
service departments (p. 742)
stores ledger (pp. 735, 739)
stores requisition (p. 739)
time ticket (p. 740)
underabsorbed factory overhead (p. 742)
underapplied (p. 742)
variable factory overhead (p. 742)
Work in Process (p. 738)
work in process inventory (p. 737)

CHAPTER 28

YEAR-END ACCOUNTING AND REPORTING PROCEDURE; PROCESS COST ACCOUNTING

CHAPTER OBJECTIVES

The objectives of this chapter are to enable you:

▶ To prepare a ten-column summary end-of-year work sheet, as well as supplementary three-column work sheets for factory overhead and operating expenses, for a small manufacturing business.

▶ To record additional types of adjusting and closing entries in a three-column general journal.

▶ To prepare the following financial statements for the annual report of a manufacturing corporation, in comparative form wherever possible, and using rounded dollars:

(1) Comparative income statement supported by comparative schedule of operating expenses.

(2) Comparative balance sheet supported by a statement of retained earnings.

(3) Statement of changes in financial position supported by a schedule of changes in working capital.

▶ To perform the steps involved in assembling the data for a statement of changes in financial position.

▶ To define, describe, and explain **process cost accounting**, and to prepare a diagram illustrating the flow of costs through the general ledger accounts that are typical of a process cost system.

▶ To describe how accounting for materials, labor, and factory overhead in a process cost system differs from similar accounting in a job-order cost system.

▶ To compute unit costs under a process cost system, including the computation of **equivalent units** and the use of a **cost of production summary**.

▶ To define **joint products**, **by-products**, and **standard costs** as they relate to particular cost accounting systems.

ACCOUNTING PROCEDURE AT YEAR END

The year-end accounting procedure for a corporation engaged in manufacturing is similar to that for a merchandising enterprise. Work sheets are used as a means of summarizing and classifying the information needed to produce certain financial statements and to assist in the process of formally adjusting and closing the accounts. Before examining the work sheets of Hartup Tool, Inc., in detail, however, it is useful to have an overall picture of the cost flows through the company's general ledger.

FLOW OF COSTS IN A JOB-ORDER MANUFACTURING BUSINESS

The cost flow diagram on the following page presents a summarized version of the effects of individual transactions on the accounts of Hartup Tool, Inc., during the fiscal year ended March 31, 19B. In the three inventory accounts (finished goods, work in process, and materials), amounts preceded by check marks represent either beginning or ending balances. The other amounts in these and other accounts (as indicated by the labels) may be explained as follows:

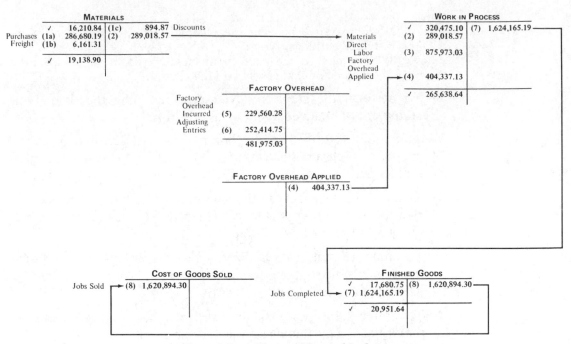

Flow of Costs Through General Ledger

(1) There are two debits to the materials inventory account for (a) the total of materials purchases for the year, $286,680.19, and (b) the total freight paid on these purchases for the year, $6,161.31. The offsetting credits would be to the vouchers payable account (not shown). The account also shows (c) a credit of $894.87 for discounts allowed on these purchases by suppliers of Hartup Tool, Inc.

(2) The debit to Work in Process and the credit to Materials for $289,018.57 show the total of direct materials requisitioned from stores during the year for use in manufacturing the company's products. The materials account thus has a balance of $19,138.90 at the end of the year.

(3) The debit to Work in Process of $875,973.03 shows the total direct factory labor cost for the year. The offsetting credits would be to the vouchers payable and accrued payroll payable accounts (not shown).

(4) The debit to Work in Process and the credit to Factory Overhead Applied for $404,337.13 show the total factory overhead applied to jobs completed during the year (applied at the rate of 55% of direct labor cost). An additional amount is charged to this account for jobs in process at year end, as explained on page 741.

(5) The debit to Factory Overhead for $229,560.28 shows the total of the costs of indirect materials, indirect labor, and other factory overhead incurred during the year. The offsetting credits would be to Materials, Accrued Payroll Payable, various tax

liability accounts, Vouchers Payable, various accumulated depreciation accounts, Prepaid Insurance, etc. (not shown).

(6) The debit to Factory Overhead for $252,414.75 shows the total of the adjustments on the factory overhead work sheet at year end. The offsetting credits would be to Factory Supplies, Prepaid Insurance, and Accumulated Depreciation — Factory Equipment and Building (not shown).

(7) The debit to Finished Goods and credit to Work in Process for $1,624,165.19 show the total cost of jobs completed during the year. The work in process account has a balance of $265,638.64 at the end of the year prior to the adjustment to apply factory overhead to jobs in process at year end, as explained on page 741.

(8) The debit to Cost of Goods Sold and credit to Finished Goods for $1,620,894.30 show the total cost of jobs sold during the year. The finished goods account has a balance of $20,951.64 at the end of the year and the total cost of goods sold is determined as a part of the ongoing accounting process.

Having examined this condensed summary of the cost flows through the Hartup Tool, Inc., general ledger, the work sheets of the company may now be considered in detail.

WORK SHEETS OF A MANUFACTURING BUSINESS

The summary work sheet prepared for Hartup Tool, Inc., for the year ended March 31, 19B[1], is shown on pages 758–759. Since the necessary adjustments affect accounts both in the factory overhead and in the operating expense ledgers as well as accounts in the general ledger, the two supplementary work sheets shown on page 760 are prepared. In order to conserve space, the summary work sheet omits the pair of Adjusted Trial Balance columns that normally follows the Adjustments columns. Following is a discussion of the steps that were involved in completing the work sheets.

Trial Balance. The first pair of amount columns of the summary work sheet contains the general ledger trial balance. The first amount column of each of the supplementary work sheets contains the trial balance of the indicated subsidiary ledger. If the general ledger trial balance totals are not the same or if the totals of the account balances in the subsidiary ledgers do not agree with the

---

[1] In the next section of this chapter, several of the financial statements and schedules are presented in comparative form; that is, the amounts for the most recent year or date are followed by the amounts for the preceding year or date in that year. To distinguish between the years, the most recent year is identified as 19B and the year before as 19A.

HARTUP
Summary
For the Year

Account	Acct. No.	Trial Balance Debit	Trial Balance Credit
First National Bank	111	62,717.67	
Petty Cash Fund	112	300.00	
Government Notes	121	10,000.00	
Accrued Interest Receivable	122		
Accounts Receivable	131	577,946.15	
Allowance for Doubtful Accounts	131.1		543.63
Finished Goods Inventory	161	20,951.64	
Work in Process Inventory	162	265,638.64	
Materials Inventory	163	19,138.90	
Office Supplies	181	3,447.68	
Factory Supplies	183	146,478.54	
Prepaid Insurance	185	53,462.21	
Land	211	38,494.93	
Building	221	265,432.91	
Accumulated Depreciation — Building	221.1		70,518.66
Factory Equipment	231	617,088.25	
Accumulated Depreciation — Factory Equipment	231.1		45,929.25
Delivery Equipment	241	5,790.96	
Accumulated Depreciation — Delivery Equipment.	241.1		2,095.00
Office Equipment	251	4,152.48	
Accumulated Depreciation — Office Equipment	251.1		1,343.90
Organization Costs	261	9,875.00	
FICA Tax Payable	311		6,316.94
FUTA Tax Payable	312		1,191.60
State Unemployment Tax Payable	313		314.07
Employees Income Tax Payable	314		6,413.83
Corporation Income Tax Payable	315		
Notes Payable	316		100,000.00
Accrued Interest Payable	317		
Vouchers Payable	318		138,010.94
Dividends Payable	319		32,000.00
Bonds Payable	421		250,000.00
Capital Stock	511		800,000.00
Retained Earnings	521		225,704.16
Sales	611		2,110,575.73
Interest Income	631		1,050.00
Factory Overhead	741	229,560.28	
Factory Overhead Applied	741.1		404,337.13
Cost of Goods Sold	811	1,620,894.30	
Operating Expenses	821	100,578.06	
Interest Expense	911	17,770.83	
Charitable Contributions Expense	921	600.00	
Income Tax Expense	931	126,025.41	
		4,196,344.84	4,196,344.84
Net Income			

Hartup Tool, Inc. —

TOOL, INC.
Work Sheet
Ended March 31, 19B

Adjustments		Income Statement		Balance Sheet	
Debit	Credit	Debit	Credit	Debit	Credit
				62,717.67	
				300.00	
				10,000.00	
(b) 150.00				150.00	
				577,946.15	
	(d) 2,346.10				2,889.73
				20,951.64	
(a) 77,448.03				343,086.67	
				19,138.90	
	(e) 1,893.57			1,554.11	
	(f) 141,502.54			4,976.00	
	(g) 42,651.96			10,810.25	
				38,494.93	
				265,432.91	
	(j) 10,574.50				81,093.16
				617,088.25	
	(j) 61,425.50				107,354.75
				5,790.96	
	(i) 1,100.00				3,195.00
				4,152.48	
	(h) 520.00				1,863.90
	(k) 1,000.00			8,875.00	
					6,316.94
					1,191.60
					314.07
				6,413.83	
	(n) 41,853.54			41,853.54	
				100,000.00	
	(c) 1,028.46				1,028.46
					138,010.94
					32,000.00
					250,000.00
					800,000.00
					225,704.16
			2,110,575.73		
	(b) 150.00		1,200.00		
(l) 252,414.75	(a) 77,448.03	481,975.03			
	(o) 189.87		481,975.03		
(o) 189.87		1,621.084.17			
(m) 10,599.42		111,177.48			
(c) 1,028.46		18,799.29			
		600.00			
(n) 41,853.54		167,878.95			
383,684.07	383,684.07	2,401,514.92	2,593,750.76	1,991,465.92	1,799,230.08
		192,235.84			192,235.84
		2,593,750.76	2,593,750.76	1,991,465.92	1,991,465.92

Summary Work Sheet

HARTUP TOOL, INC.
Factory Overhead Work Sheet
For the Year Ended March 31, 19B

Account	Acct. No.	Trial Balance Debit	Adjustments Debit		Adj. Trial Balance Debit
Indirect Labor	7401	90,213.22			90,213.22
Utilities Expense	7402	34,027.27			34,027.27
Drafting Supplies Expense	7403	4,288.69			4,288.69
Factory Supplies Expense	7404		(f)	141,502.54	141,502.54
Factory Building Maintenance	7405	25,741.40			25,741.40
Depr. of Factory Building and Equipment.	7406		(j)	72,000.00	72,000.00
Insurance Expense — Factory	7407		(g)	38,912.21	38,912.21
Real Estate Taxes — Factory	7408	8,191.19			8,191.19
Payroll Taxes — Factory	7409	59,453.41			59,453.41
Miscellaneous Factory Overhead	7411	7,645.10			7,645.10
		229,560.28	(l)	252,414.75	481,975.03

HARTUP TOOL, INC.
Operating Expenses Work Sheet
For the Year Ended March 31, 19B

Account	Acct. No.	Trial Balance Debit	Adjustments Debit		Adj. Trial Balance Debit
Office Salaries Expense	8201	42,608.20			42,608.20
Officers Salaries Expense	8202	24,000.00			24,000.00
Office Supplies Expense	8203		(e)	1,893.57	1,893.57
Depreciation of Office Equipment	8204		(h)	520.00	520.00
Office Equipment Insurance Expense	8205		(g)	178.65	178.65
Real Estate Taxes — Office	8206	615.00			615.00
Payroll Taxes — Administrative	8207	5,052.16			5,052.16
Officers Life Insurance Expense	8208		(g)	3,263.80	3,263.80
Organization Costs Amortization	8209		(k)	1,000.00	1,000.00
Miscellaneous Office Expense	8211	411.09			411.09
Sales Salaries Expense	8231	22,057.78			22,057.78
Travel Expense	8232	1,985.47			1,985.47
Advertising Expense	8233	220.00			220.00
Delivery Expense	8234	1,349.52			1,349.52
Depreciation of Delivery Equipment	8235		(i)	1,100.00	1,100.00
Delivery Equipment Insurance Expense	8236		(g)	297.30	297.30
Uncollectible Accounts Expense	8237		(d)	2,346.10	2,346.10
Payroll Taxes — Selling	8238	1,843.29			1,843.29
Miscellaneous Selling Expense	8239	435.55			435.55
		100,578.06	(m)	10,599.42	111,177.48

related general ledger control accounts (Nos. 741 and 821), the discrepancies and the errors have to be corrected before the preparation of the work sheets can proceed.

Adjusting Entries. The second pair of amount columns in the summary work sheet and the second amount column in each of the supplementary work sheets contain the entries required to adjust the account balances. Data for adjusting the accounts are indicated below:

HARTUP TOOL, INC.
Data for Adjusting the Accounts
March 31, 19B

Factory overhead to be applied to work in process ending inventory..		$ 77,448.03
Interest accruals:		
Interest receivable...		150.00
Interest payable		1,028.46
Provision for doubtful accounts (to bring balance of allowance account to ½% of accounts receivable)........................		2,346.10
Office supplies consumed..		1,893.57
Factory supplies consumed		141,502.54
Insurance expired:		
On factory building and equipment...	$38,912.21	
On office equipment	178.65	
On officers' lives..	3,263.80	
On delivery equipment...	297.30	42,651.96
Depreciation:		
Factory building		10,574.50
Delivery equipment		1,100.00
Factory equipment		61,425.50
Office equipment...		520.00
Amortization of organization costs		1,000.00
Provision for corporation income taxes		41,853.54
Underabsorbed factory overhead...		189.87

Adjustment (a)

As jobs were completed during the year, factory overhead was applied at a rate of 55% of direct labor costs on those jobs. In order to correctly state the work in process ending inventory, an appropriate amount of factory overhead must be applied based on the direct labor costs incurred on jobs in process at March 31. The job cost ledger (not shown here) indicates total direct labor costs of $140,814.60 on jobs in process at March 31. An adjustment is needed debiting Work in Process Inventory and crediting Factory Overhead Applied for 55% of these direct labor costs, $77,448.03.

Adjustment (b)

The accrued interest receivable, amounting to $150 at the end of the year, was determined by computing the interest accrued on government notes owned. The amount accrued was entered on the summary work sheet by debiting Accrued Interest Receivable, Account No. 122, and by crediting Interest Income, Account No. 631.

Adjustment (c)

The accrued interest payable, amounting to $1,028.46 at the end of the year, was determined by computing the interest accrued on notes payable and bonds payable. The amount accrued was entered on the summary work sheet by debiting Interest Expense, Account No. 911, and by crediting Accrued Interest Payable, Account No. 317.

Adjustment (d)

The estimated amount of uncollectible account losses for the year, $2,346.10 (to bring the balance of the allowance account to ½% of accounts receivable) was recorded on the operating expenses work sheet by debiting Uncollectible Accounts Expense, Account No. 8237, and by crediting Allowance for Doubtful Accounts, Account No. 131.1, on the summary work sheet. (At a later time, after all the adjustments that affect accounts in the factory overhead and operating expenses work sheets have been recorded, debit entries are made on the summary work sheet to adjust the factory overhead and operating expenses control accounts.)

Adjustments (e) and (f)

The costs of office and factory supplies consumed during the year were calculated by making a physical count of the supplies of each type that were on hand at the end of the year, determining their cost, and subtracting the amounts of these inventories from the balances of the accounts for Office Supplies, Account No. 181, and Factory Supplies, Account No. 183. On the operating expenses work sheet, Office Supplies Expense, Account No. 8203, was debited for $1,893.57. On the factory overhead work sheet, Factory Supplies Expense, Account No. 7404, was debited for $141,502.54. The proper supplies account on the summary work sheet was credited in each case.

Adjustment (g)

The amounts of expired insurance on various types of property were determined from information provided by the insurance policy files. The entry required was a debit of $38,912.21 to Insurance Expense — Factory Building and Equipment, Account No. 7407 on the factory overhead work sheet; debits of $178.65 to Office Equipment Insurance Expense, Account No. 8205, $3,263.80 to Officers Life Insurance Expense, Account No. 8208, and $297.30 to Delivery Equipment Insurance Expense, Account No. 8236, on the operating expenses work sheet; with a credit of $42,651.96 to Prepaid Insurance, Account No. 185, on the summary work sheet.

Adjustments (h), (i), and (j)

Three debits were made to record the depreciation for the year on the four types of depreciable long-term assets. On the operating expenses work sheet, Depreciation of Office Equipment, Account No. 8204, was debited for $520, and Depreciation of Delivery Equipment, Account No. 8235, was debited for $1,100. On the factory overhead work sheet, Depreciation of Factory Building and Equipment, Account No. 7406, was debited for $72,000 which is the total of $61,425.50, the depreciation of the factory equipment, and $10,574.50, the depreciation of the building. On the summary work sheet, there were proper credits to each of the four accumulated depreciation accounts.

Adjustment (k)

The company was organized several years ago. At the time of organization, it was agreed that $1,000 of the initial organization costs would be amortized each year until the balance was exhausted ($875 in the final year). Accordingly, $1,000 was written off at the end of this year. The amount was recorded by a debit to Organization Costs Amortization, Account No. 8209, on the operating expenses work sheet, and a credit to Organization Costs, Account No. 261, on the summary work sheet.

The next step is to complete the supplementary work sheets. Each of these was completed by (1) extending any amount in the first column or any amount in the second column to the third column, (2) totaling the second and third columns and, as a means of proof, checking to be sure that the sum of the totals of column 1 and column 2 is equal to the total of column three, and (3) making the rulings.

Adjustments (l) and (m)

The total of the Adjustments column of the factory overhead work sheet, $252,414.75, was entered on the summary work sheet as a debit to Factory Overhead, Account No. 741.

The total of the Adjustments column of the operating expenses work sheet, $10,599.42, was entered on the summary work sheet as a debit to Operating Expenses, Account No. 821.

Adjustment (n)

The income tax for the year just ended was determined to be $167,878.95 on the basis of the prevailing rates. The adjustment to increase Income Tax Expense to this amount was recorded on the summary work sheet by debiting Income Tax Expense, Account No. 931, and crediting Corporation Income Tax Payable, Account No. 315, for $41,853.54.

Adjustment (o)

The amount by which the balance of the factory overhead applied account is less than the adjusted balance of the factory overhead account is known as underabsorbed overhead. (If the balance of the factory overhead applied account is more than the adjusted balance of the factory overhead account, the difference is known as overabsorbed overhead.) Because this difference, $189.87, was small, it was recorded on the summary work sheet by debiting Cost of Goods Sold, Account No. 811, and crediting Factory Overhead Applied, Account No. 741.1.

Completing the Summary Work Sheet. The Adjustments columns were totaled, and the amounts in the Trial Balance columns were modified by amounts in the Adjustments columns and extended into the Adjusted Trial Balance columns (not included in the illustration on pages 758–759 to conserve space).

The amounts of sales, interest income, factory overhead, factory overhead applied, cost of goods sold, operating expenses, charitable contributions expense, and income tax expense were extended into the Income Statement columns. All of these amounts caused the total of the Credit column to exceed the total of the Debit column by $192,235.84 — the net income for the year. To balance the Income Statement columns, this amount was placed in the Debit column and was extended to the Balance Sheet Credit column.

The next step was to extend the amounts of all asset, contra-asset, liability, and stockholders' equity accounts to the Balance Sheet columns. Finally, all column totals were entered and the proper rulings were made.

ADJUSTING THE ACCOUNTS

The adjustments shown in the Adjustments columns of the work sheets for March 31 are recorded in the general journal reproduced on pages 765–766 and posted to the proper general ledger and subsidiary ledger accounts. Hartup Tool, Inc., uses a three-column general journal.

The first amount column is headed "Detail" and is used to record amounts that are to be posted to subsidiary ledger accounts. The names of the subsidiary ledger accounts to be debited are

GENERAL JOURNAL   Page 24

Date	Description	Acct. No.	Detail	√	Debit	√	Credit	√
19B								
Mar. 31	Adjusting Entries							
	Work in Process Inventory..................	162			77,448.03	√		
	Factory Overhead Applied................	741.1					77,448.03	√
	Accrued Interest Receivable................	122			150.00	√		
	Interest Income	631					150.00	√
	Interest Expense................................	911			1,028.46	√		
	Accrued Interest Payable	317					1,028.46	√
	Operating Expenses...........................	821			2,346.10	√		
	Uncollectible Accounts Expense..	8237	2,346.10	√				
	Allowance for Doubtful Accounts.....	131.1					2,346.10	√
	Operating Expenses...........................	821			1,893.57	√		
	Office Supplies Expense...............	8203	1,893.57	√				
	Office Supplies..............................	181					1,893.57	√
	Factory Overhead	741			141,502.54	√		
	Factory Supplies Expense............	7404	141,502.54	√				
	Factory Supplies	183					141,502.54	√
	Factory Overhead	741			38,912.21	√		
	Insurance Expense — Factory Building and Equipment............	7407	38,912.21	√				
	Operating Expenses...........................	821			3,739.75	√		
	Office Equipment Insurance Expense.......................................	8205	178.65	√				
	Officers Life Insurance Expense...	8208	3,263.80	√				
	Delivery Equipment Insurance Expense.......................................	8236	297.30	√				
	Prepaid Insurance.............................	185					42,651.96	√
	Operating Expenses...........................	821			520.00	√		
	Depreciation of Office Equipment	8204	520.00	√				
	Accumulated Depreciation — Office Equipment...................................	251.1					520.00	√
	Operating Expenses...........................	821			1,100.00	√		
	Depreciation of Delivery Equipment.................................	8235	1,100.00	√				
	Accumulated Depreciation — Delivery Equipment......................	241.1					1,100.00	√
	Factory Overhead	741			72,000.00	√		
	Depreciation of Factory Building and Equipment.........................	7406	72,000.00	√				
	Accumulated Depreciation — Factory Equipment......................	231.1					61,425.50	√
	Accumulated Depreciation — Building.................................	221.1					10,574.50	√
	Operating Expenses...........................	821			1,000.00	√		
	Organization Costs Amortization..	8209	1,000.00	√				
	Organization Costs	261					1,000.00	√

(continued)

GENERAL JOURNAL

Date	Description	Acct. No.	Detail	√	Debit	√	Credit	√
19B Mar. 31	Income Tax Expense............................	931			41,853.54	√		
	Corporation Income Tax payable......	315					41,853.54	√
	Cost of Goods Sold	811			189.87	√		
	Factory Overhead Applied.................	741.1					189.87	√

Hartup Tool, Inc. — Adjusting Entries *(concluded)*

placed immediately below the name of the general ledger control account to be debited. The names of subsidiary ledger accounts to be credited are placed just below the name of the general ledger control account to be credited. Note that no entries are made to the individual jobs in the job cost ledger in connection with the application of factory overhead to ending work in process. The second and the third amount columns are used to record debits and credits to general ledger accounts.

When these entries are posted, the balances in the general ledger accounts will be the same as those shown in the Adjusted Trial Balance columns of the work sheet. The total of the balances of the accounts in the factory overhead subsidiary ledger will be equal to the adjusted balance of the factory overhead control account, and the total of the balances of the accounts in the operating expense subsidiary ledger will be equal to the adjusted balance of the operating expenses control account.

CLOSING THE TEMPORARY ACCOUNTS

The preparation of closing entries is facilitated by the use of work sheets. There are five steps involved in closing the temporary accounts.

(1) The balance of the factory overhead account is transferred to Expense and Revenue Summary, Account No. 531, and the subsidiary factory overhead accounts are closed.

(2) The balances of the sales, interest income, and factory overhead applied accounts are transferred to Expense and Revenue Summary, Account No. 531.

(3) The balance of the operating expenses account is transferred to Expense and Revenue Summary, Account No. 531, and the subsidiary operating expenses accounts are closed.

(4) The balances of the cost of goods sold, interest expense, charitable contributions expense, and income tax expense accounts are transferred to Expense and Revenue Summary, Account No. 531.

(5) The balance of the expense and revenue summary account is transferred to Retained Earnings, Account No. 521.

The general journal entries to close the temporary accounts of Hartup Tool, Inc., are reproduced below and on page 768.

In posting to the expense and revenue summary account, some accountants follow the practice of posting in detail. This means that they make separate debits and credits for each item that is being transferred to the summary account, rather than posting the total of several debits or credits as shown in the journal entry. Each item is labeled in the Description column of the account. This practice makes this summary account more informative. (Factory overhead and operating expenses would not be detailed.)

POST-CLOSING TRIAL BALANCE

After all the closing entries are posted, the accounts in the subsidiary ledger, the operating expense ledger, and all the temporary and summary accounts in the general ledger will have no balances.

GENERAL JOURNAL

Date	Description	Acct. No.	Detail	√	Debit	√	Credit	√
19B Mar. 31	Closing Entries							
	Expense and Revenue Summary....	531			481,975.03	√		
	Factory Overhead	741					481,975.03	√
	Indirect Labor............................	7401	90,213.22	√				
	Utilities Expense	7402	34,027.27	√				
	Drafting Supplies Expense.......	7403	4,288.69	√				
	Factory Supplies Expense........	7404	141,502.54	√				
	Factory Building Maintenance	7405	25,741.40	√				
	Depreciation of Factory							
	Building and Equipment.......	7406	72,000.00	√				
	Insurance Expense — Factory.	7407	38,912.21	√				
	Real Estate Taxes — Factory ...	7408	8,191.19	√				
	Payroll Taxes — Factory..........	7409	59,453.41	√				
	Miscellaneous Factory							
	Overhead..............................	7411	7,645.10	√				
	Sales...	611			2,110,575.73	√		
	Interest Income................................	631			1,200.00	√		
	Factory Overhead Applied	741.1			481,975.03	√		
	Expense and Revenue Summary	531					2,593,750.76	√

(continued)

GENERAL JOURNAL

Date	Description	Acct. No.	Detail	√	Debit	√	Credit	√
19B								
Mar. 31	Expense and Revenue Summary....	531			111,177.48	√		
	Operating Expenses.....................	821					111,177.48	√
	Office Salaries Expense	8201	42,608.20	√				
	Officers' Salaries Expense	8202	24,000.00	√				
	Office Supplies Expense	8203	1,893.57	√				
	Depreciation of Office Equipment............................	8204	520.00	√				
	Office Equipment Insurance Expense................................	8205	178.65	√				
	Real Estate Taxes — Office......	8206	615.00	√				
	Payroll Taxes — Administrative........................	8207	5,052.16	√				
	Officers' Life Insurance Expense................................	8208	3,263.80	√				
	Organization Costs Amortization	8209	1,000.00	√				
	Miscellaneous Office Expense	8211	411.09	√				
	Sales Salaries Expense	8231	22,057.78	√				
	Travel Expense.........................	8232	1,985.47	√				
	Advertising Expense.................	8233	220.00	√				
	Delivery Expense......................	8234	1,349.52	√				
	Depreciation of Delivery Equipment............................	8235	1,100.00	√				
	Delivery Equipment Insurance Expense................................	8236	297.30	√				
	Uncollectible Accounts Expense................................	8237	2,346.10	√				
	Payroll Taxes — Selling...........	8238	1,843.29	√				
	Miscellaneous Selling Expense................................	8239	435.55	√				
	Expense and Revenue Summary....	531			1,808,362.41	√		
	Cost of Goods Sold	811					1,621,084.17	√
	Interest Expense...........................	911					18,799.29	√
	Charitable Contributions Expense	921					600.00	√
	Income Tax Expense....................	931					167,878.95	√
	Expense and Revenue Summary....	531			192,235.84	√		
	Retained Earnings......................	521					192,235.84	√

Hartup Tool, Inc. — Closing Entries *(concluded)*

It is customary to take a trial balance of the open accounts in the general ledger at this point. The accounts should have the same balances as those shown in the Balance Sheet columns of the summary work sheet except the balance of the retained earnings account, which will reflect the net income or net loss for the accounting period. A post-closing trial balance is, in substance, an unclassified balance sheet.

REVERSING ENTRIES

The accountant for Hartup Tool, Inc., follows the usual practice of reversing the adjusting entries for accruals after closing the books at the end of each year. In addition, the adjusting entry to apply factory overhead to Work in Process is reversed. This practice facilitates the recording of the transactions of the succeeding fiscal year in a routine manner. The reversing entries are journalized in the manner shown below.

GENERAL JOURNAL

Date	Description	Acct. No.	Detail	√	Debit	√	Credit	√
19B Apr. 1	Reversing Entries							
	Interest Income	631			150.00	√		
	Accrued Interest Receivable	122					150.00	√
	Accrued Interest Payable	317			1,028.46	√		
	Interest Expense	911					1,028.46	√
	Factory Overhead Applied	741.1			77,448.03	√		
	Work in Process Inventory	162					77,448.03	√

Hartup Tool, Inc. — Reversing Entries

BUILDING YOUR ACCOUNTING KNOWLEDGE

1. For what two types of accounts are supplementary work sheets prepared by Hartup Tool, Inc.?
2. If the general ledger trial balance totals are not the same or the totals of the subsidiary ledger account balances do not agree with the related general ledger control accounts, what should be done before preparing the work sheets?
3. What accounts are debited and credited in the two adjusting entries for interest accruals?
4. What accounts are debited and credited in the two adjusting entries for supplies consumed?
5. What accounts are debited and credited in the three adjusting entries for the depreciation of long-term assets?
6. What is the relationship between the balances of the factory overhead applied account and the factory overhead control account when the overhead is said to be underabsorbed? Overabsorbed?
7. Describe the uses of the three amount columns in the general journal format used by Hartup Tool, Inc.

8. Enumerate the five steps involved in closing the temporary accounts of Hartup Tool, Inc.

Report No. 28-1

> Complete Report No. 28-1 in the study assignments and submit your working papers for approval. Continue with the textbook discussion until Report No. 28-2 is required.

THE ANNUAL REPORT OF A MANUFACTURING BUSINESS

The primary purpose of the annual report is to provide the board of directors, officers, and stockholders of the corporation with information as to the results of operations for the year and the financial position of the company at the end of the year. The company's bondholders, general creditors, banks, and certain taxing authorities also may be interested in the annual report. The annual report of a corporation always includes an income statement, a balance sheet, and a statement of changes in financial position. A statement of retained earnings and other supporting schedules that are considered necessary may be included. The form of the statements should conform to accepted accounting practice. The nature of the business conducted and the volume of business done by the corporation may have little or no effect upon the form of the statements.

In order to make the financial statements more informative, two practices are widely followed: (1) some of the statements are shown in comparative statement form, and (2) in all of the statements, cents are omitted. In looking at an income statement, the reader most certainly would like to know how the results of the most recent year compare with the results of the year before. In looking at the most recent balance sheet, it is likely that the reader would also like to see similar data for the end of the previous fiscal year. In order to provide maximum information, accountants frequently prepare income statements and balance sheets (and, often, supplementary statements and schedules) in comparative form. In comparative statements, it is the nearly universal practice to show the most recent year first, that is, to place the amounts for the latest year to the left of the amounts for the preceding year.

Following is a discussion of the statements comprising the annual report of Hartup Tool, Inc. Most of the data relating to the year ended March 31, 19B (the year just ended) came from the work sheet reproduced on pages 758–759. The data relating to the year ended March 31, 19A came from the annual report prepared for the previous year (not reproduced).

INCOME STATEMENT

The comparative income statement of Hartup Tool, Inc., for the years ended March 31, 19B and 19A, is shown below. Note that only the total of the operating expenses for each year is shown. These totals are explained by a **comparative schedule of operating expenses** reproduced on page 772. The data for the year ended March 31, 19B, came from the operating expenses work sheet reproduced on page 760. The data for the year ended March 31, 19A, came from the statement for the preceding year.

HARTUP TOOL, INC.
Comparative Income Statement
For the Years Ended March 31, 19B and 19A

		Year Ended March 31, 19B		Year Ended March 31, 19A
Net sales...............................		$2,110,576		$1,749,428
Less cost of goods sold		1,621,084		1,343,562
Gross margin on sales..........		$ 489,492		$ 405,866
Operating expenses..............		111,178		92,023
Operating income................		$ 378,314		$ 313,843
Other revenue:				
Interest income..................		1,200		1,200
		$ 379,514		$ 315,043
Other expenses:				
Interest expense...............$18,799			$18,767	
Charitable contributions... 600		19,399	500	19,267
Income before provision for income tax.........................		$ 360,115		$ 295,776
Less corporation income tax..		167,879		137,832
Net income...........................		$ 192,236		$ 157,944

Hartup Tool, Inc. — Comparative Income Statement

BALANCE SHEET

The comparative balance sheet of Hartup Tool, Inc., as of March 31, 19B and 19A, is reproduced on page 773. The statement

HARTUP TOOL, INC.
Comparative Schedule of Operating Expenses
For the Years Ended March 31, 19B and 19A

	Year Ended March 31, 19B	Year Ended March 31, 19A
Administrative expenses:		
Office salaries expense............................	$ 42,608	$ 34,402
Officers' salaries expense	24,000	20,000
Office supplies expense	1,894	1,563
Depreciation of office equipment............	520	414
Office equipment insurance expense......	179	179
Real estate taxes — office........................	615	615
Payroll taxes — administrative.................	5,052	4,007
Officers life insurance expense	3,264	3,264
Organization costs amortization..............	1,000	1,000
Miscellaneous office expense..................	411	352
Total administrative expenses..............	$ 79,543	$ 65,796
Selling expenses:		
Sales salaries expense.............................	$ 22,058	$ 18,022
Travel expense	1,985	1,763
Advertising expense..................................	220	175
Delivery expense	1,350	1,128
Depreciation of delivery equipment	1,100	1,100
Delivery equipment insurance expense ..	297	297
Uncollectible accounts expense..............	2,346	1,939
Payroll taxes — sales...............................	1,843	1,506
Miscellaneous selling expense	436	297
Total selling expenses..........................	$ 31,635	$ 26,227
Total operating expenses............................	$111,178	$ 92,023

Hartup Tool, Inc. — Comparative Schedule of Operating Expenses

for the year ended March 31, 19B, was prepared from information found in the last two columns of the summary work sheet on pages 758–759. Note that the amount shown for retained earnings is the sum of the balance shown for the retained earnings account plus the net income for the year. The data for the year ended March 31, 19A, were copied from the balance sheet in the annual report of the preceding year. The comparative balance sheet is arranged in report form. Both assets and liabilities are classified as to current and long-term items.

STATEMENT OF RETAINED EARNINGS

The statement of retained earnings of Hartup Tool, Inc., for the year ended March 31, 19B, is reproduced on page 774. A similar

HARTUP TOOL, INC.
Comparative Balance sheet
March 31, 19B and 19A

	March 31, 19B		March 31, 19A	
Assets				
Current assets:				
Cash		$ 63,018		$ 51,148
Government notes		10,000		10,000
Accrued interest receivable		150		150
Accounts receivable	$577,946		$477,476	
Less allowance for doubtful accounts	2,890	575,056	2,387	475,089
Inventories:				
Finished goods	$ 20,951		$ 19,526	
Work in process	343,087		317,158	
Materials	19,139	383,177	17,683	354,367
Supplies and prepayments		17,340		16,249
Total current assets		$1,048,741		$ 907,003
Long term assets:				
Land		$ 38,495		$ 38,495
Building	$265,433		$265,433	
Less accumulated depreciation	81,093	184,340	70,519	194,914
Factory equipment	$617,088		$574,637	
Less accumulated depreciation	107,355	509,733	45,929	528,708
Delivery equipment	$ 5,791		$ 5,791	
Less accumulated depreciation	3,195	2,596	2,095	3,696
Office equipment	$ 4,152		$ 3,307	
Less accumulated depreciation	1,864	2,288	1,344	1,963
Organization costs		8,875		9,875
Total long-term assets		$ 746,327		$ 777,651
Total assets		$1,795,068		$1,684,654
Liabilities				
Current liabilities:				
Accrued and withheld payroll taxes	$ 14,236		$ 13,908	
Corporation income tax payable	41,853		31,973	
Notes payable	100,000		100,000	
Accrued interest payable	1,028		997	
Vouchers payable	138,011		152,072	
Dividends payable	32,000		28,000	
Total current liabilities		$ 327,128		$ 326,950
Long-term liabilities:				
Bonds payable		250,000		300,000
Total liabilities		$ 577,128		$ 626,950
Stockholders' Equity				
Capital stock (10,000 shares authorized, 8,000 shares issued)	$800,000		$800,000	
Retained earnings	417,940		257,704	
Total stockholders' equity		1,217,940		1,057,704
Total liabilities and stockholders' equity		$1,795,068		$1,684,654

Hartup Tool, Inc. — Comparative Balance sheet

statement for the year ended March 31, 19A, could have been included, but this was not considered necessary because a major reason for such a statement is to reconcile the retained earnings amounts at the start and at the close of the year to which the annual report primarily relates. The amount of retained earnings at March 31, 19A, was $257,704. The net income of $192,236, less $32,000 of cash dividends paid or declared for the year ended March 31, 19B, resulted in an increase of $160,236 ($192,236 − $32,000) in retained earnings. The amount in retained earnings at March 31, 19B, was therefore $417,940 ($257,704 + $160,236).

HARTUP TOOL, INC. Statement of Retained Earnings For the Year Ended March 31, 19B	
Balance, April 1, 19A..	$257,704
Add net income for the year (after provision for income taxes in the amount of $167,879)...	192,236
	$449,940
Less cash dividends paid or declared during the year ($4 per share)...	32,000
Balance, March 31, 19B...	$417,940

Hartup Tool, Inc. — Statement of Retained Earnings

STATEMENT OF CHANGES IN FINANCIAL POSITION

The **statement of changes in financial position** of Hartup Tool, Inc., for the year ended March 31, 19B, together with a schedule of changes in working capital, is reproduced on page 775. As in the case of the statement of retained earnings, a statement of changes in financial position for the year ended March 31, 19A, could have been included, but since a major purpose of the statement of changes in financial position is to reconcile the amounts of working capital at the start and at the close of the year to which the annual report primarily relates, such a statement for the preceding year was not considered necessary. The amount of working capital at March 31, 19A, was $580,053 (current assets, $907,003, less current liabilities, $326,950). The amount of working capital at March 31, 19B, was $721,613 (current assets, $1,048,741, less current liabilities, $327,128). The statement of changes in financial position explains the $141,560 ($721,613 − $580,053) increase.

HARTUP TOOL, INC.
Statement of Changes in Financial Position
For the Year Ended March 31, 19B

Sources of funds:		
Funds provided by operations —		
Net income (per income statement)........................	$192,236	
Add expenses not requiring funds:		
Depreciation	73,620	
Organization costs amortization........................	1,000	
Total funds provided		$266,856
Uses of funds:		
Cash dividends paid or declared	$ 32,000	
Purchase of factory equipment.................................	42,451	
Purchase of office equipment...................................	845	
Retirement of bonds	50,000	
Total funds applied...		125,296
Increase in working capital..		$141,560

Hartup Tool, Inc. — Statement of Changes in Financial Position

HARTUP TOOL, INC.
Schedule of Changes in Working Capital
For the Year Ended March 31, 19B

	March 31		Working Capital	
	19B	19A	Increase	Decrease
Cash...	$ 63,018	$ 51,148	$ 11,870	
Government notes......................	10,000	10,000		
Receivables (net).......................	575,206	475,239	99,967	
Inventories.................................	383,177	354,367	28,810	
Supplies and prepayments.......	17,340	16,249	1,091	
Payroll taxes payable	14,236	13,908		$ 328
Corporation income tax pay-				
able...	41,853	31,973		9,880
Notes and interest payable.......	101,028	100,997		31
Vouchers payable......................	138,011	152,072	14,061	
Dividends payable	32,000	28,000		4,000
			$155,799	$ 14,239
Increase in working capital.......				141,560
			$155,799	$155,799

Hartup Tool, Inc. — Schedule of Changes in Working Capital

In preparing the statement of changes in financial position, the accountant for Hartup Tool, Inc., considered all the possible sources and all the possible uses of funds. As explained in Chapter 19, the possible sources of funds are:

(1) Investments by owners.
(2) Profitable operations (including the adjustment of the calculated net income by the amount of any expenses that did not reduce working capital).
(3) Long-term borrowing.
(4) Sale of long-term assets.

The possible uses of funds are:

(1) Withdrawals by the owners (which, in the case of corporations, normally means cash dividends paid or declared).
(2) Unprofitable operations (including the adjustment of the calculated net loss by the amount of any expenses that did not reduce working capital).
(3) Repayment of long-term borrowing.
(4) Purchase of long-term assets.

Using the foregoing as a guide, each possible source and possible use of funds was considered separately to determine whether it applied to Hartup Tool, Inc., for the year ended March 31, 19B. This item-by-item analysis revealed the following:

Possible Sources

(1) Investments by owners. None. Reference to the comparative balance sheet on page 773 showed there was no change in the balance of the capital stock account during the year.
(2) Profitable operations. Yes. The income statement for the year ended March 31, 19B, showed a net income for the year of $192,236. For purposes of the statement of changes in financial position, this amount had to be increased by the amount of any expenses that did not reduce working capital. There were two types of such expenses — depreciation and organization cost amortization. Reference to the comparative balance sheet on page 773 shows that the four accumulated depreciation accounts increased, in total, $73,620. Examination of these accounts in the general ledger showed no debits to any of them (which would have occurred if any depreciated assets had been disposed of). Since there were no reductions in any of the accumulated depreciation accounts, the sum of the changes, $73,620, was the total depreciation write-off for the year. The organization costs account had been reduced $1,000 when that amount was debited to the organization costs amortization account (and to Operating Expenses in the general ledger). Accordingly, the increase in funds due to regular operations was $266,856 ($192,236 + $73,620 + $1,000).
(3) Long-term borrowing. None. The comparative balance sheet on page 773 shows that bonds payable, the only type of long-term liability, was decreased — not increased.
(4) Sale of long-term assets. None. The comparative balance sheet on page 773 shows that, except in the case of organization costs mentioned above, none of the balances of the long-term asset

accounts was reduced during the year. Examination of the general ledger accounts confirmed this. This examination of the actual accounts was made to be sure that any decreases in the accounts had not been partly or wholly offset by additions.

As a result of the foregoing analysis, it was determined that regular operations were the only source of funds during the year ended March 31, 19B.

<u>Possible Uses</u>

(1) Withdrawals by owners. Yes. The statement of retained earnings on page 774 shows that cash dividends paid or declared during the year amounted to $32,000.

(2) Unprofitable operations. Not considered since there had been net income.

(3) Repayment of long-term borrowing. Yes. The comparative balance sheet on page 773 shows that bonds payable decreased $50,000. Since the income statement for the year ended March 31, 19B, did not include any mention of gain or loss on bond retirement, and evidently no premium or discount had ever been involved in connection with these bonds, it is evident that these bonds were reacquired at face value, $50,000.

(4) Purchase of long-term assets. Yes. The comparative balance sheet shows that the amount of factory equipment increased $42,451 and that the amount of office equipment increased $845. Inquiries of company officials revealed that factory equipment and office equipment had been purchased in these amounts during the year ended March 31, 19B.

This analysis shows that there were three types (four items) of uses of funds during the year, 19B, which amounted to $125,296. Since this amount was less than the source of funds by $141,560 ($266,856 − $125,296), the increase in working capital was fully accounted for.

BUILDING YOUR ACCOUNTING KNOWLEDGE

1. What is the primary purpose of the annual report? What other parties may also be interested in the annual report?
2. What two practices are widely followed in order to make the financial statements more informative?
3. How are the totals of the operating expenses for each year as shown in the income statement explained further?
4. What two amounts from the summary work sheet will produce the amount shown for retained earnings on the balance sheet when they are added together?

5. What is a major reason for the preparation of a statement of retained earnings?
6. What is a major purpose of the statement of changes in financial position?
7. What was the only source of funds for Hartup Tool, Inc., for the year ended March 31, 19B?
8. Name the four purposes for which funds were used by Hartup Tool, Inc., during the year ended March 31, 19B.

Report No. 28-2

> *Complete Report No. 28-2 in the study assignments and submit your working papers for approval. Continue with the textbook discussion until Report No. 28-3 is required.*

PROCESS COST ACCOUNTING

If a manufacturing business is engaged in the continuous, or nearly continuous, production of a homogeneous product such as cement, chemicals, or certain foodstuffs, it may not be possible to assemble costs by jobs, lots, or batches. In such cases, the most feasible means of associating costs with units produced may be to gather costs by processes (sometimes constituting separate departments) and to assign a share of the cost to each unit passing through that process during a certain period of time — often a month. This procedure for arriving at unit costs is described as **process cost accounting**, which is an averaging device.

When more than one product is manufactured, it is possible that each product does not pass through every process. All may go through the same early processing but may follow different paths at the later stages. There are instances where the manufacture of two or more different products does not involve any of the same processing steps. This situation is described as **parallel processing**.

In an accounting sense, the heart or core of a process cost system is the account or accounts that summarize the costs associated with each process. These accounts have titles such as Work in Process — Finishing Department or just Finishing Department. Sometimes titles such as Process 43 or Work in Process — Department 29 are found. By whatever name used, such accounts are the focal points for assembling costs. These accounts are kept in the general ledger unless there are so many of them that a subsidiary ledger must be used.

ACCOUNTING FOR MATERIALS

As in job order accounting, it is likely that perpetual inventories will be used in a process cost system. If there are many different types of materials, it is probable that a subsidiary materials or stores ledger will be used. The requisition procedure may be followed, particularly if all materials do not enter into production at the same stage. In process cost accounting, the distinction between direct and indirect materials is of little or no consequence. The records must indicate the amounts to be charged to each process for the cost of materials issued to that process. Usually this is done by means of a summary entry at the end of each month.

ACCOUNTING FOR LABOR

Under a process cost accounting system, accounting for factory labor cost may be less complicated than in the case of a job order system. This is because many of the workers are likely to devote all of their time to a single process. As in the case of materials, the direct-indirect labor distinction is of minimal importance. If a worker's time is spent on activities concerned with one process, it does not matter whether the worker is a manager, a supervisor, or a "line worker" — the cost is direct labor with respect to that process. The complication that may result from overtime pay under a job order system does not arise under a process cost system.

The payroll records must provide sufficient information to make it possible to charge the proper amount of gross earnings to each process. Some labor costs may not be clearly associated with individual processes, such as the salaries of the plant manager, the staff, and custodians. Labor costs such as these will have to be apportioned among the processes in some reasonable manner. The procedure followed may involve treating such labor as factory overhead to be allocated along with other costs of an indirect nature.

ACCOUNTING FOR FACTORY OVERHEAD

A large share of total manufacturing cost can be directly associated with products under a process cost system. However, there are certain costs that are common to the entire factory or that have a seasonal variation largely unrelated to monthly production. Some procedure must be adopted that results in an equitable allocation of these costs to processes. If (1) general factory overhead is relatively small, (2) several products are not produced simultaneously, and (3) production is relatively stable throughout the year, it may be satisfactory to allocate the common costs on some basis that is reasonable with respect to each cost. For example, what are termed occupancy costs (factory rent, depreciation, insurance, property taxes, heating or cooling, lighting, cleaning, or repairing the premises) may be apportioned on the basis of the relative amount of space occupied by each processing operation. Supervision and the cost of labor fringe benefits may be apportioned in relation to the number of workers, the hours worked, or the total labor cost of each process. Sometimes an expense distribution sheet (a form of work sheet or working paper) is used to assemble the data in developing the monthly summary entries to allocate the various types of costs such as labor costs and general factory overhead costs.

Some factories — particularly large ones — have several service departments such as personnel, maintenance, accounting, production engineering and, a power plant. In the primary assignment of all factory costs (materials and labor as well as general overhead costs), the service departments as well as the producing (process) departments, are charged with costs clearly identifiable with their respective activities. Then, the costs of the service departments have to be assigned in proportion to the amount of service rendered to the other departments. The assignment and reassignment is carried out until all of the charges reach the producing departments. Predetermined rates will probably be used to provide a more reasonable monthly allocation.

The general ledger and subsidiary ledger accounts that are used will depend upon the nature and variety of products, the nature of the production processes, the volume and stability of operations, and the amount of detailed information desired.

CALCULATION OF UNIT COSTS

To illustrate the calculation of average cost per unit, assume that the costs associated with operating a mixing process for a certain month totaled $160,000. This amount represented the sum of the cost of materials put into process, the cost of labor connected with the operation, and a reasonable share of the factory overhead. During that month 100,000 units passed through the process and the average cost was determined to be $1.60 per unit ($160,000 ÷ 100,000 units). This calculation assumes that there were no partially processed units either at the start or at the end of the month.

When beginning and ending inventories do exist, the quantities and the degrees of completion of such inventories must be considered in calculating the average unit costs. To illustrate, assume the following circumstances relative to the first process in a factory:

In process, beginning of month:
    2,100 units, 100% complete as to materials content
       and 50% complete as to processing cost — i.e.,
       labor and factory overhead.
       Total cost so far assigned to the units .... $ 3,780

Materials put into process during the month:
    14,400 units @ $2.10. (In this example, the materials
       are all put into process at the start — not gradually
       or at various stages.) 30,240

Processing costs for the month:
    Labor 10,185
    Factory overhead assigned to the process................ 8,730

    Total cost to be accounted for $52,935

Completed and transferred to next process during month   15,000 units
In process, end of month (complete as to materials and
    40% complete as to processing costs)...................... 1,500 units

To be calculated:
    (1) The cost to be assigned to the 15,000 units completed and
        transferred to the next process.
    (2) The cost to be assigned to the 1,500 incomplete units.

The first step in making the calculations is to compute what is called the **equivalent units** (or **equivalent production**) with respect to the labor and factory overhead. (The sum of the costs of labor and factory overhead is called **processing cost**.) There are three components involved in the calculation:

    (1) To complete the beginning inventory of 2,100 units, work
        equivalent to fully processing 1,050 units was required since
        these 2,100 units were one-half finished last month.
    (2) 12,900 units must have been started and finished this month,
        since a total of 15,000 units were completed during the month
        and these completed units must have included the 2,100 units
        started the month before.
    (3) Since the 1,500 incomplete units are each 40 percent processed,
        the work done on them was the equivalent of fully processing
        600 units.

Thus, the equivalent production during the month was 14,550 units (1,050 + 12,900 + 600).

When the number of equivalent units has been determined, the per-unit processing cost can be calculated as follows:

Labor ($10,185 ÷ 14,550 units)............................ $ .70 per unit
Factory overhead ($8,730 ÷ 14,550 units).............. .60
Total... $1.30 per unit

The foregoing calculation can then be used to arrive at the following cost summary:

	Total	Per Unit
Cost of beginning inventory of work in process (2,100 units).......................	$ 3,780	
Cost to complete beginning inventory of work in process:		
Equivalent to 1,050 units @ $1.30....................................	1,365	
Total..	$ 5,145	$2.45
Cost to start and finish 12,900 units:		
Materials...	$27,090	$2.10
Labor..	9,030	.70
Factory overhead...	7,740	.60
Total..	$43,860	$3.40
Total cost of 15,000 units completed and transferred	$49,005	
Cost of 1,500 units incomplete at end of month:		
Materials..	$ 3,150	
Processing cost (equivalent to 600 units @ $1.30)..........	780	
Total..	$ 3,930	
Total cost accounted for..	$52,935	

FLOW OF COSTS THROUGH PROCESS COST ACCOUNTS

To illustrate the flow of costs through the accounts of a manufacturing company using a process cost accounting system, a summary is presented on page 783 showing the entries made to record costs incurred, units transferred from one process to the next, units completed, and the cost of finished products sold. The accounts are positioned to indicate the flow of costs. The illustration relates to the Prager Processing Company for September, the first month of the company's accounting year. Only transactions involving manufacturing costs are summarized and only six general ledger accounts are shown. None of these is a control account. Since only two materials enter into the manufacture of the single product produced, neither a subsidiary ledger for materials nor a subsidiary ledger for finished goods is needed. All items that comprise factory overhead are charged to the two process accounts, and frequently these costs have to be prorated between the two processes, Process 1 and Pro-

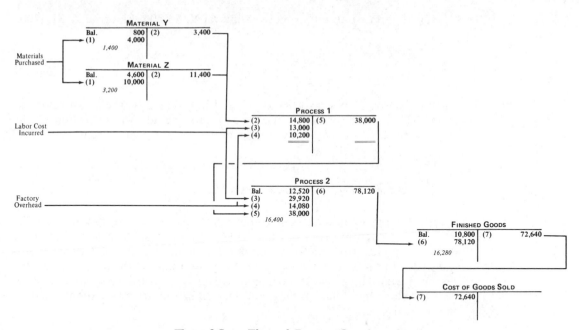

Flow of Costs Through Process Cost Accounts

cess 2. While a subsidiary factory overhead ledger could be used, the company thinks that the nature and the size of the business do not make that record necessary. The company uses a voucher system and maintains appropriate books of original entry and auxiliary records. As of September 1, the inventory accounts had the following balances:

Material Y...	$ 800
Material Z...	4,600
Process 2 (2,000 units complete as to material content and	
60% complete as to processing cost).........................	12,520
Finished goods (1,350 units @ $8)...............................	10,800

There is no inventory of work in process in Process 1 since the nature of this process is such that any work started must be finished by the end of the same day.

All of the transactions summarized are presented below and on pages 784–786 in general journal form.

(1) Materials purchases: Material Y, $4,000; Material Z, $10,000.

Material Y...	4,000	
Material Z...	10,000	
Vouchers Payable...		14,000

(2) Materials put into process: Material Y, $3,400; Material Z, $11,400.

Process 1..	14,800	
Material Y		3,400
Material Z..		11,400

(3) Factory Labor cost for the year, $42,920 ($13,000 relates to Process 1 and $29,920 to Process 2). These amounts include the proration of the gross earnings of the plant manager, janitors, security guard, etc.

Process 1..	13,000	
Process 2..	29,920	
Vouchers Payable, FICA Tax Payable, etc.		42,920

(4) Factory overhead cost (other than labor) for the month, $24,280 ($10,200 assigned to Process 1 and $14,080 to Process 2). Some of the cost such as supplies used, depreciation of equipment used by each department, and factory payroll taxes could be clearly identified with the separate processes; various other costs such as depreciation, insurance, property taxes on the factory building, utilities, and miscellaneous factory expense had to be prorated.

Process 1..	10,200	
Process 2..	14,080	
Accumulated Depreciation — Factory Building and Equipment, Prepaid Insurance, Factory Supplies, Vouchers Payable, FICA Tax Payable, etc.		24,280

(5) Cost of 10,000 units transferred from Process 1 to Process 2, $38,000. Reference to the three preceding entries, or to the Process 1 account on page 783 shows that the total was the sum of: materials put into Process 1, $14,800; labor in Process 1, $13,000; and factory overhead assigned to Process 1, $10,200.

Process 2..	38,000	
Process 1		38,000

(6) Cost of 9,000 units completed in Process 2 and transferred to finished goods stockroom, $78,120. This cost is based upon calculations in the **cost of production summary** reproduced on page 785. This report is used to summarize for each process the total costs to be accounted for, the equivalent units of production, and the accounting for the total costs.

Finished Goods	78,120	
Process 2...		78,120

(7) Cost of goods sold, $72,640. The company uses the first-in, first-out method of accounting; 8,500 units were sold during the month. The unit cost of the 1,350 units in the September inventory was $8 (see page 783). The average cost of the first 2,000 units completed in September was $8.26, and the average cost of all other units completed during the month was

PRAGER PROCESSING COMPANY
Cost of Production Summary — Process 2
For the Month of September, 19--

Work in process, September 1, 2,000 units (Complete as to Process 1 cost; 60% complete as to Process 2 cost)	$12,520
Units received from Process 1 (10,000 @ $3.80)	38,000
Labor	29,920
Factory overhead	14,080
Total cost to be accounted for	$94,520

Equivalent production for month (labor and factory overhead):

To finish units in process, September 1. Equivalent to 40% of 2,000 units	800 units
To start and finish 7,000 units	7,000
To start and 33⅓% complete, 3,000 units	1,000
Total	8,800 units

Processing costs per equivalent unit:

Labor ($29,920 ÷ 8,800 units)	$3.40
Factory overhead ($14,080 ÷ 8,800 units)	1.60
Total	$5.00

	Total	Per Unit
Cost accounted for as follows:		
Cost of beginning inventory of 2,000 units in process	$12,520	
Cost to complete. Equivalent to 800 units @ $5	4,000	
Total	$16,520	$8.26
Cost to start and finish 7,000 units:		
Previous department cost	$26,600	$3.80
Labor	23,800	3.40
Factory overhead	11,200	1.60
Total	$61,600	$8.80
Total cost of units transferred to finished goods	$78,120	
Cost of ending inventory of work in process:		
(3,000 units. Complete as to Process 1 cost; 33⅓% complete as to Process 2 cost.)		
Previous department cost (3,000 units @ $3.80)	$11,400	
Process 2 cost. Equivalent to 1,000 units @ $5	5,000	
Total cost of work in process	$16,400	
Total cost accounted for	$94,520	

Cost of Production Summary

$8.80 (see above). Accordingly, the cost of the 8,500 units sold was calculated as follows:

1,350 units @ $8.00	$10,800	
2,000 units @ $8.26	16,520	
5,150 units @ $8.80	45,320	$72,640

| Cost of Goods Sold .... | 72,640 | |
| Finished Goods .... | | 72,640 |

JOINT PRODUCTS AND BY-PRODUCTS

In many types of processing operations, it is impossible to produce one product without the emergence of some other quantity of matter. If this other matter is unwanted and must be removed or destroyed, it is called waste. If the matter has a nominal value and can be sold, it is called scrap. If the value is more than nominal, but still minor in relation to the main product, it is considered to be a by-product. If the emerging products are not widely different in value, they may be considered joint products. The terms waste, scrap, by-product, and joint product are loosely used. Their meanings overlap. There is no precise means of deciding when something has enough value to be called a joint product, or a by-product, or merely scrap.

If products with very small value are inevitable in the process of production, any revenue from their sale may be accounted for either as (1) a reduction of the total cost of the product or (2) other revenue. If the value of a particular product is more than trivial, it may be desirable to assign some of the total cost of production to that product. It is almost certain that the amount of cost assigned will be something less than the sales value of the product. (Sales value means sales price per unit times the number of units produced.) In the case of joint products, the cost to be shared may be allocated in proportion to the relative sales value of the products. For example, if the process of production inevitably results in the production of twice as many units of Product A as units of Product B, but the unit price of B is twice as great as the unit price of A, the sales value of all of the A produced will be the same as the sales value of all the B produced. If this is the case, the total production cost may be equally divided between the two products. (Their relative sales values are 1 to 1.) This practice causes the percent of gross margin to be the same when products of either type are sold. Often joint cost apportionment is complicated by the fact that not all of the cost is joint. One or all of the products may not acquire any value until further processing after the split-off point (the point at which the products can be separately identified) takes place. Any method of joint cost apportionment is arbitrary to some degree.

STANDARD COSTS

A well-established and growing practice among manufacturers is to extend their cost accounting procedures (both job order and process cost systems) to adopt standard costs. **Standard cost** is a unit concept which indicates what a unit of direct material, a unit of direct labor, or a unit of factory overhead should cost under assumed future business and economic conditions (usually for the coming year). Standard costing is a type of **budgeting** when these unit costs are multiplied by estimates for the coming year of total units of direct materials or total hours of direct labor, or an overhead rate based on estimated total direct labor hours or cost is used. An attempt is made to determine what the cost of an operation, process, or product should be under reasonably ideal conditions, and to keep records that will make it possible to determine whether costs are "out of line" and, if so, where. Standard costing is primarily a device to assist management in the control of costs.

It may have been noted that the expression "actual cost" has never been used in this chapter. Considering the variety of methods of assigning cost to materials used, of calculating depreciation, of assigning or allocating factory overhead, and of handling various matters not specifically mentioned, there is a real question as to whether there is such a thing as "actual cost" in most cases. Experienced cost accountants know that their central task is to develop costs that are meaningful, useful, sensible, and reasonable in relation to the intended use of their findings. Sometimes when a comparison is made between budgeted costs (or standard costs) and the amounts of costs as recorded, reference may be made to "budgeted versus actual," or "standard versus actual," but the accountant recognizes that "actual" is not being used in the literal sense in such cases.

BUILDING YOUR ACCOUNTING KNOWLEDGE

1. What is the heart or core of a process cost system in the accounting sense?
2. What information concerning materials should be provided by the records kept in a process cost system?
3. What information should the payroll records provide in a process cost accounting system?
4. How should occupancy costs be apportioned to the separate processes in a process cost accounting system?

5. On what basis should service department costs be assigned to producing (process) departments?
6. In calculating average unit costs, what must be considered with respect to the beginning and ending inventories of work in process?
7. What is the distinction between scrap and waste that may result from processing operation?
8. What is the primary purpose of standard costing?

Report No. 28-3

> Complete Report No. 28-3 in the study assignments and submit your working papers for approval. Continue with the textbook discussion in Chapter 29 until Report No. 29-1 is required.

EXPANDING YOUR BUSINESS VOCABULARY

What is the meaning of each of the following terms?

budgeting (p. 787)
by-product (p. 786)
comparative form (p. 757)
comparative schedule of operating expenses (p. 771)
comparative statement (p. 770)
cost flow diagram (p. 755)
cost of production summary (p. 784)
equivalent units or equivalent production (p. 781)
expense distribution sheet (p. 780)
joint products (p. 786)
occupancy costs (p. 780)
overabsorbed overhead (p. 764)
parallel processing (p. 778)
posting in detail (p. 767)
process cost accounting (p. 778)

processing cost (p. 781)
relative sales value (p. 786)
sales value (p. 786)
scrap (p. 786)
service departments (p. 780)
split-off point (p. 786)
standard cost (p. 787)
statement of changes in financial position (p. 774)
statement of retained earnings (p. 772)
summary work sheets (p. 757)
supplementary work sheets (p. 757)
three-column general journal (p. 764)
underabsorbed overhead (p. 764)
waste (p. 786)

CHAPTER 29

ANALYSIS OF FINANCIAL STATEMENTS

CHAPTER OBJECTIVES

The objectives of this chapter are to enable you:

▶ To describe **comparative analysis** of financial statements, including **horizontal analysis** and **vertical analysis** of both the income statement and the balance sheet and supporting schedules.

▶ To describe and explain **comparative ratio analysis**.

▶ To compute the following ratios:

(1) Profitability measures:
   Return on total assets
   Return on owners' equity
   Earnings per share of common stock
   Book value per share of common stock

(2) Liquidity measures:
   Quick or acid test ratio
   Current ratio
   Working capital turnover
   Receivables turnover
   Finished goods turnover
   Plant and equipment turnover

(3) Leverage measures:
   Ratio of liabilities to owners' equity
   Times interest earned ratio

Any fact, by itself, has limited significance. Meaning is added if there are related facts that permit comparison. The validity of this observation is easily demonstrated if information is needed about a business. For example, knowing that the net income of a certain corporation last year was $84,617, does not answer the following questions: Does that amount of earnings indicate a successful year or a poor one? Does the amount represent an improvement over or a decline from the year before? Is the amount large or small in relation to sales? — to assets? — to stockholders' equity? How does it compare with the net income of others in the industry? Other facts must be known if the information about last year's income is to have any real meaning.

TYPES OF COMPARISON

The financial statements of a business are intended to supply information to several interested parties such as management, present and prospective owners, present and prospective creditors, employees and their unions, government agencies, and sometimes the general public. Normally, interest centers on three aspects of the business: (1) its **profitability** (the ability to earn a satisfactory return on the investments in the business), (2) its **liquidity** or solvency (the ability to pay its debts on or before their maturity), and (3) the extent of **leverage** (the proportion of borrowed capital to owners' capital) with which it operates. The financial statements can be much more informative and meaningful if they are analyzed on a comparative basis. The following are five possible types of comparison:

(1) Comparison of the latest statements and financial relationships of the business with those of one or more previous periods.
(2) Comparison of the statements and financial relationships of the business with data for the industry as a whole.
(3) Comparison of the statements and financial relationships of the business with similar information for other businesses in the industry.
(4) Comparison of the statements and financial relationships of two or more divisions or branches of the same business.
(5) Comparison of the information in the statements with preset plans or goals (normally in the form of budgets).

Comparisons of the first type are possible for all businesses that keep accounts and prepare periodic statements. This type of comparative analysis will be illustrated using the financial statements of Hartup Tool, Inc., for the years ended March 31, 19A and 19B, which were reproduced in the preceding chapter. These statements and certain relationships that they reveal will be compared in various ways. To facilitate the comparison, certain of the statements for both years are condensed or summarized.

Comparisons of the second, third and fourth types are not possible if the business does not have divisions or branches, or if data regarding the industry or other businesses in the industry are not available. Comparisons of the fifth type require a formal budgeting procedure.

HORIZONTAL ANALYSIS

A comparison of the amounts for the same item in the financial statements of two or more periods is called horizontal analysis. The comparison is facilitated if the amount of any change and its relative size are shown. A condensed comparative income statement of Hartup Tool, Inc., for the two years under review, showing the amount and the percentage of change in each item, is shown below. In calculating the percent of change, the amount for the earlier years serves as the base. In general, the percentage of change is of greater interest than the dollar amount of change.

HARTUP TOOL, INC.
Condensed Comparative Income Statement
For the Years Ended March 31, 19B and 19A

	Year Ended		Increase or Decrease*	
	March 31, 19B	March 31, 19A	Amount	Percent
Net sales	$2,110,576	$1,749,428	$361,148	20.6
Cost of goods sold	1,621,084	1,343,562	277,522	20.7
Gross margin on sales	$ 489,492	$ 405,866	$ 83,626	20.6
Operating expenses	111,178	92,023	19,155	20.8
Operating income	$ 378,314	$ 313,843	$ 64,471	20.5
Other revenue	1,200	1,200	–0–	0.0
	$ 379,514	$ 315,043	$ 64,471	20.5
Other expenses	19,399	19,267	132	0.7
Income before income tax	$ 360,115	$ 295,776	$ 64,339	21.8
Provision for income tax	167,879	137,832	30,047	21.8
Net income	$ 192,236	$ 157,944	$ 34,292	21.7

Hartup Tool, Inc. — Condensed Comparative Income Statement

A study of the percentage change of amounts in the two income statements shows that net sales this year (19B) were 20.6 percent greater than for the year ended March 31, 19A. Cost of goods sold increased 20.7 percent. The costs of producing goods in a factory usually remain fairly constant from year to year regardless of the level of activity, but the costs of direct materials and direct labor normally vary both with production volume and with inflation. Both types of costs increased at Hartup Tool, but fortunately sales volume and unit prices kept pace with the cost increases. As a result the percent increase in gross margin was, like that of net sales, 20.6 percent.

Operating expenses advanced 20.8 percent, which was in direct proportion to the growth of sales. This combination of events (an increase in operating expenses slightly more than proportional to the increase in gross margin) had a minimal effect upon the change in operating income — an increase of 20.5 percent. The amount of other revenue was too small in both years to make any difference. Because other expenses increased only 7/10 of 1 percent, income before income tax was 21.8 percent greater. The relative amount of income tax remained virtually the same, so that net income increased by 21.7 percent.

A condensed comparative balance sheet as of March 31, 19B and 19A and a comparative schedule of current assets are presented on page 793.

The most noteworthy changes in the balance sheet are (1) the significant (15.6 percent) increase in current assets and very slight (0.05 percent) increase in current liabilities, (2) the 16.7 percent reduction in bonds payable, and (3) the sizable (62.2 percent) increase in retained earnings. The latter was due to the fact that dividends for the year, $32,000, were only about one-sixth of the earnings for the year, $192,236. (See the statement of retained earnings on page 774.) Note that the changes in the long-term assets were relatively minor. There were substantial percentage reductions in the undepreciated costs of office and delivery equipment and organization costs, but the amounts of these assets were small. The reductions of 13.7 and 10.1 percent were due primarily to depreciation and amortization — no assets of either type were sold or discarded, and only a small amount of office equipment was purchased.

The comparative schedule of current assets reveals some interesting items. The 23.2 percent increase in cash seems rather large, but the increase may be needed to support the higher level of operating activity. The 21.0 percent increase in net receivables is in line with the 20.6 increase in net sales noted earlier. The 8.2 percent increases in the materials and work in process inventories mean that a gradual buildup in those inventories is taking place presumably to

HARTUP TOOL, INC.
Condensed Comparative Balance Sheet
March 31, 19B and 19A

	March 31		Increase or Decrease*	
	19B	19A	Amount	Percent
Assets				
Current assets......................	$1,048,741	$ 907,003	$141,738	15.6
Land...	38,495	38,495	–0–	0.0
Building (net).........................	184,340	194,914	10,574*	5.4*
Factory equipment (net).......	509,733	528,708	18,975*	3.6*
Office and delivery equipment (net)................	4,884	5,659	775*	13.7*
Organization costs...............	8,875	9,875	1,000*	10.1*
Total assets	$1,795,068	$1,684,654	$110,414	6.6
Liabilities				
Current liabilities.................	$ 327,128	$ 326,950	$ 178	0.05
Bonds payable	250,000	300,000	50,000*	16.7*
Total liabilities...................	$ 577,128	$ 626,950	$ 49,822*	7.9*
Stockholders' Equity				
Capital stock	$ 800,000	$ 800,000	–0–	0.0
Retained earnings.................	417,940	257,704	$160,236	62.2
Total stockholders' equity	$1,217,940	$1,057,704	$160,236	15.1
Total liabilities and stockholders' equity...................	$1,795,068	$1,684,654	$110,414	6.6

Hartup Tool, Inc. — Condensed Comparative Balance Sheet

support the higher level of sales. The same thing is indicated by the 7.3 percent increase in finished goods inventory and the 6.7 percent increase in supplies and prepayments.

HARTUP TOOL, INC.
Comparative Schedule of Current Assets
March 31, 19B and 19A

	March 31		Increase or Decrease*	
	19B	19A	Amount	Percent
Cash...	$ 63,018	$ 51,148	$ 11,870	23.2
Government notes	10,000	10,000	–0–	0.0
Receivables (net)	575,206	475,239	99,967	21.0
Finished goods inventory.....	20,951	19,526	1,425	7.3
Work in process inventory...	343,087	317,158	25,929	8.2
Materials inventory	19,139	17,683	1,456	8.2
Supplies and prepayments ..	17,340	16,249	1,091	6.7
Total current assets..............	$1,048,741	$907,003	$141,738	15.6

Hartup Tool, Inc. — Comparative Schedule of Current Assets

A comparative schedule of current liabilities can be prepared and analyzed in the same fashion. However, since the current liabilities of Hartup Tool, Inc., are much alike in that all of the obligations must be paid in a short time, changes in the components are not of great interest. The fact that the current liabilities, in total, increased only 0.05 percent is insignificant.

VERTICAL ANALYSIS

An expression of the amount of each item in a statement as a percentage of some designated total for comparative purposes is termed vertical analysis. A maximum of information is provided if statements relating to two or more periods are vertically analyzed and the results compared or contrasted. A condensed comparative income statement of Hartup Tool, Inc., for the years ended March 31, 19B and 19A, with each item shown as a percent of the net sales for the year, is presented below. This statement reveals that there was very little difference between the two years under review in the proportionate relationship of the items.

HARTUP TOOL, INC.
Condensed Comparative Income Statement
For the Years Ended March 31, 19B and 19A

	March 31, 19B		March 31, 19A	
	Amount	Percent	Amount	Percent
Net sales....................................	$2,110,576	100.0	$1,749,428	100.0
Cost of goods sold	1,621,084	76.8	1,343,562	76.8
Gross margin on sales	$ 489,492	23.2	$ 405,866	23.2
Operating expenses	111,178	5.3	92,023	5.3
Operating income......................	$ 378,314	17.9	$ 313,843	17.9
Other revenue	1,200	0.1	1,200	0.1
	$ 379,514	18.0	$ 315,043	18.0
Other expenses..........................	19,399	0.9	19,267	1.1
Income before income tax........	$ 360,115	17.1	$ 295,776	16.9
Provision for income tax...........	167,879	8.0	137,832	7.9
Net income................................	$ 192,236	9.1	$ 157,944	9.0

Hartup Tool, Inc. — Condensed Comparative Income Statement

Vertical analysis of income statements automatically provides several important ratios relating to each statement. The analysis provides the cost of goods sold ratio (cost of goods sold to net sales), the gross margin ratio (gross margin to net sales), the operating expense ratio (operating expenses to net sales), the operating income ratio (operating income to net sales), and the net income to net sales ratio.

The vertical analysis technique can be used in connection with schedules that supplement the condensed income statement. For example, each item in a schedule of operating expenses can be shown as a percent of total operating expenses.

Balance sheets can be vertically analyzed and compared. On the asset side, each item is shown as a percent of the total assets. On the equity side, each item is shown as a percent of the total liabilities and stockholders' equity. The condensed comparative balance sheet of Hartup Tool, Inc., with vertical analysis is shown below.

HARTUP TOOL, INC.
Condensed Comparative Balance Sheet
March 31, 19B and 19A

| | March 31, 19B | | March 31, 19A | |
	Amount	Percent	Amount	Percent
Assets				
Current assets...........................	$1,048,741	58.4	$ 907,003	53.8
Land..	38,495	2.2	38,495	2.3
Building (net)	184,340	10.3	194,914	11.6
Factory equipment (net)...........	509,733	28.4	528,708	31.4
Office and delivery equipment				
(net)	4,884	0.3	5,659	0.3
Organization costs	8,875	0.4	9,875	0.6
Total assets	$1,795,068	100.0	$1,684,654	100.0
Liabilities				
Current liabilities	$ 327,128	18.2	$ 326,950	19.4
Bonds payable	250,000	13.9	300,000	17.8
Total liabilities........................	$ 577,128	32.1	$ 626,950	37.2
Stockholders' Equity				
Capital stock	$ 800,000	44.6	$ 800,000	47.5
Retained earnings	417,940	23.3	257,704	15.3
Total stockholders' equity.....	$1,217,940	67.9	$1,057,704	62.8
Total liabilities and stockholders' equity.............................	$1,795,068	100.00	$1,684,654	100.0

Hartup Tool, Inc. — Condensed Comparative Balance Sheet

Comparison of items on the balance sheet reveals that current assets were a somewhat larger share of the total assets at the end of the year ended March 31, 19B. As a share of the total equities, current liabilities decreased slightly and bonds payable were noticeably less.

As a result, total liabilities were a smaller share of total equities. Retained earnings, in amount and proportion, increased significantly.

If supporting schedules are prepared for current assets or current liabilities, either the total of the items in the schedule or the balance sheet total may be used as the base (100 percent).

COMPARATIVE RATIO ANALYSIS

The use of ratios to assess profitability, liquidity, and other aspects of business activity has been mentioned and illustrated in earlier chapters. While ratios are only a means to an end, they can be a real aid in interpreting financial statements — particularly in making comparative analyses. Any ratio by itself does not mean much, but comparisons reveal trends. To illustrate their use in comparative analysis, several of the most widely used ratios will be calculated for Hartup Tool, Inc., for the two years under review. (The ratios of certain items to net sales were determined in making the vertical analysis of the income statements. Those ratios are not repeated.)

PROFITABILITY MEASURES

Return on Total Assets. A major aim of the owners or managers of most businesses is to realize large earnings in relation to the resources of their firms. The return on total assets is a measure of the attainment of this objective. The return on total assets is calculated by dividing the net income for the year by the average assets for the year. In the case of Hartup Tool, Inc., the ratio for each year would be computed as shown below:

	Year Ended	
	March 31, 19B	March 31, 19A
Net income..	$ 192,236	$ 157,944
Total assets:		
Beginning of year	$1,684,654	$1,580,351
End of year	1,795,068	1,684,654
Average..	$1,739,861	$1,632,503
Return on total assets...	11.0%*	9.7%**

*$192,236 ÷ $1,739,861
**$157,944 ÷ $1,632,503

The 9.7 percent return for the year ended March 31, 19A, probably was considered to be barely satisfactory by the management of Hartup Tool, Inc. The 11.0 percent return for the year ended March 31, 19B, was slightly better.

Return on Owners' Equity. From the standpoint of the owners of a business, the return on owners' equity is of major interest. It is calculated by dividing the net income for the year by the average capital during the year. In the case of Hartup Tool, Inc., the ratio for each year would be computed as follows:

| | Year Ended | |
	March 31, 19B	March 31, 19A
Net income	$ 192,236	$ 157,944
Total stockholders' equity:		
Beginning of year	$1,057,704	$ 964,530
End of year	1,217,940	1,057,704
Average	$1,137,822	$1,011,117
Return on owners' equity	16.9%*	15.6%**

*$192,236 ÷ $1,137,822 = 16.9%
**$157,944 ÷ $1,011,117 = 15.6%

Because net income for the year ended March 31, 19B, was 21.7 percent greater than for the year ended March 31, 19A (see page 791), while the average stockholders' equity increased only 12.5 percent ($1,137,822 − $1,011,117 = $126,705 ÷ $1,011,117 = 12.5%), the rate of return on the stockholders' equity increased slightly.

Earnings Per Share of Common Stock. From the standpoint of an individual stockholder, the most meaningful measurement of earnings is the earnings per share. This is calculated by dividing the net income for the year by the number of outstanding shares of common stock where, as in Hartup Tool, Inc., there is only common stock. During each of the two years in question, 8,000 shares were outstanding. Thus the net earnings per share for the year ended March 31, 19A, were $19.74 ($157,944 ÷ 8,000) and, for the year ended March 31, 19B, $24.03 ($192,236 ÷ $8,000). An increase in earnings per share is considered to be an indication of overall operating improvement.

If there are preferred shares outstanding, the earnings per share of common stock is calculated by dividing net income after preferred dividend requirements by the number of outstanding shares of common stock. For example, suppose a corporation has 3,000 shares of $100 par, 8 percent preferred stock, and 6,000 shares of common stock outstanding. If the net income for the year is

$260,000, the earnings per share of common stock would be computed as follows:

Net income	$260,000
Less preferred dividend requirements (3,000 × $8)	24,000
Balance applicable to common stock	$236,000
Earnings per share of common stock ($236,000 ÷ 6,000 shares)	$39.33

Book Value Per Share of Common Stock. If a corporation has only one class of common stock outstanding, a measure of the ownership equity represented by each share, known as book value per share, can be determined by dividing the total owners' equity (i.e., assets minus liabilities) by the number of shares. Book value per share is not a measure of profitability in the direct sense, but it does indicate growth or decline in the equity of the individual stockholder, and therefore is often calculated in conjunction with earnings per share.

During both of the years under review, Hartup Tool, Inc., had 8,000 shares of common stock outstanding. The book value per share of common stock is calculated as follows:

	19B	19A
Total stockholders' equity	$1,217,940	$1,057,704
Divided by shares outstanding	8,000	8,000
Book value per share	$152.24	$132.21

When there are preferred shares outstanding, the calculation of book value per share of common stock must first take into consideration the claims or equity of the senior stock (that stock having first claim upon the assets of the business). For example, suppose that a corporation has 2,000 shares of $100 par value, preferred stock with a liquidation preference of $105 per share, and 4,000 shares of common stock outstanding. There are no dividends in arrears on the preferred stock. The total stockholders' equity of the company is $900,000. The book value per share of common stock would be calculated as follows:

Total stockholders' equity	$900,000
Less liquidation claim of preferred stock ($105 × 2,000)	210,000
Balance applicable to common stock	$690,000
Divided by shares outstanding	4,000
Book value per share of common stock	$172.50

In the calculation of book value of shares of capital stock and of certain ratios, some analysts reduce the total stockholders' equity figure by the amount of any intangible assets shown in the balance sheet. The result is called "tangible net worth." This treatment gives a more conservative book-value figure. In the case of Hartup Tool, Inc., there was only one intangible asset, organization costs, in an amount too small to have an appreciable effect upon the book value of shares of stock or upon other calculations.

In interpreting book value per share, it is important to note that book value means nothing more than what it says — value per books. The amount does not indicate what the stockholders would get for their shares in the event of the liquidation of the company. They might get more than book value; probably less.

LIQUIDITY MEASURES

Quick or Acid Test Ratio. A frequently used measure of liquidity is the quick or acid test ratio. It is calculated by dividing "quick" assets — meaning cash, temporary investments and receivables — by current liabilities. As a general rule, the ratio should be not much less than 1 to 1. The quick ratio for Hartup Tool, Inc., at the end of each year is as follows:

	March 31,	
	19B	*19A*
Quick assets:		
Cash	$ 63,018	$ 51,148
Temporary investments	10,000	10,000
Receivables (net)	575,206	475,239
Total quick assets	$648,224	$536,387
Current liabilities	$327,128	$326,950
Quick ratio	1.98 to 1*	1.64 to 1**

*$648,224 ÷ $327,128 = 1.98
**$536,387 ÷ $326,950 = 1.64

This analysis indicates that Hartup Tool, Inc., passed the acid test by a wide margin both times.

Current Ratio. The current ratio, sometimes called working capital ratio, compares total current assets to total current liabilities. It is calculated by dividing total current assets by total current liabilities. In the case of Hartup Tool, Inc., the ratio at the end of each year would be computed as shown at the top page 800. This analysis indicates that the current position of Hartup Tool, Inc., improved somewhat during the year ended March 31, 19B. There is a general rule that a current ratio of 2 to 1 or better is satisfactory, but this rule is subject to modification when applied to

	March 31,	
	19B	*19A*
Total current assets..	$1,048,741	$907,003
Total current liabilities..	327,128	326,950
Current ratio	3.2 to 1*	2.8 to 1**

*$1,048,741 ÷ $327,128 = 3.2
**$907,003 ÷ $326,950 = 2.8

certain types of businesses. In the case of Hartup Tool, Inc., their current ratio clearly is acceptable in both years.

While it is generally desirable that both the current ratio and the quick or acid test ratio be high and improving, it is possible for both of them to be too high for the good of the business. Cash and most receivables are not "earning assets" and the return on most temporary investments is not large. Inventories are expensive to hold. They take up costly space, tie up money, and are subject to loss of value from various causes. Neither too little nor too much working capital is desirable. Business management must determine and try to maintain the ideal amount of each type of asset.

Working Capital Turnover. The working capital turnover may be calculated by dividing the net sales for the year by the average working capital (current assets less current liabilities) for the year. The working capital turnover for Hartup Tool, Inc., for each year may be computed as follows:

	Year Ended	
	March 31, 19B	*March 31, 19A*
Net sales..	$2,110,576	$1,749,428
Working capital:		
Beginning of year	$ 580,053	$ 495,442
End of year..	721,613	580,053
Average...	$ 650,833	$ 537,748
Working capital turnover..	3.2*	3.3**

*$2,110,576 ÷ $650,833 = 3.2
**$1,749,428 ÷ $537,748 = 3.3

Note that there was only a slight decrease in the working capital turnover. This suggests a stable operation. On the other hand, this rate of working capital turnover is not very high, so that Hartup Tool's working capital probably could support an increased volume of business.

Receivables Turnover. It is desirable to have as little as possible invested in accounts receivable since they do not earn any income.

Carrying accounts receivable is an unavoidable consequence of selling on account, but because this may generate greater sales and net income, the disadvantage of owning receivables is accepted.

In a well-managed company, constant effort is made to see that receivables are collected promptly. A measure of the success of this effort is the accounts receivable turnover. It is calculated by dividing net sales by the average amount of net accounts receivable. The calculations for Hartup Tool, Inc., are as follows:

	Year Ended	
	March 31, 19B	March 31, 19A
Net sales..	$2,110,576	$1,749,428
Accounts receivable (net):		
Beginning of year..	$ 475,089	$ 424,977
End of year..	575,056	475,089
Average...	$ 525,073	$ 450,033
Accounts receivable turnover..	4.0*	3.9**
Average number of days..	91 days	94 days

*$2,110,576 ÷ $525,073 = 4.0
**$1,749,428 ÷ $450,033 = 3.9

Another way of examining receivables turnover is to divide 365 days by the turnover figure to get the average number of days that the accounts receivable were on the books. In the foregoing case, the result is 91 days and 94 days, respectively, for the years ended March 31, 19B and 19A, as shown on the last line of the above illustration. A slight improvement in accounts receivable turnover occurred during the most recent year. However, both these rates of collection should be of concern to management. The average number of days that receivables are on the books should not be greater than 1½ times the regular credit period allowed. Since Hartup Tool, Inc., regularly offers 30 days' credit, the average collection period should not exceed 45 days. Hartup's management, therefore, should attempt to speed up the collection process.

Finished Goods Turnover. The desirability of keeping the inventory of merchandise as small as possible has already been mentioned. Every seller of goods would like to have maximum sales and a minimum inventory. A measure of the relationship between sales and inventory is the finished goods turnover. It is calculated by dividing cost of goods sold by the average inventory of finished goods. (Cost of goods sold rather than sales is used, since the latter includes the gross margin.) The result is more accurate if an average of inventories at the end of each month is used. If this is not available, the average of the beginning-of-year and end-of-year inventories is used. In the case of Hartup Tool, Inc., the finished goods inventory turnover for each year is calculated as follows:

	Year Ended	
	March 31, 19B	March 31, 19A
Cost of goods sold	$1,621,084	$1,343,562
Finished goods inventory:		
Beginning of year	$ 19,526	$ 21,488
End of year	20,951	19,526
Average	$ 20,239	$ 20,507
Finished goods turnover	80.1*	65.5**
Average number of days	4.5 days	5.5 days

*$1,621,084 ÷ $20,239 = 80.1
**$1,343,562 ÷ $20,507 = 65.5

As with the receivables turnover, another way of examining finished goods turnover is to divide 365 days by the turnover figure to get the average number of days that the finished goods were held. In the above illustration, the goods remained in stock an average of 4.5 days and 5.5 days, respectively, for the years ended March 31, 19B and 19A.

The turnover increased slightly from the year ended March 31, 19A, to the year ended March 31, 19B, and the management of Hartup Tool, Inc., should be fairly well satisfied. Rapid turnover may be expected when an inventory includes a small number of items and production is entirely to customer order. Hartup Tool, Inc., produces only two products and its business is not unusually seasonal, so the turnover of 65 to 80 must be regarded as very rapid. Note that the finished goods inventory at March 31, 19B, is more than that at the start of that year. This recent increase seems very reasonable in light of the substantial increase in net sales for the year.

Plant and Equipment Turnover. The plant and equipment turnover may be calculated by dividing net sales for the year by the average undepreciated cost of plant and equipment during the year. The calculation of plant and equipment turnover of Hartup Tool, Inc., for each year would be as shown at the top of page 803.

Note that there was a modest improvement in the plant and equipment turnover ratio. This suggests that Hartup Tool, Inc., is making more efficient use of its plant and equipment (building and factory equipment) than it has in the recent past.

	Year Ended	
	March 31, 19B	March 31, 19A
Net sales...	$2,110,576	$1,749,428
Plant and equipment (land, building, and factory equipment (net)):		
Beginning of year...	$ 762,117	$ 761,913
End of year..	732,568	762,117
Average	$ 747,343	$ 762,015
Plant and equipment turnover	2.8*	2.3**

*$2,110,576 ÷ $747,343 = 2.8
**$1,749,428 ÷ $762,015 = 2.3

LEVERAGE MEASURES

Ratio of Liabilities to Owners' Equity. The ratio of liabilities to owners' equity is a measure of the extent of overall leverage, or proportion of borrowed capital with which a business operates. Companies in low-risk industries with fairly stable earnings often operate with a high ratio of liabilities to owners' equity. The ratio for Hartup Tool, Inc., at the end of each of the two years is calculated by dividing total liabilities by total stockholders' equity.

	Year Ended	
	March 31, 19B	March 31, 19A
Total liabilities	$ 577,128	$ 626,950
Total stockholders' equity	1,217,940	1,057,704
Ratio of liabilities to stockholders' equity	.47 to 1	.59 to 1

The ratio of liabilities to stockholders' equity was noticeably lower for the year ended March 31, 19B, than for the preceding year, apparently because of the retirement of $50,000 of bonds. The current liabilities actually increased by a small amount. In evaluating this ratio, the nature of the individual assets and liabilities is the determining factor. Commercial banks sometimes operate on ratios as high as 8 to 1. For Hartup Tool, Inc., a ratio between .5 to 1 and 1 to 1 is acceptable.

Times Interest Earned Ratio. When a business has long-term liabilities in the form of bonds payable or mortgage payable, the interest on such obligations must be paid each year. The holder of the bonds or mortgage is interested in the amount of earnings exclusive of the interest and before income tax. While the corporation is obligated to pay the interest whether or not there is net income, the size of the earnings before interest and taxes in relation to the bond interest requirement provides a measure of the security behind the obligation. The ratio of earnings before interest and taxes to the bond interest requirement is called the times interest earned ratio. For example, if the bond interest requirement is $12,000 and the income before this interest and before income tax is $48,000, the interest is said to be "four times earned" ($48,000 ÷ $12,000 = 4).

Although the bonds payable of Hartup Tool, Inc., outstanding on March 31, 19B, were $50,000 less than on March 31, 19A, the bonds outstanding during the two years were essentially the same, because the $50,000 bond retirement did not occur until late in the year 19B. Consequently, the interest expense in 19A and 19B is virtually the same.

The times interest earned ratio for each year is calculated as follows:

	Year Ended	
	March 31, 19B	March 31, 19A
Net income	$192,236	$157,944
Add back: Income tax	167,879	137,832
Bond interest	18,799	18,767
Income before bond interest and income tax	$378,914	$314,543
Bond interest	$ 18,799	$ 18,767
Number of times bond interest earned	20.2*	16.8**

*$378,914 ÷ $18,799 = 20.2
**$314,543 ÷ $18,767 = 16.8

These high and increasing times interest earned ratios would be very satisfactory to the bondholders of Hartup Tool, Inc. In many businesses, a ratio of 2 or 3 is considered adequate.

A similar computation can be made relative to dividend requirements on preferred stock. The earnings used in this computation would be after bond interest and income tax. For example, if there are 2,000 shares of $100 par, 7 percent preferred stock outstanding, the annual dividend requirements on these shares will be $14,000. If net income is $52,000, the preferred dividends will be 3.7 ($52,000 ÷ $14,000) times earned. The payment of dividends depends upon both earnings and the availability of cash. The present holder or prospective purchaser of preferred shares is very much interested in the earnings in relation to dividend requirements.

SIGNIFICANCE OF RATIO ANALYSIS

The overall financial picture of Hartup Tool, Inc., appears to have improved somewhat during the two years ended March 31,

19B. The measures of profitability that have been examined show an improving trend. The measures of liquidity show a solid position, but receivables collection needs considerable improvement and working capital could be utilized more fully. If anything, the quick ratio and the current ratio both are higher than is necessary. The measures of leverage show that exposure to risk is very slight and could safely be increased.

In summary, the management of Hartup Tool, Inc., should concentrate on the following matters:

(1) Find out why the collection of accounts receivable takes twice as long as it should, and whether the trend to build up cash and inventories is necessary or warranted.

(2) Find out why the return on total assets and on owners' equity has not shown greater improvement.

(3) Explore the use of leverage to a greater extent to (a) expand operations and (b) improve the return on owners' equity.

LIMITATIONS OF RATIO ANALYSIS

The management of Hartup Tool, inc., should not be hasty in drawing firm conclusions based on the data in the financial statements alone. A period of two consecutive years is scarcely sufficient to establish a long-term trend, either upward or downward. Published financial statements often condense information quite extensively (for example, the factory equipment item on the Hartup Tool balance sheet). The location and type of industry can, as mentioned earlier, affect operating performance. Subjective information about management performance is not included in conventional financial statements. The accounting procedures utilized by the reporting company often are not fully explained. And events like the $50,000 bond retirement made by Hartup Tool near year end in 19B can create false notions of relationships, such as leverage in this case.

For all of the above reasons, management must exercise extreme caution in using the results of financial statement analysis. Accounting is, justifiably, considered to be as much a practical art as it is a science.

BUILDING YOUR ACCOUNTING KNOWLEDGE

1. What are the three aspects of the business about which interest normally centers in financial statement analysis?

2. Describe five possible types of comparative analysis that may be made in financial statement analysis.

3. With what two factors do the costs of direct materials and direct labor in a factory normally vary?

4. Why are changes in the components of the current liabilities of Hartup Tool, Inc., not of great interest?

5. List five ratios that are automatically provided by the vertical analysis of income statements.

6. Describe four measures of profitability and growth calculated by Hartup Tool, Inc.

7. Describe six measures of liquidity calculated by Hartup Tool, Inc.

8. Describe two measures of the extent of leverage calculated by Hartup Tool, Inc.

9. Describe three areas of concern on which the management of Hartup Tool, Inc., should concentrate its attention.

10. Briefly describe six limitations of ratio analysis.

Report No. 29-1

> Complete Report 29-1 in the study assignments and submit your working papers for approval. Continue with the textbook discussion in Chapter 30 until Report No. 30-1 is required.

EXPANDING YOUR BUSINESS VOCABULARY

What is the meaning of each of the following terms?

accounts receivable turnover (p. 801)
acid test ratio (p. 799)
book value per share (p. 798)
current ratio (p. 799)
earnings per share (p. 797)
finished goods turnover (p. 801)
horizontal analysis (p. 791)
leverage (p. 790)
liquidity (p. 790)
plant and equipment turnover (p. 802)
profitability (p. 790)

quick ratio (p. 799)
ratio of liabilities to owners' equity (p. 803)
return on owners' equity (p. 797)
return on total assets (p. 796)
times interest earned ratio (p. 804)
vertical analysis (p. 794)
working capital (p. 800)
working capital turnover (p. 800)

CHAPTER 30

ACCOUNTING
FOR CHANGING PRICES

CHAPTER OBJECTIVES

The objectives of this chapter are to enable you:

▶ To explain the difference between general and specific price changes.

▶ To describe constant dollar accounting and its purpose.

▶ To prepare a constant dollar balance sheet and income statement.

▶ To describe current cost accounting and its purpose.

▶ To prepare a current cost balance sheet and income statement.

The presentation throughout the previous chapters of this text has been based on the use of an historical cost accounting system. Two important characteristics of an historical cost system are: (1) the value of the dollar is assumed to be constant (monetary unit concept), and (2) changes in asset values generally are not recognized unless a transaction occurs (historical cost concept).

During the past decade, the rate of inflation has reached levels that have made the monetary unit and historical cost concepts increasingly difficult to defend. This situation has led to various suggestions to improve the historical cost system. The most common suggestion has been to supplement historical cost financial statements with some type of partial or complete financial statements that do reflect the effects of price changes. This chapter examines two different types of supplementary financial statements with which the accounting profession is experimenting.

GENERAL PRICE CHANGES

Changes in the general level of the prices of goods and services are known as general price changes. A general price level increase of 10 percent means that the price of some broad collection of goods and services has increased by 10 percent. Some items in the collection may have increased by more than 10 percent and some by less than 10 percent. Some may even have decreased in price. But for the collection of goods and services as a whole, a price level increase of 10 percent means that it will require $110 to have the same purchasing power that $100 had before the price level change.

There are various measures of general price changes. General price levels typically are expressed in terms of indexes, with 100 as the base or initial-year index. Two of the more commonly used general price-level indexes are (1) the consumer price index (CPI) and (2) the gross national product (GNP) implicit price deflator. The latter is a more general index of price levels, but the former is more convenient for accounting purposes because it is published more frequently. These indexes are an expression of the dollar's purchasing power. For example, if the index is 100 at the end of 1982 and 115 at the end of 1983, this means that the purchasing power of the dollar has decreased by 15 percent. It will require $115 at the end of 1983 to buy what $100 would buy at the end of 1982.

SPECIFIC PRICE CHANGES

A specific price is the number of dollars required to acquire a particular good or service. Accordingly, a specific price change is a change in the price of specific goods or services. In order to determine these specific price changes, it is necessary to look to the prices at which specific exchanges occur in the market place. For example, if the cost of a new truck in 1981 was $6,000, whereas a similar new truck costs $8,000 in 1983, there has been a specific change of $2,000 (33%) in the price of this asset. In like manner, a filing cabinet which cost $500 in 1981 may cost $600 in 1983. In this case, the specific price change would amount to $100 or 20%.

Note in the examples that the percentage changes in the specific prices of the assets are quite different (33% and 20%). Furthermore, these specific price changes may have occurred during a period when the general price change was as little as 15% or as much as 40%, depending on the percentage changes in the prices of the other goods and services in the collection. Thus, while the general price index is in fact a composite of many specific price changes, neither the index of general price change nor the index of any specific price change can serve as a substitute for the other. These indexes are two very different measures.

CONSTANT DOLLAR ACCOUNTING

Constant dollar accounting is a method of reporting financial statement amounts in dollars of the same general purchasing power. This method is also known as general purchasing power accounting and price-level accounting. The purpose of constant dollar accounting is to present financial statements in terms of dollars which have the same value or meaning at a given point in time — typically as of the current balance sheet date.

The basic procedure in constant dollar accounting involves restating the asset, liability, owners' equity, revenue, and expense accounts by applying appropriate conversion factors based on a general price-level index. The affected amounts are multiplied by the following fraction:

$$\frac{\text{Index at end of current year}}{\text{Index at date of origin}}$$

The numerator of the fraction is the current price-level index at the date of restatement. The denominator is the index at the time the transaction or account arose. For example, assume that inventory on hand at year end was purchased for $1,000 at mid-year when the price level index was 140. If the index at year end is 147, the cost of this inventory expressed in terms of year-end dollars is $1,000 × 147/140, or $1,050. In other words, in terms of the purchasing power of the dollar at year end, the cost of the inventory was $1,050. Similarly, if a delivery truck was purchased for $8,000 four years ago when the index was 100, the cost of this truck expressed in terms of the purchasing power of the dollar at year end is $8,000 × 147/100, or $11,760.

MONETARY AND NONMONETARY ITEMS

Not all amounts on the financial statements are restated by means of the use of indexes. All income statement amounts are restated, but on the balance sheet a distinction must be drawn between monetary and nonmonetary items. A monetary item is cash or a right to receive or obligation to pay a fixed amount of cash. A nonmonetary item is an account balance which is not fixed in terms of the number of dollars to be received or paid. The real values of nonmonetary items can change.

Monetary items require no restatement in constant dollar financial statements, because by their very nature they are already stated in terms of current purchasing power. The dollar amount to be received or paid is fixed and properly expressed as of the current balance sheet date. On the other hand, all nonmonetary items must be restated using conversion factors like the one illustrated on page 812. This procedure is necessary in order to express each historical cost dollar amount in terms of its equivalent dollar amount of current purchasing power.

ILLUSTRATION OF CONSTANT DOLLAR ACCOUNTING

To illustrate constant dollar accounting, the historical cost comparative balance sheet of GRC Company for January 1, 1983, and December 31, 1983, and the historical cost income statement for the calendar year 1983 are reproduced on page 811. GRC Company started business on January 1, 1983, with the assets, liabilities, and stockholders' equities indicated. The following general price-level indexes are assumed:

January 1, 1983	100
Average for 1983	110
December 31, 1983......................................	120

Restatement of the Balance Sheet. The calculation of the restated balance sheet appears at the top of page 812. Each of the restatement factors is numerically coded to correspond to the following explanations of the restatements:

(1) The monetary assets and liabilities require no restatement because they are already expressed in terms of December 31, 1983 dollars. These items are extended to the right-hand column at their historical cost amounts.

(2) The year-end inventories are assumed to have been acquired evenly during the year, so the appropriate denominator in the restatement factor is 110, the average 1983 index. The appro-

GRC COMPANY
Condensed Comparative Balance Sheet — Historical Cost
January 1, 1983 and December 31, 1983

	1/1/83	12/31/83
Cash and receivables	$170,000	$240,000
Inventories	100,000	165,000
Land	80,000	80,000
Building and equipment	300,000	300,000
Less accumulated depreciation	–0–	(20,000)
Total assets	$650,000	$765,000
Accounts and notes payable	$ 50,000	$ 75,000
Bonds payable	100,000	100,000
Capital stock	500,000	500,000
Retained earnings	–0–	90,000
Total liabilities and stockholders' equity	$650,000	$765,000

GRC COMPANY
Condensed Income Statement — Historical Cost
For the Year Ended December 31, 1983

Net sales		$825,000
Cost of goods sold		450,000
Gross margin		$375,000
Operating expenses:		
Depreciation	$ 20,000	
Other operating expenses	205,000	225,000
Net income before tax		$150,000
Less corporation income tax		60,000
Net income		$ 90,000

priate numerator for this as well as each of the other restatements is 120, the December 31, 1983 index.

(3) The land was acquired when GRC started the business. The restatement factor for the land is therefore 120/100.

(4) GRC also acquired the building and equipment when it started business on January 1, 1983. The restatement factor for both the building and equipment and the related accumulated depreciation is 120/100, the same as for the land.

(5) Since the capital stock was issued at the start of business, this amount must be restated using the restatement factor, 120/100.

(6) Retained earnings typically is inserted as a balancing figure rather than as a restated amount. Thus, no restatement factor is shown for this account. Since this is the first year of business for GRC, however, the restated retained earnings corresponds to the restated net income for the year, as shown in the restated income statement at the bottom of page 812.

GRC COMPANY
Condensed Balance Sheet — Restated
December 31, 1983

	Historical Cost	Restatement Factor		Restated to 12/31/83 Dollars
Cash and receivables	$240,000		(1)	$240,000
Inventories...	165,000	120/110	(2)	180,000
Land..	80,000	120/100	(3)	96,000
Building and equipment..................	300,000	120/100	(4)	360,000
Less accumulated depreciation	(20,000)	120/100	(4)	(24,000)
Total assets	$765,000			$852,000
Accounts and notes payable............	$ 75,000		(1)	$ 75,000
Bonds payable	100,000		(1)	100,000
Capital stock	500,000	120/100	(5)	600,000
Retained earnings............................	90,000		(6)	77,000
Total liabilities and stockholders' equity...	$765,000			$852,000

Restatement of the Income Statement. The calculation of the restated income statement appears below. Each of the restatement factors is numerically coded to correspond to the following explanations of the restatements.

GRC COMPANY
Condensed Income Statement — Restated
For the Year Ended December 31, 1983

	Historical Cost	Restatement Factor		Restated to 12/31/83 Dollars
Net sales....................................	$825,000	120/110	(1)	$900,000
Cost of goods sold	450,000	(100,000 × 120/100	(2)	501,818
		+ 350,000 × 120/110)		
Gross margin............................	$375,000			$398,182
Operating expenses:				
Depreciation.........................	20,000	120/100	(3)	24,000
Other operating expenses ..	205,000	120/110	(1)	223,636
Net income before taxes	$150,000			$150,546
Less corporation income tax	60,000	120/110	(1)	65,455
Net income	$ 90,000			
Net income before purchasing power loss on net monetary items............................				$ 85,091
Purchasing power loss on net monetary items..............				(8,091)
Net income...............................				$ 77,000

(1) Sales, other operating expenses, and corporation income tax are assumed to have occurred evenly during the year. Each of these items is therefore restated using a restatement factor of 120/110.

(2) Cost of goods sold contains two components which must be restated separately: (a) Of the $450,000 total, $100,000 was the beginning inventories which were acquired at the start of the business. This amount is therefore restated using a restatement factor of 120/100, yielding $120,000. (b) The rest of the cost of goods sold, $350,000, consisted of purchases which occurred evenly during the year. This amount is restated using a restatement factor of 120/110, yielding $381,818. Adding these two restated components ($120,000 + $381,818) yields the restated cost of goods sold of $501,818.

(3) The depreciation relates to the building and equipment acquired at the start of the business. This expense therefore is restated using the same factor, 120/100, which was used in restating the building and equipment. Depreciation is always restated based on the date of acquisition of the related long-term asset.

The restated income statement on page 812 includes one additional item that does not appear in an historical cost income statement — a purchasing power loss on net monetary items.

Calculation of Purchasing Power Gain or Loss. It was explained previously that monetary items are not restated because they are already expressed in terms of current purchasing power. However, during periods of inflation a company does experience what is known as a purchasing power gain from holding net monetary liabilities, and a purchasing power loss from holding net monetary assets. A company holds net monetary assets if its monetary assets exceed its monetary liabilities. A company holds net monetary liabilities if its monetary liabilities exceed its monetary assets.

During periods of inflation, a company suffers a purchasing power loss from holding net monetary assets. Assume that a company holds net monetary assets of $1,000 for a year during which the general price level increases from 100 to 120. It would require $1,200 at the end of the year to have purchasing power equivalent to the $1,000 at the beginning the year. Yet, the company holds only $1,000 at year end. It therefore has suffered a purchasing power loss of $200 ($1,200 − $1,000).

Similarly, a company has a purchasing power gain from holding net monetary liabilities during periods of inflation. Assume that the company in the previous paragraph held net monetary liabilities rather than net monetary assets of $1,000 for the year. In terms of end-of-the-year dollars, it would require $1,200 of purchasing power to pay off these net monetary liabilities. Yet, the company only owes $1,000 at year end, because the amount owed is fixed in terms of number of dollars. The company therefore has a purchasing power gain of $200.

The calculation of the purchasing power loss of GRC Company for 1983 appears below. The procedure involves determining the number of dollars of December 31, 1983 purchasing power that would be required to equal the purchasing power of the net monetary assets actually held by GRC. The schedule shows that in historical cost dollars, GRC held net monetary assets of $20,000 at the beginning of 1983 and increased its net monetary assets during 1983 by $45,000.

GRC COMPANY
Calculation of Purchasing Power Loss
For the Year Ended December 31, 1983

	Historical Cost	Restatement Factor	Restated to 12/31/83 Dollars
Net monetary assets — January 1, 1983:			
Cash and receivables...............	$170,000		
Less: Accounts and notes payable...................	$ 50,000		
Bonds payable..............	100,000		
	$150,000		
Net monetary assets — January 1, 1983.....................................	$20,000	120/100	$24,000
Net monetary assets — December 31, 1983:			
Cash and receivables...............	$240,000		
Less: Accounts and notes payable	$ 75,000		
Bonds payable..............	100,000		
	$175,000		
Net monetary assets — December 31, 1983.......................	65,000		
Increase in net monetary assets during 1983 (assumed to occur evenly during the year)..	$45,000	120/110	49,091
Restated net monetary assets — December 31, 1983...................			$73,091
Actual net monetary assets — December 31, 1983...................			65,000
Purchasing power loss...............			$ (8,091)

To determine the purchasing power loss, it is necessary to calculate the loss from holding the $20,000 for the entire year plus the loss from holding the $45,000 increase during the year. At the end of 1983, GRC would need $24,000 in net monetary assets in order to have purchasing power equal to the $20,000 balance it held at the beginning of the year. The $24,000 appears in the right-hand column of the schedule. To calculate the purchasing power loss on the $45,000 increase, it must be determined when the net increase occurred. This could be done by examining in detail the inflows and outflows of monetary items during the year, but a common simplifying assumption is that the increase occurred evenly during the year. Applying this assumption to GRC Company, the appropriate denominator of the restatement factor is 110. As shown in the right-hand column, it would require $49,091 in year-end dollars to have purchasing power equivalent to the $45,000 increase that occurred during the year. The total number of dollars in year-end purchasing power that would be required to equal the $65,000 in net monetary assets held by GRC at December 31, 1983, is $73,091. GRC therefore has suffered a purchasing power loss of $8,091. This purchasing power loss appears as a deduction in calculating restated net income on page 812.

CURRENT COST ACCOUNTING

Current cost accounting is a method of reporting balance sheet assets and the income statement expenses associated with the use of certain assets at their current cost at the balance sheet date or at the date of use. The method is also known as replacement cost accounting. The purpose of current cost accounting is to show assets at the amounts it would currently cost to obtain them, and to show expenses at the amounts it would currently cost to operate the business.

The basic procedure in using current cost accounting is to determine the current cost of the assets held and the expenses incurred by reference to current market prices, supplier price lists, specific bids from manufacturers, or other reasonable sources of such information. The main income statement items affected by the current cost restatement are cost of goods sold and depreciation, because these items represent amounts paid at one time but not recognized as expenses until some time later. Thus, at the time these expenses are recognized, their current costs must be identified. In contrast, expenses such as wages and utilities are consumed, paid for, and recognized as expenses at virtually the same time. They are already expressed in terms of current costs.

Similarly, on the balance sheet, the main items affected are the inventories and property, plant, and equipment. Most other assets are already expressed in terms of current costs.

ILLUSTRATION OF CURRENT COST ACCOUNTING

To illustrate current cost accounting, the GRC Company example is continued. In this case, the balance sheet and income statement stated in both historical cost and current cost terms are reproduced on page 817.

Restatement of the Balance Sheet. Each of the current cost amounts which differs from the associated historical cost amount is numerically coded to correspond to the following explanations of current cost items.

(1) The current cost of the inventory on hand at December 31, 1983, is determined from supplier price lists to be $215,000. This amount therefore is included on the current cost balance sheet.

(2) The current cost of the land is determined from a real estate appraisal to be $100,000.

(3) The current cost of the building and equipment is determined from supplier price lists, specific manufacturer price estimates, and real estate appraisers to be $390,000. This amount is included in the current cost balance sheet. In addition, the current cost accumulated depreciation is calculated by applying the same depreciation rate ($6\frac{2}{3}\%$) to the current cost amount as was applied to the historical cost amount. Current cost accumulated depreciation after one year of operations is $26,000 ($390,000 × $6\frac{2}{3}\%$).

(4) The current cost retained earnings balance is the amount necessary to balance the statement. It can also be calculated as the beginning balance of retained earnings plus current cost net income for the year. Since this is the first year of operations for GRC Company, the retained earnings balance is equal to the current cost net income of $244,000 shown on page 817.

Restatement of the Income Statement. Each of the current cost items which differs in amount from the related historical cost item or is unique to the current cost income statement is numerically coded to correspond to the following explanations of the current cost items.

(1) The current cost of merchandise at the time it was sold is estimated from supplier price lists to be $550,000. This amount is the current cost of goods sold.

(2) As was explained in the discussion of the current cost balance sheet, the current cost depreciation expense of $26,000 is cal-

GRC COMPANY
Condensed Balance Sheet — Current Cost
December 31, 1981

	Historical Cost	Current Cost	
Cash and receivables...	$240,000	$240,000	
Inventories...	165,000	215,000	(1)
Land	80,000	100,000	(2)
Building and equipment...	300,000	390,000	(3)
Less accumulated depreciation...............................	(20,000)	(26,000)	(3)
Total assets...	$765,000	$919,000	
Accounts and notes payable....................................	$ 75,000	$ 75,000	
Bonds payable...	100,000	100,000	
Capital stock..	500,000	500,000	
Retained earnings...	90,000	244,000	(4)
Total liabilities and stockholders' equity	$765,000	$919,000	

GRC COMPANY
Condensed Income Statement — Current Cost
For the Year Ended December 31, 1983

	Historical Cost		Current Cost		
Net sales.................................		$825,000		$825,000	
Cost of goods sold................		450,000		550,000	(1)
Gross margin..........................		$375,000		$275,000	
Operating expenses:					
Depreciation......................	$ 20,000		$ 26,000 (2)		
Other operating expenses	205,000	225,000	205,000	231,000	
Current operating profit.......				$ 44,000	(3)
Realized holding gain:					
Inventory............................			$100,000		
Building and equipment...			6,000	106,000	(4)
Net income before income tax..		$150,000		$150,000	
Less corporation income tax..		60,000		60,000	
				$ 90,000	
Unrealized holding gain:					
Inventory............................			$ 50,000		
Land			20,000		
Building and equipment...			84,000	154,000	(5)
Net income............................		$ 90,000		$244,000	

culated by multiplying the depreciation rate of 6⅔% times the current cost of the building and equipment ($390,000).

(3) **Current operating profit** is the difference between the revenue and the current costs of the assets and services consumed in producing the revenue. The current operating profit of GRC Company is $44,000. This measurement is viewed as one of the

major benefits of current cost accounting. It represents the current profits earned by GRC solely from its *operating* activities. Any profits earned by *holding* assets are separately identified, as explained in items (4) and (5) below.

(4) The realized holding gain is the difference between the current cost and the historical cost of assets sold during the year. For GRC, there are two components of this gain: (a) Inventory which cost $450,000 had a current cost of $550,000 when it was sold. GRC realized a gain of $100,000 from holding this inventory from the date of purchase to the date of sale. (b) The building and equipment, which cost $300,000, had a current cost of $390,000 at the end of the year, a difference of $90,000. Only a portion of this $90,000 difference (the total holding gain) is considered realized in the current year. The realized portion is the $6\frac{2}{3}\%$ of the additional current cost of the building and equipment that was recognized as depreciation for the year, or $6,000 ($90,000 \times 6\frac{2}{3}\%$). This realized holding gain on the building and equipment can also be calculated as the difference between the current cost depreciation of $26,000 and the historical cost depreciation of $20,000. The total realized holding gain therefore is $106,000.

(5) The unrealized holding gain is the difference between the current cost and the historical cost of assets still on hand at the end of the year. For GRC, there are three components of this gain: (a) Ending inventory which cost $165,000 has a current cost of $215,000 at the balance sheet date. GRC therefore has an unrealized gain of $50,000 resulting from holding this inventory from the date of purchase to the balance sheet date. (b) The land, which cost $80,000, has a current cost of $100,000 at the balance sheet date. This $20,000 difference represents an unrealized holding gain. (c) The building and equipment have a net historical cost of $280,000 ($300,000 − $20,000 accumulated depreciation) and a net current cost of $364,000 ($390,000 current cost − $26,000 accumulated depreciation), a difference of $84,000. This difference also is an unrealized holding gain. The total unrealized holding gain therefore is $154,000.

The current cost net income is $244,000, consisting of current operating profit of $44,000, realized holding gain of $106,000, and unrealized holding gain of $154,000, less the corporation income tax of $60,000.

BUILDING YOUR ACCOUNTING KNOWLEDGE

1. Explain the difference between general and specific price changes.
2. What is the purpose of constant dollar accounting?

3. Why do monetary items not require restatement in preparing constant dollar financial statements?
4. How is the amount of retained earnings determined in preparing constant dollar financial statements?
5. Under what conditions does a company have a purchasing power gain? A purchasing power loss?
6. What is the purpose of current cost accounting?
7. How is the amount of current cost depreciation expense calculated?
8. What is current operating profit under current cost accounting?

Report No. 30-1

> *Complete Report 30-1 in the study assignments and submit your working papers to the instructor for approval.*

EXPANDING YOUR BUSINESS VOCABULARY

What is the meaning of each of the following terms?

constant dollar accounting (p. 809)
current cost accounting (p. 815)
current operating profit (p. 817)
general price changes (p. 808)
general purchasing power accounting (p. 809)
monetary item (p. 810)
net monetary assets (p. 813)
net monetary liabilities (p. 813)

nonmonetary item (p. 810)
price-level accounting (p. 809)
purchasing power gain (p. 813)
purchasing power loss (p. 813)
realized holding gain (p. 818)
replacement cost accounting (p. 815)
specific price (p. 808)
specific price change (p. 808)
unrealized holding gain (p. 818)

SUPPLEMENTARY PRACTICAL ACCOUNTING PROBLEMS

Problem 26-A   Home office and branch office transactions

The ledger accounts of The Carter Instruments Co. had the following balances on January 1:

Bank	$141,600	
Accounts Receivable	170,700	
Allowance for Doubtful Accounts		$ 5,280
Merchandise Inventory	118,800	
Prepaid Insurance	1,600	
Land	50,000	
Building	350,000	
Accumulated Depreciation — Building		75,000
Furniture and Fixtures	106,000	
Accumulated Depreciation — Furniture and Fixtures		48,200
Accounts Payable		99,500
Capital Stock		500,000
Retained Earnings		210,720
	$938,700	$938,700

On January 2, the company established two branches, one in the northern part of the state, called the North Branch, and another in the western part of the state, called the West Branch.

Shown below are transactions completed by the home office and by the two branches (many of the transactions are given in summary form):

(a) Home office sent $50,000 to North Branch.

(b) Home office sent $60,000 to West Branch.

(c) Total purchases of merchandise at home office, $1,500,000 (on account).

(d) Total shipments of merchandise to North Branch (at cost), $310,000.

(e) Total shipments of merchandise to West Branch (at cost), $407,000.

(f) Furniture and fixtures purchased for cash at North Branch, $35,000; insurance premium paid, $1,500.

(g) Furniture and fixtures purchased for cash at West Branch, $40,200; insurance premium paid, $1,300.

(h) Sales at home office: cash $270,000; on account, $625,000.

(i) Sales at North Branch: cash, $110,000; on account, $256,000.

(j) Sales at West Branch: cash, $90,000; on account, $330,000.

(k) Operating expenses incurred at home office, $153,600.

(l) Operating expenses incurred at North Branch, $72,100.

(m) Operating expenses incurred at West Branch, $78,600.

(n) Collected on accounts receivable at home office, $675,000; accounts written off as worthless, $5,000.

(o) Collected on accounts receivable at North Branch, $220,000.

(p) Collected on accounts receivable at West Branch, $150,000.

(q) Cash sent by North Branch to West Branch, $82,000.

(r) Cash payments on account at North Branch, $67,600.

(s) Cash payments on account at West Branch, $74,800.

(t) Cash sent to home office by North Branch, $145,000.

(u) Cash sent to home office by West Branch, $221,000.

(v) Cash payments on account at home office, $1,310,000.

Required: (1) Using two-column journal paper, journalize the foregoing transactions as they should be recorded in the books of the home office and both branch offices. Since dates are purposely omitted, it will be advisable to number each journal entry to correspond with the number of the transaction. (2) Using plain paper, 8½″ × 11″, rule 20 T account forms (eight to a page arranged in 2 columns) under the heading Home Office Ledger. In addition to the 13 accounts appearing in the trial balance at beginning of year, the following accounts will be needed: North Branch, West Branch, Purchases, Shipments to North Branch, Shipments to West Branch, Sales, and Operating Expenses. Enter the opening balances. Rule 9 T account forms under the heading North Branch ledger. Also rule 9 T account forms under the heading West Branch Ledger. In each case the following accounts are needed: Bank, Accounts Receivable, Prepaid Insurance, Furniture and Fixtures, Accounts Payable, Home Office, Sales, Shipments from Home Office, and Operating Expenses. Post the entries of the three journals to the proper T accounts in the three ledgers. Number each entry to correspond with that of the journal entry. (3) Take a trial balance as of December 31 of the accounts kept for each office.

Problem 26-B   Stock transactions — cost method; equity method

(a) On July 1, 1982 Tahan Company acquired 2,000 shares of the common stock of Tillman Company at a cost of $20,000. Tillman Company had 20,000 shares of common stock outstanding at the time of this acquisition. One year later, on July 1, 1983, Tillman Company reported a net income for the year ended June 30, 1983 of $16,000 and distributed cash dividends to its common stockholders of $10,000 (50¢ per share).

Required: Using two-column journal paper, record (1) the entry for the acquisition of the Tillman Company stock by Tahan, and (2) the entry to record the dividends received by Tahan Company from Tillman, using the cost method.

(b) On July 1, 1982, Teske Company acquired 4,500 shares of the common stock of Tichacek Company at a cost of $45,000. Tichacek Company had 10,000 shares of common stock outstanding at the time of this acquisition. One year later, on July 1, 1983, Tichacek Company reported a net income for the year ended June 30, 1983 of $28,000 and distributed cash dividends to its common stockholders of $20,000 ($2 per share).

Required: Using two-column journal paper, record (1) the entry for the acquisition of Tichacek Company stock by Teske, (2) the entry to record Teske's share of Tichacek's net income, and (3) the entry to record the dividends received by Teske Company from Tichacek, using the equity method for (2) and (3).

Problem 26-C   Consolidation work sheet for consolidated balance sheet

Pergament Company purchased 90 percent of Shimel Company's stock on July 1, 1982 for $300,000. The book value of Shimel's net assets at the time of acquisition was $306,000 (capital stock of $27,000 plus retained earnings of $279,000). The individual balance sheets of the two companies as of July 1, 1982 are shown below:

	Pergament Co.	Shimel Co.
Assets		
Cash..	$ 537,000	$ 63,000
Accounts receivable...	301,500	72,000
Inventories	373,500	216,000
Long-term assets (net)...	1,512,000	——
Investment in Shimel Co...	300,000	——
Goodwill	——	——
Total assets	$3,024,000	$351,000
Liabilities and Stockholders' Equity		
Accounts payable...	$ 135,000	$ 45,000
Capital stock — Pergament..	2,115,000	
Capital stock — Shimel..		27,000
Retained earnings — Pergament Co.	774,000	
Retained earnings — Shimel Co..		279,000
Minority interest	——	——
Total liabilities and stockholders' equity..............................	$3,024,000	$351,000

Required: Using five-column work sheet paper, prepare a consolidation work sheet for the consolidated balance sheet of Pergament Company and Shimel Company as of July 1, 1982.

Problem 27-A   Cost of goods manufactured

The following data pertain to the activities of Genell Manufacturing Company for a year just ended. The company does not keep perpetual inventories.

Work in process inventory, beginning of year..	$ 57,120
Work in process inventory, end of year..	51,200
Cost of materials used	289,680
Direct labor...	339,720
Indirect labor	45,080
Utilities expense	11,960
Factory supplies expense...	11,640
Depreciation of factory equipment...	16,800
Payroll taxes, factory	35,340
Miscellaneous factory overhead	3,250

Required: Calculate the cost of goods manufactured for the year for Genell Manufacturing Company. Show your calculations.

Problem 27-B   Inventory valuation — cost or market, whichever is lower

Fonz Company produces two products: alphs and zets. At the end of the year Fonz has on hand 5,000 alphs and 4,000 zets. On a fifo basis, 3,500 alphs cost $3 each and 1,500 alphs cost $3.10 each to produce. The 4,000 zets cost $4.00 each to produce. Production costs of alphs have been increasing steadily and have risen another 10% since the last batch was produced. In contrast, production costs of zets have declined 5% since the last batch was produced. In order to apply the lower-of-cost-or-market procedure to its ending inventory, Fonz Company must estimate the cost to replace the alphs and zets based on its latest incurred costs and the additional available information.

Required: Calculate the total amount to be assigned to the ending inventory of finished goods according to the cost or market, whichever is lower rule. Apply the rule on an individual item basis.

Problem 27-C   Job cost sheet

The Mason Manufacturing Co. produces a variety of products to customer specification. One of the jobs now underway and about to be completed is Job No. 219.

Required: Using the following information, prepare a job cost sheet similar to the one illustrated on page 738 of Chapter 27. Add a Quantity line immediately below the Description line on the form.

(a) Job No. 219; Item — Storage batteries; Quantity — 1,000; For — Emerson Electric Co.

(b) Date — July 21, 19--; Date finished — August 22, 19--.

(c) Materials requisitions:

#61B for $1,470	#124C for $1,320
#87D for 1,420	#158B for 1,480
#94A for 1,500	#173A for 1,250

(d) Daily time tickets:

July 21 — 118 hrs. — $590.00	Aug. 4 — 122 hrs. — $610.00
23 — 120 hrs. — 600.00	6 — 120 hrs. — 600.00
27 — 119.5 hrs. — 597.50	9 — 117.5 hrs. — 587.50
29 — 117 hrs. — 585.00	10 — 122 hrs. — 610.00
31 — 121 hrs. — 605.00	13 — 121 hrs. — 605.00
Aug. 2 — 120.5 hrs. — 602.50	16 — 120.5 hrs. — 602.50

(e) Factory overhead rate: 140% of direct labor cost.

Problem 27-D   Job cost system — flow of costs

The Vitcus Manufacturing Company uses a job order cost accounting system. Following are selected transactions for the current year.

(a) Materials purchases: Material A, $21,600; Material B, $54,000.

(b) Materials issued:
    Job No. 406: Material A — $ 6,200
                  Material B — $14,100
    Job No. 407: Material A — $ 5,300
                  Material B — $17,900

(c) Direct labor costs:
    Job No. 405: $ 8,300
    Job No. 406: $39,450
    Job No. 407: $41,800

(d) Factory overhead application rate: 110% of direct labor costs (applied at the completion of a job).

(e) Jobs Nos. 405 and 406 completed and transferred to finished goods. Job No. 405 is Product X and Job No. 406 is Product Y.

Required: Using as your guide the T accounts illustrated for the Stores Ledger, the Job Cost Ledger, and the Finished Goods Ledger on page 744 of Chapter 27, post each of the foregoing transactions to a similar set of T accounts and trace the flow of costs through the accounts by means of lines and arrows. Enter the following opening account balances:

Material A, $10,700; Material B, $16,800; Job No. 405, $36,400 (including $20,200 of direct labor).

Problem 28-A   End-of-year work sheet

The J. T. Reid Manufacturing Co. keeps its accounts on the calendar year basis, but the accountant prepares monthly statements. A perpetual inventory system is used. Data for adjustment of the accounts are assembled and entered on summary and supplementary work sheets at the end of each month, although adjustments of the general ledger accounts are recorded only at the end of each year. The factory overhead and operating expense accounts, however, are formally adjusted at the end of each month. These groups of accounts are kept in subsidiary ledgers, controlled by the factory overhead and operating expenses accounts in the general ledger. The trial balance on page 826 was taken on December 31 after the factory overhead adjusting entries for the month had been posted. (It will be noted that a few of the accounts have no balances. These accounts are included because they will be affected by the adjusting entries required on the work sheets.)

THE J. T. REID MANUFACTURING CO.
Trial Balance
December 31, 19--

First National Bank	111	84,575	
Petty Cash Fund	112	300	
Government Bonds	121	12,000	
Accrued Interest Receivable	122		
Accounts Receivable	131	72,199	
Allowance for Doubtful Accounts	131.1		995
Finished Goods Inventory	161	30,307	
Work in Process Inventory	162	9,408	
Materials Inventory	163	12,600	
Office Supplies	181	1,868	
Factory Supplies	182	3,448	
Prepaid Insurance	183	3,528	
Land	211	26,880	
Building	221	248,640	
Accumulated Depreciation — Building	221.1		50,400
Machinery and Equipment	231	168,000	
Accumulated Depreciation — Mach. & Equip.	231.1		52,416
Office Equipment	241	13,104	
Accumulated Depreciation — Office Equip. ...	241.1		1,250
Delivery Equipment	251	16,800	
Accumulated Depreciation — Delivery Equip.	251.1		4,200
FICA Tax Payable	311		1,620
FUTA Tax Payable	312		204
State Unemployment Tax Payable	313		626
Employees Income Tax Payable	314		2,291
Corporation Income Tax Payable	315		
Notes Payable	316		26,141
Accrued Interest Payable	317		
Vouchers Payable	318		70,493
Dividends Payable	319		3,192
Bonds Payable	421		23,520
Capital Stock ($100 par)	511		339,360
Retained Earnings	521		82,936
Sales	611		619,142
Sales Returns and Allowances	611.1	3,528	
Sales Discount	611.2	6,350	
Interest Income	631		592
Factory Overhead	741	80,314	
Factory Overhead Applied	741.1		80,314
Cost of Goods Sold	811	388,354	
Operating Expenses	821	175,829	
Interest Expense	911	1,660	
Income Tax Expense	931		
		1,359,692	1,359,692

The schedules of the balances in the factory overhead and operating expenses ledgers reproduced at the top of page 827 were prepared after posting the factory overhead adjusting entries for December. The operating expense adjusting entries had not yet been made or posted.

THE J. T. REID MANUFACTURING CO.
Schedule of Factory Overhead Ledger Account Balances
December 31, 19--

Indirect Labor	7401	31,014
Utilities Expense	7402	12,096
Maintenance and Repairs	7403	2,809
Depreciation of Factory Building and Equipment	7404	19,286
Expired Insurance on Factory Building and Equipment	7405	2,070
Payroll Taxes — Factory	7406	11,219
Miscellaneous Factory Overhead	7407	1,820
		80,314

THE J. T. REID MANUFACTURING CO.
Schedule of Operating Expenses Ledger Account Balances
For the Year Ended December 31, 19--

Officers' Salaries Expense	8201	55,776
Office Salaries Expense	8202	41,228
Office Supplies Expense	8203	
Depreciation of Office Equipment	8204	
Office Equipment Insurance Expense	8205	
Payroll Taxes — Administrative	8206	6,410
Miscellaneous Office Expense	8207	2,916
Sales Salaries Expense	8231	40,320
Advertising Expense	8232	12,210
Depreciation of Delivery Equipment	8233	
Delivery Equipment Insurance Expense	8234	
Miscellaneous Delivery Expense	8235	10,349
Uncollectible Accounts Expense	8236	
Finished Goods Insurance Expense	8237	
Payroll Taxes — Sales	8238	2,352
Miscellaneous Selling Expense	8239	4,268
		175,829

The following information is provided. (Bear in mind that the factory overhead accounts have already been adjusted.)

DATA FOR YEAR-END ADJUSTMENT OF GENERAL AND OPERATING EXPENSES LEDGER ACCOUNTS
December 31, 19--

Accruals:		
Accrued interest receivable		$ 42
Accrued interest payable		161
Office supplies expense		1,386
Depreciation of office equipment		2,433
Depreciation of delivery equipment		4,200
Insurance expense:		
On office equipment	$125	
On delivery equipment	215	
On finished goods	210	550
Provision for doubtful accounts		3,024
Provision for corporation income taxes		9,560

Required: (1) Using ten-column analysis paper, prepare a summary end-of-year work sheet as a means of summarizing and classifying the information needed in preparing financial statements. Support this summary work sheet with a three-column supplementary operating expenses work sheet. **(2)** Journalize the adjusting and closing entries. **(3)** Using four-column ledger paper, open the following accounts:

122 Accrued Interest Receivable	531 Expense and Revenue Summary
317 Accrued Interest Payable	631 Interest Income
521 Retained Earnings	911 Interest Expense

Post the adjusting and closing entries that affect these accounts. (Be sure to show any balances in these accounts before adjustment. Refer to the trial balance on page 826.) Using three-column ledger paper, open Accounts Nos. 8203, 8204, 8205, 8233, 8234, 8236, and 8237 as listed in the schedule of operating expenses on page 827 and post the detail to these accounts. **(4)** Journalize the entries required to reverse the adjusting entries for accruals and post to the accounts affected. (Retain the solution to this problem for use in solving Problem 28-B.)

Problem 28-B   Financial statements

The work sheets for The J. T. Reid Manufacturing Company, completed in Problem 28-A, are needed for the solution of this problem.

Required: (1) Prepare an income statement for the year ended December 31. **(2)** Prepare a schedule of operating expenses for the year ended December 31. **(3)** Prepare a balance sheet as of December 31 in the account form. **(4)** Prepare a statement of retained earnings for the year ended December 31. (Dividends declared during the year amount to $10,640.)

Problem 28-C   Cost of production summary

The Piston Manufacturing Company uses a process cost accounting system. The following information describes what took place with respect to the first process employed in the Piston factory during the month of July.

In process beginning of month:
400 units, complete as to material and 60% complete as to processing cost.

Total cost so far assigned	$ 3,600
Material put into process during the month:	
3,500 units @ $7.80...	27,300
Processing costs for the month:	
Labor..	13,020
Factory overhead assigned to the process..................................	9,300
Total cost to be accounted for...	$53,220
Completed and transferred to next process during month	3,100 units
In process end of month (complete as to materials and 30% complete as to processing costs)	800 units

Required: Using the foregoing information, prepare a cost of production summary similar to the one illustrated on page 785 of Chapter 28.

Problem 28-D   Process cost system — flow of costs

The Kazan Manufacturing Company uses a process cost accounting system. Following are selected transactions for the year 19––:

(a) Materials purchases: Material F, $11,880; Material G, $29,700.
(b) Materials put into Process 1: Material F, $11,140; Material G, $37,125.
(c) Factory labor cost for the year, $142,560 ($44,550 relates to Process 1 and $98,010 relates to Process 2).
(d) Factory overhead cost (other than labor) for the month $68,904 ($29,700 assigned to Process 1 and $39,204 to process 2).
(e) Cost of 10,000 units transferred from Process 1 to Process 2, $118,465.
(f) Cost of 9,000 units completed in Process 2 and transferred to finished goods stockroom, $252,230.
(g) Cost of goods sold, $240,814.

Required: Using as your guide the T accounts illustrated on page 783 of Chapter 28, post each of the foregoing transactions to a similar set of T accounts, and trace the flow of costs through the accounts by means of lines and arrows. Enter the following opening account balances:

Material F, $7,920; Material G, $13,200; Process 2, $39,865; Finished Goods, $35,640.

Problem 29-A   Comparative income statement and balance sheet

The comparative income statement (condensed) for the years 19A and 19B and the comparative balance sheet as of December 31,

19A and 19B, for The Dunning Company are presented below.

THE DUNNING COMPANY
Condensed Comparative Income Statement
For the Years Ended December 31, 19B and 19A

	19B	19A
Sales	$504,700	$497,700
Less sales returns, allowances, and discounts	3,500	3,800
Net sales	$501,200	$493,900
Cost of goods sold	285,000	276,500
Gross margin on sales	$216,200	$217,400
Administrative expenses	$ 86,000	$ 77,300
Selling expenses	94,800	89,200
Total operating expenses	$180,800	$166,500
Operating income	$ 35,400	$ 50,900
Net interest expense	5,300	5,300
Income before income tax	$ 30,100	$ 45,600
Provision for income tax	9,100	13,800
Net income	$ 21,000	$ 31,800

THE DUNNING COMPANY
Condensed Comparative Balance Sheet
December 31, 19B and 19A

Assets	19B	19A	Liabilities and Stockholders' Equity	19B	19A
Cash	$ 54,300	$ 55,000	Vouchers payable	$136,400	$118,700
Receivables (net)	152,100	142,000	Taxes payable	10,000	14,000
Inventories	220,300	197,000	Bonds payable		110,000
Supplies & prepayments	3,500	2,700	Common stock	170,000	170,000
Buildings & equipment	88,500	55,000	Preferred stock	130,000	
Less accumd. deprec.	(24,200)	(17,700)	Retained earnings	48,100	21,300
	$494,500	$434,000		$494,500	$434,000

Required: (1) Prepare a comparative income statement that shows the amount of change in each item and the percent of change relative to the first year. (A separate schedule of cost of goods sold is not required. Round off percent calculations to the nearest 1/10 of 1%.) (2) Prepare a comparative balance sheet that shows the amount of change in each item and the percent of change in relation to the amount on December 31, 19A. (The undepreciated cost of buildings and equipment, rather than both cost and accumulated depreciation, may be shown. A separate schedule of current assets is not required.) (3) Prepare a comparative income statement that shows, for both years, each amount as a percent of the net sales of that year. (4) Prepare a comparative balance sheet that shows, for both years, each amount as a percent of the total assets and equities. (5) Calculate the following ratios for each of the two years, using the data in the statements and other information that is provided:

- **(a)** Rate earned on total assets.
  (Total assets on January 1, 19A, amounted to $409,000.)
- **(b)** Rate earned on owners' equity.
  (Owners' equity on January 1, 19A, amounted to $184,500.)
- **(c)** Earnings per share of common stock.
  (There were 850 shares of common stock outstanding both years. The preferred stock was not sold and issued until late in December, 19B.)
- **(d)** Book value per share of common stock.
  (The par value of the preferred stock is $100 per share. The liquidation preference is $102 per share.)
- **(e)** Acid-test ratio.
- **(f)** Current ratio.
- **(g)** Receivables turnover.
  (The net receivables on January 1, 19A, amounted to $118,700.)
- **(h)** Inventory turnover.
  (The inventory on January 1, 19A, amounted to $175,400.)
- **(i)** Ratio of liabilities to owners' equity.
- **(j)** Times interest earned ratio.

Problem 30-A   Purchasing power loss

Febsel Company held net monetary assets of $310,000 as of January 1, 1983. As of December 31, 1983, Febsel's net monetary assets had increased to $380,000. The price level index was 100 at the beginning of 1983, and 120 at the end of 1983. The average index during the year was 110.

Required: Assuming that the increase in net monetary assets occurred evenly during the year, calculate the purchasing power loss for Febsel Company for 1983. (Round all calculations to the nearest dollar.)

Problem 30-B   Condensed current cost balance sheet

The condensed balance sheet of Leslie Company as of December 31, 1983, is presented on page 832. Assets with current costs which differ from the related historical cost amounts are as follows:

Asset	Current Cost
(1) Inventories	$251,000
(2) Land	$142,000
(3) Building and equipment	$510,000

LESLIE COMPANY
Condensed Balance Sheet
December 31, 1983

Cash and receivables.........	$190,000	Accounts and notes payable..................................	$ 95,000
Inventories..........................	210,000	Bonds payable...................	150,000
Land....................................	105,000	Capital stock......................	400,000
Building and equipment....	370,000	Retained earnings..............	156,000
Less accumulated depreciation..............................	(74,000)	Total liabilities and stockholders' equity....	
Total assets.....................	$801,000		$801,000

Required: Prepare a condensed current cost balance sheet for Leslie Company as of December 31, 1983.

INDEX